50% OFF FSOT Test Prep C

Dear Customer,

We consider it an honor and a privilege that you chose our FSOT Study Guide. As a way of showing our appreciation and to help us better serve you, we have partnered with Mometrix Test Preparation to offer you **50% off their online FSOT Prep Course.** Many Foreign Service Officer Test courses are needlessly expensive and don't deliver enough value. With their course, you get access to the best FSOT prep material, and you only pay half price.

Mometrix has structured their online course to perfectly complement your printed study guide. The FSOT Test Prep Course contains **in-depth lessons** that cover all the most important topics, over **750 practice questions** to ensure you feel prepared, more than **900 flashcards** for studying on the go, and over **150 instructional videos**.

Online FSOT Prep Course

Topics Covered:
- Writing
- Unites States Government
- United States History, Society, Customs, and Culture
- World History and Geography
- Economics
- Mathematics and Statistics
- Management Principles, Psychology, and Human Behavior
- Communications
- Computers and Internet
- And More!

Course Features:
FSOT Study Guide
- Get access to content from the best reviewed study guide available.

Track Your Progress
- Their customized course allows you to check off content you have studied or feel confident with.

4 Full-Length Practice Tests
- With 750+ practice questions and lesson reviews, you can test yourself again and again to build confidence.

FSOT Flashcards
- Their course includes a flashcard mode consisting of over 900 content cards to help you study.

To receive this discount, visit them at www.mometrix.com/university/fsot/or simply scan this QR code with your smartphone. At the checkout page, enter the discount code: **TPBFSOT50**

If you have any questions or concerns, please contact them at universityhelp@mometrix.com.

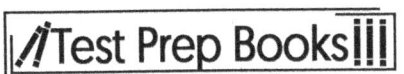 in partnership with

FREE Test Taking Tips Video/DVD Offer

To better serve you, we created videos covering test taking tips that we want to give you for FREE. **These videos cover world-class tips that will help you succeed on your test.**

We just ask that you send us feedback about this product. Please let us know what you thought about it—whether good, bad, or indifferent.

To get your **FREE videos**, you can use the QR code below or email freevideos@studyguideteam.com with "Free Videos" in the subject line and the following information in the body of the email:

    a. The title of your product

    b. Your product rating on a scale of 1-5, with 5 being the highest

    c. Your feedback about the product

If you have any questions or concerns, please don't hesitate to contact us at info@studyguideteam.com.

Thank you!

FSOT Study Guide 2023 - 2024

3 Practice Tests and Foreign Service Exam Prep [3rd Edition]

Joshua Rueda

Copyright © 2022 by TPB Publishing

All rights reserved. No part of this publication may be reproduced, distributed, or transmitted in any form or by any means, including photocopying, recording, or other electronic or mechanical methods, without the prior written permission of the publisher, except in the case of brief quotations embodied in critical reviews and certain other noncommercial uses permitted by copyright law.

Written and edited by TPB Publishing.

TPB Publishing is not associated with or endorsed by any official testing organization. TPB Publishing is a publisher of unofficial educational products. All test and organization names are trademarks of their respective owners. Content in this book is included for utilitarian purposes only and does not constitute an endorsement by TPB Publishing of any particular point of view.

Interested in buying more than 10 copies of our product? Contact us about bulk discounts:
bulkorders@studyguideteam.com

ISBN 13: 9781637750698
ISBN 10: 1637750692

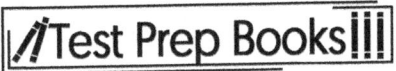

Table of Contents

Quick Overview --- 1
Test-Taking Strategies --- 2
FREE Videos/DVD OFFER --- 6
Introduction to the FSOT --- 7
Study Prep Plan for FSOT --- 9
Math Reference Sheet --- 11
Writing or Editing Reports --- 12
U.S. Government --- 45
U.S. History, Society, Customs, and Culture --- 67
World History --- 97
Geography --- 106
Economics --- 119
   Microeconomics --- 119
   Macroeconomics --- 122
Mathematics and Statistics --- 131
   Numbers Sense --- 131
   Algebra and Functions --- 147
   Measurement and Geometry --- 159
   Statistics and Data Analysis --- 186
Communications --- 206
Management Principles, Psychology, and Human Behavior 212
Computers and the internet --- 222

//Test Prep Books!!!

FSOT Oral Assessment (FSOA) ------------------------------------226
Practice Test #1 ---236
Job Knowledge --- 236
Situational Judgment -- 244
English Expression -- 254
Written Essay #1 -- 273
Answer Explanations #1 ---------------------------------------274
Job Knowledge --- 274
Situational Judgment -- 283
English Expression -- 288
Practice Test #2 ---296
Job Knowledge --- 296
Situational Judgment -- 307
English Expression -- 317
Written Essay #2 -- 337
Answer Explanations #2 ---------------------------------------338
Job Knowledge --- 338
Situational Judgment -- 346
English Expression -- 352
Practice Test #3 ---359
Job Knowledge --- 359
Situational Judgment -- 372
English Expression -- 382
Written Essay #3 -- 401
Answer Explanations #3 ---------------------------------------402

Job Knowledge -- 402
Situational Judgment --- 410
English Expression --- 415
Index --*424*

Quick Overview

As you draw closer to taking your exam, effective preparation becomes more and more important. Thankfully, you have this study guide to help you get ready. Use this guide to help keep your studying on track and refer to it often.

This study guide contains several key sections that will help you be successful on your exam. The guide contains tips for what you should do the night before and the day of the test. Also included are test-taking tips. Knowing the right information is not always enough. Many well-prepared test takers struggle with exams. These tips will help equip you to accurately read, assess, and answer test questions.

A large part of the guide is devoted to showing you what content to expect on the exam and to helping you better understand that content. In this guide are practice test questions so that you can see how well you have grasped the content. Then, answer explanations are provided so that you can understand why you missed certain questions.

Don't try to cram the night before you take your exam. This is not a wise strategy for a few reasons. First, your retention of the information will be low. Your time would be better used by reviewing information you already know rather than trying to learn a lot of new information. Second, you will likely become stressed as you try to gain a large amount of knowledge in a short amount of time. Third, you will be depriving yourself of sleep. So be sure to go to bed at a reasonable time the night before. Being well-rested helps you focus and remain calm.

Be sure to eat a substantial breakfast the morning of the exam. If you are taking the exam in the afternoon, be sure to have a good lunch as well. Being hungry is distracting and can make it difficult to focus. You have hopefully spent lots of time preparing for the exam. Don't let an empty stomach get in the way of success!

When travelling to the testing center, leave earlier than needed. That way, you have a buffer in case you experience any delays. This will help you remain calm and will keep you from missing your appointment time at the testing center.

Be sure to pace yourself during the exam. Don't try to rush through the exam. There is no need to risk performing poorly on the exam just so you can leave the testing center early. Allow yourself to use all of the allotted time if needed.

Remain positive while taking the exam even if you feel like you are performing poorly. Thinking about the content you should have mastered will not help you perform better on the exam.

Once the exam is complete, take some time to relax. Even if you feel that you need to take the exam again, you will be well served by some down time before you begin studying again. It's often easier to convince yourself to study if you know that it will come with a reward!

Test-Taking Strategies

1. Predicting the Answer

When you feel confident in your preparation for a multiple-choice test, try predicting the answer before reading the answer choices. This is especially useful on questions that test objective factual knowledge. By predicting the answer before reading the available choices, you eliminate the possibility that you will be distracted or led astray by an incorrect answer choice. You will feel more confident in your selection if you read the question, predict the answer, and then find your prediction among the answer choices. After using this strategy, be sure to still read all of the answer choices carefully and completely. If you feel unprepared, you should not attempt to predict the answers. This would be a waste of time and an opportunity for your mind to wander in the wrong direction.

2. Reading the Whole Question

Too often, test takers scan a multiple-choice question, recognize a few familiar words, and immediately jump to the answer choices. Test authors are aware of this common impatience, and they will sometimes prey upon it. For instance, a test author might subtly turn the question into a negative, or he or she might redirect the focus of the question right at the end. The only way to avoid falling into these traps is to read the entirety of the question carefully before reading the answer choices.

3. Looking for Wrong Answers

Long and complicated multiple-choice questions can be intimidating. One way to simplify a difficult multiple-choice question is to eliminate all of the answer choices that are clearly wrong. In most sets of answers, there will be at least one selection that can be dismissed right away. If the test is administered on paper, the test taker could draw a line through it to indicate that it may be ignored; otherwise, the test taker will have to perform this operation mentally or on scratch paper. In either case, once the obviously incorrect answers have been eliminated, the remaining choices may be considered. Sometimes identifying the clearly wrong answers will give the test taker some information about the correct answer. For instance, if one of the remaining answer choices is a direct opposite of one of the eliminated answer choices, it may well be the correct answer. The opposite of obviously wrong is obviously right! Of course, this is not always the case. Some answers are obviously incorrect simply because they are irrelevant to the question being asked. Still, identifying and eliminating some incorrect answer choices is a good way to simplify a multiple-choice question.

4. Don't Overanalyze

Anxious test takers often overanalyze questions. When you are nervous, your brain will often run wild, causing you to make associations and discover clues that don't actually exist. If you feel that this may be a problem for you, do whatever you can to slow down during the test. Try taking a deep breath or counting to ten. As you read and consider the question, restrict yourself to the particular words used by the author. Avoid thought tangents about what the author *really* meant, or what he or she was *trying* to say. The only things that matter on a multiple-choice test are the words that are actually in the question. You must avoid reading too much into a multiple-choice question, or supposing that the writer meant something other than what he or she wrote.

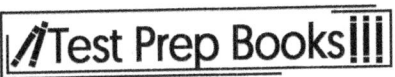

5. No Need for Panic

It is wise to learn as many strategies as possible before taking a multiple-choice test, but it is likely that you will come across a few questions for which you simply don't know the answer. In this situation, avoid panicking. Because most multiple-choice tests include dozens of questions, the relative value of a single wrong answer is small. As much as possible, you should compartmentalize each question on a multiple-choice test. In other words, you should not allow your feelings about one question to affect your success on the others. When you find a question that you either don't understand or don't know how to answer, just take a deep breath and do your best. Read the entire question slowly and carefully. Try rephrasing the question a couple of different ways. Then, read all of the answer choices carefully. After eliminating obviously wrong answers, make a selection and move on to the next question.

6. Confusing Answer Choices

When working on a difficult multiple-choice question, there may be a tendency to focus on the answer choices that are the easiest to understand. Many people, whether consciously or not, gravitate to the answer choices that require the least concentration, knowledge, and memory. This is a mistake. When you come across an answer choice that is confusing, you should give it extra attention. A question might be confusing because you do not know the subject matter to which it refers. If this is the case, don't eliminate the answer before you have affirmatively settled on another. When you come across an answer choice of this type, set it aside as you look at the remaining choices. If you can confidently assert that one of the other choices is correct, you can leave the confusing answer aside. Otherwise, you will need to take a moment to try to better understand the confusing answer choice. Rephrasing is one way to tease out the sense of a confusing answer choice.

7. Your First Instinct

Many people struggle with multiple-choice tests because they overthink the questions. If you have studied sufficiently for the test, you should be prepared to trust your first instinct once you have carefully and completely read the question and all of the answer choices. There is a great deal of research suggesting that the mind can come to the correct conclusion very quickly once it has obtained all of the relevant information. At times, it may seem to you as if your intuition is working faster even than your reasoning mind. This may in fact be true. The knowledge you obtain while studying may be retrieved from your subconscious before you have a chance to work out the associations that support it. Verify your instinct by working out the reasons that it should be trusted.

8. Key Words

Many test takers struggle with multiple-choice questions because they have poor reading comprehension skills. Quickly reading and understanding a multiple-choice question requires a mixture of skill and experience. To help with this, try jotting down a few key words and phrases on a piece of scrap paper. Doing this concentrates the process of reading and forces the mind to weigh the relative importance of the question's parts. In selecting words and phrases to write down, the test taker thinks about the question more deeply and carefully. This is especially true for multiple-choice questions that are preceded by a long prompt.

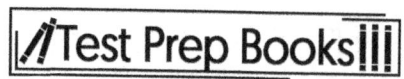

9. Subtle Negatives

One of the oldest tricks in the multiple-choice test writer's book is to subtly reverse the meaning of a question with a word like *not* or *except*. If you are not paying attention to each word in the question, you can easily be led astray by this trick. For instance, a common question format is, "Which of the following is...?" Obviously, if the question instead is, "Which of the following is not...?," then the answer will be quite different. Even worse, the test makers are aware of the potential for this mistake and will include one answer choice that would be correct if the question were not negated or reversed. A test taker who misses the reversal will find what he or she believes to be a correct answer and will be so confident that he or she will fail to reread the question and discover the original error. The only way to avoid this is to practice a wide variety of multiple-choice questions and to pay close attention to each and every word.

10. Reading Every Answer Choice

It may seem obvious, but you should always read every one of the answer choices! Too many test takers fall into the habit of scanning the question and assuming that they understand the question because they recognize a few key words. From there, they pick the first answer choice that answers the question they believe they have read. Test takers who read all of the answer choices might discover that one of the latter answer choices is actually *more* correct. Moreover, reading all of the answer choices can remind you of facts related to the question that can help you arrive at the correct answer. Sometimes, a misstatement or incorrect detail in one of the latter answer choices will trigger your memory of the subject and will enable you to find the right answer. Failing to read all of the answer choices is like not reading all of the items on a restaurant menu: you might miss out on the perfect choice.

11. Spot the Hedges

One of the keys to success on multiple-choice tests is paying close attention to every word. This is never truer than with words like *almost, most, some,* and *sometimes*. These words are called "hedges" because they indicate that a statement is not totally true or not true in every place and time. An absolute statement will contain no hedges, but in many subjects, the answers are not always straightforward or absolute. There are always exceptions to the rules in these subjects. For this reason, you should favor those multiple-choice questions that contain hedging language. The presence of qualifying words indicates that the author is taking special care with their words, which is certainly important when composing the right answer. After all, there are many ways to be wrong, but there is only one way to be right! For this reason, it is wise to avoid answers that are absolute when taking a multiple-choice test. An absolute answer is one that says things are either all one way or all another. They often include words like *every, always, best,* and *never*. If you are taking a multiple-choice test in a subject that doesn't lend itself to absolute answers, be on your guard if you see any of these words.

12. Long Answers

In many subject areas, the answers are not simple. As already mentioned, the right answer often requires hedges. Another common feature of the answers to a complex or subjective question are qualifying clauses, which are groups of words that subtly modify the meaning of the sentence. If the question or answer choice describes a rule to which there are exceptions or the subject matter is complicated, ambiguous, or confusing, the correct answer will require many words in order to be expressed clearly and accurately. In essence, you should not be deterred by answer choices that seem

Test-Taking Strategies

excessively long. Oftentimes, the author of the text will not be able to write the correct answer without offering some qualifications and modifications. Your job is to read the answer choices thoroughly and completely and to select the one that most accurately and precisely answers the question.

13. Restating to Understand

Sometimes, a question on a multiple-choice test is difficult not because of what it asks but because of how it is written. If this is the case, restate the question or answer choice in different words. This process serves a couple of important purposes. First, it forces you to concentrate on the core of the question. In order to rephrase the question accurately, you have to understand it well. Rephrasing the question will concentrate your mind on the key words and ideas. Second, it will present the information to your mind in a fresh way. This process may trigger your memory and render some useful scrap of information picked up while studying.

14. True Statements

Sometimes an answer choice will be true in itself, but it does not answer the question. This is one of the main reasons why it is essential to read the question carefully and completely before proceeding to the answer choices. Too often, test takers skip ahead to the answer choices and look for true statements. Having found one of these, they are content to select it without reference to the question above. Obviously, this provides an easy way for test makers to play tricks. The savvy test taker will always read the entire question before turning to the answer choices. Then, having settled on a correct answer choice, he or she will refer to the original question and ensure that the selected answer is relevant. The mistake of choosing a correct-but-irrelevant answer choice is especially common on questions related to specific pieces of objective knowledge. A prepared test taker will have a wealth of factual knowledge at their disposal, and should not be careless in its application.

15. No Patterns

One of the more dangerous ideas that circulates about multiple-choice tests is that the correct answers tend to fall into patterns. These erroneous ideas range from a belief that B and C are the most common right answers, to the idea that an unprepared test-taker should answer "A-B-A-C-A-D-A-B-A." It cannot be emphasized enough that pattern-seeking of this type is exactly the WRONG way to approach a multiple-choice test. To begin with, it is highly unlikely that the test maker will plot the correct answers according to some predetermined pattern. The questions are scrambled and delivered in a random order. Furthermore, even if the test maker was following a pattern in the assignation of correct answers, there is no reason why the test taker would know which pattern he or she was using. Any attempt to discern a pattern in the answer choices is a waste of time and a distraction from the real work of taking the test. A test taker would be much better served by extra preparation before the test than by reliance on a pattern in the answers.

FREE Videos/DVD OFFER

Doing well on your exam requires both knowing the test content and understanding how to use that knowledge to do well on the test. We offer completely FREE test taking tip videos. **These videos cover world-class tips that you can use to succeed on your test.**

To get your **FREE videos**, you can use the QR code below or email freevideos@studyguideteam.com with "Free Videos" in the subject line and the following information in the body of the email:

   a. The title of your product

   b. Your product rating on a scale of 1-5, with 5 being the highest

   c. Your feedback about the product

If you have any questions or concerns, please don't hesitate to contact us at info@studyguideteam.com.

Thanks again!

Introduction to the FSOT

Function of the Test

Taking the Foreign Service Officer Test (FSOT) is one step out of eight to being selected as a Foreign Service Officer (FSO). Those who have a desire to become an FSO must first choose a career track and then register for the FSOT exam. If a candidate passes the FSOT exam, they will move on to the next step in the process of being considered for an FSO.

Although there are no degrees specified in order to become an FSO, the knowledge and skills needed to understand and pass the FSOT are usually comparable to the education on the level of a Bachelor's degree. Additionally, no specific experience is required; however, it is suggested that candidates have strong leadership and negotiation skills and are able to provide sound judgment and analytical ability. Note that those who are considered to be Foreign Service Officers must be US citizens between the ages of 20 and 59. In a given year, approximately 20,000 people take the FSOT, and only 500 to 700 candidates are offered positions in the Foreign Service.

Test Administration

The FSOT is offered three times a year in February, June, and October in both domestic and overseas locations. Each month will have a testing window of eight days. The specific dates displaying when registration opens and closes is listed on the careers.state.gov website. Overseas, the FSOT is offered at Pearson Professional Centers (PPCs) or at some embassies, if available. A list of the FSOT offered in overseas cities is available on the careers.state.gov website. The FSOT will be offered at 130 on base test centers (OBTCs) in US states and territories, Europe, Asia, and the Middle East on US military installations.

Although there is no limit to how many times an individual can take the FSOT, one must wait at least 12 months before taking the test again. Note that those who need to request accommodations for the test can do so through the Pearson VUE website. Accommodations are considered on a case-by-case basis.

Test Format

At the testing center, be sure to bring a current government or state-issued ID, or a passport, depending on the location. Photos will be taken before the test begins for security purposes, and candidates will be required to sign a Candidate Rules agreement form. The testing period is around 3 hours, so be sure to take care of everything beforehand. Candidates will not be allowed to use their cell phones or leave the testing room for any reason.

The FSOT is a multiple-choice test but also includes a writing section. The multiple-choice sections are Job Knowledge, Situational Judgment, and English Expression. The fourth section is a written essay test. The Job Knowledge section tests your ability on US government, US culture, US and world history, management theory, technology, psychology, world affairs, and economics and finance. The Situational Judgment section presents scenarios that might be potential circumstances of the FSO job, and asks you

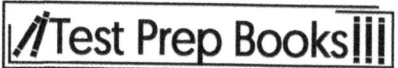

Introduction to the FSOT

to choose the best and worse responses to any given situation. The English Expression tests your knowledge of grammar as well as composition. The following table gives an outline of the test:

Section	Questions	Time
Job Knowledge	60 questions	40 minutes
Situational Judgment	28 scenarios	42 minutes
English Expression	65 questions	50 minutes
Written Essay	1 question	30 minutes

Scoring

Although the Department of State does not give information regarding scoring or passing rates on the FSOT, candidates who have taken the test in the past state that the scaled passing score on the multiple-choice portion is 154 points, and a passing score of 6 out of 12 is required on the essay.

Recent Developments

The Situational Judgment section, described above, replaced the Biographic Information Questionnaire beginning in October 2017. The Biographic Information Questionnaire asked personal questions such as work style, communication with others, and one's approach to other cultures. The Situational Judgment section asks how you would react in a given scenario related to an FSO position.

Study Prep Plan for FSOT

1 **Schedule** - Use one of our study schedules below or come up with one of your own.

2 **Relax** - Test anxiety can hurt even the best students. There are many ways to reduce stress. Find the one that works best for you.

3 **Execute** - Once you have a good plan in place, be sure to stick to it.

One Week Study Schedule

Day 1	Correct Grammar, Organization, Writing...
Day 2	U.S. History, Society, Customs, and Culture
Day 3	Mathematics and Statistics
Day 4	Communications
Day 5	Practice Tests #1 & #2
Day 6	Practice Test #3
Day 7	Take Your Exam!

Two Week Study Schedule

Day 1	Correct Grammar, Organization, Writing...	Day 8	Measurement and Geometry
Day 2	Writing Strategy	Day 9	Statistics and Data Analysis
Day 3	U.S. Government	Day 10	Communications
Day 4	U.S. History, Society, Customs, and Culture	Day 11	Practice Test #1
Day 5	Social, Economic, and Technological...	Day 12	Practice Test #2
Day 6	Geography	Day 13	Practice Test #3
Day 7	Mathematics and Statistics	Day 14	Take Your Exam!

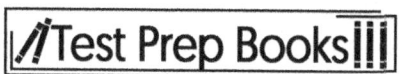

Study Prep Plan for FSOT

One Month Study Schedule

Day 1	Correct Grammar, Organization, Writing Strategy...	Day 11	Economics	Day 21	Management Principles, Psychology, and Human Behavior
Day 2	Writing Strategy	Day 12	Mathematics and Statistics	Day 22	Leadership
Day 3	Sentence Structure	Day 13	Order of Operations	Day 23	FSOT Oral Assessment (FSOA)
Day 4	U.S. Government	Day 14	Algebra and Functions	Day 24	Practice Test #1
Day 5	Civil Liberties and Civil Rights	Day 15	Measurement and Geometry	Day 25	Answer Explanations #1
Day 6	U.S. History, Society, Customs, and Culture	Day 16	Classification of Angles	Day 26	Practice Test #2
Day 7	The Civil War	Day 17	Perimeter and Area	Day 27	Answer Explanations #2
Day 8	Political Realignments from the New Deal...	Day 18	Statistics and Data Analysis	Day 28	Practice Test #3
Day 9	World History	Day 19	Making Inferences and Justifying Conclusions...	Day 29	Answer Explanations #3
Day 10	Geography	Day 20	Communications	Day 30	Take Your Exam!

Build your own prep plan by visiting:
testprepbooks.com/prep

Math Reference Sheet

Symbol	Phrase
+	added to, increased by, sum of, more than
-	decreased by, difference between, less than, take away
×	multiplied by, 3 (4, 5 . . .) times as large, product of
÷	divided by, quotient of, half (third, etc.) of
=	is, the same as, results in, as much as
x, t, n, etc.	a variable which is an unknown value or quantity
<	is under, is below, smaller than, beneath
>	is above, is over, bigger than, exceeds
≤	no more than, at most, maximum; less than or equal to
≥	no less than, at least, minimum; greater than or equal to
√	square root of, exponent divided by 2

Geometry	Description
$P = 2l + 2w$	for perimeter of a rectangle
$P = 4 \times s$	for perimeter of a square
$P = a + b + c$	for perimeter of a triangle
$A = \frac{1}{2} \times b \times h = \frac{bh}{2}$	for area of a triangle
$A = b \times h$	for area of a parallelogram
$A = \frac{1}{2} \times h(b_1 + b_2)$	for area of a trapezoid
$A = \frac{1}{2} \times a \times P$	for area of a regular polygon
$C = 2 \times \pi \times r$	for circumference (perimeter) of a circle
$A = \pi \times r^2$	for area of a circle
$c^2 = a^2 + b^2; c = \sqrt{a^2 + b^2}$	for finding the hypotenuse of a right triangle
$SA = 2xy + 2yz + 2xz$	for finding surface area
$V = \frac{1}{3}xyh$	for finding volume of a rectangular pyramid
$V = \frac{4}{3}\pi r^3; \frac{1}{3}\pi r^2 h; \pi r^2 h$	for volume of a sphere; a cone; and a cylinder

Radical Expressions	Description
$\sqrt[n]{a} = a^{\frac{1}{n}}, \sqrt[n]{a^m} = (\sqrt[n]{a})^m = a^{\frac{m}{n}}$	a is the radicand, n is the index, m is the exponent
$\sqrt{x^2} = (x^2)^{\frac{1}{2}} = x$	to convert square root to exponent
$a^m \times a^n = a^{m+n}$	multiplying radicands with exponents
$(a^m)^n = a^{m \times n}$	multiplying exponents
$(a \times b)^m = a^m \times b^m$	parentheses with exponents

Property	Addition	Multiplication
Commutative	$a + b = b + a$	$a \times b = b \times a$
Associative	$(a + b) + c = a + (b + c)$	$(a \times b) \times c = a \times (b \times c)$
Identity	$a + 0 = a; 0 + a = a$	$a \times 1 = a; 1 \times a = a$
Inverse	$a + (-a) = 0$	$a \times \frac{1}{a} = 1; a \neq 0$
Distributive	$a(b + c) = ab + ac$	

Data	Description
Mean	equal to the total of the values of a data set, divided by the number of elements in the data set
Median	middle value in an odd number of ordered values of a data set, or the mean of the two middle values in an even number of ordered values in a data set
Mode	the value that appears most often
Range	the difference between the highest and the lowest values in the set

Graphing	Description
(x, y)	ordered pair, plot points in a graph
$y = mx + b$	slope-intercept form; m represents the slope of the line and b represents the y-intercept
$f(x)$	read as f of x, which means it is a function of x
(x_2, y_2) and (x_2, y_2)	two ordered pairs used to determine the slope of a line
$m = \frac{y_2 - y_1}{x_2 - x_1}$	to find the slope of the line, m, for ordered pairs
$Ax + By = C$	standard form of an equation, also for solving a system of equations through the elimination method
$M = (\frac{x_1 + x_2}{2}, \frac{y_1 + y_2}{2})$	for finding the midpoint of an ordered pair
$y = ax^2 + bx + c$	quadratic function for a parabola
$y = a(x - h)^2 + k$	quadratic function for a parabola with vertex
$y = ab^x; y = a \times b^x$	function for exponential curve
$y = ax^2 + bx + c$	standard form of a quadratic function
$x = \frac{-b}{2a}$	for finding axis of symmetry in a parabola; given quadratic formula in standard form
$f = \sqrt{\frac{\Sigma(x - \bar{x})^2}{n - 1}}$	function for standard deviation of the sample; where $\bar{x}$ = sample mean and n = sample size

Proportions and Percentage	Description
$\frac{gallons}{cost} = \frac{gallons}{cost} : \frac{7 \text{ gallons}}{\$14.70} = \frac{x}{\$20}$	written as equal ratios with a variable representing the missing quantity
$\frac{y_1}{x_1} = \frac{y_2}{x_2}$	for direct proportions
$(y_1)(x_1) = (y_2)(x_2)$	for indirect proportions
$\frac{change}{original \ value} \times 100 = percent \ change$	for finding percentage change in value
$\frac{new \ quantity - old \ quantity}{old \ quantity} \times 100$	for calculating the increase or decrease in percentage

Writing or Editing Reports

This knowledge area encompasses English expression and language usage skills required for preparing or editing written reports, including correct grammar and good writing at the sentence and paragraph level.

Grammar

Nouns

A **noun** is a person, place, thing, or idea. All nouns fit into one of two types, common or proper.

A **common noun** is a word that identifies any of a class of people, places, or things. Examples include numbers, objects, animals, feelings, concepts, qualities, and actions. *A, an,* or *the* usually precedes the common noun. These parts of speech are called *articles*. Here are some examples of sentences using nouns preceded by articles.

A building is under construction.
The girl would like to move to *the* city.

A **proper noun** (also called a *proper name*) is used for the specific name of an individual person, place, or organization. The first letter in a proper noun is capitalized. "My name is *Mary*." "I work for *Walmart*."

Nouns sometimes serve as adjectives (which themselves describe nouns), such as "hockey player" and "state government."

An **abstract noun** is an idea, state, or quality. It is something that can't be touched, such as happiness, courage, evil, or humor.

A **concrete noun** is something that can be experienced through the senses (touch, taste, hear, smell, see). Examples of concrete nouns are birds, skateboard, pie, and car.

A **collective noun** refers to a collection of people, places, or things that act as one. Examples of collective nouns are as follows: team, class, jury, family, audience, and flock.

Pronouns

A word used in place of a noun is known as a **pronoun**. Pronouns are words like *I, mine, hers,* and *us*.

Pronouns can be split into different classifications (see below) which make them easier to learn; however, it's not important to memorize the classifications.

- **Personal pronouns**: refer to people
- **First person**: we, I, our, mine
- **Second person**: you, yours
- **Third person**: he, them
- **Possessive pronouns**: demonstrate ownership (mine, his, hers, its, ours, theirs, yours)

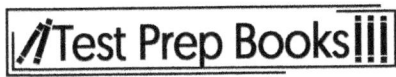

Writing or Editing Reports

- **Interrogative pronouns**: ask questions (what, which, who, whom, whose)

- **Relative pronouns**: include the five interrogative pronouns and others that are relative (whoever, whomever, that, when, where)

- **Demonstrative pronouns**: replace something specific (this, that, those, these)

- **Reciprocal pronouns**: indicate something was done or given in return (each other, one another)

- Indefinite pronouns: have a nonspecific status (anybody, whoever, someone, everybody, somebody)

Indefinite pronouns such as *anybody, whoever, someone, everybody,* and *somebody* command a singular verb form, but others such as *all, none,* and *some* could require a singular or plural verb form.

Antecedents

An **antecedent** is the noun to which a pronoun refers; it needs to be written or spoken before the pronoun is used. For many pronouns, antecedents are imperative for clarity. In particular, many of the personal, possessive, and demonstrative pronouns need antecedents. Otherwise, it would be unclear who or what someone is referring to when they use a pronoun like *he* or *this*.

Pronoun reference means that the pronoun should refer clearly to one, clear, unmistakable noun (the antecedent).

Pronoun-antecedent agreement refers to the need for the antecedent and the corresponding pronoun to agree in gender, person, and number. Here are some examples:

The *kidneys* (plural antecedent) are part of the urinary system. *They* (plural pronoun) serve several roles.

The kidneys are part of the *urinary system* (singular antecedent). *It* (singular pronoun) is also known as the renal system.

Pronoun Cases

The **subjective pronouns** —*I, you, he/she/it, we, they,* and *who*—are the subjects of the sentence.

Example: *They* have a new house.

The **objective pronouns**—*me, you* (*singular*), *him/her, us, them,* and *whom*—are used when something is being done for or given to someone; they are objects of the action.

Example: The teacher has an apple for *us*.

The **possessive pronouns**—*mine, my, your, yours, his, hers, its, their, theirs, our,* and *ours*—are used to denote that something (or someone) belongs to someone (or something).

Example: It's *their* chocolate cake.
Even Better Example: It's *my* chocolate cake!

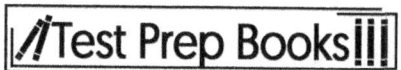

One of the greatest challenges and worst abuses of pronouns concerns *who* and *whom*. Just knowing the following rule can eliminate confusion. *Who* is a subjective-case pronoun used only as a subject or subject complement. *Whom* is only objective-case and, therefore, the object of the verb or preposition.

Hint: When using *who* or *whom*, think of whether someone would say *he* or *him*. If the answer is *he*, use *who*. If the answer is *him*, use *whom*. This trick is easy to remember because *he* and *who* both end in vowels, and *him* and *whom* both end in the letter *M*.

Verbs

A **verb** is the part of speech that describes an action, state of being, or occurrence.

A *verb* forms the main part of a predicate of a sentence. This means that the verb explains what the noun (which will be discussed shortly) is doing. A simple example is *time flies*. The verb *flies* explains what the action of the noun, *time*, is doing. This example is a *main* verb.

Helping (*auxiliary*) verbs are words like *have, do, be, can, may, should, must,* and *will*. "I *should* go to the store." Helping verbs assist main verbs in expressing tense, ability, possibility, permission, or obligation.

Particles are minor function words like *not, in, out, up,* or *down* that become part of the verb itself. "I might *not*."

Participles are words formed from verbs that are often used to modify a noun, noun phrase, verb, or verb phrase.

The *running* teenager collided with the cyclist.

Participles can also create compound verb forms.

He is *speaking*.

Verbs have five basic forms: the *base* form, the *-s* form, the *-ing* form, the *past* form, and the *past participle* form.

The *past* forms are either *regular* (*love/loved; hate/hated*) or *irregular* because they don't end by adding the common past tense suffix "-ed" (*go/went; fall/fell; set/set*).

Verb Forms

Shifting verb forms entails **conjugation**, which is used to indicate *tense, voice,* or *mood*.

Verb tense is used to show when the action in the sentence took place. There are several different verb tenses, and it is important to know how and when to use them. Some verb tenses can be achieved by changing the form of the verb, while others require the use of helping verbs (e.g., *is, was,* or *has*).

- Present tense shows the action is happening currently or is ongoing:

    I walk to work every morning.

    She is stressed about the deadline.

Writing or Editing Reports

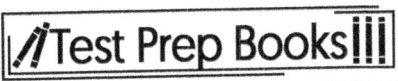

- Past tense shows that the action happened in the past or that the state of being is in the past:

    I walked to work yesterday morning.

    She was stressed about the deadline.

- Future tense shows that the action will happen in the future or is a future state of being:

    I will walk to work tomorrow morning.

    She will be stressed about the deadline.

- Present perfect tense shows action that began in the past, but continues into the present:

    I have walked to work all week.

    She has been stressed about the deadline.

- Past perfect tense shows an action was finished before another took place:

    I had walked all week until I sprained my ankle.

    She had been stressed about the deadline until we talked about it.

- Future perfect tense shows an action that will be completed at some point in the future:

    By the time the bus arrives, I will have walked to work already.

Voice

Verbs can be in the active or passive voice. When the subject completes the action, the verb is in **active voice**. When the subject receives the action of the sentence, the verb is in *passive voice*.

   Active: Jamie ate the ice cream.

   Passive: The ice cream was eaten by Jamie.

In active voice, the subject (*Jamie*) is the "do-er" of the action (*ate*). In passive voice, the subject *ice cream* receives the action of being eaten.

While passive voice can add variety to writing, active voice is the generally preferred sentence structure.

Mood

Mood is used to show the speaker's feelings about the subject matter. In English, there is *indicative mood, imperative mood,* and *subjective mood*.

Indicative mood is used to state facts, ask questions, or state opinions:

   Bob will make the trip next week.

   When can Bob make the trip?

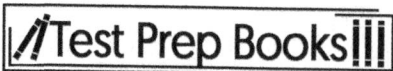

Imperative mood is used to state a command or make a request:

Wait in the lobby.

Please call me next week.

Subjunctive mood is used to express a wish, an opinion, or a hope that is contrary to fact:

If I were in charge, none of this would have happened.

Allison wished she could take the exam over again when she saw her score.

Adjectives

Adjectives are words used to modify nouns and pronouns. They can be used alone or in a series and are used to further define or describe the nouns they modify.

Mark made us a delicious, four-course meal.

The words *delicious* and *four-course* are adjectives that describe the kind of meal Mark made.

Articles are also considered adjectives because they help to describe nouns. Articles can be general or specific. The three articles in English are: a, an, and the.

Indefinite articles *(a, an)* are used to refer to nonspecific nouns. The article *a* proceeds words beginning with consonant sounds, and the article *an* proceeds words beginning with vowel sounds.

A car drove by our house.

An alligator was loose at the zoo.

He has always wanted a ukulele. (The first *u* makes a *y* sound.)

Note that *a* and *an* should only proceed nonspecific nouns that are also singular. If a nonspecific noun is plural, it does not need a preceding article.

Alligators were loose at the zoo.

The **definite article** *(the)* is used to refer to specific nouns:

The car pulled into our driveway.

Note that *the* should proceed all specific nouns regardless of whether they are singular or plural.

The cars pulled into our driveway.

Comparative adjectives are used to compare nouns. When they are used in this way, they take on positive, comparative, or superlative form.

The positive form is the normal form of the adjective:

Alicia is tall.

Writing or Editing Reports

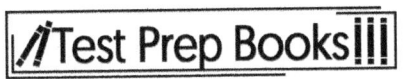

The *comparative* form shows a comparison between two things:

Alicia is taller than Maria.

Superlative form shows comparison between more than two things:

Alicia is the tallest girl in her class.

Usually, the comparative and superlative can be made by adding *–er* and *–est* to the positive form, but some verbs call for the helping verbs *more* or *most*. Other exceptions to the rule include adjectives like *bad*, which uses the comparative *worse* and the superlative *worst*.

An **adjective phrase** is not a bunch of adjectives strung together, but a group of words that describes a noun or pronoun and, thus, functions as an adjective. Very happy is an adjective phrase; so are way too hungry and passionate about traveling.

Adverbs
Adverbs have more functions than adjectives because they modify or qualify verbs, adjectives, or other adverbs as well as word groups that express a relation of place, time, circumstance, or cause. Therefore, adverbs answer any of the following questions: *How, when, where, why, in what way, how often, how much, in what condition,* and/or *to what degree*. How good looking is he? He is <u>very</u> handsome.

Here are some examples of adverbs for different situations:

- how: quickly
- when: daily
- where: there
- in what way: easily
- how often: often
- how much: much
- in what condition: badly
- what degree: hardly

As one can see, for some reason, many adverbs end in *-ly*.

Adverbs do things like emphasize (*really, simply,* and *so*), amplify (*heartily, completely,* and *positively*), and tone down (*almost, somewhat,* and *mildly*).

Adverbs also come in phrases.

The dog ran as <u>though his life depended on it.</u>

Prepositions
Prepositions are connecting words and, while there are only about 150 of them, they are used more often than any other individual groups of words. They describe relationships between other words. They are placed before a noun or pronoun, forming a phrase that modifies another word in the sentence. **Prepositional phrases** begin with a preposition and end with a noun or pronoun, the **object of the preposition**. *A pristine lake is <u>near the store</u> and <u>behind the bank</u>.*

17

Writing or Editing Reports

Some commonly used prepositions are *about, after, anti, around, as, at, behind, beside, by, for, from, in, into, of, off, on, to,* and *with*.

Complex prepositions, which also come before a noun or pronoun, consist of two or three words such as *according to, in regards to,* and *because of*.

Conjunctions

Conjunctions are vital words that connect words, phrases, thoughts, and ideas. Conjunctions show relationships between components. There are two types:

Coordinating conjunctions are the primary class of conjunctions placed between words, phrases, clauses, and sentences that are of equal grammatical rank; the coordinating conjunctions are *or, and, nor, but, or, yes,* and *so*. A useful memorization trick is to remember that all the first letters of these conjunctions collectively spell the word fanboys.

> I need to go shopping, *but* I must be careful to leave enough money in the bank.
> She wore a black, red, *and* white shirt.

Subordinating conjunctions are the secondary class of conjunctions. They connect two unequal parts, one *main* (or *independent*) and the other *subordinate* (or *dependent*). I must go to the store *even though* I do not have enough money in the bank.

> *Because* I read the review, I do not want to go to the movie.

Notice that the presence of subordinating conjunctions makes clauses dependent. *I read the movie* is an independent clause, but *because* makes the clause dependent. Thus, it needs an independent clause to complete the sentence.

Interjections

Interjections are words used to express emotion. Examples include *wow, ouch,* and *hooray*. Interjections are often separate from sentences; in those cases, the interjection is directly followed by an exclamation point. In other cases, the interjection is included in a sentence and followed by a comma. The punctuation plays a big role in the intensity of the emotion that the interjection is expressing. Using a comma or semicolon indicates less excitement than using an exclamation mark.

Subjects

Every sentence must include a subject and a verb. The **subject** of a sentence is who or what the sentence is about. It's often directly stated and can be determined by asking "Who?" or "What?" did the action:

Most sentences contain a direct subject, in which the subject is mentioned in the sentence.

> *Kelly mowed the lawn.*
>
> Who mowed the lawn? *Kelly*
>
> *The air-conditioner ran all night*
>
> What ran all night? *the air-conditioner*

Writing or Editing Reports

The subject of imperative sentences is the implied *you*, because imperative subjects are commands:

Go home after the meeting.

Who should go home after the meeting? *you* (implied)

In *expletive sentences* that start with "there are" or "there is," the subject is found after the predicate. The subject cannot be "there," so it must be another word in the sentence:

There is a cup sitting on the coffee table.

What is sitting on the coffee table? *a cup*

Simple and Complete Subjects

A **complete subject** includes the simple subject and all the words modifying it, including articles and adjectives. A **simple subject** is the single noun without its modifiers.

A warm, chocolate-chip cookie sat on the kitchen table.

Complete subject: *a warm, chocolate-chip cookie*

Simple subject: *cookie*

The words *a, warm, chocolate,* and *chip* all modify the simple subject *cookie*.

There might also be a *compound subject*, which would be two or more nouns without the modifiers.

A little girl and her mother walked into the shop.

Complete subject: *A little girl and her mother*

Compound subject: *girl, mother*

In this case, *the girl and her mother* are both completing the action of walking into the shop, so this is a *compound subject*.

Predicates

In addition to the subject, a sentence must also have a predicate. The **predicate** contains a verb and tells something about the subject. In addition to the verb, a predicate can also contain a direct or indirect object, object of a preposition, and other phrases.

The cats napped on the front porch.

In this sentence, cats is the subject because the sentence is about cats.

The **complete predicate** is everything else in the sentence: *napped on the front porch.* This phrase is the predicate because it tells us what the cats did.

This sentence can be broken down into a simple subject and predicate:

Cats napped.

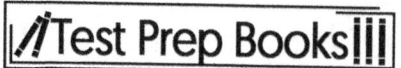

Writing or Editing Reports

In this sentence, *cats* is the simple subject, and *napped* is the **simple predicate**.

Although the sentence is very short and doesn't offer much information, it's still considered a complete sentence because it contains a subject and predicate.

Like a compound subject, a sentence can also have a **compound predicate**. This is when the subject is or does two or more things in the sentence.

> This easy chair reclines and swivels.

In this sentence, *this easy chair* is the complete subject. *Reclines and swivels* shows two actions of the chair, so this is the compound predicate.

Subject-Verb Agreement

The subject of a sentence and its verb must agree. The cornerstone rule of **subject-verb agreement** is that subject and verb must agree in number. Whether the subject is singular or plural, the verb must follow suit.

> Incorrect: The houses is new.
> Correct: The houses are new.
> Also Correct: The house is new.

In other words, a singular subject requires a singular verb; a plural subject requires a plural verb. The words or phrases that come between the subject and verb do not alter this rule.

> Incorrect: The houses built of brick is new.
> Correct: The houses built of brick are new.
>
> Incorrect: The houses with the sturdy porches is new.
> Correct: The houses with the sturdy porches are new.

The subject will always follow the verb when a sentence begins with *here* or *there*. Identify these with care.

> Incorrect: Here *is* the *houses* with sturdy porches.
> Correct: Here *are* the *houses* with sturdy porches.

The subject in the sentences above is not *here*, it is *houses*. Remember, *here* and *there* are never subjects. Be careful that contractions such as *here's* or *there're* do not cause confusion!

Two subjects joined by *and* require a plural verb form, except when the two combine to make one thing:

> Incorrect: Garrett and Jonathan is over there.
> Correct: Garrett and Jonathan are over there.
>
> Incorrect: Spaghetti and meatballs are a delicious meal!
> Correct: Spaghetti and meatballs is a delicious meal!

In the example above, *spaghetti and meatballs* is a compound noun. However, *Garrett and Jonathan* is not a compound noun.

Writing or Editing Reports

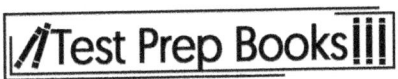

Two singular subjects joined by *or, either/or,* or *neither/nor* call for a singular verb form.

   Incorrect: Butter or syrup *are* acceptable.
   Correct: Butter or syrup *is* acceptable.

Plural subjects joined by *or, either/or,* or *neither/nor* are, indeed, plural.

   The chairs or the boxes *are* being moved next.

If one subject is singular and the other is plural, the verb should agree with the closest noun.

   Correct: The chair or the boxes *are* being moved next.
   Correct: The chairs or the box *is* being moved next.

Some plurals of money, distance, and time call for a singular verb.

   Incorrect: Three dollars *are* enough to buy that.
   Correct: Three dollars *is* enough to buy that.

For words declaring degrees of quantity such as *many of, some of,* or *most of,* let the noun that follows *of* be the guide:

   Incorrect: Many of the books *is* in the shelf.
   Correct: Many of the books *are* in the shelf.

   Incorrect: Most of the pie *are* on the table.
   Correct: Most of the pie *is* on the table.

For indefinite pronouns like anybody or everybody, use singular verbs.

   Everybody *is* going to the store.

However, the pronouns *few, many, several, all, some,* and *both* have their own rules and use plural forms.

   Some *are* ready.

Some nouns like *crowd* and *congress* are called *collective nouns* and they require a singular verb form.

   Congress *is* in session.
   The news *is* over.

Books and movie titles, though, including plural nouns such as *Great Expectations*, also require a singular verb. Remember that only the subject affects the verb. While writing tricky subject-verb arrangements, say them aloud. Listen to them. Once the rules have been learned, one's ear will become sensitive to them, making it easier to pick out what's right and what's wrong.

Direct Objects

The **direct object** is the part of the sentence that receives the action of the verb. It is a noun and can usually be found after the verb. To find the direct object, first find the verb, and then ask the question *who* or *what* after it.

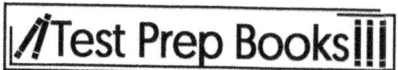

The bear climbed the tree.

What did the bear climb? *the tree*

Indirect Objects

An **indirect object** receives the direct object. It is usually found between the verb and the direct object. A strategy for identifying the indirect object is to find the verb and ask the questions *to whom/for whom* or *to what/for what*.

Jane made her daughter a cake.

For whom did Jane make the cake? *her daughter*

Cake is the direct object because it is what Jane made, and *daughter* is the indirect object because she receives the cake.

Complements

A **complement** completes the meaning of an expression. A complement can be a pronoun, noun, or adjective. A verb complement refers to the direct object or indirect object in the sentence. An object complement gives more information about the direct object:

The magician got the kids excited.

Kids is the direct object, and *excited* is the object complement.

A **subject complement** comes after a linking verb. It is typically an adjective or noun that gives more information about the subject:

The king was noble and spared the thief's life.

Noble describes the *king* and follows the linking verb *was*.

Predicate Nouns

A **predicate noun** renames the subject:

John is a carpenter.

The subject is *John*, and the predicate noun is *carpenter*.

Predicate Adjectives

A **predicate adjective** describes the subject:

Margaret is beautiful.

The subject is *Margaret*, and the predicate adjective is *beautiful*.

Writing or Editing Reports

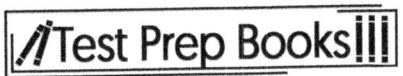

Homonyms

Homonyms are words that sound the same but are spelled differently, and they have different meanings. There are several common homonyms that give writers trouble.

There, They're, and Their

The word *there* can be used as an adverb, adjective, or pronoun:

There are ten children on the swim team this summer.

I put my book over *there*, but now I can't find it.

The word *they're* is a contraction of the words *they* and *are*:

They're flying in from Texas on Tuesday.

The word *their* is a possessive pronoun:

I store *their* winter clothes in the attic.

Its and It's

Its is a possessive pronoun:

The cat licked *its* injured paw.

It's is the contraction for the words *it* and *is*:

It's unbelievable how many people opted not to vote in the last election.

Your and You're

Your is a possessive pronoun:

Can I borrow *your* lawnmower this weekend?

You're is a contraction for the words *you* and *are*:

You're about to embark on a fantastic journey.

To, Too, and Two

To is an adverb or a preposition used to show direction, relationship, or purpose:

We are going *to* New York.

They are going *to* see a show.

Too is an adverb that means more than enough, also, and very:

You have had *too* much candy.

We are on vacation that week, *too*.

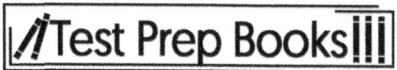

Two is the written-out form of the numeral 2:

Two of the shirts didn't fit, so I will have to return them.

New and Knew
New is an adjective that means recent:

There's a *new* customer on the phone.

Knew is the past tense of the verb *know*:

I *knew* you'd have fun on this ride.

Affect and Effect
Affect and effect are complicated because they are used as both nouns and verbs, have similar meanings, and are pronounced the same.

	Affect	**Effect**
Noun Definition	emotional state	result
Noun Example	The patient's affect was flat.	The effects of smoking are well documented.
Verb Definition	to influence	to bring about
Verb Example	The pollen count affects my allergies.	The new candidate hopes to effect change.

Independent and Dependent Clauses

Independent and *dependent* clauses are strings of words that contain both a subject and a verb. An **independent clause** *can* stand alone as complete thought, but a dependent clause *cannot*. A **dependent clause** relies on other words to be a complete sentence.

Independent clause: The keys are on the counter.
Dependent clause: If the keys are on the counter

Notice that both clauses have a subject (*keys*) and a verb (*are*). The independent clause expresses a complete thought, but the word *if* at the beginning of the dependent clause makes it *dependent* on other words to be a complete thought.

Independent clause: If the keys are on the counter, please give them to me.

This example constitutes a complete sentence since it includes at least one verb and one subject and is a complete thought. In this case, the independent clause has two subjects (*keys* & an implied *you*) and two verbs (*are* & *give*).

Independent clause: I went to the store.
Dependent clause: Because we are out of milk,

Complete Sentence: Because we are out of milk, I went to the store.
Complete Sentence: I went to the store because we are out of milk.

Writing or Editing Reports

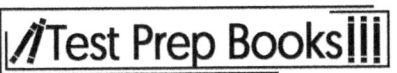

Writing Strategy

Distinguishing Between Common Modes of Writing

To distinguish between the common modes of writing, it is important to identify the primary purpose of the work. This can be determined by considering what the author is trying to say to the reader. Although there are countless different styles of writing, all written works tend to fall under four primary categories: argumentative/persuasive, informative expository, descriptive, and narrative.

The below table highlights the purpose, distinct characteristics, and examples of each rhetorical mode.

Writing Mode	Purpose	Distinct Characteristics	Examples
Argumentative	To persuade	Opinions, loaded or subjective language, evidence, suggestions of what the reader should do, calls to action	Critical reviews Political journals Letters of recommendation Cover letters Advertising
Informative	To teach or inform	Objective language, definitions, instructions, factual information	Business and scientific reports Textbooks Instruction manuals News articles Personal letters Wills Informative essays Travel guides Study guides
Descriptive	To deliver sensory details to the reader	Heavy use of adjectives and imagery, language that appeals to any of the five senses	Poetry Journal entries Often used in narrative mode
Narrative	To tell a story, share an experience, entertain	Series of events, plot, characters, dialogue, conflict	Novels Short stories Novellas Anecdotes Biographies Epic poems Autobiographies

Identifying Common Types of Writing
The following steps help to identify examples of common types within the modes of writing:

1. Identifying the audience—to whom or for whom the author is writing
2. Determining the author's purpose—why the author is writing the piece
3. Analyzing the word choices and how they are used

25

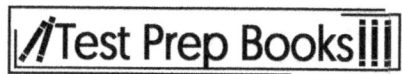

Writing or Editing Reports

To demonstrate, the following passage has been marked to illustrate *the addressee*, the author's purpose, and word choices:

> *To Whom It May Concern*:
>
> I am <u>extraordinarily excited</u> to be applying to the Master of Environmental Science program at Australian National University. I believe the richness in biological and cultural diversity, as well as Australia's close proximity to the Great Barrier Reef, would provide a <u>deeply fulfilling</u> educational experience. *I am writing to express why I believe I would be an <u>excellent</u> addition to the program.*
>
> While in college, I participated in a three-month public health internship in Ecuador, where I spent time both learning about medicine in a third world country and also about the Ecuadorian environment, including the Amazon Jungle and the Galápagos Islands. <u>My favorite experience</u> through the internship, besides swimming with sea lions in San Cristóbal, was helping to neutralize parasitic potable water and collect samples for analysis in Puyo.
>
> Though my undergraduate studies related primarily to the human body, I took several courses in natural science, including a year of chemistry, biology, and physics as well as a course in a calculus. <u>I am confident</u> that my fundamental knowledge in these fields will prepare me for the science courses integral to the Masters of Environmental Science.

Having identified the *addressee*, it is evident that this selection is a letter of some kind. Further inspection into the author's purpose, seen in *bold*, shows that the author is trying to explain why he or she should be accepted into the environmental science program, which automatically places it into the argumentative mode as the writer is trying to persuade the reader to agree and to incite the reader into action by encouraging the program to accept the writer as a candidate. In addition to revealing the purpose, the use of emotional language—extraordinarily, excellent, deeply fulfilling, favorite experience, confident—illustrates that this is a persuasive piece. It also provides evidence for why this person would be an excellent addition to the program—their experience in Ecuador and with scientific curriculum.

The following passage presents an opportunity to solidify this method of analysis and practice the steps above to determine the mode of writing:

> The biological effects of laughter have long been an interest of medicine and psychology. Laughing is often speculated to reduce blood pressure because it induces feelings of relaxation and elation. Participating students watched a series of videos that elicited laughter, and their blood pressure was taken before and after the viewings. An average decrease in blood pressure was observed, though resulting p-values attest that the results were not significant.

This selection contains factual and scientific information, is devoid of any adjectives or flowery descriptions, and is not trying to convince the reader of any particular stance. Though the audience is not directly addressed, the purpose of the passage is to present the results of an experiment to those who would be interested in the biological effects of laughter—most likely a scientific community. Thus, this passage is an example of informative writing.

Writing or Editing Reports

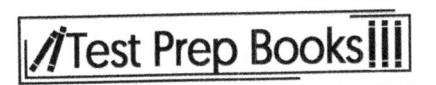

Below is another passage to help identify examples of the common writing modes, taken from *The Endeavor Journal of Sir Joseph Banks*:

10th May 1769 – THE ENGLISH CREW GET TAHITIAN NAMES

We have now got the Indian name of the Island, Otahite, so therefore for the future I shall call it. As for our own names the Indians find so much dificulty in pronouncing them that we are forcd to indulge them in calling us what they please, or rather what they say when they attempt to pronounce them. I give here the List: Captn Cooke *Toote*, Dr Solander *Torano*, Mr Hicks *Hete*, Mr Gore *Toárro*, Mr Molineux *Boba* from his Christian name Robert, Mr Monkhouse *Mato*, and myself *Tapáne*. In this manner they have names for almost every man in the ship.

This extract contains no elements of an informative or persuasive intent and does not seem to follow any particular line of narrative. The passage gives a list of the different names that the Indians have given the crew members, as well as the name of an island. Although there is no context for the selection, through the descriptions, it is clear that the author and his comrades are on an island trying to communicate with the native inhabitants. Hence, this passage is a journal that reflects the descriptive mode.

These are only a few of the many examples that can be found in the four primary modes of writing.

Determining the Appropriate Mode of Writing

The author's **primary purpose** is defined as the reason an author chooses to write a selection, and it is often dependent on their **audience**. A biologist writing a textbook, for example, does so to communicate scientific knowledge to an audience of people who want to study biology. An audience can be as broad as the entire global population or as specific as women fighting for equal rights in the bicycle repair industry. Whatever the audience, it is important that the author considers its demographics—age, gender, culture, language, education level, etc.

If the author's purpose is to persuade or inform, he or she will consider how much the intended audience knows about the subject. For example, if an author is writing on the importance of recycling to anyone who will listen, he or she will use the informative mode—including background information on recycling—and the argumentative mode—evidence for why it works, while also using simple diction so that it is easy for everyone to understand. If, on the other hand, the writer is proposing new methods for recycling using solar energy, the audience is probably already familiar with standard recycling processes and will require less background information, as well as more technical language inherent to the scientific community.

If the author's purpose is to entertain through a story or a poem, he or she will need to consider whom he/she is trying to entertain. If an author is writing a script for a children's cartoon, the plot, language, conflict, characters, and humor would align with the interests of the age demographic of that audience. On the other hand, if an author is trying to entertain adults, he or she may write content not suitable for children. The author's purpose and audience are generally interdependent.

Development

Brainstorming

One of the most important steps in writing an essay is prewriting. Before drafting an essay, it's helpful to think about the topic for a moment or two, in order to gain a more solid understanding of the task.

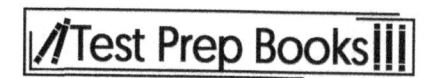

Then, spending about five minutes jotting down the immediate ideas that could work for the essay is recommended. It is a way to get some words on the page and offer a reference for ideas for when drafting. Scratch paper is provided for writers to use any prewriting techniques such as webbing, free writing, or listing. The goal is to get ideas out of the mind and onto the page.

Considering Opposing Viewpoints
In the planning stage, it's important to consider all aspects of the topic, including different viewpoints on the subject. There are more than two ways to look at a topic, and a strong argument considers those opposing viewpoints. Considering opposing viewpoints can help writers present a fair, balanced, and informed essay that shows consideration for all readers. This approach can also strengthen an argument by recognizing and potentially refuting opposing viewpoint(s).

Drawing from personal experience may help to support ideas. For example, if the goal for writing is a personal narrative, then the story should come from the writer's own life. Many writers find it helpful to draw from personal experience, even in an essay that is not strictly narrative. Personal anecdotes or short stories can help to illustrate a point in other types of essays as well.

Moving from Brainstorming to Planning
Once the ideas are on the page, it's time to turn them into a solid plan for the essay. The best ideas from the brainstorming results can then be developed into a more formal outline. An outline typically has one main point (the thesis) and at least three sub-points that support the main point. Here's an example:

<u>Main Idea</u>

- Point #1
- Point #2
- Point #3

Of course, there will be details under each point, but this approach is the best for dealing with timed writing.

Staying on Track
Basing the essay on the outline aids in both organization and coherence. The goal is to ensure that there is enough time to develop each sub-point in the essay, roughly spending an equal amount of time on each idea. Keeping an eye on the time will help. If there are fifteen minutes left to draft the essay, then it makes sense to spend about 5 minutes on each of the ideas. Staying on task is critical to success, and timing out the parts of the essay can help writers avoid feeling overwhelmed.

Writing or Editing Reports

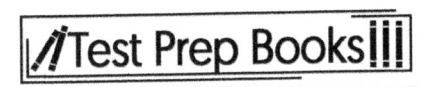

Parts of the Essay
The **introduction** has to do a few important things:

- Establish the *topic* of the essay in original wording (i.e., not just repeating the prompt)
- Clarify the significance/importance of the topic or purpose for writing (not too many details, a brief overview)
- Offer a **thesis statement** that identifies the writer's own viewpoint on the topic (typically one-two brief sentences as a clear, concise explanation of the main point on the topic)

Body paragraphs reflect the ideas developed in the outline. Three-four points is probably sufficient for a short essay, and they should include the following:

- A **topic sentence** that identifies the sub-point (e.g., a reason why, a way how, a cause or effect)

- A detailed *explanation* of the point, explaining why the writer thinks this point is valid

- Illustrative *examples*, such as personal examples or real-world examples, that support and validate the point (i.e., "prove" the point)

- A *concluding sentence* that connects the examples, reasoning, and analysis to the point being made

The **conclusion**, or final paragraph, should be brief and should reiterate the focus, clarifying why the discussion is significant or important. It is important to avoid adding specific details or new ideas to this paragraph. The purpose of the conclusion is to sum up what has been said to bring the discussion to a close.

Don't Panic!
Writing an essay can be overwhelming, and performance panic is a natural response. The outline serves as a basis for the writing and helps to keep writers focused. Getting stuck can also happen, and it's helpful to remember that brainstorming can be done at any time during the writing process. Following the steps of the writing process is the best defense against writer's block.

Timed essays can be particularly stressful, but assessors are trained to recognize the necessary planning and thinking for these timed efforts. Using the plan above and sticking to it helps with time management. Timing each part of the process helps writers stay on track. Sometimes writers try to cover too much in their essays. If time seems to be running out, this is an opportunity to determine whether all of the ideas in the outline are necessary. Three body paragraphs are sufficient, and more than that is probably too much to cover in a short essay.

More isn't always *better* in writing. A strong essay will be clear and concise. It will avoid unnecessary or repetitive details. It is better to have a concise, five-paragraph essay that makes a clear point, than a ten-paragraph essay that doesn't. The goal is to write one-two pages of quality writing. Paragraphs should also reflect balance; if the introduction goes to the bottom of the first page, the writing may be going off-track or be repetitive. It's best to fall into the one-two page range, but a complete, well-developed essay is the ultimate goal.

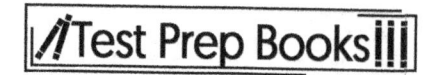

The Final Steps

Leaving a few minutes at the end to revise and proofread offers an opportunity for writers to polish things up. Putting one's self in the reader's shoes and focusing on what the essay actually says helps writers identify problems—it's a movement from the mindset of writer to the mindset of editor. The goal is to have a clean, clear copy of the essay. The following areas should be considered when proofreading:

- Sentence fragments
- Awkward sentence structure
- Run-on sentences
- Incorrect word choice
- Grammatical agreement errors
- Spelling errors
- Punctuation errors
- Capitalization errors

The Short Overview

The essay may seem challenging, but following these steps can help writers focus:

- Take one-two minutes to think about the topic.
- Generate some ideas through brainstorming (three-four minutes).
- Organize ideas into a brief outline, selecting just three-four main points to cover in the essay (eventually the body paragraphs).
- Develop essay in parts:
- Introduction paragraph, with intro to topic and main points
- Viewpoint on the subject at the end of the introduction
- Body paragraphs, based on outline
- Each paragraph: makes a main point, explains the viewpoint, uses examples to support the point
- Brief conclusion highlighting the main points and closing
- Read over the essay (last five minutes).
- Look for any obvious errors, making sure that the writing makes sense.

Organization

Good writing is not merely a random collection of sentences. No matter how well written, sentences must relate and coordinate appropriately with one another. If not, the writing seems random, haphazard, and disorganized. Therefore, good writing must be organized, where each sentence fits a larger context and relates to the sentences around it.

Transition Words

The writer should act as a guide, showing the reader how all the sentences fit together. Consider the seat belt example again:

> Seat belts save more lives than any other automobile safety feature. Many studies show that airbags save lives as well. Not all cars have airbags. Many older cars don't. Air bags aren't entirely reliable. Studies show that in 15% of accidents, airbags don't deploy as designed. Seat belt malfunctions are extremely rare.

Writing or Editing Reports

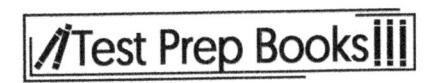

There's nothing wrong with any of these sentences individually, but together they're disjointed and difficult to follow. The best way for the writer to communicate information is through the use of transition words. Here are examples of transition words and phrases that tie sentences together, enabling a more natural flow:

- To show causality: as a result, therefore, and consequently
- To compare and contrast: *however*, *but*, and *on the other hand*
- To introduce examples: *for instance*, *namely*, and *including*
- To show order of importance: *foremost*, *primarily*, *secondly*, and *lastly*

NOTE: This is not a complete list of transitions. There are many more that can be used; however, most fit into these or similar categories. The important point is that the words should clearly show the relationship between sentences, supporting information, and the main idea.

Here is an update to the previous example using transition words. These changes make it easier to read and bring clarity to the writer's points:

> Seat belts save more lives than any other automobile safety feature. Many studies show that airbags save lives as well; however, not all cars have airbags. For instance, some older cars don't. Furthermore, air bags aren't entirely reliable. For example, studies show that in 15% of accidents, airbags don't deploy as designed, but, on the other hand, seat belt malfunctions are extremely rare.

Also, be prepared to analyze whether the writer is using the best transition word or phrase for the situation. Take this sentence for example: "As a result, seat belt malfunctions are extremely rare." This sentence doesn't make sense in the context above because the writer is trying to show the contrast between seat belts and airbags, not the causality.

Logical Sequence

Even if the writer includes plenty of information to support their point, the writing is only coherent when the information is in a logical order. First, the writer should introduce the main idea, whether for a paragraph, a section, or the entire piece. Second, they should present evidence to support the main idea by using transitional language. This shows the reader how the information relates to the main idea and to the sentences around it. The writer should then take time to interpret the information, making sure necessary connections are obvious to the reader. Finally, the writer can summarize the information in a closing section.

Though most writing follows this pattern, it isn't a set rule. Sometimes writers change the order for effect. For example, the writer can begin with a surprising piece of supporting information to grab the reader's attention, and then transition to the main idea. Thus, if a passage doesn't follow the logical order, don't immediately assume it's wrong. However, most writing usually settles into a logical sequence after a nontraditional beginning.

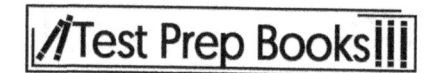

Introductions and Conclusions

Examining the writer's strategies for introductions and conclusions puts the reader in the right mindset to interpret the rest of the text. Look for methods the writer might use for introductions such as:

- Stating the main point immediately, followed by outlining how the rest of the piece supports this claim.

- Establishing important, smaller pieces of the main idea first, and then grouping these points into a case for the main idea.

- Opening with a quotation, anecdote, question, seeming paradox, or other piece of interesting information, and then using it to lead to the main point.

Whatever method the writer chooses, the introduction should make their intention clear, establish their voice as a credible one, and encourage a person to continue reading.

Conclusions tend to follow a similar pattern. In them, the writer restates their main idea a final time, often after summarizing the smaller pieces of that idea. If the introduction uses a quote or anecdote to grab the reader's attention, the conclusion often makes reference to it again. Whatever way the writer chooses to arrange the conclusion, the final restatement of the main idea should be clear and simple for the reader to interpret. Finally, conclusions shouldn't introduce any new information.

Effective Language Use

Precision

People often think of precision in terms of math, but precise word choice is another key to successful writing. Since language itself is imprecise, it's important for the writer to find the exact word or words to convey the full, intended meaning of a given situation. For example:

> The number of deaths has gone down since seat belt laws started.

There are several problems with this sentence. First, the word *deaths* is too general. From the context, it's assumed that the writer is referring only to deaths caused by car accidents. However, without clarification, the sentence lacks impact and is probably untrue. The phrase "gone down" might be accurate, but a more precise word could provide more information and greater accuracy. Did the numbers show a slow and steady decrease of highway fatalities or a sudden drop? If the latter is true, the writer is missing a chance to make their point more dramatically. Instead of "gone down" they could substitute *plummeted*, *fallen drastically*, or *rapidly diminished* to bring the information to life. Also, the phrase "seat belt laws" is unclear. Does it refer to laws requiring cars to include seat belts or to laws requiring drivers and passengers to use them? Finally, *started* is not a strong verb. Words like *enacted* or *adopted* are more direct and make the content more real. When put together, these changes create a far more powerful sentence:

> The number of highway fatalities has plummeted since laws requiring seat belt usage were enacted.

However, it's important to note that precise word choice can sometimes be taken too far. If the writer of the sentence above takes precision to an extreme, it might result in the following:

Writing or Editing Reports

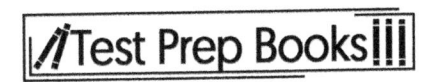

The incidence of high-speed, automobile accident related fatalities has decreased 75% and continued to remain at historical lows since the initial set of federal legislations requiring seat belt use were enacted in 1992.

This sentence is extremely precise, but it takes so long to achieve that precision that it suffers from a lack of clarity. Precise writing is about finding the right balance between information and flow. This is also an issue of conciseness (discussed in the next section).

The last thing to consider with precision is a word choice that's not only unclear or uninteresting, but also confusing or misleading. For example:

The number of highway fatalities has become hugely lower since laws requiring seat belt use were enacted.

In this case, the reader might be confused by the word *hugely*. Huge means large, but here the writer uses *hugely* to describe something small. Though most readers can decipher this, doing so disconnects them from the flow of the writing and makes the writer's point less effective.

Conciseness

"Less is more" is a good rule to follow when writing a sentence. Unfortunately, writers often include extra words and phrases that seem necessary at the time but add nothing to the main idea. This confuses the reader and creates unnecessary repetition. Writing that lacks conciseness is usually guilty of excessive wordiness and redundant phrases. Here's an example containing both of these issues:

> When legislators decided to begin creating legislation making it mandatory for automobile drivers and passengers to make use of seat belts while in cars, a large number of them made those laws for reasons that were political reasons.

There are several empty or "fluff" words here that take up too much space. These can be eliminated while still maintaining the writer's meaning. For example:

- "Decided to begin" could be shortened to "began"
- "Making it mandatory for" could be shortened to "requiring"
- "Make use of" could be shortened to "use"
- "A large number" could be shortened to "many"

In addition, there are several examples of redundancy that can be eliminated:

- "Legislators decided to begin creating legislation" and "made those laws"
- "Automobile drivers and passengers" and "while in cars"
- "Reasons that were political reasons"

These changes are incorporated as follows:

> When legislators began requiring drivers and passengers to use seat belts, many of them did so for political reasons.

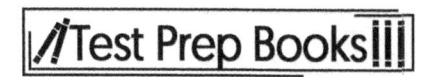

There are many general examples of redundant phrases, such as "add an additional," "complete and total," "time schedule," and "transportation vehicle." If asked to identify a redundant phrase on the test, look for words that are close together with the same (or similar) meanings.

Sentence Structure

When examining writing, be mindful of grammar, structure, spelling, and patterns. Sentences can come in varying sizes and shapes, so the point of grammatical correctness is not stamp out creativity or diversity in writing. Rather, grammatical correctness ensures that writing will be enjoyable and clear. One of the most common methods for catching errors is to mouth the words as you read them. Many typos are fixed automatically by our brain, but mouthing the words often circumvents this instinct and helps one read what's actually on the page. Often, grammar errors are caught not by memorization of grammar rules but by the training of one's mind to know whether something *sounds* right or not.

Components of Sentences
Clauses

Clauses contain a subject and a verb. An *independent clause* can function as a complete sentence on its own, but it might also be one component of a longer sentence. *Dependent clauses* cannot stand alone as complete sentences. They rely on independent clauses to complete their meaning. Dependent clauses usually begin with a subordinating conjunction. Independent and dependent clauses are sometimes also referred to as **main clauses** and **subordinate clauses**, respectively. The following structure highlights the differences:

Apiculturists raise honeybees because they love insects.

Apiculturists raise honeybees is an independent or main clause. The subject is *apiculturists*, and the verb is *raise*. It expresses a complete thought and could be a standalone sentence.

Because they love insects is a dependent or subordinate clause. If it were not attached to the independent clause, it would be a sentence fragment. While it contains a subject and verb—*they love*—this clause is dependent because it begins with the subordinate conjunction *because*. Thus, it does not express a complete thought on its own.

Another type of clause is a **relative clause**, and it is sometimes referred to as an **adjective clause** because it gives further description about the noun. A relative clause begins with a **relative pronoun**: *that, which, who, whom, whichever, whomever,* or *whoever*. It may also begin with a **relative adverb**: *where, why,* or *when*. Here's an example of a relative clause, functioning as an adjective:

The strawberries that I bought yesterday are already beginning to spoil.

Here, the relative clause is *that I bought yesterday*; the relative pronoun is *that*. The subject is *I*, and the verb is *bought*. The clause modifies the subject *strawberries* by answering the question, "Which strawberries?" Here's an example of a relative clause with an adverb:

The tutoring center is a place where students can get help with homework.

The relative clause is *where students can get help with homework*, and it gives more information about a place by describing what kind of place it is. It begins with the relative adverb *where* and contains the noun *students* along with its verb phrase *can get*.

Writing or Editing Reports

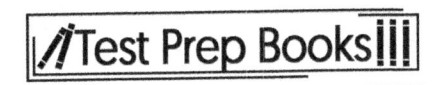

Relative clauses may be further divided into two types: essential or nonessential. *Essential clauses* contain identifying information without which the sentence would lose significant meaning or not make sense. These are also sometimes referred to as **restrictive clauses**. The sentence above contains an example of an essential relative clause. Here is what happens when the clause is removed:

> The tutoring center is a place where students can get help with homework.
>
> The tutoring center is a place.

Without the relative clause, the sentence loses the majority of its meaning; thus, the clause is essential or restrictive.

Nonessential clauses—also referred to as **non-restrictive clauses**—offer additional information about a noun in the sentence, but they do not significantly control the overall meaning of the sentence. The following example indicates a nonessential clause:

> New York City, which is located in the northeastern part of the country, is the most populated city in America.
>
> New York City is the most populated city in America.

Even without the relative clause, the sentence is still understandable and continues to communicate its central message about New York City. Thus, it is a nonessential clause.

Punctuation differs between essential and nonessential relative clauses, too. Nonessential clauses are set apart from the sentence using commas whereas essential clauses are not separated with commas. Also, the relative pronoun *that* is generally used for essential clauses, while *which* is used for nonessential clauses. The following examples clarify this distinction:

> *Romeo and Juliet* is my favorite play *that Shakespeare wrote*.

The relative clause *that Shakespeare wrote* contains essential, controlling information about the noun *play*, limiting it to those plays by Shakespeare. Without it, it would seem that *Romeo and Juliet* is the speaker's favorite play out of every play ever written, not simply from Shakespeare's repertoire.

> *Romeo and Juliet*, *which Shakespeare wrote*, is my favorite play.

Here, the nonessential relative clause—"which Shakespeare wrote"—modifies *Romeo and Juliet*. It doesn't provide controlling information about the play, but simply offers further background details. Thus, commas are needed.

Phrases

A **phrase** is a group of words that do not make a complete thought or a clause. They are parts of sentences or clauses. Phrases can be used as nouns, adjectives, or adverbs. A phrase does not contain both a subject and a verb.

A **noun phrase** consists of a noun and all its modifiers—adjectives, adverbs, and determiners. Noun phrases can serve many functions in a sentence, acting as subjects, objects, and object complements:

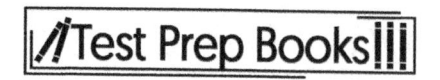

The shallow yellow bowl sits on the top shelf.

Nina just bought *some incredibly fresh organic produce*.

Prepositional Phrases

A **prepositional phrase** shows the relationship between a word in the sentence and the object of the preposition. The object of the preposition is a noun that follows the preposition.

The orange pillows are on the couch.

On is the preposition, and *couch* is the object of the preposition.

She brought her friend with the nice car.

With is the preposition, and *car* is the object of the preposition. Here are some common prepositions:

about	as	at	after
by	for	from	in
of	on	to	with

Verbals and Verbal Phrases

Verbals are forms of verbs that act as other parts of speech. They can be used as nouns, adjectives, or adverbs. Though they are verb forms, they are not to be used as the verb in the sentence. A word group that is based on a verbal is considered a *verbal phrase*. There are three major types of verbals: *participles, gerunds,* and *infinitives.*

Participles are verbals that act as adjectives. The present participle ends in *–ing*, and the past participle ends in *–d, -ed, -n*, or *-t*.

Verb	Present Participle	Past Participle
walk	walking	walked
share	sharing	shared

Participial phrases are made up of the participle and modifiers, complements, or objects.

Crying for most of an hour, the baby didn't seem to want to nap.

Having already taken this course, the student was bored during class.

Crying for most of an hour and *Having already taken this course* are the participial phrases.

Gerunds are verbals that are used as nouns and end in *–ing*. A gerund can be the subject or object of the sentence like a noun. Note that a present participle can also end in *–ing*, so it is important to distinguish between the two. The gerund is used as a noun, while the participle is used as an adjective.

Swimming is my favorite sport.

I wish I were sleeping.

Writing or Editing Reports

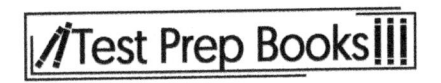

A **gerund phrase** includes the gerund and any modifiers or complements, direct objects, indirect objects, or pronouns.

> Cleaning the house is my least favorite weekend activity.

Cleaning the house is the gerund phrase acting as the subject of the sentence.

> The most important goal this year is raising money for charity.

Raising money for charity is the gerund phrase acting as the direct object.

> The police accused the woman of stealing the car.

The *gerund* phrase *stealing the car* is the object of the preposition in this sentence.

An **infinitive** is a verbal made up of the word to and a verb. Infinitives can be used as nouns, adjectives, or adverbs.

> Examples: To eat, to jump, to swim, to lie, to call, to work

An **infinitive phrase** is made up of the infinitive plus any complements or modifiers. The infinitive phrase *to wait* is used as the subject in this sentence:

> To wait was not what I had in mind.

The infinitive phrase *to sing* is used as the subject complement in this sentence:

> Her dream is to sing.

The infinitive phrase *to grow* is used as an adverb in this sentence:

> Children must eat to grow.

Appositive Phrases

An **appositive** is a noun or noun phrase that renames a noun that comes immediately before it in the sentence. An appositive can be a single word or several words. These phrases can be *essential* or *nonessential*. An essential appositive phrase is necessary to the meaning of the sentence and a nonessential appositive phrase is not. It is important to be able to distinguish these for purposes of comma use.

> Essential: My sister Christina works at a school.

Naming which sister is essential to the meaning of the sentence, so no commas are needed.

> Nonessential: My sister, who is a teacher, is coming over for dinner tonight.

Who is a teacher is not essential to the meaning of the sentence, so commas are required.

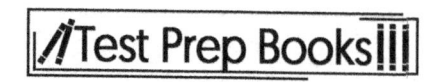

Absolute Phrases

An **absolute phrase** modifies a noun without using a conjunction. It is not the subject of the sentence and is not a complete thought on its own. Absolute phrases are set off from the independent clause with a comma.

Arms outstretched, she yelled at the sky.

All things considered, this has been a great day.

Structures of Sentences

All sentences contain the same basic elements: a subject and a verb. The **subject** is who or what the sentence is about; the **verb** describes the subject's action or condition. However, these elements, subjects and verbs, can be combined in different ways. The following graphic describes the different types of sentence structures.

Sentence Structure	Independent Clauses	Dependent Clauses
Simple	1	0
Compound	2 or more	0
Complex	1	1 or more
Compound-Complex	2 or more	1 or more

A **simple sentence** expresses a complete thought and consists of one subject and verb combination:

The children ate pizza.

The subject is *children*. The verb is *ate*.

Either the subject or the verb may be *compound*—that is, it could have more than one element:

The children and their parents ate pizza.

The children *ate pizza and watched a movie*.

All of these are still simple sentences. Despite having either compound subjects or compound verbs, each sentence still has only one subject and verb combination.

Compound sentences combine two or more simple sentences to form one sentence that has multiple subject-verb combinations:

The children ate pizza, and *their parents watched a movie*.

This structure is comprised of two independent clauses: (1) *the children ate pizza* and (2) *their parents watched a movie.* Compound sentences join different subject-verb combinations using a comma and a coordinating conjunction.

I called my mom, *but* she didn't answer the phone.

The weather was stormy, *so* we canceled our trip to the beach.

Writing or Editing Reports

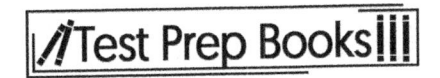

A **complex sentence** consists of an independent clause and one or more dependent clauses. Dependent clauses join a sentence using *subordinating conjunctions*. Some examples of subordinating conjunctions are *although, unless, as soon as, since, while, when, because, if,* and *before*.

> I missed class yesterday *because* my mother was ill.

> *Before* traveling to a new country, you need to exchange your money to the local currency.

The order of clauses determines their punctuation. If the dependent clause comes first, it should be separated from the independent clause with a comma. However, if the complex sentence consists of an independent clause followed by a dependent clause, then a comma is not always necessary.

A **compound-complex sentence** can be created by joining two or more independent clauses with at least one dependent clause:

> After the earthquake struck, thousands of homes were destroyed, and many families were left without a place to live.

The first independent clause in the compound structure includes a subordinating clause—*after the earthquake struck*. Thus, the structure is both complex and compound.

Types of Sentences

There isn't an overabundance of absolutes in grammar, but here is one: every sentence in the English language falls into one of four categories.

- Declarative: a simple statement that ends with a period

    The price of milk per gallon is the same as the price of gasoline.

- Imperative: a command, instruction, or request that ends with a period

    Buy milk when you stop to fill up your car with gas.

- Interrogative: a question that ends with a question mark

    Will you buy the milk?

- Exclamatory: a statement or command that expresses emotions like anger, urgency, or surprise and ends with an exclamation mark

    Buy the milk now!

Declarative sentences are the most common type, probably because they are comprised of the most general content, without any of the bells and whistles that the other three types contain. They are, simply, declarations or statements of any degree of seriousness, importance, or information.

Imperative sentences often seem to be missing a subject. The subject is there, though; it is just not visible or audible because it is *implied*. Look at the imperative example sentence.

> Buy the milk when you fill up your car with gas.

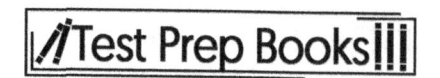

You is the implied subject, the one to whom the command is issued. This is sometimes called *the understood you* because it is understood that *you* is the subject of the sentence.

Interrogative sentences—those that ask questions—are defined as such from the idea of the word *interrogation*, the action of questions being asked of suspects by investigators. Although that is serious business, interrogative sentences apply to all kinds of questions.

To exclaim is at the root of **exclamatory sentences**. These are made with strong emotions behind them. The only technical difference between a declarative or imperative sentence and an exclamatory one is the exclamation mark at the end. The example declarative and imperative sentences can both become an exclamatory one simply by putting an exclamation mark at the end of the sentences.

> The price of milk per gallon is the same as the price of gasoline!
> Buy milk when you stop to fill up your car with gas!

After all, someone might be really excited by the price of gas or milk, or they could be mad at the person that will be buying the milk! However, as stated before, exclamation marks in abundance defeat their own purpose! After a while, they begin to cause fatigue! When used only for their intended purpose, they can have their expected and desired effect.

Punctuation

Capitalization

Here's a non-exhaustive list of things that should be capitalized:

- The first word of every sentence
- The first word of every line of poetry
- The first letter of proper nouns (World War II)
- Holidays (Valentine's Day)
- The days of the week and months of the year (Tuesday, March)
- The first word, last word, and all major words in the titles of books, movies, songs, and other creative works (In the novel, *To Kill a Mockingbird*, note that *a* is lowercase since it's not a major word, but *to* is capitalized since it's the first word of the title.)
- Titles when preceding a proper noun (President Roberto Gonzales, Aunt Judy)

When simply using a word such as president or secretary, though, the word is not capitalized.

> Officers of the new business must include a *president* and *treasurer*.

Seasons—spring, fall, etc.—are not capitalized.

North, *south*, *east*, and *west* are capitalized when referring to regions but are not when being used for directions. In general, if it's preceded by *the* it should be capitalized.

> I'm from the South.
> I drove south.

Writing or Editing Reports

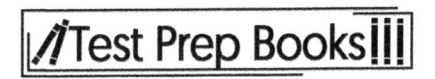

Ellipses

An **ellipsis (…)** is used to show that there is more to the quoted text than is necessary for the current discussion. Writers use them in place of words, lines, phrases, list content, or paragraphs that might just as easily have been omitted from a passage of writing. This can be done to save space or to focus only on the specifically relevant material.

> Exercise is good for some unexpected reasons. Watkins writes, "Exercise has many benefits such as…reducing cancer risk."

In the example above, the ellipsis takes the place of the other benefits of exercise that are more expected.

The ellipsis may also be used to show a pause in sentence flow.

> "I'm wondering…how this could happen," Dylan said in a soft voice.

Commas

A **comma (,)** is the punctuation mark that signifies a pause—breath—between parts of a sentence. It denotes a break of flow. As with so many aspects of writing structure, authors will benefit by memorizing all of the different ways in which commas can be used so as not to abuse them.

In a complex sentence—one that contains a subordinate (dependent) clause or clauses—the use of a comma is dictated by where the subordinate clause is located. If the subordinate clause is located before the main clause, a comma is needed between the two clauses.

> Because I don't have enough money, I will not order steak.

Generally, if the subordinate clause is placed after the main clause, no punctuation is needed.

> I did well on my exam because I studied two hours the night before.

Notice how the last clause is dependent because it requires the earlier independent clauses to make sense.

Use a comma on both sides of an interrupting phrase.

> I will pay for the ice cream, *chocolate and vanilla,* and I will eat it all myself.

The words forming the phrase in italics are nonessential (extra) information. To determine if a phrase is nonessential, try reading the sentence without the phrase and see if it's still coherent.

A comma is not necessary in this next sentence because no interruption—nonessential or extra information—has occurred. Read sentences aloud when uncertain.

I will pay for his chocolate and vanilla ice cream and I will eat it all myself.

If the nonessential phrase comes at the beginning of a sentence, a comma should only go at the end of the phrase. If the phrase comes at the end of a sentence, a comma should only go at the beginning of the phrase.

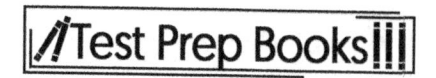

Other types of interruptions include the following:

- interjections: Oh no, I am not going.
- abbreviations: Barry Potter, M.D., specializes in heart disorders.
- direct addresses: Yes, Claudia, I am tired and going to bed.
- parenthetical phrases: His wife, lovely as she was, was not helpful.
- transitional phrases: Also, it is not possible.

The second comma in the following sentence is called an Oxford comma.

> I will pay for ice cream, syrup, and pop.

It is a comma used after the second-to-last item in a series of three or more items. It comes before the word *or* or *and*. Not everyone uses the **Oxford comma**; it is optional, but many believe it is needed. The comma functions as a tool to reduce confusion in writing. So, if omitting the Oxford comma would cause confusion, then it's best to include it.

Commas are used in math to mark the place of thousands in numerals, breaking them up so they are easier to read. Other uses for commas are in dates (*March 19, 2016*), letter greetings (*Dear Sally,*), and in between cities and states (*Louisville, KY*).

Semicolons

The **semicolon (;)** might be described as a heavy-handed comma. Take a look at these two examples:

> I will pay for the ice cream and I will pay for the syrup, but I will not pay for the steak.
> I will pay for the ice cream and I will pay for the syrup; I will not pay for the steak.

What's the difference? The first example has a comma and a conjunction separating the two independent clauses. The second example does not have a conjunction, but there are two independent clauses in the sentence. So something more than a comma is required. In this case, a semicolon is used.

Two independent clauses can only be joined in a sentence by either a comma and conjunction or a semicolon. If one of those tools is not used, the sentence will be a run-on. Remember that while the clauses are independent, they need to be closely related in order to be contained in one sentence.

Another use for the semicolon is to separate items in a list when the items themselves require commas.

> The family lived in Phoenix, Arizona; Oklahoma City, Oklahoma; and Raleigh, North Carolina.

Colons

Colons have many miscellaneous functions. Colons can be used to precede further information or a list. In these cases, a colon should only follow an independent clause.

> Humans take in sensory information through five basic senses: sight, hearing, smell, touch, and taste.

Writing or Editing Reports

The meal includes the following components:

- Caesar salad
- spaghetti
- garlic bread
- cake

The family got what they needed: a reliable vehicle.

While a comma is more common, a colon can also precede a formal quotation.

He said to the crowd: "Let's begin!"

The colon is used after the greeting in a formal letter.

Dear Sir:
To Whom It May Concern:

In the writing of time, the colon separates the minutes from the hour (*4:45 p.m.*). The colon can also be used to indicate a ratio between two numbers (*50:1*).

Hyphens

The **hyphen (-)** is a little hash mark that can be used to join words to show that they are linked.

Hyphens can connect two words that work together as a single adjective (a *compound adjective*).

honey-covered biscuits

Some words always require hyphens even if not serving as an adjective.

merry-go-round

Hyphens always go after certain prefixes like *anti-* & *all-*.

Hyphens should also be used when the absence of the hyphen would cause a strange vowel combination (*semi-engineer*) or confusion. For example, *re-collect* should be used to describe something being gathered twice rather than being written as *recollect*, which means to remember.

Parentheses and Dashes

Parentheses are half-round brackets that look like this: ( ). They set off a word, phrase, or sentence that is an afterthought, explanation, or side note relevant to the surrounding text but not essential. A pair of commas is often used to set off this sort of information, but parentheses are generally used for information that would not fit well within a sentence or that the writer deems not important enough to be structurally part of the sentence.

The picture of the heart (see above) shows the major parts you should memorize.
Mount Everest is one of three mountains in the world that are over 28,000 feet high (K2 and Kanchenjunga are the other two).

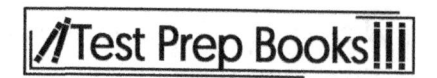

See how the sentences above are complete without the parenthetical statements? In the first example, *see above* would not have fit well within the flow of the sentence. The second parenthetical statement could have been a separate sentence, but the writer deemed the information not pertinent to the topic.

The **em-dash (—)** is a mark longer than a hyphen used as a punctuation mark in sentences and to set apart a relevant thought. Even after plucking out the line separated by the dash marks, the sentence will be intact and make sense.

> Looking out the airplane window at the landmarks—Lake Clarke, Thompson Community College, and the bridge—she couldn't help but feel excited to be home.

The dashes use is similar to that of parentheses or a pair of commas. So, what's the difference? Many believe that using dashes makes the clause within them stand out while using parentheses is subtler. It's advised to not use dashes when commas could be used instead.

Quotation Marks
Quotation marks ("") are used in a number of ways. Here are some instances where quotation marks should be used: to indicate a quote that was taken from somewhere else, either from a verbal or written source...

- Dialogue for characters in narratives. When characters speak, the first word should always be capitalized, and the punctuation goes inside the quotes. For example:

    Janie said, "The tree fell on my car during the hurricane."

- Around titles of songs, short stories, essays, and chapters in books
- To emphasize a certain word
- To refer to a word as the word itself

Apostrophes
This punctuation mark, the **apostrophe (')**, is a versatile little mark. It has a few different functions:

- Quotes: Apostrophes are used when a second quote is needed within a quote.

    In my letter to my friend, I wrote, "The girl had to get a new purse, and guess what Mary did? She said, 'I'd like to go with you to the store.' I knew Mary would buy it for her."

- Contractions: Another use for an apostrophe in the quote above is a contraction. *I'd* is used for *I would*.

- Possession: An apostrophe followed by the letter *s* shows possession (*Mary's* purse). If the possessive word is plural, the apostrophe generally just follows the word.

    The trees' leaves are all over the ground.

U.S. Government

United States Government and Politics

Constitutional Underpinnings

The **role of government** is to maintain a society and provide public services through its formal institutions, protect the citizens of the state, and regulate the economic system. To determine how a government should perform these functions and to protect the rights and liberties of the citizens, states enact a **constitution**, a written document that typically establishes the form of government and delegation of powers within the government, delineates limits on government, and defines protected rights, liberties, and privileges.

The many underpinnings, or foundations, upon which the *Constitution* of the United States was founded include:

Articles of Confederation (1781-1789)

The **Articles of Confederation** established a formal agreement or confederation between the original thirteen states. The Articles of Confederation established a central government composed of a unicameral legislative assembly in which each state was granted a single representative. Passing a bill required votes from nine of the thirteen representatives. Under the Articles of Confederation, the centralized government, the Continental Congress, was granted very limited powers, rendering it largely ineffective. Those powers included:

- Borrowing money from states or foreign government
- Creating post offices
- Appointing military offices
- Declaring war
- Signing treaties with foreign states

The weak central government established under the Articles of Confederation lacked the power to impose taxes, enforce a draft to staff the new army and navy, regulate trade, or enforce the laws enacted in Congress. As such, the sovereignty remained primarily with the states. Under the Articles, the states reserved the powers to impose taxes upon each other and the citizens of their states, regulate trade within their states, coin and print money, and sign treaties with foreign states. The states also often ignored the laws enacted by the Congress because there was no executive branch to enforce the law.

This imbalance of power between the central government and the states led to crisis within the states, resulting in economic difficulties and violence. The lack of common currency and investment in interstate infrastructure greatly hindered economic growth. In the years 1786 and 1787, farmers in several states staged a series of protests over local tax and debt collection imposed on struggling farms, commonly known as Shay's Rebellion.

Constitutional Convention, 1787

The failures of the Articles of Confederation to effectively govern on a national level directly led to the Constitutional Convention, and those experiences influenced the founders' decision to include a more robust federal government in the United States Constitution. The Constitutional Convention faced several challenges, including disputes over representation between large and small states, tension between the southern and northern states over slavery, differing visions of how power would be delegated within the government, and opposition to ceding states' sovereignty to a national federal government.

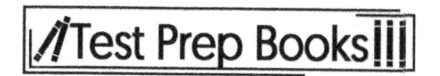

New Jersey Plan

Led by **William Patterson**, the **New Jersey Plan** called for a unicameral legislature that would grant each state a single vote. It proposed a plural executive power selected by the legislature, which would possess no veto power over the legislature, as well as judges appointed by the executive power for the duration of their lives.

The Virginia Plan

Drafted by **James Madison**, the **Virginia Plan** featured a bicameral legislature with two houses. The representatives of the lower house were to be selected by the people, and then the lower house would elect the upper house. The number of representatives of each house would be based upon population or the amount of money contributed to the federal government by each state; thus, large states supported the Virginia Plan. In this plan, the legislature could appoint judges and select a single executive with veto power.

Compromises

Connecticut Compromise

This compromise included aspects of both the New Jersey Plan and Virginia Plan in a bicameral legislature. Representation in the House of Representatives was proportional to a state's population, and in the Senate, states enjoyed equal representation with two senators per state.

Slavery Compromises

Several other compromises were made during the Convention, including the **Three-Fifths Compromise**, which, in an effort to appease both the South states who wanted slaves to be counted as part of the population for the purpose of representation but not counted for the purpose of taxes, and the North, who demanded slaves be counted for taxes but not representation, the framers of the Constitution determined that three-fifths of the slave population of each state would be counted for the purpose of both taxes and representation. In an additional compromise called the **Commerce and Slave Trade Compromise**, Congress agreed not to tax exports from states or ban the trading of slaves for twenty years. This eased Southerners' fears that if the Northern states controlled the federal government, then they could enforce antislavery policies.

Constitution vs. Articles of Confederation

The Constitution addressed the weaknesses of the Articles of Confederation in the following ways:

- Unlike the sovereign states under the Articles of Confederation, the people are now the sovereign, and they bestow sovereignty to both the states and federal government, according to principles of Federalism.

- The Constitution creates a robust central government with many specific and implied powers.

- The Constitution empowers the federal government to levy taxes against the states.

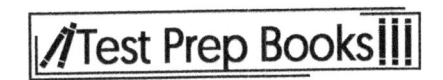

- The Constitution establishes an executive branch of the federal government to enforce the laws; it is led by a president who serves as the commander-in-chief.

- The Constitution establishes a federal judiciary branch with a Supreme Court and lower courts to interpret the laws enacted by the legislative branch.

- The Constitution removes the states' power to coin and print money and establishes a national currency; Congress may regulate interstate and international commerce.

- The Constitution specifies representation in Congress based on population and equal representation for each state in the Senate.

- The Constitution requires a simple majority in both houses to enact laws rather than a vote of at least nine out of thirteen, as specified in the Articles of Confederation. In addition, senators vote separately under the Constitution, while states vote as a single bloc in the Constitution.

- The Constitution requires a two-thirds majority vote in the House of Representatives and a two-thirds majority in the Senate to amend the Constitution, while the Articles of Confederation required a unanimous vote.

Federalism

To strengthen the central government, while still appeasing the individual states who preferred to remain sovereign over their territories, the framers of the Constitution based the new government upon the principles of **Federalism**—a compound government system that divides powers between a central government and various regional governments. The Constitution clearly defined the roles of both the state governments and the new federal government, specifying the limited power of the federal government and reserving all other powers not specifically granted by the Constitution to the federal government to the states in the **Tenth Amendment to the Constitution**, commonly referred to as the Reservation Clause.

The Constitution establishes the specific powers granted to the federal and state governments.

- **Delegated powers**: the specific powers granted to the federal government by the Constitution
- **Implied powers**: the unstated powers that can be reasonably inferred from the Constitution
- **Inherent powers**: the reasonable powers required by the government to manage the nation's affairs and maintain sovereignty
- **Reserved powers**: the unspecified powers belonging to the state that are not expressly granted to the federal government or denied to the state by the Constitution
- **Concurrent powers**: the powers shared between the federal and state governments

The Constitution would delegate the following expanded powers to the federal government:

- Coin money
- Declare war
- Establish federal courts
- Sign foreign treaties
- Expand the territories of the United States, and admit new states into the union

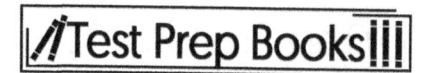

- Regulate immigration
- Regulate interstate commerce

The following powers were reserved for the states:

- Establish local governments
- Hold elections
- Implement welfare and benefit programs
- Create public school systems
- Establish licensing standards and requirements
- Regulate state corporations
- Regulate commerce within the state

The *concurrent* powers granted to both the federal and state governments in the Constitution include:

- The power to levy taxes
- The power to borrow money
- The power to charter corporations

Ratifying the Constitution

The framers of the Constitution signed the Constitution on September 17, 1787, but the Articles of Confederation required nine of the thirteen states to ratify the document. Conventions were held in all thirteen states and sparked heated debates between those who supported and those who opposed the new system of government. The Federalists supported the expansion of the federal government, and the anti-Federalists feared that a stronger central government would weaken the states. The anti-Federalists also sought additional protection for civil liberties. The debates between these two parties continued for two years and inspired a series of essays known as the **Federalist Papers** and **Anti-Federalist Papers** authored anonymously by leaders of their respective party.

Notable Federalists and authors of the *Federalist Papers* include:

- **Alexander Hamilton**: founder of the Federalist Party and advocate for a centralized financial system

- **George Washington**: commander-in-chief of the Continental Army and future first president of the United States

- **James Madison**: one of the primary drafters of the Constitution and the future fourth president of the United States

- **John Jay**: president of the Continental Congress and future first chief justice of the United States

- **John Adams**: future second president of the United States

Notable anti-Federalists and authors of the *Anti-Federalist Papers* include:

- **Thomas Jefferson**: primary author of the Declaration of Independence and future third president of the United States

U.S. Government

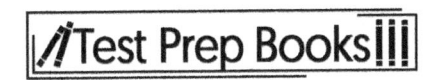

- **Patrick Henry**: governor of Virginia (1776–1779, 1784–1786)

- **Samuel Adams**: governor of Massachusetts (1794–1797), lieutenant governor of Massachusetts (1789–1794), and president of the Massachusetts Senate (1782–1785, 1787–1788)

- **George Mason**: one of only three delegates who did not sign the Constitution at the Constitutional Convention and author of Objections to This Constitution of Government (1787) and the Virginia Declaration of Rights of 1776, which served as the basis for the Bill of Rights

The first state to ratify the Constitution was Delaware in a unanimous vote on December 7, 1787. Several other states followed, and eventually, after ten months, New Hampshire became the ninth state to ratify the Constitution in June 1788. However, some states still remained divided between Federalist and anti-Federalist sentiments and had yet to approve the document, including the two most populous states, Virginia and New York. To reconcile their differing views, the Federalists agreed to include a bill of rights if anti-Federalists supported the new Constitution. Federalist sentiment prevailed, and the remaining states approved the document. On May 29, 1790, the last holdout, Rhode Island, ratified the Constitution by two votes. As promised, the **Bill of Rights**—the first 10 amendments to the Constitution—was added in 1791, providing expanded civil liberty protection and due process of law.

Powers, Structure, and Processes of National Political Institutions

A **political institution** is an organization created by the government to enact and enforce laws, act as a mediator during conflict, create economic policy, establish social systems, and carry out some power. These institutions maintain a rigid structure of internal rules and oversight, especially if the power is delegated, like agencies under the executive branch.

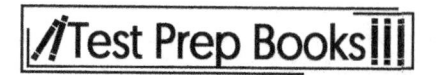

The Constitution established a federal government divided into three branches: legislative, executive, and judicial.

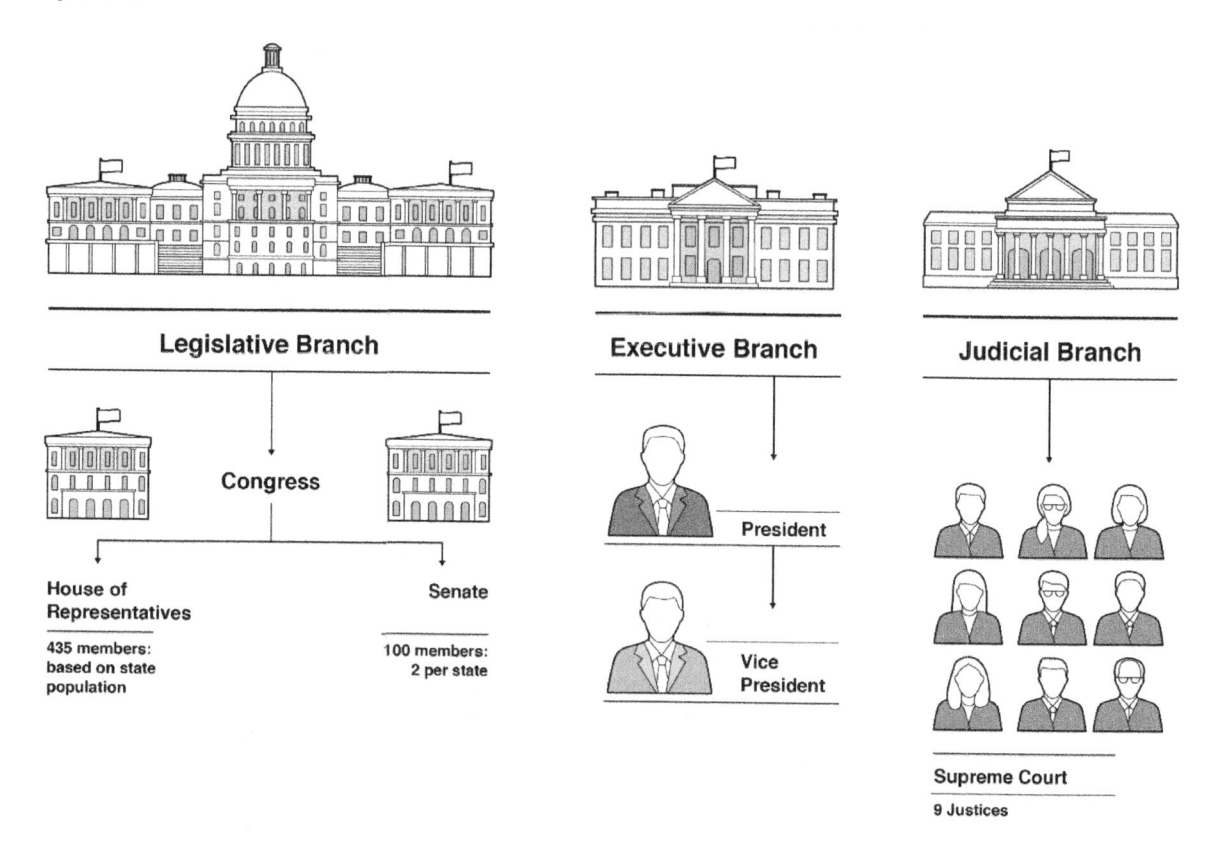

Legislative Branch

Congress

House of Representatives
435 members: based on state population

Senate
100 members: 2 per state

Executive Branch

President

Vice President

Judicial Branch

Supreme Court
9 Justices

Executive Branch

The **executive branch** is responsible for enforcing the laws. The executive branch consists of the president, the vice president, the president's cabinet, and federal agencies created by Congress to execute some delegated.

The **president** of the United States:

- Serves a four-year term and is limited to two terms in office
- Is the chief executive officer of the United States and commander-in-chief of the armed forces
- Is elected by the Electoral College
- Appoints cabinet members, federal judges, and the heads of federal agencies
- Vetoes or signs bills into law
- Handles foreign affairs, including appointing diplomats and negotiating treaties
- Must be thirty-five years old, a natural-born U.S. citizen, and have lived in the United States for at least fourteen years

The **vice president**:

- Serves four-year terms alongside and at the will of the president
- Acts as president of the Senate

U.S. Government

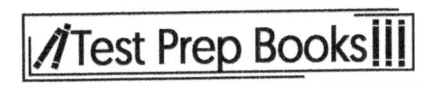

- Assumes the presidency if the president is incapacitated
- Assumes any additional duties assigned by the president

The **cabinet members**:

- Are appointed by the president
- Act as heads for the fifteen executive departments
- Advise the president in matters relating to their departments and carry out delegated power

Note that the president can only sign and veto laws and cannot initiate them himself. As head of the executive branch, it is the responsibility of the president to execute and enforce the laws passed by the legislative branch.

Although Congress delegates their legislative authority to agencies in an enabling statute, they are located in the executive branch because they are tasked with executing their delegating authority. The president enjoys the power of appointment and removal over all federal agency workers, except those tasked with quasi-legislative or quasi-judicial powers.

Legislative Branch

The **legislative branch** is responsible for enacting federal laws. This branch possesses the power to declare war, regulate interstate commerce, approve or reject presidential appointments, and investigate the other branches. The legislative branch is **bicameral**, meaning it consists of two houses: the lower house, called the **House of Representatives**, and the upper house, known as the **Senate**. Both houses are elected by popular vote.

Members of both houses are intended to represent the interests of the constituents in their home states and to bring their concerns to a national level. Ideas for laws, called bills, are proposed in one chamber and then are voted upon according to the body's rules; should the bill pass the first round of voting, the other legislative chamber must approve it before it can be sent to the president.

The two houses (or chambers) are similar though they differ on some procedures such as how debates on bills take place.

House of Representatives

The **House of Representatives** is responsible for enacting bills relating to revenue, impeaching federal officers including the president and Supreme Court justices, and electing the president in the case of no candidate reaching a majority in the Electoral College.

In the House of Representatives:

- Each state's representation in the House of Representatives is determined proportionally by population, with the total number of voting seats limited to 435.

- There are six nonvoting members from Washington, D.C., Puerto Rico, American Samoa, Guam, Northern Mariana Islands, and the U.S. Virgin Islands.

- The **Speaker of the House** is elected by the other representatives and is responsible for presiding over the House. In the event that the president and vice president are unable to fulfill their duties, the Speaker of the House will succeed to the presidency.

- The representatives of the House serve two-year terms.
- The requirements for eligibility in the House include:
  - Must be twenty-five years of age
  - Must have been a U.S. citizen for at least seven years
  - Must be a resident of the state they are representing by the time of the election

Senate

The **Senate** has the exclusive powers to confirm or reject all presidential appointments, ratify treaties, and try impeachment cases initiated by the House of Representatives.

In the Senate:

- The number of representatives is one hundred, with two representatives from each state.
- The vice president presides over the Senate and breaks the tie, if necessary.
- The representatives serve six-year terms.
- The requirements for eligibility in the Senate include:
  - Must be thirty years of age
  - Must have been a U.S. citizen for the past nine years
  - Must be a resident of the state they are representing at the time of their election

Legislative Process

Although all members of the houses make the final voting, the senators and representatives serve on committees and subcommittees dedicated to specific areas of policy. These committees are responsible for debating the merit of bills, revising bills, and passing or killing bills that are assigned to their committee. If it passes, they then present the bill to the entire Senate or House of Representatives (depending on which they are a part of). In most cases, a bill can be introduced in either the Senate or the House, but a majority vote of both houses is required to approve a new bill before the president may sign the bill into law.

Judicial Branch

The **judicial branch**, though it cannot pass laws itself, is tasked with interpreting the law and ensuring citizens receive due process under the law. The judicial branch consists of the Supreme Court, the highest court in the country, overseeing all federal and state courts. Lower federal courts are the district courts and court of appeals.

The Supreme Court:

- Judges are appointed by the president and confirmed by the Senate.
- Judges serve until retirement, death, or impeachment.
- Judges possess sole power to judge the constitutionality of a law.
- Judges set precedents for lower courts based on their decisions.
- Judges try appeals that have proceeded from the lower courts.

Checks and Balances

Notice that a system of checks and balances between the branches exists. This is to ensure that no branch oversteps its authority. They include:

U.S. Government

- Checks on the Legislative Branch:
    - The president can veto bills passed by Congress.
    - The president can call special sessions of Congress.
    - The judicial branch can rule legislation unconstitutional.
- Checks on the Executive Branch:
    - Congress has the power to override presidential vetoes by a two-thirds majority vote.
    - Congress can impeach or remove a president, and the chief justice of the Supreme Court presides over impeachment proceedings.
    - Congress can refuse to approve presidential appointments or ratify treaties.
- Checks on the Judicial Branch:
    - The president appoints justices to the Supreme Court, as well as district court and court of appeals judges.
    - The president can pardon federal prisoners.
    - The executive branch can refuse to enforce court decisions.
    - Congress can create federal courts below the Supreme Court.
    - Congress can determine the number of Supreme Court justices.
    - Congress can set the salaries of federal judges.
    - Congress can refuse to approve presidential appointments of judges.
    - Congress can impeach and convict federal judges.

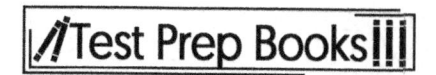

The three branches of government operate separately, but they must rely on each other to create, enforce, and interpret the laws of the United States.

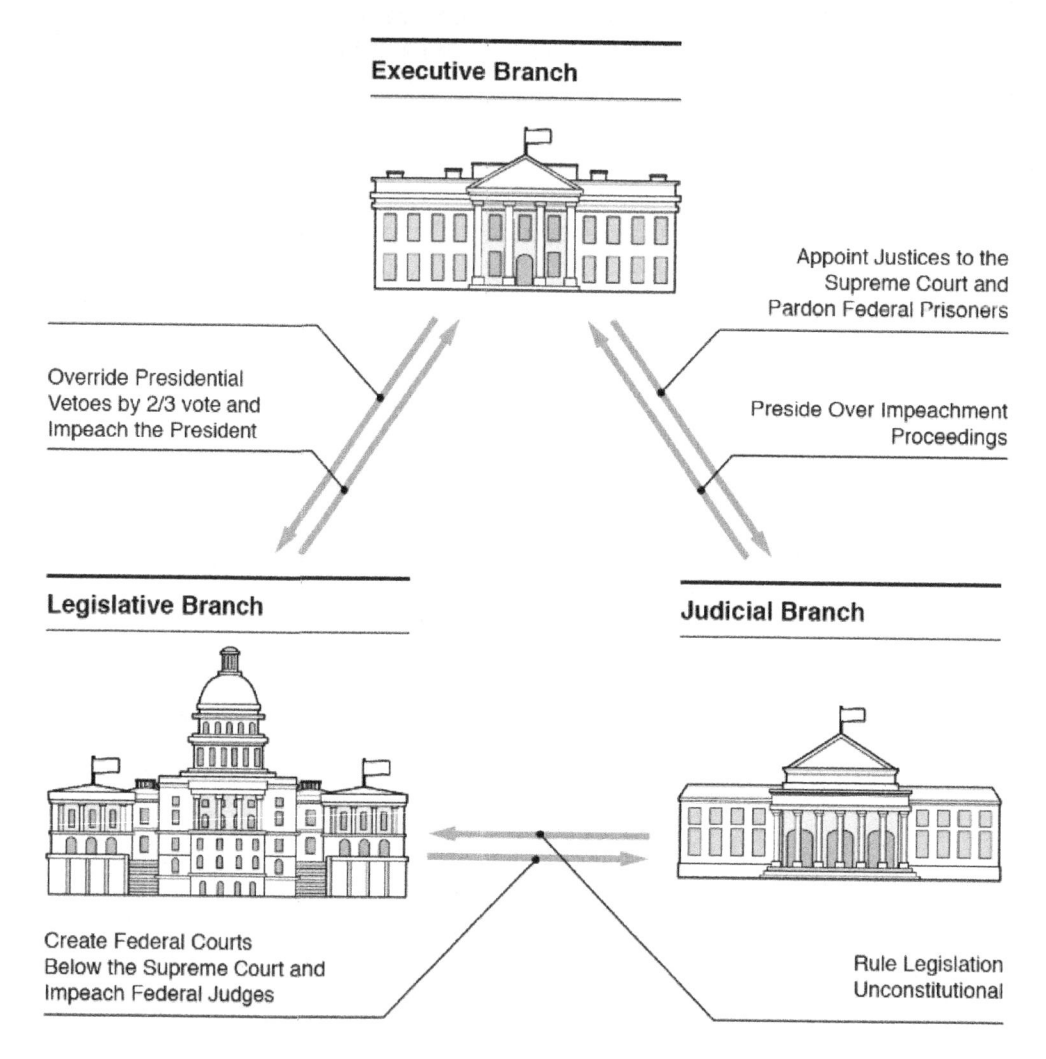

Executive Branch

Appoint Justices to the Supreme Court and Pardon Federal Prisoners

Override Presidential Vetoes by 2/3 vote and Impeach the President

Preside Over Impeachment Proceedings

Legislative Branch

Judicial Branch

Create Federal Courts Below the Supreme Court and Impeach Federal Judges

Rule Legislation Unconstitutional

How Laws are Enacted and Enforced

To enact a new law:

- The bill is introduced to Congress.
- The bill is sent to the appropriate committee for review and revision.
- The approved bill is sent to the Speaker of the House and the majority party leader of the Senate, who places the bill on the calendar for review.
- The houses debate the merits of the bill and recommend amendments.

    - In the House of Representatives, those who wish to debate about a bill are allowed only a few minutes to speak, and amendments to the bill are limited.

    - In the Senate, debates and amendments are unlimited, and those who wish to postpone a vote may do so by filibuster, refusing to stop speaking.

U.S. Government

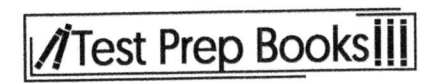

- The approved bill is revised in both houses to ensure identical wording in both bills.
- The revised bill is returned to both houses for final approval.
- The bill is sent to the president, who may
    - Sign the bill into law
    - Veto the bill
    - Take no action, resulting in the bill becoming law if Congress remains in session for ten days or dying if Congress adjourns before ten days have passed

The Role of State Government

While the federal government manages the nation as a whole, state governments address issues pertaining to their specific territory. In the past, states claimed the right, known as nullification, to refuse to enforce federal laws that they considered unconstitutional. However, conflicts between state and federal authority, particularly in the South in regard to first, slavery, and later, discrimination, have led to increased federal power, and states cannot defy federal laws. Even so, the **Tenth Amendment** limits federal power to those powers specifically granted in the Constitution, and the rest of the powers are retained by the states and citizens. Therefore, individual state governments are left in charge of decisions with immediate effects on their citizens, such as state laws and taxes.

In this way, the powers of government are separated both horizontally between the three branches of government (executive, legislative, and judicial) and vertically between the levels of government (federal, state, and local).

Like the federal government, state governments consist of executive, judicial, and legislative branches, but the exact configuration of those branches varies between states. For example, while most states follow the bicameral structure of Congress, Nebraska has only a single legislative chamber. Additionally, requirements to run for office, length of terms, and other details vary from state to state. State governments have considerable authority within their states, but they cannot impose their power on other states.

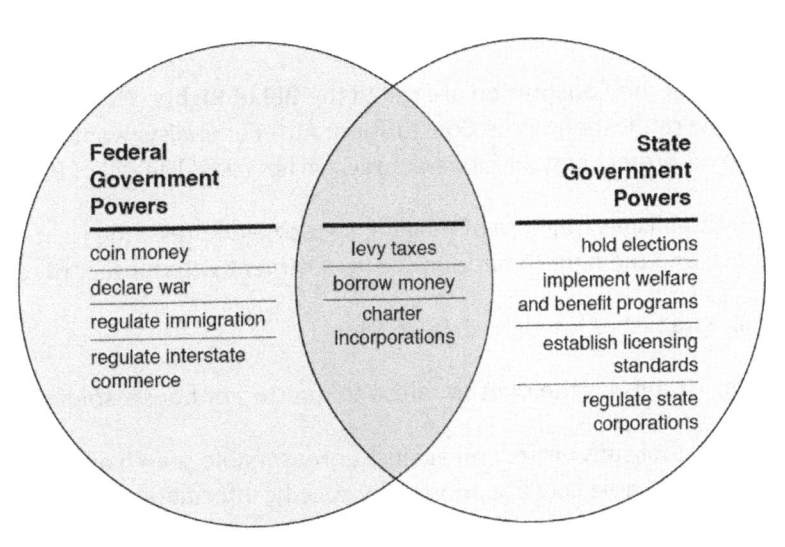

Federal Government Powers	(Shared)	State Government Powers
coin money	levy taxes	hold elections
declare war	borrow money	implement welfare and benefit programs
regulate immigration	charter incorporations	establish licensing standards
regulate interstate commerce		regulate state corporations

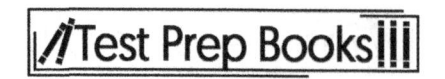

The Role of Local Government

Local governments, which include town governments, county boards, library districts, and other agencies, are especially variable in their composition. They often reflect the overall views of their state governments but also have their own values, rules, and structures. Generally, local governments function in a democratic fashion, although the exact form of government depends on its role. Depending on the location within the state, local government may have considerable or minimal authority based on the population and prosperity of the area; some counties may have strong influence in the state, while others may have a limited impact.

Native American Tribes

Native American tribes are treated as dependent nations that answer to the federal government but may be immune to state jurisdiction. As with local governments, the exact form of governance is left up to the tribes, which ranges from small councils to complex systems of government. Other U.S. territories, including the District of Columbia (site of Washington, D.C.) and acquired islands, such as Guam and Puerto Rico, have representation within Congress, but their legislators cannot vote on bills.

Civil Liberties and Civil Rights

The protection of *civil liberties* is one of the most important political values upon which American society is based. Though the terms **civil liberties** and **civil rights** are commonly used interchangeably, they describe two very distinct types of protections. Civil liberties refer to the legal protections afforded to U.S. citizens against government action, while civil rights refer to equal treatment under the law, especially in relation to minority groups, like women, African Americans, and Hispanics.

Civil Liberties

A **civil liberty** is a protection from legal action by the government. Civil liberties are granted by the Constitution in the first ten amendments, collectively known as the Bill of Rights, which were added to the Constitution in 1791. Civil liberties are conditional and do not afford protection from government action in every scenario. They can be restricted when they infringe on the rights of others; for example, with defamation, child pornography, or "fighting words." They also may be suspended with just cause, such as in the case of limiting the freedom of press to protect national security.

The Bill of Rights

The first ten amendments of the Constitution are called the **Bill of Rights**. They were passed to win over anti-Federalists during the ratification of the Constitution. Anti-Federalists wanted assurances that the federal government would protect certain fundamental civil liberties. The Bill of Rights includes:

- **Amendment I**: Establishes freedom of religion, speech, and press; the right to assemble in peaceful protest; and the right to petition the government without fear of reprisal

- **Amendment II**: Establishes the right to bear arms

- **Amendment III**: Establishes the right to refuse to quarter, or house, soldiers in time of war

- **Amendment IV**: Establishes protection against unreasonable search and seizure and requires a warrant based on probable cause supported by specific information

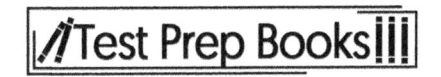

- **Amendment V**: Protects against self-incrimination in criminal trials, except in cases of military court martial; protects against being tried more than once for the same crime, known as double jeopardy; and protects against seizure of private property for public use without compensation

- **Amendment VI**: Establishes extensive set of rights to protect defendants in a criminal trial—the right to a speedy and timely trial before a judge and impartial jury of peers, the right to be informed of criminal accusations, the right to present and compel witnesses in defense of the accused, the right to confront witnesses against the accused, and the right to assistance of counsel

- **Amendment VII**: Protects the right to a trial by jury in civil cases exceeding a dollar amount of $20

- **Amendment VIII**: Protects against cruel and unusual punishment and excessive fines

- **Amendment IX**: Establishes the existence of additional fundamental rights unnamed in the Constitution; protects those rights that are not enumerated

- **Amendment X**: Reserves all powers that are not specified to the federal government or prohibited to the states or the people, establishing the principles of separation of powers and Federalism

Civil Rights

Civil rights concern who is protected, while *civil liberties* concern what is protected. Civil rights refer to protection against unfair treatment based on characteristics such as gender, race, ethnicity, religion, sexual orientation, and disability. The struggle for civil rights has a long history in the United States. Following the Civil War, the ratification of three amendments—Thirteenth, Fourteenth, and Fifteenth, collectively known as the Reconstruction Amendments—expanded the constitutional protection of equal civil rights.

The **Thirteenth Amendment** abolished slavery and involuntary servitude, except as punishment for a crime. The issue of slavery was no longer in the states' hands. Although the **Emancipation Proclamation** freed slaves in the Confederacy, the status of former slaves remained uncertain as the war neared its conclusion. Many Northerners did not hold strong views on slavery, but most wanted to punish the South and resolve the primary cause of the bloody Civil War. The Northern states all immediately ratified the amendment, and in December 1865, enough reconstructed Southern states ratified the amendment for it to be adopted into law.

The **Fourteenth Amendment** prohibited states from depriving life, liberty, or property without due process and from violating equal protection based on race, color, or previous condition of servitude. Now, all persons born or naturalized in the United States were considered legal citizens. Although revolutionary for the theoretical rights of all American citizens, newly freed or otherwise, the Fourteenth Amendment did not provide actual federally enforced equal protection until the Civil Rights Act of 1964.

The **Fifteenth Amendment** prohibits the government from denying a citizen the right to vote for reasons of race, color, or previous condition of servitude. Adopted in 1870, the last of the Reconstruction Amendments, the Fifteenth Amendment sought to protect newly freed slaves' right to vote. As discussed below, most states interpreted the amendment to only apply to male suffrage. In addition,

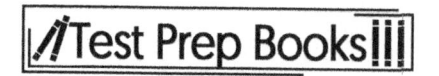

Southern states passed a series of laws to systematically disenfranchise African Americans, like poll taxes, literacy tests, and residency rules. The use of violence and intimidation for political purpose was also common. Meaningful change did not occur until the Civil Rights Movement, nearly one hundred years later. In 1964, the Twenty-Fourth Amendment prohibited the states and federal government from charging a poll tax or fee to vote. Later, the Voting Rights Act of 1965 empowered the federal government to enforce the Fifteenth Amendment on the states for the first time.

Women's Suffrage

The Fourteenth Amendment specified equal treatment for all citizens; however, it did not establish women's right to vote in elections, known as **women's suffrage**. Although landowning women were allowed to vote in New Jersey in the late eighteenth century, the right was removed in 1807. The fight for women's suffrage continued in the middle of the nineteenth century. Famous women's rights activists include **Susan B. Anthony**, **Lucy Stone**, and **Elizabeth Cady Stanton**, who authored the **Declaration of Rights and Sentiments**, which demanded access to the civil liberties granted to all men. Women gained the right to vote in 1869 in Wyoming and 1870 in Utah.

The women's suffrage movement gained momentum in the early twentieth century after their increased participation in the economy during World War I when much of the workforce went overseas to fight. The National Women's Party picketed outside the White House and led a series of protests in Washington, resulting in the imprisonment of the party's leader, Alice Paul. In 1918, Woodrow Wilson declared his support for women's suffrage despite earlier opposition, and in 1920, Congress passed the Nineteenth Amendment, which made it illegal for states to withhold voting rights based on gender.

Jim Crow Laws

Southern states circumvented the Fourteenth Amendment and imposed what were referred to as **Jim Crow laws**, which established racial segregation of public facilities. These "separate but equal" facilities included the military, workplaces, public schools, restaurants, restrooms, transportation, and recreational facilities. Despite the label of "separate but equal," most facilities reserved for African Americans were considerably inferior.

In 1896, the Supreme Court handed down a decision in the case of **Plessy vs. Ferguson**, in which **Homer Plessy**, a Louisiana man of mixed race, attempted to board a railway car reserved for "whites only" and was charged for violating the separate car law. Plessy subsequently filed suit against the state, claiming they violated his Fourteenth Amendment rights. The Supreme Court decided in favor of the state, ruling that the law was not unconstitutional. The Supreme Court upheld separate but equal laws until the 1954 case of *Brown vs. the Board of Education of Topeka* where the Supreme Court ruled that racial segregation of public schools violated the Fourteenth Amendment.

Civil Rights Movement

Brown vs. the Board of Education prohibited segregation in 1954, but the Civil Rights Movement, led by the **National Association for the Advancement of Colored People (NAACP)** and such famous activists as Martin Luther King Jr. and Malcolm X, did not secure the enforcement of the Fourteenth Amendment until the passage of the Civil Rights Act of 1964, which outlawed discrimination based on gender, race, ethnicity, and religion. African American and Native American women, however, did not gain the right to vote until the Voting Rights Act of 1965, which enforced the voting rights articulated in the Fourteenth Amendment and Fifteenth Amendment. Section 5 of the Voting Rights Act prevented states with a history of discrimination from altering their voting laws without getting approval from the attorney general or a federal district court.

Political Beliefs and Behaviors

Political beliefs are the beliefs held by the citizens of a nation about the government, leaders, policies, and the related political issues of their state. Political beliefs differ among individual citizens, but in America, a strong basis of democracy shapes the political beliefs, behaviors, and attitudes.

Democratic Values

The foundation of democratic values upon which the United States is based include:

- The people are sovereign, and they elect a representative government to exercise that sovereignty.
- The citizens of the nation are equal under the law.
- The peaceful transition of power is valued regardless of election results.
- The private property of individuals cannot be taken by force by the government without due process or fair compensation.
- The civil liberties of the citizens of the state cannot be abridged or violated by the government without due process.
- The government should be accountable to the citizenry.

Political Socialization

American citizens undergo a process of *political socialization* from early childhood to adulthood during which they develop their individual sense of political identity and civic pride. Children learn about politics in the home from an early age, whether from the views, opinions, and facts of family and friends, or through the media to which they are exposed.

In school, they learn about the nation's political history, basic politics, and democratic values, as well as the ideals of patriotism and the processes of government. As they grow older, they join interest groups, labor unions, religious groups, and political organizations that further influence their political beliefs. This socialization shapes not only the political beliefs and values of individual citizens and groups but the political ideals of the nation and public opinion.

Public Opinion

Public opinion is the shared political ideals, opinions, and attitudes of the people of a state regarding the politics, current events, and social issues that influence policy and shape the political atmosphere of a state. Public opinion is the result of political beliefs, socialization, and current events. Political scientists measure public opinion through:

- Distribution of opinion across demographics such as age, race, gender, and religion
- Strength of the opinion
- Stability of the opinion over time

Public opinion refers to the majority opinion in a democratic state. Citizens express public opinion through the interest groups they join, the media they consume and interact with, and the leaders they elect. To measure public opinion, scientists use polls to gather data. Accurate polling requires:

- Random sampling of representative populations

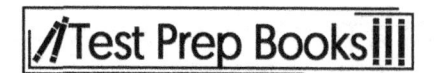

- Unbiased questions
- Clear instructions for how to answer questions
- Controlled procedures such as the use of telephone, mail, Internet, or in-person interviews with an unbiased pollster
- Accurate reporting of the results, including information about methods, inconsistencies, respondents, and possible sources and degree of error

Political Participation

Citizens express their political beliefs and public opinion through participation in politics. The conventional ways citizens can participate in politics in a democratic state include:

- Obeying laws
- Voting in elections
- Running for public office
- Staying interested in and informed of current events
- Learning U.S. history
- Attending public hearings to be informed and to express opinions on issues, especially on the local level
- Forming interest groups to promote common goals
- Forming political action committees (PACs) that raise money to influence policy decisions
- Petitioning government to create awareness of issues
- Campaigning for a candidate
- Contributing to campaigns
- Using mass media to express political ideas, opinions, and grievances

Voting

In a democratic state, the most common way to participate in politics is by voting for candidates in an election. **Voting** allows the citizens of a state to influence policy by selecting the candidates who share their views and make policy decisions that best suit their interests, or candidates who they believe are most capable of leading the country. In Canada, all citizens over 18—regardless of gender, race, or religion—are allowed to vote.

Since the Progressive movement and the increased social activism of the 1890s to the 1920s that sought to eliminate corruption in government, direct participation in politics through voting has increased. Citizens can participate by voting in the following types of elections:

- **Direct primaries**: Citizens can nominate candidates for public office.

- **National, state, and municipal elections**: Citizens elect their representatives in government.

- **Recall elections**: Citizens can petition the government to vote an official out of office before their term ends.

- **Referendums**: Citizens can vote directly on proposed laws or amendments to the state constitution.

- **Voter initiatives**: Citizens can petition their local or state government to propose laws that will be approved or rejected by voters.

U.S. Government

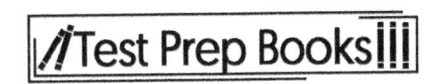

Electoral Process, Political Parties, and Interest Groups

As members of a Constitutional Republic with certain aspects of a **democracy**, U.S. citizens are empowered to elect most government leaders, but the process varies between branch and level of government. Presidential elections at the national level use the **Electoral College system**. Rather than electing the president directly, citizens cast their ballots to select *electors* that represent each state in the college.

Legislative branches at the federal and state level are also determined by elections. In some areas, judges are elected, but in other states judges are appointed by elected officials. The U.S. has a **two-party system**, meaning that most government control is under two major parties: the Republican Party and the Democratic Party. It should be noted that the two-party system was not designed by the Constitution but gradually emerged over time.

Electoral Process

During the **electoral process**, the citizens of a state decide who will represent them at the local, state, and federal level. Different political officials that citizens elect through popular vote include but are not limited to:

- City mayor
- City council members
- State representative
- State governor
- State senator
- House member
- U.S. Senator
- President

The Constitution grants the states the power to hold their own elections, and the voting process often varies from city to city and state to state.

While a popular vote decides nearly all local and state elections, the president of the United States is elected by the **Electoral College**, rather than by popular vote. Presidential elections occur every four years on the first Tuesday after the first Monday in November.

The electoral process for the president of the United States includes:

Primary Elections and Caucuses

In a presidential election, *nominees* from the two major parties, as well as some third parties, run against each other. To determine who will win the nomination from each party, the states hold *primary elections* or *caucuses*.

During the primary elections, the states vote for who they want to win their party's nomination. In some states, primary elections are closed, meaning voters may only vote for candidates from their registered party, but other states hold **open primaries** in which voters may vote in either party's primary.

Some states hold **caucuses** in which the members of a political party meet in small groups, and the decisions of those groups determine the party's candidate.

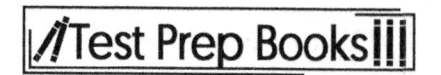

Each state holds a number of delegates proportional to its population, and the candidate with the most delegate votes receives the domination. Some states give all of their delegates (*winner-take-all*) to the primary or caucus winner, while some others split the votes more proportionally.

Conventions

The two major parties hold national conventions to determine who will be the nominee to run for president from each party. The **delegates** each candidate won in the primary elections or caucuses are the voters who represent their states at the national conventions. The candidate who wins the most delegate votes is given the nomination. Political parties establish their own internal requirements and procedures for how a nominee is nominated.

Conventions are typically spread across several days, and leaders of the party give speeches, culminating with the candidate accepting the nomination at the end.

Campaigning

Once the nominees are selected from each party, they continue campaigning into the national election. Prior to the mid-1800s, candidates did not actively campaign for themselves, considering it dishonorable to the office, but campaigning is now rampant. Modern campaigning includes, but is not limited to:

- Raising money
- Meeting with citizens and public officials around the country
- Giving speeches
- Issuing policy proposals
- Running internal polls to determine strategy
- Organizing strategic voter outreach in important districts
- Participating in debates organized by a third-party private debate commission
- Advertising on television, through mail, or on the Internet

General Election

On the first Tuesday after the first Monday in November of an election year, every four years, the people cast their votes by secret ballot for president in a **general election**. Voters may vote for any candidate, regardless of their party affiliation. The outcome of the popular vote does not decide the election; instead, the winner is determined by the Electoral College.

Electoral College

When the people cast their votes for president in the general election, they are casting their votes for the *electors* from the *Electoral College* who will elect the president. In order to win the presidential election, a nominee must win 270 of the 538 electoral votes. The number of electors is equal to the total number of senators and representatives from each state plus three electoral votes for Washington D.C. which does not have any voting members in the legislative branch.

The electors typically vote based on the popular vote from their states. Although the Constitution does not require electors to vote for the popular vote winner of their state, no elector voting against the popular vote of their state has ever changed the outcome of an election. Due to the Electoral College, a nominee may win the popular vote and still lose the election.

For example, let's imagine that there are only two states — Wyoming and New Mexico — in a presidential election. Wyoming has three electoral votes and awards them all to the winner of the election by majority vote. New Mexico has five electoral votes and also awards them all to the winner of the election by majority vote. If 500,000 people in Wyoming vote and the Republican candidate wins by a vote of 300,000 to 200,000, the Republican candidate will win the three electoral votes for the state. If the same number of people vote in New Mexico, but the Republican candidate loses the state by a vote of 249,000 to 251,000, the Democratic candidate wins the five electoral votes from that state. This means the Republican candidate will have received 549,000 popular votes but only three electoral votes, while the Democratic candidate will have received 451,000 popular votes but will have won five electoral votes. Thus, the Republican won the popular vote by a considerable margin, but the Democratic candidate will have been awarded more electoral votes, which are the only ones that matter.

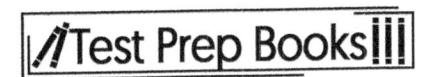

	Wyoming	New Mexico	Total # of Votes
Republican Votes	300,000	249,000	**549,000**
Democratic Votes	200,000	251,000	**451,000**
Republican Electoral Votes	3	0	**3**
Democratic Electoral Votes	0	5	**5**

If no one wins the majority of electoral votes in the presidential election, the House of Representatives decides the presidency, as required by the Twelfth Amendment. They may only vote for the top three candidates, and each state delegation votes as a single bloc. Twenty-six votes, a simple majority, are required to elect the president. The House has only elected the president twice, in 1801 and 1825.

Here how many electoral votes each state and the District of Columbia have:

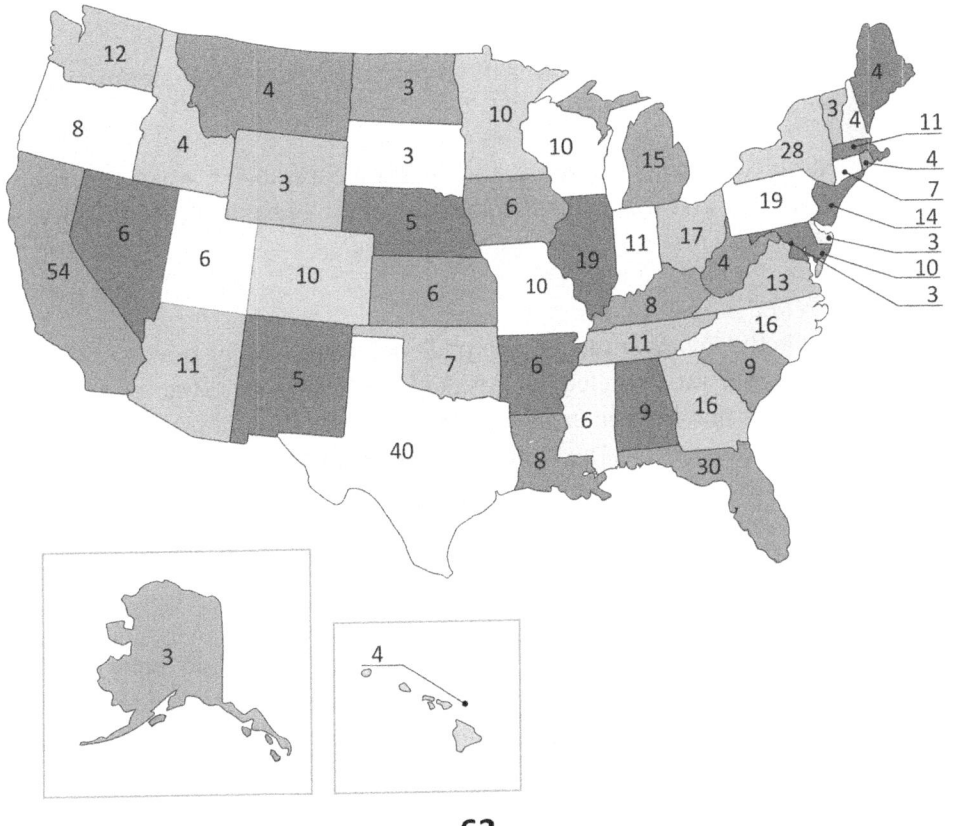

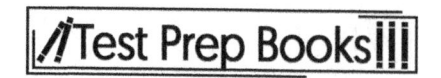

Political Parties

A **political party** is an organized group of voters who share the same political values and support or oppose the same policies. Members of a political party vote for the candidates from their party who they believe share their values and will approve or reject the policies they support or oppose. Political parties often determine the positions party members take on issues of policy, such as the economy, taxation, and social services.

The Founding Fathers of the United States opposed the divisiveness they associated with political parties, and **President George Washington** railed against the evil of political parties in his Farewell Address. However, the ratification of the Constitution led to the creation of the first two American political parties, the Federalists and the anti-Federalist Democratic-Republican Party. When **Andrew Jackson** became the seventh president of the United States as a Democrat, his opposition organized under the Whig Party. The Whigs asserted Congress' supremacy over the president and primarily focused on economic concerns, like banking and violations.

Slavery divided the nation and created unrest among the political parties, as members took opposing views and splintered into separate sects of the party or started new parties with members who shared their views. The Whig Party, so divided by the differing views of the members, collapsed. Former Whigs joined or formed the following parties:

- **Constitutional Union Party**: Devoted itself to a single-issue platform of preserving the Union and recognizing the Constitution as the supreme rule of law. The party did not take a firm issue on slavery, but vigorously opposed secession.

- **Democratic Party**: Divided into northern and southern factions over slavery, but the Democrats sought to compromise and remain unified.

- **Know-Nothing Party**: Advocated for an anti-immigration single-party platform, especially immigrants from Catholic countries.

- **Republican Party**: Formed in response to the Kansas-Nebraska Act, which threatened to extend slavery into new territories, called for the abolition of slavery and argued for a more modernized economy.

Modern Political Parties

The defeat of the South in the Civil War resulted in the Republicans holding power until the 1930s, when **Franklin D. Roosevelt**, a Democrat, was elected president. Roosevelt instituted the New Deal, which included many social policies that built an expansive social welfare program to provide financial support to citizens during the Great Depression. The Republican Party opposed this interference by the government, and the two parties became more strongly divided. The political landscape again shifted during the Civil Rights Movement, as Southern Democrats fled to the Republican Party over their opposition to enforcing federal civil rights onto states. This strengthened the modern coalition between economic conservatives and social conservatives.

Today, the Democrats and Republicans are still the two major parties, though many third parties have emerged. The Republicans and Democrats hold opposing views on the degree of state intervention into private business, taxation, states' rights, and government assistance.

U.S. Government

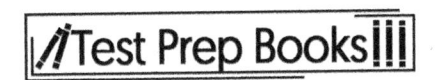

The ideals of these parties include:

Republican (or the Grand Old Party [GOP])
- Founded by abolitionists
- Support capitalism, free enterprise, and a policy of noninterference by the government
- Support strong national defense
- Support deregulation and restrictions of labor unions
- Advocate for states' rights
- Oppose abortion
- Support traditional values, often based on Judeo-Christian foundations, including considerable opposition to same-sex marriage

Democrat
- Founded by anti-Federalists and rooted in classical Liberalism
- Promote civil rights, equal opportunity and protection under the law, and social justice
- Support government-instituted social programs and safety nets
- Support environmental issues
- Support government intervention and regulation, and advocate for labor unions
- Support universal health care

Some prominent third parties include:

- Reform Party: support political reform of the two-party system
- Green Party: support environmental causes
- Libertarian Party: support a radical policy of nonintervention and small, localized government

Interest Groups
An **interest group** is an organization with members who share similar social concerns or political interests. Members of political interest groups work together to influence policy decisions that benefit a particular segment of society or cause. Interest groups might include:

- Activist groups, like the NAACP, American Civil Liberties Union (ACLU), or People for the Ethical Treatment of Animals (PETA)
- Corporations, like pharmaceutical companies or banks
- Small-business advocates
- Religious groups, like the Concerned Women PAC and the Muslim Public Affairs Council
- Unions, such as the Association of Teacher Educators and International Brotherhood of Electrical Workers

Lobbyists
To promote their causes and influence policy in their favor, many interest groups employ **lobbyists**, paid advocates who work to influence lawmakers. Lobbying is a controversial practice, but it is sanctioned and protected as free speech. Lobbying from interest groups has a powerful impact on many policy decisions made in the United States. Examples of lobbyist groups include American Israel Public Affairs Committee (AIPAC) and Pharmaceutical Research and Manufacturers of America.

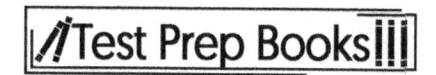

Foreign Policy

Foreign policy refers to a state's international policy governing and informing their interactions with other states. A state's foreign policy typically defines the methods they employ to safeguard the state against foreign states, the social and economic goals of the state, and how the state will achieve these goals in the global arena through their relations with foreign states. Foreign policy is typically an executive function, either through the head of state or delegated to the foreign minister.

A state's foreign policy is influenced by several factors, including:

- Public opinion
- Economic and domestic stability
- Current events
- Social and humanitarian interests

The foreign policy of the United States has changed dramatically since the Founding Fathers established a policy of isolationism, which persisted well into the nineteenth century. After World War II, the United States emerged alongside the Soviet Union as the lone remaining global support powers. The United States led Europe and her allies during the Cold War's fight against the spread of Communism. When the Cold War ended after the collapse of the Soviet Union, the United States was left as the only true superpower, enjoying an unrivaled military and one of the world's most productive economies. American foreign policy shifted toward funding sustainable development economic projects in struggling countries and supporting democracy across the globe. The United States remains the leader of the NATO and has entered into several free trade agreements, most notably the North American Free Trade Association between Mexico, America, and Canada.

The president and secretary of state of the United States determine and enforce the U.S. foreign policy. The goals of U.S. foreign policy include:

- Maintain national security
- Promote world peace
- Promote civil rights and democracy
- Ally with other states to solve international problems
- Promote global cooperation and trade

To accomplish these goals, the State Department:

- Employs foreign diplomats to meet and talk with officials from foreign countries
- Maintains U.S. embassies in foreign nations from which to practice diplomacy
- Joins and supports international organizations such as:
    - NATO
    - WTO
    - United Nations

U.S. History, Society, Customs, and Culture

Origins of the American Revolution and Founding of the United States

The French colonies in Canada also threatened the British settlements. France and Britain had been enemies for centuries. Religious differences reinforced their hostility; the British were Protestant and the French were mostly Catholic. Far fewer colonists settled in "New France," but they often clashed with the British, especially over the lucrative fur trade. Both the British and French sought to dominate the trade in beaver pelts, which were used to make hats in Europe. The British and French fought a series of colonial wars between 1689 and 1748 that failed to resolve the struggle for dominance in North America.

Eventually, the contest culminated in the **French and Indian War** (which was part of the Seven Years' War), which ended in 1763. The French initially enjoyed the upper hand because they were able to persuade more Native American tribes to support them. The Native Americans felt the French were less likely to encroach on their territory than the land-hungry British. The Native Americans launched devastating raids along the British colonial frontier. However, the British eventually emerged victorious after they blockaded the French colonies in Canada. This prevented the French from bringing in reinforcements or from resupplying their Native American allies with gunpowder and ammunition. Native American raids subsided and eventually the French surrendered almost all of their colonial possessions in North America. Some historians consider this war the first global conflict because battles were also fought in Europe, Asia, and Africa.

The French defeat radically altered the balance of power in North America. Previously, Native Americans had been able to play the French and British against each other, but now they were without many of their French allies. In addition, the French and Indian War also set the stage for the American Revolution. Although victorious, the British monarchy spent an enormous amount of money and the war doubled the national debt. In order to pay off the debts, King George III began imposing taxes upon the North American colonies, which eventually led to revolution.

Since 1651, the British crown had tried to control trade within its empire, which eventually led to tension and discontent in the North American colonies. That year, the monarchy introduced the Navigation Acts, which prevented the North American colonies from trading directly with other European powers—all goods had to be shipped to Britain first. This was an attempt to keep wealth within the British Empire and to prevent other empires from profiting from their colonies. This was an example of mercantilism—an economic policy that formed the foundation of Britain's empire. Mercantilism called for government regulation in the form of tariffs, a tax on imports from other countries. This raised prices on foreign goods and encouraged British imperial subjects to purchase goods made in Britain or the colonies. This reduced imports and maximized exports, thus enriching the British Empire.

The **Molasses Act in 1731** was another outgrowth of mercantilism. This law imposed a higher tax on the molasses that colonists purchased from the Dutch, French, or Spanish colonies. The tax was unpopular with the colonists and British imperial officials eventually decided not to enforce the tax. The Molasses Act had threatened to disrupt the pattern of triangular trade that had emerged in the Atlantic world. First, ships from Britain's North American colonies carried rum to Africa where it was traded for slaves and gold. Then, the ships took the slaves to French and Spanish colonies in the Caribbean and exchanged them for sugar or molasses. In the last part of the triangular trade system, merchants sailed back to North America where the sugar and molasses was used to make rum, and the cycle could start over again.

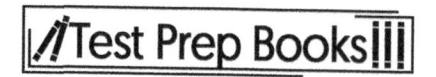

In addition to economic connections, many other bonds also bridged the Atlantic Ocean. Most colonists shared a common language, common religion, and common culture. However, as the colonies grew in population, they began to develop local institutions and a separate sense of identity. For example, it became common for ministers to receive their education at seminaries in North America rather than Britain. Newspapers also began to focus on printing more local news as well. Perhaps most importantly, the colonies began to exercise more control over their own political affairs. The British government retained control over international issues, such as war and trade, but the colonists controlled their own domestic affairs. Colonies began to form their own political assemblies and elect landowners who represented local districts. In addition, communications between the colonies and Britain were very slow because it took months for a ship to cross the Atlantic and return with a response.

A number of political acts by the British monarchy also led to more discontent among the colonies. After the French and Indian War ended in 1763, the king declared that the colonists could not settle west of the Appalachian Mountains. This was known as the Proclamation of 1763. Many colonists were frustrated because they had expected this territory would be open for expansion after the French had been defeated.

Additionally, taxes were imposed in an effort to help reduce the debt Britain amassed during the French and Indian War. In 1764, Parliament passed the **Sugar Act**, which reduced the tax on molasses but also provided for greater enforcement powers. Some colonists protested by organizing boycotts on British goods. One year later, in 1765, Parliament passed the **Quartering Act**, which required colonists to provide housing and food to British troops. This law was also very unpopular and led to protests in the North American colonies.

The **Stamp Act of 1765** required the colonists to pay a tax on legal documents, newspapers, magazines and other printed materials. Colonial assemblies protested the tax and petitioned the British government in order to have it repealed. Merchants also organized boycotts and established correspondence committees in order to share information. Eventually, Parliament repealed the Stamp Act but simultaneously reaffirmed the Crown's right to tax the colonies.

In 1767, Parliament introduced the **Townshend Acts**, which imposed a tax on goods the colonies imported from Britain, such as tea, lead, paint, glass, and paper. The colonies protested again and British imperial officials were assaulted in some cases. The British government sent additional troops to North America to restore order. The arrival of troops in Boston only led to more tension that eventually culminated in the Boston Massacre in 1770, where five colonists were killed and eight were wounded. Except for the duty on tea, all of the Townshend Act taxes were repealed after the Boston Massacre.

Parliament passed the **Tea Act in 1773** and, although it actually reduced the tax on tea, it was another unpopular piece of legislation. The Tea Act allowed the British East India Company to sell its products directly, effectively cutting out colonial merchants and stirring more Anglo-American anger and resentment. This resulted in the **Boston Tea Party in 1773**, an incident in which colonial tea merchants disguised themselves as Indians before storming several British ships that were anchored in Boston harbor. Once aboard, the disguised colonists dumped more than 300 chests of tea into the water.

U.S. History, Society, Customs, and Culture

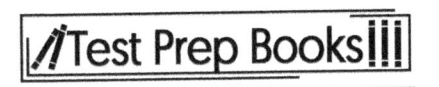

Because the British government was unable to identify the perpetrators, Parliament passed a series of laws that punished the entire colony of Massachusetts. These acts were known as the **Coercive or Intolerable Acts**. The first law closed the port of Boston until the tea had been paid for (an estimated $1.7 million in today's currency). The second act curtailed the authority of Massachusetts' colonial government. Instead of being elected by colonists, most government officials were now appointed by the king. In addition, the act restricted town meetings, the basic form of government in Massachusetts, and limited most villages to one meeting per year. This act angered colonists throughout the thirteen colonies because they feared their rights could be stripped away as well. A third act allowed for British soldiers to be tried in Britain if they were accused of a crime. The fourth act once again required colonists to provide food and shelter to British soldiers.

Colonists responded by forming the **First Continental Congress in 1774**, and all the colonies except for Georgia sent delegates. The delegates sought a compromise with the British government instead of launching an armed revolt. The First Continental Congress sent a petition to King George III affirming their loyalty but demanding the repeal of the Intolerable Acts. The delegates organized a boycott of imports from and exports to Britain until their demands were met.

The colonists began to form militias and gather weapons and ammunition. The first battle of the revolution began at Lexington and Concord in April 1775 when British troops tried to seize a supply of gunpowder and were confronted by about eighty Minutemen. A brief skirmish left eight colonists dead and ten wounded. Colonial reinforcements poured in and harassed the British force as they retreated to Boston. Although the battle did not result in many casualties, it marked the beginning of war.

A month later, the Second Continental Congress convened in Philadelphia. The delegates formed an army and appointed George Washington as commander in chief. Delegates were still reluctant to repudiate their allegiance to King George III and did not do so until they issued the Declaration of Independence on July 4, 1776. The Declaration drew on the ideas of the Enlightenment and declared that the colonists had the right to life, liberty, and the pursuit of happiness. The Declaration stated that the colonists had to break away from Britain because King George III had violated their rights.

After the Battle of Lexington and Concord, British troops retreated to Boston and the colonial militias laid siege to the city. Colonists built fortifications on Bunker Hill outside the city and British troops attacked the position in June 1775. The colonists inflicted heavy casualties on the British and killed a number of officers. However, the defenders ran out of ammunition and British troops captured Bunker Hill on the third assault. Although it was a defeat for the colonists, the Battle of Bunker Hill demonstrated that they could stand and fight against the disciplined and professional British army.

The British army initially had the upper hand and defeated colonial forces in a number of engagements. The Americans did not achieve a victory until the Battle of Trenton in December 1776. Washington famously crossed the Delaware River on Christmas Day and launched a surprise attack against Hessian mercenaries. They captured more than 1,000 soldiers and suffered very minimal casualties. The victory at Trenton bolstered American morale and showed that they could defeat professional European soldiers.

The **Battle of Saratoga** in New York in the fall of 1777 was an important turning point in the **American War for Independence**. American troops surrounded and captured more than 6,000 British soldiers. This victory convinced the French king to support the revolutionaries by sending troops, money, weapons, and ships to the American continent. French officers who fought alongside the Patriots brought back many ideas with them that eventually sparked a revolution in France in 1789.

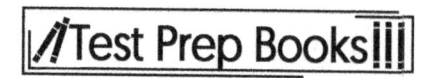

French support was very important in the last major battle of the revolution at Yorktown, Virginia, in 1781. American troops laid siege to General Cornwallis's British forces at Yorktown. The French fleet defeated a British naval squadron sent to relieve Cornwallis. French and American troops began attacking the British fortifications in Yorktown; a sustained artillery bombardment by American guns eventually forced Cornwallis to surrender. This ended the Revolutionary War, and in 1783 the British signed the Treaty of Paris. Britain recognized the United States as an independent country and set the Mississippi River as the nation's western border. However, British troops continued to occupy several forts in the Great Lakes region.

In addition, tens of thousands of colonists who remained loyal to the British Empire fled the United States after the war. They were known as loyalists and many thousands had joined militias and fought against the patriots. Some loyalists fled to Canada or Britain but many remained in the United States. Many Native American tribes had sided with the British as well in an attempt to curb western expansion. No Native American leaders signed the Treaty of Paris and they refused to give up their territories, which led to further conflict as the new American nation began to expand westward.

Adoption of the Constitution and Bill of Rights

America's first system of government was actually laid out in the Articles of Confederation, and not the Constitution. The Articles of Confederation were ratified during the Revolutionary War and went into effect in 1781. The Articles of Confederation created a relatively weak central government and allowed individual states to retain most of the power. Under this system, the national government did not have a president or judiciary. Each state had only one vote in the Confederation Congress and most major decisions required unanimous approval by all thirteen states. Despite this requirement, the Confederation Congress did pass some important legislation, including the Northwest Ordinance, which organized the land west of Appalachian Mountains. The territories eventually became the states of Ohio, Indiana, Michigan, Illinois, Wisconsin, and Minnesota. However, Congress did not have the power to tax and could only request money from the states without any way to enforce its demands. A Revolutionary War veteran named Daniel Shays led an armed insurrection in western Massachusetts in 1787. Although Shay's Rebellion was defeated, it drew attention to the weaknesses of the Articles of Confederation.

The Constitutional Convention met in Philadelphia a few months after the rebellion in order to create a stronger federal government. However, delegates disagreed over how to structure the new system. The Virginia Plan was one proposal that included a bicameral legislature where states were awarded representation based on their population size. This would benefit more populous states at the expense of smaller states. The other main proposal was the New Jersey Plan, which retained many elements of the Articles of Confederation, including a unicameral legislature with one vote per state. This plan would put states on an equal footing regardless of population.

Eventually, delegates agreed to support the Connecticut Compromise (also known as the Great Compromise), which incorporated elements from both the Virginia and New Jersey Plans. Under the new Constitution, Congress would be a bicameral body. In the House of Representatives, states would be allocated seats based on population, but in the Senate each state would have two votes. The Constitution also included a president and judiciary that would each serve to check the power of other

U.S. History, Society, Customs, and Culture

branches of government. In addition, Congress had the power to tax and had more enforcement powers.

Slavery was another contentious issue during the Constitutional Convention. Slavery was more common in the Southern states and less common in the North. The Southern states wanted slaves to be counted when calculating representation in Congress but not when it came to assessing taxes. Northern states wanted the opposite and eventually the two sides agreed to the **Three-Fifths Compromise** where slaves were counted as three-fifths of a person for the purposes of both taxation and representation. The Constitution also included a provision that allowed slave owners to recover slaves who had escaped and permitted the international slave trade to continue until 1808.

Once the Constitution had been drafted, nine of the thirteen states had to ratify it. Vigorous debate erupted over whether or not the Constitution should be approved. Two different political factions emerged. The Federalists supported the Constitution because they felt a stronger central government was necessary in order to promote economic growth and improve national security. Several leading federalists, including Alexander Hamilton, John Jay, and James Madison, published a series of articles urging voters to support the Constitution. However, the Anti-Federalists, including Thomas Jefferson and Patrick Henry, felt that the Constitution took too much power away from the states and gave it to the national government. They also thought there weren't enough protections for individual rights and lobbied for the addition of a Bill of Rights that guaranteed basic liberties. Ultimately, the Constitution was ratified in 1788 and the Bill of Rights was approved a year later.

The Electoral College unanimously elected George Washington as the nation's first president in 1789. Despite this appearance of unity, deep political divisions led to the formation of the nation's first party system. Washington supported the Federalist ideology and appointed several Federalists to his cabinet, including Alexander Hamilton as secretary of the treasury. The Anti-Federalist faction evolved into the Democratic-Republican Party and favored stronger state governments instead of a powerful federal government. As settlers moved into the new Northwest Territories, Washington helped pacify Indians who opposed further expansion. He also successfully put down a rebellion in western Pennsylvania by farmers opposed to a federal tax on whiskey.

A number of different issues divided the Federalists and the Democratic-Republicans, including the French Revolution, which began in 1789. Initially, many Americans supported the French effort to replace their monarchy and create a republican government. However, the French Revolution quickly became more violent, as thousands of suspected opponents of the revolution were executed during the Reign of Terror. The Federalists, including Washington, were horrified by the violence, while Jefferson and the Democratic-Republicans thought the United States should help its former ally. Washington ensured that the country remain officially neutral.

Washington declined to seek a third term and another Federalist, John Adams, became our second president. Adams signed the Alien and Sedition Acts, which made it a criminal offense to criticize the government, and allowed the president to deport aliens suspected of treason. Adams and the Federalists argued that the laws were necessary in order to improve security as Europe became embroiled in a war against the new French republic. Jefferson and the Democratic-Republicans said the laws restricted free speech. Jefferson made the acts an important topic in 1800 when he successfully ran for president.

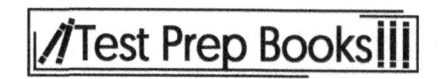

Jefferson's victory marked a turning point in the political system because the Democratic-Republicans gained more power while the Federalists went into decline. He repealed the **Alien and Sedition Acts** when he was elected. The Federalists were further weakened when Hamilton was killed in a duel in 1804.

Jefferson accomplished several significant achievements during his presidency, and one of the most important was the Louisiana Purchase in 1803. For $15 million, Jefferson bought French territory west of the Mississippi River that doubled the size of the United States. He then appointed Meriwether Lewis and William Clark to lead an expedition to explore the vast new territory and study its geography, vegetation, and plant life. Clark also brought his African-American slave, York, on the journey. York helped hunt and even saved Clark's life during a flood. The expedition was also aided by Sacagawea, a Shoshone woman, who acted as a guide and interpreter. The explorers also established relations with Native American tribes and set the stage for further western expansion in the 1800s.

Several key Supreme Court decisions were also issued during this time. The case of **Marbury vs. Madison** established the policy of judicial review, which declared that the Supreme Court could rule whether or not an act of Congress was constitutional. The case of **McCullough vs. Maryland** affirmed that Congress had the power to pass laws that were "necessary and proper" in order to carry out its other duties. The case also upheld the supremacy of federal laws over state laws when they came into conflict.

War between the United States and Britain broke out in 1812 because the United States was drawn into a conflict between Britain and France. Britain refused to stop interfering with American ships bound for France and had begun forcibly recruiting American citizens into the British navy. Furthermore, the British still occupied several forts near the Great Lakes and continued to encourage Indians to attack American settlements in the Northwest Territories.

This led to war in 1812, and many Native American leaders allied themselves with the British, including the Shawnee warrior Tecumseh. Tecumseh temporarily united several tribes but his confederacy fell apart when he was killed in battle. This further weakened Native American resistance and facilitated American settlement in the Northwest Territory after the war.

The United States also achieved a victory at the Battle of Lake Erie where several American ships routed a British squadron. However, an American attempt to invade Canada failed, and the British humiliated the nation by invading Washington D.C. and burning down several public buildings, including the White House. The United States did achieve another victory after hostilities had ceased when future president Andrew Jackson repulsed a British attack at New Orleans. The war did not result in any major territorial gains or losses, but it did reaffirm American independence and gave America its national anthem, the **"Star Spangled Banner."** It also led to the collapse of the Federalist Party, which had opposed the war. The Democratic-Republicans dominated politics for the next decade, which was known as the **"Era of Good Feelings,"** thus marking the end of the first party system.

Causes and Consequences of Territorial Expansion

Constant immigration meant that land prices in the eastern United States rose, and people sought new economic opportunities on the frontier where land was cheaper. The United States government tried purchasing land from Native Americans, but most refused to relinquish their territories. Native Americans continued to defend their land until the Shawnee chief Tecumseh, who had formed a

U.S. History, Society, Customs, and Culture

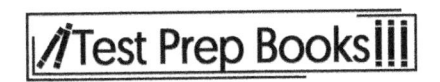

confederacy of Native American tribes to establish a self-governing Indian nation and oppose U.S. expansion into the Northwest Territory, was defeated and killed in the War of 1812. This defeat helped secure the Northwest Territory, and more settlers began pouring in. After the Louisiana Purchase, Lewis and Clark paved the way for expansion into the Great Plains and further west.

The Cherokee, Chickasaw, Choctaw, Creek, and Seminole tribes of the Southeastern United States were known as the "**Five Civilized Tribes**" because they had developed a written language and many members had become Christians. Nevertheless, Andrew Jackson signed the Indian Removal Act of 1830, which gave him the power to continue buying land from various tribes. The Cherokee filed a lawsuit to protect their territory and won their arguments before the Supreme Court. However, President Andrew Jackson ignored the ruling and eventually used troops to force many tribes off their land and sent them west to Oklahoma during the 1830s. This was known as the "**Trail of Tears**" because thousands of Native Americans died from starvation, exposure, and disease along the way.

Furthermore, the concept of Manifest Destiny emerged during the 1800s and introduced the idea that God wanted Americans to civilize and control the entire North American continent. This led to conflict when the province of Texas declared its independence from Mexico and asked to be annexed by the United States. **President James K. Polk** tried to buy Texas, but when Mexico refused, he sent troops into the disputed territory. Mexican troops responding by attacking an American unit, which led to war in 1846.

The **Mexican-American War** (1846-1848) began over a border dispute. The Republic of Texas declared its independence from Mexico in 1836 and applied to join the United States. However, in a desire to avoid war with Mexico, the administration of **President Martin van Buren** decided not to annex Texas. Two administrations later, **President John Tyler**, with the support of President-Elect James K. Polk, was able to pass a bill to annex Texas right before he left office in 1845, which Polk then signed. The Texas and Mexican governments disagreed on where the Texas border ended. Polk sent in the U.S. Army under Zachary Taylor to occupy the disputed territory. After a failed attempt to purchase the disputed territory from Mexico, the United States declared war on Mexico in 1846.

The American troops won several battles although the Mexican army usually outnumbered them. The Mexican troops were poorly armed and trained, and the Americans made use of their highly skilled artillery force. The Americans eventually captured Mexico City in 1847 and forced the Mexican government to sign the Treaty of Guadalupe-Hidalgo in 1848. The treaty recognized American control over Texas and also ceded California, Utah, Colorado, Arizona, New Mexico, and Nevada in exchange for $15 million. Tens of thousands of prospectors flooded into California when gold was discovered there in 1849. The prospectors often encroached on Native American lands, which led to further conflict. In 1854, the United States also acquired additional territories as part of the Gadsden Purchase. The acquisition of so much new territory sparked a debate over whether the land would be open or closed to slavery.

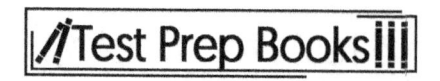

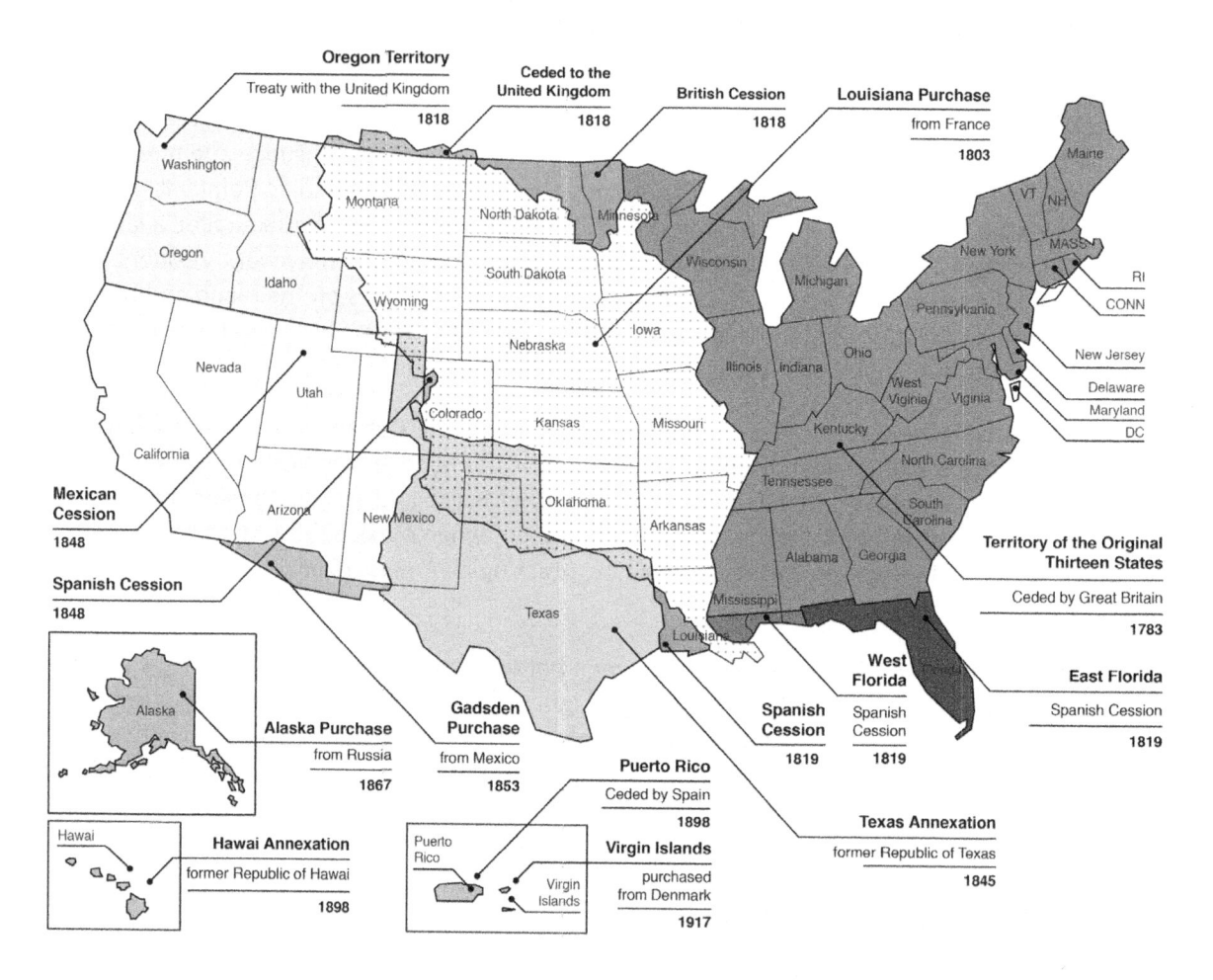

Manifest Destiny also sparked a desire to expand American influence into Central and South America. Adventurers launched several unsuccessful attempts to invade Nicaragua and Cuba.

Several important laws also stimulated western expansion during the second half of the 19th century. Congress passed the Homestead Act in 1862, which allowed citizens to claim 160 acres for only $1.25 per acre. The settler also had to live on the land for five years and make improvements. That same year, Congress also passed the Pacific Railroad Act, which supported the construction of a transcontinental railroad. The United States government provided land and financial support to railroad companies and the first transcontinental link was established in 1869. This facilitated trade and communication between the eastern and western United States.

As Americans poured westward, conflict again broke out between settlers and Native Americans. The discovery of gold in the Black Hills of South Dakota caused prospectors to flood into the area although the U.S. government had recognized the territory belonged to the Sioux. General George Armstrong Custer brought in troops to try and take possession of the Black Hills. This led to disaster when Custer and more than 250 soldiers died at the Battle of Little Big Horn in 1876.

U.S. History, Society, Customs, and Culture

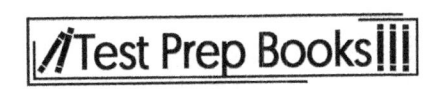

The U.S. government continued its efforts to control Native American tribes. The Dawes Act of 1887 encouraged Native Americans to settle on reservations and become farmers in exchange for U.S. citizenship. Chief Joseph was a leader of the Nez Perce tribe who refused to live on a reservation and tried to flee to Canada. However, the U.S. captured Chief Joseph and his tribe and forced them onto a reservation. Reformers also required Native Americans to send their children to boarding schools where they had to speak English and dress like Caucasians instead of maintaining their traditional culture. The schools were often crowded, and students were also subjected to physical and sexual abuse.

In 1890, the Lakota Indians tried to preserve their traditional beliefs by performing a special ceremony called a Ghost Dance. U.S. government officials felt threatened and sent soldiers to try and disarm the Lakota. This led to the **Massacre at Wounded Knee** in 1890 where at least 150 Lakota, including many women and children, were slaughtered. It was the last major conflict between Native Americans and U.S. forces.

The United States purchased Alaska from Russia in 1867 for $7.2 million. At the time, the purchase was unpopular with the public, but seal hunting became very profitable and gold was discovered in 1896. Alaska became a state in 1959.

In 1893, American businessmen launched an armed coup, overthrew the queen of Hawaii, and asked Congress to annex Hawaii. The businessmen owned sugar plantations and feared the queen's attempts to enact reform would threaten their political influence. Hawaii became a U.S. territory in 1898 and a state in 1959.

The last phase of American territorial expansion occurred as a result of the Spanish-American War in 1898. New ideas arose in the late 19th century that helped justify further expansion. Some intellectuals applied Charles Darwin's ideas of "survival of the fittest" to the human race and called this new concept Social Darwinism. They used this idea to justify why stronger groups of people colonized and exploited weaker groups. In addition, imperialists also used the idea of the White Man's Burden to justify further expansion. They claimed that Caucasians were obligated to civilize and govern groups thought to be less advanced.

These ideas were used to justify America's new status as a colonial power as a result of the Spanish-American War. Although Spain had once been a powerful empire, it had been in decline. The United States went to war against Spain in 1898 when the American battleship USS Maine exploded in Havana Harbor and killed more than 250 sailors. The U.S. Navy defeated the Spanish fleet in several engagements and then the Army followed up with a victory at San Juan Hill, which included the famous charge by Teddy Roosevelt and the Rough Riders.

The war lasted less than four months and made the United States a world power. The U.S. also acquired several Spanish colonies, including Puerto Rico, Guam, and the Philippines. Guam became an important refueling station for American naval forces in the Pacific and remains a U.S. territory today, along with Puerto Rico. When the United States occupied the Philippines, the Filipino people launched a rebellion in order to obtain their independence. The U.S. Army put down the insurrection, but in doing so, they committed many atrocities against the Filipino people. The Philippines would remain an American territory until 1946.

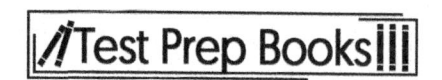

Causes and Consequences of 19th-Century Sectionalism, the Civil War, and Reconstruction

In the early 1800s, political and economic differences between the North and South became more apparent. Politically, a small but vocal group of abolitionists emerged in the North who demanded a complete end to slavery throughout the United States. William Lloyd Garrison edited the abolitionist newspaper **The Liberator** and vehemently denounced the brutality of slavery. His criticism was so vicious that the legislature of Georgia offered a $5,000 bounty to anyone who could capture Garrison and deliver him to state authorities. Other activists participated in the **Underground Railroad**—a network that helped fugitive slaves escape to the Northern United States or Canada.

Economic differences emerged as the North began to industrialize, especially in the textile industry where factories increased productivity. However, the Southern economy remained largely agricultural and focused on labor-intensive crops such as tobacco and cotton. This meant that slavery remained an essential part of the Southern economy. In addition, the North built more roads, railroads, and canals, while the Southern transportation system lagged behind. The Northern economy was also based on cash, while many Southerners still bartered for goods and services. This led to growing sectional tension between the North and South as their economies began to diverge further apart.

These economic differences led to political tension as well, especially over the debate about the expansion of slavery. This debate became more important as the United States expanded westward into the Louisiana Purchase and acquired more land after the Mexican-American War. Most Northerners were not abolitionists. However, many opposed the expansion of slavery into the western territories because it would limit their economic opportunities. If a territory was open to slavery, it would be more attractive to wealthy slave owners who could afford to buy up the best land. In addition, the presence of slave labor would make it hard for independent farmers, artisans, and craftsman to make a living, because they would have to compete against slaves who did not earn any wages. For their part, Southerners felt it was essential to continue expanding in order to strengthen the southern economy and ensure that the Southern way of life survived. As intensive farming depleted the soil of nutrients, Southern slave owners sought more fertile land in the west.

Both the North and South also feared losing political power as more states were admitted to the nation. For example, neither side wanted to lose influence in the United States senate if the careful balance of free and slave state representation was disrupted. Several compromises were negotiated in Congress, but they only temporarily quieted debate. The first such effort, called the Missouri Compromise, was passed in 1820, and it maintained political parity in the U.S. Senate by admitting Missouri as a slave state and Maine as a free state. The Missouri Compromise banned slavery in the portion of the Louisiana Purchase that was north of the 36°30' parallel and permitted slavery in the portion south of that line as well as Missouri.

However, the slavery debate erupted again after the acquisition of new territory during the Mexican-American War. The Compromise of 1850 admitted California as a free state and ended the slave trade, but not slavery itself, in Washington D.C., in order to please Northern politicians. In return, Southern politicians were able to pass a stronger fugitive slave law and demanded that New Mexico and Utah be allowed to vote on whether or not slavery would be permitted in their state constitutions. This introduced the idea of popular sovereignty where the residents of each new territory, and not the federal government, could decide whether or not they would become a slave state or a free state. This

U.S. History, Society, Customs, and Culture

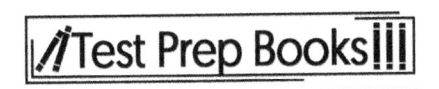

essentially negated the **Missouri Compromise of 1820**. The enhanced fugitive slave law also angered many Northerners, because it empowered federal marshals to deputize anyone, even residents of a free state, and force them to help recapture escaped slaves. Anyone who refused would be subject to a $1,000 fine (equivalent to more than $28,000 in 2015).

The debate over slavery erupted again only a few years later when the territories of Kansas and Nebraska were created in 1854. The application of popular sovereignty meant that pro- and anti-slavery settlers flooded into these two territories to ensure that their faction would have a majority when it came time to vote on the state constitution. Tension between pro- and anti-slavery forces in Kansas led to an armed conflict known as "**Bleeding Kansas**."

John Brown was a militant abolitionist who fought in "Bleeding Kansas" and murdered five pro-slavery settlers there in 1856. He returned to the eastern United States and attacked the federal arsenal at Harper's Ferry, Virginia, in 1859. He hoped to seize the weapons there and launch a slave rebellion, but federal troops killed or captured most of Brown's accomplices and Brown was executed. The attack terrified Southerners and reflected the increasing hostility between North and South.

The sectional differences that emerged in the last several decades culminated in the presidential election of 1860. Abraham Lincoln led the new Republican Party, which opposed slavery on moral and economic grounds. The question of how best to expand slavery into new territories split the Democratic Party into two different factions that each nominated a presidential candidate. A fourth candidate also ran on a platform of preserving the union by trying to ignore the slavery controversy.

Lincoln found little support outside of the North but managed to win the White House since the Democratic Party was divided. Southern states felt threatened by Lincoln's anti-slavery stance and feared he would abolish slavery throughout the country. South Carolina was the first Southern state to secede from the Union and ten more eventually followed. Lincoln declared that the Union could not be dissolved and swore to defend federal installations. The Civil War began when Confederate troops fired on Fort Sumter in Charleston in 1861.

The Civil War

The **First Battle of Bull Run** (also known as the First Battle of Manassas) in 1861 was the first major infantry engagement of the Civil War. Both the Northern and Southern troops were inexperienced and although they had equal numbers, the Confederates emerged victorious. Many had thought the war would be short, but it continued for another four years.

The Union navy imposed a blockade on the Confederacy and captured the port of New Orleans in 1862. The Union navy was much stronger than the Confederate fleet and prevented the Southern states from selling cotton to foreign countries or buying weapons.

In 1862, Union forces thwarted a Confederate invasion of Maryland at the Battle of Antietam. This engagement was the single bloodiest day of the war and more than 23,000 men on both sides were killed or wounded. Union troops forced the Confederates to retreat, and that gave Lincoln the political capital he needed to issue the Emancipation Proclamation in 1863. This declaration did not abolish slavery, but it did free slaves in Southern territory. It also allowed African Americans to join the Union navy and about 200,000 did so. The 54th Massachusetts Infantry was a famous unit of African American soldiers who led an assault on Fort Wagner in South Carolina in 1863. Although the attack failed, the 54th Massachusetts witnessed African American troops fighting bravely under fire.

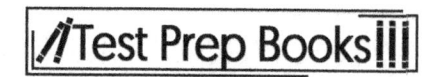

The **Siege of Vicksburg in 1863** was a major Union victory because they gained control of the Mississippi River and cut the Confederacy in half. This made it difficult the Confederacy to move troops around and communicate with their forces. Grant commanded the Northern forces in the siege and eventually became the Union army's top general.

The Battle of Gettysburg in 1863 marked the turning point of the Civil War. **Robert E. Lee** led Confederate troops into Pennsylvania, but in three days of heavy fighting, the Union army forced them to retreat. The victory bolstered Northern morale and weakened Southern resolve. Never again would Confederate forces threaten Northern territory.

In 1864, Union general **William T. Sherman** captured Atlanta and then marched more than 200 miles to Savannah. Along the way, he destroyed anything that could support the Southern war effort, such as railroads and cotton mills. At this point, the Southern economy was beginning to collapse. The North had more manpower than the South and could afford to sustain more casualties. The North also had more industrial capacity to produce weapons and supplies and more railroads to transport men and equipment.

Eventually, Robert E. Lee surrendered to **Ulysses S. Grant** at Appomattox, Virginia, on April 9, 1865. Five days later, **John Wilkes Booth** assassinated Lincoln in Washington, D.C. **Vice President Andrew Johnson**, a Democrat, succeeded him and soon came into conflict with Republicans in Congress about how to reintegrate Southern states into the nation. This process was known as **Reconstruction** and lasted from 1865 to 1877.

Reconstruction

Johnson opposed equal rights for African Americans and pardoned many Confederate leaders. However, many Congressional Republicans wanted to harshly punish Southerners for their attempts to secede from the Union. They were known as Radical Republicans because they also wanted to give former slaves equal rights.

Johnson vetoed bills that were designed to protect the rights of freed slaves, but Congress overrode his vetoes. This led to increasing conflict between Johnson and Congress, which eventually caused Radical Republicans to impeach him. Although Johnson was acquitted in 1868, he had very little power, and Radical Republicans took control of the Reconstruction process.

Republicans passed three important constitutional amendments as part of the Reconstruction process. The 13th amendment was ratified in 1865, and it abolished slavery throughout the country. The 14th Amendment was ratified in 1868 and gave equal rights to all citizens. The 15th Amendment was ratified in 1870 and specifically granted all men the right to vote regardless of race.

Southerners resisted these demands and passed laws that prohibited freed slaves from owning weapons or testifying against whites. They also formed militias and vigilante groups, such as the Ku Klux Klan, in order to intimidate African Americans who tried to vote. Congress sent federal troops into Southern states in order to enforce the law and prevent vigilante violence.

After the much-disputed election of 1876, the Democrats offered to let the Republicans have the White House if they agreed to end Reconstruction. After the Republicans agreed, federal troops were withdrawn and African Americans in the South were subjected to discrimination until the Civil Rights

U.S. History, Society, Customs, and Culture

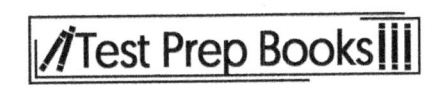

movement of the 1960s. Scholars often consider the Reconstruction era the beginning of Jim Crow and a transition into a new form of "institutionalized racism" that still pervades much of modern U.S. society.

Relationships Among Industrialization, Urbanization, and Immigration in the Late 19th and Early 20th Centuries

After the end of the Civil War, America experienced a period of intense industrialization, immigration, and urbanization, and all three trends were interrelated. The process of industrialization had begun before the Civil War but expanded into more sectors of the economy in the later part of the century. This era is often called the Second Industrial Revolution and included growth in the chemical, petroleum, iron, steel, and telecommunications industries. For example, the Bessemer process made it much easier to produce high quality steel by removing impurities during the smelting process.

The writer **Mark Twain** called the late 19th century the **Gilded Age** because the era was also one of extreme social inequality. Some corporations expanded and began to control entire industries. For example, by 1890, the Standard Oil Company produced 88 percent of all the refined oil in the nation. This made a few individuals, such as John D. Rockefeller who owned Standard Oil, extremely wealthy. On the other hand, many workers earned low wages and began to form labor unions, such as the American Federation of Labor in 1886, in order to demand better working conditions and higher pay.

Strikes were one of the most common ways workers could express their dissatisfaction, and the Pullman Strike of 1894 was one of the largest such incidents in the 19th century. Workers went on strike after the Pullman Company, which manufactured railroad cars, cut wages by about 25 percent. More than 125,000 workers around the country walked off the job and attacked workers hired to replace them. Federal troops were sent in to end the strike, and more than eighty workers were killed or wounded during confrontations. The strike was unsuccessful, but Congress passed a law making Labor Day a federal holiday in order to placate union members.

Immigration also played an important part in the economic and social changes that occurred during the late 19th century. Immigration patterns changed during this time and immigrants from Southern and Eastern Europe, such as Italy and Poland, began to surpass the number of arrivals from Northern and Western Europe. The immigrants sought economic opportunity in the United States because wages for unskilled workers were higher than in their home countries. Some Americans resented the influx of immigrants because they spoke different languages and practiced Catholicism. In 1924, Congress passed a law that restricted immigration from Southern and Eastern Europe.

Increased urbanization was the last factor that contributed to the rapid changes of the Gilded Age. Factories were located near cities in order to draw upon a large pool of potential employees. Immigrants flooded into cities in search of work, and new arrivals often settled in the same neighborhoods where their compatriots lived. Between 1860 and 1890, the urbanization rate increased from about 20 percent to 35 percent. Cities struggled to keep up with growing populations, and services such as sanitation and water often lagged behind demand. Immigrants often lived in crowded living conditions that facilitated the spread of diseases.

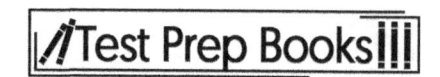

Political, Economic, Social, and Cultural Developments from the Progressive Era Through the New Deal

The social inequalities and economic abuses of the Gilded Age did not go unnoticed, and in the 1890s many reformers began to demand change. This period was called the Progressive Era and included activists in both the Democratic and Republican parties. The Progressives wanted to use scientific methods and government regulation to improve society. For example, they advocated the use of initiative, referendum, and recall to make government more responsive to its citizens. Progressives also argued that it was necessary to breakup large monopolies (known as trust busting) in order to promote equal economic competition. In 1911, Rockefeller's Standard Oil was split up into thirty-four different companies in order to promote competition, and the Federal Trade Commission was established in 1914 in order to prevent other monopolies from forming. Many Progressives also supported several constitutional amendments that were ratified in early 20th century, including the 17th amendment, which established the direct election of U.S. Senators in 1913 (previously state legislatures had elected senators). They also favored the prohibition of alcohol that went into effect with the 18th Amendment in 1919. Progressives also advocated for women's rights and backed the 19th Amendment, which gave women the right to vote in 1920.

Many journalists who supported the reform movement of the Progressives were known as **Muckrakers** because they helped expose political corruption and social inequality. Upton Sinclair wrote a novel in 1906 called "The Jungle," which exposed poor working conditions and health violations in the Chicago meatpacking industry. His exposé led to the passages of the Pure Food and Drug Act in 1906, which authorized the federal government to inspect the purity of foodstuffs and medicines. Jacob Riis was a photographer who documented the crowded and unhealthy living conditions that many immigrants and poor workers endured.

World War I, from 1914 to 1918, led to a communist revolution in Russia in 1917. Many Americans wanted to prevent political radicals from gaining influence in the United States. A number of strikes and bombings around the country led the federal government to crack down on anarchists, socialists, and communists in an event known as the First Red Scare. In 1919, U.S. Attorney General A. Mitchell Palmer launched a series of raids and arrested resident aliens suspected of belonging to radical groups. About 500 resident aliens were eventually deported.

In 1933, President Franklin D. Roosevelt introduced the New Deal, which was a series of executive orders and laws passed by Congress in response to the Great Depression. The programs focused on relief, recovery, and reform, and were enacted until 1938. The second New Deal from 1935-1938 promoted the Social Security Act, labor unions, and aided tenant farmers and migrant workers who were struggling from the economic devastation of the Great Depression.

Social Developments

With the ratification of the 19th Amendment in 1920, women obtained the right to vote. This achievement was partly due to women's contributions on the home front during World War I. Women served as Army nurses and worked in factories to help produce weapons, ammunition, and equipment. As more women entered the workforce, they became more financially independent and began to socialize without being supervised by a chaperone, as was the norm during the 19th century. Overall, women during this period, known as **"New Women,"** took on a more active role in public life, pursued higher education in greater numbers, and sought more sexual freedom. During the 1920s, women,

U.S. History, Society, Customs, and Culture

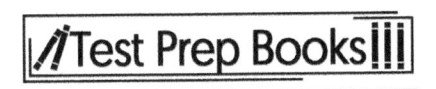

known as **"flappers,"** began to flaunt social conventions by wearing short skirts, bobbing hair, smoking cigarettes, and driving automobiles. Nevertheless, a **"glass ceiling"** still remains in place decades after women's suffrage in regards to a gender wage gap.

Millions of African Americans also moved north during and after World War I in search of work in a phenomenon known as the Great Migration. This led to increased racial tension as whites and blacks competed for jobs and housing. This culminated in a wave of race riots that swept across the country in the summer of 1919. In Chicago, conflict broke out between whites and blacks at a segregated beach, which led to five days of violence during which thirty-eight people were killed and more than 500 injured. The impact of the Great Migration can still be seen in contemporary, heavily segregated Rust Belt cities such as Gary, IN and Milwaukee, WI.

The invention of the automobile also contributed to social change. Henry Ford applied the method of assembly line construction and scientific management to the automobile manufacturing industry. This made it much cheaper to manufacture cars and allowed more people to purchase them. Automobiles allowed young men and women to socialize and date without adult supervision. Automobiles also improved transportation, increased mobility, and spawned the first suburbs.

Cultural Developments

Motion picture cameras were invented in the late 19th century, and the film industry experienced significant growth in the early 20th century. Because the first movies were silent, dialogue was displayed on intertitles and a live orchestra usually performed during a screening. "Birth of a Nation," by D.W. Griffith, was one of the first major cinema blockbusters, and it portrayed the Ku Klux Klan in a heroic light. Millions of Americans saw the film, which helped the Klan spread throughout the Northern and Western United States.

The Great Migration also led to cultural changes during the 1920s known as the **Harlem Renaissance**. The movement was based in the neighborhood of Harlem and led to a rebirth of black literature, art, music, and fashion. Jazz was an important feature of the Harlem Renaissance and challenged musical conventions by emphasizing improvisation and spontaneity. Jazz became very popular with both whites and blacks during the 1920s. Langston Hughes was a poet of the Harlem Renaissance who encouraged his readers to take pride in their black identity.

Economic Developments

The **Panic of 1893** was a worldwide economic depression that devastated the American economy. Businesses went bankrupt, banks collapsed, and unemployment rose to approximately 17 percent. The economy began to recover by 1897, and the beginning of World War I boosted the U.S. economy as European nations bought American goods.

In 1918, the United States emerged from World War I as a major economic power because it had helped finance the Allied war effort and produced large amounts of weapons and equipment. The American agricultural sector also prospered because European farms had been devastated by the war. This sent crop prices up, and farmers used the money to buy more land and equipment. Although the 1920s is usually depicted as an era of economic prosperity, agricultural prices fell after World War I, and farmers were unable to pay back their debts.

Stock market speculation increased during the 1920s, and investors borrowed money in order to purchase shares. This did not cause any concern as long as the stock market went up, but it led to disaster when stock prices fell sharply in October 1929 and investors were unable to repay their loans. The stock market crash may have triggered the **Great Depression**, but it did not cause it. The Great Depression spread around the globe as nations stopped trading with each other. In the United States, families lost their savings when banks failed because there was no federal insurance. The economy went into a downward spiral because as more people lost their jobs, they had little money to spend, which led to further layoffs and more economic contraction.

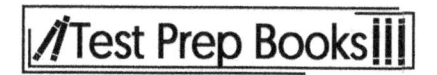

Unemployment peaked at 25 percent between 1932 and 1933.

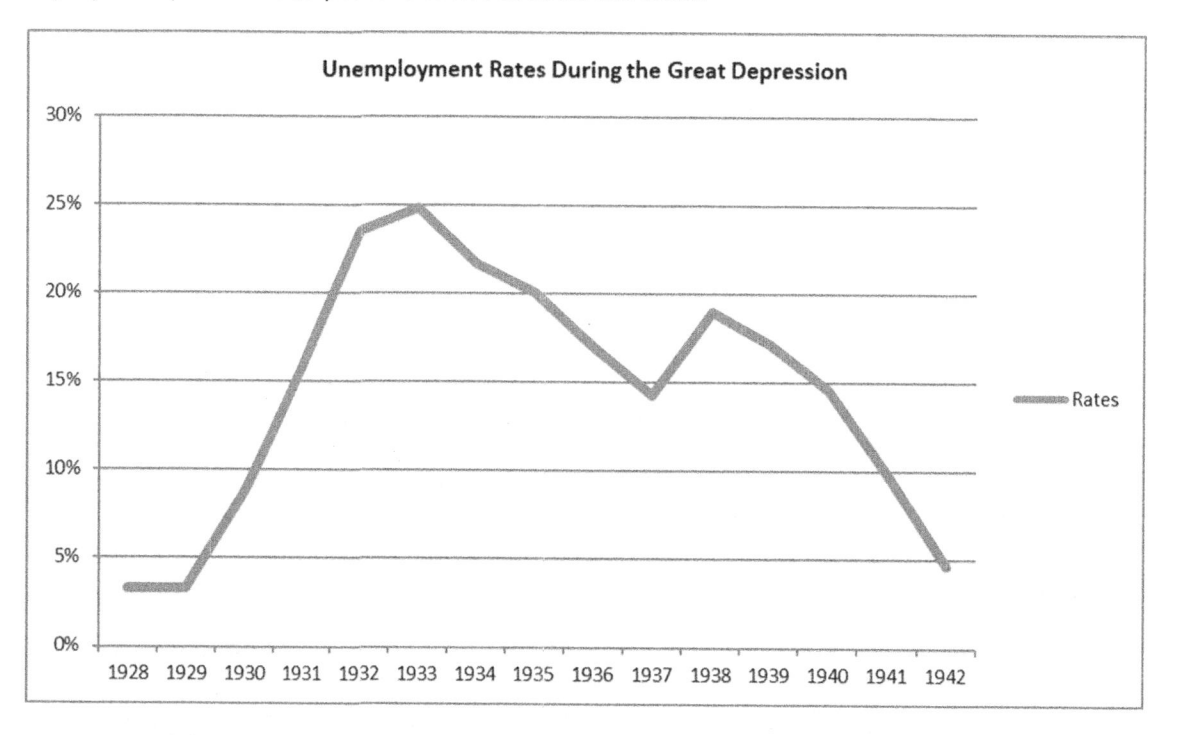

Unemployment Rates During the Great Depression

Democratic candidate Franklin D. Roosevelt was elected president in 1932 on his promise to help the economy recover by increasing government spending. After taking office in 1933, Roosevelt introduced a barrage of proposals, called the New Deal, that he hoped would boost employment, stimulate demand, and increase government regulation. Some elements of the New Deal were temporary, such as the Civilian Conservation Corps, which put young men to work improving parks between 1933 and 1942.

Other New Deal programs endure to this day, such as the Social Security Administration, which has provided pensions to retirees, temporary payments to unemployed workers, and benefits to handicapped individuals since 1935. In addition, the Securities and Exchange Commission was created in 1934 and continues to regulate stock markets and investment companies. The **Wagner Act of 1935** was also an important part of the New Deal because it guaranteed the right of workers to unionize and go on strike. The 21st Amendment was ratified in 1933 and repealed Prohibition, which had been hard to enforce and was unpopular. Roosevelt also hoped it would create jobs and stimulate spending. The New Deal helped reduce unemployment, but the economy did not completely recover until America entered World War II and production increased in order to support the war efforts.

U.S. History, Society, Customs, and Culture

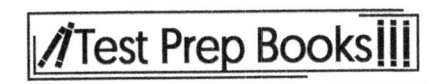

Causes and Consequences of American Participation in World War I & II

World War I began in 1914 with the assassination of **Franz Ferdinand**, the apparent heir of the Austro-Hungarian Empire. A network of secret alliances meant that most European nations were quickly drawn into the conflict, although **President Woodrow Wilson** initially tried to keep the United States neutral. The war involved two major European alliances: the Triple Entente of Britain, France, and Russia, and the Central Powers, which included Germany and Austria-Hungary. The British implemented a naval blockade that was very successful, and the Germans retaliated by launching submarine attacks. German submarines attacked any ship carrying supplies to the Triple Entente, including the passenger ship RMS Lusitania in 1915. About 1,200 people died, including more than 100 Americans.

The Germans temporarily halted their unrestricted submarine campaign, but eventually resumed the attacks in 1917. In addition, in 1917, Germany asked Mexico to attack the United States in a communiqué known as the Zimmerman telegram. These events led the United States to join the Triple Entente in 1917, although significant numbers of American troops did not arrive in Europe until 1918. American reinforcement helped the British and French, who had been fighting continuously since 1914, launch a final offensive that defeated Germany in 1918. American forces suffered about 320,000 casualties. As previously noted, World War I also led to significant changes on the home front as women took on new responsibilities, and thousands of African Americans migrated north in search of work. World War I also led to a communist revolution that transformed Russia into the USSR in 1922.

After Germany was defeated in 1918, Wilson made a proposal known as the Fourteen Points and argued that the best way to resolve the conflict was by promoting free trade and democracy. For instance, Wilson wanted nations to respect the right to navigate in international waters and create a League of Nations that would resolve future disputes. Some of his suggestions, such as the League of Nations, were adopted, but many were not. In 1919, Germany was forced to sign the Treaty of Versailles, which imposed harsh economic penalties and restricted the German military. Ultimately, the Treaty of Versailles created resentment in Germany that lead to World War II. America emerged as an important player in world affairs after World War I because the American economy had supplied the Triple Entente with arms and equipment and American soldiers helped to achieve victory.

In the period between the world wars, fascism became popular in many European countries that were ravaged by the Great Depression. **Fascism** is a political ideology that advocates for a dictatorship in order to provide stability and unity. **Adolf Hitler** emerged as a prominent fascist leader in Germany and eventually brought the Nazi party to power in 1933. Germany, Italy, and Japan formed an alliance called the Axis and began to threaten other countries. The League of Nations could not diffuse the conflict. World War II broke out when Germany invaded Poland in 1939. Hitler quickly conquered most of Europe, except for Britain, and attacked the USSR in 1941. The United States sent military equipment and weapons to Britain and the USSR, but did not formally join the war until the Japanese attacked Pearl Harbor on December 7, 1941. Again, women played an important role on the home front by working in factories to build guns, tanks, planes, and ships. African Americans, Native Americans, and Japanese Americans also contributed by fighting on the front lines.

American forces first landed in North Africa where they, along with British and French troops, defeated German and Italian forces in 1942. In 1943, Allied forces invaded Italy, and Soviet troops began to push the German army back out of the USSR. Allied troops landed in France in 1944 and the Soviets began to advance on Germany as well. By May 1945, Hitler had committed suicide and Germany had been defeated.

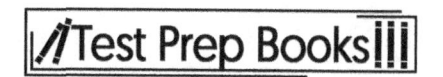

This also brought about an end to the Holocaust. The Holocaust was a genocide committed by Hitler's Nazi Germany and collaborators that resulted in the deaths of more than 6 million Jews and 5 million Romanis, Gypsies, Afro-Europeans, disabled citizens, and homosexuals. A network of facilities in Germany and its territories were used to house victims for slave labor and mass murder, among other heinous crimes. The Nuremberg trials were part of the aftermath of the **Holocaust**, which served to prosecute important members of Nazi Germany leadership.

In the Pacific theater, American naval forces defeated the Japanese fleet in several key engagements, including the battle of Midway in 1942. American troops began recapturing territory in the Pacific as well and eventually pushed the Japanese back to their home islands in 1945. The Japanese refused to surrender until American planes dropped atomic bombs on the cities of Nagasaki and Hiroshima in August 1945.

Because World War II devastated most of Europe, the United States and the USSR emerged as the only superpowers when it ended. However, the erstwhile allies were suspicious of each other, which led to the Cold War.

Origins, Developments, and Consequences of the Cold War

Although the United States and the USSR worked together to defeat the Axis powers during World War II, the alliance quickly fell apart. As previously discussed, Americans had been afraid of communist influence since the Russian revolution in 1917. The USSR viewed the United States as a capitalist and imperialist power that threatened Soviet security. The USSR and United States divided Europe into spheres of influence, and this mutual hostility led to the Cold War. For example, the Soviets built a wall around the portion of Berlin, Germany that they occupied. The United States formed a military alliance, called the North Atlantic Treaty Organization, with its allies in Western Europe.

The Soviets responded with their own defensive alliance in Eastern Europe, known as the **Warsaw Pact**. **President Harry Truman** announced that the United States would try to contain communist influence and would assist countries threatened by communist aggression. The domino theory predicted that once one country succumbed to communism, neighboring nations would also be at risk (thus following like a stack of dominoes). A resurgence of anti-communist sentiment occurred in the early 1950s when Senator Joseph McCarthy pledged to root out spies within the federal government. Known as the **Second Red Scare** in American history, McCarthy's communist "witch hunts" produced little evidence of his allegations and was censored in 1954 when he refused to reign in his attacks.

The resistance to communism led to a number of indirect conflicts around the globe between the United States and the USSR and China, which had become a communist regime in 1949. For example, Korea was divided into two portions after World War II (at the 38th parallel). When the communist regime in North Korea invaded South Korea in 1950, the United States sent troops to defend South Korea. The USSR and China sent troops, weapons, and equipment to support North Korea. The war ended in a stalemate in 1953, and Korea remains divided to this day. Today, it is divided at a unique demarcation line close to the original 38th parallel separation.

Vietnam was also partitioned into northern and southern regions after World War II. The United States supported South Vietnam and sent troops in ever-increasing numbers. The conflict intensified when North Vietnamese gunboats allegedly attacked a U.S. navy ship in 1964. However, U.S. forces were unable to defeat the Vietnamese communists, who preferred to use guerrilla troops and ambush tactics.

U.S. History, Society, Customs, and Culture

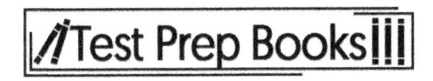

The support for the war evaporated in United States as casualties mounted and the draft was unpopular as well. American troops also killed at least 300 civilians in the Vietnamese village of My Lai in 1968. National Guardsmen shot and killed four students and wounded nine others during an anti-war protest at Kent State University in 1970. These scandals made the war extremely unpopular. American troops withdrew in 1973, and South Vietnam was defeated in 1975.

The U.S. and USSR also vied for influence in South America and Africa as well. Some nations refused to pick sides and instead formed the Non-Aligned Movement.

The nuclear arms race and the space race were also important arenas in the Cold War. The Soviets took an early lead in the space race and successfully launched the first satellite into orbit in 1957. The Soviets also put the first man, cosmonaut Yuri Gagarin, into space in 1961. However, the United States surpassed the Soviet Union by landing the first man, Neil Armstrong, on the Moon in 1969.

The United States was the only nuclear power for a brief period after World War II, but the Soviets quickly caught up and detonated their own nuclear bomb in 1949. Both sides developed nuclear missiles during the 1950s. This became a very dramatic issue during the Cuban Missile Crisis. In 1962, President John F. Kennedy learned that the Soviets were installing nuclear missiles in Cuba, which had become a communist regime. The U.S. navy imposed a blockade, and tensions rose as the Soviets refused to back down. Eventually, negotiations ended the crisis and the Soviets agreed to withdraw the missiles in Cuba if the U.S. agreed to withdraw missiles from Turkey that threatened the USSR. Although tensions remained, the nuclear arms race slowed during the 1970s when the U.S. and USSR entered into negotiations. Both the U.S. and USSR promised to reduce nuclear weapons tests and limit their nuclear arsenals. Throughout the Cold War, a concept known as **"Mutually Assured Destruction"** (MAD) helped prevent nuclear war. Both the United States and the USSR each had thousands of warheads and MAD predicted that no matter who struck first, the other side would have enough surviving firepower to destroy the aggressor.

During the Cold War, a number of protests and demonstrations occurred in the Soviet satellites in Eastern Europe, including Hungary in 1956 and in Czechoslovakia in 1968. The uprisings were suppressed, but demands for reform continued and, in 1985, Mikhail Gorbachev became the leader of the USSR. He promised to make political and economic reforms, but protestors wanted change to occur more rapidly. Revolutions swept through Eastern Europe in 1989, and the communist regimes in Poland, Romania, and elsewhere crumbled. The Berlin Wall fell in 1989, and the Cold War ended when the USSR collapsed in 1991. This left the United States as the sole superpower, although other countries, such as India and China, have become more powerful. Recent scholars, however, are questioning whether the Cold War is once again beginning to heat up with the most recent tensions between Russia and the United States in the early 2000s.

Social, Economic, and Technological Changes Between 1950 and 2000

The post-World War II era led to a number of social, economic, and technological changes in the United States. The counter-culture phenomenon was one of the most powerful social movements in the latter half of the twentieth century in the U.S. The counter-culture movement challenged social norms and rejected traditional authority figures. The movement began in the 1950s with the beatniks, a group of non-conformist writers and artists who were dissatisfied with society. The beatniks sought inspiration in African and Asian cultures and many eschewed materialism.

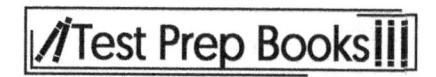

The **counter-culture movement** became more popular during the 1960s as millions of children from the Baby Boomers generation entered into adulthood. Veterans came home after World War II and started families, and, by the 1960s, many of these young adults also felt disaffected and rebellious. Their parents criticized them because they began to wear colorful clothing and the boys let their hair grow out. Many members of the counter-culture movement, now called **hippies**, inherited the beatnik's interest in African and Asian cultures. Writer Ken Kesey traveled around the country on a bus encouraging people to experiment with psychedelic drugs, such as LSD. The counter-culture movement influenced musicians and avant-garde artists.

The counter-culture movement was also closely connected to other protest movements during the 1960s, including the Civil Rights movement. Many members of the counter-culture movement during the 1960s also opposed the war in Vietnam. The Baby Boomers could be conscripted to fight in Vietnam whether they wanted to or not. In 1965, young men began burning their draft cards, which was a criminal offense, in protest. Massive demonstrations against the war occurred around the country, especially on college campuses, but many other people also refused to support the war effort, including clergymen and even some veterans who had fought in Vietnam. The counter-culture movement disappeared during the 1970s but had a lasting impact on the social and cultural history of the United States.

Economic Changes

America emerged as one of the most powerful economies in the world after 1945. The US economy, especially manufacturing, was very prosperous during the 1950s and 1960s. The economy successfully switched from wartime production, and consumer demand was very high. During the Great Depression, few families had disposable income. Although most workers earned good wages during World War II, they had little to spend it on because most goods were rationed. Once production of consumer goods resumed, families used their savings to buy cars, household appliances, and televisions. This was good for the economy, and unemployment remained below 5 percent for most of the 1950s and 1960s. However, during the latter part of the 20th century, the manufacturing base in the North and Midwest began to crumble and the area became known as the Rust Belt. Manufacturing jobs began to move from the North and Midwest to states in the South and West, known as the Sun Belt, where land was cheap and wages were low.

The world economy also became increasingly interconnected during the post-World War II era. This accelerated the process of globalization, which is the integration of ideas and products from different cultures. This benefitted the United States economically because businesses, such as McDonald's and Coca-Cola, found many consumers around the world who were eager to consume American goods. However, the process works both ways, and many aspects of foreign culture, such as Japanese cartoons and animation, have become very popular in the United States. Many critics also point out that globalization has hurt the American economy in recent decades because manufacturing jobs have gone overseas to countries in South America and Asia where wages are low.

Technological Changes

Several technological changes have had a significant impact on the U.S. economy as well. The Cold War led to advances in nuclear power and aerospace engineering. The development of computers, in particular, has helped accelerate the transition to a post-industrial economy where information technology and other services have replaced traditional manufacturing jobs. The first computers were used to break coded messages during World War II and had very limited computing power. The invention of transistor technology in 1947 made computers cheaper, smaller, and more reliable. The invention of integrated circuits in the 1960s and 1970s increased computing power and gave birth to the first personal computers. The Internet was created in 1969, but widespread use in business and academia did not begin until the 1980s. These developments have made it much easier to share information and have increased economic opportunities. But, the increasing use of robots, especially in the manufacturing industry, have also made the economy more efficient while also causing layoffs.

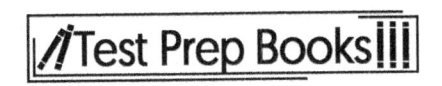

Political Realignments from the New Deal and Great Society Through the Rise of Conservatism

President Franklin D. Roosevelt created the **New Deal** in order to stimulate the economy and improve government regulation. The New Deal also marked an important shift in American politics because the Democratic Party began to favor government intervention while Republicans opposed it. This was a reversal of the parties' previous platforms. The Democratic Party relied on a coalition of labor unions, Catholics, African Americans, and other minorities. The Republican Party included conservatives, evangelicals, and business leaders.

The Great Society was another major government program that the Democratic Party supported. **President Lyndon B. Johnson** sought to end poverty and improve education. For example, he raised the minimum wage and created programs to provide poor Americans with job training. **The Great Society** also implemented a number of Civil Rights laws that will be discussed in greater detail later.

The presidential election of 1980 was another watershed moment. Republican nominee Ronald Reagan carried forty-three states, and the Republicans won a majority in the U.S. Senate after twenty-eight years of Democratic control. Reagan presented an optimistic message and broadcasted a television advertisement that proclaimed "It's morning again in America." He promised to restore America's military power, cut government regulations, and reduce taxes. Reagan enjoyed the support of resurgent conservative Christian evangelicals, who wanted to restore morality to American society. They were particularly concerned about issues such as abortion. The **Moral Majority**, founded by Baptist minister **Jerry Falwell** in 1979, was one key group that helped Reagan win the election. This coalition helped realign party loyalties, as more liberal Republicans and conservative Democrats shifted their allegiance.

Impact of Race, Gender, and Ethnicity Throughout American History

Race, gender, and ethnicity have been important themes in American history from the colonial era to the present. Individuals from different races, ethnicities, and genders have had very different experiences throughout the same historical events or eras. It is important to distinguish between race and ethnicity: **race** refers to a group of people with common ancestry, while **ethnicity** refers to cultural background, such as language and tradition.

Race played an important part in colonial America because both Caucasians and Africans occupied positions of servitude. White immigrants who could not purchase passage to the New World sometimes agreed to become indentured servants. Their employers paid for their passage across the Atlantic, and in exchange, the indentured servant agreed to work without wages for at least five years. However, African slaves were rarely able to free themselves. The strong connection between slavery and race meant that all blacks, whether free or enslaved, were viewed as inferior. After the American Revolution, most free blacks, even those living in northern states, were denied the right to vote. Although the Civil

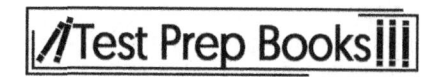

Rights Movement in the 1960s made great gains, many activists claim more must be done in order to overcome the legacy of racial inequality in America.

Japanese Americans experienced discrimination during and after World War II, specifically with the implementation of Japanese internment camps in America. This forced 110,000 to 120,000 Japanese Americans into camps, 62 percent of which were United States citizens.

Discrimination against certain ethnicities is also prominent throughout American history as well. For example, many Americans resented the arrival of German and Irish immigrants during the 1800s because they spoke a different language or practiced different religions. Hispanics were also subject to discrimination, and in 1943, a number of Hispanic youths were attacked during the Zoot Suit Riots.

Gender differences in the United States have also been impossible to ignore. For example, until the 1840s, most married women in the United States were unable to enter into contracts, own property, or retain their own wages. As previously discussed, women were unable to vote until the 19th Amendment was ratified in 1920. The Women's Rights Movement in the U.S. ranged from 1848 to 1920. This movement called for a woman's right to vote, the right to bodily autonomy, freedom from sexual violence, the right to hold public office, the right to work, the right to fair wages and equal pay, and the right to own property and obtain an education.

How Participants in the Political Process Engage in Politics and Shape Policy

The Constitution provides for a series of checks and balances between the legislative, executive, and judicial branches of the federal government. Members of Congress debate and vote on legislation, although the president may request that legislators consider a certain proposal. The president may veto legislation that he or she disagrees with, but Congress can override the veto with a two-thirds majority

U.S. History, Society, Customs, and Culture

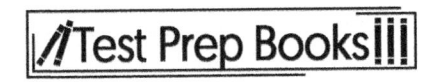

in both chambers. The Supreme Court may review legislation and declare it unconstitutional. The president selects nominees to the Supreme Court but the Senate must confirm them.

Branch	Role	Checks & Balances on Other Branches	
Executive	Carries out the laws	**Legislative Branch** • Proposes laws • Vetoes laws • Calls special sessions of Congress • Makes appointments • Negotiates foreign treaties	**Judicial Branch** • Appoints federal judges • Grants pardons to federal offenders
Legislative	Makes the laws	**Executive Branch** • Has the ability to override a President's veto • Confirms executive appointments • Ratifies treaties • Has the ability to declare war • Appropriates money • Has the ability to impeach and remove President	**Judicial Branch** • Creates lower federal courts • Has the ability to impeach and remove judges • Has the ability to propose amendments to overrule judicial decisions • Approves appointments of federal judges
Judicial	Interprets the laws	**Executive Branch** • Has the ability to declare executive actions unconstitutional	**Legislative Branch** • Has the ability to declare acts of Congress unconstitutional

Constituents, businesses, professional associations, civic organizations, and other interest groups may lobby members of Congress and ask them to propose legislation or support a certain proposal. Interest groups may also lobby the president and other executive branch officials in order to try and influence policies. The president appoints fifteen men and women to head a variety of executive departments, including defense, transportation, education, and many others. These officials are known as the president's cabinet, and they advise the president on various matters. These discussions are used to help formulate policies, and the cabinet members are responsible for putting the decisions into action. The president may also issue executive orders that instruct federal employees how to enforce certain policies. For example, in 1948, President Harry S. Truman issued an executive order that established racial integration within the armed forces.

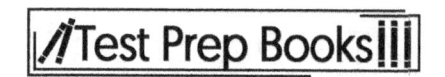

Elections are an essential part of our democracy. Although members of Congress are prohibited from accepting gifts, individuals and interest groups can make campaign contributions during elections, which occur every two years in the House, four years for the White House, and six years in the Senate. Individuals can give a maximum of $2,700 per year to individual candidates. Since 2010, individuals, corporations, labor unions, and other contributors can give an unlimited amount to organizations known as super PACs (**Political Action Committees**). Super PACs may not give money to candidates or parties but can air commercials that support a specific issue.

Although President George Washington warned against creating political parties in his farewell address in 1796, they have been a part of American politics since the founding of our country. The Republicans and Democrats hold conventions to nominate candidates for state and national elections. The parties also create a platform, which is a set of goals and principles, at each convention in order to set priorities and inform members about issues. During elections, parties also organize rallies and urge voters to support their candidates and issues. Some Americans belong to either the Republican or Democratic Party, but voters who belong to neither party are known as independents.

Emergence of the United States as a World Power and the Evolving Role of United States in the World

The United States gained prestige and international status after the Spanish-American War of 1898, because the United States defeated Spain and acquired several colonies. American participation in World War I made the United States an economic and financial leader as well. The United States loaned money to Britain and France and supplied weapons and equipment that helped the Triple Entente achieve victory. The United States and USSR emerged from World War II as the only surviving superpowers because so much of the rest of the world had been devastated. This system was described as bipolar because there were two centers of power.

The United States was the leader of the free world during the Cold War and formed military and economic alliances with other nations. With the collapse of the USSR in 1991, the United States was the only surviving world power. This era was a unipolar system because there were no other major powers that could rival the United States.

Although the U.S. was still considered a world power, September 11, 2001 demonstrated that America was nevertheless vulnerable to attacks. The attacks on 9/11 killed more than 3,000 civilians and first-responders. Although American troops have been stationed in Iraq and Afghanistan for more than a decade, both nations are still unstable, and the lack of progress has damaged American prestige. Furthermore, new economic and military powers have risen to challenge American dominance in world affairs. The Chinese economy has grown significantly, and the Chinese government has expanded and improved its armed forces. India has also boosted its manufacturing industry and has purchased new fighter jets and an aircraft carrier. The European Union, Russia, and Brazil have also emerged as potential rivals that might create a multipolar environment. However, the United States is still the world's largest economy and remains a cultural leader.

The Influence of Religion Throughout American History

Religion has also been an important, albeit divisive, theme in American history since the colonial period. The British colonies in North America attracted settlers from many different religions, including Catholics in Maryland, Quakers in Pennsylvania, Puritans in New England, and Anglicans in Virginia. This led to conflict and tension. For example, **Puritans** in New England expelled dissenters and even executed four Quakers between 1659 and 1661.

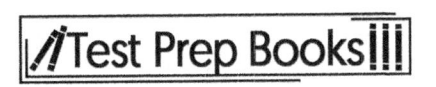

In the 1730s and 1740s, a religious revival known as the **First Great Awakening** swept through the British colonies in North America. This movement emphasized a more personal connection to Christ, and some Protestant preachers, such as Jonathan Edwards, began to present their sermons in a more passionate and emotional style. This "fire and brimstone" form of religious dissemination became the cornerstone of the First Great Awakening. These passionate sermons—and the emotions that they stirred—caused divisions within Protestant congregations. Those who supported the Great Awakening were known as New Lights while those who opposed it were called **Old Lights**. The Baptists and Methodists became more popular during the revival because they embraced this new style of preaching.

The **Second Great Awakening** occurred in the early 1800s and urged Protestants to work not only for their own salvation but for the salvation of others as well. This helped fuel a social reform movement that promoted the abolition of slavery, temperance, and prison reform. The question of slavery caused schisms in the Baptist and Methodist churches during the 1840s. The Second Great Awakening, much like the First Great Awakening, inaugurated the creation of several **New Religious Movements** (NRMs) in the United States, especially in the southern states.

A third revival occurred in the late 1800s that emphasized temperance. As previously discussed, the religious right emerged after World War II and began to play an important part in American politics, especially during the election of President Ronald Reagan in 1980.

Although Catholics were a minority during the colonial period of American history, Catholicism has become the largest religious denomination in the United States. Many colonial governments actually banned Catholicism, but the American Revolution brought more toleration. However, anti-Catholic sentiment renewed in the 1800s as immigrants from Ireland and Germany, many of whom were Catholic, arrived in ever-increasing numbers. The arrival of Italian immigrants in the late 1800s and early 1900s also increased Protestant-Catholic tension in America. Many Americans feared that Catholic immigrants would be more loyal to Pope than they would be to the Constitution. This led to the creation of the Know-Nothings who sought to limit immigration and physically attacked Catholics. Anti-Catholic sentiment remained an issue even until the presidential election of 1960 when John F. Kennedy, a Catholic, won the Democratic nomination. Kennedy helped allay fears by promising to respect the separation of church and state. Since then, anti-Catholicism has largely disappeared.

Small numbers of Jews immigrated to the U.S. during the colonial period, but large numbers of Jews from Eastern Europe began to arrive in the late 19th and early 20th centuries. Jews contributed to the American economy in many different ways but drew criticism from anti-Semites because of their prominence in the financial industry. The Anti-Defamation League was founded in 1913 to combat anti-Semitic sentiments. In the 1920s, the resurgent Ku Klux Klan revived anti-Semitism. The Anti-Defamation League sponsored events after World War II to commemorate the Holocaust and repudiate Holocaust deniers. Anti-Semitism has declined, but the **Anti-Defamation League** reported that more than 900 anti-Semitic incidents occurred across the country in 2014.

Muslim immigration in the 1800s remained modest. The first mosque was not constructed in the United States until the 20th century. In the latter part of the 20th century, more Muslims, especially from Pakistan, began arriving in the United States. In the wake of the 9/11 attacks, Islamophobic incidents increased, and Muslims were victims of harassment, intimidation, and assaults. The United States' current battle with ISIS in the Middle East, North Africa, and Europe has also increased Islamophobia.

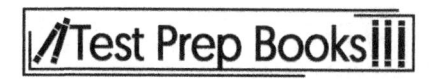

Major Economic Transformations in the United States

The American economy has changed dramatically since the 1700s, a century where agriculture was the main economic activity. The First Industrial Revolution began in the early 1800s when steam-powered machines were used to increase productivity, especially in the textile industry. The invention of steamboats and railroads made it much cheaper and faster to ship goods across the country in the mid-1800s as well. After the Civil War, the Second Industrial Revolution led to increased productivity and efficiency in the many industries, including metallurgy, chemicals, telecommunications, and energy. This led to significant social changes as immigration and urbanization increased. Workers began to form labor unions in order to demand better wages and working conditions, which led to strikes and conflict with law enforcement officials.

In the early 20th century, Henry Ford introduced the moving assembly line to the automobile manufacturing industry, which made it easier for middle- and working-class families to buy cars. Other industries adopted Ford's methods, which led to lower prices for many consumer goods. The stock market crash in 1929 helped trigger the Great Depression, which resulted in a vicious downward economic spiral. Franklin D. Roosevelt introduced the New Deal to try and boost the economy, but only the outbreak of World War II led to full employment. The United States emerged from World War II as the world's largest economy and pent-up consumer demand fueled prosperity during the post-war era.

The development of computers in the latter part of the 20th century improved communications and led to greater economic efficiency. However, it also marked the beginning of the post-industrial economy in the United States. Traditional manufacturing jobs began to disappear as robots replaced unskilled workers. On the other hand, careers in the information technology sector grew and became a key component of the new high-tech economy. Many unskilled manufacturing jobs also went overseas to countries in Asia and South America as the global economy became more interconnected.

The Causes and Consequences of Changing Immigration Patterns

Immigration has always played an important role in American history, although patterns have changed over time. Most immigrants came to the United States in search of better economic opportunities, although some have sought religious and political freedom as well. During the colonial period, most immigrants came from Britain, but during the mid-1800s that began to change. In the 1840s, a fungus destroyed the potato crop in Ireland, which led to widespread famine. Many Irish starved, but millions also emigrated, with many heading to the United States. A wave of revolutions also swept across Europe in 1848 and many participants, especially Germans, fled to the United States when the movements failed. This shift led to tension and conflict between immigrants and those born in America. Native-born Americans resented the immigrants' cultural differences and the increased competition for jobs. In the late 1800s, immigration patterns changed again and arrivals from Southern and Eastern Europe began to increase. In 1924, Congress passed an act that limited immigration from these areas.

In 1965, immigration patterns changed again when Congress passed the **Immigration and Nationality Act of 1965** act that changed the way immigration quotas were calculated. Immigrants from Central and South America, as well as Asia, became very numerous. Like their predecessors, most came in search of jobs. Recently, many refugees are fleeing violence that erupted from revolutions that swept through the

U.S. History, Society, Customs, and Culture

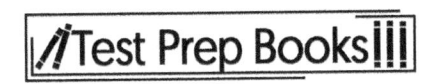

Middle East between 2010 and 2012. Cultural differences and economic competition between immigrants and native-born American citizens continue.

Internal Migration

Migration within the United States has also been an important theme since the colonial period. During the 18th and 19th centuries, the focus was on westward expansion because settlers sought cheap land. This often led to violence between settlers and Native Americans who refused to relinquish their territory.

The 19th century also saw an increase in migration from rural areas to cities as individuals sought employment in factories. This trend continued until the late 20th century and more than 80 percent of Americans now live in cities. World War I led to the Great Migration of African Americans from the South to the North. This influx also created more competition for jobs and housing and resulted in a wave of race riots in 1919.

Struggles and Achievements for Political and Civil Rights

Although the **Declaration of Independence** declared "all men are created equal," blacks, women, and other minorities struggled for more than a century to make this dream a reality. The U.S. Constitution legalized slavery, and it was not abolished until the 13th Amendment was ratified in 1865. The 14th Amendment, ratified in 1868, granted African Americans citizenship, and the 15th Amendment, ratified in 1870, explicitly granted them the right to vote. However, white Southerners passed laws, known as the Jim Crow system, that prevented blacks from exercising their rights and, when that failed, they relied on violence and intimidation to oppress African Americans. For example, many Southern states required voters to pass literacy tests and used them to prevent blacks from casting a ballot. Whites were either exempt from the test or were held to much lower standards. Blacks who protested their oppression could be assaulted and even killed with impunity. In the 1896 decision **Plessy vs. Ferguson**, the U.S. Supreme Court ruled that "separate but equal" schools for white and black students were permissible. In reality, black schools were almost always inferior to white schools.

The emergence of the Civil Rights Movement after World War II finally destroyed the Jim Crow system. In the 1954 decision **Brown vs. Board of Education**, the Supreme Court reversed the "separate but equal" doctrine and declared that separate schools were inherently unequal because they stigmatized African American students. In 1957, **President Dwight D. Eisenhower** used federal troops to force the high school in Little Rock, Arkansas, to integrate and accept nine black students. This encouraged civil rights activists to demand additional reforms. In 1955, Rosa Parks refused to give up her seat on a bus in Montgomery, Alabama, which led to a boycott. **Martin Luther King Jr.** led the bus boycott and became a national leader in the Civil Rights Movement. In 1960, four students in Greensboro, North Carolina, launched a peaceful sit-in at a segregated lunch counter, which sparked similar protests around the country. White activists from the North went south to help blacks register to vote, and in 1964 three activists were murdered in Mississippi. That same year, King led 250,000 protesters in a march on Washington D.C. where he delivered his famous "**I Have a Dream Speech**."

Although King advocated for peaceful protests, many other civil rights activists disagreed with him. For example, **Malcolm X** believed that blacks should use violence to defend themselves. Furthermore, King worked with white activists while Malcom X rejected any cooperation. Malcolm X was assassinated in 1965, and, despite his reputation as a non-violent leader, King was also gunned down in 1968.

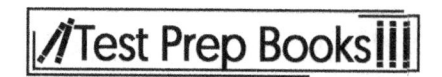

Under mounting pressure, Congress passed several important pieces of legislation. The **1964 Civil Rights Act** banned discrimination based on race, color, religion, sex, or national origin. The **Voting Rights Act of 1965** prohibited the use of poll taxes or literacy tests to prohibit voting. The **Civil Rights Act of 1968** banned housing discrimination. In 1967, **Carl Stokes** became the first black mayor of a major American city, Cleveland. That same year, Thurgood Marshall became the first African American to serve on the Supreme Court. President Gerald Ford declared February to be black history month. In 1989, **Colin Powell** became the first black chairman of the Joint Chiefs of Staff. Despite these reforms, activists claim institutional racism is still a problem in the 21st century. The Civil Rights movement inspired women, Latinos, and other groups to make similar demands for equal rights.

Women

In 1776, **Abigail Adams** urged her husband, founding father John Adams, to advocate for women's rights, but it would take more than a century before women could vote. In 1848, activists organized a convention in Seneca Falls, New York, to organize the women's suffrage movement, and their efforts slowly gained momentum. The ratification of the **19th Amendment** in 1920 finally gave women the right to vote.

Although women had achieved political equality, they continued to demand reform throughout the 20th century. In the early 1900s, Margaret Sanger provided women with information about birth control, which was illegal at the time. Women entered the industrial workforce in large numbers during World War II, but when the war ended, they were fired so that veterans would have jobs when they came home. Many women were frustrated when told they had to return to their domestic lives. Simone de Beauvoir, a French writer, published her book "The Second Sex" after World War II, and an English translation was published in 1953.

It highlighted the unequal treatment of women throughout history and sparked a feminist movement in the United States. In 1963, Betty Friedan published a book, called "The Feminine Mystique," that revealed how frustrated many suburban wives were with the social norms that kept them at home. During the 1960s, women participated in the sexual revolution and exerted more control over their own sexuality. In 1972, Congress passed **Title IX**, which prohibited sexual discrimination in education and expanded women's sports programs. In the 1970s, women's rights activists also pushed for greater access to birth control, and in 1973 the Supreme Court issued the landmark decision **Roe vs. Wade** which removed many barriers to abortion services. Women also demanded greater protection from domestic abuse and greater access to divorce.

During the 20th century, many American women made notable achievements, including Amelia Earhart, who was the first woman to cross the Atlantic in an airplane in 1928. In 1981, Sandra Day O'Connor became the first woman to serve on the Supreme Court. In 1983, Sally Ride became the first female astronaut. In 1984, Geraldine Ferraro became the first woman to run for vice-president, although she was unsuccessful. However, many activists continue to demand reform in the 21st century. For example, women only account for 20 percent of the U.S. Senate and House of Representatives. Furthermore, women only earn 79 percent of what men in similar jobs are paid. In 1980, President Jimmy Carter declared March to be women's history month.

Hispanics

After World War II, many Hispanics also began to demand greater equality. In 1949, veterans protested a refusal by a Texas town to bury a Mexican American soldier, who died during World War II, in the local cemetery, because only whites could be buried there. Activists called themselves Chicanos, a term that

U.S. History, Society, Customs, and Culture

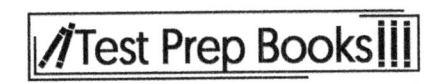

previously was used as a pejorative to describe Mexican Americans. **Cesar Chavez** was a labor union activist who organized transient Hispanic agricultural workers in an effort to obtain better working conditions in the 1960s and 1970s. Activists encouraged a sense of pride in Chicano identity, especially in arts and literature. In 1968, President Lyndon B. Johnson declared **National Hispanic Heritage Month** would run from mid-September to mid-October.

In 1959, biochemist **Severo Ochoa** became the first Hispanic to win a Nobel Prize. **Franklin Chang-Diaz** became the first Hispanic astronaut in 1986, and he flew a total of seven space shuttle missions. In 1990, **Oscar Hijuelos** became the first Hispanic American to win the Pulitzer Prize. **Sonja Sotomayor** became the first Hispanic to serve on the Supreme Court in 2009.

Native Americans

Native Americans suffered centuries of oppression at the hands of European colonists, and later American settlers as they pushed further west. Native Americans resisted attempts to encroach on their lands but were pushed onto smaller and smaller reservations. The **Massacre at Wounded Knee** in 1890 was the last major conflict between Native Americans and U.S. forces. However, American officials continued to try and force Native Americans to assimilate into white culture.

In 1968, a group of Native Americans formed the American Indian Movement in order to combat racism and demand greater independence. Between 1969 and 1971, a group of Native American activists occupied the federal prison on Alcatraz Island near San Francisco, although it had been closed since 1963. The activists offered to buy back the island for $9.40 in order to draw attention to how the federal government had forced tribes to sell their lands at low prices. Other activists disrupted Thanksgiving Day ceremonies aboard a replica of the Mayflower in Boston in 1970. In 1971, Native American activists also occupied Mount Rushmore, which is located on ground the Native Americans consider sacred. Violence broke out between activists and law enforcement officials in 1973 when Native Americans occupied the town of Wounded Knee, sight of the famous massacre.

In 1970, **President Richard Nixon** granted Native American tribes more autonomy. In 1978, Congress passed the American Indian Religious Freedom Act, which guaranteed Native Americans' rights to practice their religious ceremonies and visit sacred sites. In 1990, President George H.W. Bush declared November Native American History Month. In 1969, Navarre Scott Momaday became the first Native American to win a Pulitzer Prize for his book "House Made of Dawn." In 2014, **Diane Humetewa**, a member of the Hopi tribe, became the first Native American woman to serve as a federal judge. However, many Native American communities still suffer from high rates of unemployment, alcoholism, and domestic abuse.

Asian Americans

Asian Americans also faced discrimination throughout American history and in 1882, Congress passed a law banning all Chinese immigrants. During World War II, more than 100,000 Japanese Americans were interned in concentration camps. In 1982, two American autoworkers beat Vincent Chin to death with a baseball bat because his assailants blamed him for the loss of jobs in the automotive manufacturing industry.

In the 1960s, activists demanded that the term "Asian American" replace the word "oriental," because it carried a stigma. Asian Americans also promoted a sense of pride in their cultural identity and successfully pushed for the creation of ethnic studies programs. Ellison Onizuka became the first Asian American astronaut in 1985, although he perished in the space shuttle Challenger disaster. In 1990,

President George H.W. Bush declared May **Asian Pacific American Heritage Month** and **Sheryl WuDunn** became the first Asian American to win a Pulitzer Prize that same year.

World History

The Major Causes and Consequences of Revolutions, Nationalism, and Imperialism in the Period 1750 CE to 1914 CE

While the colonies were increasing in population and production over their first 150 years, British oversight was loose, and the colonies enjoyed extensive self-government. However, in the mid-1700s, England, in need of revenue, began to enforce laws and create new ones that restricted the freedoms in trade the colonies enjoyed. Starting in 1764, the prime minister of England, Lord George Grenville, began to impose acts that the American colonies resented and protested, including the Sugar Act, the Quartering Act, and the Stamp Act. Groups were formed in protest, such as the Sons of Liberty, and even the colonial governments threatened to refuse to obey the acts. A spirit of nationalism swept through the colonies, who began to view themselves as a collective entity.

In 1765, believing that the colonies had the only right to tax colonists, nine colonies banded together to form the Stamp Act Congress, also known as the **First Congress of the American Colonies**. The Stamp Act Congress sent their grievances to King George III of England. Though the Stamp Act was repealed, Parliament issued a law making it clear that the colonies were under the British government's rule. More laws were enacted to tax the colonies, further stirring discontent in the British colonies.

In an attempt to punish and subdue the American colonies, Parliament issued further acts called the **Coercive Acts**, or the **Intolerable Acts**, as they were known in America. These acts only served to unify the colonies and, as a result, the First Continental Congress in 1774 issued another formal complaint. The response from King George III and Parliament was to increase troops in the colonies. In the Second Continental Congress, the colonies again petitioned the king, sending the Olive Branch Petition to King George III. On July 4, 1776, after the failed diplomatic attempts, the Declaration of Independence was adopted, and after the war, it would herald a radical form of self-government never before seen in world history.

Unlike the United States' revolution against a ruler across the ocean, the French Revolution was an internal fight. In 1789, tension between the lower class (peasants) and middle class (bourgeois) and the extravagant wealthy upper class of France came to a head. The Old Regime, headed by the monarchy, was overthrown, and the Third Estate, made up of the bourgeois class, seized power. The American Revolution, overtaxation, years of bad harvests, drastic income inequality, and the Enlightenment influenced the French Revolution. In August 1789, the National Constituent Assembly, a democratic assembly formed during the French Revolution, passed the Declaration of the Rights of Man and of the Citizen, which defined the natural right of men to be free and equal under the law.

France radically changed the government from a monarchy to a democracy with provisions for civil rights, religious freedoms, and decriminalization of various morality crimes, like same-sex relationships. Two political powers emerged: liberal republicans called Girondists and radical revolutionaries, known as *Jacobins*. Conflict between the parties resulted in the Reign of Terror—a period of mass executions— and eventually the rise of Napoleon who set up a nationalist military dictatorship. During the revolution, Napoleon Bonaparte consolidated power after becoming famous for his heroism during the revolutionary wars against Britain, Austria, and other monarchies that sought to retain their right of royal rule. However, by 1804, Napoleon declared himself emperor and remilitarized France, and he conquered most of Europe in a series of global conflicts collectively known as the *Napoleonic Wars*, starting in 1803 and continuing until Napoleon's defeat at the Battle of Waterloo in 1815.

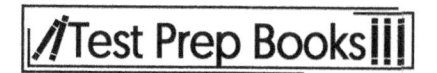

After the chaos sparked by the French Revolution that fanned across Europe during the revolutionary wars, European powers met at the Congress of Vienna in November 1814 to June 1815 to rebalance power and restore old boundaries. The Congress of Vienna carved out new territories, changing the map of Europe. France lost all of its conquered territories, while Prussia, Austria, and Russia expanded their own. With the restoration of a balance of power, Europe enjoyed nearly fifty years of peace.

Fueled by the successful American Revolution, Napoleon's rise to power, and the writings of the Enlightenment, a spirit of revolution swept across the Americas. The French colony in Haiti was the first major revolution occurring in 1791. The Haitian Revolution was the largest slave uprising since the Roman Empire, and it holds a unique place in history because it is the only slave uprising to establish a slave-free nation ruled by nonwhites and former slaves. In 1804, the Haitians achieved independence and became the first independent nation in Latin America.

When Napoleon conquered Spain in 1808, Latin American colonies refused to recognize his elder brother, Joseph Bonaparte, as the new Spanish monarch and advocated for their own independence. Known as the **Latin American Wars of Independence**, Venezuela, Colombia, Ecuador, Argentina, Uruguay, Paraguay, Chile, Peru, and Bolivia all achieved independence between 1810 and 1830. In 1824, Mexico declared itself a republic when, after several attempts by the lower classes of Mexico to revolt, the wealthier classes joined and launched a final and successful revolt. When Napoleon overtook Portugal, King John VI fled to Brazil and set up court. Later he left his son Pedro behind to rule. Pedro launched a revolution that saw him crowned emperor.

By the mid-1800s, the revolutions of Latin America ceased, and only a few areas remained under European rule. The U.S. President James Monroe issued the Monroe Doctrine (1823), which stated that the Americas could no longer be colonized. It was an attempt to stop European nations, especially Spain, from colonizing areas or attempting to recapture areas. England's navy contributed to the success of the doctrine, as they were eager to increase trade with the Americas and establish an alliance with the United States.

Industrial Revolution

While Europe was in the midst of colonization and revolutions, they experienced an industrial revolution that would impact the social and economic fabric of life. Starting in the 1760s, with humble origins in England's textile economy, it lasted until the 1820s and changed the way people worked and lived. The revolution brought new scientific developments and improvements to agriculture and textile manufacturing. It was also a time of great invention in steam- and water-powered engines, machines, tools, chemicals, transportation, factories, lighting, glass, cement, medicines, and many more.

In some ways, it improved people's standard of living, but in many ways, it made life harder. Falling prices on goods made nutrition levels improve and allowed people more buying power. Medicines and better transportation also improved the quality of life for many. However, crowded living quarters in the booming urban centers were often appalling, as were the diseases brought on by working in factory conditions. The use of child labor eventually brought about reform, and labor unions had an effect on working conditions, but it took many years for either of these problems to be properly addressed.

World History

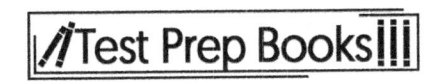

Nationalism and Imperialism

With most revolutions, nationalism, or the devotion to one's country, plays a central role. The American and French revolutions, along with the revolutions of Latin America, were fought with the desire to improve the prosperity and position of its civilians. After the Napoleonic Wars and the Congress of Vienna, the years of undisturbed peace resulted in a buildup of nationalism. Countries like Italy and Poland resented Austrian and Russian rule as much as they had disliked French occupation. A rise in nationalism in Germany was a constant threat to Austria, as it tried to govern multiple cultures and languages across a wide geographic area. The precarious situation would remain hostile to some degree until the outbreak of World War I. The Industrial Revolution had made the lower and middle classes restless for change and improvements. By 1848, uprisings began to spring up all over Europe, beginning with France. Many who had nationalistic leanings toward a country that was either no longer in existence or had been forced into another country were able to separate from other nations. The Hungarians broke with Vienna, though they were forced back soon after, the Romans split from papal power, and the Italians threatened rebellion.

The development of imperialism began in the mid-nineteenth century and lasted until the twentieth century, with much of the imperialized world gaining freedom after World Wars I and II. The spread of imperialism that was to follow the revolutions of the eighteenth and nineteenth centuries can be traced, in part, to the idea of nationalism. Some countries believed they were doing a good, and even a moral, thing by conquering and colonizing new territory to spread their culture, traditions, religion, and government. However, a darker side of nationalism—the feeling of superiority and right—caused the takeover of areas and the enforcement of foreign rules and laws.

The British Empire stretched across the world, and at one point had over 450 million people under its rule. With the loss of its American colonies, England began to focus on other areas of the world. In the mid-1700s, India was the first target of British imperialism. Opposition to the ruling Mughal Empire allowed the British army an inroad at the Battle of Plassey in 1757, where General Robert Clive and his army overtook Bengal in northeast India. Next, the British forced the Mughal emperor to give all tax-collecting rights to England. In 1784, Parliament passed the **East India Company Act**, also known as **Pitt's India Act**, which brought the East India Company's rule in India under control of the British government.

Railway systems to expedite the shipment of goods to Great Britain were built, and a new government called the **British Raj** was established. Indians were educated to work in the government and, at first, used their education to promote reform in India. Many of these civil service workers would take on the mantle of nationalism and advocate for India's independence. Great Britain further expanded its empire into areas of Africa and solidified its rule in Australia, capitalizing on exports from Australia and Canada. It also had what is seen as an informal empire in China and other nations due to its ability to dominate trade and influence economic policy.

Imperialism was also seen in Japan, a country that moved from a primitive and feudal system to a strong empire quickly and overtook Taiwan, Korea, many islands in the Pacific Ocean, and parts of China. It was not until the end of World War II that Japan was forced to surrender control of its accumulated empire. Germany, Russia, and the Ottoman Empire also gained land through imperialism during the years before World War I, most of which was lost by the end of the Great War. The United States was initially against imperialism after having been a colony itself and even solidified these ideas in the Monroe Doctrine; however, by the late nineteenth and early twentieth centuries, the United States defeated Spain in the Spanish-American War and annexed Hawaii, Guam, and the Philippines.

World History

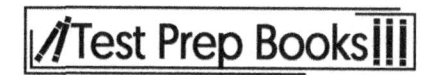

The Major Ideological, Economic, and Political Causes and Consequences of the First and Second World Wars and the Cold War

First World War

The onset of World War I began with the precarious balance of power and the geographic divisions written by the Napoleonic Wars' Vienna Congress.

Austria-Hungary's large empire was diverse in culture and included various peoples of several nationalities, languages, and beliefs. However, minorities in their lands in the Balkans grew tired of foreign control. This was especially true in Bosnia, which was all but under control by the nationalistic secret military society, the Black Hand. This nationalistic sentiment grew until, in 1914, **Gavrilo Princip**, a Serb patriot and member of the Black Hand, assassinated Archduke Franz Ferdinand, heir presumptive to the throne of Austria-Hungary. In response, **Emperor Franz Joseph I** of Austria-Hungary declared war on the kingdom of Serbia, officially launching the First World War.

Europe had tied itself into a tangled web of alliances and mutual protection pacts. Germany and Austria-Hungary were allies. Russia promised protection to France and Serbia, and England maintained a tacit support to its past allies throughout the mainland. Each of the Allies soon mobilized to support each other. Germany had already planned for declarations of war, however, and was nervous about fighting a two-border war against both France and Russia, so it developed the **Schlieffen Plan**—a strategy to quickly demolish French resistance before turning around to fight Russia on the Eastern Front. However, this plan relied on the neutrality of England; after Germany invaded Belgium to attack France, England's declaration of war ensured that a long war would be inevitable.

The Great War lasted from 1914 to 1918 and was the deadliest war in European history until World War II, with approximately 16 million combatants and civilians dying in the conflict. The carnage was largely a result of technological innovation outpacing military tactics. World War I was the first military conflict to deploy millions of soldiers and the first war to involve telephones, tanks, aircrafts, chemical weapons, and heavy artillery. These twentieth-century technological innovations were deployed alongside outdated military tactics, particularly trench warfare. As a result, hundreds of thousands of troops would die during battles without achieving any meaningful strategic gains. Countries were devastated by the loss of the male population and struggled to cope with a depleted workforce, and widows and orphans struggled to regain any degree of normalcy.

Due to the high death tolls, the Allies' need of the financial support, and the anger associated with the war, the Treaty of Versailles harshly punished Germany, who the Allies blamed for the war. The Allies coerced Germany into signing the treaty that was a death sentence to their country's economy. It contained a "guilt clause," which, unlike the Congress of Vienna's terms for the similarly belligerent France, made oppressive demands on Germany. The treaty took German lands, enforced a heavy reparations debt that was impossible to pay, and stripped Germany of its colonies. After suffering enormous losses during the war itself, the Treaty of Versailles ensured that no national recovery would be possible.

In the aftermath, Russia, Italy, and Germany turned to totalitarian governments, and colonies of Europe started to have nationalistic, anticolonial movements. The Russian Revolution of 1917 led to a civil war in which the Bolsheviks, or Communists, took control under the guidance of Communist revolutionary Vladimir Lenin and established the Soviet Union. The Communist government turned into a dictatorship when Stalin emerged as leader in 1924. Stalin ruled with an iron fist and executed all of his political

World History

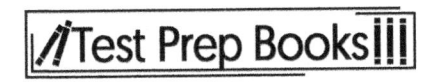

opponents, including the Bolsheviks. Dissatisfaction with the treaty in Italy led to the rise of fascist leader Benito Mussolini. Germany suffered through several small revolutions, splintering political parties, and class division; this, combined with wartime debt and hyperinflation—a result of the Treaty of Versailles—caused many to become desperate, especially during the throes of the Great Depression.

Adolf Hitler, a popular leader in the **National Socialist German Workers' Party** (Nazi Party), organized street violence against Communists. In the 1932 parliamentary elections, the Nazis emerged as the largest party in the **Reichstag** (German Parliament), but the Nazis did not have enough votes to name Hitler as chancellor. The street violence against Communists and Jews continued unabated, and on January 30, 1933, political pressure led to President von Hindenburg naming Adolf Hitler the chancellor of Germany. Hitler immediately expelled Communists, the second most popular political party, from the *Reichstag*, and coerced the *Reichstag* to pass the Enabling Act of 1933, effectively creating a dictatorship.

The start of decolonization in India occurred after World War I, with the Government of India Act of 1919. While the war was raging, Britain promised India more self-rule if they supported the war effort. However, the act did not grant freedom in taxation, foreign policy, or justice and only went as far as allowing local matters to be addressed by native-born citizens. For the Indian National Congress, India's largest political party, this fell short of what they had expected. In the 1920s, Mahatma Gandhi, leader of the Indian National Congress, protested using civil disobedience. In August 1947, England granted independence to India and split the British Indian Empire into India and Pakistan.

Second World War

Nazi Germany had risen to power through the 1920s and 1930s, with Hitler's belief that Germany would only recover its honor if it had a resounding military victory over Europe. Nazi ideology adhered to an extreme nationalism advocating for the superiority of the German people and the necessity of expanding their lands into an empire. Jews, Communists, and other nonconformists were banned from political and social participation.

In 1936, German troops violated the Treaty of Versailles by moving outside Germany's borders, with a remilitarization of the Rhineland. The Rome-Berlin Axis, an alliance between Germany and Italy, was forged in the same year. Germany was the only European power to support Italy's invasion and annexation of Ethiopia, and in exchange, Italy supported Germany's annexation of Austria. In 1936, a civil war broke out in Spain between Spanish nationalist rebels and the government of the Spanish Republic. Mussolini and Hitler supported the Spanish nationalist general Francisco Franco and used the Spanish Civil War as a testing ground for their new alliance. The Allies did not respond to these actions, and when Germany demanded the return of the Sudetenland, a territory in Czechoslovakia, France and Great Britain agreed in hopes of an appeasement despite the protests of the Czech government. Hitler then moved into more areas farther afield, which prompted the Soviet Union to sign a nonaggression pact with Germany. On September 1, 1939, Germany invaded Poland, and on September 3, 1939, France and Great Britain declared war on Germany, jumpstarting the deadliest conflict in world history.

Aside from the incredible casualties resulting from intense fighting and bombings of cities, World War II is marked by the worst war crimes in human history. Germany conducted a systematic genocide of six million Jewish people during the Holocaust, sending two-thirds of Europe's Jewish population to be executed in death camps. Millions of non-Jews were also exterminated during the Holocaust, including Slavs, Poles, Romani, people of color, Communists, homosexuals, and disabled people, among others. It is estimated that anywhere between six and eleven million people were executed in the Holocaust.

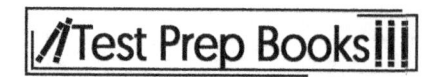

Although less discussed than the Holocaust, the Japanese military committed similar war crimes across Asia, executing between three and ten million Chinese and Koreans, among others, between 1937 and 1945. In one event, the **Rape of Nanking**, Japanese soldiers captured Nanking and brutally murdered 300,000 civilians. An additional twenty thousand women, children, and elderly were raped during the massacre. Japanese newspapers closely covered a contest between two Japanese officers to see who could kill more people with a sword during the Rape of Nanking. Stalin also committed heinous war crimes during World War II, with estimates ranging from four to ten million deaths as a result of executions and sentences to the Gulag. The United States has also faced criticism for its decision to drop two nuclear bombs on the Japanese cities of Hiroshima and Nagasaki, killing more than 129,000 civilians, leveling both cities, and ending the war. The American government justified the use of nuclear weapons as the only way to avoid a ground invasion of Japan that would have cost more Japanese and American lives than the bombs.

Towns and cities had been leveled, civilian and soldier death tolls were crippling to economies, and countries struggled well into the 1950s to recover economically. It became a breeding ground for Communism, and in China, the end of the war meant a reprisal of the civil war between Mao Zedong's Communists and nationalists that had been interrupted by world war. Another result of the war was a changed map of the world, as countries were divided or newly formed, and the end of most of Britain's colonialism occurred as a result of the empire's economic and military losses. Following the war, Great Britain, France, Portugal, Belgium, Italy, the Netherlands, and Japan had either granted freedom to colonies or lost areas during the war. Many African and Middle Eastern countries would be granted their independence; however, the newly formed countries' borders were drawn according to those of the former colonies, creating ethnic and religious tensions that still exist today.

In an effort to stop a world war from occurring again, the Allies created the United Nations to be a safeguard and upholder of peace. This proved especially important, yet difficult, as the world was divided between a capitalist Western bloc and a Communist Eastern bloc. Germany was divided between the United States and Soviet Union to maintain peace and to better control the reconstruction of Germany; occupation zones were established, with East Germany occupied by the Soviet Union and West Germany occupied by Great Britain, France, and the United States.

Cold War

Within two years of World War II, the world was involved in a different kind of war—a **Cold War**—that pitted capitalism and Communism against each other. World War II left Europe on the brink of collapse, leaving the United States and Soviet Union as the world's undisputed remaining superpowers. The United States and its Allies embarked on a campaign of containment in an attempt to keep Communism from spreading to other countries. After World War II, the United States offered European countries the Marshall Plan—a grant of American subsidies to help Europe and Japan recover economically. The largest recipients were England, France, and West Germany. Aside from sincere humanitarian desires, the Marshall Plan also served the interests of the United States by ensuring that Europe's citizens did not resort to Communism out of desperation. In turn, the Soviet Union developed their own plan, the Molotov Plan, to help their Communist Allies' recovery.

In the 1940s, U.S. president Harry S. Truman, in an effort to contain Communism, offered U.S. military and economic protection to any nation threatened by Communist takeover. By 1949, the United States, Canada, and ten European nations agreed to the same idea in an alliance known as the **North Atlantic Treaty Organization (NATO)**. When West Germany was invited into NATO in 1955, the Soviet Union responded with a similar alliance known as the *Warsaw Pact*. The Warsaw Pact and NATO were vehicles for the United States and Soviet Union to flex their military might. In addition to conventional arms, the two superpowers competed in a nuclear arms race throughout the Cold War. The nuclear arms race created a situation where each country could destroy the world many times over at the push of a button. There were several close calls during the conflict due to mixed signals, misunderstandings, or provocation—the most notorious being the Cuban Missile Crisis when the Soviet Union placed nuclear missiles in Cuba, ninety miles away from Florida.

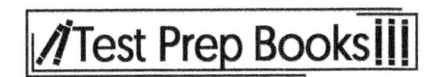

In China, **Mao Zedong**, the chairman of the Communist Party and leader of the People's Republic of China, attempted to quickly transform China into a Communist state through an ineffective and devastating economic program known as the **Great Leap Forward**, which abolished private ownership of property and featured collective communes. The Great Leap Forward caused a humanitarian disaster, resulting in tens of millions of deaths, due to inefficient economic planning under a poorly devised Communist system.

The United States fought a series of proxy wars against the Soviet Union to prevent the spread of Communism. The Korean War (1950–1953) was an attempt to keep Communism from spreading into Korea. China and the Soviet Union joined together to fight the United States and Allies until an armistice was signed that divided Korea into a Communist North and a democratic South along the thirty-eighth parallel. The **thirty-eighth parallel** was an important demarcation during the war itself, as America was cautious to pursue the North Koreans back across the parallel or else risk escalating the proxy war into a conventional one against the Soviets. **The Vietnam Conflict** (1955–1975) was another proxy war pitting the United States against Communism.

China and the Soviet Union provided extensive aid to the Communist Viet Cong guerilla fighters and the more conventional North Vietnamese army. Although the United States was the superior conventional military force, the American military struggled mightily against the guerillas using the dense jungle as cover. As intense opposition to the war mounted in the United States, the United States withdrew (1973) and the North Vietnamese captured Saigon in April 1975. The Soviet Union similarly struggled against guerilla forces backed by the United States during the Soviet-Afghan War, which lasted between 1979 and 1989. The United States provided military and financial support to the Afghans during the conflict, many of whom would later found al-Qaeda or join the Taliban to fight the United States, including Osama bin Laden.

Protests and new leaders gave some economic freedom and recovery to these European nations after WWII, but East Germany was excluded. In 1961, a wall was built to separate East and West Germany in an attempt to keep people from fleeing the Soviet-controlled East. However, in 1985, Mikhail Gorbachev became the Soviet leader and began to change politics in the Soviet Union, with *glasnost*—a policy of government transparency and openness—and **perestroika**, a government reform. He allowed the Eastern European satellite countries more economic freedom and limited self-government. The Soviet economy could not keep up with the United States, especially when President Reagan increased American military spending. Pushed to the brink of economic collapse, the Soviet Union could no longer maintain control over their satellites and Allies, who were increasingly agitated for complete autonomy. On November 9, 1989, the Soviet Union ordered the Berlin Wall to be knocked down, an important step toward thawing the Cold War. On December 26, 1991, the Soviet Union officially collapsed and broke up into fifteen distinct countries.

The Major Developments of the Post-Cold War

The collapse of the Soviet Union left the United States as the sole world superpower. In addition, Communism no longer represented a viable political ideology, cementing the market economy as the leading economic system, which is later discussed in greater detail in the section "The Major Economic Transformations that Have Affected World Societies." In the mid-1990s, the Internet emerged as a driving force in globalization, connecting people across the world and providing instantaneous access to vast stores of information. Globalization further presented itself in the form of supranational governance. In 1992, the European Union was established for the purpose of creating a common market for goods and capital. Other supranational political entities would lead the way toward the creation of a globalized economy.

Founded in 1995, the World Trade Organization is a supranational organization composed of 164 member states, and it establishes regulations, norms, and dispute resolution to govern trade agreements between countries. Trade agreements between two entities are referred to as **bilateral agreements**, and any larger type of agreement is classified as **multilateral**. The entity entering into the trade agreement can be either a single nation-state or a trade bloc—an informal group of countries who negotiate as a single entity. The most common type of trade agreement is free trade, which offers preferential treatment through the elimination of trade restrictions, like tariffs and quotas. Trade agreements force countries to rely on the economic health of their trade partners, which naturally leads to interdependence. Examples of trade agreements include the North America Free Trade Agreement and Association of Southeast Asian Nations.

Trade agreements form the basis of a globalized economy as countries seek to maximize the economic principle of economies of scale, which defines how countries can function most efficiently within markets and vis-à-vis competitors. It encourages countries to specialize in what they do best and devote the bulk of their resources to maximizing that specialty. In theory, increasing production will make the output more efficient and cost effective. Incentivizing countries to boost their production and pursue their competitive advantage inherently leads to greater economic interdependence and globalization; trading countries are necessarily dependent on their partners to meet some need. For example, in the North America Free Trade Agreement, the United States provides technology and white-collar skills, while Mexico primarily focuses on manufacturing.

Despite the trend toward supranational political and economic entities, nationalism has reemerged as a powerful force in the post-Cold War Era. Nationalism is best understood as people seeking independence for some collective reason, like geographical proximity or cultural similarities. In addition, nationalism is primarily expressed via its opposition to external influences. Just as nationalism served as a rallying cry for colonial people fighting to gain their independence, nationalism has come back into vogue as the means for people to advocate for greater local control.

The Yugoslav Wars of 1991 to 2001 and eventual collapse of Yugoslavia illustrate how ethnic nationalism exists as a powerful countervailing force to globalization trends. The former Socialist Federal Republic of Yugoslavia contained several republics that consisted of distinct ethnic groups, including Bosnia and Herzegovina, Croatia, Macedonia, Serbia, and Slovenia. Additionally, Serbia was further divided between Kosovo and Vojvodina. After the death of Yugoslavia's founding authoritarian ruler, Josip Broz Tito, the country eventually collapsed under separatist nationalist movements. Following a series of bloody wars and war crimes, collectively known as the Yugoslav Wars, seven newly independent states emerged out of Yugoslavia—Bosnia and Herzegovina, Croatia, Kosovo, Macedonia, Montenegro, Serbia, and Slovenia.

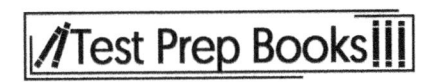

Nationalism is also on the rise in Western democracies as people grapple with the consequences of a globalized economy and greater involvement of supranational political entities beyond their control. In June 2016, the United Kingdom held a referendum on the country's membership in the European Union, and British citizens voted to withdraw, which is commonly referred to as the "Brexit" (British exit). Nationalism greatly influenced British citizens' reluctance to cede any degree of sovereignty, pay taxes, or follow regulations from the European Union.

Religious fundamentalism has increased dramatically in the post-Cold War Era. Specifically, the globalized economy has directly resulted in cultural clashes between the West and Islamic fundamentalism. The most infamous modern terrorist attack occurred on September 11, 2001, when terrorists associated with al-Qaeda hijacked four commercial airliners and flew two into the World Trade Center, one into the U.S. Pentagon, and one into a field. The 9/11 attack initially led to the United States' invasion of Afghanistan and later contributed to the decision to invade Iraq.

Additionally, the Arab Spring created a spirit of unrest in many Middle Eastern countries with a history of authoritarian rule. Following the Americans' withdrawal from Iraq and uprisings in neighboring Syria, the religious extremists declared an Islamic State in the region, known as the *Islamic State of Iraq and Levant,* ensuring the proliferation of Islamic fundamentalism and terrorism for the foreseeable future.

Geography

Locating and Using Sources of Geographic Data

Geographic data is essential to fully understanding both the spatial and human realms of geography. For instance, geographers can use data and comparative analysis to determine the different factors that affect quality of life, such as population density, infant mortality rates, and literacy rates. In addition, organizations such as the **Population Reference Bureau** and the **Central Intelligence Agency** provide incredible amounts of demographic data that are readily accessible for anyone.

The **CIA World Factbook** is an indispensable resource for anyone interested in geography. Providing information about land area, literacy rates, birth rates, and economics, this resource is one of the most comprehensive on the Internet. In addition, the **Population Reference Bureau (PRB)** provides students of geography with an abundant supply of information. The PRB provides a treasure trove of analyses related to human populations including HIV rates, immigration rates, poverty rates, and more.

Furthermore, the United States Census Bureau provides similar information about the dynamics of the American population. Not only does this source focus on the data geographers need to understand the world, but it also provides information about upcoming classes, online workshops, and even includes an online library of resources for both students and teachers.

Websites for each source can be found below:

- Population Reference Bureau: http://www.prb.org/
- United States Census Bureau: http://www.census.gov/
- CIA World Factbook: https://www.cia.gov/library/publications/the-world-factbook/

Spatial Concepts

Location is the central theme in understanding spatial concepts. In geography, there are two primary types of location: relative and absolute. Relative location involves locating objects by their proximity to another object. For example, a person giving directions may refer to well-known landmarks, highways, or intersections along the route to provide a better frame of reference. Absolute location is the exact latitudinal and longitudinal position on the globe. A common way of identifying **absolute location** is through the use of digital, satellite-based technologies such as **GPS (Global Positioning System),** which uses sensors that interact with satellites orbiting the Earth. Coordinates correspond with positions on a manmade grid system using imaginary lines known as **latitude** (also known as **parallels**) and **longitude** (also known as **meridians**).

Geography

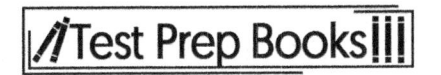

Lines of latitude run parallel to the **Equator** and measure distance from north to south. Lines of longitude run parallel to the **Prime Meridian** and measure distance from east to west.

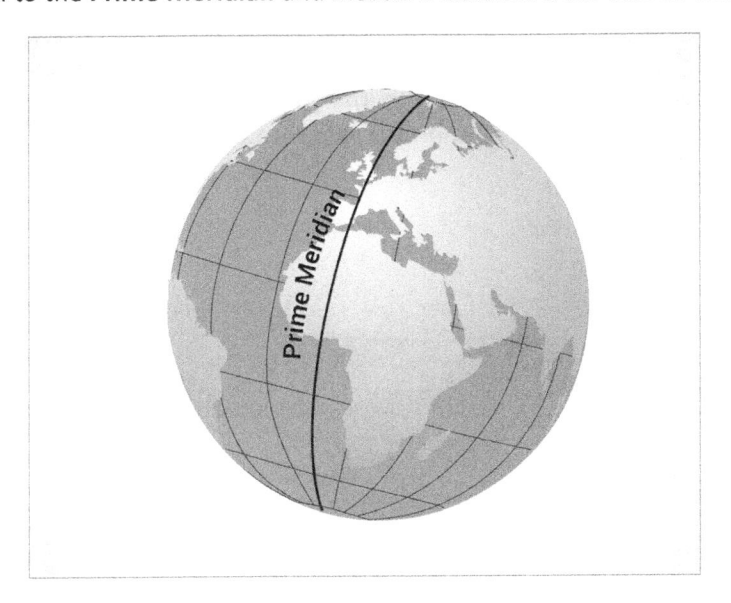

The Equator and the Prime Meridian serve as anchors of the grid system and create the basis for absolute location. They also divide the Earth into **hemispheres**. The Equator divides the Earth into the northern and southern hemispheres, while the Prime Meridian establishes the eastern and western hemispheres. Lines of latitude are measured by degrees from 0 at the Equator to 90 at the North and South Poles. Lines of longitude are measured by degrees from 0 at the Prime Meridian to 180 at the International Date Line. Coordinates are used to express a specific location using its latitude and longitude and are always expressed in the following format: degree north or south followed by degree east or west (for example, 40°N, 50°E). Since there is great distance between lines of latitude and longitude, absolute locations are often found in between two lines. In those cases, degrees are broken down into *minutes* and *seconds*, which are expressed in this manner: (40° 53' 44" N, 50° 22' 65" E).

Other major lines of latitude include the Tropics of Cancer (23.5 degrees north) and Capricorn (23.5 degrees south). These lines correspond with the **Earth's tilt** and mark the positions on the Earth where the sun is directly overhead on the solstices. The tilt and rotation of the earth determine the seasons (or lack thereof) in a given location. For example, the northern hemisphere is tilted toward the sun from June 21 to September 21, which creates the summer season in that part of the world. Conversely, the southern hemisphere is tilted away from the direct rays of the sun and experiences winter during those same months.

The area between the **Tropic of Cancer** and the **Tropic of Capricorn** (called the tropics) has more direct exposure to the sun, tends to be warmer year-round, and experiences fewer variations in seasonal temperatures. Most of the Earth's population lives in the area between the Tropic of Cancer and the Arctic Circle (66.5 degrees north), which is one of the middle latitudes. In the Southern Hemisphere, the middle latitudes exist between the Tropic of Capricorn and the Antarctic Circle (66.5 degrees south). In both of these places, indirect rays of the sun strike the Earth. Therefore, seasons are more pronounced, and milder temperatures generally prevail. The final region, known as the **high latitudes**, is found north of the Arctic Circle and south of the Antarctic Circle. These regions generally tend to be cold all year, and experience nearly twenty-four hours of sunlight during their respective **summer solstice** and twenty-four hours of darkness during the **winter solstice**.

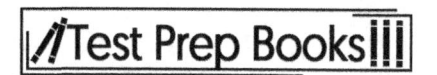

Seasons in the Southern Hemispheres are opposite of those in the Northern Hemisphere due to the position of the Earth as it rotates around the sun. An **equinox** occurs when the sun's rays are directly over the Equator, and day and night are of almost equal length throughout the world. Equinoxes occur twice a year; the autumnal equinox occurs around September 22nd, while the spring equinox occurs around March 20th. Since the Northern and Southern hemispheres experience opposite seasons, the season names vary based on location (i.e. when the Northern Hemisphere is experiencing summer, the Southern Hemisphere is in winter).

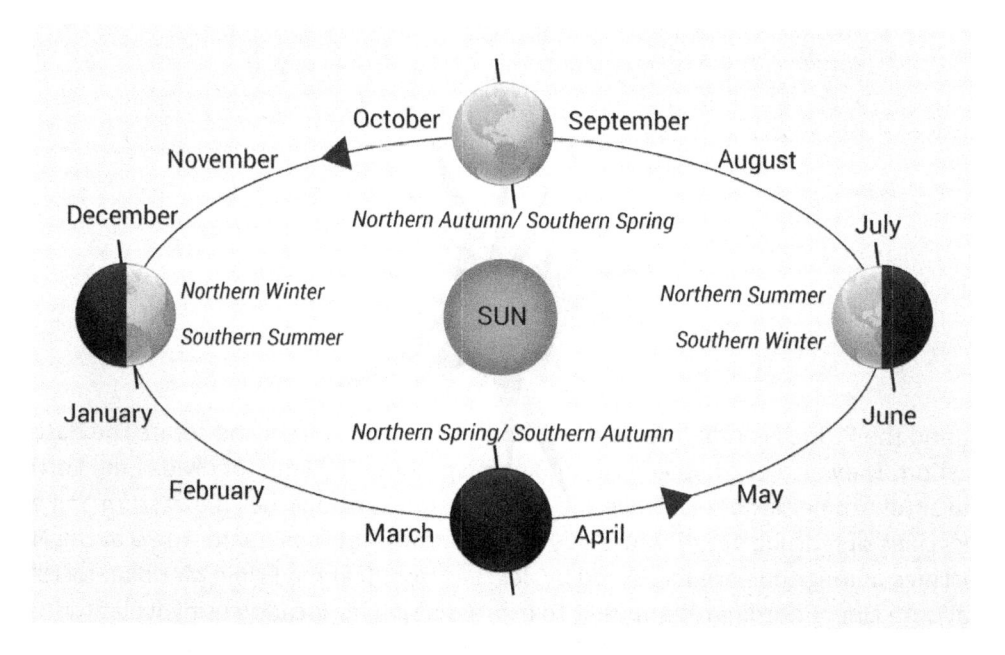

Place
While absolute and relative location identify where something is, the concept of place identifies the distinguishing physical and human characteristics of specific locations. People use **toponyms**, names of locations, to define and further orient themselves with their sense of place. Toponyms may be derived from geographical features, important historical figures in the area, or even wildlife commonly found there. For example, many cities in the state of Texas are named in honor of military leaders who fought in the Texas Revolution (such as Houston and Austin), while Mississippi and Alabama got their toponyms from Native American words.

Regions
Geographers divide the world into regions to help them understand differences inherent within the world, its people, and its environment. As mentioned previously, lines of latitude and longitude divide the Earth into solar regions relative to the amount of sunlight they receive. Additionally, geographers identify formal and functional regions.

Formal regions are spatially defined areas that have overarching similarities or some level of **homogeneity** or **uniformity.** Although not exactly alike, a formal region generally has at least one characteristic that is consistent throughout the entire area. For example, the United States could be classified as one massive formal region because English is the primary language spoken in all fifty states. Even more specifically, the United States is a linguistic region—a place where everyone generally speaks the same language.

Geography

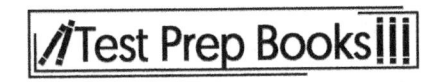

Functional regions are areas that also have similar characteristics but do not have clear boundaries. Large cities and their metropolitan areas form functional regions, as people from outside the official city limit must travel into the city regularly for work, entertainment, restaurants, etc. Other determining factors of a functional region could be a sports team, a school district, or a shopping center. For example, New York City has two professional baseball, basketball, and football teams. As a result, its citizens may have affinities for different teams even though they live in the same city. Conversely, a citizen in rural Idaho may cheer for the Seattle Seahawks, even though they live over 500 miles from Seattle.

Effects of Physical Processes, Climate Patterns, and Natural Hazards on Human Societies

The Earth's surface, like many other things in the broader universe, does not remain the same for long; in fact, it changes daily. The Earth's surface is subject to a variety of physical processes that continue to shape its appearance. Water, wind, temperature, or sunlight play a role in continually altering the Earth's surface.

Erosion involves the movement of soil from one place to another and can be caused by a variety of stimuli including ice, snow, water, wind, and ocean waves. Wind erosion occurs in generally flat, dry areas with loose topsoil. Over time, the persistent winds can dislodge significant amounts of soil into the air, reshaping the land and wreaking havoc on those who depend on agriculture for their livelihoods. Water can also cause erosion. For example, erosion caused by the Colorado River helped to form the Grand Canyon. Over time, the river moved millions of tons of soil, cutting a huge gorge in the Earth along the way. In water erosion, material carried by the water is referred to as **sediment**. With time, some sediment can collect at the mouths of rivers, forming **deltas,** which become small islands of fertile soil. This process of detaching loose soils and transporting them to a different location where they remain for an extended period of time is referred to as **deposition**, which is the end result of the erosion process.

In contrast to erosion, **weathering** does not involve the movement of any outside stimuli. Instead, the surface of the Earth is broken down physically or chemically. **Physical weathering** involves the effects of atmospheric conditions such as water, ice, heat, or pressure. For example, when ice forms in the cracks of large rocks or pavement, it can break down or split open the material. **Chemical weathering** generally occurs in warmer climates and involves organic material that breaks down rocks, minerals, or soil. Scientists believe this process led to the creation of fossil fuels such as oil, coal, and natural gas.

Climate Patterns
Weather is the condition of the Earth's atmosphere at a particular time. *Climate* is different; instead of focusing on one particular day, climate is the relative pattern of weather in a place for an extended period of time. For example, the city of Atlanta, Georgia generally has a humid subtropical climate; however, it also occasionally experiences snowstorms in the winter months. Over time, geographers, meteorologists, and other Earth scientists have determined these patterns that are indicative to north Georgia. Almost all parts of the world have predictable climate patterns, which are influenced by the surrounding geography.

The Central Coast of California is an example of a place with a predictable climate pattern. Santa Barbara, California, one of the region's larger cities, has almost the same temperature for most of the year, with only minimal fluctuation during the winter months. The temperatures there, which average between 75° and 65° Fahrenheit regardless of the time of year, are influenced by a variety of different climatological factors including elevation, location relative to the mountains and ocean, and ocean currents.

Other factors affecting climate include elevation, prevailing winds, vegetation, and latitudinal position on the globe.

Natural hazards also affect human societies. In tropical and subtropical climates, hurricanes and typhoons that form over warm water can have devastating effects. Additionally, tornadoes, which are powerful cyclonic windstorms, are responsible for widespread destruction in many parts of the world. Earthquakes, caused by shifting plates along faults deep below the Earth's surface, also bring widespread devastation, particularly in nations with poor infrastructure. For example, San Francisco, which experiences earthquakes regularly due to its position near the San Andreas Fault, saw relatively little destruction and death as a result of a major earthquake in 1989. However, in 2010, an earthquake of similar magnitude reportedly killed over 200,000 people in the Western Hemisphere's poorest nation, Haiti. Although a variety of factors may be responsible for the disparity, modern engineering methods and better building materials most likely helped to minimize destruction in San Francisco. Other natural hazards, such as tsunamis, mudslides, avalanches, forest fires, dust storms, flooding, volcanic eruptions, and blizzards also affect human societies throughout the world.

Characteristics and Spatial Distribution of Earth's Ecosystems

Earth is an incredibly large place filled with a variety of land and water ecosystems. *Marine ecosystems* cover over 75 percent of the Earth's surface and contain over 95 percent of the Earth's water. Marine ecosystems can be broken down into two primary subgroups: **freshwater ecosystems**, which only encompass around 2 percent of the earth's surface; and **ocean ecosystems**, which make up over 70 percent. Terrestrial ecosystems vary based on latitudinal distance from the equator, elevation, and proximity to mountains or bodies of water. For example, in the high latitudinal regions north of the Arctic Circle and south of the Antarctic Circle, frozen **tundra** dominates. Tundra, which is characterized by low temperatures, short growing seasons, and minimal vegetation, is only found in regions that are far away from the direct rays of the sun.

In contrast, **deserts** can be found throughout the globe and are created by different ecological factors. For example, the world's largest desert, the Sahara, is almost entirely within the tropics; however, other deserts like the Gobi in China, the Mojave in the United States, and the Atacama in Chile, are close to mountain ranges such as the Himalayas, the Sierra Nevada, and the Andes, respectively. In the United States, temperate deciduous forests dominate the southeastern region. The midwestern states such as Nebraska, Kansas, and the Dakotas, are primarily grasslands. The states of the Rocky Mountains can have decidedly different climates relative to elevation. Denver, Colorado, will often see snowfalls well into April or May due to colder temperatures, whereas cities in the eastern part of the state, with much lower elevations, may see their last significant snowfall in March.

The tropics generally experience warmer temperatures due to their position on the Earth in relation to the sun. However, like most of the world, the tropics also experience a variety of climatological regions. In Brazil, Southeast Asia, Central America, and even Northern Australia, tropical rainforests are common. These forests, which are known for abundant vegetation, daily rainfall, and a wide variety of animal life, are essential to the health of the world's ecosystems. For example, the Amazon Rain Forest's billions of trees produce substantial amounts of oxygen and absorb an equivalent amount of carbon dioxide—the

Geography

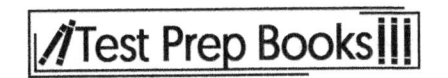

substance that many climatologists assert is causing climate change or global warming. Unlike temperate deciduous forests whose trees lose their leaves during the fall and winter months, **tropical rain forests** are always lush, green, and warm. In fact, some rainforests are so dense with vegetation that a few indigenous tribes have managed to exist within them without being influenced by any sort of modern technology, virtually maintaining their ancient way of life in the modern era.

The world's largest land ecosystem, the taiga, is found primarily in high latitudinal areas, which receive very little direct sunlight. These forests are generally made up of **coniferous** trees, which do not lose their leaves at any point during the year as **deciduous** trees do. **Taigas** are cold-climate regions that make up almost 30 percent of the world's land area. These forests dominate the northern regions of Canada, Scandinavia, and Russia, and provide the vast majority of the world's lumber.

Climates are influenced by five major factors: elevation, latitude, proximity to mountains, ocean currents, and wind patterns. For example, the cold currents off the coast of California provide the West Coast of the United States with pleasant year-round temperatures. Conversely, Western Europe, which is at the nearly the same latitude as most of Canada, is influenced by the warm waters of the **Gulf Stream**, an ocean current that acts as a conveyor belt, moving warm tropical waters to the icy north. In fact, the Gulf Stream's influence is so profound that it even keeps Iceland—an island nation in the far North Atlantic—relatively warm.

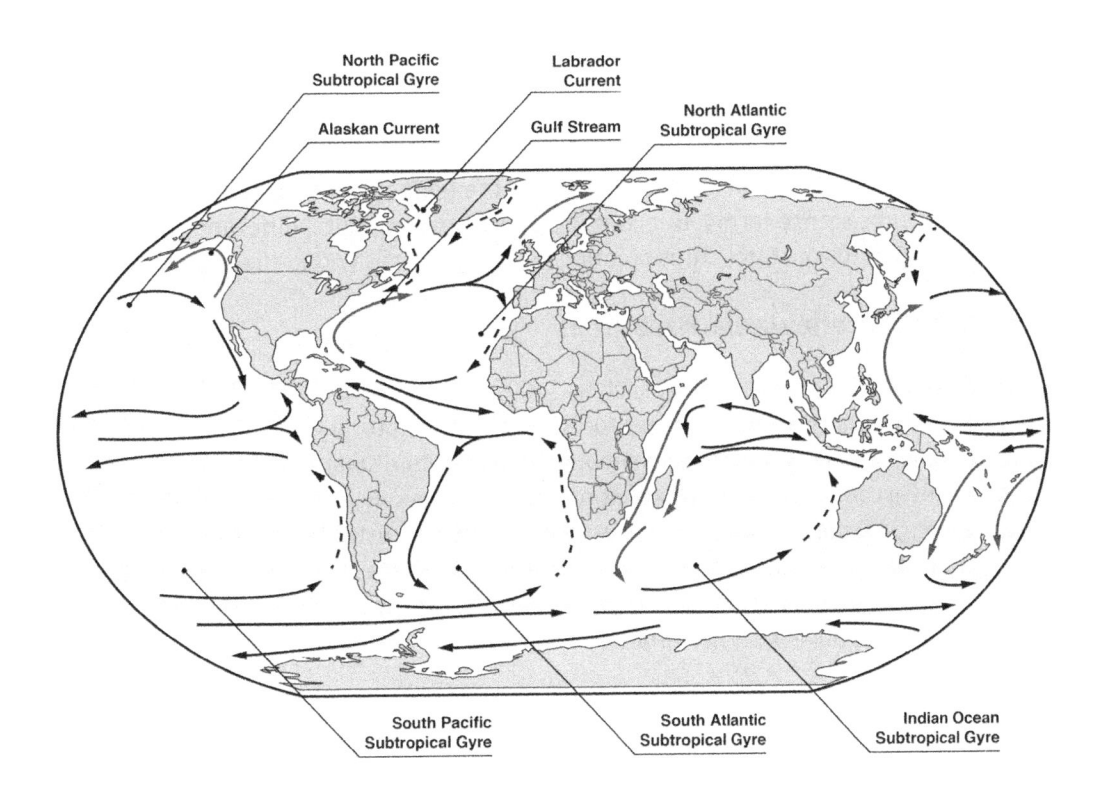

Interrelationships Between Humans and Their Environment

Humans both adapt themselves to their environment and adapt their environment to suit their needs. Humans create social systems with the goal of providing people with access to what they need to live more productive, fulfilling, and meaningful lives. Sometimes, humans create destructive systems, but generally speaking, humans tend to leverage their environments to make their lives easier. For example, in warmer climates, people tend to wear lighter clothing such as shorts, linen shirts, and hats. In the excessively sun-drenched nations of the Middle East, both men and women wear flowing white clothing complete with both a head and neck covering in order to prevent the blistering effects of exposure to the sun. Likewise, the native Inuit peoples of northern Canada and Alaska use the thick furs from the animals they kill to insulate their bodies against the bitter cold.

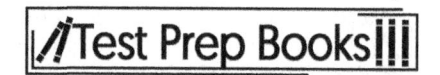

Humans must also manipulate their environments to ensure that they have sufficient access to food and water. In locations where water is not readily available, humans have had to invent ways to redirect water for drinking or agriculture. For example, the city of Los Angeles, America's second most populous city, did not have adequate freshwater resources to sustain its population. However, city and state officials realized that abundant water resources existed approximately three hundred miles to the east. Rather than relocating some of its population to areas with more abundant water resources, the State of California undertook one of the largest construction projects in the history of the world, the Los Angeles Aqueduct, which is a massive water transportation system that connects water-rich areas with the thirsty citizens of Los Angeles.

Farming is another way in which humans use the environment for their advantage. The very first permanent British Colony in North America, Jamestown, VA, was characterized by a hot and humid climate with fertile soil. Consequently, its inhabitants engaged in agriculture for both food and profit. Twelve years after Jamestown's founding in 1607, it was producing millions of dollars of tobacco each year. In order to sustain this booming industry, millions of African slaves and indentured servants from Europe were imported to provide labor. Conversely, poor soil in the New England colonies did not allow for widespread cash crop production, and the settlers there generally only grew enough food for themselves on small subsistence farms. Due in part to this environmental difference, slavery failed to take a strong foothold in these states, thus creating distinct cultures within the same country.

Renewable and Nonrenewable Resources

Renewable resources are self-replenishing, such as solar, wind, water, and geothermal energy. Nonrenewable resources, also known as fossil fuels, such as oil, natural gas, and coal, take much longer to replenish but are generally abundant and cheaper to use. While solar energy is everywhere, the actual means to convert the sun's rays into energy is not. Conversely, coal-fired power plants and gasoline-powered engines, older technologies used during the industrial revolution, remain quite common throughout the world. Reliance on nonrenewable resources continues to grow due to availability and existing infrastructure, but use of renewable energy is also increasing as it becomes more economically competitive with nonrenewable resources.

In addition to sources of energy, nonrenewable resources also include any materials that can be exhausted, such as precious metals, precious stones, and freshwater underground aquifers. Although abundant, most nonrenewable sources of energy are not sustainable because their replenishment takes so long. While renewable resources are sustainable, their use must be properly overseen so that they remain renewable. For example, the beautiful African island of Madagascar is home to some of the most amazing rainforest trees in the world. Logging companies cut, milled, and sold thousands of them in order to make quick profits without planning how to ensure the continued health of the forests. In this way, renewable resources were mismanaged and thus essentially became nonrenewable due to the length of time it takes for replacement trees to grow. In contrast, many United States paper companies that harvest pine trees must utilize planning techniques to ensure that mature pine trees will always be available. In this manner, these resources remain renewable for human use in a sustainable fashion.

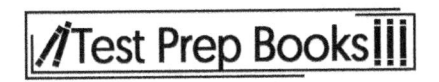

Renewable sources of energy are relatively new in the modern economy. Even though electric cars, wind turbines, and solar panels are becoming more common, they still do not provide enough energy to power the world's economy. As a result, reliance on older forms of energy continues, which can have a devastating effect on the environment. Beijing, China, which has seen a massive boom in industrial jobs, is also one of the most polluted places on Earth. Furthermore, developing nations with very little modern infrastructure also rely heavily on fossil fuels due to the ease in which they are converted into usable energy. Even the United States, which has one of the most developed infrastructures in the world, still relies almost exclusively on fossil fuels, with only ten percent of the required energy coming from renewable sources.

Spatial Patterns of Cultural and Economic Activities

Spatial patterns refer to where things are in the world. Elements of both physical and human geography have spatial patterns regarding where they appear on Earth.

Ethnicity

An ethnic group, or **ethnicity**, is essentially a group of people with a common language, society, culture, or ancestral heritage. Different ethnicities developed over centuries through historical forces, the impact of religious traditions, and other factors. Thousands of years ago, it was more common for ethnic groups to remain in one area with only occasional interaction with outside groups. In the modern world, different ethnicities interact on a regular basis due to better transportation resources and the processes of globalization. For example, in countries like the United States and Canada, it is not uncommon for schools, workplaces, or communities to have people of Asian, African, Caucasian, European, Indian, or Native descent. In less developed parts of the world, travel is limited due to the lack of infrastructure.

Consequently, ethnic groups develop in small areas that can differ greatly from other people just a few miles away. For example, on the Balkan Peninsula in southeastern Europe, a variety of different ethnic groups live in close proximity to one another. Croats, Albanians, Serbs, Bosnians, and others all share the same land but have very different worldviews, traditions, and religious influences. Unfortunately, this diversity has not always been a positive characteristic, such as when Bosnia was the scene of a horrible genocide against Albanians in an "ethnic cleansing" effort that continued throughout the late 20th century.

Linguistics

Linguistics, or the study of language, groups certain languages together according to their commonalities. For example, the Romance languages—French, Spanish, Italian, Romanian, and Portuguese—all share language traits from Latin. These languages, also known as **vernaculars**, or more commonly spoken **dialects**, evolved over centuries of physical isolation on the European continent. The Spanish form of Latin emerged into today's Spanish language. Similarly, the Bantu people of Africa travelled extensively and spread their language, now called Swahili, which became the first Pan-African language. Since thousands of languages exist, it is important to have a widespread means of communication that can interconnect people from different parts of the world. One way to do this is through a lingua franca, or a common language used for business, diplomacy, and other cross-national relationships. English is a primary lingua franca around the world, but there are many others in use as well.

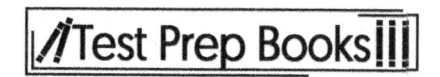

Religion

Religion has played a tremendous role in creating the world's cultures. Devout Christians crossed the Atlantic in hopes of finding religious freedom in New England, Muslim missionaries and traders travelled to the Spice Islands of the East Indies to teach about the Koran, and Buddhist monks traversed the Himalayan Mountains into Tibet to spread their faith. In some countries, religion helps to shape legal systems. These nations, termed **theocracies**, have no separation of church and state and are more common in Islamic nations such as Saudi Arabia, Iran, and Qatar. In contrast, even though religion has played a tremendous role in the history of the United States, its government remains **secular**, or nonreligious, due to the influence of European Enlightenment philosophy at the time of its inception. Like ethnicity and language, religion is a primary way that individuals and people groups self-identify. As a result, religious influences can shape a region's laws, architecture, literature, and music. For example, when the Ottoman Turks, who are Muslim, conquered Constantinople, which was once the home of the Eastern Orthodox Christian Church, they replaced Christian places of worship with mosques. Additionally, they replaced different forms of Roman architecture with those influenced by Arabic traditions.

Economics

Economic activity also has a spatial component. Nations with few natural resources generally tend to import what they need from nations willing to export raw materials to them. Furthermore, areas that are home to certain raw materials generally tend to alter their environment in order to maintain production of those materials. In the San Joaquin Valley of California, an area known for extreme heat and desert-like conditions, local residents have engineered elaborate drip irrigation systems to adequately water lemon, lime, olive, and orange trees, utilizing the warm temperatures to constantly produce citrus fruits. Additionally, other nations with abundant petroleum reserves build elaborate infrastructures in order to pump, house, refine, and transport their materials to nations who require gasoline, diesel, or natural gas. Essentially, inhabitants of different spatial regions on Earth create jobs, infrastructure, and transportation systems to ensure the continued flow of goods, raw materials, and resources out of their location so long as financial resources keep flowing into the area.

Patterns of Migration and Settlement

Migration is governed by two primary causes: **push factors** that cause someone to leave an area, and **pull factors** that lure someone to a particular place. These two factors often work in concert with one another. For example, the United States of America has experienced significant **internal migration** from the industrial states in the Northeast (such as New York, New Jersey, Connecticut) to the Southern and Western states. This massive migration, which continues into the present-day, is due to high rents in the northeast, dreadfully cold winters, and lack of adequate retirement housing, all of which are push factors. These push factors lead to migration to the *Sunbelt*, a term geographers use to describe states with warm climates and less intense winters.

International migration also takes place between countries, continents, and other regions. The United States has long been the world's leading nation in regard to **immigration**, the process by which people permanently relocate to a new nation. Conversely, developing nations that suffer from high levels of poverty, pollution, warfare, and other violence all have significant push factors, which cause people to leave and move elsewhere. This process, known as **emigration**, is when people in a particular area leave in order to seek a better life in a different—usually better—location.

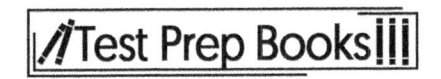

The Development and Changing Nature of Agriculture

Since the genesis of farming as a means of food production, agriculture has been essential to human existence. Humans no longer had to forage and hunt for food, and more consistent food supplies allowed societies to stabilize and grow. In modern times, farming has changed drastically in order to keep up with the increasing world population.

Until the twentieth century, the vast majority of people on Earth engaged in **subsistence farming**, the practice of growing only enough food to feed oneself and one's family. Inventions such as the steel plow, the mechanical reaper, and the seed drill allowed farmers to produce more crops on the same amount of land. As food became cheaper and easier to obtain, populations grew, but fewer people farmed. After the advent of mechanized farming in developed nations, small farms became less common, and many were either abandoned or absorbed by massive commercial farms producing staple crops and cash crops.

In recent years, agricultural practices have undergone further changes in order to keep up with the rapidly growing population. Due in part to the **Green Revolution**, which introduced the widespread use of fertilizers to produce massive amounts of crops, farming techniques and practices continue to evolve. For example, **genetically modified organisms**, or **GMOs,** are plants or animals whose genetic makeup has been modified using different strands of DNA in hopes of producing more resilient strains of staple crops, livestock, and other foodstuffs. This process, which is a form of **biotechnology**, attempts to solve the world's food production problems through the use of genetic engineering. Although these crops are abundant and resistant to pests, drought, or frost, they are also the subject of intense scrutiny. For example, the international food company, Monsanto, has faced an incredible amount of criticism regarding its use of GMOs. Many activists assert that such artificial food production processes are inherently problematic and that the resulting food products are dangerous to human health. Despite the controversy, GMOs and biotechnologies continue to change the agricultural landscape and the world's food supply.

Agribusinesses exist throughout the world and produce food for human consumption as well as farming equipment, fertilizers, agrichemicals, and breeding and slaughtering services for livestock. These companies are generally headquartered near the product they produce, like the cereal manufacturer General Mills in the Midwestern United States located near its supply of wheat and corn—the primary ingredients in its cereals.

Contemporary Patterns and Impacts of Development, Industrialization, and Globalization

As mentioned previously, developing nations are those that are struggling to modernize their economy, infrastructure, and government systems. Many of these nations may have difficulty providing basic services to their citizens like clean water, adequate roads, or even police protection. Furthermore, government corruption makes life even more difficult for these countries' citizens. In contrast, developed nations are those that have relatively high **Gross Domestic Products (GDP)**, or the total value of all goods and services produced in the nation in a given year. The United States, one of the wealthiest nations on Earth, has a GDP of over twenty-one trillion dollars, while Haiti, one of the poorest nations in the Western Hemisphere, has a GDP of over fourteen billion dollars. This comparison is not intended to disparage Haiti or other developing nations, but rather to show that extreme inequities exist in very close proximity to one another, and it may be difficult for developing nations to meet the needs of their citizens and move their economic infrastructure forward toward modernization.

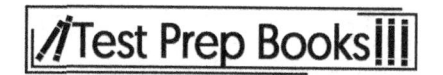

In the modern world, industrialization is the initial key to modernization and development. For developed nations, the process of industrialization took place centuries ago. England, where the Industrial Revolution began, actually began to utilize factories in the early 1700s. Later, the United States and some Western European nations followed suit, using raw materials brought in from their colonies abroad to make finished products. For example, elaborate weaving machines spun cotton into fabric, allowing for the mass production of textiles. As a result, nations that perfected the textile process were able to sell their products around the world, which produced enormous profits. Over time, those nations were able to accumulate wealth, improve their nation's infrastructure, and provide more services for their citizens. Nations throughout the world are undergoing a similar process in modern times. China exemplifies this concept. While agriculture is still a dominant sector of the Chinese economy, millions of citizens are flocking to major cities like Beijing, Shanghai, and Hangzhou due to the availability of factory jobs that allow workers a certain element of social mobility, or the ability to rise up to a better socioeconomic situation.

Due to improvements in transportation and communication, the world has become figuratively smaller. For example, university students now compete directly with others all over the world to obtain the skills that employers desire. Additionally, many corporations in developed nations have begun to *outsource* labor to nations with high levels of educational achievement but lower wage expectations. **Globalization**, the process of opening the marketplace to all nations throughout the world, has only just started to take hold in the modern economy. As industrial sites shift to the developing world, more opportunities become available for those nation's citizens as well. However, due to the massive amounts of pollution produced by factories, the process of globalization also has had significant ecological impacts. The most widely known impact, **climate change**, which most climatologists assert is caused by an increase of carbon dioxide in the atmosphere, remains a serious problem that has posed challenges for developing nations, who need industries in order to raise their standard of living, and developed nations, whose citizens use a tremendous amount of fossil fuels to run their cars, heat their homes, and maintain their ways of life.

Demographic Patterns and Demographic Change

Demography, the study of human populations, investigates a variety of factors related to the human experience. For instance, several variables impact the geographical movement of people, such as economics, climate, natural disasters, or internal unrest. A recent example of this phenomenon is found in the millions of Syrian immigrants who have moved as far away as possible from the danger in their war-torn homeland. As previously mentioned, people tend to live near reliable sources of food and water and away from extreme temperatures. Furthermore, the vast majority of people live in the Northern Hemisphere because more land lies in that part of the Earth. In keeping with these factors, human populations tend to be greater where human necessities are easily accessible, or at least more readily available. In other words, such areas have a greater chance of having a higher population density than places without such characteristics.

Demographic patterns on earth are not always stagnant. In contrast, people move and will continue to move as both push and pull factors fluctuate along with the flow of time. While thousands of Europeans fled their homelands in the 1940s due to the impact of the Second World War, the opposite is true today as thousands of migrants arrive on European shores each month due to conflicts in the Levant and difficult economic conditions in Northern Africa. Furthermore, people tend to migrate to places with a greater economic potential for themselves and their families. As a result, developed nations such as the United States, Germany, Canada, and Australia have a net gain of migrants, while developing nations such as Somalia, Zambia, and Cambodia generally tend to see thousands of their citizens seek better lives elsewhere.

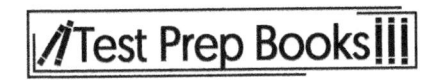

Religion and religious conflict also play a role in determining the composition and location of human populations. For example, the Nation of Israel won its independence in 1948 and has since attracted thousands of Jewish people from all over the world. Additionally, the United States has long been a popular destination due to its promise of religious freedom inherent within its own Constitution. In contrast, nations like Saudi Arabia and Iran do not typically tolerate different religions, resulting in a decidedly uniform religious—and oftentimes ethnic—composition. Other factors such as economic opportunity, social unrest, and cost of living also play a vital role in demographic composition.

Basic Concepts of Political Geography

Nation, state, and nation-state are terms with very similar meanings, but knowing the differences aids in a better understanding of geography. A nation is an area with similar cultural, linguistic, and historical experiences. A **state** is a political unit with sovereignty, or the ability to make its own decisions within defined borders. A **nation-state** is both a nation and a sovereignly governed state. For example, in the United States, the state of Texas is not an independent nation-state. Instead, it is part of the United States and thus, is subject to its laws.

The United Kingdom encompasses four member states: England, Wales, Northern Ireland, and Scotland. Although citizens of those countries may consider themselves to be sovereign, or self-governing, the reality is that they cannot make decisions regarding international trade, declarations of war, or other important decisions regarding the rest of the world. Instead, they are **semi-autonomous**, meaning that they can make some decisions regarding how their own state is run but must yield more major powers to a centralized authority. In the United States, this sort of system is called **Federalism**, or the sharing of power among Local, State, and Federal entities, each of whom is assigned different roles in the overall system of government.

Nation-states and their boundaries are not always permanent. For example, after the fall of the Soviet Union in 1991, new nations emerged that had once been a part of the larger entity called the Union of Soviet Socialists Republics. These formerly sovereign nations were no longer forced to be a part of a unifying communist government, and as a result, they regained their autonomy and became newly independent nations that were no longer *satellite nations* of the Soviet Union. In a historical sense, the United States can be seen as a prime example of how national boundaries change. After the conclusion of the American Revolution in 1781, the **Treaty of Paris** defined the United States' western boundary as the Mississippi River; today, after a series of conflicts with Native American groups, the Mexican government, Hawaiian leadership, the Spanish, and the purchase of Alaska from the Russians, the boundaries of the United States have changed drastically. In a similar fashion, nations in Europe, Africa, and Asia have all shifted their boundaries due to warfare, cultural movements, and language barriers.

In the modern world, boundaries continue to change. For example, the Kurds, an ethnic minority in the Middle East, are still fighting for the right to control their people's' right to *self-determination*, but have not yet been successful in establishing a nation for themselves. In contrast, the oil-rich region of South Sudan, which has significant cultural, ethnic, and religious differences from Northern Sudan, successfully won its independence in a bloody civil war, which established the nation's newest independent nation. In recent years, Russia has made the world nervous by aggressively annexing the Crimean Peninsula, which has been part of Ukraine since the end of the Cold War. Even the United Kingdom and Canada have seen their own people nearly vote for their own rights to self-determination. In 1995, Quebec narrowly voted against becoming a sovereign state through a tightly contested referendum. Similarly, Scotland voted to remain part of the Crown even though many Scots see themselves as inherently different from other regions within the UK.

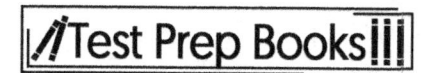

Decolonization, or the removal of dependency on colonizers, has altered the political landscape of Africa, allowed more autonomy for the African people, and redefined the boundaries of the entire continent. Essentially, political geography across the globe is constantly changing.

Economics

The term **economy** is used to describe and calculate the supply and demand of goods and services. Economics is the study of human behavior in response to the production, consumption, and distribution of assets or wealth. It is a multi-tiered dynamic; people need to make personal choices about their own individual spending, while governments must make judgments that shape a whole society. Economics is divided into two subgroups: microeconomics and macroeconomics.

Microeconomics is the study of individual or small group behaviors and patterns related to markets of goods and services. It specifically looks at single factors that could affect these behaviors and decisions. For example, the use of coupons in a grocery store could affect an individual's product choice, quantity purchased, and overall savings that could be directed to a different purchase. **Microeconomics** encompasses the study of many things, including scarcity, choice, opportunity costs, economics systems, factors of production, supply and demand, market efficiency, the role of government, distribution of income, and product markets.

Macroeconomics examines a much larger scale of the economy. It focuses on how aggregate factors such as demand, output, and spending habits affect the people in a society or nation. For example, if a national company moves its production overseas to save on costs, how will production, labor, and capital be affected? Macroeconomics analyzes all aggregate indicators and the microeconomic factors that influence the economy. Governments and corporations use macroeconomic models to help formulate economic policies and strategies.

Economic activity is cyclical with periods of booms and busts, which are typically prompted by extreme changes in the economy. **Booms** are cycles of increased activity resulting in new businesses, technologies, and jobs. However, these are often followed by periods of economic slowdowns, or *busts*, which can lead to recessions and even depressions. For example, the **Wall Street Crash of 1929** triggered the Great Depression of the 1930s. During the Great Depression, New York Stock Market share prices dropped dramatically, causing the world's economic output to decrease by one-third and prompting a spike in unemployment levels of 25 percent or greater among global economies.

Microeconomics

Scarcity

People have different needs and wants, and the question arises, are the resources available to supply those needs and wants? Limited resources and high demand create scarcity. When a product is **scarce**, there is a short supply of it. For example, when the newest version of a cellphone is released, people line up to buy the phone or put their name on a wait list if the phone is not immediately available. The new cellphone may become a scarce commodity. In turn, the phone company may raise their prices, knowing that people may be willing to pay more for an item in such high demand. If a competing company lowers the cost of the phone but has contingencies, such as extended contracts or hidden fees, the buyer will still have the opportunity to purchase the scarce product. Limited resources and extremely high demand create scarcity and, in turn, cause companies to acquire opportunity costs.

Choice and Opportunity Costs

On a large scale, governments and communities have to assess different opportunity costs when it comes to using taxpayers' money. Should the government build a new school, repair roads, or allocate funds to local hospitals? Each choice has a tradeoff, and decision makers must choose which option they think is best.

Economic Systems

Economic systems determine what is being produced, who is producing it, who receives the product, and the money generated by the sale of the product. There are two basic types of economic systems: **market economies** (including free and competitive markets), and planned or **command economies**.

- Market Economies are characterized by:

    o Privately owned businesses, groups, or individuals provide goods or services based on demand.

    o Demand determines the types of goods and services produced (supply).

    o Two types: competitive market and free market.

Competitive Market	Free Market
Due to the large number of both buyers and sellers, there is no way any one seller or buyer can control the market or price.	Voluntary private trades between buyers and sellers determine markets and prices without government intervention or monopolies.

- Planned or Command Economies:

    o Government or central authority determines market prices of goods and services.

    o Government or central authority determines what is being produced and the quantity of production.

    o Advantage: large number of shared goods such as public services (transportation, schools, or hospitals).

    o Disadvantages of command economies include wastefulness of resources.

Factors of Production

There are four factors of production:

1. **Land**: both renewable and nonrenewable resources
2. **Labor**: effort put forth by people to produce goods and services
3. **Capital**: the tools used to create goods and services
4. **Entrepreneurs**: persons who combine land, labor, and capital to create new goods and services

Economics

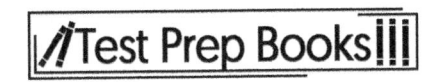

The four factors of production are used to create goods and services to make economic profit. All four factors strongly impact one another.

Supply and Demand

Supply and demand are the most important concepts of economics in a market economy. **Supply** is the amount of a product that a market can offer. **Demand** is the quantity of a product needed or desired by buyers. The price of a product is directly related to supply and demand. The price of a product and the demand for that product go hand in hand in a market economy. For example, when there are a variety of treats at a bakery, certain treats are in higher demand than others. The bakery can raise the cost of the more demanded items as supplies get limited. Conversely, the bakery can sell the less desirable treats by lowering the cost of those items as an incentive for buyers to purchase them.

Market Efficiency and the Role of Government

Market efficiency is directly affected by supply and demand. The government can help the market stay efficient by either stepping in when the market is inefficient and/or providing the means necessary for markets to run properly. For example, society needs two types of infrastructure: physical (bridges, roads, etc.) and institutional (courts, laws, etc.). The government may impose taxes, subsidies, and price controls to increase revenue, lower prices of goods and services, ensure product availability for the government, and maintain fair prices for goods and services.

The Purpose of Taxes, Subsidies, and Price Controls

Taxes	Subsidies	Price Controls
-Generate government revenue -Discourage purchase or use of "bad" products such as alcohol or cigarettes	-Lower the price of goods and services -Reassure the supply of goods and services -Allow opportunities to compete with overseas vendors	-Act as emergency measures when government intervention is necessary -Set a minimum or maximum price for goods and services

Distribution of Income

Distribution of income refers to how wages are spread across a society or segments of a society. If everyone made the same amount of money, the distribution of income would be equal. That is not the case in most societies. Wealth varies among people and companies. Income inequality gaps are present in America and many other nations. Taxes provide an option to redistribute income or wealth because they provide revenue to build new infrastructure and provide cash benefits to some of the poorest members in society.

Product Markets

Product markets are where goods and services are bought and sold. Product markets provide a place for sellers to offer goods and services and for consumers to purchase them. The annual value of goods and services exchanged throughout the year is measured by the **Gross Domestic Product (GDP)**, a monetary measure of goods and services made either quarterly or annually. Department stores, gas stations, grocery stores, and other retail stores are all examples of product markets. However, product markets do not include any raw or unfinished materials.

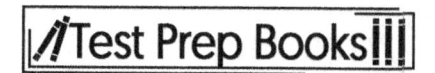

Theory of the Firm

The **behavior of firms** is composed of several theories varying between short- and long-term goals. There are four basic firm behaviors: perfect competition, profit maximization, short run, and long run. Each firm follows a pattern, depending on its desired outcome. **Theory of the Firm** posits that firms, after conducting market research, make decisions that will maximize their profits.

- Perfect competition:
    - In perfect competition, several businesses are selling the same product simultaneously.
    - There are so many businesses and consumers that none will directly impact the market.
    - Each business and consumer is aware of the competing businesses and markets.
- Profit maximization:
    - Firms decide the quantity of a product that needs to be produced in order to receive maximum profit gains. Profit is the total amount of revenue made after subtracting costs.
- Short run:
    - A short amount of time where fixed prices cannot be adjusted
    - The quantity of the product depends on the varying amount of labor. Less labor means less product.
- Long run:
    - An amount of time where fixed prices can be adjusted
    - Firms try to maximize production while minimizing labor costs.

Overall, microeconomics operates on a small scale, focusing on how individuals or small groups use and assign resources.

Macroeconomics

Macroeconomics analyzes the economy as a whole. It studies unemployment, interest rates, price levels, and national income, which are all factors that can affect the nation as a whole, and not just individual households. Macroeconomics studies all large factors to determine how, or if, they will affect future trend patterns of production, consumption, and economic growth.

Types of Productive Resources and the Role of Money as a Resource

Productive resources are the means used by a society to succeed and survive. The four types are:

1. **Natural resources**—the raw materials taken from the land, such as corn, beef, lumber, water, oil, and iron.

2. **Human resources**—the human labor, both mental and physical, that are required to produce goods.

3. **Capital resources**—the man-made physical resources used to create products, such as machinery, tools, buildings, and equipment.

Economics

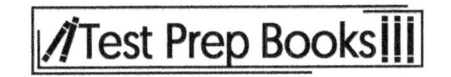

4. **Entrepreneurship**—the capability and motivation to cultivate, organize, and oversee the other three resources into a business venture.

Money functions as a method of exchange to obtain goods or services. It replaced the barter system, which was often considered inefficient and disorganized. Economists referred to the **barter system** as a double coincidence of wants since trades between parties were not always considered equal. Prices of goods are determined by supply and demand. **Inflation** occurs when people have money to spend, but not enough goods can be produced or imported to meet their demand for a product, which causes prices to rise. The amount of money issued by government-controlled central banks and the prices of leading commodities, such as oil, can also affect inflation. **Deflation** is when people save their money and spend less, leaving stores with surplus goods, which causes prices to drop.

Measures of Economic Performance

Measurements of economic performance determine if an economy is growing, stagnant, or deteriorating. To measure the growth and sustainability of an economy, several indicators can be used. Economic indicators provide data that economists can use to determine if there are faulty processes or if some form of intervention is needed.

One of the main indicators of a country's economic performance is the Gross Domestic Product (GDP). GDP growth provides important information that can be used to determine fiscal or financial policies. The GDP does not measure income distribution, quality of life, or losses due to natural disasters. For example, if a community lost everything to a hurricane, it would take a long time to rebuild the community and stabilize its economy. That is why there is a need to take into account more balanced performance measures when factoring overall economic performance.

Other indicators used to measure economic performance are unemployment or employment rates, inflation, savings, investments, surpluses and deficits, debt, labor, trade terms, the HDI (Human Development Index), and the HPI (Human Poverty Index).

Unemployment

Unemployment occurs when an individual does not have a job, is actively trying to find employment, and is not getting paid. Official unemployment rates do not factor in the number of people who have stopped looking for work, but true unemployment rates do.

There are three types of unemployment: cyclical, frictional, and structural.

Cyclical
Comes as a result of the regular economic cycle and variations in supply and demand; This usually occurs during a recession.
Frictional
When workers voluntarily leave their jobs; An example would be a person changing careers.
Structural
When companies' needs change and a person no longer possesses the skills needed

Given the nature of a market economy and the fluctuations of the labor market, a 100 percent employment rate is impossible to reach.

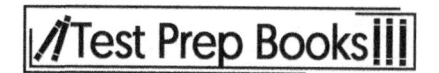

Inflation

Inflation is when the value of money decreases and the cost of goods and services increases over time. Supply, demand, and money reserves all affect inflation. Generally, inflation is measured by the **Consumer Price Index (CPI)**, a tool that tracks price changes of goods and services. The CPI measures goods and services such as gasoline, cars, clothing, and food. When the cost of goods and services increase, manufacturers may reduce the quantity they produce due to lower demand. This decreases the purchasing power of the consumer. Basically, as more money is printed, it holds less and less value in purchasing power. When inflation occurs, consumers spend and save less because their currency is worth less. However, if inflation occurs steadily over time, the people can better plan and prepare for future necessities.

Inflation can vary from year to year, usually never fluctuating more than 2 percent. Central banks try to prevent drastic increases or decreases of inflation to prohibit prices from rising or falling too far. Inflation can also vary based on different monetary currencies. Although rare, any country's economy may experience hyperinflation (when inflation rates increase to over 50 percent), while other economies may experience deflation (when the cost of goods and services decrease over time). Deflation occurs when the inflation rate drops below zero percent.

Business Cycle

A **business cycle** is when the Gross Domestic Product (GDP) moves downward and upward over a long-term growth trend. These cycles help determine where the economy currently stands, as well as where it could be heading. Business cycles usually occur almost every six years and have four phases: expansion, peak, contraction, and trough. Here are some characteristics of each phase:

- Expansion:
    - Increased employment rates and economic growth
    - Production and sales increase
    - On a graph, expansion is where the lines climb.
- Peak:
    - Employment rates are at or above full employment and the economy is at maximum productivity.
    - On a graph, the peak is the top of the hill, where expansion has reached its maximum.
- Contraction:
    - When growth starts slowing
    - Unemployment is on the rise.
    - On a graph, contraction is where the graph begins to slide back down or contract.
- Trough:
    - The cycle has hit bottom and is waiting for the next cycle to start again.
    - On a graph, the trough is the bottom of the contraction prior to when it starts to climb back up.

When the economy is expanding or "booming," the business cycle is going from a trough to a peak. When the economy is headed down and toward a recession, the business cycle is going from a peak to a trough.

Economics

Four phases of a business cycle:

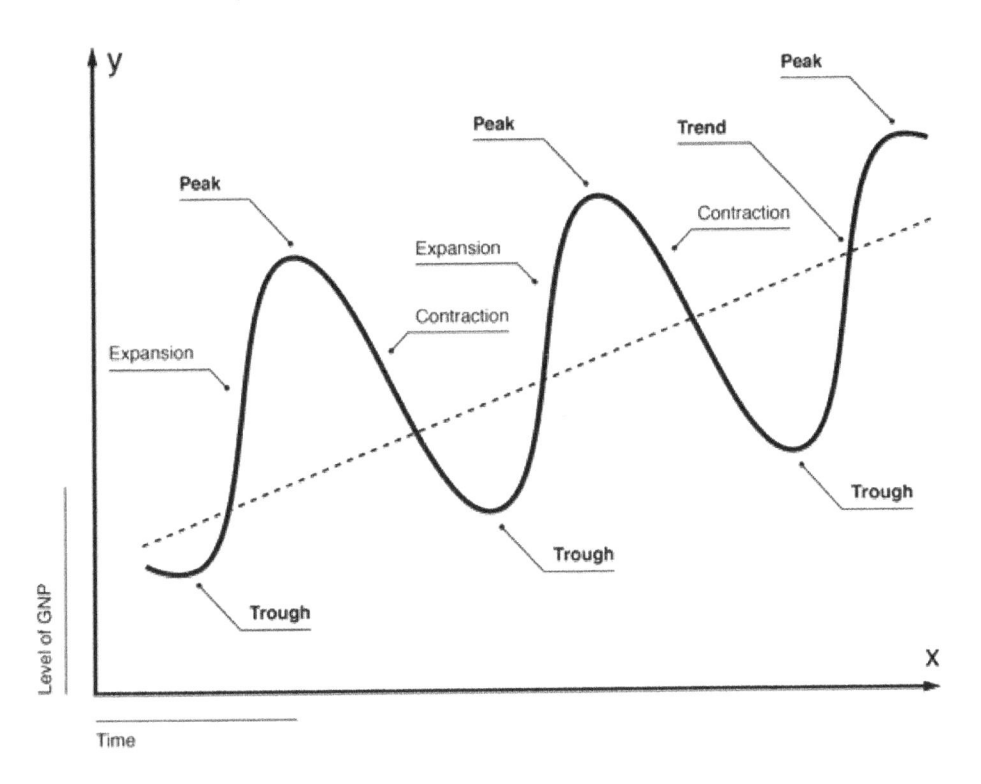

Business cycle diagram showing Level of GNP on y-axis and Time on x-axis, with labeled phases: Expansion, Peak, Contraction, Trough (repeating), and a Trend line.

Fiscal Policy

Fiscal policy refers to how the government adjusts spending and tax rates to influence the functions of the economy. Fiscal policies can either increase or decrease tax rates and spending. These policies represent a tricky balancing act, because if the government increases taxes too much, consumer spending and monetary value will decrease. Conversely, if the government lowers taxes, consumers will have more money in their pockets to buy more goods and services, which increases demand and the need for companies to supply those goods and services. Due to the higher demand, suppliers can add jobs to fulfill that demand. While increases in supply, demand, and jobs are positive for the overall economy, they may result in a devaluation of the dollar and less purchasing power.

Money and Banking

Money is a means of exchange that provides a convenient way for sellers and consumers to understand the value of their goods and services. As opposed to **bartering** (when sellers and consumers exchange goods or services as equal trades), money is convenient for both buyers and sellers.

There are three main forms of money: commodity, fiat, and bank. Here are characteristics of each form:

- **Commodity money**: a valuable good, such as precious metals or tobacco, used as money
- **Fiat money**: currency that has no intrinsic value but is recognized by the government as valuable for trade, such as paper money
- **Bank money**: Money that is credited by a bank to those who deposit it into bank accounts, such as checking and savings accounts or credit

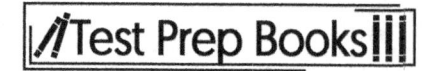

While price levels within the economy set the demand for money, most countries have central banks that supply the actual money. Essentially, banks buy and sell money. Borrowers can take loans and pay back the bank, with interest, providing the bank with extra capital.

A **central bank** has control over the printing and distribution of money. Central banks serve three main purposes: manage monetary growth to help steer the direction of the economy, be a backup to commercial banks that are suffering, and provide options and alternatives to government taxation.

The Federal Reserve is the central bank of the United States. The **Federal Reserve** controls banking systems and determines the value of money in the United States. Basically, the Federal Reserve is the bank for banks.

All Western economies have to keep a minimum amount of protected cash called **required reserve**. Once banks meet those minimums, they can then lend or loan the excess to consumers. The required reserves are used within a fractional reserve banking system (fractional because a small portion is kept separate and safe). Not only do banks reserve, manage, and loan money, but they also help form monetary policies.

Monetary Policy

The central bank and other government committees control the amount of money that is made and distributed. The money supply determines monetary policy. Three main features sustain monetary policy:

> 1. Assuring the minimum amount held within banks (bank reserves): when banks are required to hold more money in reserve funds, they are less willing to lend money to help control inflation.

> 2. Adjusting interest rates: raising interest rates makes borrowing more costly, which can slow down unsustainable growth and lower inflation. Lowering interest rates encourages borrowing and can stimulate struggling economies.

> 3. Purchasing and selling bonds (open market operations): Controlling the money supply by buying bonds to increase it and selling bonds to reduce it.

In the United States, the Federal Reserve maintains monetary policy. There are two main types of monetary policy: expansionary and contractionary.

- Expansionary monetary policy:
    - Increases the money supply
    - Lowers unemployment
    - Increases consumer spending
    - Increases private sector borrowing
    - Possibly decreases interest rates to very low levels, even near zero
    - Decreases reserve requirements and federal funds
- Contractionary monetary policy:
    - Decreases the money supply
    - Helps control inflation
    - Possibly increases unemployment due to slowdowns in economic growth
    - Decreases consumer spending

Economics

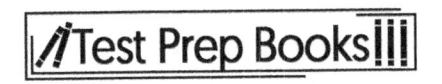

　　　o　Decreases loans and/or borrowing

The Federal Reserve uses monetary policy to try to achieve maximum employment and secure inflation rates. Because the Federal Reserve is the "bank of banks," it truly strives to be the last-resort option for distressed banks. This is because once these kinds of institutions begin to rely on the Federal Reserve for help, all parts of the banking industry—such as those dealing with loans, bonds, interest rates, and mortgages—are affected.

International Trade and Exchange Rates

International trade is when countries import and export goods and services. Countries often want to deal in terms of their own currency. Therefore, when importing or exporting goods or services, consumers and businesses need to enter the market using the same form of currency. For example, if the United States would like to trade with China, the U.S. may have to trade in China's form of currency, the *Yuan*, versus the dollar, depending on the business.

The **exchange rate** is what one country's currency will exchange for another. The government and the market (supply and demand) determine the exchange rate. There are two forms of exchange rates: fixed and floating. **Fixed exchange** rates involve government interventions (like central banks) to help keep the exchange rates stable. **Floating, or "flexible," exchange rates** constantly change because they rely on supply and demand needs. While each type of exchange rate has advantages and disadvantages, the rate truly depends on the current state of each country's economy. Therefore, each exchange rate may differ from country to country.

Advantages and Disadvantages of Fixed Versus Floating Exchange Rates			
Fixed Exchange Rate: government intervention to help keep exchange rates stable		Floating or "Flexible" Exchange Rate: Supply and demand determines the exchange rate	
Advantages	*Disadvantages*	*Advantages*	*Disadvantages*
-Stable prices -Stable foreign exchange rates -Exports are more competitive and in turn more profitable	-Requires a large amount of reserve funds -Possibly mispricing currency values -Inflation increases	-Central bank involvement is not needed. -Facilitates free trade	-Currency speculation -Exchange rate risks -Inflation increases

Countries may have differing economic statuses and exchange rates, but they rely on one another for goods and services. Prices of imports and exports are affected by the strength of another country's currency. For example, if the United States dollar is at a higher value than another country's currency, imports will be less expensive because the dollar will have more value than that of the country selling its good or service. On the other hand, if the dollar is at a low value compared to the currency of another country, importers will tend to avoid buying international items from that country. However, U.S. exporters to that country could benefit from the low value of the dollar.

Economic Growth

The most common tool for measuring economic growth is the **Gross Domestic Product (GDP)**. The increase of goods and services over time indicates positive movement in economic growth. The quantity of goods and services produced is not always an indicator of economic growth, however; the value of the goods and services produced matters more than the quantity.

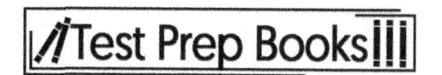

There are many causes of economic growth, which can be short- or long-term. In the short term, if aggregate demand (the total demand for goods and services produced at a given time) increases, then the overall GDP increases as well. As the GDP increases, interest rates may decrease, which may encourage greater spending and investing. Real estate prices may also rise, and there may be lower income taxes. All of these short-term factors can stimulate economic growth.

In the long term, if aggregate supply (the total supply of goods or services in a given time period) increases, then there is potential for an increase in capital as well. With more working capital, more infrastructure and jobs can be created. With more jobs, there is an increased employment rate, and education and training for jobs will improve. New technologies will be developed, and new raw materials may be discovered. All of these long-term factors can also stimulate economic growth.

Other causes of economic growth include low inflation and stability. Lower inflation rates encourage more investing as opposed to higher inflation rates that cause market instability. Stability encourages businesses to continue investing. If the market is unstable, investors may question the volatility of the market.

Potential Costs of Economic Growth:

- Inflation: When economic growth occurs, inflation tends to be high. If supply cannot keep up with demand, then the inflation rate may be unmanageable.

- Economic booms and recessions: The economy goes through cycles of booms and recessions. This causes inflation to fluctuate over time, which puts the economy into a continuous cycle of rising and falling.

- Account inefficiencies: When the economy grows, consumers and businesses increase their import spending. The increase of import spending affects the current account and causes a shortage.

- Environmental costs: When the economy is growing, there is an abundance of output, which may result in more pollutants and a reduction in quality of life.

- Inequalities: Growth occurs differently among members of society. While the wealthy may be getting richer, those living in poverty may just be getting on their feet. So, while economic growth is happening, it may happen at very different rates.

While these potential costs could affect economic growth, if the growth is consistent and stable, then it can occur without severe inflation swings. As technology improves, new ways of production can reduce negative environmental factors as well.

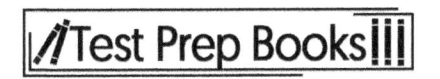

Major Sectors of the United States Economy

Economies consist of the following four business sectors, or parts, that share similar products or services:

- Primary sector—gathers natural resources, including industries such as farming, fishing, and oil and gas drilling.

- Secondary sector—develops raw materials from the primary sector into finished goods through enhancement, manufacture, or construction, including industries such as car manufacturing, food processing, and steelworks.

- Tertiary sector—provides consumer or business services, including industries such as entertainment, travel and tourism, and banking.

- Quaternary sector—provides informational and knowledge services, including industries such as universities, consultancies, and research and development companies.

These sectors function like interconnected links in a chain, with each one passing its production along to the next sector. Service industries typically increase as a country develops and constitute the largest sector of both the U.S. and global economies. The U.S. is the leading global economy in terms of size and significance providing twenty percent of the world's total production of goods and services. About eighty percent of this output comes from its innovative, technically advanced services sector, and fifteen percent comes from manufacturing.

Economists often use the circular flow model to describe the movement of supply, demand, and payment between businesses and consumers (also referred to as sectors). Functioning as an interdependent continuous loop, consumers obtain income, goods, and services from business producers. These producers then receive profits and the ability to buy necessary supplies. Money flows one way, and the goods and productive resources flow in the opposite direction. Each sector relies on the other.

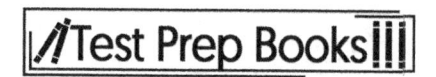

Here's an illustration of that:

Circular Flow Model

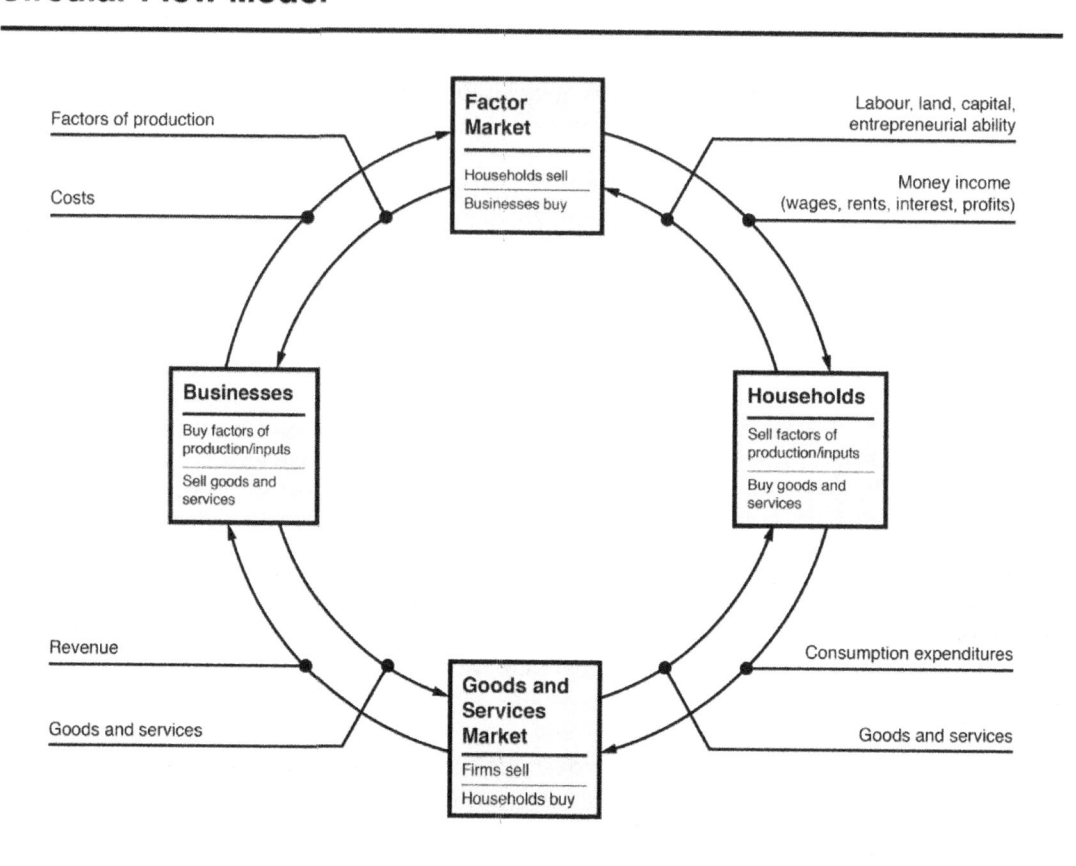

```
                        Factor
Factors of production   Market          Labour, land, capital,
                        Households sell entrepreneurial ability
Costs                   Businesses buy
                                        Money income
                                        (wages, rents, interest, profits)

Businesses                              Households
Buy factors of                          Sell factors of
production/inputs                       production/inputs
Sell goods and                          Buy goods and
services                                services

Revenue                                 Consumption expenditures
                        Goods and
                        Services
Goods and services      Market          Goods and services
                        Firms sell
                        Households buy
```

Costs and Benefits of Personal Spending and Savings Choices

Individuals earn an income by trading their labor – both mental and physical – for pay. They then budget their money through spending or saving it. As consumers, every choice has an opportunity cost since they must choose which goods and services they want to buy with a limited income. By purchasing one good or service, they give up the chance to purchase another.

Additionally, consumers have the choice to save money when they don't have enough money to purchase what they want, or when they want to utilize a savings account to use during emergencies or periods of economic difficulty. People also choose to save for **retirement**, a time when they will no longer be working and drawing a salary. Saving money by putting it in a bank is considered low-risk—the bank will pay the saver a low interest rate to keep it safe, but it will not increase much in value. A riskier path is investing money through the purchase of valuable items (or **assets**) in the hopes that they will increase in worth over time and yield returns (or **profits**). **Assets** can include shares in companies, real estate or land investments, or capital such as money, equipment, and structures used to create wealth.

Mathematics and Statistics

Numbers Sense

Place Value of a Given Digit

The number system that is used consists of only ten different digits or characters. However, this system is used to represent an infinite number of values. The place value system makes this infinite number of values possible. The position in which a digit is written corresponds to a given value. Starting from the decimal point (which is implied, if not physically present), each subsequent place value to the left represents a value greater than the one before it. Conversely, starting from the decimal point, each subsequent place value to the right represents a value less than the one before it.

The names for the place values to the left of the decimal point are as follows:

Billions	Hundred-Millions	Ten-Millions	Millions	Hundred-Thousands	Ten-Thousands	Thousands	Hundreds	Tens	Ones

*Note that this table can be extended infinitely further to the left.

The names for the place values to the right of the decimal point are as follows:

Decimal Point (.)	Tenths	Hundredths	Thousandths	Ten-Thousandths	...

*Note that this table can be extended infinitely further to the right.

When given a multi-digit number, the value of each digit depends on its place value. Consider the number 682,174.953. Referring to the chart above, it can be determined that the digit 8 is in the ten-thousands place. It is in the fifth place to the left of the decimal point. Its value is 8 ten-thousands or 80,000. The digit 5 is two places to the right of the decimal point. Therefore, the digit 5 is in the hundredths place. Its value is 5 hundredths or $\frac{5}{100}$ (equivalent to .05).

Base-10 System

Value of Digits
In accordance with the **base-10 system**, the value of a digit increases by a factor of ten each place it moves to the left. For example, consider the number 7. Moving the digit one place to the left (70), increases its value by a factor of 10 ($7 \times 10 = 70$). Moving the digit two places to the left (700) increases its value by a factor of 10 twice ($7 \times 10 \times 10 = 700$). Moving the digit three places to the left (7,000) increases its value by a factor of 10 three times ($7 \times 10 \times 10 \times 10 = 7,000$), and so on.

Conversely, the value of a digit decreases by a factor of ten each place it moves to the right. (Note that multiplying by $\frac{1}{10}$ is equivalent to dividing by 10). For example, consider the number 40. Moving the digit one place to the right (4) decreases its value by a factor of 10 ($40 \div 10 = 4$). Moving the digit two places to the right (0.4), decreases its value by a factor of 10 twice ($40 \div 10 \div 10 = 0.4$) or

$(40 \times \frac{1}{10} \times \frac{1}{10} = 0.4)$. Moving the digit three places to the right (0.04) decreases its value by a factor of 10 three times $(40 \div 10 \div 10 \div 10 = 0.04)$ or $(40 \times \frac{1}{10} \times \frac{1}{10} \times \frac{1}{10} = 0.04)$, and so on.

Exponents to Denote Powers of 10

The value of a given digit of a number in the base-10 system can be expressed utilizing powers of 10. A **power of 10** refers to 10 raised to a given exponent such as $10^0, 10^1, 10^2, 10^3$, etc. For the number 10^3, 10 is the base and 3 is the exponent. A base raised by an exponent represents how many times the base is multiplied by itself. Therefore, $10^1 = 10$, $10^2 = 10 \times 10 = 100$, $10^3 = 10 \times 10 \times 10 = 1,000$, $10^4 = 10 \times 10 \times 10 \times 10 = 10,000$, etc. Any base with a zero exponent equals one.

Powers of 10 are utilized to decompose a multi-digit number without writing all the zeroes. Consider the number 872,349. This number is decomposed to $800,000 + 70,000 + 2,000 + 300 + 40 + 9$. When utilizing powers of 10, the number 872,349 is decomposed to $(8 \times 10^5) + (7 \times 10^4) + (2 \times 10^3) + (3 \times 10^2) + (4 \times 10^1) + (9 \times 10^0)$. The power of 10 by which the digit is multiplied corresponds to the number of zeroes following the digit when expressing its value in standard form. For example, 7×10^4 is equivalent to 70,000 or 7 followed by four zeros.

Comparing, Classifying, and Ordering Rational Numbers

A **rational number** is any number that can be written as a fraction or ratio. Within the set of rational numbers, several subsets exist that are referenced throughout the mathematics topics. Counting numbers are the first numbers learned as a child. Counting numbers consist of 1,2,3,4, and so on. Whole numbers include all counting numbers and zero (0,1,2,3,4,...). Integers include counting numbers, their opposites, and zero (..., -3, -2, -1, 0, 1, 2, 3, ...). Rational numbers are inclusive of integers, fractions, and decimals that terminate, or end (1.7, 0.04213) or repeat ($0.136\bar{5}$).

When comparing or ordering numbers, the numbers should be written in the same format (decimal or fraction), if possible. For example, $\sqrt{49}$, 7.3, and $\frac{15}{2}$ are easier to order if each one is converted to a decimal, such as 7, 7.3, and 7.5 (converting fractions and decimals is covered in the following section). A number line is used to order and compare the numbers. Any number that is to the right of another number is greater than that number. Conversely, a number positioned to the left of a given number is less than that number.

Structure of the Number System

The mathematical number system is made up of two general types of numbers: real and complex. **Real numbers** are those that are used in normal settings, while **complex numbers** are those composed of both a real number and an imaginary one. Imaginary numbers are the result of taking the square root of -1, and $\sqrt{-1} = i$.

The real number system is often explained using a Venn diagram similar to the one below. After a number has been labeled as a real number, further classification occurs when considering the other groups in this diagram. If a number is a never-ending, non-repeating decimal, it falls in the irrational category. Otherwise, it is rational. More information on these types of numbers is provided in the previous section. Furthermore, if a number does not have a fractional part, it is classified as an integer,

Mathematics and Statistics

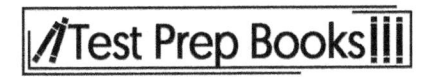

such as -2, 75, or 0. Whole numbers are an even smaller group that only includes positive integers and 0. The last group of natural numbers is made up of only positive integers, such as 2, 56, or 12.

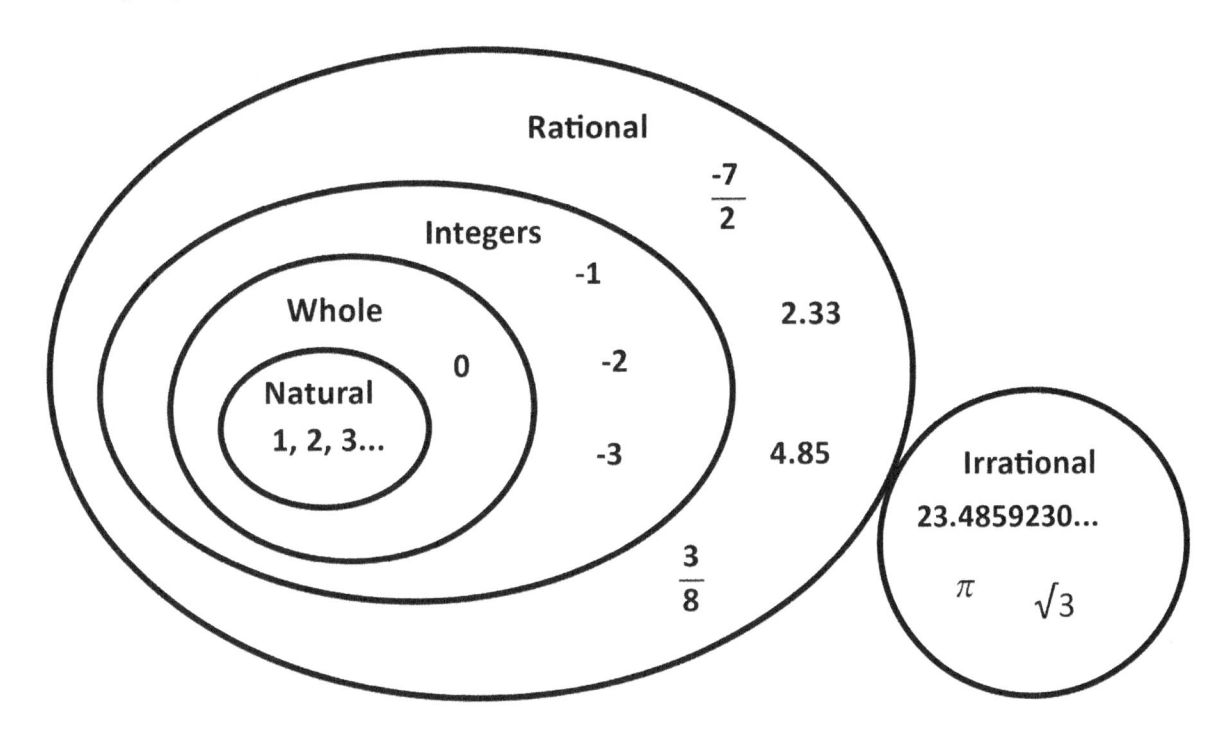

Real numbers can be compared and ordered using the number line. If a number falls to the left on the real number line, it is less than a number on the right. For example, $-2 < 5$ because -2 falls to the left of 0, and 5 falls to the right. Numbers to the left of zero are negative while those to the right are positive.

Complex numbers are made up of the sum of a real number and an imaginary number. Some examples of complex numbers include $6 + 2i$, $5 - 7i$, and $-3 + 12i$. Adding and subtracting complex numbers is similar to collecting like terms. The real numbers are added together, and the imaginary numbers are added together. For example, if the problem asks to simplify the expression $6 + 2i - 3 + 7i$, the 6 and -3 are combined to make 3, and the $2i$ and $7i$ combine to make $9i$. Multiplying and dividing complex numbers is similar to working with exponents. One rule to remember when multiplying is that $i * i = -1$. For example, if a problem asks to simplify the expression $4i(3 + 7i)$, the $4i$ should be distributed throughout the 3 and the $7i$. This leaves the final expression $12i - 28$. The 28 is negative because $i * i$ results in a negative number. The last type of operation to consider with complex numbers is the conjugate. The *conjugate* of a complex number is a technique used to change the complex number into a real number. For example, the conjugate of $4 - 3i$ is $4 + 3i$. Multiplying $(4 - 3i)(4 + 3i)$ results in $16 + 12i - 12i + 9$, which has a final answer of $16 + 9 = 25$.

The order of operations—PEMDAS—simplifies longer expressions with real or imaginary numbers. Each operation is listed in the order of how they should be completed in a problem containing more than one operation. Parenthesis can also mean grouping symbols, such as brackets and absolute value. Then, exponents are calculated. Multiplication and division should be completed from left to right, and addition and subtraction should be completed from left to right.

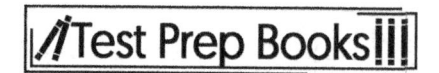

Simplification of another type of expression occurs when radicals are involved. As explained previously, root is another word for radical. For example, the following expression is a radical that can be simplified: $\sqrt{24x^2}$. First, the number must be factored out to the highest perfect square. Any perfect square can be taken out of a radical. Twenty-four can be factored into 4 and 6, and 4 can be taken out of the radical. $\sqrt{4} = 2$ can be taken out, and 6 stays underneath. If $x > 0$, x can be taken out of the radical because it is a perfect square. The simplified radical is $2x\sqrt{6}$. An approximation can be found using a calculator.

There are also properties of numbers that are true for certain operations. The **commutative property** allows the order of the terms in an expression to change while keeping the same final answer. Both addition and multiplication can be completed in any order and still obtain the same result. However, order does matter in subtraction and division. The **associative property** allows any terms to be "associated" by parenthesis and retain the same final answer. For example, $(4 + 3) + 5 = 4 + (3 + 5)$. Both addition and multiplication are associative; however, subtraction and division do not hold this property. The **distributive property** states that $a(b + c) = ab + ac$. It is a property that involves both addition and multiplication, and the a is distributed onto each term inside the parentheses.

Integers can be factored into prime numbers. To **factor** is to express as a product. For example, $6 = 3 \times 2$, and $6 = 6 \times 1$. Both are factorizations, but the expression involving the factors of 3 and 2 is known as a **prime factorization** because it is factored into a product of two **prime numbers**—integers which do not have any factors other than themselves and 1. A **composite number** is a positive integer that can be divided into at least one other integer other than itself and 1, such as 6. Integers that have a factor of 2 are even, and if they are not divisible by 2, they are odd. Finally, a **multiple** of a number is the product of that number and a counting number—also known as a **natural number**. For example, some multiples of 4 are 4, 8, 12, 16, etc.

Properties of Exponents

Exponents are used in mathematics to express a number or variable multiplied by itself a certain number of times. For example, x^3 means x is multiplied by itself three times. In this expression, x is called the **base**, and 3 is the **exponent**. Exponents can be used in more complex problems when they contain fractions and negative numbers.

Fractional exponents can be explained by looking first at the inverse of exponents, which are *roots*. Given the expression x^2, the square root can be taken, $\sqrt{x^2}$, cancelling out the 2 and leaving x by itself, if x is positive. Cancellation occurs because $\sqrt{x}$ can be written with exponents, instead of roots, as $x^{\frac{1}{2}}$. The numerator of 1 is the exponent, and the denominator of 2 is called the root (which is why it's referred to as **square root**). Taking the square root of x^2 is the same as raising it to the $\frac{1}{2}$ power. Written out in mathematical form, it takes the following progression: $\sqrt{x^2} = (x^2)^{\frac{1}{2}} = x$.

From properties of exponents, $2 \times \frac{1}{2} = 1$ is the actual exponent of x. Another example can be seen with $x^{\frac{4}{7}}$. The variable x, raised to four-sevenths, is equal to the seventh root of x to the fourth power: $\sqrt[7]{x^4}$. In general, $x^{\frac{1}{n}} = \sqrt[n]{x}$ and $x^{\frac{m}{n}} = \sqrt[n]{x^m}$.

Mathematics and Statistics

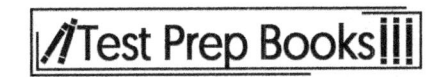

Negative exponents also involve fractions. Whereas y^3 can also be rewritten as $\frac{y^3}{1}$, y^{-3} can be rewritten as $\frac{1}{y^3}$. A negative exponent means the exponential expression must be moved to the opposite spot in a fraction to make the exponent positive. If the negative appears in the numerator, it moves to the denominator. If the negative appears in the denominator, it is moved to the numerator. In general, $a^{-n} = \frac{1}{a^n}$, and a^{-n} and a^n are reciprocals.

Take, for example, the following expression:

$$\frac{a^{-4}b^2}{c^{-5}}$$

Since a is raised to the negative fourth power, it can be moved to the denominator. Since c is raised to the negative fifth power, it can be moved to the numerator. The b-variable is raised to the positive second power, so it does not move. The simplified expression is as follows:

$$\frac{b^2 c^5}{a^4}$$

In mathematical expressions containing exponents and other operations, the order of operations must be followed. **PEMDAS** states that exponents are calculated after any parenthesis and grouping symbols but before any multiplication, division, addition, and subtraction.

Ratios and Proportions

Ratios are used to show the relationship between two quantities. The ratio of oranges to apples in the grocery store may be 3 to 2. That means that for every 3 oranges, there are 2 apples. This comparison can be expanded to represent the actual number of oranges and apples, such as 36 oranges to 24 apples. Another example may be the number of boys to girls in a math class. If the ratio of boys to girls is given as 2 to 5, that means there are 2 boys to every 5 girls in the class. Ratios can also be compared if the units in each ratio are the same. The ratio of boys to girls in the math class can be compared to the ratio of boys to girls in a science class by stating which ratio is higher and which is lower.

Rates are used to compare two quantities with different units. *Unit rates* are the simplest form of rate. With unit rates, the denominator in the comparison of two units is one. For example, if someone can type at a rate of 1,000 words in 5 minutes, then their unit rate for typing is $\frac{1,000}{5} = 200$ words in one minute or 200 words per minute. Any rate can be converted into a unit rate by dividing to make the denominator one. 1000 words in 5 minutes has been converted into the unit rate of 200 words per minute.

Ratios and rates can be used together to convert rates into different units. For example, if someone is driving 50 kilometers per hour, that rate can be converted into miles per hour by using a ratio known as the **conversion factor**. Since the given value contains kilometers and the final answer needs to be in miles, the ratio relating miles to kilometers needs to be used. There are 0.62 miles in 1 kilometer. This, written as a ratio and in fraction form, is $\frac{0.62 \text{ miles}}{1 \text{ km}}$. To convert 50km/hour into miles per hour, the following conversion needs to be set up:

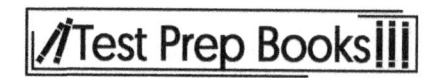

$$\frac{50 \text{ km}}{\text{hour}} \times \frac{0.62 \text{ miles}}{1 \text{ km}} = 31 \text{ miles per hour}$$

The ratio between two similar geometric figures is called the **scale factor**. For example, a problem may depict two similar triangles, A and B. The scale factor from the smaller triangle A to the larger triangle B is given as 2 because the length of the corresponding side of the larger triangle, 16, is twice the corresponding side on the smaller triangle, 8. This scale factor can also be used to find the value of a missing side, x, in triangle A. Since the scale factor from the smaller triangle (A) to larger one (B) is 2, the larger corresponding side in triangle B (given as 25) can be divided by 2 to find the missing side in A ($x = 12.5$). The scale factor can also be represented in the equation $2A = B$ because two times the lengths of A gives the corresponding lengths of B. This is the idea behind similar triangles.

Much like a scale factor can be written using an equation like $2A = B$, a **relationship** is represented by the equation $Y = kX$. X and Y are proportional because as values of X increase, the values of Y also increase. A relationship that is inversely proportional can be represented by the equation $Y = \frac{k}{X}$, where the value of Y decreases as the value of x increases and vice versa.

Proportional reasoning can be used to solve problems involving ratios, percentages, and averages. Ratios can be used in setting up proportions and solving them to find unknowns. For example, if a student completes an average of 10 pages of math homework in 3 nights, how long would it take the student to complete 22 pages? Both ratios can be written as fractions. The second ratio would contain the unknown. The following proportion represents this problem, where x is the unknown number of nights:

$$\frac{10 \text{ pages}}{3 \text{ nights}} = \frac{22 \text{ pages}}{x \text{ nights}}$$

Solving this proportion entails cross-multiplying and results in the following equation: $10x = 22 * 3$. Simplifying and solving for x results in the exact solution: $x = 6.6$ nights. The result would be rounded up to 7 because the homework would actually be completed on the 7th night.

The following problem uses ratios involving percentages:

If 20% of the class is girls and 30 students are in the class, how many girls are in the class?

To set up this problem, it is helpful to use the common proportion: $\frac{\%}{100} = \frac{is}{of}$. Within the proportion, % is the percentage of girls, 100 is the total percentage of the class, *is* is the number of girls, and *of* is the total number of students in the class. Most percentage problems can be written using this language. To solve this problem, the proportion should be set up as $\frac{20}{100} = \frac{x}{30}$, and then solved for x. Cross-multiplying results in the equation $20 \times 30 = 100x$, which results in the solution $x = 6$. There are 6 girls in the class.

Mathematics and Statistics

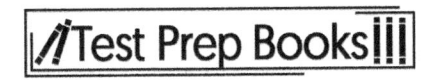

Problems involving volume, length, and other units can also be solved using ratios. For example, a problem may ask for the volume of a cone to be found that has a radius, $r = 7$ m and a height,

$$h = 16 \text{ m}$$

Referring to the formulas provided on the test, the volume of a cone is given as: $V = \pi r^2 \frac{h}{3}$, where r is the radius, and h is the height. Plugging $r = 7$ and $h = 16$ into the formula, the following is obtained: $V = \pi(7^2)\frac{16}{3}$. Therefore, the volume of the cone is found to be approximately 821 m³. Sometimes, answers in different units are sought. If this problem wanted the answer in liters, 821 m³ would need to be converted. Using the equivalence statement 1 m³ = 1,000 L, the following ratio would be used to solve for liters: $821 \text{ m}^3 \times \frac{1,000 \text{ L}}{1 \text{ m}^3}$. Cubic meters in the numerator and denominator cancel each other out, and the answer is converted to 821,000 liters, or 8.21×10^5 L.

Other conversions can also be made between different given and final units. If the temperature in a pool is 30°C, what is the temperature of the pool in degrees Fahrenheit? To convert these units, an equation is used relating Celsius to Fahrenheit. The following equation is used: $T_{°F} = 1.8 T_{°C} + 32$. Plugging in the given temperature and solving the equation for T yields the result: $T_{°F} = 1.8(30) + 32 = 86°F$. Units in both the metric system and U.S. customary system are widely used.

Scientific Notation

Scientific Notation is used to represent numbers that are either very small or very large. For example, the distance to the sun is approximately 150,000,000,000 meters. Instead of writing this number with so many zeros, it can be written in scientific notation as 1.5×10^{11} meters. The same is true for very small numbers, but the exponent becomes negative. If the mass of a human cell is 0.000000000001 kilograms, that measurement can be easily represented by 1.0×10^{-12} kilograms. In both situations, scientific notation makes the measurement easier to read and understand. Each number is translated to an expression with one digit in the tens place times an expression corresponding to the zeros.

When two measurements are given and both involve scientific notation, it is important to know how these interact with each other:

- In addition and subtraction, the exponent on the ten must be the same before any operations are performed on the numbers. For example, $(1.3 \times 10^4) + (3.0 \times 10^3)$ cannot be added until one of the exponents on the ten is changed. The 3.0×10^3 can be changed to 0.3×10^4, then the 1.3 and 0.3 can be added. The answer comes out to be 1.6×10^4.

- For multiplication, the first numbers can be multiplied and then the exponents on the tens can be added. Once an answer is formed, it may have to be converted into scientific notation again depending on the change that occurred.

  - The following is an example of multiplication with scientific notation: $(4.5 \times 10^3) \times (3.0 \times 10^{-5}) = 13.5 \times 10^{-2}$. Since this answer is not in scientific notation, the decimal is moved over to the left one unit, and 1 is added to the ten's exponent. This results in the final answer: 1.35×10^{-1}.

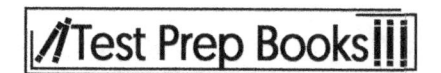

- For division, the first numbers are divided, and the exponents on the tens are subtracted. Again, the answer may need to be converted into scientific notation form, depending on the type of changes that occurred during the problem.

- **Order of magnitude** relates to scientific notation and is the total count of powers of 10 in a number. For example, there are 6 orders of magnitude in 1,000,000. If a number is raised by an order of magnitude, it is multiplied times 10. Order of magnitude can be helpful in estimating results using very large or small numbers. An answer should make sense in terms of its order of magnitude.
  - For example, if area is calculated using two dimensions with 6 orders of magnitude, because area involves multiplication, the answer should have around 12 orders of magnitude. Also, answers can be estimated by rounding to the largest place value in each number. For example, $5,493,302 \times 2,523,100$ can be estimated by $5 \times 3 = 15$ with 12 orders of magnitude.

Basic Concepts of Number Theory

Prime and Composite Numbers

Whole numbers are classified as either prime or composite. A prime number can only be divided evenly by itself and one. For example, the number 11 can only be divided evenly by 11 and one; therefore, 11 is a prime number. A helpful way to visualize a prime number is to use concrete objects and try to divide them into equal piles. If dividing 11 coins, the only way to divide them into equal piles is to create 1 pile of 11 coins or to create 11 piles of 1 coin each. Other examples of prime numbers include 2, 3, 5, 7, 13, 17, and 19.

A composite number is any whole number that is not a prime number. A composite number is a number that can be divided evenly by one or more numbers other than itself and one. For example, the number 6 can be divided evenly by 2 and 3. Therefore, 6 is a composite number. If dividing 6 coins into equal piles, the possibilities are 1 pile of 6 coins, 2 piles of 3 coins, 3 piles of 2 coins, or 6 piles of 1 coin. Other examples of composite numbers include 4, 8, 9, 10, 12, 14, 15, 16, 18, and 20.

To determine if a number is a prime or composite number, the number is divided by every whole number greater than one and less than its own value. If it divides evenly by any of these numbers, then the number is composite. If it does not divide evenly by any of these numbers, then the number is prime. For example, when attempting to divide the number 5 by 2, 3, and 4, none of these numbers divide evenly. Therefore, 5 must be a prime number.

Factors and Multiples of Numbers

The factors of a number are all integers that can be multiplied by another integer to produce the given number. For example, 2 is multiplied by 3 to produce 6. Therefore, 2 and 3 are both factors of 6. Similarly, $1 \times 6 = 6$ and $2 \times 3 = 6$, so 1, 2, 3, and 6 are all factors of 6. Another way to explain a factor is to say that a given number divides evenly by each of its factors to produce an integer. For example, 6 does not divide evenly by 5. Therefore, 5 is not a factor of 6.

Multiples of a given number are found by taking that number and multiplying it by any other whole number. For example, 3 is a factor of 6, 9, and 12. Therefore, 6, 9, and 12 are multiples of 3. The multiples of any number are an infinite list. For example, the multiples of 5 are 5, 10, 15, 20, and so on.

Mathematics and Statistics

This list continues without end. A list of multiples is used in finding the least common multiple, or LCM, for fractions when a common denominator is needed. The denominators are written down and their multiples listed until a common number is found in both lists. This common number is the LCM.

Prime factorization breaks down each factor of a whole number until only prime numbers remain. All composite numbers can be factored into prime numbers. For example, the prime factors of 12 are 2, 2, and 3 ($2 \times 2 \times 3 = 12$). To produce the prime factors of a number, the number is factored, and any composite numbers are continuously factored until the result is the product of prime factors only. A factor tree, such as the one below, is helpful when exploring this concept.

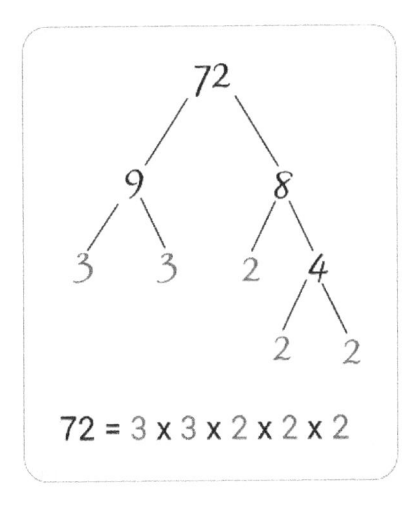

$$72 = 3 \times 3 \times 2 \times 2 \times 2$$

Number Relationships

The set of natural numbers can be separated into a variety of different types such as odds, evens, perfect squares, cubes, primes, composite, Fibonacci, etc. Number theory concepts can be used to prove relationships between these subsets of natural numbers. One of the main goals of number theory is to discover relationships between different subsets and prove that they are true. For example, some number theory proofs involve showing that the sum of two odd numbers is even and the sum of two even numbers is even.

Order of Operations

When solving equations with multiple operations, special rules apply. These rules are known as the **Order of Operations**. The order is as follows: Parentheses, Exponents, Multiplication and Division from left to right, and Addition and Subtraction from left to right. A popular mnemonic device to help remember the order is **Please Excuse My Dear Aunt Sally (PEMDAS)**. Evaluate the following two problems to understand the Order of Operations:

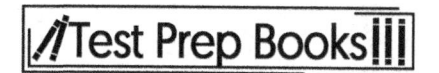

1) $4 + (3 \times 2)^2 \div 4$

> First, solve the operation within the parentheses: $4 + 6^2 \div 4$.
> Second, solve the exponent: $4 + 36 \div 4$.
> Third, solve the division operation: $4 + 9$.
> Fourth, finish the operation with addition for the answer, 13.

2) $2 \times (6 + 3) \div (2 + 1)^2$

> $2 \times 9 \div (3)^2$
> $2 \times 9 \div 9$
> $18 \div 9$
> 2

Positive and Negative Numbers

Signs

Aside from 0, numbers can be either positive or negative. The sign for a positive number is the plus sign or the + symbol, while the sign for a negative number is the minus sign or the – symbol. If a number has no designation, then it's assumed to be positive.

Absolute Values

Both positive and negative numbers are valued according to their distance from 0. Look at this number line for +3 and -3:

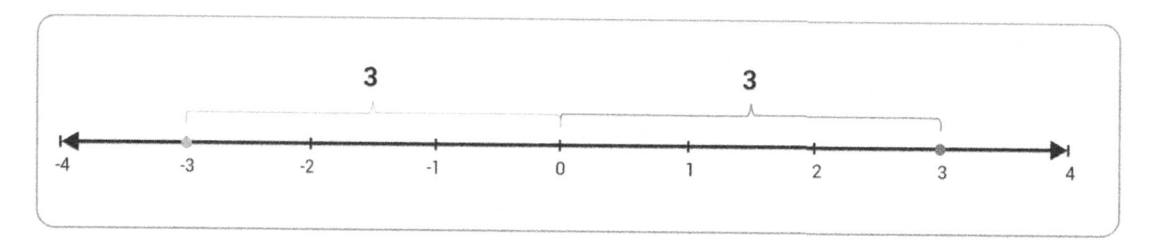

Both 3 and -3 are three spaces from 0. The distance from 0 is called its absolute value. Thus, both -3 and 3 have an absolute value of 3 since they're both three spaces away from 0.

An **absolute number** is written by placing | | around the number. So, |3| and |−3| both equal 3, as that's their common absolute value.

Implications for Addition and Subtraction

For addition, if all numbers are either positive or negative, simply add them together. For example, $4 + 4 = 8$ and $-4 + -4 = -8$. However, things get tricky when some of the numbers are negative, and some are positive.

Mathematics and Statistics

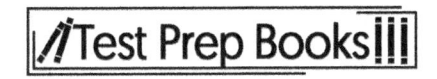

Take $6 + (-4)$ as an example. First, take the absolute values of the numbers, which are 6 and 4. Second, subtract the smaller value from the larger. The equation becomes $6 - 4 = 2$. Third, place the sign of the original larger number on the sum. Here, 6 is the larger number, and it's positive, so the sum is 2.

Here's an example where the negative number has a larger absolute value: $(-6) + 4$. The first two steps are the same as the example above. However, on the third step, the negative sign must be placed on the sum, as the absolute value of (-6) is greater than 4. Thus, $-6 + 4 = -2$.

The absolute value of numbers implies that subtraction can be thought of as flipping the sign of the number following the subtraction sign and simply adding the two numbers. This means that subtracting a negative number will in fact be adding the positive absolute value of the negative number. Here are some examples:

$$-6 - 4 = -6 + -4 = -10$$

$$3 - -6 = 3 + 6 = 9$$

$$-3 - 2 = -3 \pm 2 = -5$$

Implications for Multiplication and Division

For multiplication and division, if both numbers are positive, then the product or quotient is always positive. If both numbers are negative, then the product or quotient is also positive. However, if the numbers have opposite signs, the product or quotient is always negative.

Simply put, the product in multiplication and quotient in division is always positive, unless the numbers have opposing signs, in which case it's negative. Here are some examples:

$$(-6) \times (-5) = 30$$

$$(-50) \div 10 = -5$$

$$8 \times |-7| = 56$$

$$(-48) \div (-6) = 8$$

If there are more than two numbers in a multiplication or division problem, then whether the product or quotient is positive or negative depends on the number of negative numbers in the problem. If there is an odd number of negatives, then the product or quotient is negative. If there is an even number of negative numbers, then the result is positive.

Here are some examples:

$$(-6) \times 5 \times (-2) \times (-4) = -240$$

$$(-6) \times 5 \times 2 \times (-4) = 240$$

Strategies and Algorithms to Perform Operations on Rational Numbers

A **rational number** is any number that can be written in the form of a ratio or fraction. Integers can be written as fractions with a denominator of 1 ($5 = \frac{5}{1}$; $-342 = \frac{-342}{1}$; etc.). Decimals that terminate and/or repeat can also be written as fractions ($47 = \frac{47}{100}$; $0.\overline{33} = \frac{1}{3}$). For more on converting decimals to fractions, see the section *Converting Between Fractions, Decimals,* and *Percent*.

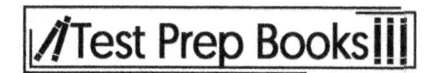

When adding or subtracting fractions, the numbers must have the same denominators. In these cases, numerators are added or subtracted, and denominators are kept the same. For example, $\frac{2}{7} + \frac{3}{7} = \frac{5}{7}$ and $\frac{4}{5} - \frac{3}{5} = \frac{1}{5}$. If the fractions to be added or subtracted do not have the same denominator, a common denominator must be found. This is accomplished by changing one or both fractions to a different but equivalent fraction. Consider the example $\frac{1}{6} + \frac{4}{9}$. First, a common denominator must be found. One method is to find the least common multiple (LCM) of the denominators 6 and 9. This is the lowest number that both 6 and 9 will divide into evenly. In this case the LCM is 18. Both fractions should be changed to equivalent fractions with a denominator of 18. To obtain the numerator of the new fraction, the old numerator is multiplied by the same number by which the old denominator is multiplied. For the fraction $\frac{1}{6}$, 6 multiplied by 3 will produce a denominator of 18. Therefore, the numerator is multiplied by 3 to produce the new numerator:

$$\frac{1 \times 3}{6 \times 3} = \frac{3}{18}$$

For the fraction $\frac{4}{9}$, multiplying both the numerator and denominator by 2 produces $\frac{8}{18}$. Since the two new fractions have common denominators, they can be added:

$$\frac{3}{18} + \frac{8}{18} = \frac{11}{18}$$

When multiplying or dividing rational numbers, these numbers may be converted to fractions and multiplied or divided accordingly. When multiplying fractions, all numerators are multiplied by each other and all denominators are multiplied by each other. For example:

$$\frac{1}{3} \times \frac{6}{5} = \frac{1 \times 6}{3 \times 5} = \frac{6}{15}$$

$$\frac{-1}{2} \times \frac{3}{1} \times \frac{11}{100}$$

$$\frac{-1 \times 3 \times 11}{2 \times 1 \times 100} = \frac{-33}{200}$$

When dividing fractions, the problem is converted by multiplying by the reciprocal of the divisor. This is done by changing division to multiplication and "flipping" the second fraction, or divisor. For example, $\frac{1}{2} \div \frac{3}{5} \to \frac{1}{2} \times \frac{5}{3}$ and $\frac{5}{1} \div \frac{1}{3} \to \frac{5}{1} \times \frac{3}{1}$. To complete the problem, the rules for multiplying fractions should be followed.

Note that when adding, subtracting, multiplying, and dividing mixed numbers (ex. $4\frac{1}{2}$), it is easiest to convert these to improper fractions (larger numerator than denominator). To do so, the denominator is kept the same. To obtain the numerator, the whole number is multiplied by the denominator and added

Mathematics and Statistics

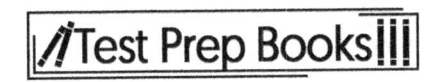

to the numerator. For example, $4\frac{1}{2} = \frac{9}{2}$ and $7\frac{2}{3} = \frac{23}{3}$. Also, note that answers involving fractions should be converted to the simplest form.

Converting Between Fractions, Decimals, and Percent

To convert a fraction to a decimal, the numerator is divided by the denominator. For example, $\frac{3}{8}$ can be converted to a decimal by dividing 3 by 8 ($\frac{3}{8} = 0.375$). To convert a decimal to a fraction, the decimal point is dropped, and the value is written as the numerator. The denominator is the place value farthest to the right with a digit other than zero. For example, to convert .48 to a fraction, the numerator is 48, and the denominator is 100 (the digit 8 is in the hundredths place). Therefore, $0.48 = \frac{48}{100}$. Fractions should be written in the simplest form, or reduced. To reduce a fraction, the numerator and denominator are divided by the largest common factor. In the previous example, 48 and 100 are both divisible by 4. Dividing the numerator and denominator by 4 results in a reduced fraction of $\frac{12}{25}$.

To convert a decimal to a percent, the number is multiplied by 100. To convert .13 to a percent, .13 is multiplied by 100 to get 13 percent. To convert a fraction to a percent, the fraction is converted to a decimal and then multiplied by 100. For example, $\frac{1}{5} = 0.20$ and 0.20 multiplied by 100 produces 20 percent.

To convert a percent to a decimal, the value is divided by 100. For example, 125 percent is equal to 1.25 ($\frac{125}{100}$). To convert a percent to a fraction, the percent sign is dropped, and the value is written as the numerator with a denominator of 100. For example, $80\% = \frac{80}{100}$. This fraction can be reduced ($\frac{80}{100} = \frac{4}{5}$).

Representing Rational Numbers and Their Operations

Concrete Models

Concrete objects are used to develop a tangible understanding of operations of rational numbers. Tools such as tiles, blocks, beads, and hundred charts are used to model problems. For example, a hundred chart (10×10) and beads can be used to model multiplication. If multiplying 5 by 4, beads are placed across 5 rows and down 4 columns producing a product of 20. Similarly, tiles can be used to model division by splitting the total into equal groups. If dividing 12 by 4, 12 tiles are placed one at a time into 4 groups. The result is 4 groups of 3. This is also an effective method for visualizing the concept of remainders.

Representations of objects can be used to expand on the concrete models of operations. Pictures, dots, and tallies can help model these concepts. Utilizing concrete models and representations creates a foundation upon which to build an abstract understanding of the operations.

Rational Numbers on a Number Line

A **number line** typically consists of integers (...3, 2, 1, 0, -1, -2, -3...), and is used to visually represent the value of a rational number. Each rational number has a distinct position on the line determined by comparing its value with the displayed values on the line. For example, if plotting -1.5 on the number line below, it is necessary to recognize that the value of -1.5 is .5 less than -1 and .5 greater than -2. Therefore, -1.5 is plotted halfway between -1 and -2.

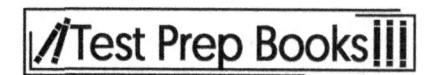

Number lines can also be useful for visualizing sums and differences of rational numbers. Adding a value indicates moving to the right (values increase to the right), and subtracting a value indicates moving to the left (numbers decrease to the left). For example, $5 - 7$ is displayed by starting at 5 and moving to the left 7 spaces, if the number line is in increments of 1. This will result in an answer of -2.

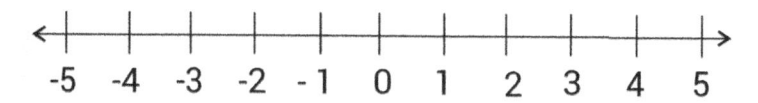

Multiplication and Division Problems

Multiplication and division are inverse operations that can be represented by using rectangular arrays, area models, and equations. **Rectangular arrays** include an arrangement of rows and columns that correspond to the factors and display product totals.

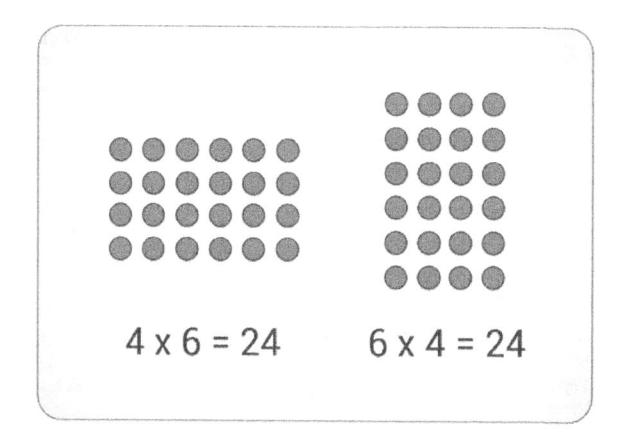

Another method of multiplication can be done with the use of an *area model*. An **area model** is a rectangle that is divided into rows and columns that match up to the number of place values within each number. Take the example 29×65. These two numbers can be split into simpler numbers: $29 = 25 + 4$ and $65 = 60 + 5$. The products of those 4 numbers are found within the rectangle and then summed up to get the answer. The entire process is:

$$(60 \times 25) + (5 \times 25) + (60 \times 4) + (5 \times 4)$$

$$1{,}500 + 125 + 240 + 20$$

$$1{,}885$$

Mathematics and Statistics

Here is the actual area model:

	25	4
60	60x25 1,500	60x4 240
5	5x25 125	5x4 20

```
  1,500
    240
    125
+    20
  -----
  1,885
```

Dividing a number by a single digit or two digits can be turned into repeated subtraction problems. An area model can be used throughout the problem that represents multiples of the divisor. For example, the answer to $8580 \div 55$ can be found by subtracting 55 from 8580 one at a time and counting the total number of subtractions necessary.

However, a simpler process involves using larger multiples of 55. First, $100 \times 55 = 5{,}500$ is subtracted from 8,580, and 3,080 is leftover. Next, $50 \times 55 = 2{,}750$ is subtracted from 3,080 to obtain 330. $5 \times 55 = 275$ is subtracted from 330 to obtain 55, and finally, $1 \times 55 = 55$ is subtracted from 55 to obtain zero. Therefore, there is no remainder, and the answer is $100 + 50 + 5 + 1 = 156$.

Here is a picture of the area model and the repeated subtraction process:

$$8580 \div 55$$

	55
100	5500
50	2750
5	275
1	55

```
  55 ) 8580
      -5500   (100 x 55)
       ----
       3080
      -2750   (50 x 55)
       ----
        330
       -275   (5 x 55)
       ----
         55
        -55   (1 x 55)
        ---
          0
```

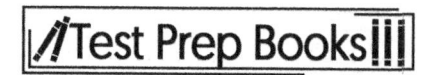

Determining the Reasonableness of Results

When solving math word problems, the solution obtained should make sense within the given scenario. The step of checking the solution will reduce the possibility of a calculation error or a solution that may be *mathematically* correct but not applicable in the real world. Consider the following scenarios:

A problem states that Lisa got 24 out of 32 questions correct on a test and asks to find the percentage of correct answers. To solve the problem, a student divided 32 by 24 to get 1.33, and then multiplied by 100 to get 133 percent. By examining the solution within the context of the problem, the student should recognize that getting all 32 questions correct will produce a perfect score of 100 percent. Therefore, a score of 133 percent with 8 incorrect answers does not make sense, and the calculations should be checked.

A problem states that the maximum weight on a bridge cannot exceed 22,000 pounds. The problem asks to find the maximum number of cars that can be on the bridge at one time if each car weighs 4,000 pounds. To solve this problem, a student divided 22,000 by 4,000 to get an answer of 5.5. By examining the solution within the context of the problem, the student should recognize that although the calculations are mathematically correct, the solution does not make sense. Half of a car on a bridge is not possible, so the student should determine that a maximum of 5 cars can be on the bridge at the same time.

Mental Math Estimation

Once a result is determined to be logical within the context of a given problem, the result should be evaluated by its nearness to the expected answer. This is performed by approximating given values to perform mental math. Numbers should be rounded to the nearest value possible to check the initial results.

Consider the following example: A problem states that a customer is buying a new sound system for their home. The customer purchases a stereo for $435, 2 speakers for $67 each, and the necessary cables for $12. The customer chooses an option that allows him to spread the costs over equal payments for 4 months. How much will the monthly payments be?

After making calculations for the problem, a student determines that the monthly payment will be $145.25. To check the accuracy of the results, the student rounds each cost to the nearest ten (440 + 70 + 70 + 10) and determines that the total is approximately $590. Dividing by 4 months gives an approximate monthly payment of $147.50. Therefore, the student can conclude that the solution of $145.25 is very close to what should be expected.

When rounding, the place-value that is used in rounding can make a difference. Suppose the student had rounded to the nearest hundred for the estimation. The result (400 + 100 + 100 + 0 = 600; 600 ÷ 4 = 150) will show that the answer is reasonable but not as close to the actual value as rounding to the nearest ten.

Precision and Accuracy

Precision and accuracy are used to describe groups of measurements. **Precision** describes a group of measures that are very close together, regardless of whether the measures are close to the true value. **Accuracy** describes how close the measures are to the true value.

Mathematics and Statistics

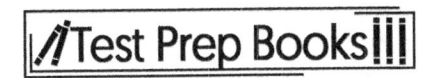

Since **accuracy** refers to the closeness of a value to the true measurement, the level of accuracy depends on the object measured and the instrument used to measure it. This will vary depending on the situation. If measuring the mass of a set of dictionaries, kilograms may be used as the units. In this case, it is not vitally important to have a high level of accuracy. If the measurement is a few grams away from the true value, the discrepancy might not make a big difference in the problem.

In a different situation, the level of accuracy may be more significant. Pharmacists need to be sure they are very accurate in their measurements of medicines that they give to patients. In this case, the level of accuracy is vitally important and not something to be estimated. In the dictionary situation, the measurements were given as whole numbers in kilograms. In the pharmacist's situation, the measurements for medicine must be taken to the milligram and sometimes further, depending on the type of medicine.

When considering the accuracy of measurements, the error in each measurement can be shown as absolute and relative. **Absolute error** tells the actual difference between the measured value and the true value. The **relative error** tells how large the error is in relation to the true value. There may be two problems where the absolute error of the measurements is 10 grams. For one problem, this may mean the relative error is very small because the measured value is 14,990 grams, and the true value is 15,000 grams. Ten grams in relation to the true value of 15,000 is small: 0.06%. For the other problem, the measured value is 290 grams, and the true value is 300 grams. In this case, the 10-gram absolute error means a high relative error because the true value is smaller. The relative error is 10/300=0.03, or 3%.

Algebra and Functions

Number Patterns

Given a sequence of numbers, a mathematical rule can be defined that represents the numbers if a pattern exists within the set. For example, consider the sequence of numbers 1, 4, 9, 16, 25, etc. This set of numbers represents the positive integers squared, and an explicitly defined sequence that represents this set is $f_n = n^2$. An important mathematical concept is recognizing patterns in sequences and translating the patterns into an explicit formula. Once the pattern is recognized and the formula is defined, the sequence can be extended easily. For example, the next three numbers in the sequence are 36, 49, and 64.

Predicting Values

In a similar sense, patterns can be used to make conjectures, predictions, and generalizations. If a pattern is recognized in a set of numbers, values can be predicted that aren't originally provided. For example, if an experiment results in the sequence of numbers 1, 4, 9, 16, and 25, where 1 represents the first trial, 2 represents the second trial, etc., one expects the tenth trial to result in a value of 100 because that value is equal to the square of the trial number.

Recursively Defined Functions

Similar to recursively defined sequences, recursively defined functions are not explicitly defined in terms of a variable. A recursive function builds on itself and consists of a smaller argument, such as $f(0)$ or

$f(1)$ and the actual definition of the function. For example, a recursively defined function is the following:

$$f(0) = 3$$

$$f(n) = f(n-1) + 2n$$

Contrasting an explicitly defined function, a recursively defined function must be evaluated in order. The first five terms of this function are $f(0) = 3, f(1) = 5, f(2) = 9, f(3) = 15$, and $f(4) = 23$. Some recursively defined functions have an explicit counterpart and, like sequences, they can be used to model real-life applications. The Fibonacci numbers can also be thought of as a recursively defined function if $f(n) = f_n$.

Closed-Form Functions

A **closed-form function** can be evaluated using a finite number of operations such as addition, subtraction, multiplication, and division. An example of a function that's not a closed-form function is one involving an infinite sum. For example, $y = \sum_{n=1}^{\infty} x$ isn't a closed-form function because it consists of a sum of infinitely many terms. Many recursively defined functions can be expressed as a closed-form expression. To convert to a closed-form expression, a formula must be found for the nth term. This means that the recursively defined sequence must be converted to its explicit formula.

Translating Between Verbal and Symbolic Forms

Being able to translate verbal scenarios into symbolic forms is a critical skill in mathematics. This idea is seen mostly when solving word problems. First, the problem needs to be read carefully several times until one can state clearly what is being sought. Then, variables that represent the unknown quantities need to be defined. Equations can be defined using those variables that model the verbal conditions of the given problem. The equations then need to be solved to answer the problem's questions. The problem-solving skills learned in these types of problems is an invaluable skill, and is ultimately more important than finding the answer to each individual problem.

Solving Problems by Quantitative Reasoning

Dimensional analysis is the process of converting between different units using equivalent measurement statements. For instance, running 5 kilometers is approximately the same as running 3.1 miles. This conversion can be found by knowing that 1 kilometer is equal to approximately 0.62 miles.

When setting up the dimensional analysis calculations, the original units need to be opposite one another in each of the two fractions: one in the original amount (essentially in the numerator) and one in the denominator of the conversion factor. This enables them to cancel after multiplying, leaving the converted result.

Calculations involving formulas, such as determining volume and area, are a common situation in which units need to be interpreted and used. However, graphs can also carry meaning through units. The graph below is an example. It represents a graph of the position of an object over time. The y-axis represents the position or the number of meters the object is from the starting point at time s, in seconds. Interpreting this graph, the origin shows that at time zero seconds, the object is zero meters away from the starting point. As the time increases to one second, the position increases to five meters away. This trend continues until 6 seconds, where the object is 30 meters away from the starting position. After this point in time—since the graph remains horizontal from 6 to 10 seconds—the object must have stopped moving.

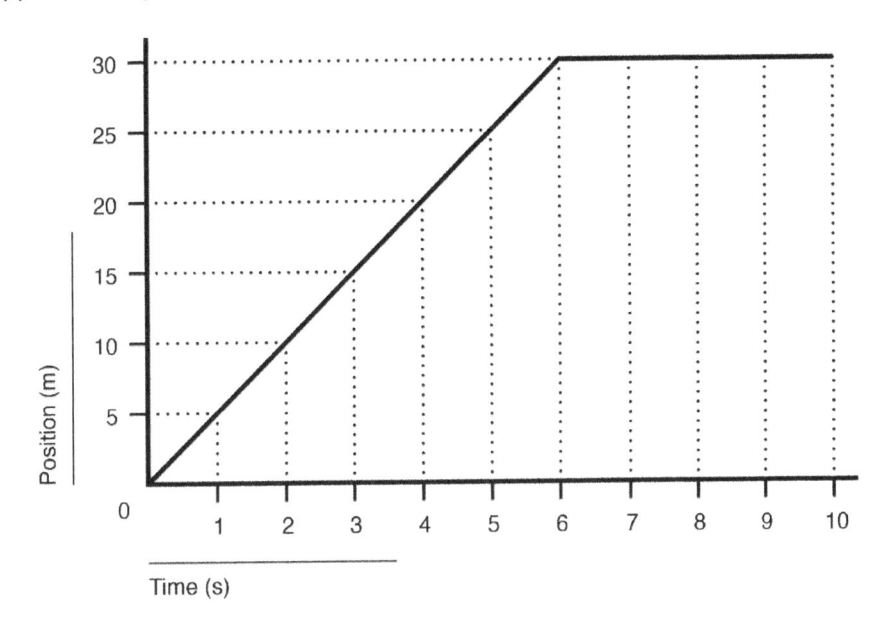

When solving problems with units, it's important to consider the reasonableness of the answer. If conversions are used, it's helpful to have an estimated value to compare the final answer to. This way, if the final answer is too distant from the estimate, it will be obvious that a mistake was made.

Functions

A **function** is defined as a relationship between inputs and outputs where there is only one output value for a given input. As an example, the following function is in function notation: $f(x) = 3x - 4$. The $f(x)$ represents the output value for an input of x. If $x = 2$, the equation becomes:

$$f(2) = 3(2) - 4 = 6 - 4 = 2$$

The input of 2 yields an output of 2, forming the ordered pair $(2, 2)$. The following set of ordered pairs corresponds to the given function: $(2, 2), (0, -4), (-2, -10)$. The set of all possible inputs of a function is its **domain**, and all possible outputs is called the **range**. By definition, each member of the domain is paired with only one member of the range.

Functions can also be defined recursively. In this form, they are not defined explicitly in terms of variables. Instead, they are defined using previously-evaluated function outputs, starting with either $f(0)$ or $f(1)$. An example of a recursively-defined function is $f(1) = 2, f(n) = 2f(n-1) + 2n, n > 1$. The domain of this function is the set of all integers.

Domain and Range

The domain and range of a function can be found visually by its plot on the coordinate plane. In the function $f(x) = x^2 - 3$, for example, the domain is all real numbers because the parabola stretches as far left and as far right as it can go, with no restrictions. This means that any input value from the real number system will yield an answer in the real number system. For the range, the inequality $y \geq -3$

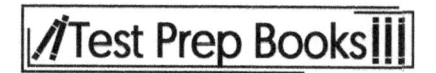

would be used to describe the possible output values because the parabola has a minimum at $y = -3$. This means there will not be any real output values less than -3 because -3 is the lowest value it reaches on the y-axis.

These same answers for domain and range can be found by observing a table. The table below shows that from input values $x = -1$ to $x = 1$, the output results in a minimum of -3. On each side of $x = 0$, the numbers increase, showing that the range is all real numbers greater than or equal to -3.

x (domain/input)	y (range/output)
-2	1
-1	-2
0	-3
-1	-2
2	1

Finding the Zeros of a Function

The zeros of a function are the points where its graph crosses the x-axis. At these points, $y = 0$. One way to find the zeros is to analyze the graph. If given the graph, the x-coordinates can be found where the line crosses the x-axis. Another way to find the zeros is to set $y = 0$ in the equation and solve for x. Depending on the type of equation, this could be done by using opposite operations, by factoring the equation, by completing the square, or by using the quadratic formula. If a graph does not cross the x-axis, then the function may have complex roots.

Rate of Change

Rate of change for any line calculates the steepness of the line over a given interval. Rate of change is also known as the slope or rise/run. The rates of change for nonlinear functions vary depending on the interval being used for the function. The rate of change over one interval may be zero, while the next interval may have a positive rate of change. The equation plotted on the graph below, $y = x^2$, is a quadratic function and non-linear.

Mathematics and Statistics

The average rate of change from points $(0, 0)$ to $(1, 1)$ is 1 because the vertical change is 1 over the horizontal change of 1. For the next interval, $(1, 1)$ to $(2, 4)$, the average rate of change is 3 because the slope is $\frac{3}{1}$.

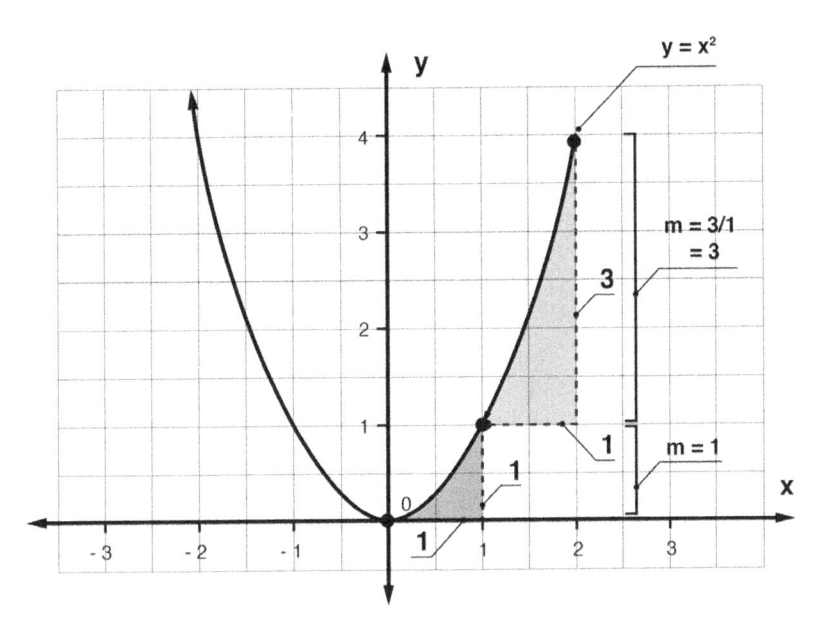

The rate of change for a linear function is constant and can be determined based on a few representations. One method is to place the equation in slope-intercept form: $y = mx + b$. Thus, m is the slope, and b is the y-intercept. In the graph below, the equation is $y = x + 1$, where the slope is 1 and the y-intercept is 1. For every vertical change of 1 unit, there is a horizontal change of 1 unit. The x-intercept is -1, which is the point where the line crosses the x-axis.

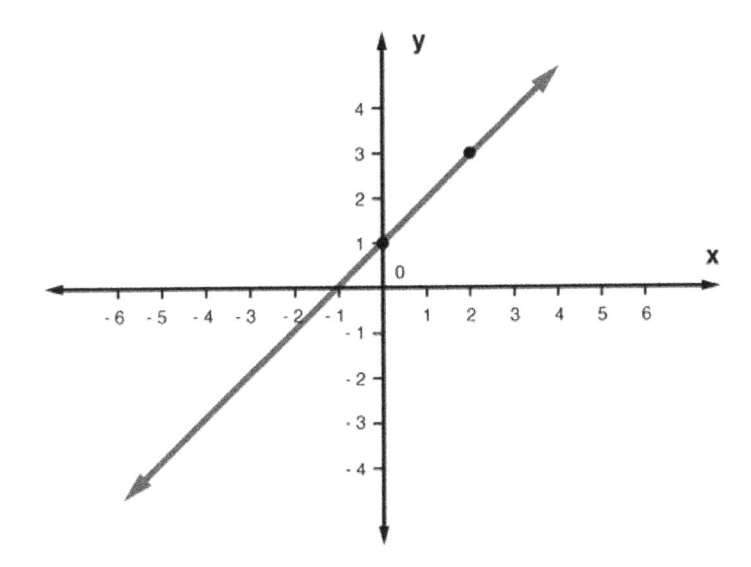

Solving Line Problems

Two lines are parallel if they have the same slope and a different intercept. Two lines are perpendicular if the product of their slope equals -1. **Parallel lines** never intersect unless they are the same line, and perpendicular lines intersect at a right angle. If two lines aren't parallel, they must intersect at one point. Determining equations of lines based on properties of parallel and perpendicular lines appears in word problems. To find an equation of a line, both the slope and a point the line goes through are necessary.

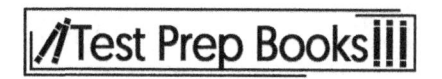

Therefore, if an equation of a line is needed that's parallel to a given line and runs through a specified point, the slope of the given line and the point are plugged into the point-slope form of an equation of a line. Secondly, if an equation of a line is needed that's perpendicular to a given line running through a specified point, the negative reciprocal of the slope of the given line and the point are plugged into the point-slope form. Also, if the point of intersection of two lines is known, that point will be used to solve the set of equations. Therefore, to solve a system of equations, the point of intersection must be found. If a set of two equations with two unknown variables has no solution, the lines are parallel.

Rewriting Expressions

Algebraic expressions are made up of numbers, variables, and combinations of the two, using mathematical operations. Expressions can be rewritten based on their factors. For example, the expression $6x + 4$ can be rewritten as $2(3x + 2)$ because 2 is a factor of both $6x$ and 4. More complex expressions can also be rewritten based on their factors. The expression $x^4 - 16$ can be rewritten as $(x^2 - 4)(x^2 + 4)$. This is a different type of factoring, where a difference of squares is factored into a sum and difference of the same two terms. With some expressions, the factoring process is simple and only leads to a different way to represent the expression. With others, factoring and rewriting the expression leads to more information about the given problem.

In the following quadratic equation, factoring the binomial leads to finding the zeros of the function: $x^2 - 5x + 6 = y$. This equations factors into $(x - 3)(x - 2) = y$, where 2 and 3 are found to be the zeros of the function when y is set equal to zero. The zeros of any function are the x-values where the graph of the function on the coordinate plane crosses the x-axis.

Factoring an equation is a simple way to rewrite the equation and find the zeros, but factoring is not possible for every quadratic. Completing the square is one way to find zeros when factoring is not an option. The following equation cannot be factored: $x^2 + 10x - 9 = 0$. The first step in this method is to move the constant to the right side of the equation, making it $x^2 + 10x = 9$. Then, the coefficient of x is divided it by 2 and squared. This number is then added to both sides of the equation, to make the equation still true. For this example, $\left(\frac{10}{2}\right)^2 = 25$ is added to both sides of the equation to obtain:

$$x^2 + 10x + 25 = 9 + 25$$

This expression simplifies to $x^2 + 10x + 25 = 34$, which can then be factored into $(x + 5)^2 = 34$. Solving for x then involves taking the square root of both sides and subtracting 5. This leads to two zeros of the function: $x = \pm\sqrt{34} - 5$. Depending on the type of answer the question seeks, a calculator may be used to find exact numbers.

Given a quadratic equation in standard form—$ax^2 + bx + c = 0$—the sign of a tells whether the function has a minimum value or a maximum value. If $a > 0$, the graph opens up and has a minimum value. If $a < 0$, the graph opens down and has a maximum value. Depending on the way the quadratic equation is written, multiplication may need to occur before a max/min value is determined.

Mathematics and Statistics

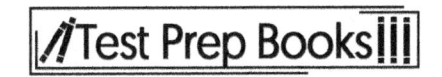

Exponential expressions can also be rewritten, just as quadratic equations. Properties of exponents must be understood. Multiplying two exponential expressions with the same base involves adding the exponents:

$$a^m a^n = a^{m+n}$$

Dividing two exponential expressions with the same base involves subtracting the exponents:

$$\frac{a^m}{a^n} = a^{m-n}$$

Raising an exponential expression to another exponent includes multiplying the exponents: $(a^m)^n = a^{mn}$. The zero power always gives a value of 1: $a^0 = 1$. Raising either a product or a fraction to a power involves distributing that power:

$$(ab)^m = a^m b^m \text{ and } \left(\frac{a}{b}\right)^m = \frac{a^m}{b^m}$$

Finally, raising a number to a negative exponent is equivalent to the reciprocal including the positive exponent:

$$a^{-m} = \frac{1}{a^m}$$

Polynomial Identities

Difference of squares refers to a binomial composed of the difference of two squares. For example, $a^2 - b^2$ is a difference of squares. It can be written $(a)^2 - (b)^2$, and it can be factored into $(a - b)(a + b)$. Recognizing the difference of squares allows the expression to be rewritten easily because of the form it takes. For some expressions, factoring consists of more than one step. When factoring, it's important to always check to make sure that the result cannot be factored further. If it can, then the expression should be split further. If it cannot be, the factoring step is complete, and the expression is completely factored.

A sum and difference of cubes is another way to factor a polynomial expression. When the polynomial takes the form of addition or subtraction of two terms that can be written as a cube, a formula is given. The following graphic shows the factorization of a difference of cubes:

$$a^3 - b^3 = (a - b)(a^2 + ab + b^2)$$

same sign (↑↑)
opposite sign
always + (↑)

This form of factoring can be useful in finding the zeros of a function of degree 3. For example, when solving $x^3 - 27 = 0$, this rule needs to be used. $x^3 - 27$ is first written as the difference two cubes, $(x)^3 - (3)^3$ and then factored into $(x - 3)(x^2 + 3x + 9)$. This expression may not be factored any further. Each factor is then set equal to zero. Therefore, one solution is found to be $x = 3$, and the other two solutions must be found using the quadratic formula. A sum of squares would have a similar process. The formula for factoring a sum of squares is $a^3 + b^3 = (a + b)(a^2 - ab + b^2)$.

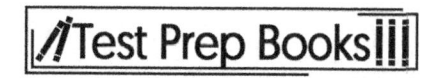

The opposite of factoring is multiplying. Multiplying a square of a binomial involves the following rules: $(a + b)^2 = a^2 + 2ab + b^2$ and $(a - b)^2 = a^2 - 2ab + b^2$. The binomial theorem for expansion can be used when the exponent on a binomial is larger than 2, and the multiplication would take a long time. The binomial theorem is given as:

$$(a+b)^n = \sum_{k=0}^{n} \binom{n}{k} a^{n-k} b^k$$

where $\binom{n}{k} = \dfrac{n!}{k!(n-k)!}$

The **Remainder Theorem** can be helpful when evaluating polynomial functions $P(x)$ for a given value of x. A polynomial can be divided by $(x - a)$, if there is a remainder of 0. This also means that $P(a) = 0$ and $(x - a)$ is a factor of $P(x)$. In a similar sense, if P is evaluated at any other number b, $P(b)$ is equal to the remainder of dividing $P(x)$ by $(x - b)$.

Zeros of Polynomials

Finding the zeros of polynomial functions is the same process as finding the solutions of polynomial equations. These are the points at which the graph of the function crosses the x-axis. As stated previously, factors can be used to find the zeros of a polynomial function. The degree of the function shows the number of possible zeros. If the highest exponent on the independent variable is 4, then the degree is 4, and the number of possible zeros is 4. If there are complex solutions, the number of roots is less than the degree.

Given the function $y = x^2 + 7x + 6$, y can be set equal to zero, and the polynomial can be factored. The equation turns into $0 = (x + 1)(x + 6)$, where $x = -1$ and $x = -6$ are the zeros. Since this is a quadratic equation, the shape of the graph will be a parabola. Knowing that zeros represent the points where the parabola crosses the x-axis, the maximum or minimum point is the only other piece needed to sketch a rough graph of the function. By looking at the function in standard form, the coefficient of x

Mathematics and Statistics

is positive; therefore, the parabola opens *up*. Using the zeros and the minimum, the following rough sketch of the graph can be constructed:

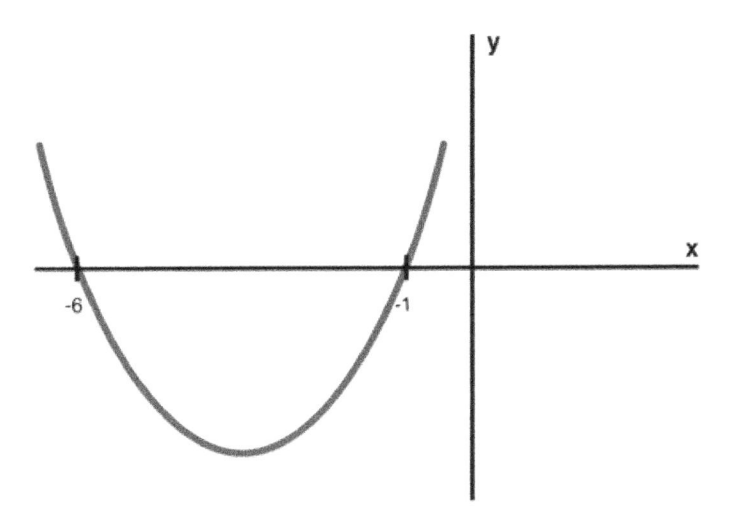

Operations with Polynomials

Addition and subtraction operations can be performed on polynomials with like terms. **Like terms** refer to terms that have the same variable and exponent. The two following polynomials can be added together by collecting like terms:

$$(x^2 + 3x - 4) + (4x^2 - 7x + 8)$$

The x^2 terms can be added as:

$$x^2 + 4x^2 = 5x^2$$

The x terms can be added as $3x + -7x = -4x$, and the constants can be added as $-4 + 8 = 4$. The following expression is the result of the addition: $5x^2 - 4x + 4$. When subtracting polynomials, the same steps are followed, only subtracting like terms together.

Multiplication of polynomials can also be performed. Given the two polynomials, $(y^3 - 4)$ and $(x^2 + 8x - 7)$, each term in the first polynomial must be multiplied by each term in the second polynomial. The steps to multiply each term in the given example are as follows:

$$(y^3 \times x^2) + (y^3 \times 8x) + (y^3 \times -7) + (-4 \times x^2) + (-4 \times 8x) + (-4 \times -7)$$

Simplifying each multiplied part, yields $x^2 y^3 + 8xy^3 - 7y^3 - 4x^2 - 32x + 28$. None of the terms can be combined because there are no like terms in the final expression. Any polynomials can be multiplied by each other by following the same set of steps, then collecting like terms at the end.

Equations and Inequalities

The sum of a number and 5 is equal to -8 times the number. To find this unknown number, a simple equation can be written to represent the problem. Key words such as difference, equal, and times are used to form the following equation with one variable: $n + 5 = -8n$. When solving for n, opposite operations are used. First, n is subtracted from $-8n$ across the equals sign, resulting in $5 = -9n$.

155

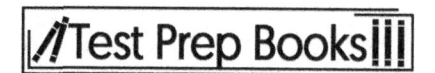

Then, -9 is divided on both sides, leaving $n = -\frac{5}{9}$. This solution can be graphed on the number line with a dot as shown below:

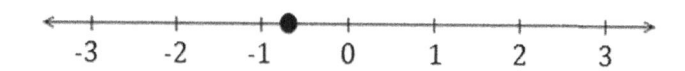

If the problem were changed to say, "The sum of a number and 5 is greater than -8 times the number," then an inequality would be used instead of an equation. Using key words again, *greater than* is represented by the symbol >. The inequality $n + 5 > -8n$ can be solved using the same techniques, resulting in $n < -\frac{5}{9}$. The only time solving an inequality differs from solving an equation is when a negative number is either multiplied times or divided by each side of the inequality. The sign must be switched in this case. For this example, the graph of the solution changes to the following graph because the solution represents all real numbers less than $-\frac{5}{9}$. Not included in this solution is $-\frac{5}{9}$ because it is a *less than* symbol, not *equal to*.

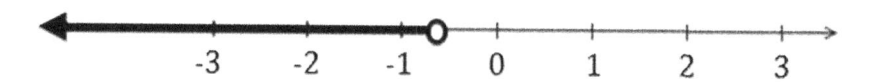

Equations and inequalities in two variables represent a relationship. Jim owns a car wash and charges $40 per car. The rent for the facility is $350 per month. An equation can be written to relate the number of cars Jim cleans to the money he makes per month. Let x represent the number of cars and y represent the profit Jim makes each month from the car wash. The equation $y = 40x - 350$ can be used to show Jim's profit or loss. Since this equation has two variables, the coordinate plane can be used to show the relationship and predict profit or loss for Jim. The following graph shows that Jim must wash at least nine cars to pay the rent, where $x = 9$. Anything nine cars and above yield a profit shown in the value on the y-axis.

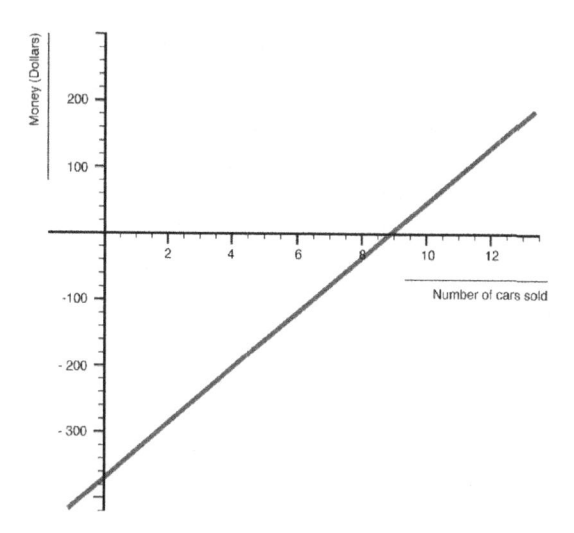

With a single equation in two variables, the solutions are limited only by the situation the equation represents. When two equations or inequalities are used, more constraints are added. For example, in a system of linear equations, there is often—although not always—only one answer. The point of intersection of two lines is the solution. For a system of inequalities, there are infinitely many answers.

Mathematics and Statistics

The intersection of two solution sets gives the solution set of the system of inequalities. In the following graph, the darker shaded region with the swirls where the shading for the two inequalities overlap. Any set of x and y found in that region satisfies both inequalities. The line with the positive slope is solid, meaning the values on that line are included in the solution. The with the negative line is dotted, so the coordinates on that line are not included.

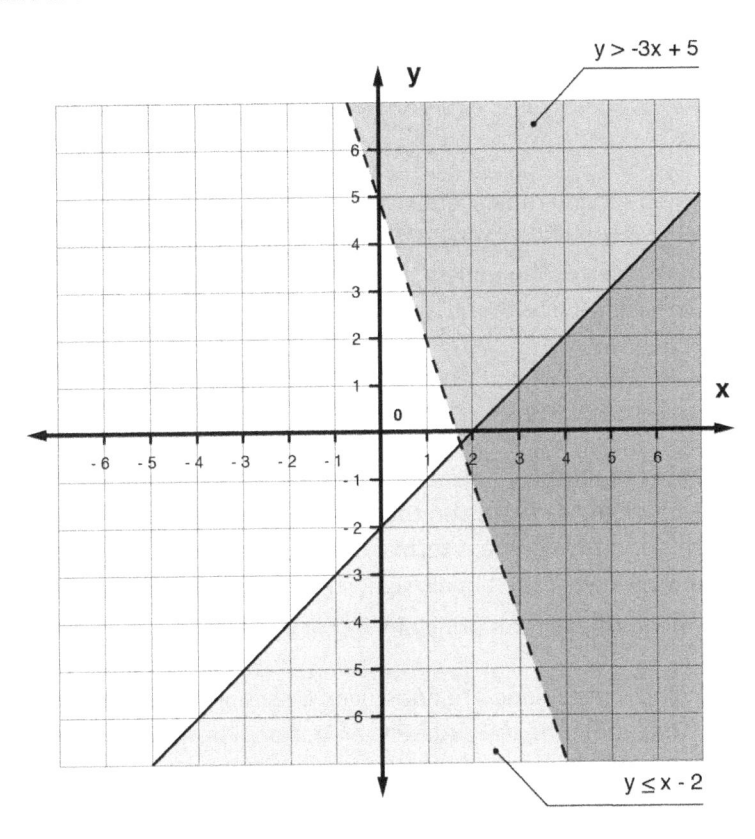

Formulas with two variables are equations used to represent a specific relationship. For example, the formula $d = rt$ represents the relationship between distance, rate, and time. If Bob travels at a rate of 35 miles per hour on his road trip from Westminster to Seneca, the formula $d = 35t$ can be used to represent his distance traveled in a specific length of time. Formulas can also be used to show different roles of the variables, transformed without any given numbers. Solving for r, the formula becomes $\frac{d}{t} = r$. The t is moved over by division so that *rate* is a function of distance and time.

Solving Equations

Solving equations in one variable is the process of isolating that variable on one side of the equation. For example, in $3x - 7 = 20$, the variable x needs to be isolated. Using opposite operations, the -7 is moved to the right side of the equation by adding seven to both sides: $3x - 7 + 7 = 20 + 7$, resulting in $3x = 27$. Dividing by three on each side, $\frac{3x}{3} = \frac{27}{3}$, results in isolation of the variable. It is important to note that if an operation is performed on one side of the equals sign, it has to be performed on the other side to maintain equality. The solution is found to be $x = 9$. This solution can be checked for accuracy by plugging $x=7$ in the original equation. After simplifying the equation, $20 = 20$ is found, which is a true statement.

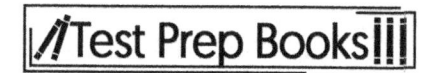

When solving radical and rational equations, extraneous solutions must be accounted for when finding the answers. For example, the equation $\frac{x}{x-5} = \frac{3x}{x+3}$ has two values that create a 0 denominator: $x \neq 5, -3$. When solving for x, these values must be considered because they cannot be solutions. In the given equation, solving for x can be done using cross-multiplication, yielding the equation $x(x + 3) = 3x(x - 5)$. Distributing results in the quadratic equation $x^2 + 3x = 3x^2 - 15x$; therefore, all terms must be moved to one side of the equals sign. This results in $2x^2 - 18x = 0$, which in factored form is $2x(x - 9) = 0$. Setting each factor equal to zero, the apparent solutions are $x = 0$ and $x = 9$. These two solutions are neither 5 nor -3, so they are viable solutions. Neither 0 nor 9 create a 0 denominator in the original equation.

A similar process exists when solving radical equations. One must check to make sure the solutions are defined in the original equations. Solving an equation containing a square root involves isolating the root and then squaring both sides of the equals sign. Solving a cube root equation involves isolating the radical and then cubing both sides. In either case, the variable can then be solved for because there are no longer radicals in the equation.

Methods for Solving Equations

Equations with one variable can be solved using the addition principle and multiplication principle. If $a = b$, then $a + c = b + c$, and $ac = bc$. Given the equation $2x - 3 = 5x + 7$, the first step is to combine the variable terms and the constant terms. Using the principles, expressions can be added and subtracted onto and off both sides of the equals sign, so the equation turns into $-10 = 3x$. Dividing by 3 on both sides through the multiplication principle with $c = \frac{1}{3}$ results in the final answer of $x = \frac{-10}{3}$.

Some equations have a higher degree and are not solved by simply using opposite operations. When an equation has a degree of 2, completing the square is an option. For example, the quadratic equation $x^2 - 6x + 2 = 0$ can be rewritten by completing the square. The goal of completing the square is to get the equation into the form $(x - p)^2 = q$. Using the example, the constant term 2 first needs to be moved over to the opposite side by subtracting. Then, the square can be completed by adding 9 to both sides, which is the square of half of the coefficient of the middle term $-6x$. The current equation is $x^2 - 6x + 9 = 7$. The left side can be factored into a square of a binomial, resulting in $(x - 3)^2 = 7$. To solve for x, the square root of both sides should be taken, resulting in $(x - 3) = \pm\sqrt{7}$, and $x = 3 \pm \sqrt{7}$.

Other ways of solving quadratic equations include graphing, factoring, and using the quadratic formula. The equation $y = x^2 - 4x + 3$ can be graphed on the coordinate plane, and the solutions can be observed where it crosses the x-axis. The graph will be a parabola that opens up with two solutions at 1 and 3.

The equation can also be factored to find the solutions. The original equation, $y = x^2 - 4x + 3$ can be factored into $y = (x - 1)(x - 3)$. Setting this equal to zero, the x-values are found to be 1 and 3, just as on the graph. Solving by factoring and graphing are not always possible. The quadratic formula is a method of solving quadratic equations that always results in exact solutions. The formula is:

$$x = \frac{-b \pm \sqrt{b^2 - 4ac}}{2a}$$

Mathematics and Statistics

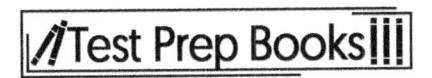

a, b, and c are the coefficients in the original equation in standard form $y = ax^2 + bx + c$. For this example:

$$x = \frac{4 \pm \sqrt{(-4)^2 - 4(1)(3)}}{2(1)} = \frac{4 \pm \sqrt{16-12}}{2} = \frac{4 \pm 2}{2} = 1, 3$$

The expression underneath the radical is called the *discriminant*. Without working out the entire formula, the value of the discriminant can reveal the nature of the solutions. If the value of the discriminant $b^2 - 4ac$ is positive, then there will be two real solutions. If the value is zero, there will be one real solution. If the value is negative, the two solutions will be imaginary or complex. If the solutions are complex, it means that the parabola never touches the x-axis. An example of a complex solution can be found by solving the following quadratic: $y = x^2 - 4x + 8$.

By using the quadratic formula, the solutions are found to be:

$$x = \frac{4 \pm \sqrt{(-4)^2 - 4(1)(8)}}{2(1)} = \frac{4 \pm \sqrt{16-32}}{2} = \frac{4 \pm \sqrt{-16}}{2} = 2 \pm 2i$$

The solutions both have a real part, 2, and an imaginary part, $2i$.

Measurement and Geometry

Points, Lines, Planes, and Angles

A point is a place, not a thing, and therefore has no dimensions or size. A set of points that lies on the same line is called collinear. A set of points that lies on the same plane is called coplanar.

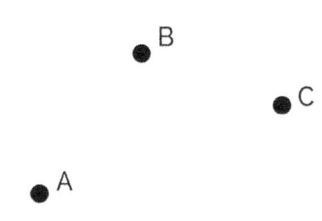

•B

•C

•A

The image above displays point A, point B, and point C.

A line is as series of points that extends in both directions without ending. It consists of an infinite number of points and is drawn with arrows on both ends to indicate it extends infinitely. Lines can be named by two points on the line or with a single, cursive, lower case letter. The lines below are named: line AB or line BA or $\overleftrightarrow{AB}$ or $\overleftrightarrow{BA}$; and line m.

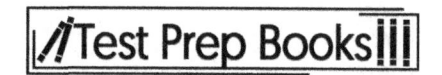

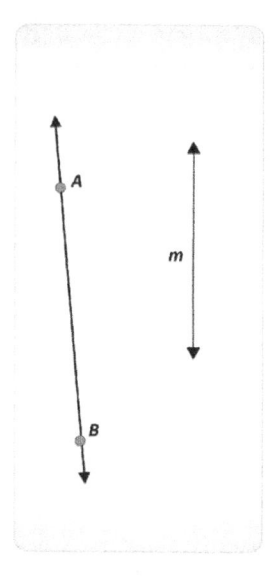

Two lines are considered parallel to each other if, while extending infinitely, they will never intersect (or meet). Parallel lines point in the same direction and are always the same distance apart. Two lines are considered perpendicular if they intersect to form right angles. Right angles are 90°. Typically, a small box is drawn at the intersection point to indicate the right angle.

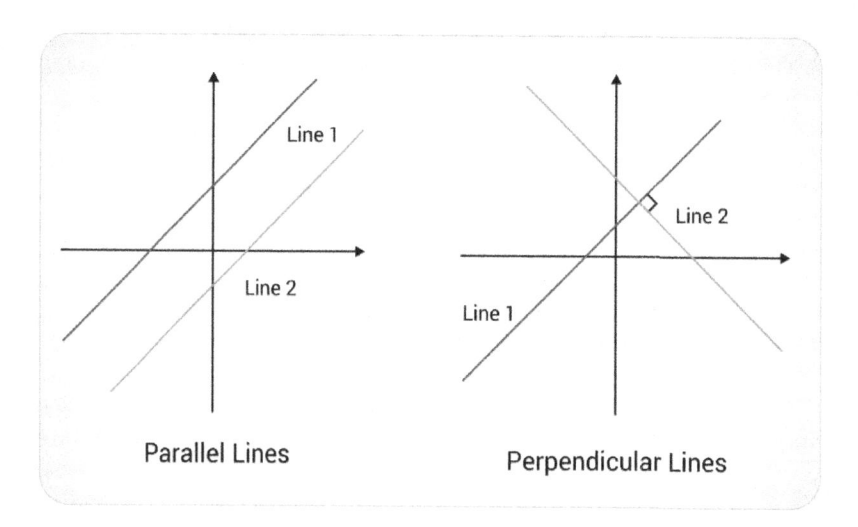

Parallel Lines

Perpendicular Lines

Line 1 is parallel to line 2 in the left image and is written as line 1 || line 2. Line 1 is perpendicular to line 2 in the right image and is written as line 1 ⊥ line 2.

Mathematics and Statistics

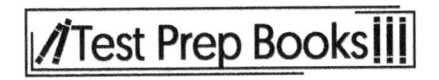

A **ray** has a specific starting point and extends in one direction without ending. The endpoint of a ray is its starting point. Rays are named using the endpoint first, and any other point on the ray. The following ray can be named ray AB and written $\overrightarrow{AB}$.

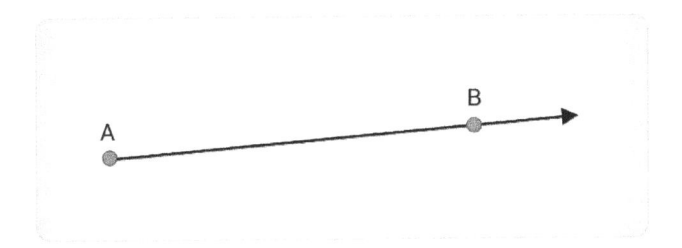

A **line segment** has specific starting and ending points. A line segment consists of two endpoints and all the points in between. Line segments are named by the two endpoints. The example below is named segment GH or segment HG, written $\overline{GH}$ or $\overline{HG}$.

Two- and Three-Dimensional Shapes

A **polygon** is a closed geometric figure in a single plane (flat surface) consisting of at least 3 sides formed by line segments. These are often defined as two-dimensional shapes. Common two-dimensional shapes include circles, triangles, squares, rectangles, pentagons, and hexagons. Note that a circle is a two-dimensional shape without sides.

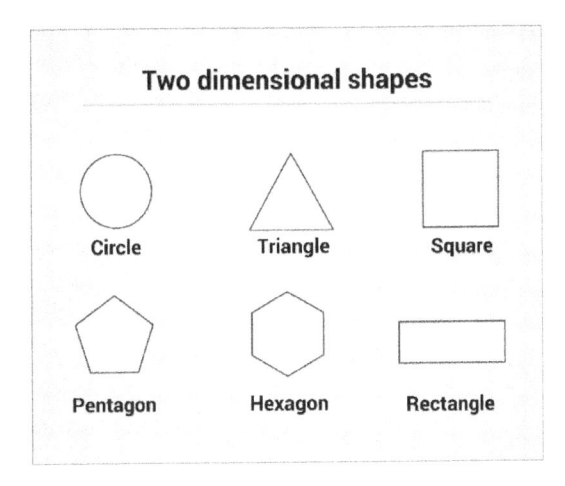

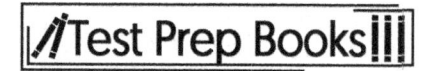

A **solid figure**, or simply solid, is a figure that encloses a part of space. Some solids consist of flat surfaces only while others include curved surfaces. Solid figures are often defined as three-dimensional shapes. Common three-dimensional shapes include spheres, prisms, cubes, pyramids, cylinders, and cones.

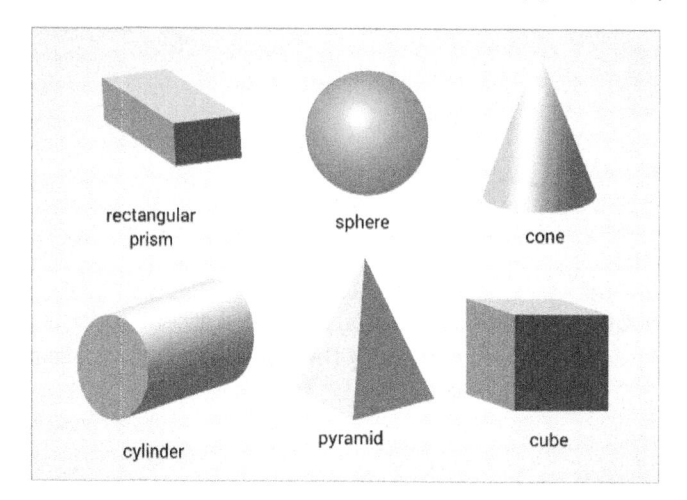

Composing two- or three-dimensional shapes involves putting together two or more shapes to create a new larger figure. For example, a semi-circle (half circle), rectangle, and two triangles can be used to compose the figure of the sailboat shown below.

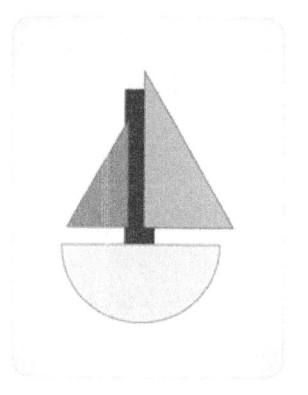

Similarly, solid figures can be placed together to compose an endless number of three-dimensional objects.

Mathematics and Statistics

Decomposing two- and three-dimensional figures involves breaking the shapes apart into smaller, simpler shapes. Consider the following two-dimensional representations of a house:

This complex figure can be decomposed into the following basic two-dimensional shapes: large rectangle (body of house); large triangle (roof); small rectangle and small triangle (chimney). Decomposing figures is often done more than one way. To illustrate, the figure of the house could also be decomposed into: two large triangles (body); two medium triangles (roof); two smaller triangles of unequal size (chimney).

Polygons and Solids

A **polygon** is a closed two-dimensional figure consisting of three or more sides. Polygons can be either convex or concave. A polygon that has interior angles all measuring less than 180° is convex. A concave polygon has one or more interior angles measuring greater than 180°. Examples are shown below.

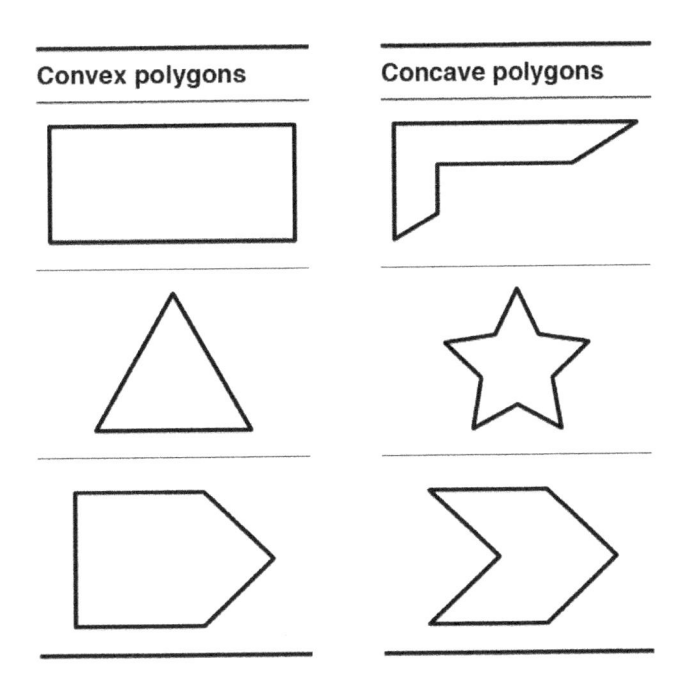

Polygons can be classified by the number of sides (also equal to the number of angles) they have. The following are the names of polygons with a given number of sides or angles:

# of Sides	Name of Polygon
3	Triangle
4	Quadrilateral
5	Pentagon
6	Hexagon
7	Septagon (or heptagon)
8	Octagon
9	Nonagon
10	Decagon

Equiangular polygons are polygons in which the measure of every interior angle is the same. The sides of equilateral polygons are always the same length. If a polygon is both equiangular and equilateral, the polygon is defined as a regular polygon. Examples are shown below.

Triangles can be further classified by their sides and angles. A triangle with its largest angle measuring 90° is a **right triangle**. A triangle with the largest angle less than 90° is an **acute triangle**. A triangle with the largest angle greater than 90° is an **obtuse triangle**.

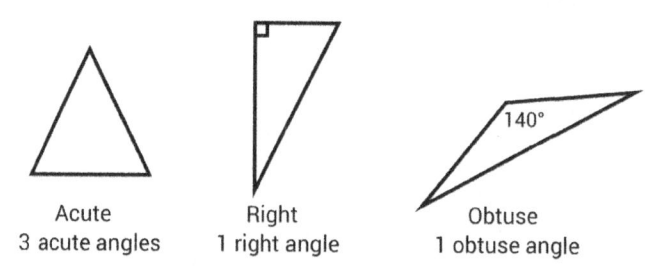

Acute
3 acute angles

Right
1 right angle

Obtuse
1 obtuse angle

A triangle consisting of two equal sides and two equal angles is an **isosceles triangle**. A triangle with three equal sides and three equal angles is an **equilateral triangle**. A triangle with no equal sides or angles is a **scalene triangle**.

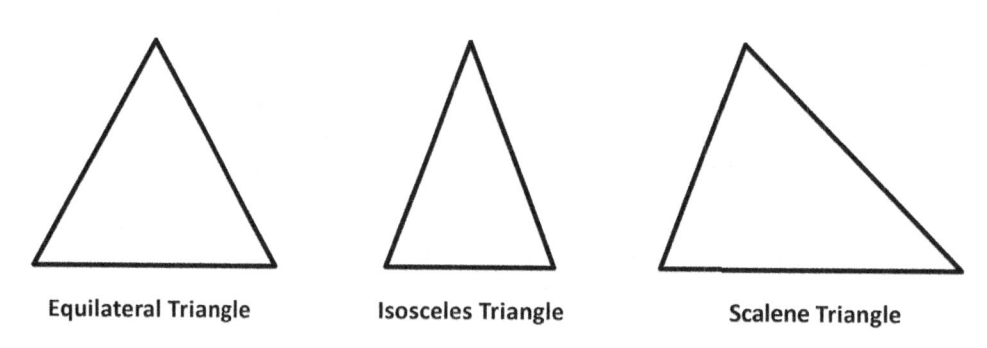

Equilateral Triangle

Isosceles Triangle

Scalene Triangle

Mathematics and Statistics

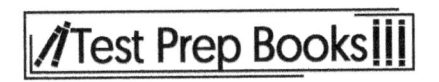

Quadrilaterals can be further classified according to their sides and angles. A quadrilateral with exactly one pair of parallel sides is called a trapezoid. The parallel sides are known as bases, and the other two sides are known as legs. If the legs are congruent, the trapezoid can be labelled an **isosceles trapezoid.** An important property of a trapezoid is that their diagonals are congruent. Also, the median of a trapezoid is parallel to the bases, and its length is equal to half of the sum of the base lengths.

A quadrilateral that shows both pairs of opposite sides parallel is a parallelogram. Parallelograms include rhombuses, rectangles, and squares. A **rhombus** has four equal sides. A **rectangle** has four equal angles (90° each). A **square** has four 90° angles and four equal sides. Therefore, a square is both a rhombus and a rectangle.

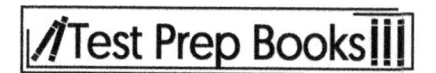

A parallelogram has six important properties:

- Opposite sides are congruent.
- Opposite angles are congruent.
- Within a parallelogram, consecutive angles are supplementary, so their measurements total 180 degrees.
- If one angle is a right angle, all of them have to be right angles.
- The diagonals of the angles bisect each other.
- These diagonals form two congruent triangles.

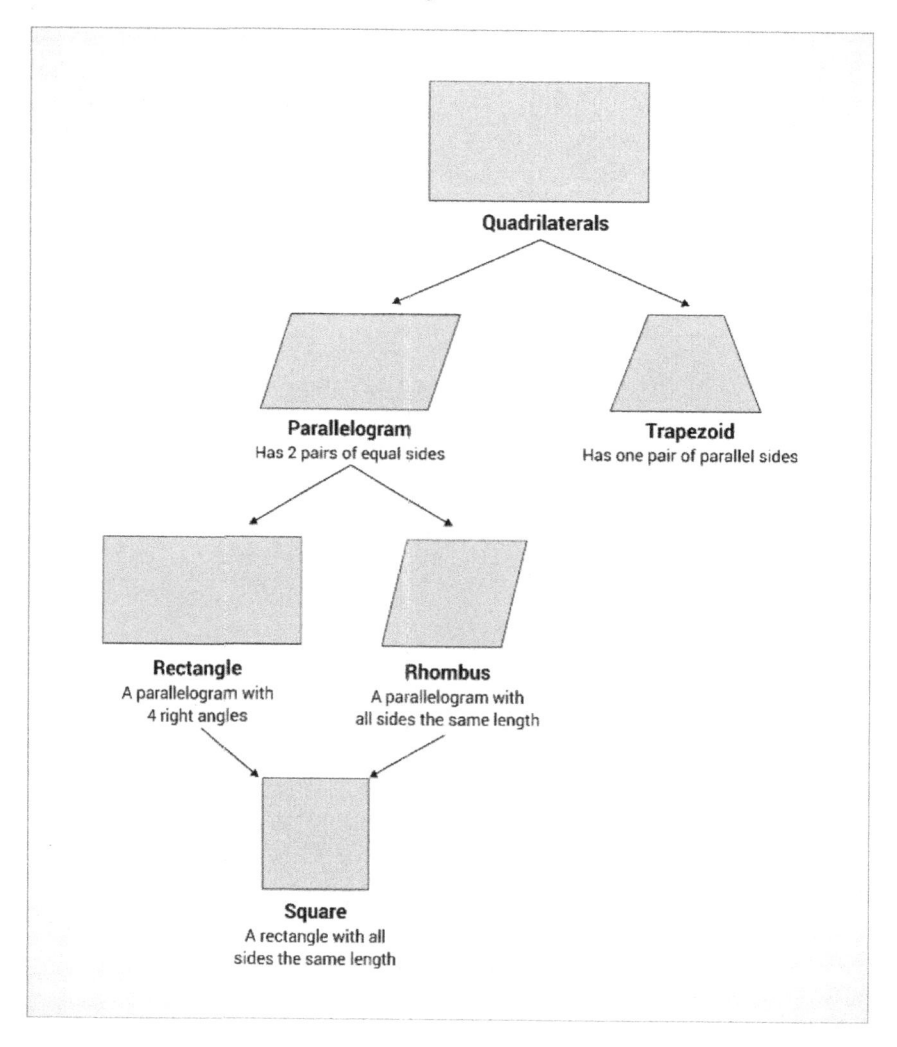

Quadrilaterals

Parallelogram
Has 2 pairs of equal sides

Trapezoid
Has one pair of parallel sides

Rectangle
A parallelogram with 4 right angles

Rhombus
A parallelogram with all sides the same length

Square
A rectangle with all sides the same length

A **solid** is a three-dimensional figure that encloses a part of space. Solids consisting of all flat surfaces that are polygons are called polyhedrons. The two-dimensional surfaces that make up a polyhedron are called faces. Types of polyhedrons include prisms and pyramids. A **prism** consists of two parallel faces that are congruent (or the same shape and same size), and lateral faces going around (which are parallelograms). A prism is further classified by the shape of its base, as shown below:

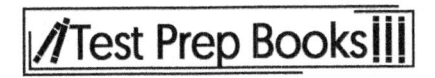

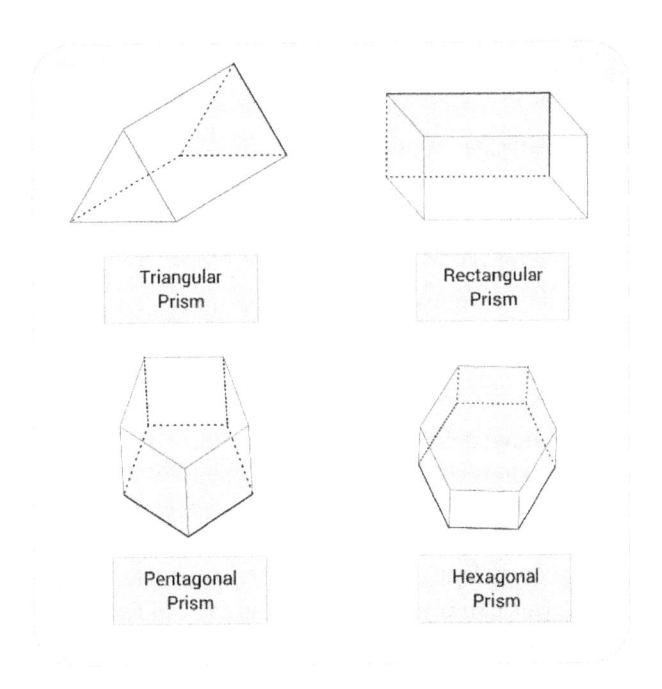

Triangular Prism

Rectangular Prism

Pentagonal Prism

Hexagonal Prism

A **pyramid** consists of lateral faces (triangles) that meet at a common point called the vertex and one other face that is a polygon, called the base. A pyramid can be further classified by the shape of its base, as shown below.

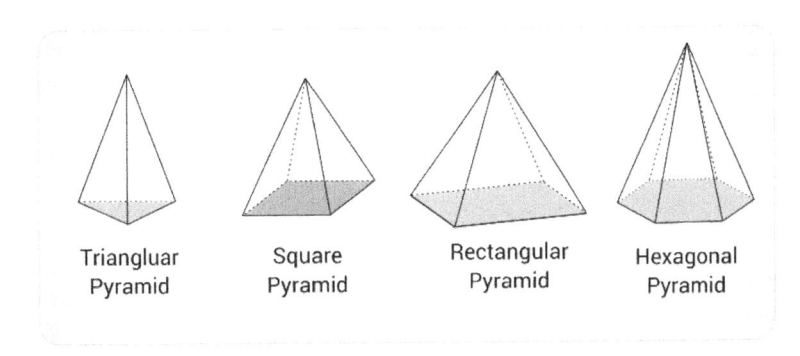

Triangluar Pyramid

Square Pyramid

Rectangular Pyramid

Hexagonal Pyramid

A **tetrahedron** is another name for a triangular pyramid. All the faces of a tetrahedron are triangles.

Solids that are not polyhedrons include spheres, cylinders, and cones. A **sphere** is the set of all points a given distance from a given center point. A sphere is commonly thought of as a three-dimensional circle. A cylinder consists of two parallel, congruent (same size) circles and a lateral curved surface. A **cone** consists of a circle as its base and a lateral curved surface that narrows to a point called the **vertex**.

Similar polygons are the same shape but different sizes. More specifically, their corresponding angle measures are congruent (or equal) and the length of their sides is proportional. For example, all sides of one polygon may be double the length of the sides of another. Likewise, similar solids are the same shape but different sizes. Any corresponding faces or bases of similar solids are the same polygons that are proportional by a consistent value.

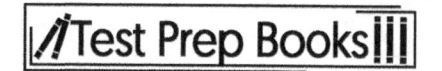

Properties of certain polygons allow that the perimeter may be obtained by using formulas. A rectangle consists of two sides called the length (l), which have equal measures, and two sides called the width (w), which have equal measures. Therefore, the perimeter (P) of a rectangle can be expressed as $P = l + l + w + w$. This can be simplified to produce the following formula to find the perimeter of a rectangle: $P = 2l + 2w$ or $P = 2(l + w)$.

A **regular polygon** is one in which all sides have equal length and all interior angles have equal measures, such as a square and an equilateral triangle. To find the perimeter of a regular polygon, the length of one side is multiplied by the number of sides. For example, to find the perimeter of an equilateral triangle with a side of length of 4 feet, 4 feet is multiplied by 3 (number of sides of a triangle). The perimeter of a regular octagon (8 sides) with a side of length of $\frac{1}{2}$ cm is $\frac{1}{2}$ cm $\times 8 = 4$ cm.

Classification of Angles

An angle consists of two rays that have a common endpoint. This common endpoint is called the **vertex of the angle**. The two rays can be called **sides of the angle**. The angle below has a vertex at point B and the sides consist of ray BA and ray BC. An angle can be named in three ways:

1. Using the vertex and a point from each side, with the vertex letter in the middle.
2. Using only the vertex. This can only be used if it is the only angle with that vertex.
3. Using a number that is written inside the angle.

The angle below can be written ∠ABC (read angle ABC), ∠CBA, ∠B, or ∠1.

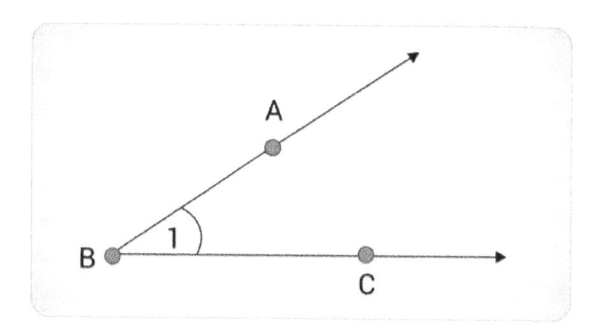

An angle divides a plane, or flat surface, into three parts: the angle itself, the interior (inside) of the angle, and the exterior (outside) of the angle. The figure below shows point M on the interior of the angle and point N on the exterior of the angle.

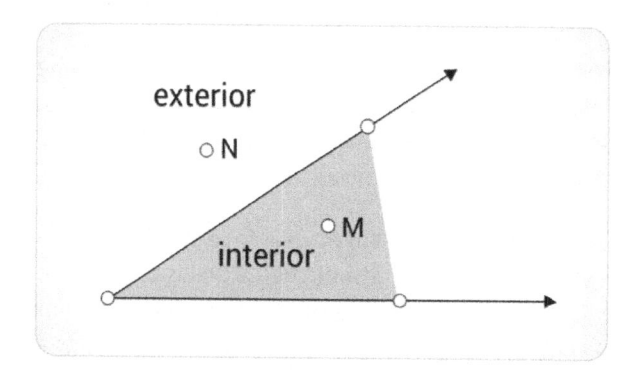

Mathematics and Statistics

Angles can be measured in units called **degrees**, with the symbol °. The degree measure of an angle is between 0° and 180° and can be obtained by using a protractor.

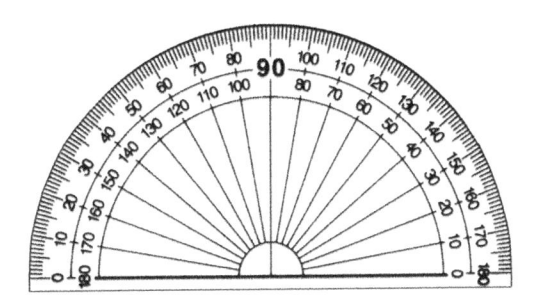

A **straight angle** (or simply a line) measures exactly 180°. A right angle's sides meet at the vertex to create a square corner. A **right-angle** measures exactly 90° and is typically indicated by a box drawn in the interior of the angle. An **acute angle** has an interior that is narrower than a right angle. The measure of an acute angle is any value less than 90° and greater than 0°. For example, 89.9°, 47°, 12°, and 1°. An **obtuse angle** has an interior that is wider than a right angle. The measure of an obtuse angle is any value greater than 90° but less than 180°. For example, 90.1°, 110°, 150°, and 179.9°.

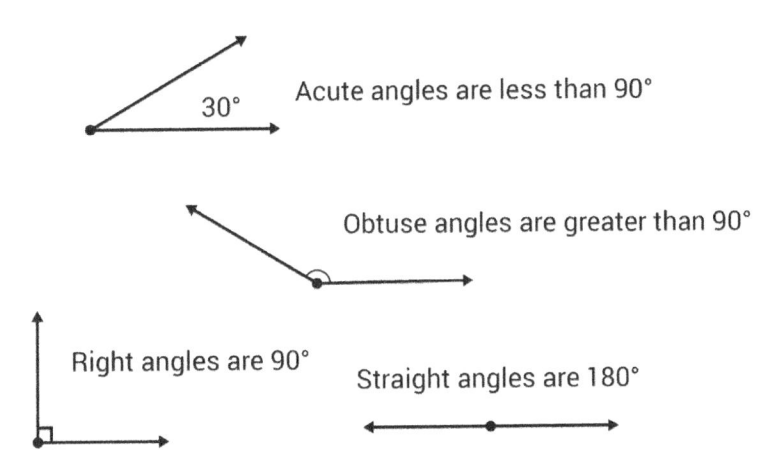

30° Acute angles are less than 90°

Obtuse angles are greater than 90°

Right angles are 90°   Straight angles are 180°

Solving Line Problems

Two lines are parallel if they have the same slope and a different intercept. Two lines are perpendicular if the product of their slope equals -1. Parallel lines never intersect unless they are the same line, and perpendicular lines intersect at a right angle. If two lines aren't parallel, they must intersect at one point. Determining equations of lines based on properties of parallel and perpendicular lines appears in word problems. To find an equation of a line, both the slope and a point the line goes through are necessary.

Therefore, if an equation of a line is needed that's parallel to a given line and runs through a specified point, the slope of the given line and the point are plugged into the point-slope form of an equation of a line. Secondly, if an equation of a line is needed that's perpendicular to a given line running through a specified point, the negative reciprocal of the slope of the given line and the point are plugged into the point-slope form. Also, if the point of intersection of two lines is known, that point will be used to solve the set of equations. Therefore, to solve a system of equations, the point of intersection must be found. If a set of two equations with two unknown variables has no solution, the lines are parallel.

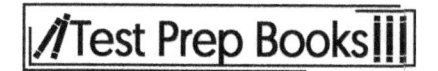

Solving Problems with Parallel and Perpendicular Lines

Two lines can be parallel, perpendicular, or neither. If two lines are parallel, they have the same slope. This is proven using the idea of similar triangles. Consider the following diagram with two parallel lines, L1 and L2:

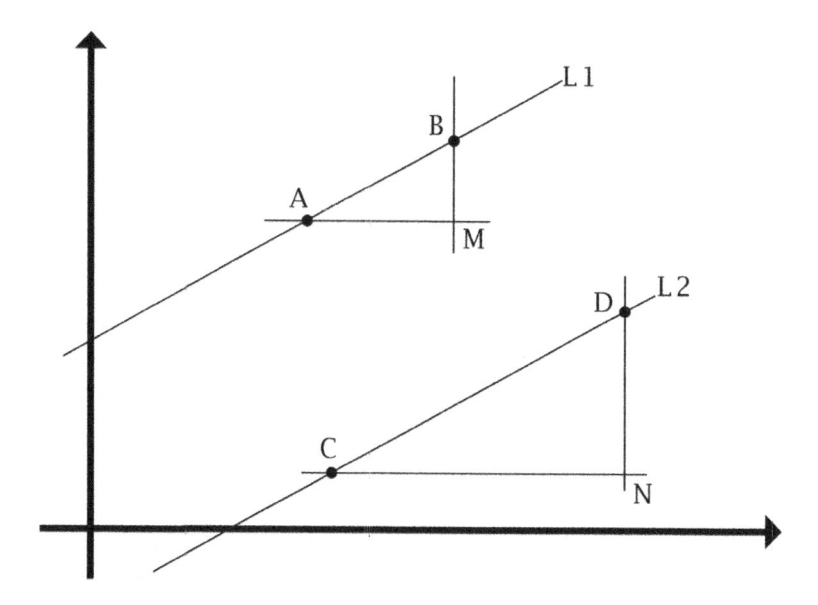

A and B are points on L1, and C and D are points on L2. Right triangles are formed with vertex M and N where lines BM and DN are parallel to the y-axis and AM and CN are parallel to the x-axis. Because all three sets of lines are parallel, the triangles are similar. Therefore, $\frac{BM}{DN} = \frac{MA}{NC}$. This shows that the rise/run is equal for lines L1 and L2. Hence, their slopes are equal.

Mathematics and Statistics

Secondly, if two lines are perpendicular, the product of their slopes equals -1. This means that their slopes are negative reciprocals of each other. Consider two perpendicular lines, l and n:

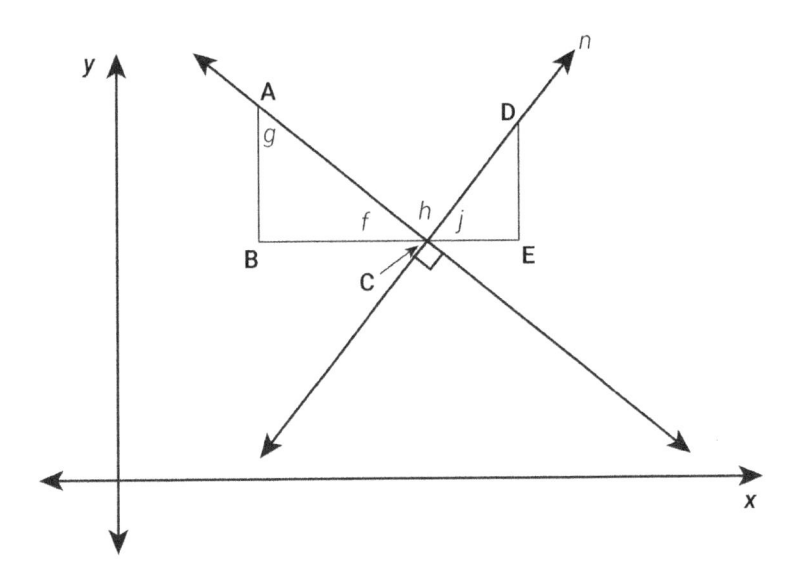

Right triangles ABC and CDE are formed so that lines BC and CE are parallel to the x-axis, and AB and DE are parallel to the y-axis. Because line BE is a straight line, angles $f + h + i = 180$ degrees. However, angle h is a right angle, so $f + j = 90$ degrees. By construction, $f + g = 90$, which means that $g = j$. Therefore, because angles $B = E$ and $g = j$, the triangles are similar and $\frac{AB}{BC} = \frac{CE}{DE}$. Because slope is equal to rise/run, the slope of line l is $-\frac{AB}{BC}$ and the slope of line n is $\frac{DE}{CE}$. Multiplying the slopes together gives:

$$-\frac{AB}{BC} \times \frac{DE}{CE} = -\frac{CE}{DE} \times \frac{DE}{CE} = -1$$

This proves that the product of the slopes of two perpendicular lines equals -1. Both parallel and perpendicular lines can be integral in many geometric proofs, so knowing and understanding their properties is crucial for problem-solving.

Effects of Changes to Dimensions on Area and Volume

Similar polygons are figures that are the same shape but different sizes. Likewise, similar solids are different sizes but are the same shape. In both cases, corresponding angles in the same positions for both figures are congruent (equal), and corresponding sides are proportional in length. For example, the triangles below are similar. The following pairs of corresponding angles are congruent: $\angle A$ and $\angle D$; $\angle B$ and $\angle E$; $\angle C$ and $\angle F$. The corresponding sides are proportional: $\frac{AB}{DE} = \frac{6}{3} = 2, \frac{BC}{EF} = \frac{9}{4.5} = 2, \frac{CA}{FD} = \frac{10}{5} = 2$.

In other words, triangle ABC is the same shape but twice as large as triangle DEF.

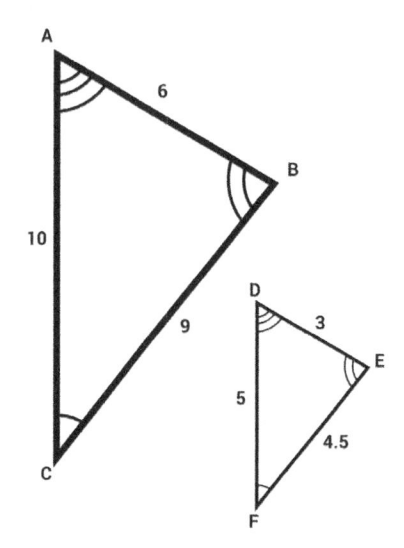

An example of similar triangular pyramids is shown below.

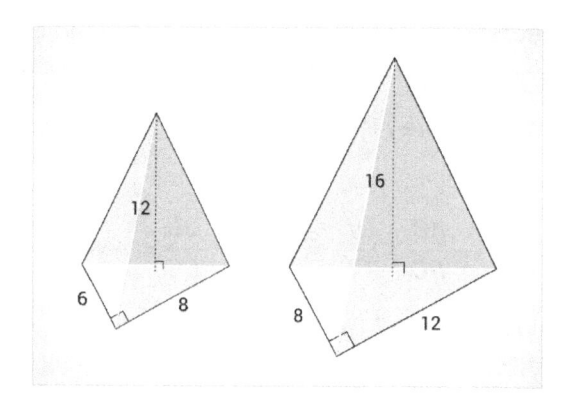

Given the nature of two- and three-dimensional measurements, changing dimensions by a given scale (multiplier) does not change the area of volume by the same scale. Consider a rectangle with a length of 5 centimeters and a width of 4 centimeters. The area of the rectangle is 20 cm². Doubling the dimensions of the rectangle (multiplying by a scale factor of 2) to 10 centimeters and 8 centimeters *does not* double the area to 40 cm². Area is a two-dimensional measurement (measured in square units). Therefore, the dimensions are multiplied by a scale that is squared (raised to the second power) to determine the scale of the corresponding areas. For the previous example, the length and width are multiplied by 2. Therefore, the area is multiplied by 2^2, or 4. The area of a 5 cm × 4 cm rectangle is 20 cm². The area of a 10 cm × 8 cm rectangle is 80 cm².

Volume is a three-dimensional measurement, which is measured in cubic units. Therefore, the scale between dimensions of similar solids is cubed (raised to the third power) to determine the scale between their volumes. Consider similar right rectangular prisms: one with a length of 8 inches, a width of 24 inches, and a height of 16 inches; the second with a length of 4 inches, a width of 12 inches, and a height of 8 inches. The first prism, multiplied by a scalar of $\frac{1}{2}$, produces the measurement of the second prism. The volume of the first prism, multiplied by $(\frac{1}{2})^3$, which equals $\frac{1}{8}$, produces the volume of the second prism. The volume of the first prism is 8 in × 24 in × 16 in which equals 3,072 in^3. The volume of the second prism is 4 in × 12 in × 8 in which equals 384 in^3 (3,072 in^3 × $\frac{1}{8}$ = 384 in^3).

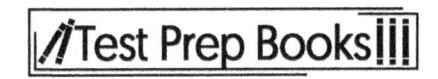

The rules for squaring the scalar for area and cubing the scalar for volume only hold true for similar figures. In other words, if only one dimension is changed (changing the width of a rectangle but not the length) or dimensions are changed at different rates (the length of a prism is doubled and its height is tripled) the figures are not similar (same shape). Therefore, the rules above do not apply.

Trigonometric Ratios in Right Triangles

Trigonometric Functions

Within similar triangles, corresponding sides are proportional, and angles are congruent. In addition, within similar triangles, the ratio of the side lengths is the same. This property is true even if side lengths are different. Within right triangles, trigonometric ratios can be defined for the acute angle within the triangle. The functions are defined through ratios in a right triangle. Sine of acute angle, A, is opposite over hypotenuse, cosine is adjacent over hypotenuse, and tangent is opposite over adjacent. Note that expanding or shrinking the triangle won't change the ratios. However, changing the angle measurements will alter the calculations.

Complementary Angles

Angles that add up to 90 degrees are **complementary**. Within a right triangle, two complementary angles exist because the third angle is always 90 degrees. In this scenario, the **sine** of one of the complementary angles is equal to the **cosine** of the other angle. The opposite is also true. This relationship exists because sine and cosine will be calculated as the ratios of the same side lengths.

The Pythagorean Theorem

The **Pythagorean theorem** is an important relationship between the three sides of a right triangle. It states that the square of the side opposite the right triangle, known as the **hypotenuse** (denoted as c^2), is equal to the sum of the squares of the other two sides ($a^2 + b^2$). Thus, $a^2 + b^2 = c^2$.

Both the trigonometric functions and the Pythagorean theorem can be used in problems that involve finding either a missing side or a missing angle of a right triangle. To do so, one must look to see what sides and angles are given and select the correct relationship that will help find the missing value. These relationships can also be used to solve application problems involving right triangles. Often, it's helpful to draw a figure to represent the problem to see what's missing.

Congruence and Similarity in Terms of Transformations

Rigid Motion

A **rigid motion** is a transformation that preserves distance and length. Every line segment in the resulting image is congruent to the corresponding line segment in the pre-image. **Congruence** between two figures means a series of transformations (or a rigid motion) can be defined that maps one of the figures onto the other. Basically, two figures are congruent if they have the same shape and size.

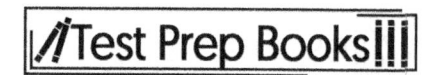

Dilation

A shape is dilated, or a **dilation** occurs, when each side of the original image is multiplied by a given scale factor. If the scale factor is less than 1 and greater than 0, the dilation contracts the shape, and the resulting shape is smaller. If the scale factor equals 1, the resulting shape is the same size, and the dilation is a rigid motion. Finally, if the scale factor is greater than 1, the resulting shape is larger and the dilation expands the shape. The **center of dilation** is the point where the distance from it to any point on the new shape equals the scale factor times the distance from the center to the corresponding point in the pre-image. Dilation isn't an isometric transformation because distance isn't preserved. However, angle measure, parallel lines, and points on a line all remain unchanged. The following figure is an example of translation, rotation, dilation, and reflection:

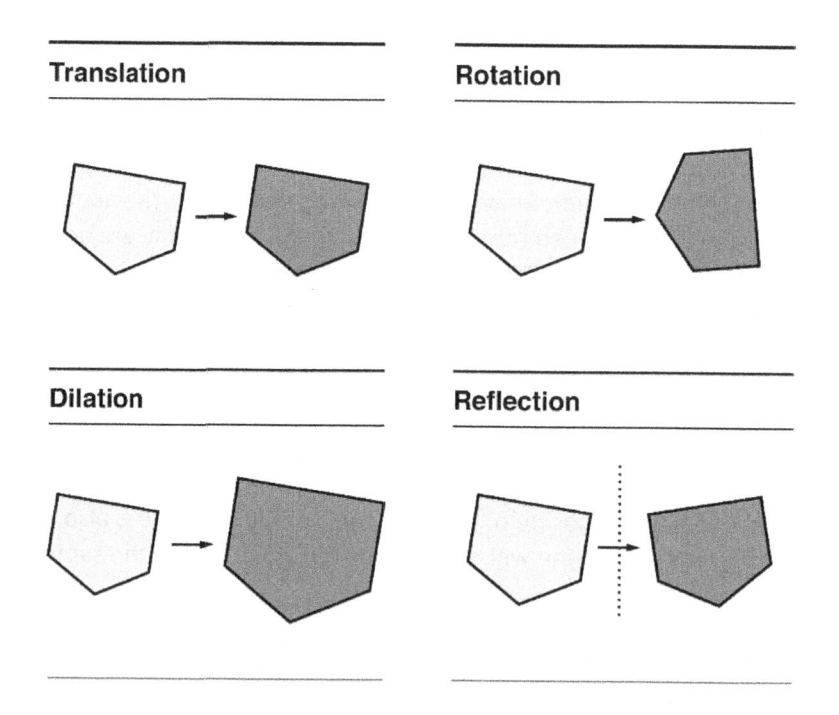

Determining Congruence

Two figures are congruent if there is a rigid motion that can map one figure onto the other. Therefore, all pairs of sides and angles within the image and pre-image must be congruent. For example, in triangles, each pair of the three sides and three angles must be congruent. Similarly, in two four-sided figures, each pair of the four sides and four angles must be congruent.

Similarity

Two figures are *similar* if there is a combination of translations, reflections, rotations, and dilations, which maps one figure onto the other. The difference between congruence and similarity is that dilation can be used in similarity. Therefore, side lengths between each shape can differ. However, angle measure must be preserved within this definition. If two polygons differ in size so that the lengths of corresponding line segments differ by the same factor, but corresponding angles have the same measurement, they are similar.

Mathematics and Statistics

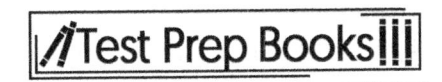

Triangle Congruence

There are five theorems to show that triangles are congruent when it's unknown whether each pair of angles and sides are congruent. Each theorem is a shortcut that involves different combinations of sides and angles that must be true for the two triangles to be congruent. For example, **side-side-side (SSS)** states that if all sides are equal, the triangles are congruent. **Side-angle-side (SAS)** states that if two pairs of sides are equal and the included angles are congruent, then the triangles are congruent. Similarly, **angle-side-angle (ASA)** states that if two pairs of angles are congruent and the included side lengths are equal, the triangles are similar.

Angle-angle-side (AAS) states that two triangles are congruent if they have two pairs of congruent angles and a pair of corresponding equal side lengths that aren't included. Finally, **hypotenuse-leg (HL)** states that if two right triangles have equal hypotenuses and an equal pair of shorter sides, then the triangles are congruent. An important item to note is that **angle-angle-angle (AAA)** is not enough information to have congruence. It's important to understand why these rules work by using rigid motions to show congruence between the triangles with the given properties. For example, three reflections are needed to show why *SAS* follows from the definition of congruence.

Similarity for Two Triangles

If two angles of one triangle are congruent with two angles of a second triangle, the triangles are similar. This is because, within any triangle, the sum of the angle measurements is 180 degrees. Therefore, if two are congruent, the third angle must also be congruent because their measurements are equal. Three congruent pairs of angles mean that the triangles are similar.

Proving Congruence and Similarity

The criteria needed to prove triangles are congruent involves both angle and side congruence. Both pairs of related angles and sides need to be of the same measurement to use congruence in a proof. The criteria to prove similarity in triangles involves proportionality of side lengths. Angles must be congruent in similar triangles; however, corresponding side lengths only need to be a constant multiple of each other. Once similarity is established, it can be used in proofs as well. Relationships in geometric figures other than triangles can be proven using triangle congruence and similarity. If a similar or congruent triangle can be found within another type of geometric figure, their criteria can be used to prove a relationship about a given formula. For instance, a rectangle can be broken up into two congruent triangles.

Relationships between Angles

Supplementary angles add up to 180 degrees. **Vertical angles** are two nonadjacent angles formed by two intersecting lines. **Corresponding angles** are two angles in the same position whenever a straight line (known as a **transversal**) crosses two others. If the two lines are parallel, the corresponding angles are equal.

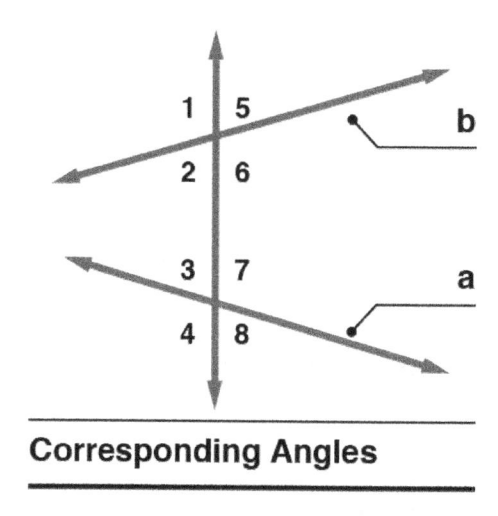

Corresponding Angles

Alternate interior angles are also a pair of angles formed when two lines are crossed by a transversal. They are opposite angles that exist inside of the two lines. In the corresponding angles diagram above, angles 2 and 7 are alternate interior angles, as well as angles 6 and 3. **Alternate exterior angles** are opposite angles formed by a transversal but, in contrast to interior angles, exterior angles exist outside the two original lines. Therefore, angles 1 and 8 are alternate exterior angles and so are angles 5 and 4. Finally, **consecutive interior angles** are pairs of angles formed by a transversal. These angles are located on the same side of the transversal and inside the two original lines. Therefore, angles 2 and 3 are a pair of consecutive interior angles, and so are angles 6 and 7. These definitions are instrumental in solving many problems that involve determining relationships between angles.

Medians, Midpoints, and Altitudes

A **median** of a triangle is the line drawn from a vertex to the midpoint on the opposite side. A triangle has three medians, and their point of intersection is known as the **centroid**. An **altitude** is a line drawn from a vertex perpendicular to the opposite side. A triangle has three altitudes, and their point of intersection is known as the **orthocenter**. An altitude can actually exist outside, inside, or on the triangle depending on the placement of the vertex. Many problems involve these definitions. For example, given one endpoint of a line segment and the midpoint, the other endpoint can be determined by using the midpoint formula. In addition, area problems heavily depend on these definitions. For example, it can be proven that the median of a triangle divides it into two regions of equal areas. The actual formula for the area of a triangle depends on its altitude.

Special Triangles

An **isosceles triangle** contains at least two equal sides. Therefore, it must also contain two equal angles and, subsequently, contain two medians of the same length. An isosceles triangle can also be labelled as an **equilateral triangle** (which contains three equal sides and three equal angles) when it meets these conditions. In an equilateral triangle, the measure of each angle is always 60 degrees. Also, within an equilateral triangle, the medians are of the same length. A **scalene triangle** can never be an equilateral or an isosceles triangle because it contains no equal sides and no equal angles. Also, medians in a scalene triangle can't have the same length. However, a **right triangle**, which is a triangle containing a 90-degree angle, can be a scalene triangle. There are two types of special right triangles. The *30-60-90 right triangle* has angle measurements of 30 degrees, 60 degrees, and 90 degrees. Because of the nature of this triangle, and through the use of the Pythagorean theorem, the side lengths have a special relationship.

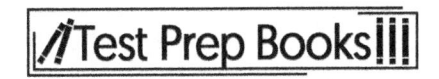

If x is the length opposite the 30-degree angle, the length opposite the 60-degree angle is $\sqrt{3}x$, and the hypotenuse has length $2x$. The 45-45-90 right triangle is also special as it contains two angle measurements of 45 degrees. It can be proven that, if x is the length of the two equal sides, the hypotenuse is $x\sqrt{2}$. The properties of all of these special triangles are extremely useful in determining both side lengths and angle measurements in problems where some of these quantities are given and some are not.

Diagonals and Angles

Diagonals are lines (excluding sides) that connect two vertices within a polygon. **Mutually bisecting diagonals** intersect at their midpoints. Parallelograms, rectangles, squares, and rhombuses have mutually bisecting diagonals. However, trapezoids don't have such lines. **Perpendicular diagonals** occur when they form four right triangles at their point of intersection. Squares and rhombuses have perpendicular diagonals, but trapezoids, rectangles, and parallelograms do not. Finally, **perpendicular bisecting diagonals** (also known as **perpendicular bisectors**) form four right triangles at their point of intersection, but this intersection is also the midpoint of the two lines. Both rhombuses and squares have perpendicular bisecting angles, but trapezoids, rectangles, and parallelograms do not. Knowing these definitions can help tremendously in problems that involve both angles and diagonals.

Polygons with More Than Four Sides

A **pentagon** is a five-sided figure. A six-sided shape is a **hexagon**. A seven-sided figure is classified as a **heptagon**, and an eight-sided figure is called an **octagon**. An important characteristic is whether a polygon is regular or irregular. If it's *regular*, the side lengths and angle measurements are all equal. An *irregular* polygon has unequal side lengths and angle measurements. Mathematical problems involving polygons with more than four sides usually involve side length and angle measurements. The sum of all internal angles in a polygon equals $180(n - 2)$ degrees, where n is the number of sides. Therefore, the total of all internal angles in a pentagon is 540 degrees because there are five sides so $180(5 - 2) = 540$ degrees. Unfortunately, area formulas don't exist for polygons with more than four sides. However, their shapes can be split up into triangles, and the formula for area of a triangle can be applied and totaled to obtain the area for the entire figure.

Perimeter and Area

Perimeter is the measurement of a distance around something. Think of perimeter as the length of the boundary, like a fence. In contrast, area is the space occupied by a defined enclosure, like a field enclosed by a fence.

Mathematics and Statistics

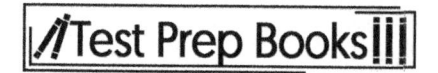

The perimeter of a polygon is the distance around the outside of the two-dimensional figure. Perimeter is a one-dimensional measurement and is therefore expressed in linear units such as centimeters (cm), feet (ft), and miles (mi). The perimeter (P) of the figure below is calculated by:

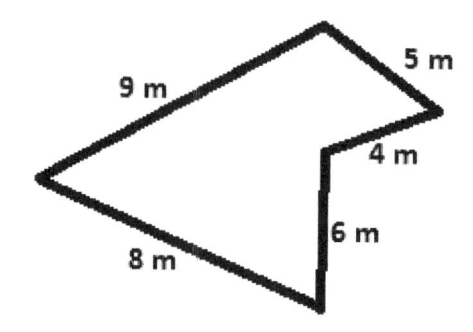

$$P = 9\text{ m} + 5\text{ m} + 4\text{ m} + 6\text{ m} + 8\text{ m} \rightarrow P = 32\text{ m}$$

The perimeter of a square is measured by adding together all of the sides. Since a square has four equal sides, its perimeter can be calculated by multiplying the length of one side by 4. Thus, the formula is $P = 4 \times s$, where s equals one side. The area of a square is calculated by squaring the length of one side, which is expressed as the formula $A = s^2$.

Like a square, a rectangle's perimeter is measured by adding together all of the sides. But as the sides are unequal, the formula is different. A rectangle has equal values for its lengths (long sides) and equal values for its widths (short sides), so the perimeter formula for a rectangle is $P = l + l + w + w = 2l + 2w$, where l equals length and w equals width. The area is found by multiplying the length by the width, so the formula is $A = l \times w$.

A triangle's perimeter is measured by adding together the three sides, so the formula is $P = a + b + c$, where a, b, and c are the values of the three sides. The area is calculated by multiplying the length of the base times the height times $\frac{1}{2}$, so the formula is $A = \frac{1}{2} \times b \times h = \frac{bh}{2}$. The base is the bottom of the triangle, and the height is the distance from the base to the peak. If a problem asks to calculate the area of a triangle, it will provide the base and height.

A circle's perimeter—also known as its circumference—is measured by multiplying the diameter (the straight line measured from one end to the direct opposite end of the circle) by π, so the formula is $\pi \times d$. This is sometimes expressed by the formula $C = 2 \times \pi \times r$, where r is the radius of the circle. These formulas are equivalent, as the radius equals half of the diameter. The area of a circle is calculated through the formula $A = \pi \times r^2$. The test will indicate either to leave the answer with π attached or to calculate to the nearest decimal place, which means multiplying by 3.14 for π.

The perimeter of a parallelogram is measured by adding the lengths and widths together. Thus, the formula is the same as for a rectangle, $P = l + l + w + w = 2l + 2w$. However, the area formula differs

Mathematics and Statistics

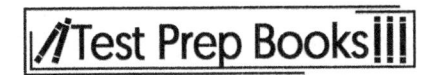

from the rectangle. For a parallelogram, the area is calculated by multiplying the length by the height: $A = h \times l$

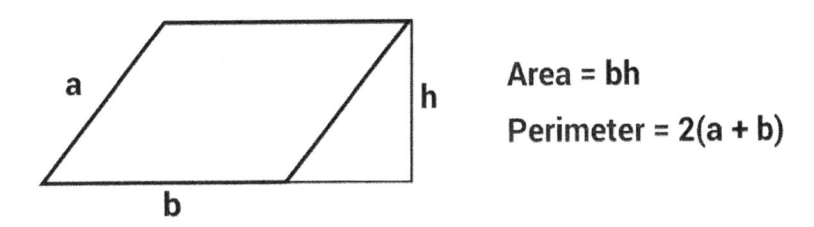

Area = bh
Perimeter = 2(a + b)

The perimeter of a trapezoid is calculated by adding the two unequal bases and two equal sides, so the formula is $P = a + b_1 + c + b_2$. Although unlikely to be a test question, the formula for the area of a trapezoid is $A = \frac{b_1 + b_2}{2} \times h$, where h equals height, and b_1 and b_2 equal the bases.

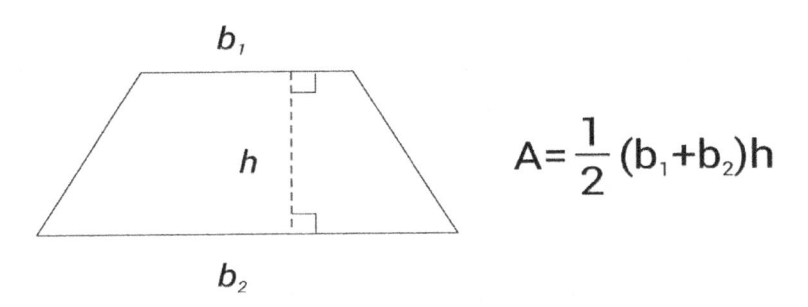

$$A = \frac{1}{2}(b_1 + b_2)h$$

Irregular Shapes

The perimeter of an irregular polygon is found by adding the lengths of all of the sides. In cases where all of the sides are given, this will be very straightforward, as it will simply involve finding the sum of the provided lengths. Other times, a side length may be missing and must be determined before the perimeter can be calculated. Consider the example below:

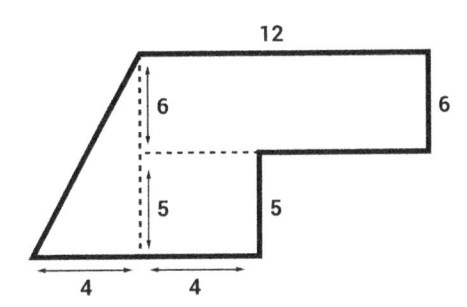

All of the side lengths are provided except for the angled side on the left. Test takers should notice that this is the hypotenuse of a right triangle. The other two sides of the triangle are provided (the base is 4 and the height is $6 + 5 = 11$). The Pythagorean Theorem can be used to find the length of the hypotenuse, remembering that $a^2 + b^2 = c^2$.

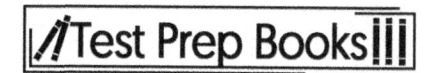

Substituting the side values provided yields $(4)^2 + (11)^2 = c^2$.

Therefore, $c = \sqrt{16 + 121} = 11.7$

Finally, the perimeter can be found by adding this new side length with the other provided lengths to get the total length around the figure: $4 + 4 + 5 + 8 + 6 + 12 + 11.7 = 50.7$. Although units are not provided in this figure, remember that reporting units with a measurement is important.

The area of an irregular polygon is found by decomposing, or breaking apart, the figure into smaller shapes. When the area of the smaller shapes is determined, these areas are added together to produce the total area of the area of the original figure. Consider the same example provided before:

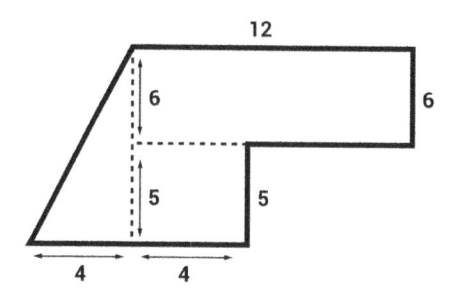

The irregular polygon is decomposed into two rectangles and a triangle. The area of the large rectangle ($A = l \times w \to A = 12 \times 6$) is 72 square units. The area of the small rectangle is 20 square units ($A = 4 \times 5$). The area of the triangle ($A = \frac{1}{2} \times b \times h \to A = \frac{1}{2} \times 4 \times 11$) is 22 square units. The sum of the areas of these figures produces the total area of the original polygon: $A = 72 + 20 + 22 \to A = 114$ square units.

Surface Area of Three-Dimensional Figures

The area of a **two-dimensional figure** refers to the number of square units needed to cover the interior region of the figure. This concept is similar to wallpaper covering the flat surface of a wall. For example, if a rectangle has an area of 21 square centimeters (written $21cm^2$), it will take 21 squares, each with sides one centimeter in length, to cover the interior region of the rectangle. Note that area is measured in square units such as: square feet or ft^2; square yards or yd^2; square miles or mi^2.

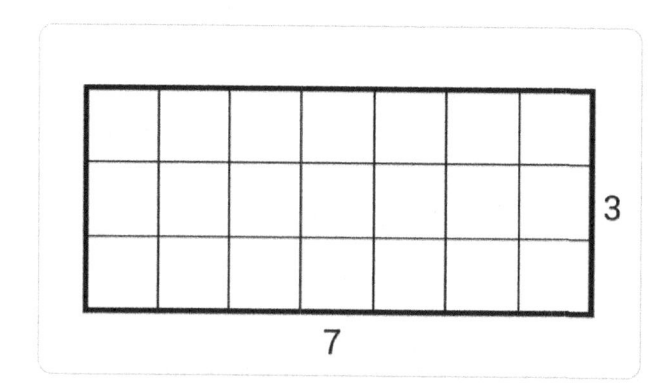

The surface area of a **three-dimensional figure** refers to the number of square units needed to cover the entire surface of the figure. This concept is similar to using wrapping paper to completely cover the

Mathematics and Statistics

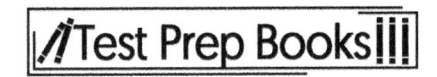

outside of a box. For example, if a triangular pyramid has a surface area of 17 square inches (written 17 in²), it will take 17 squares, each with sides one inch in length, to cover the entire surface of the pyramid. Surface area is also measured in square units.

Many three-dimensional figures (solid figures) can be represented by nets consisting of rectangles and triangles. The surface area of such solids can be determined by adding the areas of each of its faces and bases. Finding the surface area using this method requires calculating the areas of rectangles and triangles. To find the area (A) of a rectangle, the length (l) is multiplied by the width (w) → $A = l \times w$. The area of a rectangle with a length of 8 cm and a width of 4 cm is calculated:

$$A = (8 \text{ cm}) \times (4 \text{ cm}) \rightarrow A = 32 \text{ cm}^2$$

To calculate the area (A) of a triangle, the product of $\frac{1}{2}$, the base (b), and the height (h) is found → $A = \frac{1}{2} \times b \times h$. Note that the height of a triangle is measured from the base to the vertex opposite of it forming a right angle with the base. The area of a triangle with a base of 11 cm and a height of 6 cm is calculated: $A = \frac{1}{2} \times (11 \text{ cm}) \times (6 \text{ cm}) \rightarrow A = 33 \text{ cm}^2$.

Consider the following triangular prism, which is represented by a net consisting of two triangles and three rectangles.

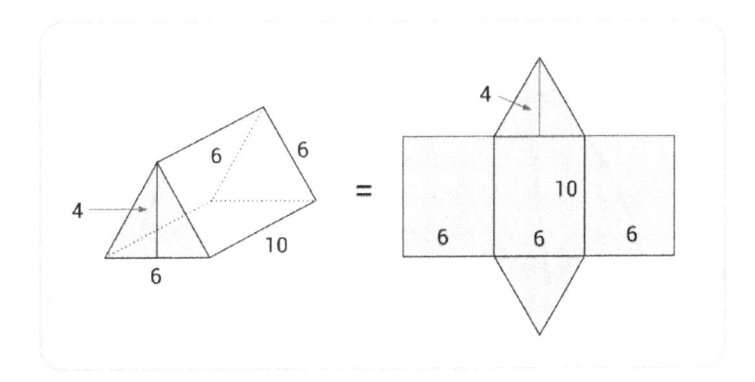

The surface area of the prism can be determined by adding the areas of each of its faces and bases. The surface area:

$$SA = \text{area of triangle} + \text{area of triangle} + \text{area of rectangle}$$
$$+ \text{area of rectangle} + \text{area of rectangle}$$

$$SA = \left(\frac{1}{2} \times b \times h\right) + \left(\frac{1}{2} \times b \times h\right) + (l \times w) + (l \times w) + (l \times w)$$

$$SA = \left(\frac{1}{2} \times 6 \times 4\right) + \left(\frac{1}{2} \times 6 \times 4\right) + (6 \times 10) + (6 \times 10) + (6 \times 10)$$

$$SA = (12) + (12) + (60) + (60) + (60)$$

$$SA = 204 \text{ square units}$$

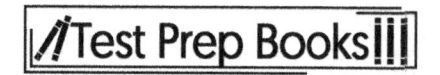

Circles

Circle Angles

The **radius** of a circle is the distance from the center of the circle to any point on the circle. A *chord* of a circle is a straight line formed when its endpoints are allowed to be any two points on the circle. Many angles exist within a circle. A **central angle** is formed by using two radii as its rays and the center of the circle as its vertex. An **inscribed angle** is formed by using two chords as its rays and its vertex is a point on the circle itself.

Finally, a **circumscribed angle** has a vertex that is a point outside the circle and rays that intersect with the circle. Some relationships exist between these types of angles, and, in order to define these relationships, arc measure must be understood. An **arc** of a circle is a portion of the circumference. Finding the **arc measure** is the same as finding the degree measure of the central angle that intersects the circle to form the arc. The measure of an inscribed angle is half the measure of its intercepted arc. It's also true that the measure of a circumscribed angle is equal to 180 degrees minus the measure of the central angle that forms the arc in the angle.

Quadrilateral Angles

If a quadrilateral is inscribed in a circle, the sum of its opposite angles is 180 degrees. Consider the quadrilateral $ABCD$ centered at the point O:

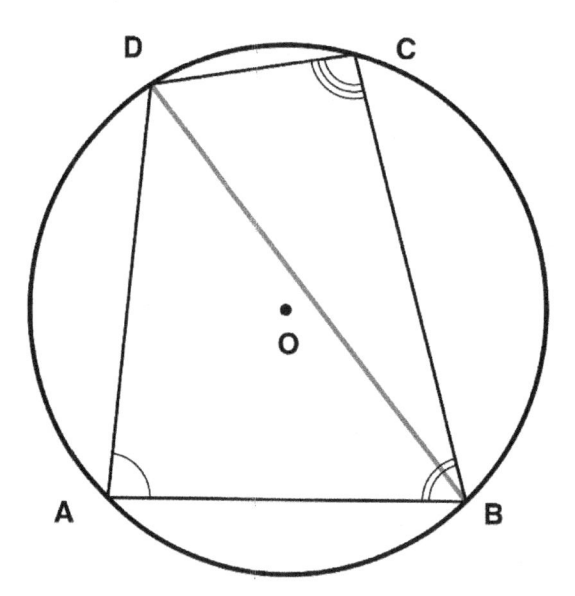

Each of the four line segments within the quadrilateral is a chord of the circle. Consider the diagonal DB. Angle DAB is an inscribed angle leaning on the arc DCB. Therefore, angle DAB is half the measure of the arc DCB. Conversely, angle DCB is an inscribed angle leaning on the arc DAB. Therefore, angle DCB is half the measure of the arc DAB. The sum of arcs DCB and DAB is 360 degrees because they make up the entire circle. Therefore, the sum of angles DAB and DCB equals half of 360 degrees, which is 180 degrees.

Circle Lines

A **tangent line** is a line that touches a curve at a single point without going through it. A **compass** and a **straightedge** are the tools necessary to construct a tangent line from a point P outside the circle to the

Mathematics and Statistics

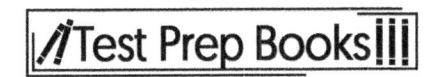

circle. A tangent line is constructed by drawing a line segment from the center of the circle O to the point P, and then finding its midpoint M by bisecting the line segment. By using M as the center, a compass is used to draw a circle through points O and P. N is defined as the intersection of the two circles. Finally, a line segment is drawn through P and N. This is the tangent line. Each point on a circle has only one tangent line, which is perpendicular to the radius at that point. A line similar to a tangent line is a **secant line**. Instead of intersecting the circle at one point, a secant line intersects the circle at two points. A **chord** is a smaller portion of a secant line.

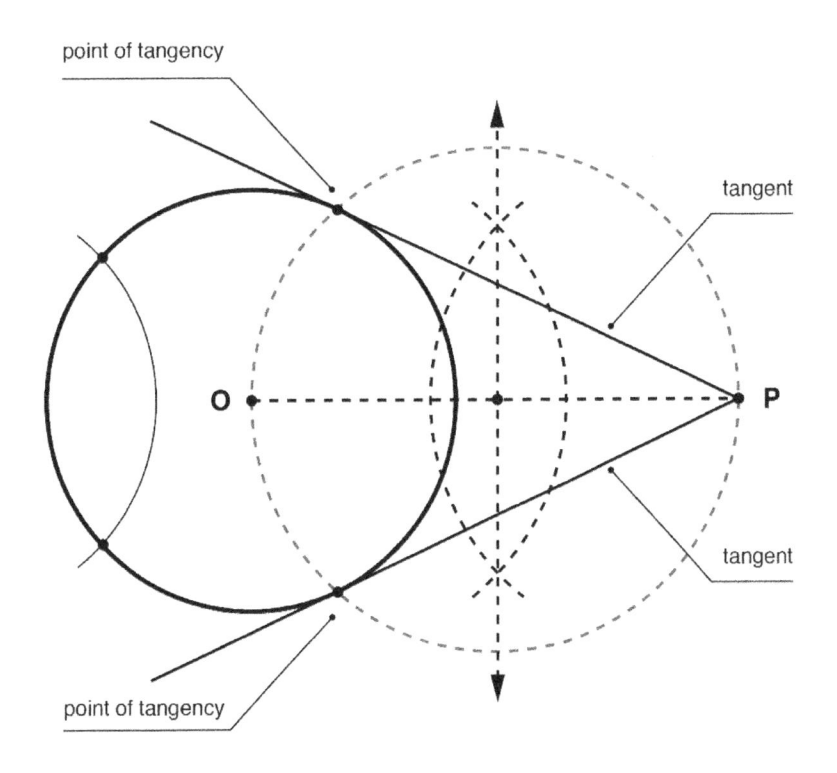

Applying Geometric Concepts to Real-World Situations

Real-World Geometry

Many real-world objects can be compared to geometric shapes. Describing certain objects using the measurements and properties of two- and three-dimensional shapes is an important part of geometry. For example, basic ideas such as angles and line segments can be seen in real-world objects. The corner of any room is an angle, and the intersection of a wall with the floor is like a line segment. Building upon this idea, entire objects can be related to both two- and three-dimensional shapes. An entire room can be thought of as square, rectangle, or a sum of a few three-dimensional shapes. Knowing what properties and measures are needed to make decisions in real life is why geometry is such a useful branch of mathematics. One obvious relationship between a real-life situation and geometry exists in construction. For example, to build an addition onto a house, several geometric measurements will be used.

Density

The **density** of a substance is the ratio of mass to area or volume. It's a relationship between the mass and how much space the object actually takes up. Knowing which units to use in each situation is crucial. Population density is an example of a real-life situation that's modeled by using density concepts. It involves calculating the ratio of the number of people to the number of square miles. The amount of material needed per a specific unit of area or volume is another application. For example, estimating the number of BTUs per cubic foot of a home is a measurement that relates to heating or cooling the house based on the desired temperature and the house's size.

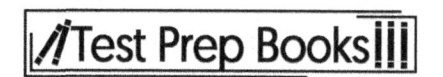

Solving Design Problem

Design problems are an important application of geometry (e.g., building structures that satisfy physical constraints and/or minimize costs). These problems involve optimizing a situation based on what's given and required. For example, determining what size barn to build, given certain dimensions and a specific budget, uses both geometric properties and other mathematical concepts. Equations are formed using geometric definitions and the given constraints. In the end, such problems involve solving a system of equations and rely heavily on a strong background in algebra. *Typographic grid systems* also help with such design problems. A grid made up of intersecting straight or curved lines can be used as a visual representation of the structure being designed. This concept is seen in the blueprints used throughout the graphic design process.

Converting Within and Between Standard and Metric Systems

American Measuring System

The measuring system used today in the United States developed from the British units of measurement during colonial times. The most typically used units in this customary system are those used to measure weight, liquid volume, and length, whose common units are found below. In the customary system, the basic unit for measuring weight is the ounce (oz); there are 16 ounces (oz) in 1 pound (lb) and 2000 pounds in 1 ton. The basic unit for measuring liquid volume is the ounce (oz); 1 ounce is equal to 2 tablespoons (tbsp) or 6 teaspoons (tsp), and there are 8 ounces in 1 cup, 2 cups in 1 pint (pt), 2 pints in 1 quart (qt), and 4 quarts in 1 gallon (gal). For measurements of length, the inch (in) is the base unit; 12 inches make up 1 foot (ft), 3 feet make up 1 yard (yd), and 5280 feet make up 1 mile (mi). However, as there are only a set number of units in the customary system, with extremely large or extremely small amounts of material, the numbers can become awkward and difficult to compare.

Common Customary Measurements		
Length	**Weight**	**Capacity**
1 foot = 12 inches	1 pound = 16 ounces	1 cup = 8 fluid ounces
1 yard = 3 feet	1 ton = 2,000 pounds	1 pint = 2 cups
1 yard = 36 inches		1 quart = 2 pints
1 mile = 1,760 yards		1 quart = 4 cups
1 mile = 5,280 feet		1 gallon = 4 quarts
		1 gallon = 16 cups

Metric System

Aside from the United States, most countries in the world have adopted the metric system embodied in the International System of Units (SI). The three main SI base units used in the metric system are the meter (m), the kilogram (kg), and the liter (L); meters measure length, kilograms measure mass, and liters measure volume.

Mathematics and Statistics

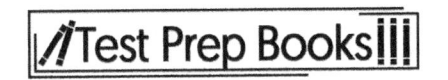

These three units can use different prefixes, which indicate larger or smaller versions of the unit by powers of ten. This can be thought of as making a new unit, which is sized by multiplying the original unit in size by a factor.

These prefixes and associated factors are:

Metric Prefixes			
Prefix	Symbol	Multiplier	Exponential
kilo	k	1,000	10^3
hecto	h	100	10^2
deca	da	10	10^1
no prefix		1	10^0
deci	d	0.1	10^{-1}
centi	c	0.01	10^{-2}
milli	m	0.001	10^{-3}

The correct prefix is then attached to the base. Some examples:

1 milliliter equals .001 liters.

1 kilogram equals 1,000 grams.

Choosing the Appropriate Measuring Unit

Some units of measure are represented as square or cubic units depending on the solution. For example, perimeter is measured in linear units, area is measured in square units, and volume is measured in cubic units.

Also be sure to use the most appropriate unit for the thing being measured. A building's height might be measured in feet or meters while the length of a nail might be measured in inches or centimeters. Additionally, for SI units, the prefix should be chosen to provide the most succinct available value. For example, the mass of a bag of fruit would likely be measured in kilograms rather than grams or milligrams, and the length of a bacteria cell would likely be measured in micrometers rather than centimeters or kilometers.

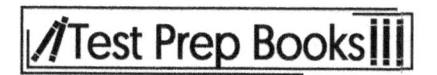

Conversion

Converting measurements in different units between the two systems can be difficult because they follow different rules. The best method is to look up an English to Metric system conversion factor and then use a series of equivalent fractions to set up an equation to convert the units of one of the measurements into those of the other. The table below lists some common conversion values that are useful for problems involving measurements with units in both systems:

English System	Metric System
1 inch	2.54 cm
1 foot	0.3048 m
1 yard	0.914 m
1 mile	1.609 km
1 ounce	28.35 g
1 pound	0.454 kg
1 fluid ounce	29.574 mL
1 quart	0.946 L
1 gallon	3.785 L

Consider the example where a scientist wants to convert 6.8 inches to centimeters. The table above is used to find that there are 2.54 centimeters in every inch, so the following equation should be set up and solved: $6.8 \text{ in} \times \frac{2.54 \text{ cm}}{1 \text{ in}} = 17.272 \text{ cm}$. Notice how the inches in the numerator of the initial figure and the denominator of the conversion factor cancel out. (This equation could have been written simply as $6.8 \text{ in} \times 2.54 \text{ cm} = 17.272 \text{ cm}$, but it was shown in detail to illustrate the steps). The goal in any conversion equation is to set up the fractions so that the units you are trying to convert from cancel out and the units you desire remain.

For a more complicated example, consider converting 2.15 kilograms into ounces. The first step is to convert kilograms into grams and then grams into ounces:

$$2.15 \text{ kg} \times \frac{1{,}000 \text{ g}}{\text{kg}} = 2{,}150 \text{ g}$$

Then, use the conversion factor from the table to convert grams to ounces:

$$2{,}150 \text{ g} \times \frac{1 \text{ oz}}{28.35 \text{ g}} = 75.8 \text{ oz}$$

Statistics and Data Analysis

Interpreting Displays of Data

A set of data can be visually displayed in various forms allowing for quick identification of characteristics of the set. Histograms, such as the one shown below, display the number of data points (vertical axis) that fall into given intervals (horizontal axis) across the range of the set. Suppose the histogram below displays IQ scores of students. Each rectangle represents the number of students with scores between a given ten-point span. For example, the furthest bar to the right indicates that five students scored between 130 and 140.

Mathematics and Statistics

Histograms can describe the center, spread, shape, and any unusual characteristics of a data set.

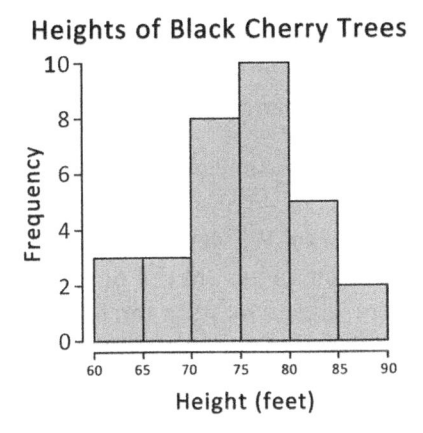

Heights of Black Cherry Trees

A **box plot**, also called a box-and-whisker plot, divides the data points into four groups and displays the five-number summary for the set as well as any outliers. The five-number summary consists of:

- The lower extreme: the lowest value that is not an outlier
- The higher extreme: the highest value that is not an outlier
- The median of the set: also referred to as the second quartile or Q_2
- The first quartile or Q_1: the median of values below Q_2
- The third quartile or Q_3: the median of values above Q_2

To construct a box (or box-and-whisker) plot, the five-number summary for the data set is calculated as follows: the second quartile (Q_2) is the median of the set. The first quartile (Q_1) is the median of the values below Q_2. The third quartile (Q_3) is the median of the values above Q_2. The upper extreme is the highest value in the data set if it is not an outlier (greater than 1.5 times the interquartile range $Q_3 - Q_1$). The lower extreme is the least value in the data set if it is not an outlier (more than 1.5 times lower than the interquartile range). To construct the box-and-whisker plot, each value is plotted on a number line, along with any outliers. The box consists of Q_1 and Q_3 as its top and bottom and Q_2 as the dividing line inside the box. The whiskers extend from the lower extreme to Q_1 and from Q_3 to the upper extreme.

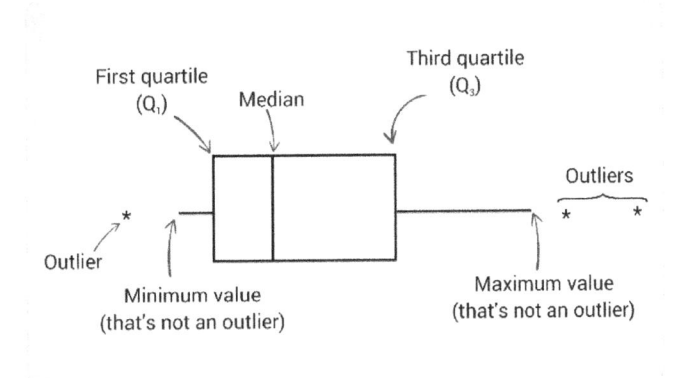

Suppose the box plot displays IQ scores for 12th grade students at a given school. The five-number summary of the data consists of: lower extreme (67); upper extreme (127); Q_2 or median (100); Q_1 (91);

Q_3 (108); and outliers (135 and 140). Although all data points are not known from the plot, the points are divided into four quartiles each, including 25% of the data points. Therefore, 25% of students scored between 67 and 91, 25% scored between 91 and 100, 25% scored between 100 and 108, and 25% scored between 108 and 127. These percentages include the normal values for the set and exclude the outliers. This information is useful when comparing a given score with the rest of the scores in the set.

A **scatter plot** is a mathematical diagram that visually displays the relationship or connection between two variables. The independent variable is placed on the *x*-axis, or horizontal axis, and the dependent variable is placed on the *y*-axis, or vertical axis. When visually examining the points on the graph, if the points model a linear relationship, or if a line of best-fit can be drawn through the points with the points relatively close on either side, then a correlation exists. If the line of best-fit has a positive slope (rises from left to right), then the variables have a positive correlation. If the line of best-fit has a negative slope (falls from left to right), then the variables have a negative correlation. If a line of best-fit cannot be drawn, then no correlation exists. A positive or negative correlation can be categorized as strong or weak, depending on how closely the points are graphed around the line of best-fit.

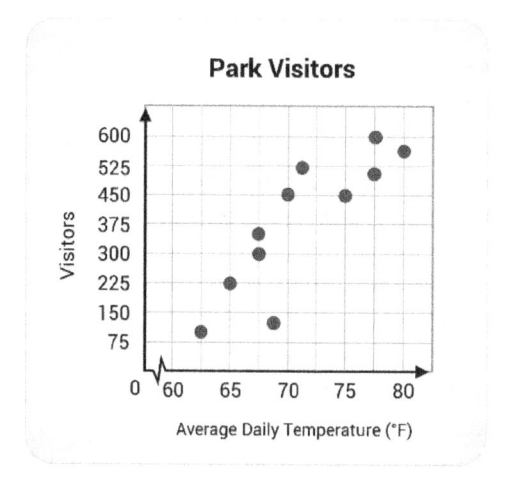

Park Visitors

Graphical Representation of Data

Like a scatter plot, a **line graph** compares variables that change continuously, typically over time. Paired data values (ordered pairs) are plotted on a coordinate grid with the x- and y-axis representing the

Mathematics and Statistics

variables. A line is drawn from each point to the next, going from left to right. The line graph below displays cell phone use for given years (two variables) for men, women, and both sexes (three data sets).

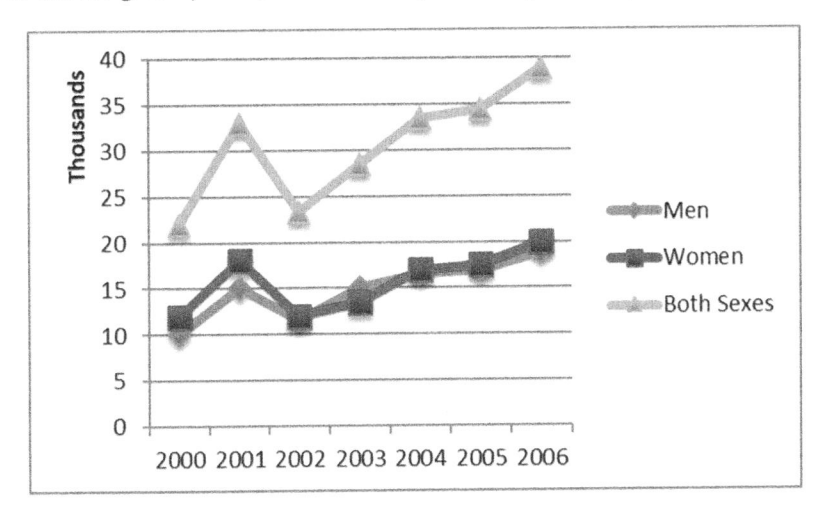

A **line plot**, also called dot plot, displays the frequency of data (numerical values) on a number line. To construct a line plot, a number line is used that includes all unique data values. It is marked with x's or dots above the value the number of times that the value occurs in the data set.

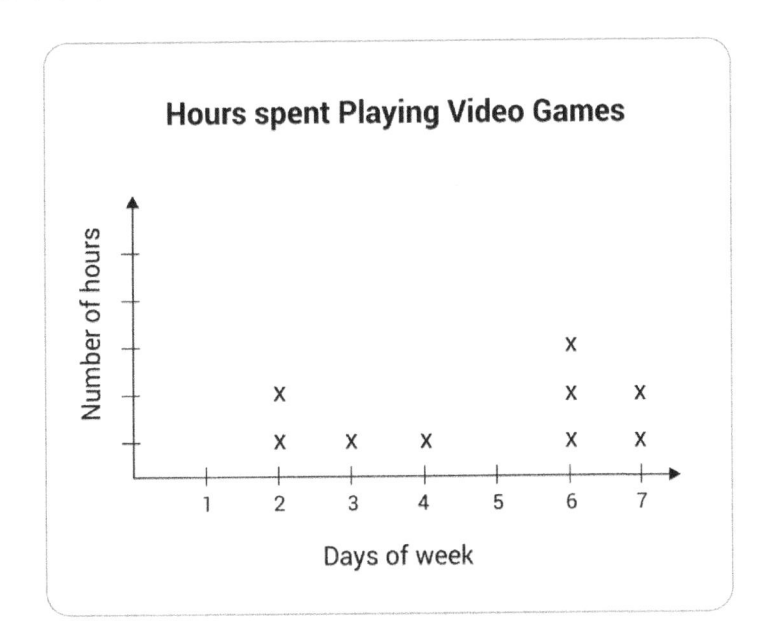

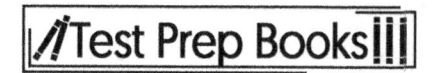

A **bar graph** is a diagram in which the quantity of items within a specific classification is represented by the height of a rectangle. Each type of classification is represented by a rectangle of equal width. Here is an example of a bar graph:

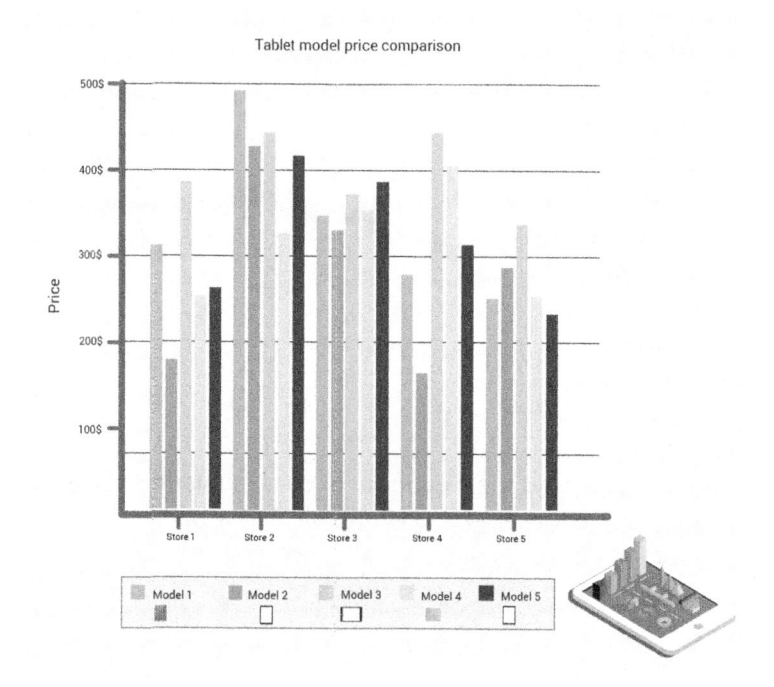

A circle graph, also called a pie chart, shows categorical data with each category representing a percentage of the whole data set. To make a circle graph, the percent of the data set for each category must be determined. To do so, the frequency of the category is divided by the total number of data points and converted to a percent. For example, if 80 people were asked what their favorite sport is and 20 responded basketball, basketball makes up 25% of the data ($\frac{20}{80} = 0.25 = 25\%$). Each category in a data set is represented by a *slice* of the circle proportionate to its percentage of the whole.

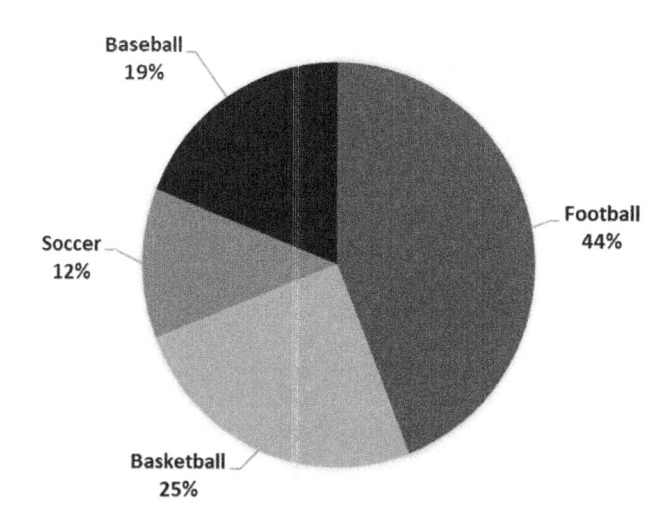

FAVORITE SPORT

- Baseball 19%
- Football 44%
- Soccer 12%
- Basketball 25%

Mathematics and Statistics

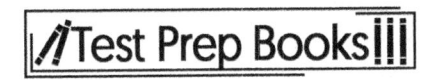

Choice of Graphs to Display Data

Choosing the appropriate graph to display a data set depends on what type of data is included in the set and what information must be displayed. Histograms and box plots can be used for data sets consisting of individual values across a wide range. Examples include test scores and incomes. Histograms and box plots will indicate the center, spread, range, and outliers of a data set. A histogram will show the shape of the data set, while a box plot will divide the set into quartiles (25% increments), allowing for comparison between a given value and the entire set.

Scatter plots and line graphs can be used to display data consisting of two variables. Examples include height and weight, or distance and time. A correlation between the variables is determined by examining the points on the graph. Line graphs are used if each value for one variable pairs with a distinct value for the other variable. Line graphs show relationships between variables.

Line plots, bar graphs, and circle graphs are all used to display categorical data, such as surveys. Line plots and bar graphs both indicate the frequency of each category within the data set. A line plot is used when the categories consist of numerical values. For example, the number of hours of TV watched by individuals is displayed on a line plot. A bar graph is used when the categories consists of words. For example, the favorite ice cream of individuals is displayed with a bar graph. A circle graph can be used to display either type of categorical data. However, unlike line plots and bar graphs, a circle graph does not indicate the frequency of each category. Instead, the circle graph represents each category as its percentage of the whole data set.

Describing a Set of Data

A set of data can be described in terms of its center, spread, shape and any unusual features. The center of a data set can be measured by its mean, median, or mode. The **spread of a data set** refers to how far the data points are from the center (mean or median). The spread can be measured by the range or by the quartiles and interquartile range. A data set with all its data points clustered around the center will have a small spread. A data set covering a wide range of values will have a large spread.

When a data set is displayed as a histogram or frequency distribution plot, the shape indicates if a sample is normally distributed, symmetrical, or has measures of skewness or kurtosis. When graphed, a data set with a normal distribution will resemble a bell curve.

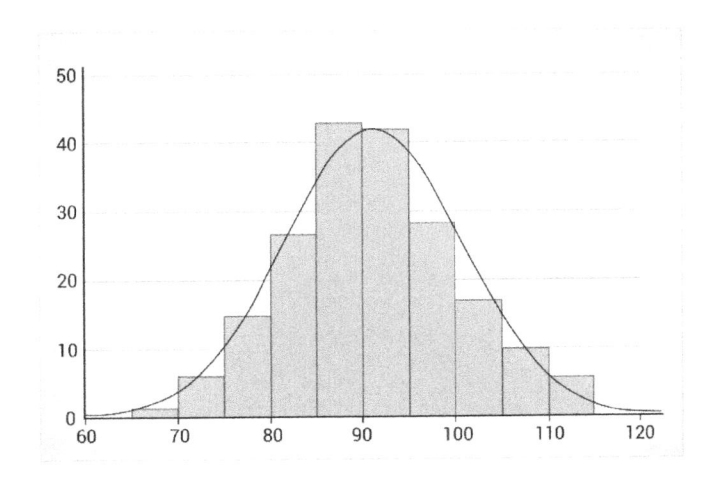

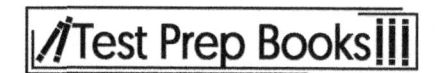

If the data set is symmetrical, each half of the graph when divided at the center is a mirror image of the other. If the graph has fewer data points to the right, the data is skewed right. If it has fewer data points to the left, the data is skewed left.

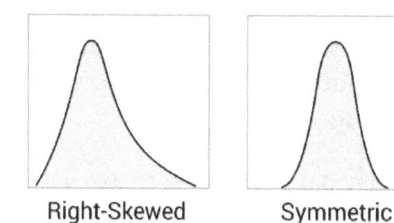

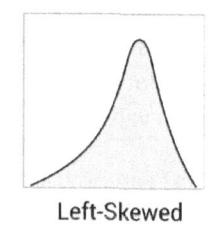

Right-Skewed   Symmetric   Left-Skewed

Kurtosis is a measure of whether the data is heavy-tailed with a high number of outliers, or light-tailed with a low number of outliers.

A description of a data set should include any unusual features such as gaps or outliers. A gap is a span within the range of the data set containing no data points. An outlier is a data point with a value either extremely large or extremely small when compared to the other values in the set.

Normal Distribution

A **normal distribution** of data follows the shape of a bell curve. In a normal distribution, the data set's median, mean, and mode are equal. Therefore, 50 percent of its values are less than the mean and 50 percent are greater than the mean. Data sets that follow this shape can be generalized using normal distributions. Normal distributions are described as **frequency distributions** in which the data set is plotted as percentages rather than true data points. A **relative frequency distribution** is one where the y-axis is between 0 and 1, which is the same as 0% to 100%.

Within a standard deviation, 68 percent of the values are within 1 standard deviation of the mean, 95 percent of the values are within 2 standard deviations of the mean, and 99.7 percent of the values are within 3 standard deviations of the mean. The number of standard deviations that a data point falls from the mean is called the *z-score*. The formula for the z-score is $Z = \frac{x-\mu}{\sigma}$, where μ is the mean, σ is the standard deviation, and x is the data point. This formula is used to fit any data set that resembles a

Mathematics and Statistics

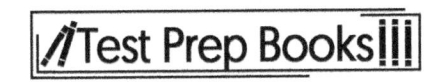

normal distribution to a standard normal distribution in a process known as **standardizing**. Here is a normal distribution with labeled z-scores:

Normal Distribution with Labelled Z-Scores

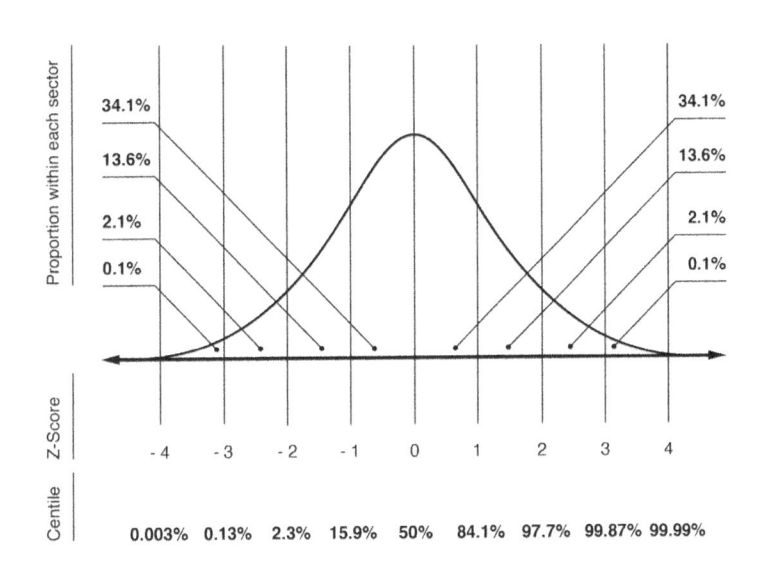

Population percentages can be estimated using normal distributions. For example, the probability that a data point will be less than the mean, or that the z-score will be less than 0, is 50%. Similarly, the probability that a data point will be within 1 standard deviation of the mean, or that the z-score will be between -1 and 1, is about 68.2%. When using a z-table, the left column states how many standard deviations (to one decimal place) away from the mean the point is, and the row heading states the second decimal place. The entries in the table corresponding to each column and row give the probability, which is equal to the area.

Measures of Center and Range

The center of a set of data (statistical values) can be represented by its mean, median, or mode. These are sometimes referred to as measures of central tendency. The **mean** is the average of the data set. The mean can be calculated by adding the data values and dividing by the sample size (the number of data points). Suppose a student has test scores of 93, 84, 88, 72, 91, and 77. To find the mean, or average, the scores are added and the sum is divided by 6 because there are 6 test scores:

$$\frac{93 + 84 + 88 + 72 + 91 + 77}{6} = \frac{505}{6} = 84.17$$

Given the mean of a data set and the sum of the data points, the sample size can be determined by dividing the sum by the mean. Suppose you are told that Kate averaged 12 points per game and scored a total of 156 points for the season. The number of games that she played (the sample size or the number of data points) can be determined by dividing the total points (sum of data points) by her average (mean of data points): $\frac{156}{12} = 13$. Therefore, Kate played in 13 games this season.

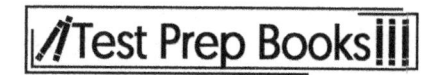

If given the mean of a data set and the sample size, the sum of the data points can be determined by multiplying the mean and sample size. Suppose you are told that Tom worked 6 days last week for an average of 5.5 hours per day. The total number of hours worked for the week (sum of data points) can be determined by multiplying his daily average (mean of data points) by the number of days worked (sample size): $5.5 \times 6 = 33$. Therefore, Tom worked a total of 33 hours last week.

The **median** of a data set is the value of the data point in the middle when the sample is arranged in numerical order. To find the median of a data set, the values are written in order from least to greatest. The lowest and highest values are simultaneously eliminated, repeating until the value in the middle remains. Suppose the salaries of math teachers are: $35,000; $38,500; $41,000; $42,000; $42,000; $44,500; $49,000. The values are listed from least to greatest to find the median. The lowest and highest values are eliminated until only the middle value remains. Repeating this step three times reveals a median salary of $42,000. If the sample set has an even number of data points, two values will remain after all others are eliminated. In this case, the mean of the two middle values is the median. Consider the following data set: 7, 9, 10, 13, 14, 14. Eliminating the lowest and highest values twice leaves two values, 10 and 13, in the middle. The mean of these values $\left(\frac{10+13}{2}\right)$ is the median. Therefore, the set has a median of 11.5.

The **mode** of a data set is the value that appears most often. A data set may have a single mode, multiple modes, or no mode. If different values repeat equally as often, multiple modes exist. If no value repeats, no mode exists. Consider the following data sets:

- A: 7, 9, 10, 13, 14, 14
- B: 37, 44, 33, 37, 49, 44, 51, 34, 37, 33, 44
- C: 173, 154, 151, 168, 155

Set A has a mode of 14. Set B has modes of 37 and 44. Set C has no mode.

The **range** of a data set is the difference between the highest and the lowest values in the set. The range can be considered the span of the data set. To determine the range, the smallest value in the set is subtracted from the largest value. The ranges for the data sets A, B, and C above are calculated as follows: A: $14 - 7 = 7$; B: $51 - 33 = 18$; C: $173 - 151 = 22$.

Best Description of a Set of Data

Measures of central tendency, namely mean, median, and mode, describe characteristics of a set of data. Specifically, they are intended to represent a *typical* value in the set by identifying a central position of the set. Depending on the characteristics of a specific set of data, different measures of central tendency are more indicative of a typical value in the set.

When a data set is grouped closely together with a relatively small range and the data is spread out somewhat evenly, the mean is an effective indicator of a typical value in the set. Consider the following data set representing the height of sixth grade boys in inches: 61 inches, 54 inches, 58 inches, 63 inches, 58 inches. The mean of the set is 58.8 inches. The data set is grouped closely (the range is only 9 inches) and the values are spread relatively evenly (three values below the mean and two values above the mean). Therefore, the mean value of 58.8 inches is an effective measure of central tendency in this case.

Mathematics and Statistics

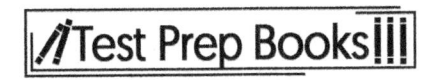

When a data set contains a small number of values either extremely large or extremely small when compared to the other values, the mean is not an effective measure of central tendency. Consider the following data set representing annual incomes of homeowners on a given street: $71,000; $74,000; $75,000; $77,000; $340,000. The mean of this set is $127,400. This figure does not indicate a typical value in the set, which contains four out of five values between $71,000 and $77,000. The median is a much more effective measure of central tendency for data sets such as these. Finding the middle value diminishes the influence of outliers, or numbers that may appear out of place, like the $340,000 annual income. The median for this set is $75,000 which is much more typical of a value in the set.

The mode of a data set is a useful measure of central tendency for categorical data when each piece of data is an option from a category. Consider a survey of 31 commuters asking how they get to work with results summarized below.

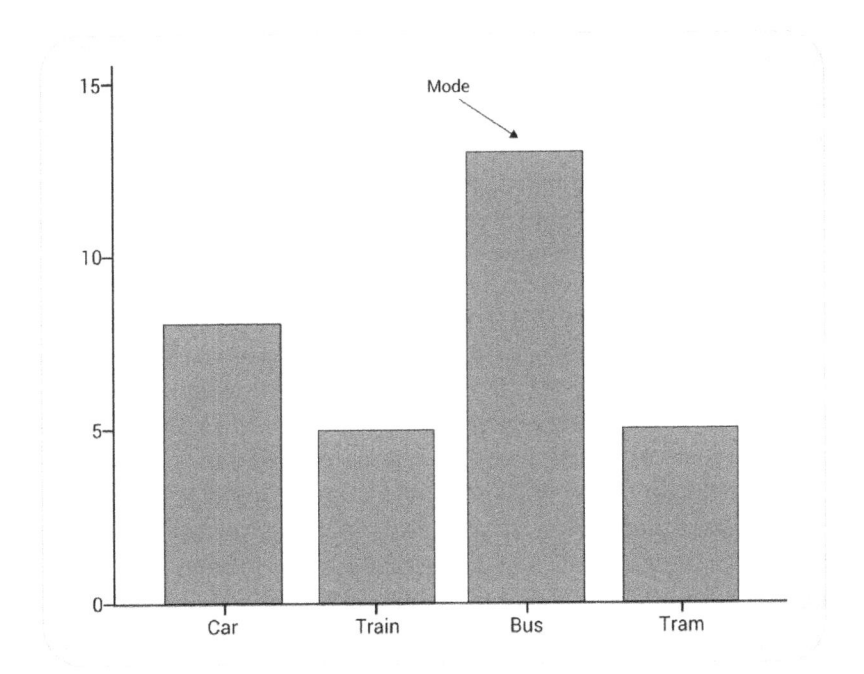

The mode for this set represents the value, or option, of the data that repeats most often. This indicates that the bus is the most popular method of transportation for the commuters.

Effects of Changes in Data

Changing all values of a data set in a consistent way produces predictable changes in the measures of the center and range of the set. A **linear transformation** changes the original value into the new value by either adding a given number to each value, multiplying each value by a given number, or both. Adding (or subtracting) a given value to each data point will increase (or decrease) the mean, median, and any modes by the same value. However, the range will remain the same due to the way that range is calculated. Multiplying (or dividing) a given value by each data point will increase (or decrease) the mean, median, and any modes, and the range by the same factor.

Consider the following data set, call it set P, representing the price of different cases of soda at a grocery store: $4.25, $4.40, $4.75, $4.95, $4.95, $5.15. The mean of set P is $4.74. The median is $4.85. The mode of the set is $4.95. The range is $0.90. Suppose the state passes a new tax of $0.25 on every case of soda sold. The new data set, set T, is calculated by adding $0.25 to each data point from set P. Therefore, set T consists of the following values: $4.50, $4.65, $5.00, $5.20, $5.20, $5.40. The mean of set T is $4.99. The median is $5.10. The mode of the set is $5.20. The range is $.90. The mean, median and mode of set T is equal to $0.25 added to the mean, median, and mode of set P. The range stays the same.

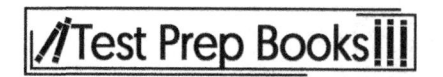

Now suppose, due to inflation, the store raises the cost of every item by 10 percent. Raising costs by 10 percent is calculated by multiplying each value by 1.1. The new data set, set I, is calculated by multiplying each data point from set T by 1.1. Therefore, set I consists of the following values: $4.95, $5.12, $5.50, $5.72, $5.72, $5.94. The mean of set I is $5.49. The median is $5.61. The mode of the set is $5.72. The range is $0.99. The mean, median, mode, and range of set I is equal to 1.1 multiplied by the mean, median, mode, and range of set T because each increased by a factor of 10 percent.

Comparing Data

Data sets can be compared by looking at the center and spread of each set. Measures of central tendency involve median, mean, midrange, and mode. The **mode** of a data set is the data value or values that appears the most frequently. The **midrange** is equal to the maximum value plus the minimum value divided by two. The **median** is the value that is halfway into each data set; it splits the data into two intervals. The **mean** is the sum of all data values divided by the number of data points. Two completely different sets of data can have the same mean.

For example, a data set having values ranging from 0 to 100 and a data set having values ranging from 44 to 46 could both have means equal to 50. The first data set would have a much wider range, which is known as the *spread* of the data. It measures how varied the data is within each set. Spread can be defined further as either interquartile range or standard deviation. The **interquartile range (IQR)** is the range of the middle fifty percent of the data set. The **standard deviation**, s, quantifies the amount of variation with respect to the mean. A lower standard deviation shows that the data set does not differ much from the mean. A larger standard deviation shows that the data set is spread out farther away from the mean. The formula used for standard deviation depends on whether it's being used for a population or a sample (a subset of a population). The formula for sample standard deviation is:

$$s = \sqrt{\frac{\Sigma(x - \bar{x})^2}{n - 1}}$$

In this formula, s represents the standard deviation value, x is each value in the data set, $\bar{x}$ is the sample mean, and n is the total number of data points in the set. Note that sample standard deviations use *one less than the total* in the denominator. The population standard deviation formula is similar:

$$\sigma = \sqrt{\frac{\Sigma(x - \mu)^2}{N}}$$

For population standard deviations, **sigma** (σ) represents the standard deviation, x represents each value in the data set, mu (μ) is the population mean, and N is the total number of data points for the population. A data set can have outliers, and measures of central tendency that are not affected by outliers are the mode and median. Those measures are labeled as resistant measures of center.

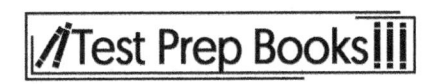

Making Inferences and Justifying Conclusions from Samples, Experiments, and Observational Studies

Data Gathering Techniques

Statistics involves making decisions and predictions about larger sets of data based on smaller data sets. The information from a small subset can help predict what happens in the entire set. The smaller data set is called a **sample** and the larger data set for which the decision is being made is called a **population**. The three most common types of data gathering techniques are sample surveys, experiments, and observational studies. **Sample surveys** involve collecting data from a random sample of people from a desired population. The measurement of the variable is only performed on this set of people. To have accurate data, the sampling must be unbiased and random. For example, surveying students in an advanced calculus class on how much they enjoy math classes is not a useful sample if the population should be all college students based on the research question. There are many methods to form a random sample, and all adhere to the fact that every sample that could be chosen has a predetermined probability of being chosen. Once the sample is chosen, statistical experiments can then be carried out to investigate real-world problems.

An **experiment** is the method by which a hypothesis is tested using a controlled process called the scientific method. A cause and the effect of that cause are measured, and the hypothesis is accepted or rejected. Experiments are usually completed in a controlled environment where the results of a control population are compared to the results of a test population. The groups are selected using a randomization process in which each group has a representative mix of the population being tested. Finally, an **observational study** is similar to an experiment. However, this design is used when circumstances prevent or do not allow for a designated control group and experimental group (e.g., lack of funding or unrealistic expectations). Instead, existing control and test populations must be used, so this method has a lack of randomization.

Interpreting Statistical Information

To make decisions concerning populations, data must be collected from a sample. The sample must be large enough to be able to make conclusions. A common way to collect data is via surveys and polls. Every survey and poll must be designed so that there is no bias. An example of a biased survey is one with loaded questions, which are either intentionally worded or ordered to obtain a desired response. Once the data is obtained, conclusions should not be made that are not justified by statistical analysis. One must make sure the difference between correlation and causation is understood. Correlation implies there is an association between two variables, and correlation does not imply causation.

Population Mean and Proportion

Both the population mean and proportion can be calculated using data from a sample. The **population mean (μ)** is the average value of the parameter for the entire population. Due to size constraints, finding the exact value of μ is impossible, so the mean of the sample population is used as an estimate instead. The larger the sample size, the closer the sample mean gets to the population mean. An alternative to finding μ is to find the *proportion* of the population, which is the part of the population with the given characteristic. The proportion can be expressed as a decimal, a fraction, or a percentage, and can be given as a single value or a range of values. Because the population mean and proportion are both estimates, there's a **margin of error**, which is the difference between the actual value and the expected value.

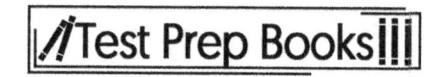

T-Tests

A **randomized experiment** is used to compare two treatments by using statistics involving a **t-test**, which tests whether two data sets are significantly different from one another. To use a t-test, the test statistic must follow a normal distribution. The first step of the test involves calculating the t value, which is given as $t = \frac{\bar{x}_1 - \bar{x}_2}{s_{\bar{x}_1 - \bar{x}_2}}$, where $\bar{x}_1$ and $\bar{x}_2$ are the averages of the two samples. Also,

$$s_{\bar{x}_1 - \bar{x}_2} = \sqrt{\frac{s_1^2}{n_1} + \frac{s_2^2}{n_2}}$$

s_1 and s_2 are the standard deviations of each sample and n_1 and n_2 are their respective sample sizes. The **degrees of freedom** for two samples are calculated as $df = \frac{(n_1 - 1) + (n_2 - 1)}{2}$ rounded to the lowest whole number. Also, a significance level α must be chosen, where a typical value is $\alpha = 0.05$. Once everything is compiled, the decision is made to use either a **one-tailed test** or a **two-tailed test**. If there's an assumed difference between the two treatments, a one-tailed test is used. If no difference is assumed, a two-tailed test is used.

Analyzing Test Results

Once the type of test is determined, the t-value, significance level, and degrees of freedom are applied to the published table showing the t distribution. The row is associated with degrees of freedom and each column corresponds to the probability. The t-value can be exactly equal to one entry or lie between two entries in a row. For example, consider a t-value of 1.7 with degrees of freedom equal to 30. This **test statistic** falls between the p-values of 0.05 and 0.025. For a one-tailed test, the corresponding p-value lies between 0.05 and 0.025. For a two-tailed test, the p-values need to be doubled so the corresponding p-value falls between 0.1 and 0.05. Once the probability is known, this range is compared to α. If $p < \alpha$, the hypothesis is rejected. If $p > \alpha$, the hypothesis isn't rejected. In a two-tailed test, this scenario means the hypothesis is accepted that there's no difference in the two treatments. In a one-tailed test, the hypothesis is accepted, indicating that there's a difference in the two treatments.

Evaluating Completed Tests

In addition to applying statistical techniques to actual testing, evaluating completed tests is another important aspect of statistics. Reports can be read that already have conclusions, and the process can be evaluated using learned concepts. For example, deciding if a sample being used is appropriate. Other things that can be evaluated include determining if the samples are randomized or the results are significant. Once statistical concepts are understood, the knowledge can be applied to many applications.

Sample Statistics

A **point estimate** is a single value used to approximate a population parameter. The sample proportion is the best point estimate of the population proportion. It is used because it is an **unbiased estimator**, meaning that it is a statistic that targets the value of the population parameter by assuming the mean of the sampling distribution is equal to the mean of the population distribution. Other unbiased estimators include the mean and variance. **Biased estimators** do not target the value of the population parameter, and such values include median, range, and standard deviation. A **confidence interval** consists of a range of values that is utilized to approximate the true value of a population parameter. The **confidence**

Mathematics and Statistics

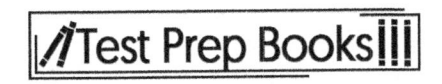

level is the probability that the confidence interval does contain the population parameter, assuming the estimation process is repeated many times.

Population Inferences Using Distributions

Samples are used to make inferences about a population. The sampling distribution of a sample mean is a distribution of all sample means for a fixed sample size, n, which is part of a population. Depending on different criteria, either a binomial, normal, or geometric distribution can be used to determine probabilities. A **normal distribution** uses a continuous random variable, and is bell-shaped and symmetric. A **binomial distribution** uses a discrete random variable, has a finite number of trials, and only has two possible outcomes: a success and a failure. A **geometric distribution** is very similar to a binomial distribution; however, the number of trials does not have to be finite.

Creating and Interpreting Linear Regression Models

Linear Regression

Regression lines are a way to calculate a relationship between the independent variable and the dependent variable. A straight line means that there's a linear trend in the data. The average daily temperature example above is one in which a straight line represented the data because the shape of the scatterplot resembles a straight line. Technology can be used to find the equation of this line (e.g., a graphing calculator or Microsoft Excel®). In either case, all of the data points are entered, and a line is "fit" that best represents the shape of the data. Other functions used to model data sets include quadratic and exponential models.

Estimating Data Points

Regression lines can be used to estimate data points not already given. For example, if an equation of a line is found that fit the temperature and beach visitor data set, its input is the average daily temperature and its output is the projected number of visitors. Thus, the number of beach visitors on a 100-degree day can be estimated. The output is a data point on the regression line, and the number of daily visitors is expected to be greater than on a 96-degree day because the regression line has a positive slope.

Plotting and Analyzing Residuals

Once the function is found that fits the data, its accuracy can be calculated. Therefore, how well the line fits the data can be determined. The difference between the actual dependent variable from the data set and the estimated value located on the regression line is known as a **residual**. Therefore, the residual is known as the predicted value $\hat{y}$ minus the actual value y. A residual is calculated for each data point and can be plotted on the scatterplot. If all the residuals appear to be approximately the same distance from the regression line, the line is a good fit. If the residuals seem to differ greatly across the board, the line isn't a good fit.

Interpreting the Regression Line

The formula for a regression line is $y = mx + b$, where m is the slope and b is the y-intercept. Both the slope and y-intercept are found in the *Method of Least Squares*, which is the process of finding the equation of the line through minimizing residuals. The slope represents the rate of change in y as x gets larger. Therefore, because y is the dependent variable, the slope actually provides the predicted values given the independent variable. The y-intercept is the predicted value for when the independent variable equals 0. In the temperature example, the y-intercept is the expected number of beach visitors for a very cold average daily temperature of 0 degrees.

Correlation Coefficient

The **correlation coefficient (r)** measures the association between two variables. Its value is between -1 and 1, where -1 represents a perfect negative linear relationship, 0 represents no relationship, and 1 represents a perfect positive linear relationship. A *negative linear relationship* means that as x-values increase, y-values decrease. A **positive linear relationship** means that as x-values increase, y-values increase. The formula for computing the correlation coefficient is:

$$r = \frac{n(\sum xy) - (\sum x)(\sum y)}{\sqrt{n(\sum x^2) - (\sum x)^2}\sqrt{n(\sum y^2) - (\Sigma y)^2}}$$

n is the number of data points

Both Microsoft Excel® and a graphing calculator can evaluate this easily once the data points are entered. A correlation greater than 0.8 or less than -0.8 is classified as "strong" while a correlation between -0.5 and 0.5 is classified as "weak."

Correlation Versus Causation

Correlation and causation have two different meanings. If two values are correlated, there is an association between them. However, correlation doesn't necessarily mean that one variable causes the other. **Causation** (or "cause and effect") occurs when one variable causes the other. Average daily temperature and number of beachgoers are correlated and have causation. If the temperature increases, the change in weather causes more people to go to the beach. However, alcoholism and smoking are correlated but don't have causation. The more someone drinks the more likely they are to smoke but drinking alcohol doesn't cause someone to smoke.

Regression Models

Regression lines are straight lines that calculate a relationship between nonlinear data involving an independent variable and a dependent variable. A regression line is of the form $y = mx + b$, where m is the slope and b is the y-intercept. Both the slope and y-intercept are found using the *Method of Least Squares*, which involves minimizing residuals – the difference between the dependent variable from the data set and the estimated value located on the regression line. The slope represents the rate of change in y as x increases. The y-intercept is the predicted value when the independent variable is equal to 0. Technology, such as a graphing calculator or Microsoft Excel®, can also be utilized to find the equation of this line. In either case, the data points are entered, and a line is "fit" that best represents the shape of the data.

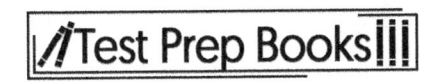

Here is an example of a data set and its regression line:

The Regression Line is the Line of Best Fit

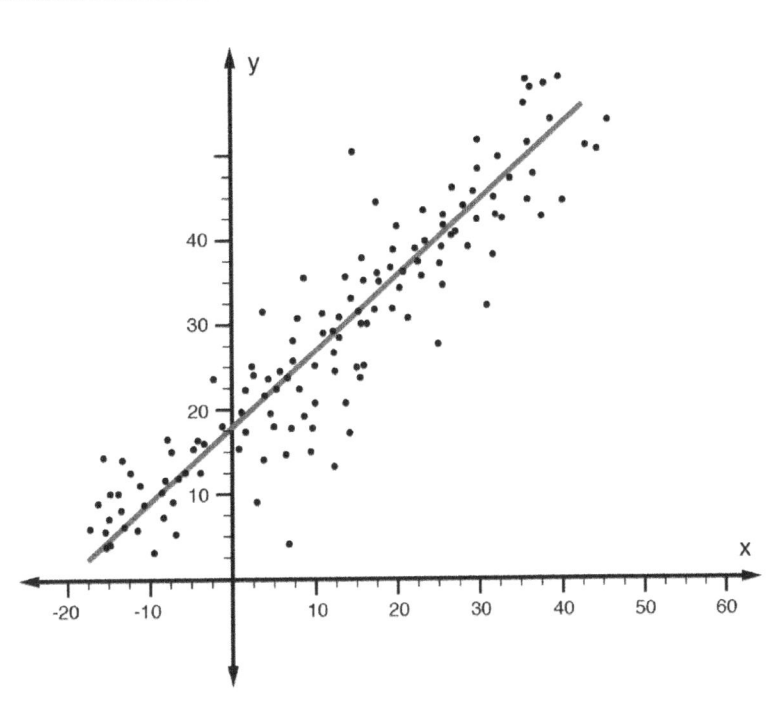

Regression models are highly used for forecasting, and linear regression techniques are the simplest models. If the nonlinear data follows the shape of exponential, logarithmic, or power functions, those types of functions can be used to more accurately model the data rather than lines.

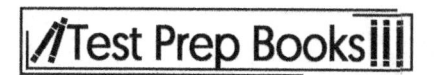

Here is an example of both an exponential regression and a logarithmic regression model:

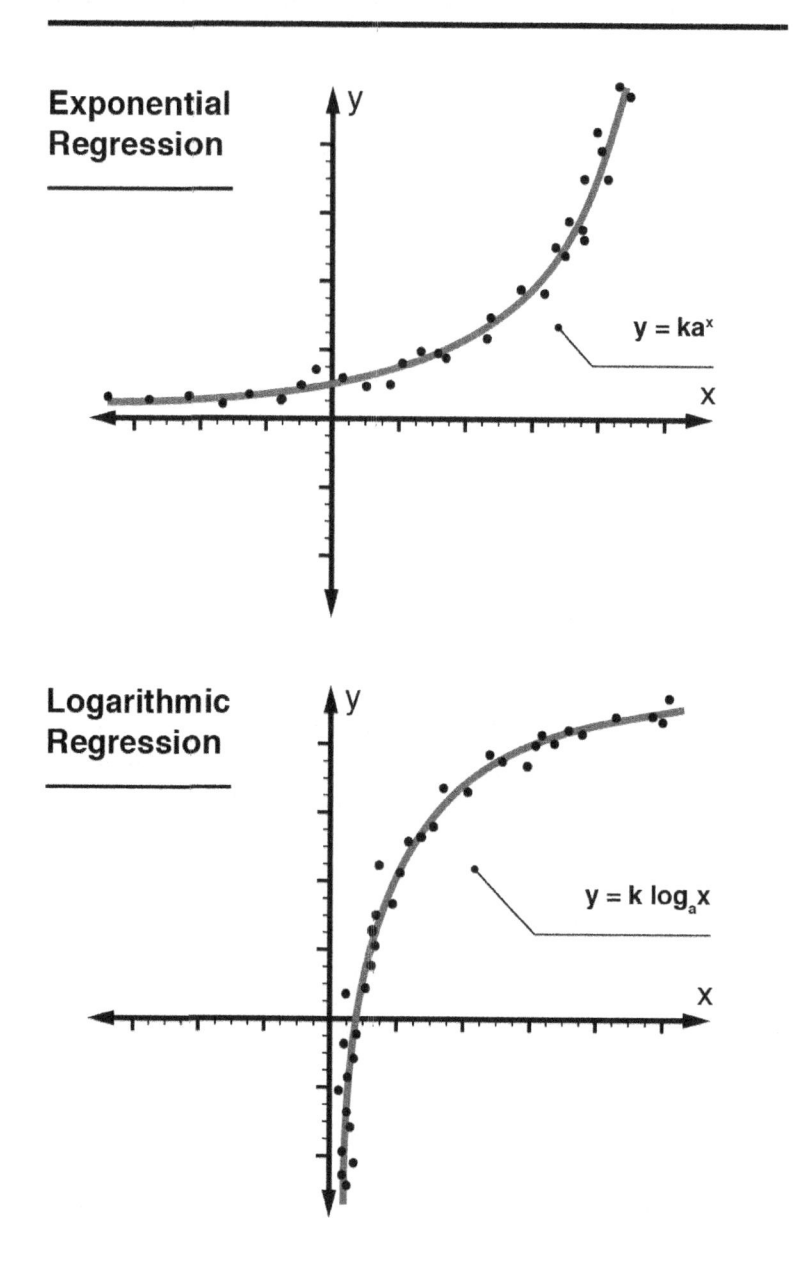

Nonlinear Regression

Exponential Regression

$y = ka^x$

Logarithmic Regression

$y = k \log_a x$

The Law of Large Numbers and the Central Limit Theorem

The **Law of Large Numbers** states that as the number of experiments increase, the actual ratio of outcomes will approach the theoretical probability. The **Central Limit Theorem** states that through using a sufficiently large sample size N, meaning over 30, the sampling distribution of the mean approaches a normal distribution with a mean of μ and variance of σ^2/N. The variance of the actual population is σ^2 and its mean is μ. In other words, as the sample size increases, the distribution will behave normally.

Mathematics and Statistics

Estimating Parameters

A point estimate of a population parameter is a single statistic. For example, the sample mean is a point estimate of the population mean. Once all calculations are made, a confidence interval is used to express the accuracy of the sampling method used. The confidence interval consists of a confidence level, the statistic, and a margin of error. A 95% confidence level indicates that 95% of all confidence intervals will contain the population parameter. Also, the margin of error gives a range of values above and below the sample statistic, which helps to form a confidence interval.

The Principles of Hypotheses Testing

The **P-value approach** to hypothesis testing involves assuming a null hypothesis is true and then determining the probability of a test statistic in the direction of the alternative hypothesis. The test statistic is defined as the t-statistic, $t^* = \frac{\bar{x} - \mu}{s/\sqrt{n}}$, which follows a t-distribution with $n-1$ degrees of freedom. The P-value is then calculated as the probability that if the null hypothesis is true, a more extreme test statistic in the direction of the alternative hypothesis would be observed. A significance level, α, is set (usually at 0.05 or 0.001) and the P-value is compared to α. If $P \leq \alpha$, one rejects the null hypothesis and accepts the alternative hypothesis. If $P > \alpha$, one accepts the null hypothesis.

Measuring Probabilities with Two-Way Frequency Tables

When measuring event probabilities, two-way frequency tables can be used to report the raw data and then used to calculate probabilities. If the frequency tables are translated into relative frequency tables, the probabilities presented in the table can be plugged directly into the formulas for conditional probabilities. By plugging in the correct frequencies, the data from the table can be used to determine if events are independent or dependent.

Differing Probabilities

The probability that event A occurs differs from the probability that event A occurs given B. When working within a given model, it's important to note the difference. $P(A|B)$ is determined using the formula $P(A|B) = \frac{P(A \text{ and } B)}{P(B)}$ and represents the total number of A's outcomes left that could occur after B occurs. $P(A)$ can be calculated without any regard for B. For example, the probability of a student finding a parking spot on a busy campus is different once class is in session.

Uniform and Non-Uniform Probability Models

A **uniform probability model** is one where each outcome has an equal chance of occurring, such as the probabilities of rolling each side of a die. A **non-uniform probability model** is one where each outcome has an unequal chance of occurring. In a uniform probability model, the conditional probability formulas for $P(B|A)$ and $P(A|B)$ can be multiplied by their respective denominators to obtain two formulas for $P(A \text{ and } B)$. Therefore, the multiplication rule is derived as $P(A \text{ and } B) = P(A)P(B|A) = P(B)P(A|B)$. In a model, if the probability of either individual event is known and the corresponding conditional probability is known, the multiplication rule allows the probability of the joint occurrence of A and B to be calculated.

Binomial Experiments

In statistics, a **binomial experiment** is where each trial can have only two possible outcomes: a success or a failure. An example of a binomial experiment is rolling a die 10 times with the goal of rolling a 5. Rolling a 5 is a success while any other value is a failure. In a binomial experiment, each event is independent of the others, and the probability of success is constant in every event. In this example, each roll of the die has nothing do to with the others and the probability of rolling a 5 is $\frac{1}{6}$. In any binomial experiment, x is the number of resulting successes, n is the number of trials, P is the probability of success in each trial, and $Q = 1 - P$ is the probability of failure within each trial. The probability of obtaining x successes within n trials is $\binom{n}{x} P^x (1-P)^{n-x}$, where $\binom{n}{x} = \frac{n!}{x!(n-x)!}$ is the **binomial coefficient**. Within its calculation, $n!$ is n factorial that's defined as $n \times (n-1) \times (n-2) \cdots 2 \times 1$. Therefore, the probability of obtaining four rolls of a 5 in 10 trials is $\binom{10}{4} \left(\frac{1}{6}\right)^4 \left(\frac{5}{6}\right)^6$.

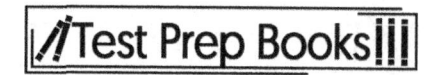

Statistical Questions

A statistical question is answered by collecting data with variability. Data consists of facts and/or statistics (numbers), and **variability** refers to a tendency to shift or change. Data is a broad term, inclusive of things like height, favorite color, name, salary, temperature, gas mileage, and language. Questions requiring data as an answer are not necessarily statistical questions. If there is no variability in the data, then the question is not statistical in nature. Consider the following examples: what is Mary's favorite color? How much money does your mother make? What was the highest temperature last week? How many miles did your car get on its last tank of gas? How much taller than Bob is Ed?

None of the above are statistical questions because each case lacks variability in the data needed to answer the question. The questions on favorite color, salary, and gas mileage each require a single piece of data, whether a fact or statistic. Therefore, variability is absent. Although the temperature question requires multiple pieces of data (the high temperature for each day), a single, distinct number is the answer. The height question requires two pieces of data, Bob's height and Ed's height, but no difference in variability exists between those two values. Therefore, this is not a statistical question. Statistical questions typically require calculations with data.

Consider the following statistical questions:

How many miles per gallon of gas does the 2016 Honda Civic get? To answer this question, data must be collected. This data should include miles driven and gallons used. Different cars, different drivers, and different driving conditions will produce different results. Therefore, variability exists in the data. To answer the question, the mean (average) value could be determined.

Are American men taller than German men? To answer this question, data must be collected. This data should include the heights of American men and the heights of German men. All American men are not the same height and all German men are not the same height. Some American men are taller than some German men and some German men are taller than some American men. Therefore, variability exists in the data. To answer the question, the median values for each group could be determined and compared.

The following are more examples of statistical questions: What proportion of 4th graders have a favorite color of blue? How much money do teachers make? Is it colder in Boston or Chicago?

Statistical Processes

Samples and Populations

Statistics involves making decisions and predictions about larger data sets based on smaller data sets. Basically, the information from one part or subset can help predict what happens in the entire data set

Mathematics and Statistics

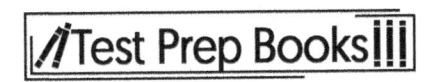

or population at large. The entire process involves guessing, and the predictions and decisions may not be 100 percent correct all of the time; however, there is some truth to these predictions, and the decisions do have mathematical support. The smaller data set is called a **sample** and the larger data set (in which the decision is being made) is called a **population.** A **random sample** is used as the sample, which is an unbiased collection of data points that represents the population as well as it can. There are many methods of forming a random sample, and all adhere to the fact that every potential data point has a predetermined probability of being chosen.

Goodness of Fit

Goodness of fit tests show how well a statistical model fits a given data set. They allow the differences between the observed and expected quantities to be summarized to determine if the model is consistent with the results. The **Chi-Squared Goodness of Fit Test** (or *Chi-Squared Test* for short) is used with one categorical variable from one population, and it concludes whether or not the sample data is consistent with a hypothesized distribution. Chi-Squared is evaluated using the following formula: $\chi^2 = \sum \frac{(O-E)^2}{E}$, where O is the observed frequency value and E is the expected frequency value. Also, the **degree of freedom** must be calculated, which is the number of categories in the data set minus one. Then a Chi-Squared table is used to test the data. The **degree of freedom value** and a **significance value**, such as 0.05, are located on the table. The corresponding entry represents a critical value.

If the calculated χ^2 is greater than the critical value, the data set does not work with the statistical model. If the calculated χ^2 is less than the critical value, the statistical model can be used.

Communications

This knowledge area encompasses a general understanding of the principles of effective communication and public-speaking techniques, as well as general knowledge of public media, media relations, and the goals and techniques of public diplomacy and their use to support work functions.

Principles of Effective Communication

Good public speakers all have several characteristics in common. It is not enough to simply write a speech, but it must also be delivered in a manner that is both engaging and succinct. The following qualities are inherent to good public speaking.

Confidence is possibly the most important attribute a speaker can have. It instills trust in the listener that the person knows what he or she is talking about and that he or she is credible and competent. Confidence is displayed by making brief eye contact—about 2-3 seconds—with different members of the audience to demonstrate that the speaker is engaged. It is also displayed in their tone of voice—strong, light-hearted, and natural. A nervous speaker can easily be identified by a small, quivering voice. Confidence is also conveyed by the speaker facing the audience; turning one's back may demonstrate insecurity.

Authenticity is another quality of an effective speaker, as it makes a person more relatable and believable to the audience. Speeches that are memorized word-for-word can give the impression of being inauthentic as the monologue does not flow quite naturally, especially if the speaker accidentally fumbles or forgets. Memorizing speeches can also lead to a monotonous tone, which is sure to put the audience to sleep, or worse, a misinterpreted tone, which can cause the audience to stop listening entirely or even become offended. Therefore, speeches should be practiced with a natural intonation and not be memorized mechanically.

Connection with the audience is another important aspect of public speaking. Speakers should engage with their listeners by the use of storytelling and visual or auditory aids, as well as asking questions that the audience can participate in. Visual and auditory aids could range from an interesting PowerPoint presentation to a short video clip to physical objects the audience can pass around to a soundtrack. The use of appropriate humor also allows the audience to connect with the speaker on a more personal level and will make the speech sound more like a conversation than a one-sided lecture. Speakers who are passionate about their subject inspire their listeners to care about what they're saying; they transfer their energy into the audience. This level of connection will encourage their listeners to want to be there.

Succinctness and *purposeful repetition* ensures that the audience's attention remains focused on the message at hand. Repeating the overall point of the speech in different ways helps listeners remember what the speaker is trying to tell them, even when the speech is over. A speech that is longer than necessary will cause listeners to become bored and stop absorbing information. Keeping the speech short and sweet and leaving more time for questions at the end will ensure that the audience stays engaged.

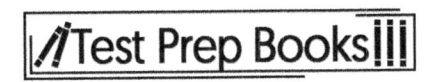

There are many different styles a speaker can utilize, but the most important thing speakers should keep in mind is maintaining a connection with the audience. This will help ensure that the audience will remain open and focused enough to hear and absorb the message.

Public Speaking

All information should be presented with a clear beginning, middle, and end. Distinct organization always makes any work more clear, concise, and logical. For a presentation, this should involve choosing a primary topic and then discussing it in the following format:

- Introducing the speaker and the main topic
- Providing evidence, supporting details, further explanation of the topic in the main body
- Concluding it with a firm resolution and repetition of the main point

The beginning, middle, and end should also be linked with effective transitions that make the presentation flow well. For example, a presentation should always begin with an introduction by the speaker, including what he/she does and what he/she is there to present. Good transitional introductions may begin with statements such as *For those who do not know me, my name is...*, *As many of you know, I am...* or *Good morning everyone, my name is ___, and I am the new project manager*. A good introduction grabs the attention and interest of the audience.

After an introduction has been made, the speaker will then want to state the purpose of the presentation with a natural transition, such as *I am here to discuss the latest editions to our standard of procedure...* or *This afternoon, I would like to present the results of our latest findings*. Once the purpose has been identified, the speaker will want to adhere to the main idea announced. The presenter should be certain to keep the main idea to one sentence as too much information can confuse an audience; an introduction should be succinct and to the point.

Supporting information should always be presented in concise, easy-to-read formats such as bullet points or lists—if visual aids are presented during the presentation. Good transitions such as *Let's begin with...* or *Now to look at...* make the presentation flow smoothly and logically, helping listeners to keep ideas organized as they are presented. Keeping the material concise is extremely important in a presentation, and visual aids should be used only to emphasize points or explain ideas. All the supporting information should relate back to the main idea, avoiding unnecessary tangents.

Finally, a firm conclusion involves repeating the main point of the presentation by either inspiring listeners to act or by reiterating the most important points made in the speech. It should also include an expression of gratitude to the audience as well as transition to opening the floor for questions.

Public Media

Mass media refers to the various methods by which the majority of the general public receives news and information. Mass media includes television, newspapers, radio, magazines, online news outlets, and social media networks. The general public relies on mass media for political knowledge and cultural socialization, as well as the majority of their knowledge of current events, social issues, and political news.

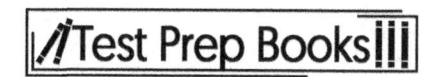

Evolution of Mass Media

- Until the end of the nineteenth century, print media such as newspapers and magazines was the only form of mass communication.

- In the 1890s, after the invention of the radio, broadcast media become a popular form of communication, particularly among illiterate people.

- In the 1940s, television superseded both print and broadcast media as the most popular form of mass media.

- In 1947, President Harry Truman gave the first political speech on television.

- In 1952, Dwight Eisenhower was the first political candidate to air campaign ads on television.

- Today, the internet is the most widespread mass media technology, and citizens have instant access to news and information, as well as interactive platforms on which they can communicate directly with political leaders or share their views through social media, blogs, and independent news sites.

Influence of Mass Media on Politics

Mass media has a powerful effect on public opinion and politics. Mass media:

- Shapes public interests

- Enables candidates to reach voters wherever they are

- Determines what is and is not considered important in society based on how it prioritizes events and issues

- Provides the context in which to report events

- Is paid for by advertisers who may pressure news outlets to suppress or report information in their own interests

Media Relations

Media relations is the relationship between the media and an organization. Organizations work with the media in order to build credibility with the public and inform the public on certain decisions being made within the organization, from policies to proposals. More specifically, media relations involve the specific relationships between journalists and the organization itself. The risk involved in creating media relations through an organization is that the organization has no control over what the media puts out. Thus, it's important to develop a positive relationship between the media and the organization. Usually, an organization will have one person or a media relations personnel to deal with journalists, editors, and/or reporters regarding what the story or information involves.

Media relations personnel should be knowledgeable of different media outlets, such as blogs, television, and radio, and must be informed of the angle of different news sources, their relationships with the public, and the types of stories they like to produce. Knowledge of this type of information will ensure that the personnel will find the most appropriate media source for their purposes. Personnel must also

Communications

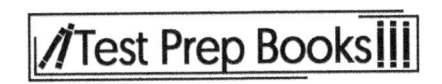

be aware what audience each media outlet has and thus choose the media with the knowledge of that particular audience in mind.

Purposes for an organization to use media relations may include ways to boost the organization's presence in the public, information that's important to public interest, launch of products or services, engagement in community service or activities, or simply negative publicity that is going to come out anyway.

Again, developing a positive relationship with the media is important for media relations; one of the main goals of using media relations is so that the organization will be viewed in a positive light by the public. Some of the mediums used in relations are named in the following list:

Newspaper: Newspapers are popular for local ads and news. They usually rely on people paying for the newspaper or payment from businesses purchasing ad space. Newspapers are a great way to reach a dedicated local audience.

Internet: The internet is a media source used to reach a global platform. The internet has multiple mediums to reach different kinds of audiences. These include online articles from reputable news companies, video games, blogs, websites, etc. The following is a list of common types of tools used for digital media:

- Smartphones/apps
- Email
- Microsoft Office
- iMovie
- Skype
- Twitter
- Facebook
- Instagram
- Google Drive
- Various blogging websites
- Online bulletin boards
- Wikis
- Podcasts

Broadcasting: Broadcasting is used in film or radio, and it's considered a sequencing of radio or film shows that are put in a particular order for an audience. Through broadcasting, multiple shows can be put out at the same time, or sometimes a broadcasting network will be split or shared between two networks.

Television: Television is another popular form of media communications, as many channels feature news programs on air. Some journalists must work with both television and social media and make sure their message is appropriate for both mediums. The intermingling of social media and television is a new phenomenon that should not be ignored by media relations personnel.

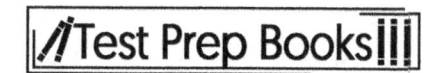

Diplomacy

States conduct diplomacy to negotiate compromises between states; accomplish militaristic, economic, environmental, and humanitarian goals; and garner allies in case of future crisis or conflict.

Diplomacy remains front and center to any efforts within a country or between countries to minimize conflict and, in many cases, maximize cooperation. Both cooperation and conflict are necessary in order for diplomacy to truly prosper; if there is no conflict, there is no need for diplomacy, and if there is no cooperation, there can be no common ground for establishing any diplomatic efforts.

Diplomacy is thought of as a management of international relations by way of negotiations, typically carried out by ambassadors or diplomats. It is regarded as a machine for action in times of conflict, and is used as the first line of defense in disagreements. Diplomacy is usually defined in bilateral terms, but given the increase in power of international conferences and organizations, diplomacy measures are characterized by a semblance of plurality, thus becoming multilateral in nature. Concerning the means of diplomacy, there are six main devices:

- Persuasion: This is clearly the first line of defense in that logical cases can be presented without overhead or other bargaining devices

- Rewards: A state can offer another state goods or services in exchange for accepting their policy measures

- Promise of rewards and concessions: Diplomats can offer reassurance that, if their policy measures are accepted, then the country will match their investment

- Threat of use of force: Diplomacy, by its very definition, cannot preclude violence; however, there can be ultimatum, boycotts, walkouts, or even threat of war should the parties continue to disagree

- Non-violent punishment: The opposite of rewarding, punishment can come in the form of non-violence.

- Use of pressure: Diplomatic efforts that fall under the use of pressure include propaganda, exploitation of events, and creation of scenes or situations that seek to change opposing parties' views

Public Diplomacy

Diplomacy is the act of meeting with officials from foreign states to discuss matters of international interest, foster harmonious relationships, organize international partnerships, broker agreements, and resolve disputes. **Public diplomacy** is different in that it is designed to circulate information to a foreign public in order to advance goals of foreign or national policy. Public diplomacy is done in a transparent way as possible, and is often called "people's diplomacy." Countries will conduct public diplomacy in such a way as to send a positive image of their country to a receiving country's public.

For example, Canada participated in public diplomacy in 2015 when they worked with a certain story within the media to showcase the acceptance of Syrian refugees into their country. Millions of Syrians witnessing a devastating civil war sought refuge in countries elsewhere, only to find themselves and

Communications

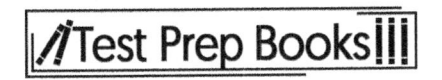

their families turned away from sanctuary. Canada's actions, however, led by Prime Minister Justin Trudeau, welcomed the Syrians into their country, charming many countries in the process.

Public diplomacy uses many different mediums, such as educational exchange programs, language training, visitor programs, broadcasting, and certain cultural exchanges.

Management Principles, Psychology, and Human Behavior

Basic Management and Supervisory Techniques and Methods (PHR)

Generally speaking, there are four basic functions of management: planning, organizing, directing, and controlling. Let's consider all four in greater detail. Before everything, an organization must develop a plan. An organization's plan is its roadmap to success, pinpointing its future goals and recommending the best course of action to reach them. In order to carry out the plan, careful organizing is essential. Organizing involves structuring tasks, locating and acquiring sufficient resources (human resources, financial resources, etc.) to complete tasks, and allocating those resources appropriately. Next is directing, also known as leading or commanding. Directing is people management: giving clear direction, feedback, and motivation to staff so that employees know what is expected of them and can complete their work as effectively as possible. The last function of management is controlling, which is when management evaluates performance by establishing standards, measuring performance based on these standards, and making adjustments as necessary.

Establishing Relationships: Organization and Individuals

In order to best serve its organization, HR must have good relationships with other departments and individuals within the organization. The key to any relationship is communication. HR should maintain open dialogue with other departments and help managers with any employee-related issues. While HR must ensure that departments comply with company policies, it's better to coach and educate managers about following policy rather than complaining about every mistake. When HR is a team player and not just a distant authority figure, it's easier for managers to approach HR and solve problems together.

In this way, HR can also demonstrate its usefulness in aiding organization decisions. Any change in the organization will inevitably affect employees, so HR can help balance the needs of the organization with the needs of workers and advise on decisions that will satisfy everyone. HR also acts as a bridge between executive decisions in the organization and how those decisions will be translated into new policies and procedures.

Managing Organizational Change

In order to remain competitive, adopt industry best practices, and adapt to changing markets, an organization will undergo change at many points. Change might be undertaken to benefit company shareholders and increase the profitability of the company. Change can also occur to reduce costs and increase efficiency. However, especially from an HR perspective, it's important to keep in mind how change affects employees. The truth is that most people don't like change. Also, work force changes in particular (such as outsourcing or downsizing) are certain to be met with employee resistance. Even more minor changes like revised vacation policies may go through an unpopular adjustment period. Change management helps to smooth over these difficulties.

Change Management

Change is inevitable for any organization, especially in fields affected by global markets and technological innovation. Change management seeks to aid organizations through significant transitions in resource allocation, operations, business processes, or any other large-scale changes. Careful change management helps the organization to function effectively even while undergoing a major evolution.

Management Principles, Psychology, and Human Behavior

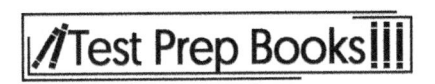

Implementing Change

How should an organization implement change? The classic 1961 text *The Planning of Change* tackles this question. The book outlines three strategies for managing change: the empirical-rational strategy, the normative-reductive strategy, and the power-coercive strategy.

The empirical-rational strategy assumes that people are rational and will naturally follow any course that's in their self-interest. Therefore, they are likelier to accept change when they think it will directly benefit them. To implement change in line with this strategy, an organization must either 1) demonstrate the benefit of the change or 2) demonstrate the harm of the status quo (or both). One way of accomplishing this is to incentivize change. For example, a growing company is gaining new employees, but it doesn't want to expand its available parking. The company decides to limit the number of parking spots and encourage public transportation use. Employees are reluctant to give up the freedom to drive, so the company holds an educational seminar about how to save money by using public transportation and also offers monthly reimbursement for employees who use public transportation.

The next approach proposed in *The Planning of Change* is the normative-reductive strategy. This strategy assumes that people will closely follow social norms and expectations. In order to implement change, it's necessary to first change people's idea of what is socially acceptable. This is the strategy that harnesses the power of advertising. For example, think of anti-tobacco advertising campaigns over the past few decades. Throughout most of the twentieth century, smoking was socially acceptable just about anywhere. However, especially in the 1990s and 2000s, aggressive anti-smoking advertisements attacked the tobacco industry and started anti-smoking education programs for students. The social norm turned *against* smoking in most public places, and now there are more anti-smoking laws than ever before.

Finally, the power-coercive strategy assumes that people are followers who will listen to authority and do as they are told. This approach to change is basically, "My way or the highway!" Where the empirical-rational strategy seeks to demonstrate how change will benefit employees, the power-coercive strategy says that *not* following change will be *harmful* to employees, who might be punished or even fired for failure to comply. For example, a factory undergoes an intense safety inspection and decides to completely renovate its safety standards. Employees now have new dress code requirements. If they don't follow the dress code, they aren't allowed to work that day; after the third dress code violation, they will be fired.

Deciding which strategy to employ depends on the overall character of the organization (for example, an otherwise friendly and collegial office might respond negatively to usage of the power-coercive strategy) as well as the importance and sensitivity of the change (the power-coercive strategy would be useful for changes with clear legal or financial liabilities, such as when an organization must follow new government regulations).

Reinforcing Value and Expectations

HR is responsible for formulating and enforcing policies about employee behavior. Of course, HR must first educate employees about the organization's expectations. Let's look at some approaches to developing desired behaviors.

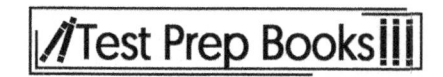

Communication

The first step of any business interaction is communication. No matter how carefully an idea is researched and planned, it could all fall apart if it isn't properly communicated to those who must carry it out. For this reason, all HR policies must be clearly communicated to employees, particularly when new policies are enacted or when the same HR issues occur often. Communication can occur in a variety of ways, such as through e-mail, individual interviews, or department meetings.

Modeling

Modeling provides a hands-on approach to teaching new behaviors. Some can learn quickly from reading a book or listening to a presentation. For others, the easiest way to learn is by doing—or by watching other people. Employees can learn new behaviors and skills by watching a manager or trainer perform them first. However, while training situations may involve formal modeling, employees also learn from informal modeling as they observe the behavior of other workers. So it's important to enforce HR policies at all levels of an organization, including upper management. If managers are getting away with unacceptable behaviors like sneaking out of work early or using abusive language in the office, other employees can learn from that modeled undesirable behavior. Both formal and informal modeling should provide positive examples for workers.

Coaching

HR coaching helps employees achieve their potential and continue to develop their skills, matching them with the needs of the organization. Through evaluations and employee self-assessments, HR can nurture strengths while providing training to overcome weaknesses. Coaching can also help employees progress on their career path by identifying areas for advancement within the organization. This gives employees an incentive to stay with the organization and pursue self-improvement goals.

Human Psychology and Behavior

There are many different theoretical perspectives to explain human behavior. The following are some of the most prevalent approaches to understanding human behavior.

The **systems approach** seeks to evaluate and explain human behavior as the individual interacts with the different social systems that they are a part of, including the family, community, and work environment. The systems approach emphasizes the importance of a person's perceived role in society or family, such as father, wife, or student. The **Stanford Prison Experiment of 1971** confirmed the importance of social roles, when students—who were given the roles of guards and prisoners in a simulated prison experience—began to dramatically and even dangerously adopt those roles.

Another important theory to explain human behavior is the **conflict theory**, which focuses on division of power, oppression, and conflict between social groups and within social systems, and what happens when groups or people have competing interests. Recently in social work, with an increased emphasis on social justice, the conflict theory has gained more influence as it looks at dominant and privileged groups as contrasted with oppressed and underprivileged populations.

The **rational choice** or **social exchange perspective** explains human behavior in the context of the social give and take of resources. Each person is making rational choices in their interactions with others, primarily motivated by selfish reasons and with the desire to minimize costs to themselves, while maximizing the benefits received.

Management Principles, Psychology, and Human Behavior

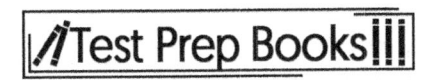

The **social constructionist perspective** has to do with how people derive meaning from their world and how they analyze and classify society around them. Socially and culturally, shared understandings are developed about people and their places in the world, which leads to an ever-changing social construct.

The **psychodynamic theory,** built on Freud's work, emphasizes the unconscious and internal drives and motives that rule human behavior. Some other important components of the psychodynamic perspective are the significance of childhood experiences and the use of defense mechanisms as a means of protection from unacceptable feelings and impulses.

As previously discussed, the **developmental perspective** looks at how humans grow and change throughout the lifespan and the impact that this has on human behavior. At each stage of life, there are different emotional, physical, and psychological changes that occur, and there are different developmental tasks that must be overcome.

Another way of explaining human behavior is the **social learning perspective**, built on the idea that people learn how to behave as they interact with their environment. This learning may take place through classical conditioning, which is the development of automatic responses to stimuli in the environment, or operant conditioning, in which the behaviors that are rewarded increase, and the behaviors that are punished decrease. The third form of learning is observational learning, which explains how people learn the behaviors that are modeled for them.

Finally, *the* **humanistic approach** emphasizes the uniqueness, individuality, free will, and value of each human being. Human behavior is viewed as an attempt to reach toward self-actualization and to find a sense of purpose and fulfillment. Abraham Maslow, a renowned humanist psychologist, developed his hierarchy of needs to explain the human progression from having basic needs met to becoming self-transcendent.

Strengths-Based and Resilience Theories

Rather than focusing on problems and pathology, the strengths perspective (or **strengths-based approach**) in social work encourages social workers to focus on a client's strengths or assets and to build upon the client's inherent resiliency and positive characteristics. Outcome studies regarding use of the strengths perspective are limited. However, it is posited that a strength-based approach could help to remove some of the stigma attached to groups or to conditions (e.g., mental illness, poverty).

Defense Mechanisms and Human Behavior

Sigmund Freud's psychoanalytic theory focused on the conflicts, drives, and unacceptable desires in the unconscious mind and how they affect a person. One method of dealing with unconscious conflicts is through *defense mechanisms*, which are the mind's way of protecting a person from unacceptable thoughts. Here are some of the most common defense mechanisms:

- **Repression** is when a person suppresses thoughts or memories that are too difficult to handle. They are pushed out of the conscious mind, and a person may experience memory loss or have psychogenic amnesia related to those memories.

- **Displacement** takes place when someone displaces the feelings they have toward one person, such as anger, and puts it on another person who may be less threatening. For example, someone may express anger toward a spouse, even if they are really angry with a boss.

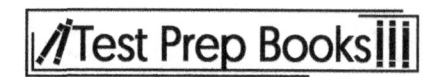

- **Sublimation** is when the socially unacceptable thought is transformed into healthy, acceptable creativity in another direction. Pain may become poetry, for example.

- **Rationalization** is when unacceptable feelings or thoughts are rationally and logically explained and defended.

- **Reaction formation** occurs when the negative feeling is covered up by a false or exaggerated version of its opposite. In such a case, a person may display strong feelings of affection toward someone, though internally and unconsciously hate that person.

- **Denial** is refusing to accept painful facts or situations and instead acting as if they are not true or have not happened.

- **Projection** is putting one's own feelings onto someone else and acting as if they are the one who feels that way instead of oneself.

Group Theories

The following is a list of groups in social work that individuals use for greater social functioning and fellowship in order to learn better coping skills.

The **Mutual Aid Model** is derived from theoretical work by social work pioneer, **William Schwartz**. This model is also referred to as self-help or support groups. Clients within the group need and help each other as they tackle problems that are common across group members. This model is commonly used with groups focused on substance abuse.

Cognitive-behavioral group work utilizes cognitive-behavioral therapy (CBT) interventions, initially used in individual work and applies those interventions to a group setting. Although mutual aid is not emphasized or a core component, group discussion is valued, and group members do interact with each other. The focus is on learning skills and changing behavior in order for individuals to function more effectively.

Systems-Centered therapy groups are based on the work of Yvonne Agazarian (*Theory of Living Human Systems*). Human systems have energy and use that energy for survival, development, and mastery of the environment. Group members use functional subgrouping to work together, explore similarities and differences, learn perspective taking, and resolve conflicts.

Interpersonal Learning Groups were made well known by Irvin Yalom, a pioneer in group theory and practice. This approach uses group interaction as the mechanism for achieving awareness, insight, and change. The leader of the group must facilitate interpersonal learning.

Systems and Ecological Perspectives

Systems Theory in social work refers to the view that human behavior is explained by the influences of the various systems to which individuals belong. When evaluating and conceptualizing an individual's behavior, that behavior must be considered in the context of the individual's family, society, and other systems.

- All systems are seen as possessing interrelated parts and exerting influence on each other.

- There are many iterations of the premise of the basic systems theory.

Management Principles, Psychology, and Human Behavior

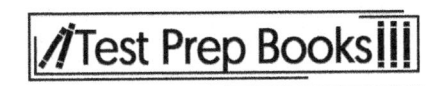

- In practice, systems theory allows a social worker to understand the dynamics of a client's systems better, while also creating an appropriate intervention approach.

- The originator of systems theory in social work was Ludwig von Bertalanffy, a biologist, who was influenced by sociologists Max Weber and Emile Durkheim.

Talcott Parsons expanded on earlier work with his framework of *structural functionalism,* which proposes that a system is defined by its function in its social environment.

Four states of social systems:

- Adaptation to the social environment
- Goal attainment
- Integration with other systems
- Latency or homeostasis (social patterns and norms are maintained)

Designations of social systems in social work:

- **Microsystems**: small systems (e.g., an individual or a couple)
- **Mezzosystems**: medium-sized systems (e.g., extended families, groups to which the individual belongs)
- **Macrosystems**: large systems (e.g., organizations, communities)

The **ecological systems perspective** is concerned with the transactions between systems:

- People and families must be considered within cultural and societal contexts, which also necessitates examining the events that have occurred in an individual's life.

- Changes made by the individual that cause the entire system to shift must also be considered.

Common interventions based on systems theory:

- Strengthening a part of the system in order to improve the whole system

- Creating a genogram: a family tree constructed with a client in order to improve understanding of the familial relationships and to identify recurring patterns

- Connecting clients to organizations or individuals who can help them to function better within and between their systems

- Developing an ecomap: an Illustration of client's systems, such as family and community and how it changes over time

Person-in-Environment
Carel Germain described person-in environment interaction based upon earlier work in systems theory. This perspective takes into consideration an individual's environmental and systemic influences. It is specific to social work, which differentiates it from other like professions.

- **Life stress**: the normal tension that occurs as the result of both external demands and internal experiences. What is experienced as stressful varies across people and their perceptions. For example, two people placed in the same environment may have completely different experiences due to the ways in which they experience and perceive the situation.

- **Adaptation**: when the environment and the individual change in response to the interaction with each other

- **Coping**: individual use of one's own strengths and problem-solving abilities to navigate life stress and develop self-esteem and hope

- **Power**: a source of stress to the individual and the larger system misused by groups

- **Human relatedness**: the ability of individuals to cultivate relationships

- Three related concepts are *self-direction*, *competence*, and *self-esteem*. These attributes are interdependent and occur cross-culturally.

Impact of Social Institutions on Society

Social institutions exist to meet the needs of individuals, promote pro-social behavior, define social norms, and create order.

There are five major social institutions:

Family
- Regulates sexual behavior
- Creates and provides for new society members
- Socializes new society members

Religion
- Provides explanations for the unexplainable
- Supports societal norms and values
- Provides a means of coping with life situations

Government
- Institutionalizes norms (by creating laws)
- Enforces laws
- Protects members of society
- Provides a means of resolving conflict

Education
- Prepares society members to contribute to the society in specified roles
- Teaches skills necessary to function within the society

Economics
- Produces and distributes goods needed by society members
- Provides services necessary to the society

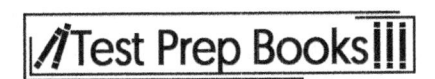

Social Change and Community Development Theories

Community development theory focuses on oppressed people who are in the process of overcoming social problems that were imposed upon them by external forces. In the process of community development, members of a community learn how to improve that community and gain control of their local environment. **Community-level change** brings people together and demonstrates the power of solidarity. This theory also acknowledges the reality that many problems are at the social, rather than individual, level. An implication of the theory is that therapy addresses only the symptoms of a problem and not the underlying causes.

The Influence of Social Context on Behavior

There are many ways in which a social context can influence individual behavior, either positively or negatively. Social psychology looks at the person-environment interaction and explores the many ways the social setting influences a person's attitudes and actions.

Attitudes toward, and influenced by, those around play a major role in a person's behaviors. **Attribution theory** has to do with how one views the behavior of others, whether attributing their behaviors to disposition or situation. If one wrongly attributes someone's negative action to their disposition—the **fundamental attribution error**—then one may think more negatively about others than is deserved.

The concept of **conformity**—the tendency for a person to conform personal behaviors to the behaviors of those around them—helps explain everything from style trends to mass genocide. **Solomon Asch** performed a study that showed that people tend to conform to the people around them, even if it means giving an answer they know is false. The phenomenon of conformity stems from the idea that people act in a way to get approval from others and to avoid disapproval, called **normative social influence**. Another impact of the social sphere that people live in is **deindividuation**, in which a person loses a sense of personal responsibility or individualism. This may happen in crowds at a concert or sports event, or a riot, leading people to behave in ways they would not normally behave if they did not feel anonymous and emotionally charged by the social setting.

People tend to automatically form groups, often developing the in-group and out-group concepts. The *in-group* consists of those who are part of the group, who share its identity and unifying characteristics. The **out-group** consists of those outside the group, particularly those who may be in opposition or share opposite beliefs to those in the in-group. This in-group and out-group concept may lead to patriotism or working together towards a common goal, but it may also lead to prejudice and discrimination. Groups also tend to engage in *group think*, where no one is willing to share an opinion contrary to the group, or **group polarization**, in which people in the group become stronger and stronger in their opinions as they spend time with others who have similar beliefs.

Some other key concepts related to the effects of social context on behavior are social loafing and social facilitation. **Social loafing** happens in a context of shared responsibility for a task. In this case, there is a tendency for some people to abdicate responsibility, assuming that others will fulfill the obligations of the work. **Social facilitation**, on the other hand, is when having an audience inspires people to perform tasks they do well even better. Alternatively, it can also cause them to do worse in tasks they find more difficult or challenging.

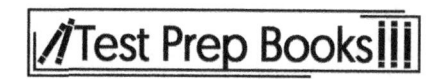

Leadership

Quality leadership skills are essential to any organization, and thus, leadership training is typically provided to mid and upper management. Signs of effective leadership skills are strategic thinking, solving problems as they come, and managing time in the most financially responsible manner. While these skills are essential, there are also more human characteristics that must be mentioned. A successful leader must have the ability to: build confidence within their team or organization, obtain the trust of others, inspire others, and engender a sense of pride and purpose within their company.

Management and Leadership Development

Management and leadership development is a critical component for organizations to invest in. For this practice to be effective, managers must exercise their capacities to establish objectives and means of attainment. Concurrently, management and leadership development is designed to equip the workforce with the requisite tools and skills to compete in a functional organization. The primary purpose of management and leadership development is to provide a holistic approach for individuals, managers, and leadership. Individuals are able to increase their skills and knowledge working within an organizational apparatus. Managers find more efficient ways to execute predetermined objectives. Leaders improve their ability in a decision-making process that incorporates creative input from the organization's members and accomplishes mutually shared goals.

Motivational Strategies

Foreign Service Officers (FSOs) are motivated individuals driven to serve others. Just like in any other leadership position, FSOs possess the ability to provide emotional support and are aware of strategies dealing with effective communication and supporting team members. The following sections contain ideas on how to motivate others in the workplace.

Empowerment

Empowering others is a valuable tool for the FSO to learn. To empower someone else means having the ability to inspire in the other person a sense of control and efficacy over their own life and work. Empowerment not only means inspiring someone, but also advocating for them, their ideas, and their career. Empowerment is a key tool for an effective leader as well as an effective team.

Empowerment should begin with a trustworthy relationship between a manager and employee or a team member and their peers. To gain trust, an individual must be trustworthy, so it's important for an FSO to apply the principle of honesty in everything they do. Developing trust among team members also means allowing them to have the opportunity to make their own decisions without correcting them or trying to control the process or outcome. Even if mistakes are made, it's important for the other person to make the mistakes themselves (if the mistake is not harmful to others) and to let the process happen organically. Trust will commence out of giving the other person total freedom to do their best work.

Communication

One characteristic of people who succeed in motivating others is effective communication. Effective communication among team members and between a manager and employee must be easy and accessible in order for the job to get done correctly. If coworkers or employees are unclear or confused about their job duties, frustration or errors occur as a result. One helpful tip is that if one is unsure whether someone knows how to do something or not, assume that they don't. Withholding valuable information will hinder growth within employees and the organization.

Management Principles, Psychology, and Human Behavior

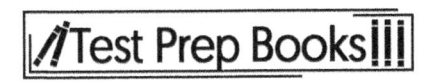

Setting boundaries is an important part of communication; everyone should be clear on what their own role is in relation to everyone else's, as well as what's expected of them. Effective communication will aid in the organization's health as a whole as well as the health of its employees. Good communication is a necessity for helping with diversity within a workplace as well. It's important for us to learn about cultures other than our own and find out if or how their communication is different from our own. Paying attention to cultural differences is key to effective communication. If our listeners or audience is turned off by the way we are communicating, we must be willing to change our methods.

Rewards Systems

Rewards systems are a way to encourage employees and let them know that they are valued within the company. Rewards can come in the form of external rewards, which are things like bonuses, paid time off, or a raise, while internal rewards are the satisfaction that employees get from doing their jobs. Internal rewards are different from external rewards in that internal rewards can only come from the person experiencing joy in their work and cannot come from external validation.

It's also important to remember what kinds of rewards are appropriate. Rewards should go beyond satisfying the basic needs of employees. It may also help to look to other successful organizations to see what kinds of rewards they offer their employees, and how their employees value these rewards. Rewards should be fair for all employees involved based on their skill and position, and they should also be among a wide range of benefits: money, time, and flexibility are all reward-worthy notions that can be dispersed among employees who have earned them.

Equal Employment Practices

Equal employment practices (EEP) are ways employers and human resource administrators can ensure best practices are put to use when hiring, training, and retaining employees. Equal employment opportunity was first put into place to prevent discrimination against race or color. Furthering equal employment opportunity was the Executive Order 11246 signed by Lyndon B. Johnson in order to prohibit discrimination against race, sex, creed, religion, color, or national origin. More protected classes have been added to the order, including age and Americans with disabilities, among others.

The U.S. government has an Equal Opportunity Commission website with a list on how to prevent discrimination. On the site, it mentions that human resource managers should train employees on EEO laws, encourage an inclusive culture, and foster open communication in order to prevent and manage disputes. They also promote hiring workers from a diverse pool of applicants and that the criteria in selecting an employee should not disproportionately exclude a certain race, unless "the criteria are valid predictors of successful job performance and meet the employer's business needs." All employees should have equal access to workplace networks, and compensation practices should be monitored by the employers to ensure fair ratings.

Computers and the internet

Word Processing

For companies that work with creating or manipulating documents or any other text, word processing is an essential application to have available. Word processing software provides a medium to write text and format that text with different fonts, colors, sizes, margins, page breaks, section headers, formulas, and more. There are also features like spell-check, which automatically proofs spelling as well as errors at the sentence level. Note that spell check will even pick up awkward syntax. Microsoft Word™ processors often come with built-in thesauruses as well as their own collection of images and shapes for the user to insert into the document if they wish. Among other important features, some word processor applications are able to create tables, charts, and graphs for those who need visual support in their documents. There are many kinds of word processing software. The best-known word processing software is Microsoft Word, but here is a list of some other word processing software:

- Microsoft Word™
- Google Docs™
- Pages (for Mac) ™
- WordPerfect™
- OpenOffice™
- AbiWord™
- WordPad™
- WordStar™
- Apache Open Office™

Databases

A **database** is a collection of data that is organized inside a computer. A database management system (DBMS) is the system required in order to view and manage data. Databases are used quite frequently in the modern world, and perhaps without us even realizing it. When we go to the doctor, chances are all of our information will be stored in their database system so that they can access information already recorded from us. The same situation happens in banks, pharmacies, or universities—we will find that our information is stored inside a large database for easy access through text or numbers.

Social media also has databases that are for extremely large systems—Facebook™, Twitter™, Google™, and Amazon™ use NOSQL systems, storage systems known as "big data." These large databases are needed in order to hold the capacity of information that is coming through them—posts, pictures, texts, and videos from millions of users are all part of this system. These databases are fairly new technology designed specifically for the mass amounts of data we've begun to accumulate as a technological society. We also, as a society, have the option to participate in various systems of cloud storage, which are database programs designed by companies like Google™ or Apple™ to hold our personal information online. Cloud storage can hold photos, videos, music, and documents, and are usually accessible through applications as long as the user has an internet connection.

Computers and the internet

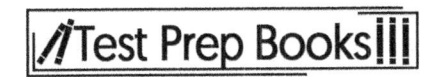

Spreadsheets

Spreadsheets are tabular documents that contain columns and rows, which are adjustable to the number of columns and rows suitable for the user's purposes. Spreadsheets contain cells created by the intersections of columns and rows that are capable of holding text or numbers. Some cells, if formatted properly, can even be the result of calculations from cells above or beside it. Spreadsheets are used in producing graphs and charts, making budgets, and for sorting through data. It can also act as an inventory for a small business or to keep track of storage information for other purposes. The most popular spreadsheet currently in use is Microsoft Excel™, followed closely by Open Office™ and Google Documents™.

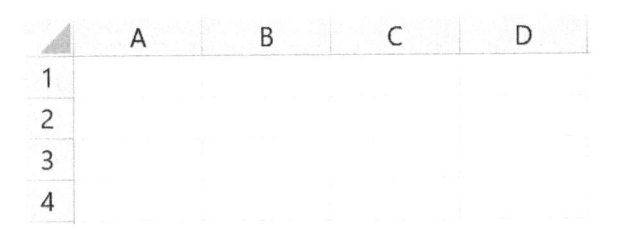

	A	B	C	D
1				
2				
3				
4				

Email and the internet

Email

Known as **electronic mail**, "email" is one of the fastest and most efficient ways to communicate electronically in the twenty-first century. Having sufficient knowledge of email is crucial in today's working atmosphere. It's important for communication, and it's also imperative that an email is written with all the following things kept in mind:

Tone

Every distinct piece of writing has its own tone; whether serious or funny, tragic or happy, the author usually creates a tone for their text with specific word and syntax choices. Within an email, it's important to identify the audience before getting started on any kind of text. Is your audience a busy executive? Are they a government official? A coworker? A friend? Audience is important to know when determining what kind of tone to use for your electronic communication. Let's look at the following emails below written to a government official and gauge which one is the better email to send.

Email 1:

> Dear Mr. Badeaux,
>
> Thank you for allowing me to come in tomorrow evening to present my proposal to you about clean water in the Ichetucknee River. This proposal is very important to us over here at Clean Water International, and we hope we are able to answer any questions you may have regarding the subject. Please let us know if you need anything from us before we arrive at your place of operation tomorrow. Looking forward to seeing you then.
>
>
> Best Regards,
>
> Clean Water International

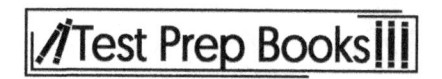

Email 2:

Hey Mr. Badeaux,

We're going to come in tomorrow to see y'all over there about the proposal. Don't forget about us. We can't wait to talk to you and hear what you have to say regarding our proposal to you! We're going to need about two hours of your time. Thanks so much.

Clean Water International

Let's look at the two emails closely. All emails should begin with a greeting. The first greeting, "Dear," is more appropriate for the audience, who is probably a busy executive. "Hey" is more of an informal tone used towards a friend or acquaintance. Next, it's always considered good form to start by thanking the recipient for their time, especially since our audience is someone who will be giving their time to Clean Water International by listening to one of their proposals. The first email thanks Mr. Badeaux, but the second email skips this part.

Also, notice that the second email uses "y'all," which is appropriate for an informal conversation, but not for a formal business transaction. Additionally, the first email uses "serving" language, asking what they can do to serve the other person rather than what the other person can do for them. The second email states "We can't wait to hear...what you have to say regarding our proposal" and "We're going to need..." which is more of a demanding tone rather than an attitude of service. When identifying your audience, tone is one of the most important aspects of written communication to ensure a positive reception from your audience.

Internet

The **internet** is a system designed to connect computers across an interconnected web of networks. The idea of an internet began in the 1960s, but a modern use of connected networks for commercial purposes did not come into fruition until the 1990s. Today, the internet infiltrates almost every aspect of modern existence. We are connected on a global scale with smart phones, TVs, cable, computers, and cars.

Social media is a modern phenomenon that allows people to stay connected with their family and friends. Through social media sites like Facebook™ and Twitter™, users can follow anyone they choose depending on their personal preference. For example, many people follow political posts on Facebook™ or Twitter™ to get caught up on the latest news. Some people follow their favorite celebrities or sites with funny animal videos that are posted daily. On social media, there is something for everyone. Social media not only allows people to stay connected, but also gives a platform to those who are struggling for independence and have no way else to reach a global audience. This example can be seen in the Arab Spring beginning in 2010, where the revolutionaries used social media to gain awareness, organize groups, and call for protests through Facebook™ and Twitter™.

The internet is also used as hub for research and academia. Sites like Jstor™ and Europeana™, among others, are digital library collections that have stored thousands of books and articles for the purpose of preserving texts digitally. Google Scholar™ is also a useful tool for researchers because it provides a way to search through many library databases at the same time using specific keywords or dates. Other sites list literary or scientific text that is now in the public domain, such as *Public Domain Review* and *Project*

Computers and the internet

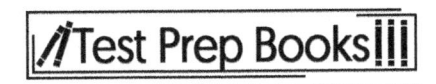

Gutenberg. Many libraries are converting to digital databases as a way to preserve digital texts as well as gain easy access to information through key words and phrases.

FSOT Oral Assessment (FSOA)

Depending on the anticipated hiring needs, the Department of State invites a variable number of qualified candidates who have passed the FSOT to take the Oral Assessment (FSOA). This raw number, as well as the percentage, fluctuates over time based on the current and projected open positions and hiring targets at the Department of State. It should be noted that the selection process is highly competitive and even those candidates with excellent qualifications may not receive invitations or may need to repeat the process when more positions become available.

Candidates who receive an Oral Assessment invitation will travel to Washington, DC, or potentially San Francisco to test, depending on the Department of State's budget and schedule for a given year. Oral Assessments occur twice annually. It is recommended that candidates make travel and lodging plans as soon as their FSOA is scheduled and confirmed. Additionally, candidates requiring "Reasonable Accommodations" at the test center for FSOA administration should email ReasonableAccommodations@state.gov as soon as their testing appointment is confirmed to request the appropriate provisions.

The following tips can help when making travel arrangements:

- Plan to arrive at least a day or two early, particularly if traveling across time zones. The FSOA can be stressful and demanding, so being well rested can not only make the experience more manageable for candidates, but also help them feel sharper during test day.

- Schedule travel with a time cushion for unanticipated delays and inevitable travel challenges. Doing so can help prevent a candidate from facing last minute scrambling, or worse, missing the testing appointment. Delayed flights, traffic jams, difficulty navigating public transportation, and other mishaps are frequent issues during any travel. Planning what feels like an excessive amount of time for each step of the travel logistics can ensure these obstacles are navigated without compromising timeliness to the testing appointment.

- The test day often ends as late as 7:00pm local time, so candidates should make return travel arrangements accordingly.

- Pack professional attire. Essentially, the FSOA is a job interview and candidates need to dress as such. Footwear should be neat, but comfortable.

- Arrive to the assessment center early. Candidates are required to arrive by 6:45am on their scheduled test day, but arriving at least 30 minutes prior to that is recommended. Late arrivals are not accepted, and candidates will be turned away. Not all candidates follow the same schedule on test day, which is a tightly organized affair with many moving parts to accommodate all candidates and components of the FSOA. As such, it is imperative that candidates follow their own test day schedule and not rely on fellow test takers for the next set of directions or timetable.

- Get your bearings. The address of the assessment center in Washington, DC is 1800 G Street, NW, which is at the intersection of 18th and G Street. The address of the testing center in San Francisco is revealed to candidates scheduled there approximately 30 days

FSOT Oral Assessment (FSOA)

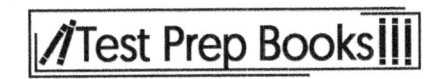

before their scheduled FSOA. It is wise to rehearse commuting to the assessment center the day before test day so that any difficulties finding the site are encountered and eliminated prior to the rushed morning of the test.

- Ensure all of the required documents, which are listed on Department of State's website under downloads, are packed for travel and for test day. To facilitate the process of medical clearance, overseas candidates who are traveling with family members should have an available list of the dates of birth and Social Security numbers of those in their party.

- Pack and bring snacks and drinks for test day. Sandwiches, snacks, and nonalcoholic beverages from outside are permitted and a 45-minute lunch break is built into the test day schedule. Water is available at the test center along with a secure area for coats, bags, and personal belongings. It should be noted that some test takers will have gaps of time between modules of the FSOA, so reading or other quiet activities are usually permitted and can help pass the time.

The Dimensions Measured by the Oral Assessment

The different exercises that comprise the FSOA are designed to measure the candidate's aptitude in the following 13 dimensions:

1. Composure: maintaining self-control and poise during challenging or stressful situations, and being flexible and adaptable to changes and unforeseen circumstances.

2. Cultural Adaptability: respecting and working amicably with those of different races, cultures, beliefs, economic status, value systems, etc.

3. Experience and Motivation: effectively applying previously obtained knowledge and skills and demonstrating unwavering motivation to work in the Foreign Service.

4. Information Integration and Analysis: absorbing and retaining complex information presented in different formats, remembering details unaided by notes, drawing sound conclusions, and critically analyzing and using resources.

5. Initiative and Leadership: identifying and taking responsibility for needed tasks, following through on work until completion, influencing and motivating others positively, etc.

6. Judgment: exercising sound decisions that are appropriate, fair, and reasonable, and prioritizing competing needs and responsibilities in a rational way.

7. Objectivity and Integrity: conducting oneself in an honest, fair, and unbiased manner.

8. Oral Communication: speaking eloquently, precisely, and intelligently using language that is grammatically correct, appropriate for the situation, persuasive, and accurate.

9. Planning and Organizing: effectively prioritizing demands in a way that makes logical sense in terms of urgency, resources, time, and ability, and keeping track of responsibilities, details, data, etc.

10. Quantitative Analysis: efficiently and correctly analyzing and manipulating quantitative data.

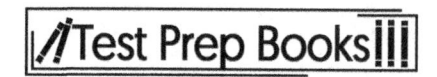

11. Resourcefulness: devising innovative solutions and demonstrating flexibility and adaptability when changes occur or crises arise.

12. Working with Others: communicating and collaborating with others in an efficient, productive, and respectful manner using appropriate verbal and nonverbal language.

13. Written Communication: adhering to the conventions of standard English language in writing that is clear, precise, professional, effective, and produced efficiently.

Each candidate's aptitude in these thirteen dimensions are assessed by four Foreign Service Officers drawn from different career tracks, roles, and geographic areas. The assessments and situations that candidates undergo are designed to demonstrate their performance in the various dimensions. The evaluators are specially trained on objectively conducting and scoring performance assessments.

A candidate's performance is evaluated against established standards rather than the other candidates undergoing the same assessments. In this way, the FSOA is not a direct competition between candidates for the "best" performance. The Department of State has an established cutoff or minimum score that candidates must obtain to move forward in the application process. Theoretically, on any given test day, all or none of the candidates might achieve that score and move forward.

There are three distinct activities that comprise the Oral Assessment. Prior to participating in any of the activities, each candidate must sign a Non-Disclosure Agreement.

1. The Group Exercise

There are four phases that together comprise the Group Exercise.

Preparation Phase
In the first exercise encountered on test day, groups of three to six candidates come together to form an Embassy task force. The goal of the task force is to decide how to allocate different resources to competing projects occurring in their assigned host country. Candidates are given 30 minutes to independently read a packet containing information about the task force prior to beginning the exercise. The packet contains common background materials that all members receive, as well five pages detailing candidate-specific information. During this preparation phase, candidates are monitored in their group rooms to ensure that they work alone; communication with others is not permitted. The common materials that all candidates receive include:

- General instructions

- A memo written from the point of view of one of the fictitious countries' senior U.S. Embassy officials that appoints the candidate to a task force charged with evaluating proposals for allocations of scarce resources

- The United States' objectives and plans

- Background information and a map of the host country

- Lists of the important and/or relevant government officials in the U.S. Embassy of the host country

FSOT Oral Assessment (FSOA)

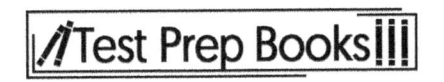

In addition, each candidate receives five pages of candidate-specific information, which details a specific project that he or she will present and advocate for.

Presentation Phase

After the 30-minute preparation phase, four BEX assessors, who still know nothing about the candidates, enter the group room and sit in the corners to observe. The candidates are briefed on the ground rules by the head assessor and then given the go-ahead to begin presenting their individual projects in a group-determined, unassigned order. It is important for candidates to listen carefully to all the instructions. Each candidate must present all of the relevant aspects (such as the necessary resources and U.S. interests) of their individual project to the other group members in no more than six minutes. It is wise for candidates to leave time at the end of each presentation for the presenting candidate to solicit questions from the others.

Discussion Phase

Once all members have presented their individual projects, the head assessor signals the start of the discussion phase and provides additional instructions pertinent to the tasks to accomplish. The discussion phases lasts 20-25 minutes, depending on the number of members in the group. During this time, candidates have two goals: to advocate for their assigned project and to help the group reach a consensus on how they recommend the Ambassador allocate the limited resources amongst the various vying projects. Assessors will be observing the manner in which each candidate describes and advocates for their projects, works with others, communicates, and helps lead group members to an agreed upon proposal for the Ambassador.

Tips and notable rules for the discussion phase are as follows:

- The limited resource is not necessarily money, so "funding" a project is not always the most appropriate vernacular for candidates to use while advocating for their project or competing ones.

- It is forbidden for candidates to alter the project they were assigned in any way, nor may they make up additional information besides what was given. Likewise, candidates cannot create their own project to use in lieu of the one they were given, even if they dislike their assigned one.

- Candidates are not allowed to strengthen their arguments or provide "evidence" with real life facts or situations.

- After listening to all presentations and considering the positive and negative aspects of each member's project, a candidate may opt to relinquish their project in favor of another.

- Candidates may take notes, but they cannot use the notes during the subsequent briefing stage.

The Ambassador's Briefing

After the discussion phase, each candidate must meet privately with two assessors and explain the group's consensus in three to four minutes. The time for candidates to prepare for this is limited, so it is important that candidates hone their briefing skills and fully understand the results of the group's deliberations and rationale. One assessor serves as the Ambassador and asks follow-up questions that the candidate must address after their briefing.

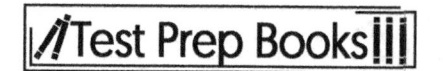

The four phases of the group exercise are designed to demonstrate and evaluate the following dimensions: composure, planning and organizing, objectivity and integrity, integration and analysis, working with others, initiative and leadership, oral communication, and judgment. It is critical that candidates are active participants in all phases so that the assessors can have a means on which to evaluate them. The most successful candidates display behaviors, explanations, and motivations that are consistent with the exercise's objective, which is to assist the Ambassador's decision on how to best apportion the U.S. government's limited resources among different deserving projects. They also demonstrate strong leadership skills by inciting motivation in all group members to bring their best ideas, negotiation skills, and diplomacy and helping the group reach a consensus in a timely fashion. Strong candidates remain calm and composed when others disagree with their ideas and help diffuse arguments and reconcile differences in the group, bridging members together rather than allowing factions to form. Effective candidates can advocate for their project, but integrate the needs and merits of the other projects and explain their rationale clearly and logically. They may suggest creative solutions, unique ideas, and demonstrate listening and negotiating skills.

2. The Structured Interview

For the Structured Interview portion of the FSOA, candidates meet individually with two assessors. Unlike in the Group Exercise where assessors have no background information on the candidates they are observing, the assessors review portions of each candidate's application, preferred career track, and Statement of Interest prior to the interview. However, they do not read the personal narratives. Assessors will pose questions to the candidate they are interviewing about their experience, background, and interest in becoming a Foreign Service Officer.

The following tips and pointers can assist candidates in having a successful Structured Interview:

- Should it directly apply to an answer solicited by the assessors, candidates can draw upon experiences and motivations cited in their personal narratives since the assessors have not reviewed this material prior to the interview.

- It is important that candidates respond to the specific questions they are asked instead of simply providing a response that better highlights their qualifications or motivations.

- The assessors are trained to conduct the interviews in a completely neutral manner, without providing verbal or non-verbal feedback regarding a candidate's performance. This lack of emotional expression can shake a candidate's confidence should he or she not be prepared for such a stoic interaction. Candidates should not worry that they are underwhelming or disappointing the assessors; assessors intentionally maintain this neutrality throughout all interviews.

- Candidates should expect to be interrupted, cut short, or even seemingly ignored while assessors shuffle papers or otherwise seem unimpressed. Again, these actions do not signal positive or negative reactions, but rather that the assessors likely feel they have acquired all they need about a given subject from the candidate's responses. Because there is limited time for the Structured Interview and three components to get through, it behooves the assessors (and certainly the candidate) to move on as soon as possible to ensure there is sufficient time to get through all of the questions and components.

FSOT Oral Assessment (FSOA)

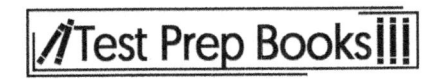

The Structured Interview lasts about one hour and is comprised of three distinct portions.

1. Experience and Motivation Interview: questions will address a candidate's personality, education and work experience, understanding of the Foreign Service and reasons for applying, specific applicable skills and traits, and responses to previous opportunities and setbacks. The questions are designed to help assessors determine the candidate's potential to be a successful Foreign Service Officer, particularly in their selected career track. The following tips can help candidates in this module of the Structured Interview:

   - Providing persuasive, succinct, and direct answers allows candidates to showcase their qualifications in an efficient manner so that there is ample time for all questions.

   - Candidates should ensure that they are well-versed in general information regarding the Foreign Service, their desired career track, and the attributes and experience that would be helpful for FSOs before participating in the interview.

   - As long as it is appropriate for a given question, it is better for candidates to flesh out their answers with a justification or rationale (the "why" or "how") rather than just give the "what" response. For example, instead of just describing an experience interning at the United Nations Headquarters in New York City, the candidate should comment on what was learned and how the opportunity uniquely prepares themselves or is indicative for success as a Foreign Service Officer.

   - Candidates should expect to be interrupted to move forward, or to provide clarification or details during responses.

   - Candidates should practice and determine stories and scenarios from their past that demonstrates each of the 13 dimensions so that they can easily pull these out during their responses.

2. Hypothetical Scenarios: a series of hypothetical, though realistic, scenarios posed that are intended to assess the candidate's situational judgment as it pertains to commonly encountered situations as a Foreign Service Officer. Assessors provide the candidate with a short reading that gives background information on the hypothetical situation such as the candidate's Embassy role in the country in the scenario and facts about that country. The following tips can help candidates in this module of the Structured Interview:

   - Candidates will not necessarily receive hypothetical situations and questions that pertain to their selected career track. It is primarily the candidate's judgment and sensibility of their proposed solutions that are assessed rather than their specific knowledge of Embassy operations or specific governmental regulations.

   - The hypothetical scenario module requires candidates to demonstrate their critical thinking skills, creativity and ingenuity, decision-making under time- and pressure-constraints, flexibility and ability in considering alternative approaches, and capacity to explain their thinking effectively and maturely. Candidates should answer the questions associated with the scenarios as thoroughly as possible, addressing both the short- and long-term ramifications of their proposed ideas.

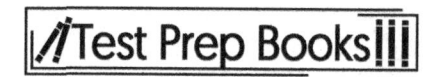

- Candidates should aim to be clear and complete, by addressing the main points quickly before being cut off by an assessor. They should still be able to verbalize their rationale, assumptions, train of thought and alternatives they considered.

- When devising a solution, candidates should consider their assigned fictitious position in the Embassy and use this information to inform their actions. For example, they should exercise their level authority to the fullest, and refrain from pawning the task onto someone else, unless it exceeds their "role's" power or expertise.

- Composure, Cultural Adaptability, Judgment, Information Integration and Analysis, Initiation and Leadership, Objectivity and Integrity, Planning and Organizing, Resourcefulness, and Working with Others are the dimensions scored during this module.

3. Past Behavior Interview: candidates receive a sheet of questions pertaining to the various dimensions this module evaluates. The sheet has two questions per dimension, and candidates have five minutes to review the options, select one question per dimension, and formulate their responses. A research-informed job analysis helped determine the attributes that successful Foreign Service Officers embody. These serve as the dimensions addressed in the questions, for questions designed to elicit examples from the candidates' own experiences in specific areas. The questions for each dimension will focus on specific examples from the candidates' past experiences. The following tips can help candidates in this module of the Structured Interview:

- Candidates should give concrete examples that directly relate to the intended dimension. Scores for responses that do not explicitly answer the posed question are penalized.

- Candidates should select examples from their past experiences that best highlight their positive qualities in the attribute and refrain from citing examples that showcase "failures" or weaknesses.

- This module is not the time to be modest. Even if discussing a group project or achievement, candidates should assert their valuable contributions and instrumental role in facilitating the success of the project.

- Composure, Cultural Adaptability, Objectivity and Integrity, Oral Communication, Planning and Organizing, Initiative and Leadership, and Working with Others are the dimensions evaluated in this module.

3. Case Management Exercise

The Case Management Exercises last 90 minutes and is designed to assess writing and management skills. Assessors provide the candidate with a memo listing the necessary tasks for the assignment. It also contains a summary of the primary problem and ongoing issues, email correspondences between employees describing their thoughts about the issues, a staff performance review, an organizational chart, and applicable rules and ordinances. Calculations with the data are required and must be completed manually on paper or mentally; calculators are prohibited. Candidates must read and analyze the provided information, and then prepare a written memo in response that takes into account the quantitative and qualitative data provided to offer sound recommendations.

FSOT Oral Assessment (FSOA)

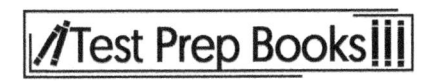

Most candidates consider the Case Management Exercise to be the most difficult portion of the FSOA. It requires quick reading, analytical skills, critical considerations, an understanding of what might be in the best interest for the United States, and persuasive writing all under a time crunch. Candidates often receive a binder chocked full of material to review and they must consider the merit and relevancy of the information provided. The most successful candidates keep the primary goal in mind—providing a wise recommendation that prioritized the United States' best interests. Of the mountain of provided materials, those that are factual should usually take precedence over subjective sources. Candidates should ensure that their written responses justify their decisions, explain their rationale, and end with a strong, persuasive summary.

It is recommended that candidates budget 10-15 minutes for reviewing, revising, and editing their work after writing before the 90 minutes has elapsed. Assessors are expecting candidates to demonstrate skilled data analysis, as well as high-quality writing that adheres to the conventions of the English language, is clear, and is of a certain level of professionalism.

Information Integration and Analysis, Judgment, Objectivity and Integrity, Written Communication and Quantitative Skills, and Working with Others are the dimensions measured in the Case Management exercise.

Final Tips for Overall Success

In addition to the tips and guidance provided in the previous section, the following advice can be applied in general for a successful FSOA administration:

- Spend time reviewing the 13 dimensions. While the terms are commonly used in daily life, the specific meaning and qualities ascribed to the title for each dimension is somewhat unique. Assessors are evaluating candidates on these dimensions, so a fluent and comprehensive understanding, rather than just familiarity, is a crucial strategy for optimizing one's score.

- Review the different career tracks offered in the Foreign Service. Although candidates will select the track that interests them most, for the Hypothetical Situations module, knowledge of the offered tracks and the responsibilities of the roles under those tracks can help candidates speak from a more informed position and thus craft stronger responses.

- Practice speaking and writing. It may seem obvious that practicing speaking for an oral assessment is important, but a surprisingly low percentage of FSOA candidates actually dedicate some of their study and preparation time explicitly to this work. Candidates must be able to converse fluently, confidently, and intelligently under high pressure situations with minimal time to prepare or think. It is critical that they get right to the point by listening carefully to the question posed and responding in a direct and concise manner. Several of the modules require argumentative and persuasive responses, which is a skill that takes practice and time to hone. Additionally, the need to be able to communicate effectively in writing is equally important, especially in the Case Management Exercise. Successful candidates practice their writing, revising, and editing skills and review the important tenants of standard English grammar, spelling, and writing.

- Don't allow other candidates to rattle you. It's human nature to compare oneself to others, especially in situations where they are being evaluated. However, it is important for candidates to remember that the FSOA is not an adversarial process. Each candidate merely needs to achieve the minimum passing score and candidates are not scored relative to one another. It is likely that on any given test day, one or more candidates has previously taken the FSOA and is retesting. He or she may appear more practiced and calm. Other candidates may come across as more experienced either in the testing process itself or in terms of their education and background. It behooves the candidates to stay within themselves and refrain from comparisons as this often increases anxiety and feelings of inferiority, shakes confidence, and ultimately negatively impacts the candidate. The Oral Assessment is not a direct competition; candidates should focus on themselves and doing their personal best.

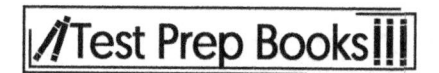

- During the group exercise, offer to go first when sharing individual projects. This demonstrates leadership, courage, and confidence. However, it should be noted that the person who goes first sets the standard for the day. Although candidates are not scored relative to one another, the person who goes first misses out on the opportunity to listen to their colleagues present and consider strengths, weaknesses, the most relevant information, and forgotten omissions of their explanation. These drawbacks of presenting first can be minimized by ample practice.

- Respect and abide by the rules and directions. If the Case Management Exercise states that candidates cannot exceed two pages in their response, do *not* exceed two pages, even by one word, as this can cause even an otherwise outstanding response to earn zero points. Similarly, if instructed to provide a briefing in two to three minutes, talk for at least two, but no more than three, minutes. Part of the assessment process is simply evaluating whether candidates can follow explicit directions.

- Stay informed. Many of the modules and questions (particularly in the Case Management Exercise and Hypothetical Situations) may address current or common Embassy issues. Even though hypothetical, candidates who can speak knowledgeably about these types of current affairs come across as dedicated, smart, and suited for work as a Foreign Service Officer.

- Present yourself warmly and expressively, even though the assessors will be flat. As mentioned, assessors are instructed to remain neutral and expressionless. Particularly during the Structured Interview, this can cause candidates to speak in monotone and wear blank facial expressions as there is no energy return from the other side of the conversation. However, the motivation, passion, commitment, and personality of candidates will fail to be conveyed if they fall prey to this tendency.

- Appear confident even if you are nervous. Sit up straight, smile, make eye contact, give assessors your undivided attention when they are speaking, and otherwise stay as engaged, professional, and poised as possible.

Scoring

While candidates participate in each module of the Oral Assessment, the assessors carefully observe and take copious notes on their performance. Upon completion of each module, the assessors personally enter the score they've assigned to a candidate into the computer. A candidate's overall score is found by taking the average of the individual scores. The overall score ranges from a low of 1 to a high of 7. Each of the three distinct exercises that comprise the Oral Assessment contribute equally to the overall

FSOT Oral Assessment (FSOA)

total score. A minimum score of 5.25 is needed for a candidate to move forward in the application process.

Practice Test #1

Job Knowledge

1. Which political concept describes a ruling body's ability to influence the actions, behaviors, or attitudes of a person or community?
    a. Authority
    b. Sovereignty
    c. Power
    d. Legitimacy

2. What were the consequences of the Spanish-American War?
    a. The U.S. acquired colonies in the Caribbean and Pacific oceans.
    b. The U.S. acquired large swaths of territory in the Southwestern United States.
    c. It led to the formation of the League of Nations.
    d. It ended the Great Depression.

3. Which political theorist considered violence necessary in order for a ruler to maintain political power and stability?
    a. John Locke
    b. Jean-Jacques Rousseau
    c. Karl Marx
    d. Niccolo Machiavelli

4. What consequences did the Great Migration have?
    a. It led to conflict with Native Americans in the West in the 1800s.
    b. It led to increased racial tension in the North in the early 1900s.
    c. It led to increased conflict with Mexican immigrants in the 1900s.
    d. It led to increased conflict with Irish and German immigrants in the 1800s.

5. Which political orientation emphasizes maintaining traditions and stability over progress and change?
    a. Socialism
    b. Liberalism
    c. Conservatism
    d. Libertarianism

6. All EXCEPT which of the following are true of an area with an extremely high population density?
    a. Competition for resources is intense
    b. Greater strain on public services exists
    c. More people live in rural areas
    d. More people live in urban areas

Practice Test #1 | Job Knowledge

7. Which political orientation emphasizes a strong central government and promotes violence as a means of suppressing dissent?
    a. Communism
    b. Socialism
    c. Nationalism
    d. Fascism

8. What determines the exchange rate in a "floating" or "flexible" exchange?
    a. The government
    b. Taxes
    c. The Federal Reserve
    d. The market

9. Under Federalism, which is considered a concurrent power held by both the states and the federal government?
    a. Hold elections
    b. Regulate immigration
    c. Expand the territories of a state
    d. Pass and enforce laws

10. Two cards are drawn from a shuffled deck of 52 cards. What's the probability that both cards are kings if the first card isn't replaced after it's drawn?
    a. $\frac{1}{169}$
    b. $\frac{1}{221}$
    c. $\frac{1}{13}$
    d. $\frac{4}{13}$

11. Which part of the legislative process differs in the House and the Senate?
    a. Who may introduce the bill
    b. How debates about a bill are conducted
    c. Who may veto the bill
    d. What wording the bill contains

12. Which of the following statements best describes the relationship, if any, between the revolutions in America and France?
    a. The French Revolution inspired the American Revolution.
    b. The American Revolution inspired the French Revolution.
    c. They both occurred simultaneously.
    d. There was no connection between the French and American revolutions.

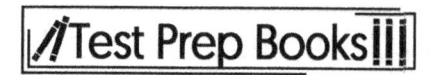

13. Which political party was founded to advocate for the abolition of slavery?
    a. Constitutional Union
    b. Southern Democrat
    c. Republican
    d. Libertarian

14. What is one advantage that the North had over the South during the Civil War?
    a. The North was defending their homes from damage.
    b. The North had free labor at home.
    c. The North had a larger navy.
    d. The North had more experienced military leaders.

15. Which of the following is NOT a power of the mass media?
    a. Ability to shape public opinion
    b. Ability to regulate communications
    c. Ability to influence the importance of events in society
    d. Ability to determine the context in which to report events

16. Which of the following could be considered a pull factor for a particular area?
    a. High rates of unemployment
    b. Low GDP
    c. Educational opportunity
    d. High population density

17. Which form of government most limits the civil liberties of the people?
    a. Authoritarianism
    b. Communism
    c. Socialism
    d. Federal monarchy

18. Which of the following correctly lists the factors of production?
    a. Land, labor, material, entrepreneurship
    b. Land, labor, capital, equity
    c. Land, a building, capital, labor
    d. Land, labor, capital, entrepreneurship

19. The U.S. foreign policy currently includes all but which of the following goals?
    a. Prevent the spread of Communism
    b. Solve international problems
    c. Promote global cooperation
    d. Maintain national security

20. For a group of 20 men, the median weight is 180 pounds and the range is 30 pounds. If each man gains 10 pounds, which of the following would be true?
    a. The median weight will increase, and the range will remain the same.
    b. The median weight and range will both remain the same.
    c. The median weight will stay the same, and the range will increase.
    d. The median weight and range will both increase.

21. Which practice of international relations most limits the sovereignty of a state?
    a. Diplomacy
    b. Foreign aid
    c. Treaty
    d. Cooperation

22. Which form of economic exchange allowed the Chinese to maintain political control over their empire?
    a. Potlatches
    b. Tribute
    c. Bartering
    d. All of the above

23. Which of the following best describes a principle of Realism in international relations?
    a. It supports international cooperation for mutual benefit.
    b. It seeks to establish international organizations and values the contributions of nongovernmental organizations.
    c. All states are interested in advancing their self-interests by expanding their power.
    d. It seeks to reduce the net conflict in the world.

24. What did Radical Republicans hope to accomplish during Reconstruction?
    a. Equal rights for freed slaves.
    b. Leniency for former Confederates.
    c. Acquittal of President Johnson during impeachment.
    d. Effective segregation laws.

25. Which of the following is the primary problem with map projections?
    a. They are not detailed
    b. They do not include physical features
    c. They distort areas near the poles
    d. They only focus on the Northern Hemisphere

26. Which of the following is the subgroup of economics that studies large-scale economic issues such as unemployment, interest rates, price levels, and national income?
    a. Microeconomics
    b. Macroeconomics
    c. Scarcity
    d. Supply and demand

27. A pair of dice is thrown, and the sum of the two scores is calculated. What's the expected value of the roll?
    a. 5
    b. 6
    c. 7
    d. 8

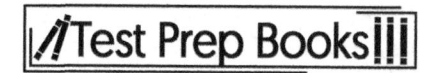

28. Which of the following civilizations developed the first democratic form of government?
    a. Roman Empire
    b. Ancient Greece
    c. Achaemenid Empire
    d. Zhou dynasty

29. Which of the following documents outlawed slavery throughout the United States?
    a. U.S. Constitution
    b. Compromise of 1850
    c. Emancipation Proclamation
    d. 13th Amendment

30. In which manner is absolute location expressed?
    a. The cardinal directions (north, south, east, and west)
    b. Through latitudinal and longitudinal coordinates
    c. Location nearest to a more well-known location
    d. Hemispherical position on the globe

31. Which kind of market does not involve government interventions or monopolies while trades are made between suppliers and buyers?
    a. Free
    b. Command
    c. Gross
    d. Exchange

32. Which measure for the center of a small sample set is most affected by outliers?
    a. Mean
    b. Median
    c. Mode
    d. None of the above

33. The Silk Roads had which of the following results?
    a. Spread of Buddhism from India to China
    b. The devastation of European economies
    c. Introduction of the Bubonic Plague to the New World
    d. The Great War

34. Which constitutional amendment gave women the right to vote in the United States?
    a. 15th
    b. 18th
    c. 19th
    d. 20th

35. Literacy rates are more likely to be higher in which area?
    a. Developing nations
    b. Northern Hemispherical Nations
    c. Developed Nations
    d. Near centers of trade

Practice Test #1 | Job Knowledge

36. In a business cycle, a recession occurs between which cycles?
    a. Expansion, peak
    b. Peak, contraction
    c. Contraction, trough
    d. Trough, expansion

37. What is the probability of randomly picking the winner and runner-up from a race of four horses and distinguishing which is the winner?
    a. $\frac{1}{4}$
    b. $\frac{1}{2}$
    c. $\frac{1}{16}$
    d. $\frac{1}{12}$

38. Which of the following statements most accurately describes the Mongol Empire?
    a. The Mongol army was largely a cavalry force.
    b. Mongol rulers did not tolerate other religions.
    c. Mongol rulers neglected foreign trade.
    d. The Mongol Empire is known for its discouragement of literacy and the arts.

39. Which Supreme Court decision struck down the "separate but equal" doctrine?
    a. *Roe vs. Wade*
    b. *Brown vs. Board of Education*
    c. *Plessy vs. Ferguson*
    d. *Marbury vs. Madison*

40. All of the following are negative demographic indicators EXCEPT which of the following?
    a. High Infant Mortality Rates
    b. Low Literacy Rates
    c. High Population Density
    d. Low Life Expectancy

41. Which option does NOT sustain monetary policies?
    a. Closed market operations
    b. Open market operations
    c. Assuring bank reserves
    d. Adjusting interest rates

42. What is the solution to the following system of equations?
$$x^2 - 2x + y = 8$$
$$x - y = -2$$
    a. $(-2, 3)$
    b. There is no solution.
    c. $(-2, 0) (1, 3)$
    d. $(-2, 0) (3, 5)$

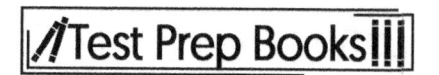

43. Renaissance scholars and artists were inspired by which classical civilization?
    a. Ancient Greece
    b. Ancient Egypt
    c. The Zhou Dynasty
    d. The Ottoman Empire

44. Which event(s) contributed to increasing sectional tension before the Civil War?
    a. Malcom X's death
    b. The "Bleeding Kansas" conflict
    c. The 13th Amendment
    d. Shay's Rebellion

45. Which of the following is NOT a factor in a location's climate?
    a. Latitudinal position
    b. Elevation
    c. Longitudinal position
    d. Proximity to mountains

46. Which statement is true about inflation and purchasing power?
    a. As inflation decreases, purchasing power increases.
    b. As inflation increases, purchasing power decreases.
    c. As inflation increases, purchasing power increases.
    d. As inflation decreases, purchasing power decreases.

47. Mom's car drove 72 miles in 90 minutes. How fast did she drive in feet per second?
    a. 0.8 feet per second
    b. 48.9 feet per second
    c. 0.009 feet per second
    d. 70.4 feet per second

48. Which of the following statements best describes King Louis XIV of France?
    a. He abdicated his throne during the French Revolution.
    b. He supported the American Revolution.
    c. He was the ultimate example of an absolute monarch.
    d. He created the concept of the Mandate of Heaven.

49. What consequences did World War II have?
    a. It led to the creation of the League of Nations.
    b. It led to a communist revolution in Russia.
    c. It made the U.S. the only superpower in the world.
    d. None of the above.

50. Which of the following is true regarding the physical process of weathering?
    a. It is the same as erosion.
    b. It involves wind and rain.
    c. It does not involve moving particles.
    d. It is only a problem in cold climates.

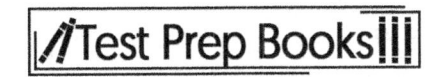

51. Which of the following refers to the value of a good set by supply and demand rather than the actual value it represents?
    a. Commodity money
    b. Fiat money
    c. Bank money
    d. Reserve money

52. The area of a given rectangle is 24 square centimeters. If the measure of each side is multiplied by 3, what is the area of the new figure?
    a. 48 cm²
    b. 72 cm²
    c. 216 cm²
    d. 13,824 cm²

53. Which of the following consequences did NOT result from the discovery of the New World in 1492 CE?
    a. Proof that the world was round instead of flat
    b. The deaths of millions of Native Americans
    c. Biological exchange between Europe and the New World
    d. The creation of new syncretic religions

54. What consequences did the Neolithic Revolution have?
    a. Native Americans domesticated cattle and horses.
    b. Native Americans began to grow crops.
    c. Native Americans developed steel weapons and tools.
    d. Native Americans began to emigrate to Canada.

55. A developing nation is more likely to have which of the following?
    a. Complex highway networks
    b. Higher rates of subsistence farmers
    c. Stable government systems
    d. Little economic instability

56. Which of the following lists all four phases of the business cycle?
    a. Expansion, crest, peak, trough
    b. Expansion, contraction, peak, trench
    c. Peak, trough, contraction, expansion
    d. Peak, rise, trough, decline

57. Which of the following was a consequence of industrialization in Europe during the 1800s?
    a. The birth of the working class
    b. The expansion of European empires in Africa and Asia
    c. Improved transportation and economic efficiency
    d. All of the above

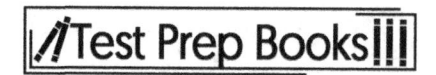

58. What consequences did the New Deal have?
   a. It established a number of federal agencies and programs that continue to function in the 21st century.
   b. It led to a third political party.
   c. It established a two-term limit in the White House.
   d. It led to the Great Depression.

59. Which is NOT true of nonrenewable resources?
   a. They tend to be used more frequently than renewables.
   b. They are thought to be responsible for climate change.
   c. They are relied upon heavily in developing economies.
   d. They have slowed industrial growth.

60. How is economic growth measured?
   a. By the rise in the inflation of a country
   b. By the amount of reserves that a country holds
   c. By the amount of exports that a country has
   d. By the GDP of a country

Situational Judgment

The Situational Judgment Test (SJT) is designed to determine an individual's ability to select the most and least effective way to handle a situation.

Situation 1

You have an innovative plan for your unit that, in your opinion, will improve performance. Not everyone in the unit is of the same opinion, and some downright oppose your plan. Even though the plan has not been put in motion, someone has already written a letter of complaint and sent it to your superior.

What would you do?
   a. Don't worry about anyone else's opinion, and implement the plan.
   b. Ignore the letter of complaint, and push forward with the plan.
   c. Have a meeting with the unit, including the person who wrote the complaint to your superior, and explain to everyone again the chain-of-command and how it is to be used.
   d. Discipline the person who wrote the letter of complaint so that no one else in the unit will break the chain-of-command in the future.
   e. Give up your plan in the wake of opposition, and see what the unit would like to do.

Situation 2

You have had a successful working relationship with an aide assigned to you. On a personal level, you dislike the assignee based on your opinion that they are arrogant and too critical of others. A senior officer is thinking of giving the aide a promotion, which would greatly benefit their future and put the aide on a fast track for future promotions.

Practice Test #1 | Situational Judgment

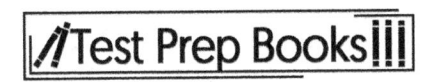

What would you do?
    a. Attempt to dissuade the senior officer by sharing your personal feelings about the aide.
    b. You want the aide to just go away, so you give a recommendation for promotion.
    c. You do not want the aide to be rewarded, so you recommend that the senior officer give it to someone else.
    d. Other than expressing your opinion of the aide, you do not interfere with the selection process.
    e. List your complaints about the aide in an anonymous letter to the senior officer.

Situation 3

A coworker, who is another officer in your division, has to give an important speech in a few days. The officer has spent a great deal of time and effort on the report, but is still nervous about presenting it. After being asked by the officer to look over the report, you find some items that you feel need to be changed. You discuss these items with the other officer, who disagrees with you. You are positive that the changes you identified need to be made.

What would you do?
    a. Mention the conversation to a senior officer prior to the speech as a way to make yourself look better, since you are right and the other officer wouldn't listen to you.
    b. Do everything you can to convince the officer to review the report and supporting information and make the changes you have recommended.
    c. Avoid going to the speech if at all possible.
    d. Attempt to get a senior officer involved to order that the report be changed.
    e. Do not say or do anything. You are not giving the speech.

Situation 4

You have been teamed up with another FSO on an important one-month assignment to draft a report. Unfortunately, early in the project, your coworker has become ill and is required to be on leave. The illness keeps him/her out of the office much longer than expected. At the one-month mark on the report, your coworker is still ill and remains on leave. There is no way of knowing when your coworker will return to work and their expertise is needed to complete the assignment.

What would you do?
    a. Order a subordinate onto the project in an attempt to complete the report.
    b. To the best of your ability, put in as many hours as it takes to finish it yourself.
    c. Don't give any details; just ask for the deadline to be extended.
    d. Relay the situation to your superior and request help to finish the report.
    e. Wait indefinitely for the coworker to return without regard to the timeline for the report.

Situation 5

After a long day at work, you are at home and you realize you forgot to sign documents that need to go on to another unit for completion. The documents cannot move forward without your signature. While the documents are not urgent in nature, your oversight will cause another officer to be delayed and have to stay at work later than usual.

What would you do?
 a. Go back to work and sign the papers.
 b. The documents are not urgent, so you wait until the next day to sign them.
 c. Show up to work early the next day to sign the documents, get them moving first thing in the morning, and hope the other officer won't have to stay late.
 d. Get a subordinate at your office to sign your name on the documents so they can move forward.
 e. Call the officer that this will impact and explain that the documents will be late in arriving.

Situation 6

You are a Consular Officer. A week before you are about to be transferred to a new unit you receive a message from the officer in charge of that unit. The officer explains you are entering the unit at a critical time, as they are leading training exercises for evacuating Americans in the case of a disaster. The message goes on to indicate that you are expected to be a valuable contributor from the moment you arrive, with minimal assistance. However, your experience in this area is minimal.

What would you do?
 a. Send a courteous thank you message in return and attempt to study for the new position.
 b. Send no response to the email. You should have no problem taking on this new position.
 c. Discreetly ask one of the officers in the new unit if he/she will be able to train you upon arrival.
 d. You think you should remain with your current unit, so you request that your transfer be cancelled.
 e. Respond to the senior officer's message with a request for a meeting, where you can discuss the transition into the new position.

Situation 7

A coworker, who is another officer, has lied about their time off. The officer had requested leave for a week to visit an ailing family member. The request for leave was granted. Through social media, you learned the officer was at the beach on vacation, hundreds of miles away from the ailing family member he/she was supposedly visiting.

What would you do?
 a. Go see the commanding officer immediately to relay what you just discovered.
 b. Anonymously send the social media evidence of the officer's actions to the commanding officer.
 c. Since you now have a bargaining chip, you tell the officer you will keep this information to yourself in exchange for him taking on part of your weekly workload.
 d. Tell the officer if he/she does anything unethical like that again you will have no choice but to report it.
 e. You mind your own business and do nothing.

Practice Test #1 | Situational Judgment

Situation 8

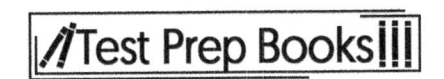

After being in the same unit and performing the same job for two years, you are beginning to feel burned out. Even though you are successful in your current position, you wonder what other options may be available. You have been asking around to people in other units to gauge their experiences. Within a month the rumors in your unit have started that are you are looking for a transfer.

What would you do?
  a. Address the concerns that are brought up and refocus on your current position.
  b. Ask for a leave of absence so you can find a way to handle the situation.
  c. Send a formal request for transfer to your senior officer, acknowledging the truth of the rumors.
  d. Refocus on your position and ignore the rumors, even though they are true.
  e. Continue looking for a new unit to transfer to, but deny the rumors that are circulating.

Situation 9

Your current workload has you extremely busy, but you are managing to meet your deadlines and are producing quality work. A senior officer has asked if you would perform an additional assignment in conjunction with the work you are performing. While you would like to impress the senior officer and take on the additional work, you are already pushing yourself with your current workload. If you took on the extra work, the quality of work on both assignments would suffer.

What would you do?
  a. Tell the senior officer that you would be glad to do the work, and then pass it on to a coworker to complete.
  b. Apologize to the senior officer, and say you are too busy and that you cannot do the extra assignment.
  c. Ask for a few days to think about it.
  d. You can't say no so you take the assignment; you will just have to find a way to complete the work as quickly as possible.
  e. Present an offer to pass the assignment to another qualified coworker, but inform the senior officer that unfortunately you are unable to complete the work yourself at this time.

Situation 10

While assigned to a field office, you become aware that a coworker is extremely overworked with assignments being sent from other offices. The coworker's senior officers do not seem to notice that this person is overworked because your coworker does an excellent job, but they need to work extra hours to get the tasks completed.

What would you do?
  a. You do nothing. That situation has nothing to do with you.
  b. Sympathize with the coworker about their workload.
  c. Assist the coworker and help with their workload as much as possible.
  d. Request a meeting with the coworker's senior officer to inform the officer of the situation.
  e. Task one of your subordinates to assist this person in the workload.

Situation 11

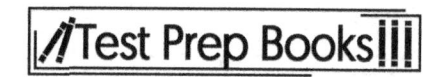

You are in attendance at a meeting where two officers get in a heated dispute over policy changes. It is considered common knowledge around work that these two officers do not like each other on a personal level, but no one is sure why. Unable to come to an agreement on the policy, they ask you to settle the disagreement.

What would you do?
   a. Resolve the dispute on the side of the officer that you favor.
   b. Resolve the dispute on the side of the officer who can benefit your career the most in the future.
   c. Put all personal feelings aside and choose what you believe is the best option.
   d. Point out the officers' blatant issues with each other as the reason they cannot agree, and then remove yourself from the situation.
   e. Disregard the request to settle the dispute on the policy; this is a good time to lecture these two on the importance of teamwork and cooperation when working for the United States Foreign Service.

Situation 12

You are working on reports for your senior officers with a coworker. The reports are used by the officers to track the training and readiness of soldiers for the most hazardous and difficult missions. You noticed your coworker appears to be manipulating these numbers, and they are not being entered correctly. If the soldiers are reported as having a higher amount of training than is required for these missions and then chosen, this could pose a huge risk to the missions and put lives in jeopardy.

What would you do?
   a. Do nothing yet, but monitor the coworker to see what is going on.
   b. Report this issue to your senior officer right away.
   c. Review your coworker's numbers and correct them yourself.
   d. Leave an anonymous note to your coworker to stop changing the numbers in the report and make sure what is turned in is accurate.
   e. Wait for coworker to finish assignment, and then you will have proof of what is going on.

Situation 13

A senior officer asks you in private how you feel about your supervisor. Your supervisor reports to this senior officer. You feel the officer in question overall does a good job, but could do better in a certain aspect of their job.

What would you do?
   a. Express just that: They do a good job overall, but could use improvement in this one area.
   b. Refuse to answer the question.
   c. Give the supervisor a glowing review, without mentioning their weak area.
   d. Discuss the solutions to improving the area where the officer is weak.
   e. Write a note that explains your thoughts about the officer.

Practice Test #1 | Situational Judgment

Situation 14

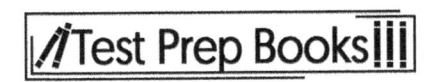

You are serving on a board of three officers interviewing three candidates for promotion. Candidate 1 is a known family friend of your commanding officer, but is the most impressive of the three candidates through the interview process. Candidate 2 seems to be another good choice for the position. Candidate 3 did not do well in the interview process and does not seem like a good choice for promotion at this point. The other two officers on the board have voted, one for each of the first two candidates. You have the deciding vote.

What would you do?
   a. You cast your vote for the second candidate, to avoid the appearance of favoritism.
   b. You remove yourself from the board so that you do not have to vote.
   c. You vote for Candidate 3, so you do not have to decide who gets the promotion.
   d. You vote for Candidate 1, because that candidate is most qualified.
   e. You refrain from the vote and ask for a new group of candidates.

Situation 15

You are given an important assignment that involves working with an officer from a different unit. This officer appears to already have "one foot out the door," as retirement is near. The officer does not put much effort into the assignment, leaving you to do the bulk of the work.

What would you do?
   a. Explain your feelings to your new coworker. Point out that the situation is not fair to you and that the work is very important and should be shared equally.
   b. Put in a request for a new partner on the assignment.
   c. Say nothing and do all the work necessary to successfully complete the assignment.
   d. Just do the best you can with the realization the assignment will likely be unsuccessful due to lack of participation of your coworker.
   e. Inform your senior officer of the situation.

Situation 16

You have had a feeling that one of your subordinates may have an ambitious agenda and be deliberately undermining your work. Other officers have discussed that this subordinate wants to take your job.

What would you do?
   a. Publicly attempt to humiliate the subordinate and reprimand him/her.
   b. Do nothing and the situation may just go away.
   c. Discuss the situation with the subordinate and explain that you expect their cooperation and support.
   d. Ask for another officer to step in and discuss the problem with your subordinate.
   e. File a report for insubordination to your senior officer.

Situation 17

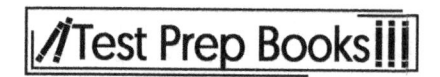

Recently it has come to your attention that office supplies are disappearing from the supply closet at a much faster rate than usual. There is no apparent reason that would account for the change in supply usage. Your gut is telling you that the officer that is last to leave the office may be taking items with him/her after everyone else has left. You do not have any evidence of your suspicion, but it does seem like things disappear on the shifts for which this officer is the last to leave.

What would you do?
  a. Report your suspicions to a senior officer.
  b. Secretly set up hidden cameras in an attempt to catch the thief.
  c. Discuss your suspicions with the officer you suspect and ask for an explanation.
  d. Discuss with fellow officers to see what they think is going on.
  e. Don't do anything.

Situation 18

You are a Political Officer. Rumors have been circulating that your office in your host country is going to be shut down due to budgetary restraints. You are in attendance at a meeting between local community leaders and senior officers from your unit. The community leaders are willing to lobby to keep the office open in return for the support from policy makers in Washington, D.C. for the local military leadership in new initiatives, specifically disaster-relief coordination efforts. A community leader asks your opinion on the matter being discussed.

What would you do?
  a. Answer the question honestly to the best of your ability, but explain you are not a senior officer.
  b. Tell the leader you are not a senior officer and cannot give your opinion.
  c. Defer the question to a senior officer without giving your opinion.
  d. Give a thorough answer even though you have little knowledge on this topic.
  e. Answer the question, but keep it positive; do not mention any possible negative result of what is being proposed.

Situation 19

A subordinate in your unit has recently been showing signs of burnout and seems frustrated with their current position over the last month. You notice this coincides with a decline in the quality and quantity of their work. This negative attitude has been affecting the overall work environment with the fellow officers in the unit.

What would you do?
  a. Report the situation to your senior officer.
  b. Do nothing and hope the situation will improve on its own.
  c. Point out this behavior and bad performance in a meeting with the entire unit.
  d. Meet with the subordinate to discuss these issues, along with the effects on the unit, and present possible solutions.
  e. Reassign the subordinate to alleviate the problem in your unit.

Situation 20

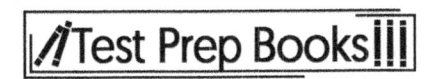

In your current position, one of your many responsibilities is to brief a small team of some activities that are confidential in nature. You have accidentally sent an email containing some of this confidential information to an officer that is not on this team, and who does not have the security clearance to have access to the information you sent.

What would you do?
    a. Immediately email this person and request they destroy the information you just sent. Then, immediately inform your supervisor of your mistake.
    b. Tell your supervisor what happened and let him/her handle it.
    c. Do nothing. Wait and see what happens.
    d. Ask your senior officer if they can request that the individual be cleared for a higher security level since they have been presented with the material.
    e. Send an email to the same person saying your email was hacked and to disregard any previous messages.

Situation 21

You are a Public Diplomacy Officer. Officers in the U.S. Embassy in your host country have been awaiting training to serve as a contact for local reporters seeking accurate and current facts about U.S. policy and culture. A request was made to be in the next training cycle, but officers from the U.S. Embassy in a neighboring country were chosen for the next block of training—even though they had not been waiting as long and the informant position is in your host country, not the neighboring one. You have no evidence, but you have a feeling your unit may not have been given the training block requested due to the training director disliking you on a personal level.
What would you do?
    a. Ask the director if your Public Diplomacy Officers can attend the same training along with the other soldiers selected.
    b. Meet with the training director to determine the reason you Public Diplomacy Officers in the U.S. Embassy in your host country were passed over, and emphasize the importance of this training to your officers.
    c. Do nothing; the decision has been made.
    d. Send a critical letter to the director and your senior officer over this perceived injustice.
    e. Discuss the situation with the other country's U.S. Embassy's senior Public Diplomacy Officer to see if they would give up their training spots so your officers could have them.

Situation 22

You are a Management Officer. When you joined a new unit within the management section of the Embassy a couple of months ago, the leader of the office was very helpful. You were given a great deal of training to carry out the duties and responsibilities of your new position. You are now feeling pretty confident in your abilities, but still have not been given the freedom to work your position independently.

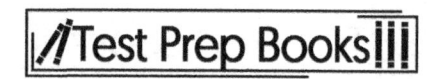

What would you do?
a. Tell the unit leader's supervisor that they need to back off and give you the leeway to do your job.
b. Provide evidence and demonstrate your competence so the leader will leave you alone.
c. Meet with the leader, thank him for all the assistance and guidance, and discuss that you feel ready to work more independently.
d. Try to avoid the leader as much as possible and maybe the situation will correct itself.
e. Request another officer be assigned to your unit so that the leader will need to refocus attention on someone else.

Situation 23

Almost two months ago you were assigned to a new unit. In that brief amount of time you have identified numerous deficiencies in existing operations and have developed solutions for these problems. The majority of the people you have discussed these issues with agree with your proposed solutions. However, the senior officer believes the solutions are too risky and may cause more harm than good.

What would you do?
a. Implement your proposed solutions, believing the senior officer will come around once he/she witnesses their success.
b. Accept the senior officer's decision and work within the current structure without making your changes.
c. Using the majority support of the unit, again confront the senior officer with your solutions.
d. In detail, create a comprehensive report on the benefits of implementing your proposed solutions. Deliver your report and subsequently accept your senior officer's decision either way.
e. Accept the senior officer's decision, then keep a log of the ways your solutions could have improved performance.

Situation 24

You have always excelled in your work, and you received a promotion six months ago. Recent budget cuts have affected the quality of your work over the last few weeks. The budget cuts prevented you from having what you needed to perform your job efficiently and in the proper way. Your senior officer, however, is unaware of the budget effects and has expressed that you are the problem, your work is not up to par, and the performance drop is a result of poor management on your part.

What would you do?
a. Ask for advice or ideas from other officers who are dealing with the same issues resulting from budget problems.
b. Tell your senior officer the problem lies with your subordinates.
c. Get a list of complaints from your senior officer.
d. Ask for time off to get some perspective.
e. Defend your position and remind the senior officer of the budget cuts.

Practice Test #1 | Situational Judgment

Situation 25

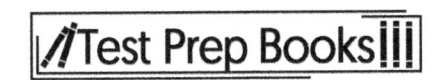

Supply and delivery logistics are maintained in a foreign U.S. Embassy's computer program. While you are coordinating a long line of deliveries, the computer system crashes. You are advised by computer support the problem may take an hour or more to fix. The delivery drivers are already getting impatient. What would you do?

   a. Request guidance from a senior officer.
   b. Ask the drivers if they have any other deliveries they could make in the meantime and return later.
   c. Try to avoid the drivers by going on a break.
   d. Ask for assistance in advising all drivers of the issue and the possible wait time, and accommodate them in whatever way you can.
   e. Receive the deliveries anyway.

Situation 26

You and your direct supervisor get along very well. She is considerate and motivated and works well with your entire team. However, while online one day, you discover that she hosts a radical political podcast. You are concerned that the views she expresses could severely damage the political relationship between your home country and the country you are assigned to.

What would you do?

   a. Confront your supervisor and demand she discontinue the podcast.
   b. Decide that you agree with her political views and ask to be a guest speaker on the podcast.
   c. Take your concerns to your supervisor's boss and let them deal with the situation.
   d. Discuss your concerns about the podcast with HR.
   e. Publicly condemn your supervisor and post the clips that you are most concerned about online.

Situation 27

Over the course of a few weeks, you notice that the snacks in the breakroom are being depleted much more rapidly than normal. After that, you realize that several people are missing personal food from the communal refrigerator. While working late one night, you see the janitor taking the food. When you confront him, he explains that his brother was injured at work and that he has taken on the responsibility of caring for his brother's children until he recovers, but his paycheck cannot feed the additional people.

What would you do?

   a. Denounce the janitor to HR; he should be fired, regardless of why he was stealing.
   b. Help the janitor find appropriate social services to help him and his brother until his brother recovers.
   c. Ask maintenance to install locks on the cabinets and refrigerator so this can't happen again.
   d. Suggest that your coworkers stop bringing food into work until the janitor's brother recovers.
   e. Start an office-wide food drive to assist the janitor until his brother recovers.

Situation 28

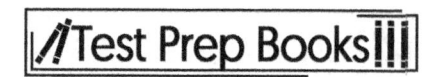

Your office has a fairly strict dress code in place to comply with the religious ethics of the country you are assigned to. However, a new member of the team you supervise repeatedly comes to work dressed in clothing that is appropriate for your home country but does not meet the office dress code.

What would you do?
   a. Pull your team member aside and privately explain the importance of meeting the dress code.
   b. Mock your team member in a meeting for their inability to follow the rules.
   c. File a complaint with HR.
   d. Recommend that your team member be fired for their obvious inability to respect the culture of the country they are assigned to.
   e. Do nothing; it is not your job to supervise your team members' clothing choices.

English Expression

For the answer choices below in response to the passages, choose the option that is most consistent with standard English in the underlined section.

Read the following passage and answer Questions 1–7.

I have to admit that when my father bought a recreational vehicle (RV), I thought he was making a huge mistake. I didn't really know anything about RVs, but I knew that my dad was as big a "city slicker" as there was. (1) In fact, I even thought he might have gone a little bit crazy. On trips to the beach, he preferred to swim at the pool, and whenever he went hiking, he avoided touching any plants for fear that they might be poison ivy. Why would this man, with an almost irrational fear of the outdoors, want a 40-foot camping behemoth?

(2) The RV was a great purchase for our family and brought us all closer together. Every morning (3) we would wake up, eat breakfast, and broke camp. We laughed at our own comical attempts to back The Beast into spaces that seemed impossibly small. (4) We rejoiced as "hackers." When things inevitably went wrong and we couldn't solve the problems on our own, we discovered the incredible helpfulness and friendliness of the RV community. (5) We even made some new friends in the process.

(6) Above all, it allowed us to share adventures. While traveling across America, which we could not have experienced in cars and hotels. Enjoying a campfire on a chilly summer evening with the mountains of Glacier National Park in the background, or waking up early in the morning to see the sun rising over the distant spires of Arches National Park are memories that will always stay with me and our entire family. (7) Those are also memories that my siblings and me have now shared with our own children.

Practice Test #1 | English Expression

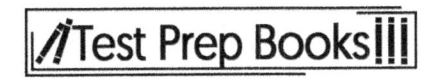

1. Which of the following would be the best choice for this sentence (reproduced below)?

    In fact, I even thought he might have gone a little bit crazy.

    a. (No change; best as written.)
    b. Move the sentence so that it comes before the preceding sentence.
    c. Move the sentence to the end of the first paragraph.
    d. Omit the sentence.

2. In context, which is the best version of the underlined portion of this sentence (reproduced below)?

    The RV was a great purchase for our family and brought us all closer together.

    a. The RV
    b. Not surprisingly, the RV
    c. Furthermore, the RV
    d. As it turns out, the RV

3. Which is the best version of the underlined portion of this sentence (reproduced below)?

    Every morning we would wake up, eat breakfast, and broke camp.

    a. we would wake up, eat breakfast, and broke camp.
    b. we would wake up, eat breakfast, and break camp.
    c. would we wake up, eat breakfast, and break camp?
    d. we are waking up, eating breakfast, and breaking camp.

4. Which is the best version of the underlined portion of this sentence (reproduced below)?

    We rejoiced as "hackers."

    a. We rejoiced as "hackers."
    b. To a nagging problem of technology, we rejoiced as "hackers."
    c. We rejoiced when we figured out how to "hack" a solution to a nagging technological problem.
    d. To "hack" our way to a solution, we had to rejoice.

5. Which is the best version of the underlined portion of this sentence (reproduced below)?

    We even made some new friends in the process.

    a. We even made some new friends in the process.
    b. In the process was the friends we were making.
    c. We are even making some new friends in the process.
    d. We will make new friends in the process.

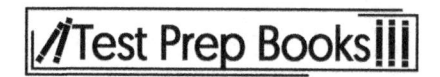

6. Which is the best version of the underlined portion of this sentence (reproduced below)?

Above all, it allowed us to share adventures. While traveling across America, which we could not have experienced in cars and hotels.

a. Above all, it allowed us to share adventures. While traveling across America,
b. Above all, it allowed us to share adventures while traveling across America,
c. Above all, it allowed us to share adventures; while traveling across America,
d. Above all, it allowed us to share adventures—while traveling across America,

7. Which is the best version of the underlined portion of this sentence (reproduced below)?

Those are also memories that my siblings and me have now shared with our own children.

a. Those are also memories that my siblings and me
b. Those are also memories that me and my siblings
c. Those are also memories that my siblings and I
d. Those are also memories that I and my siblings

Read the following passage and answer Questions 8–20.

Fred Hampton desired to see lasting social change for African American people through nonviolent means and community recognition. (8) In the meantime, he became an African American activist during the American Civil Rights Movement and led the Chicago chapter of the Black Panther Party.

Hampton's Education

Hampton was born and raised (9) in Maywood of Chicago, Illinois in 1948. Gifted academically and a natural athlete, he became a stellar baseball player in high school. (10) After graduating from Proviso East High School in 1966, he later went on to study law at Triton Junior College. While studying at Triton, Hampton joined and became a leader of the National Association for the Advancement of Colored People (NAACP). As a result of his leadership, the NAACP gained more than 500 members. Hampton worked relentlessly to acquire recreational facilities in the neighborhood and improve the educational resources provided to the impoverished black community of Maywood.

The Black Panthers

The Black Panther Party (BPP) (11) was another that formed around the same time as and was similar in function to the NAACP. Hampton was quickly attracted to the (12) Black Panther Party's approach to the fight for equal rights for African Americans. Hampton eventually joined the chapter and relocated to downtown Chicago to be closer to its headquarters.

His charismatic personality, organizational abilities, sheer determination, and rhetorical skills (13) enable him to quickly rise through the chapter's ranks. Hampton soon became the leader of the Chicago chapter of the BPP where he organized rallies, taught political education classes, and established a free medical clinic. (14) He also took part in the community police supervision project. He played an instrumental role in the BPP breakfast program for impoverished African American children.

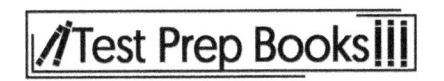

Hampton's (15) greatest acheivement as the leader of the BPP may be his fight against street gang violence in Chicago. In 1969, (16) Hampton was held by a press conference where he made the gangs agree to a nonaggression pact known as the Rainbow Coalition. As a result of the pact, a multiracial alliance between blacks, Puerto Ricans, and poor youth was developed.

Assassination

(17) As the Black Panther Party's popularity and influence grew, the Federal Bureau of Investigation (FBI) placed the group under constant surveillance. In an attempt to neutralize the party, the FBI launched several harassment campaigns against the BPP, raided its headquarters in Chicago three times, and arrested over one hundred of the group's members. Hampton was shot during such a raid that occurred on the morning of December 4th, 1969.

(18) In 1976; seven years after the event, it was revealed that William O'Neal, Hampton's trusted bodyguard, was an undercover FBI agent. (19) O'Neal will provide the FBI with detailed floor plans of the BPP's headquarters, identifying the exact location of Hampton's bed. It was because of these floor plans that the police were able to target and kill Hampton.

The assassination of Hampton fueled outrage amongst the African American community. It was not until years after the assassination that the police admitted wrongdoing. (20) The Chicago City Council now are commemorating December 4th as Fred Hampton Day.

8. In context, which is the best version of the underlined portion of this sentence (reproduced below)?

In the meantime, he became an African American activist during the American Civil Rights Movement and led the Chicago chapter of the Black Panther Party.

   a. In the meantime,
   b. Unfortunately,
   c. Finally,
   d. As a result,

9. Which is the best version of the underlined portion of this sentence (reproduced below)?

Hampton was born and raised *in Maywood of Chicago, Illinois in 1948.*

   a. in Maywood of Chicago, Illinois in 1948.
   b. in Maywood, of Chicago, Illinois in 1948.
   c. in Maywood of Chicago, Illinois, in 1948.
   d. in Chicago, Illinois of Maywood in 1948.

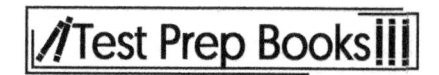

10. Which of the following sentences, if any, should begin a new paragraph?

After graduating from Proviso East High School in 1966, he later went on to study law at Triton Junior College. While studying at Triton, Hampton joined and became a leader of the National Association for the Advancement of Colored People (NAACP). As a result of his leadership, the NAACP gained more than 500 members.

a. (No change; best as written.)
b. After graduating from Proviso East High School in 1966, he later went on to study law at Triton Junior College.
c. While studying at Triton, Hampton joined and became a leader of the National Association for the Advancement of Colored People (NAACP).
d. As a result of his leadership, the NAACP gained more than 500 members.

11. Which of the following facts would be the most relevant to include here?

The Black Panther Party (BPP) was another that formed around the same time as and was similar in function to the NAACP.

a. was another that
b. was another activist group that
c. had a lot of members that
d. was another school that

12. Which is the best version of the underlined portion of this sentence (reproduced below)?

Hampton was quickly attracted to the Black Panther Party's approach to the fight for equal rights for African Americans.

a. Black Panther Party's approach
b. Black Panther Parties approach
c. Black Panther Partys' approach
d. Black Panther Parties' approach

13. Which is the best version of the underlined portion of this sentence (reproduced below)?

His charismatic personality, organizational abilities, sheer determination, and rhetorical skills enable him to quickly rise through the chapter's ranks.

a. enable him to quickly rise
b. are enabling him to quickly rise
c. enabled him to quickly rise
d. will enable him to quickly rise

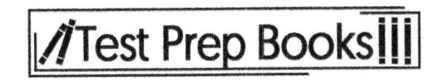

14. Which is the best version of the underlined portion of this sentence (reproduced below)?

He also took part in the community police supervision project. He played an instrumental role in the BPP breakfast program for impoverished African American children.

   a. He also took part in the community police supervision project. He played an instrumental role
   b. He also took part in the community police supervision project but played an instrumental role
   c. He also took part in the community police supervision project, he played an instrumental role
   d. He also took part in the community police supervision project and played an instrumental role

15. Which of these, if any, is misspelled?

Hampton's greatest acheivement as the leader of the BPP may be his fight against street gang violence in Chicago.

   a. (No change; best as written.)
   b. greatest
   c. acheivement
   d. leader

16. Which is the best version of the underlined portion of this sentence (reproduced below)?

In 1969, Hampton was held by a press conference where he made the gangs agree to a nonaggression pact known as the Rainbow Coalition.

   a. Hampton was held by a press conference
   b. Hampton held a press conference
   c. Hampton, holding a press conference
   d. Hampton to hold a press conference

17. Which is the best version of the underlined portion of this sentence (reproduced below)?

As the Black Panther Party's popularity and influence grew, the Federal Bureau of Investigation (FBI) placed the group under constant surveillance.

   a. (No change; best as written)
   b. The Federal Bureau of Investigation (FBI) placed the group under constant surveillance as the Black Panther Party's popularity and influence grew.
   c. Placing the group under constant surveillance, the Black Panther Party's popularity and influence grew.
   d. As their influence and popularity grew, the FBI placed the group under constant surveillance.

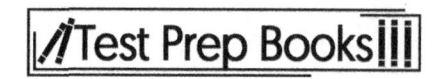

18. Which is the best version of the underlined portion of this sentence (reproduced below)?

In 1976; seven years after the event, it was revealed that William O'Neal, Hampton's trusted bodyguard, was an undercover FBI agent.

a. In 1976; seven years after the event
b. In 1976, seven years after the event,
c. In 1976 seven years after the event,
d. In 1976. Seven years after the event,

19. Which is the best version of the underlined portion of this sentence (reproduced below)?

O'Neal will provide the FBI with detailed floor plans of the BPP's headquarters, identifying the exact location of Hampton's bed.

a. O'Neal will provide
b. O'Neal provides
c. O'Neal provided
d. O'Neal, providing

20. Which is the best version of the underlined portion of this sentence (reproduced below)?

The Chicago City Council now are commemorating December 4th as Fred Hampton Day.

a. The Chicago City Council now are commemorating December 4th as Fred Hampton Day.
b. Fred Hampton Day by the Chicago City Council, December 4, is now commemorated.
c. Now commemorated December 4th is Fred Hampton Day.
d. The Chicago City Council now commemorates December 4th as Fred Hampton Day.

Read the following passage and answer Questions 21–35.

Early in my career, (21) a master's teacher shared this thought with me "Education is the last bastion of civility." While I did not completely understand the scope of those words at the time, I have since come to realize the depth, breadth, truth, and significance of what he said. (22) Education provides society with a vehicle for (23) raising it's children to be civil, decent, human beings with something valuable to contribute to the world. It is really what makes us human and what (24) distinguishes us as civilised creatures.

Being "civilized" humans means being "whole" humans. Education must address the mind, body, and soul of students. (25) It would be detrimental to society, only meeting the needs of the mind, if our schools were myopic in their focus. As humans, we are multi-dimensional, multi-faceted beings who need more than head knowledge to survive. (26) The human heart and psyche have to be fed in order for the mind to develop properly, and the body must be maintained and exercised to help fuel the working of the brain. Education is a basic human right, and it allows us to sustain a democratic society in which participation is fundamental to its success. It should inspire students to seek better solutions to world problems and to dream of a more equitable society. Education should never discriminate on any basis, and it should create individuals who are self-sufficient, patriotic, and tolerant of (27) others' ideas.

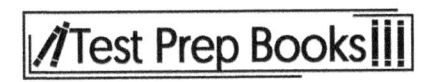

(28) All children can learn. Although not all children learn in the same manner. All children learn best, however, when their basic physical needs are met and they feel safe, secure, and loved. Students are much more responsive to a teacher who values them and shows them respect as individual people. Teachers must model at all times the way they expect students to treat them and their peers. If teachers set high expectations for (29) there students, the students will rise to that high level. Teachers must make the well-being of students their primary focus and must not be afraid to let students learn from their own mistakes.

In the modern age of technology, a teacher's focus is no longer the "what" of the content, (30) but more importantly, the 'why.' Students are bombarded with information and have access to ANY information they need right at their fingertips. Teachers have to work harder than ever before to help students identify salient information (31) so to think critically about the information they encounter. Students have to (32) read between the lines, identify bias, and determine who they can trust in the milieu of ads, data, and texts presented to them.

Schools must work in consort with families in this important mission. While children spend most of their time in school, they are dramatically and indelibly shaped (33) with the influences of their family and culture. Teachers must not only respect this fact, (34) but must strive to include parents in the education of their children and must work to keep parents informed of progress and problems. Communication between classroom and home is essential for a child's success.

Humans have always aspired to be more, do more, and to better ourselves and our communities. This is where education lies, right at the heart of humanity's desire to be all that we can be. Education helps us strive for higher goals and better treatment of ourselves and others. I shudder to think what would become of us if education ceased to be the "last bastion of civility." (35) We must be unapologetic about expecting excellence from our students? Our very existence depends upon it.

21. Which is the best version of the underlined portion of this sentence (reproduced below)?

Early in my career, a master's teacher shared this thought with me "Education is the last bastion of civility."

   a. a master's teacher shared this thought with me "Education is the last bastion of civility."
   b. a master's teacher shared this thought with me: "Education is the last bastion of civility."
   c. a master's teacher shared this thought with me: "Education is the last bastion of civility".
   d. a master's teacher shared this thought with me. "Education is the last bastion of civility."

22. Which is the best version of the underlined portion of this sentence (reproduced below)?

Education provides society with a vehicle

   a. Education provides
   b. Education provide
   c. Education will provide
   d. Education providing

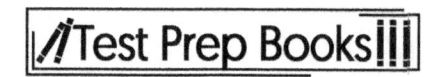

23. Which is the best version of the underlined portion of this sentence (reproduced below)?

for <u>raising it's children to be</u> civil, decent, human beings with something valuable to contribute to the world.

   a. raising it's children to be
   b. raises its children to be
   c. raising its' children to be
   d. raising its children to be

24. Which of these, if any, is misspelled?

It is really what makes us human and what <u>distinguishes</u> us as <u>civilised</u> <u>creatures.</u>

   a. (No change; best as written.)
   b. distinguishes
   c. civilised
   d. creatures

25. Which is the best version of the underlined portion of this sentence (reproduced below)?

<u>It would be detrimental to society, only meeting the needs of the mind, if our schools were myopic in their focus.</u>

   a. (No change; best as written.)
   b. It would be detrimental to society if our schools were myopic in their focus, only meeting the needs of the mind.
   c. Only meeting the needs of our mind, our schools were myopic in their focus, detrimental to society.
   d. Myopic is the focus of our schools, being detrimental to society for only meeting the needs of the mind.

26. Which of these sentences, if any, should begin a new paragraph?

<u>The human heart and psyche have to be fed in order for the mind to develop properly, and the body must be maintained and exercised to help fuel the working of the brain. Education is a basic human right, and it allows us to sustain a democratic society in which participation is fundamental to its success. It should inspire students to seek better solutions to world problems and to dream of a more equitable society.</u>

   a. (No change; best as written.)
   b. The human heart and psyche have to be fed in order for the mind to develop properly, and the body must be maintained and exercised to help fuel the working of the brain.
   c. Education is a basic human right, and it allows us to sustain a democratic society in which participation is fundamental to its success.
   d. It should inspire students to seek better solutions to world problems and to dream of a more equitable society.

Practice Test #1 | English Expression

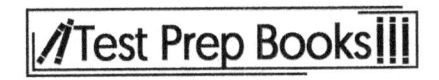

27. Which is the best version of the underlined portion of this sentence (reproduced below)?

    Education should never discriminate on any basis, and it should create individuals who are self-sufficient, patriotic, and tolerant of <u>others' ideas.</u>

    a. others' ideas.
    b. other's ideas
    c. others ideas
    d. others's ideas

28. Which is the best version of the underlined portion of this sentence (reproduced below)?

    <u>All children can learn. Although not all children learn in the same manner.</u>

    a. All children can learn. Although not all children learn in the same manner.
    b. All children can learn although not all children learn in the same manner.
    c. All children can learn although, not all children learn in the same manner.
    d. All children can learn, although not all children learn in the same manner.

29. Which is the best version of the underlined portion of this sentence (reproduced below)?

    If teachers set high expectations for <u>there students</u>, the students will rise to that high level.

    a. there students
    b. they're students
    c. their students
    d. thare students

30. Which is the best version of the underlined portion of this sentence (reproduced below)?

    In the modern age of technology, a teacher's focus is no longer the "what" of the content, <u>but more importantly, the 'why.'</u>

    a. but more importantly, the 'why.'
    b. but more importantly, the "why."
    c. but more importantly, the 'why'.
    d. but more importantly, the "why".

31. Which is the best version of the underlined portion of this sentence (reproduced below)?

    Teachers have to work harder than ever before to help students identify salient information <u>so to think critically</u> about the information they encounter.

    a. so to think critically
    b. and to think critically
    c. but to think critically
    d. nor to think critically

32. Which is the best version of the underlined portion of this sentence (reproduced below)?

Students have to <u>read between the lines, identify bias, and determine</u> who they can trust in the milieu of ads, data, and texts presented to them.

   a. read between the lines, identify bias, and determine
   b. read between the lines, identify bias, and determining
   c. read between the lines, identifying bias, and determining
   d. reads between the lines, identifies bias, and determines

33. Which is the best version of the underlined portion of this sentence (reproduced below)?

While children spend most of their time in school, they are dramatically and indelibly shaped <u>with the influences</u> of their family and culture.

   a. with the influences
   b. for the influences
   c. to the influences
   d. by the influences

34. Which is the best version of the underlined portion of this sentence (reproduced below)?

Teachers must not only respect this fact, <u>but must strive</u> to include parents in the education of their children and must work to keep parents informed of progress and problems.

   a. but must strive
   b. but to strive
   c. but striving
   d. but strived

35. Which is the best version of the underlined portion of this sentence (reproduced below)?

<u>*We must be unapologetic about expecting excellence from our students? Our very existence depends upon it.*</u>

   a. We must be unapologetic about expecting excellence from our students? Our very existence depends upon it.
   b. We must be unapologetic about expecting excellence from our students, our very existence depends upon it.
   c. We must be unapologetic about expecting excellence from our students—our very existence depends upon it.
   d. We must be unapologetic about expecting excellence from our students our very existence depends upon it.

Read the following passage and answer Questions 36–40.

Although many Missourians know that Harry S. Truman and Walt Disney hailed from their great state, probably far fewer know that it was also home to the remarkable George Washington

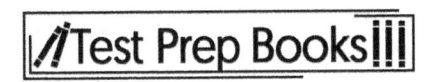

Carver. (36) As a child, George was driven to learn, and he loved painting. At the end of the Civil War, Moses Carver, the slave owner who owned George's parents, decided to keep George and his brother and raise them on his farm.

He even went on to study art while in college but was encouraged to pursue botany instead. He spent much of his life helping others (37) by showing them better ways to farm, his ideas improved agricultural productivity in many countries. One of his most notable contributions to the newly emerging class of Black farmers was to teach them the negative effects of agricultural monoculture, i.e. (38) growing the same crops in the same fields year after year, depleting the soil of much needed nutrients and results in a lesser yielding crop.

Carver was an innovator, always thinking of new and better ways to do things, and is most famous for his over three hundred uses for the peanut. Toward the end of his career, (39) Carver returns to his first love of art. Through his artwork, he hoped to inspire people to see the beauty around them and to do great things themselves. (40) Because Carver died, he left his money to help fund ongoing agricultural research. Today, people still visit and study at the George Washington Carver Foundation at Tuskegee Institute.

36. Which of the following would be the best choice for this sentence (reproduced below)?

As a child, George was driven to learn, and he loved painting.

   a. (No change; best as is)
   b. Move to the end of the first paragraph.
   c. Move to the beginning of the first paragraph.
   d. Move to the end of the second paragraph.

37. Which is the best version of the underlined portion of this sentence (reproduced below)?

He spent much of his life helping others by showing them better ways to farm, his ideas improved agricultural productivity in many countries.

   a. by showing them better ways to farm, his ideas improved agricultural productivity
   b. by showing them better ways to farm his ideas improved agricultural productivity
   c. by showing them better ways to farm...his ideas improved agricultural productivity
   d. by showing them better ways to farm; his ideas improved agricultural productivity

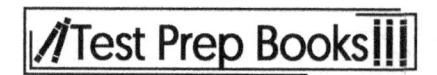

38. Which is the best version of the underlined portion of this sentence (reproduced below)?

One of his most notable contributions to the newly emerging class of Black farmers *was to teach them the negative effects of agricultural monoculture, i.e. growing the same crops in the same fields year after year, depleting the soil of much needed nutrients and results in a lesser yielding crop.*

a. growing the same crops in the same fields year after year, depleting the soil of much needed nutrients and results in a lesser yielding crop.
b. growing the same crops in the same fields year after year, depleting the soil of much needed nutrients and resulting in a lesser yielding crop.
c. growing the same crops in the same fields year after year, depletes the soil of much needed nutrients and resulting in a lesser yielding crop.
d. grows the same crops in the same fields year after year, depletes the soil of much needed nutrients and resulting in a lesser yielding crop.

39. Which is the best version of the underlined portion of this sentence (reproduced below)?

Toward the end of his career, Carver returns to his first love of art.

a. Carver returns
b. Carver is returning
c. Carver returned
d. Carver was returning

40. Which is the best version of the underlined portion of this sentence (reproduced below)?

Because Carver died, he left his money to help fund ongoing agricultural research.

a. Because Carver died,
b. Although Carver died,
c. When Carver died,
d. Finally Carver died,

Read the following passage and answer Questions 41–42.

(41) Christopher Columbus is often credited for discovering America. This is incorrect. First, it is impossible to "discover" something where people already live; however, Christopher Columbus did explore places in the New World that were previously untouched by Europe, (42) so the ships set sail from Palos, Spain. Another correction must be made, as well: Christopher Columbus was not the first European explorer to reach the Americas! Rather, it was Leif Erikson who first came to the New World and contacted the natives, nearly five hundred years before Christopher Columbus.

Practice Test #1 | English Expression

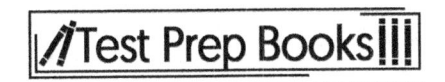

41. Which is the best version of the underlined portion of this sentence (reproduced below)?

Christopher Columbus is often credited for discovering America. This is incorrect.

   a. Christopher Columbus is often credited for discovering America. This is incorrect.
   b. Christopher Columbus is often credited for discovering America this is incorrect.
   c. Christopher Columbus is often credited for discovering America, this is incorrect.
   d. Christopher Columbus is often credited for discovering America: this is incorrect.

42. Which of the following facts would be the most relevant to include here?

however, Christopher Columbus did explore places in the New World that were previously untouched by Europe, so the ships set sail from Palos, Spain.

   a. so the ships set sail from Palos, Spain.
   b. so Columbus discovered Watling Island in the Bahamas.
   c. so the ships were named them the Santa María, the Pinta, and the Niña.
   d. so the term "explorer" would be more accurate.

Sentence Selection: Select the one sentence that best meets the requirements of standard written English.

Questions 43–47

43.
   a. Accompanied by a master's degree in advanced engineering or business administration is a bachelor's degree in aircraft engineering.
   b. A bachelor's degree in aircraft engineering is commonly accompanied by a master's degree in advanced engineering or business administration.
   c. In advanced engineering or business administration you get a master's degree and in aircraft engineering you get a bachelor's degree and one follows the other.
   d. A bachelor's degree in aircraft engineering are commonly accompanied by a master's degree in advanced engineering or business administration.

44.
   a. In May 2015, the United States Bureau of Labor Statistics (BLS) reported that the median annual salary of aircraft engineers was $107,830.
   b. In May 2015, the United States Bureau of Labor Statistics (BLS) reported that the median annual salary of aircraft engineers is $107,830.
   c. In May of 2015 the United States Bureau of Labor Statistics (BLS) reported that the median annual salary of aircraft engineers was $107,830.
   d. In May, 2015, the United States Bureau of Labor Statistics (BLS) reported that the median annual salary of aircraft engineers was $107,830.

45.
   a. Ancient civilizations have reported seeing Bigfoot as well including Native Americans.
   b. Ancient civilizations have reported seeing Bigfoot, Native Americans as well.
   c. Ancient civilizations have reported seeing Bigfoot also the Native Americans.
   d. Ancient civilizations have reported seeing Bigfoot, including Native Americans.

46.
   a. In 1020, seventeen years later. The legendary Viking died.
   b. In 1020, seventeen years later; the legendary Viking died.
   c. In 1020 seventeen years later the legendary Viking died.
   d. In 1020, seventeen years later, the legendary Viking died.

47.
   a. There are stories of Thor destroying mountains, defeating scores of giants and lifting up the world's largest creature the Midgard Serpent.
   b. There are stories of Thor destroying mountains, defeating scores of giants, and lifting up the world's largest creature, the Midgard Serpent.
   c. There are stories of Thor destroying mountains, defeating scores of giants, and lifting up the world's largest creature the Midgard Serpent.
   d. There are stories of Thor destroying mountains, defeating scores, of giants, and lifting up the world's largest creature the Midgard Serpent.

Sentence Correction: For the next eight questions, select the answer choice that needs to be used in place of the underlined text to make the sentence correct, or indicate that the underlined text is not in error.

Questions 48–55

48. They fear that the melting of icebergs will cause the <u>oceans levels</u> to rise and flood coastal regions.
   a. NO ERROR
   b. ocean levels
   c. ocean's levels
   d. levels of the oceans

49. <u>Although often associated with devastation, not all flooding results</u> in adverse circumstances.
   a. NO ERROR
   b. Although often associated with devastation not all flooding results in adverse circumstances.
   c. Although often associated with devastation. Not all flooding results in adverse circumstances.
   d. While often associated with devastation, not all flooding results in adverse circumstances.

50. The flooding of such rivers <u>is caused</u> nutrient-rich silts to be deposited on the floodplains.
   a. NO ERROR
   b. Cause
   c. Causing
   d. Causes

Practice Test #1 | English Expression

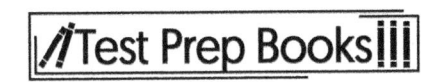

51. Such technologies can also be used to project the severity of an anticipated flood.
    a. NO ERROR
    b. Projecting
    c. Project
    d. Projected

52. He had to conceal himself in order to achieve revenge.
    a. NO ERROR
    b. To be concealed
    c. Conceals
    d. Concealing

53. Myths continue to help us understood ancient cultures while still helping us connect to real-world lessons through narrative.

    a. NO ERROR
    b. understand ancient cultures
    c. understood ancient cultures,
    d. understanding ancient cultures

54. Other accounts describes clashes where the Skraelings defeated the Viking explorers with long spears, while still others claim the Vikings dominated the natives.
    a. NO ERROR
    b. Other account's describe
    c. Other accounts describe
    d. Others account's describes

55. During their time in present-day Newfoundland, Leif's expedition made contact with the natives, whom they referred to as Skraelings (which translates to 'wretched ones' in Norse).
    a. NO ERROR
    b. (which translates to "wretched ones" in Norse.)
    c. (which translates to 'wretched ones' in Norse.)
    d. (which translates to "wretched ones" in Norse).

Paragraph Organization: For each item in this section, select the ordering of sentences that results in the most organized paragraph.

Questions 56–60

56. Sentence 1: Many students entering college may shy away from a major because they don't know much about it.

Sentence 2: For example, many students won't opt for a career as an actuary, because they aren't exactly sure what it entails.

Sentence 3: When selecting a career path, it's important to explore the various options available.

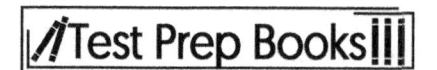

Sentence 4: They would be missing out on a career that is very lucrative and in high demand.

    a. 1, 2, 3, 4
    b. 2, 3, 1, 4
    c. 3, 1, 2, 4
    d. 4, 1, 2, 3

57. Sentence 1: One solution is to install a water softener to reduce the mineral content of water, but this can be costly.

Sentence 2: Hard water has a high mineral count, including calcium and magnesium.

Sentence 3: Hard water can stain dishes, ruin clothes, and reduce the life of any appliances it touches, such as hot water heaters, washing machines, and humidifiers.

Sentence 4: The mineral deposits from hard water can stain hard surfaces in bathrooms and kitchens as well as clog pipes.

    a. 2, 4, 3, 1
    b. 1, 2, 4, 3
    c. 4, 3, 2, 1
    d. 3, 2, 1, 4

58. Sentence 1: A famous children's author recently published a historical fiction novel under a pseudonym; however, it did not sell as many copies as her children's books.

Sentence 2: In her earlier years, she had majored in history and earned a graduate degree in Antebellum American History, which is the time frame of her new novel.

Sentence 3: In fact, her new novel was nominated for the prestigious Albert J. Beveridge Award but still isn't selling like her children's books, which fly off the shelves because of her name alone.

Sentence 4: Critics praised this newest work far more than the children's series that made her famous.

    a. 2, 3, 4, 1
    b. 1, 2, 3, 4
    c. 3, 2, 4, 1
    d. 1, 2, 4, 3

59. Sentence 1: Addiction is defined as a compulsion to seek the substance despite negative consequences.

Sentence 2: However, more than 85 percent of those who struggle with addiction will not achieve their goal.

Sentence 3: According to the National Institute of Drug Abuse, nearly 35 million smokers expressed a desire to quit smoking in 2015.

Practice Test #1 | English Expression

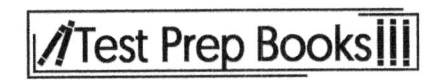

Sentence 4: Cigarettes contain a drug called nicotine, one of the most addictive substances known.

    a. 1, 2, 4, 3
    b. 4, 1, 3, 2
    c. 2, 1, 3, 4
    d. 1, 2, 3, 4

60. Sentence 1: It has recently been brought to my attention that most people believe that 75% of your body heat is lost through your head.

Sentence 2: I had certainly heard this before, and am not going to attempt to say I didn't believe it when I first heard it.

Sentence 3: It is natural to be gullible to anything said with enough authority.

Sentence 4: But the "fact" that the majority of your body heat is lost through your head is a lie.

    a. 4, 3, 2, 1
    b. 1, 2, 3, 4
    c. 1, 2, 4, 3
    d. 3, 4, 1, 2

Paragraph Revision: This section consists of different paragraphs. Read each paragraph carefully, and then answer the questions that follow it.

Questions 61–65

Sentence 1: Thus far the protective work of the Audubon Association has been successful.

Sentence 2: Now there are twenty colonies, which contain all told, about 5,000 egrets and about 120,000 herons and ibises which are guarded by the Audubon wardens.

Sentence 3: Today, the plume hunters <u>who does</u> not dare to raid the guarded rookeries are trying to study out the lines of flight of the birds, to and from their feeding-grounds, and shoot them in transit.

Sentence 4: Their motto is—"Anything to beat the law, and get the plumes." It is there that the state of Florida should take part in the war.

61. The writer discovers the following sentence has been left out of the paragraph: "One of the most important is on Bird Island, a mile out in Orange Lake, central Florida, and it is ably defended by Oscar E. Baynard." Which sentence is this sentence most likely to be placed after?
    a. Sentence 1
    b. Sentence 2
    c. Sentence 3
    d. Sentence 4

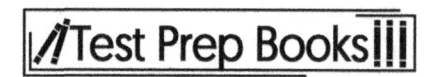

62. Choose the best choice for the underlined text in Sentence 3. If you think the text is correct as-is, choose Choice A.
  a. who does
  b. whom does
  c. who do
  d. whom do

Sentence 1: <u>Cynthia keeps</u> to a strict vegetarian diet.

Sentence 2: <u>Keeping this diet are part</u> of her religion.

Sentence 3: She cannot have any meat or fish dishes.

Sentence 4: This is more than a preference.

63. The writer discovers the following sentence has been left out of the paragraph: "Her body has never developed the enzymes to process meat or fish, so she becomes violently ill if she accidentally eats any of the offending foods." Which sentence is this sentence most likely to be placed after?
  a. Sentence 1
  b. Sentence 2
  c. Sentence 3
  d. Sentence 4

64. Choose the best choice for the underlined text in Sentence 1. If you think the text is correct as-is, choose Choice A.
  a. Cynthia keeps
  b. Cynthia keeping
  c. Cynthia keep
  d. Cynthia has keeping

65. Choose the best choice for the underlined text in Sentence 2. If you think the text is correct as-is, choose Choice A.
  a. Keeping this diet are part
  b. Keeping this diet is part
  c. Keeping this diets are part
  d. Keeping this diets is part

Written Essay #1

On the FSOT, you will be presented with multiple essay topics to choose from. The test allows you seven minutes to choose the topic before you get started. If you don't choose a topic before seven minutes, they will choose one for you. Then, you will have twenty-five minutes to develop and write your essay. Reviewers of your essay will look for a clear, organized essay with grammatically correct sentences. You will have 2800 characters, or spaces, to write your essay, then the screen will time out.

The following is an example topic essay:

> Some people feel that sharing their lives on social media sites such as Facebook, Instagram, and Snapchat is fine. They share every aspect of their lives, including pictures of themselves and their families, what they ate for lunch, who they are dating, and when they are going on vacation. They even say that if it's not on social media, it didn't happen. Other people believe that sharing so much personal information is an invasion of privacy and could prove dangerous. They think sharing personal pictures and details invites predators, cyberbullying, and identity theft.

Write an essay to someone who is considering whether to participate in social media. Take a side on the issue and argue whether or not he/she should join a social media network. Use specific examples to support your argument.

Answer Explanations #1

Job Knowledge

1. C: Power is the ability of a ruling body or political entity to influence the actions, behavior, and attitude of a person or group of people. Authority, Choice *A*, is the right and justification of the government to exercise power as recognized by the citizens or influential elites. Similarly, legitimacy, Choice *D*, is another way of expressing the concept of authority. Sovereignty, Choice *B*, refers to the ability of a state to determine and control their territory without foreign interference.

2. A: The Spanish-American War of 1898 made the U.S. a colonial power because it acquired many former Spanish colonies. The Mexican-American War of 1846-48 led to the acquisition of California, Nevada, Utah, Arizona, and New Mexico, Choice *B*. World War I led to the formation of the League of Nations in 1919, Choice *C*. The Great Depression ended when Americans joined World War II in 1941, Choice *D*.

3. D: In his book, *The Prince*, Niccolo Machiavelli advocated that a ruler should be prepared to do whatever is necessary to remain in power, including using violence and political deception as a means to coerce the people of a state or eliminate political rivals. John Locke, Choice *A*, contributed and advocated liberal principles, most prominently the right to life, liberty, and health. Jean-Jacques Rousseau, Choice *B*, heavily influenced the French Revolution and American Revolution by advocating individual equality, self-rule, and religious freedom. Karl Marx, Choice *C*, wrote that the struggle between the bourgeois (ruling class) and the proletariat (working class) would result in a classless society in which all citizens commonly owned the means of production.

4. B: More than one million African Americans in the South went north in search of jobs during and after World War I. The Great Migration led to increased racial tension as blacks and whites competed for housing and jobs in northern cities. The Great Migration also led to the Harlem Renaissance.

5. C: Conservatism emphasizes maintaining traditions and believes political and social stability is more important than progress and reform. In general, Socialism, Choice *A*, seeks to establish a democratically elected government that owns the means of production, regulates the exchange of commodities, and distributes the wealth equally among citizens. Liberalism, Choice *B*, is based on individualism and equality, supporting the freedoms of speech, press, and religion, while Libertarian ideals, Choice *D*, emphasize individual liberties and freedom from government interference.

6. C: Population density, which is the total number of people divided by the total land area, generally tends to be much higher in urban areas than rural ones. This is true due to high-rise apartment complexes, sewage and freshwater infrastructure, and complex transportation systems, allowing for easy movement of food from nearby farms. Consequently, competition among citizens for resources is certainly higher in high-density areas, as are greater strains on infrastructure within urban centers.

7. D: Fascism considers a strong central government, martial law, and violent coercion as necessary means to maintain political stability and strengthen the state. Neither the politics of Communism, a society in which the people own the means of production, nor Socialism, a society in which the government owns the means of production, promote violence but instead advocate a classless society that eliminates the class struggle. Thus, Choices *A* and *B* are incorrect. Nationalism, Choice *C*,

Answer Explanations #1 | Job Knowledge

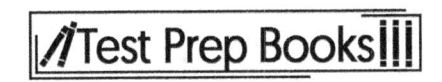

emphasizes preserving a nation's culture, often to the exclusion of other cultures, but violence is not officially promoted as a means for suppressing dissent, as is the case with Fascism.

8. D: The market. The market, through supply and demand, determines the exchange rate with a "flexible" or "floating" exchange rate. The government, Choice A, is not the correct answer because it is involved in "fixed" exchange rates to help keep exchange rates stable. Taxes, Choice B, is also incorrect because they create government revenue. The Federal Reserve, Choice C, is the bank of banks.

9. D: Both the states and the federal government may propose, enact, and enforce laws. States pass legislation that concerns the states in their state legislative houses, while the federal government passes federal laws in Congress. Only states may hold elections and determine voting procedures, even for federal offices such as the president of the United States, and only the federal government may expand any state territory, change state lines, admit new states into the nation, or regulate immigration and pass laws regarding naturalization of citizens.

10. B: For the first card drawn, the probability of a king being pulled is $\frac{4}{52}$. Since this card isn't replaced, if a king is drawn first, the probability of a king being drawn second is $\frac{3}{51}$. The probability of a king being drawn in both the first and second draw is the product of the two probabilities:

$$\frac{4}{52} \times \frac{3}{51} = \frac{12}{2,652}$$

This fraction, when divided by $\frac{12}{12}$, equals $\frac{1}{221}$.

11. B: The process by which the House and Senate may debate a bill differs. In the House, how long a speaker may debate a bill is limited, while in the Senate, speakers may debate the bill indefinitely and delay voting on the bill by filibuster—a practice in which a speaker refuses to stop speaking until a majority vote stops the filibuster or the time for the vote passes. In both the House and the Senate, anyone may introduce a bill. Only the president of the United States may veto the bill, so neither the House nor Senate holds that power. Before the bill may be presented to the president to be signed, the wording of the bill must be identical in both houses. Another procedural difference is that the number of amendments is limited in the House but not the Senate; however, this does not appear as an answer choice.

12. B: The American Revolution occurred first in 1775, and a number of European soldiers fought for the patriots. The American Revolution, in part, inspired the French Revolution. The Marquis de Lafayette came to America in 1777 and was wounded during the Battle of Brandywine. He returned to France after the American Revolution and became a leader in the French Revolution in 1789.

13. C: The Republican Party emerged as the abolitionist party during the antebellum period and succeeded in abolishing slavery after the North's victory in the Civil War. The Constitutional Union Party supported slavery but opposed Southern secession, while the Southern Democrats supported slavery and secession. The Whig Party splintered in the 1850s as a result of tension over slavery, leading to the creation of the Republican Party and Constitutional Union Party.

14. C: The North had a population of about 18.5 million while the South had only 5.5 million citizens and 3.5 million slaves. This meant the Union could more easily replace men while the Confederacy could not. The South was defending their homes from damage, since most of the war happened in the South, so

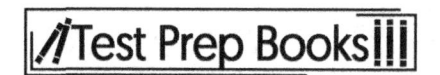

Choice A is incorrect. Choice B is incorrect—the South had free labor at home, so they didn't have to worry about leaving their farms to go to war. Finally, Choice D is incorrect; the South had more experienced military leaders due to their participation in the Mexican-American War.

15. B: The mass media does not have the ability to regulate communications. The mass media has the ability to shape public opinion, making Choice A incorrect. Mass media selects which events to report on and thereby influences the perceived importance of events in society and determines the context in which to report events, making Choices C and D incorrect. Only the federal government may regulate communications through agencies such as the Federal Communications Commission (FCC).

16. C: Pull factors are reasons people immigrate to a particular area. Obviously, educational opportunities attract thousands of people on a global level and on a local level. For example, generally areas with strong schools have higher property values, due to the relative demand for housing in those districts. The same is true for nations with better educational opportunities. Unemployment, low GDP, and incredibly high population densities may serve to deter people from moving to a certain place and can be considered push factors.

17. A: An authoritarian government is ruled by a single party that holds complete control over the powerful central government. Authoritarian governments limit political freedom and civil liberties to diminish any opposition. Communism, Choice B, is one in which the class struggle between the ruling and working classes is eliminated because the means of production belongs to the people. Similarly, Socialism, Choice C, is classless, but in this type of government, the government owns the means of production and is often democratic. Unlike a regular monarchy, a federal monarchy, Choice D, is a federal government in which political power is divided between the monarch (head of state) and regional governments, resulting in checks and balances of power.

18. D: The factors of production are land, labor, capital, and entrepreneurship. The other choices all include at least one option that is not a factor of production.

19. A: Since the Cold War ended, the U.S. foreign policy no longer centers on preventing the spread of Communism but instead focuses on promoting the ideals of democracy, promoting global cooperation through diplomacy and international organizations, and solving international problems through those channels. The U.S. foreign policy considers national security as the nation's most important goal.

20. A: If each man gains 10 pounds, every original data point will increase by 10 pounds. Therefore, the man with the original median will still have the median value, but that value will increase by 10. The smallest value and largest value will also increase by 10 and, therefore, the difference between the two won't change. The range does not change in value and, thus, remains the same.

21. C: A treaty is an agreement between states or groups of states that functions like a contract by binding the participants to the agreed-upon terms. Examples of treaties include peace treaties, trade agreements, and military defense pacts. Participating states give up some degree of sovereignty, as they are bound to the terms of the treaty until it's revoked, in exchange for the desired benefit. Cooperation and diplomacy, Choices A and D, are essential for the formation of treaties, but they do not involve the same degree of limiting the ability to govern within the state. Foreign aid, Choice B, is a voluntary transfer of resources between countries. Although the foreign aid might be attached to terms restricting the aid beneficiary's government, treaties always involve exchanging some degree of internal sovereignty for the treaty's intended mutual benefit; thus, treaties is the best answer.

Answer Explanations #1 | Job Knowledge

22. B: The Chinese required other countries to pay tribute in order to establish trade relations. Foreign emissaries also had to prostrate themselves before the Chinese emperor. Potlatches, Choice A, were a Native American form of gift giving. Bartering, Choice C, was a common form of economic exchange, but it had no political significance.

23. C: Realism focuses on how states pursue their self-interest and asserts that the international system inevitably leads to conflict. Realism necessarily assumes that all states are interested in advancing their self-interests by expanding their power. In contrast, Liberalism advocates for equality between states and supports international and nongovernmental organizations' role in international relations. Choices A and B describe principles of Liberalism. Choice D is factually incorrect and more closely associated with Liberalism.

24. A: Radical Republicans wanted to ensure that recently freed slaves had the economic and political rights that would enable them to achieve self-sufficiency in the post-Civil War era. Democrats, such as Andrew Johnson, preferred leniency towards the South while Radical Republicans wanted a harsher punishment, making Choice B incorrect. This led to conflict between Johnson and Radical Republicans who almost succeeded in having him impeached in 1868.

25. C: Map projections, such as the Mercator Projection, are useful for finding positions on the globe, but they attempt to represent a spherical object on a flat surface. As a result, they distort areas nearest the poles, which misrepresent the size of Antarctica, Greenland, and other high latitudinal locations. Map projects can include great detail; some illustrate the physical features in an area, and most include both the northern and southern hemispheres.

26. B: Macroeconomics. Macroeconomics studies the economy on a large scale and focuses on issues such as unemployment, interest rates, price levels, and national income. Microeconomics, Choice A, studies more individual or small group behaviors such as scarcity or supply and demand. Scarcity, Choice C, is not correct because it refers to the availability of goods and services. Supply and demand, Choice D, is also incorrect because it refers to the quantity of goods and services that is produced and/or needed.

27. C: To find the expected value, take the product of each individual sum and the probability of rolling the sum, then add together the products for each sum. There are 36 possible rolls:

The probability of rolling a 2 is $\frac{1}{36}$.

The probability of rolling a 3 is $\frac{2}{36}$.

The probability of rolling a 4 is $\frac{3}{36}$.

The probability of rolling a 5 is $\frac{4}{36}$.

The probability of rolling a 6 is $\frac{5}{36}$.

The probability of rolling a 7 is $\frac{6}{36}$.

The probability of rolling an 8 is $\frac{5}{36}$.

The probability of rolling a 9 is $\frac{4}{36}$.

The probability of rolling a 10 is $\frac{3}{36}$.

The probability of rolling an 11 is $\frac{2}{36}$.

Finally, the probability of rolling a 12 is $\frac{1}{36}$.

Each possible outcome is multiplied by the probability of it occurring. Like this:

$$2 \times \frac{1}{36} = a$$

$$3 \times \frac{2}{36} = b$$

$$4 \times \frac{3}{36} = c$$

And so forth.

Then, all of those results are added together:

$$a + b + c \ldots = expected\ value$$

In this case, it equals 7.

28. B: Ancient Greeks created many of the cultural and political institutions that form the basis of modern western civilization. Athens was an important Greek democracy, and all adult men could participate in politics after they had completed their military service. The Roman Empire, Choice A, evolved from the Roman Republic, but it was not democratic. The Achaemenid Empire and Zhou Dynasty, Choices C and D, were imperial monarchies that did not allow citizens to have much, if any, political voice.

29. D: 13th Amendment. The U.S. Constitution, Choice A, actually legalized slavery by counting slaves as three-fifths of a person. The Compromise of 1850, Choice B, banned the slave trade in Washington D.C. but also created a stronger fugitive slave law. The Emancipation Proclamation, Choice C, only banned slavery in the Confederacy. The 13th Amendment finally banned slavery throughout the country.

30. B: Latitudinal and longitudinal coordinates delineate absolute location. In contrast to relative location, which describes a location as compared to another, better-known place, absolute location provides an exact place on the globe through the latitude and longitude system. Choice A, cardinal directions (north, south, east, west) are used in absolute location, but coordinates must be added in order to have an absolute location. Using other, better-known locations to find a location, Choice C, is referred to as relative location, and absolute location is far more precise than simply finding hemispherical position on the globe.

31. A: Free. A free market does not involve government interventions or monopolies while trading between buyers and suppliers. However, in a command market, the government determines the price of

Answer Explanations #1 | Job Knowledge

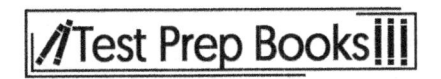

goods and services. Gross and exchange markets refer to situations where brokers and traders make exchanges in the financial realm.

32. A: An outlier is a data value that is either far above or far below the majority of values in a sample set. The mean is the average of all the values in the set. In a small sample set, a very high or very low number could drastically change the average (or mean) of the data points. Outliers will have no more of an effect on the median (the middle value when arranged from lowest to highest) than any other value above or below the median. If the same outlier does not repeat, outliers will have no effect on the mode (value that repeats most often).

33. A: The Silk Roads were a network of trade routes between Asia and the Mediterranean. Merchants and Pilgrims traveled along the Silk Roads and brought new ideas and technologies, as well as trade goods. For example, Buddhism spread from India to China. Chinese technologies also spread westward, including gunpowder and the printing press. The Silk Roads also spread the Bubonic Plague to Europe, but it did not arrive in the New World until Columbus landed there in 1492.

34. C: The 19th amendment gave women the right to vote. The 15th Amendment, Choice A, gave blacks the right to vote. The 18th Amendment, Choice B, introduced alcohol prohibition. The 20th amendment, Choice D, repealed prohibition.

35. C: Developed Nations have better infrastructural systems, which can include government, transportation, financial, and educational institutions. Consequently, its citizens tend to have higher rates of literacy, due to the sheer availability of educational resources and government sanctioned educational systems. In contrast, developing nations, Choice A, struggle to provide educational resources to their citizens. Nations in the Northern Hemisphere, Choice B, have no greater availability to educational resources than those in the Southern Hemisphere, and centers of trade, Choice D, don't necessarily equate to higher levels of education, as many may exist in poorer nations with fewer resources.

36. C: Contraction and trough. A recession occurs between the contraction and trough phases of the business cycle. Between expansion and peak phases, employment and productivity are on the rise, causing a "boom." Between the peak and contraction, unemployment rates are starting to fall, but have not yet hit an all-time low. Between trough and expansion phases, the economy is getting back on its feet and starting to increase employment again.

37. D: $\frac{1}{12}$. The probability of picking the winner of the race is $\frac{1}{4}$, or $\left(\frac{number\ of\ favorable\ outcomes}{number\ of\ total\ outcomes}\right)$. Assuming the winner was picked on the first selection, three horses remain from which to choose the runner-up (these are dependent events). Therefore, the probability of picking the runner-up is $\frac{1}{3}$. To determine the probability of multiple events, the probability of each event is multiplied:

$$\frac{1}{4} \times \frac{1}{3} = \frac{1}{12}$$

38. A: The Mongol army was largely a cavalry force. The Mongols were a nomadic people who trained as horsemen from a young age. They used their highly mobile army to build a huge empire in Asia, the Middle East, and Eastern Europe. Mongol rulers were relatively tolerant of other religions because they wanted to reduce conflict within their empire, making Choice B incorrect. They also encouraged trade because they produced few of their own goods, making Choice *C* incorrect. The Mongol rulers also encouraged literacy and appreciated visual art, making Choice *D* incorrect.

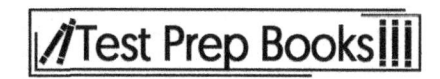

39. B: *Brown vs. Board of Education* ruled that separate schools for blacks and whites were inherently unequal and sparked demands for more civil rights. *Roe v. Wade* in 1973, Choice *A*, increased access to abortion. *Plessy vs. Ferguson*, Choice *C*, established the "separate but equal" doctrine. *Marbury vs. Madison* in 1803, Choice *D*, established the doctrine of judicial review.

40. C: Although it can place a strain on some resources, population density is not a negative demographic indicator. For example, New York City, one of the most densely populated places on Earth, enjoys one of the highest standards of living in the world. Other world cities such as Tokyo, Los Angeles, and Sydney also have tremendously high population densities and high standards of living. High infant mortality rates, low literacy rates, and low life expectancies are all poor demographic indicators that suggest a low quality of life for the citizens living in those areas.

41. A: Closed market operations. Monetary policies are sustained by assuring bank reserves, adjusting interest rates, and open market operations. Closed market operations do NOT uphold monetary policies.

42. D: This system of equations involves one quadratic function and one linear function, as seen from the degree of each equation. One way to solve this is through substitution.

Solving for y in the second equation yields:

$$y = x + 2$$

Plugging this equation in for the y of the quadratic equation yields:

$$x^2 - 2x + x + 2 = 8$$

Simplifying the equation, it becomes:

$$x^2 - x + 2 = 8$$

Setting this equal to zero and factoring, it becomes:

$$x^2 - x - 6 = 0 = (x - 3)(x + 2)$$

Solving these two factors for x gives the zeros:

$$x = 3, -2$$

To find the y-value for the point, each number can be plugged in to either original equation. Solving each one for y yields the points $(3, 5)$ and $(-2, 0)$.

43. A: Renaissance scholars and artists sought to emulate classical Greek and Roman culture. They translated Greek and Roman political philosophers and literature. They also copied classical architecture. Europeans had little direct contact with China until the thirteenth century, which was long after the Zhou Dynasty collapsed, making Choice *C* incorrect. The Renaissance Era occurred within the continent of Europe and drew from other European styles, so nations of northern Africa and the Middle East, such as ancient Egypt and the Ottoman Empire, had little to no inspiration on Renaissance scholars and artists at that time. Therefore, Choices *B* and *D* are incorrect.

Answer Explanations #1 | Job Knowledge

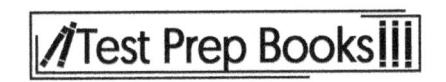

44. B: The "Bleeding Kansas" conflict contributed to sectional tension before the Civil War. The application of popular sovereignty in Kansas led to conflict as free-soil and pro-slavery forces rushed into the territory. Malcolm X's death, Choice A, was in 1965, almost 100 years after the Civil War ended. The 13th Amendment, Choice C, was ratified in 1865 and was approved at the very end of the Civil War. Shay's Rebellion, Choice D, was an uprising during 1786 and 1787 in Massachusetts.

45. C: Longitudinal position, or a place's location either east or west, has no bearing on the place's climate. In contrast, a place's latitudinal position, or its distance away from the direct rays of the sun in the Tropics, greatly affects its climate. Additionally, proximity to mountains, which can block wind patterns, and elevation, which generally lowers temperature by three degrees for every one thousand feet gained, also impact climate.

46. B: As inflation increases, purchasing power decreases. As more money is printed, the monetary value of the dollar drops and, in turn, decreases the purchasing power of goods and services. So, as inflation increases, consumers are not spending as much and the value of the dollar is low.

47. D: This problem can be solved by using unit conversion. The initial units are miles per minute. The final units need to be feet per second. Converting miles to feet uses the equivalence statement 1 mi = 5,280 ft. Converting minutes to seconds uses the equivalence statement 1 min = 60 s. Setting up the ratios to convert the units is shown in the following equation:

$$\frac{72 \text{ mi}}{90 \text{ min}} \times \frac{1 \text{ min}}{60 \text{ s}} \times \frac{5,280 \text{ ft}}{1 \text{ mi}} = 70.4 \frac{\text{ft}}{\text{s}}$$

The initial units cancel out, and the new units are left.

48. C: Louis the XIV was an absolute monarch who ruled during the sixteenth century. He concentrated power on the throne by forcing nobles to spend most of their time at the royal court. The French Revolution occurred about two hundred years after he died. Absolute monarchs like Louis the XIV bolstered their prestige by claiming they were appointed by God. The Mandate of Heaven was a similar concept, but it was developed by the Zhou Dynasty in China about two thousand years before Louis XIV was born.

49. D: World War I led to the League of Nations and the communist revolution in Russia, Choices A and B. The USSR and U.S. both emerged as two rival superpowers after World War II. It was thus a bipolar, rather than unipolar, world. The tension and mistrust between the U.S. and USSR eventually led to the Cold War, which ended in 1991.

50. C: Unlike erosion, which is caused by moving particles from water or wind, weathering occurs due to fluctuations in temperatures, the impact of long-term sun exposure, or exposure to chemicals that break down rocks, trees, or soil. Over time, the effects of freezing temperatures can break down massive rocks or lead to other significant changes in the landscape. Weathering does not involve wind and rain, since those particles are constantly moving to exact change on the earth's surface. Also, weathering takes place in all climates, not just cold ones.

51. B: Fiat money. Commodity money, Choice A, refers to a good that has value, such as a precious metal. Bank money, Choice C, is money that is credited by a bank to those people who have their money deposited there. The term Reserve money, Choice D, does not refer to anything.

52. C: 216 cm^2. Because area is a two-dimensional measurement, the dimensions are multiplied by a scale factor that is squared to determine the scale factor of the corresponding areas. The dimensions of the rectangle are multiplied by a scale factor of 3. Therefore, the area is multiplied by a scale factor of 3^2 (which is equal to 9):

$$24 \text{ cm}^2 \times 9 = 216 \text{ cm}^2$$

53. A: Most scholars already knew the world was round by 1492. On the other hand, the arrival of Europeans in North and South America introduced deadly diseases that killed millions of native peoples. Europeans had developed immunity to diseases such as smallpox, while Native Americans had not. In addition, Europeans introduced a number of new plants and animals to the New World, but they also adopted many new foods as well, including potatoes, tomatoes, chocolate, and tobacco. Finally, Europeans tried to convert Native Americans to Christianity, but Indians did not completely give up their traditional beliefs. Instead, they blended Christianity with indigenous and African beliefs to create new syncretic religions.

54. B: Native Americans began to grow crops. During the Neolithic Revolution, Native Americans began to cultivate beans, squash, chilies, and other vegetables. However, they did not domesticate many large animals, Choice A—only the dog in North America and the llama in Central America. Horses and cattle only arrived in North America as a result of European exploration. Native Americans also did not develop steel or iron, Choice C—Native Americans only obtained these items by trading with Europeans. Despite these limits, Native Americans did develop a semi-sedentary lifestyle, formed social hierarchies, and created new religious beliefs.

55. B: Developing nations tend to have higher levels of impoverished citizens. As a result, many of their citizens must rely on subsistence farming, or producing enough food to feed their families, in order to survive. In contrast, developed nations tend to produce surpluses of food and very few, if any, of its citizens engage in subsistence farming. Developing nations are less likely to have complex highway systems, stable governments, and economic stability due to financial pressures.

56. C: The four phases of the business cycle are peak, trough, expansion, contraction. The other answer choices include at least one wrong phase.

57. D: The Industrial Revolution is probably one of the most important turning points in world history. The United States and Western Europe, especially Britain, were the first areas to industrialize. Steam engines were used to improve economic and transportation efficiency. They also gave western empires a military advantage over less developed countries in Asia and Africa. Finally, industrialization required large amounts of unskilled labor, which created the working class.

58. A: The New Deal introduced a number of programs designed to increase regulation and boost the economy. Many of them remain in effect today, such as the Social Security Administration and the Securities and Exchange Commission. The New Deal also led to the Republican and Democratic parties to reverse their ideological positions on government intervention. It did not lead to a third party, Choice B. President Franklin D. Roosevelt was actually elected to four terms in office and the official two-term limit was not established until the 22nd Amendment was ratified in 1951. Until then, the two-term limit had been an informal custom established by President George Washington when he left office in 1797. Thus, Choice C is incorrect. Choice D is also incorrect. The Great Depression led to the New Deal, and not the other way around.

Answer Explanations #1 | Situational Judgment

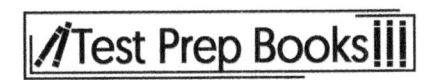

59. D: Most nonrenewable resources are easier to harness and utilize than renewable sources. That may sound counterintuitive, but the reality is that it is harder to develop solar, wind, and geothermal infrastructure than it is to build a coal-fired power plant for the production of electricity. Consequently, developing nations tend to rely on these reliable sources in order to fuel their equally developing economy.

60. D: The GDP is used to measure an economy's growth. The inflation of a country doesn't tell us anything about their growth. A country may hold a lot of money in reserves but this does not tell us if they are growing or not. The same can be said for having a lot of exports. It does indicate that an economy is necessarily growing.

Situational Judgment

Situation 1:

Most Effective - C: Having an open meeting with everyone would reemphasize the importance of the chain-of-command and resolve problems at the lowest possible level.

Least Effective - E: Giving up your position because of opposition would demonstrate weakness as a leader and lead to similar actions in future decisions.

Situation 2:

Most Effective - D: This is a case of "integrity first." It is fine to voice your opinion to the aid, but better to refrain from interfering with the selection process based on personal feelings.

Least Effective - B or E: Giving a recommendation to make the aide go away would not uphold the core value of integrity. An honest opinion should always be given. The same could be said for an anonymous letter. Officers should always be forthright and honest when giving recommendations.

Situation 3:

Most Effective - B: Part of being a good officer is to help peers. Try and point out what you would change in the speech and include why you would do it.

Least Effective - A: Never go to a superior with the intention of trying to make yourself look better by slandering a coworker. This is an integrity violation and will erode your credibility as an officer.

Situation 4:

Most Effective - D: Situations come up in every unit that can impact the mission. In this situation, notify your supervisor immediately so they can get someone to replace the ill coworker and accomplish the mission.

Least Effective - B: Do not try to finish the project by yourself. Notify your supervisor immediately any time a situation arises that may impact completing the mission on time.

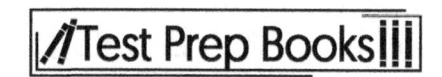

Situation 5:

Most Effective - A: Be a professional and return to work. Sign the documents so that you are not causing another officer to work late due to your honest mistake.

Least Effective - D: Having a subordinate forge the documents puts your integrity and that of the subordinate at risk. Do not let a minor mistake like forgetting to sign a piece of paper ruin your credibility.

Situation 6:

Most effective - E: A response to the new commander's email would be the best solution to this scenario. Let him know that you are excited to take the new position and that you would like to set up a date and time to discuss the new role. This will help ensure a smooth transition.

Least Effective - B: Always take the opportunity to respond to an email from your new commander. It is the professional thing to do and will allow time to discuss what is expected of the new position, answer any questions, and learn how to excel.

Situation 7:

Most Effective - D: This is an opportunity to teach, coach, and mentor a fellow officer by discussing the Air Force core values. By talking to the coworker and not telling their superior officer, you offer this person a chance to grow from the mistake without hurting their career.

Least Effective - C: Resorting to blackmail would make you just as guilty as your peer and would put your integrity on the line.

Situation 8:

Most Effective - C: It is normal to reach a plateau in assignments. Let your senior officer know, and express that you are looking for a more challenging assignment to further your career and benefit the Air Force.

Least Effective - E: Remember, integrity first. Be honest in everything you do and no one can question your integrity.

Situation 9:

Most effective - E: Be honest with the officer and let him/her know that you are already dealing with a maximum workload. In addition, you have offered a solution to the problem by offering to distribute the work to another qualified coworker.

Least Effective - D: Taking on additional work without sufficient time will cause the quality of both projects to diminish.

Situation 10:

Most Effective - D: Inform the senior officer of the situation and see if the projects can be redistributed to help alleviate stress for coworkers that are overwhelmed.

Answer Explanations #1 | Situational Judgment

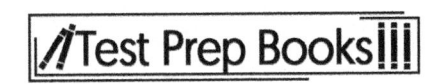

Least Effective - A: You were attentive to notice the situation; this is a good time to put service before self and offer a solution to the problem.

Situation 11:

Most Effective - C: They asked you to resolve the dispute, so be the professional and make a decision.

Least Effective - E: Giving a lecture to both officers that asked you to settle the dispute would probably turn both of them against you. They must value your opinion, or they would not have asked for your assistance.

Situation 12:

Most Effective - B: Safety issues need to be addressed immediately. It is your duty as an officer to notify the senior officer in charge if a coworker is manipulating numbers that could lead to an accident or incident.

Least Effective - A: It is your responsibility to speak up in this scenario. Again, integrity first. Anyone can prevent an accident.

Situation 13:

Most Effective - A: If the senior officer asks the question, they want an answer. Be honest, and offer a candid assessment in the area in which he/she could improve.

Least Effective - B: Again, if a senior officer asks the question, he/she is looking for an answer. Refusing makes you and your supervisor look bad.

Situation 14:

Most Effective - D: Make the correct decision and vote for the most qualified candidate.

Least Effective - C: By voting for Candidate 3, you are not being honest. Remember the honest decision is not always going to be the easiest. If you are always honest, no one will ever question your integrity.

Situation 15:

Most Effective - A: Let your new coworker know that you want to do your best on this project, you value their help, and you think the work should be shared equally. In addition, offer congratulations on the coworker's upcoming retirement and encourage him/her to finish strong.

Least Effective - D: Do not have the frame of mind that the project is going to be mediocre or it will. Talk to your new coworker and come up with a plan to share the workload and develop a quality product.

Situation 16:

Most Effective - C: Talk with the subordinate and let him/her know what you have heard and that you need their support in accomplishing the unit's mission.

Least Effective - B: Something has to be done in this scenario. If not, the situation is going to get worse.

Situation 17:

Most Effective - C: The best action to take in this scenario would be to question the last officer to leave the supply room. This would allow him/her to explain the situation without directly accusing him/her of stealing, and it would be an initial step in the investigative process.

Least Effective - E: If no action is taken, supplies are going to keep disappearing, and the situation is not going to get any better.

Situation 18:

Most Effective - A: Give an honest opinion on the subject, and explain you are not a subject-matter expert. In addition, refer to media and to the Embassy's public affairs office for further information.

Least Effective - B: Not answering the question could portray a negative opinion of the officer.

Situation 19:

Most Effective - D: Meet with the unit and discuss the issue that has been presented. Offer a solution to the problem, stay positive, and make sure there is an opportunity for subordinates to take a break.

Least Effective - A: Always try and solve the problem before going to senior leadership. This would create distrust among subordinates and show senior officers a lack of leadership and inability to handle simple unit challenges.

Situation 20:

Most Effective - A: Be honest and admit your mistake. The person receiving the email will be more than willing to delete the material. Your supervisor will appreciate the honesty and inform the chain-of-command.

Least Effective - E: Do not lie about the situation. All classified email chains are monitored, and covering up this mistake could lead to revocation of a security clearance.

Situation 21:

Most Effective - B: Meeting with the training director may open up an opportunity for training in the near future. It also shows the commanding officer cares about the mission of the U.S. Embassy in the host country.

Least Effective - D: Sending out letters would be perceived as a false accusation, damage your reputation, and could have an effect on future requests for training.

Situation 22:

Most Effective - C: The leader may not have realized they were creating this environment. Meeting with the superior will clear the air, and it should afford an opportunity to work more independently.

Least Effective - A: Telling the supervisor to back off would create animosity and make the situation worse.

Situation 23:

Answer Explanations #1 | Situational Judgment

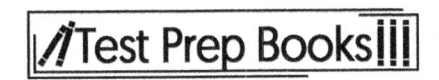

Most Effective - D: Ultimately, the boss has the final decision. A well thought out plan with actions and contingencies may sway their decision.

Least Effective - A: This would be insubordination no matter how the plan worked out. Either way, the boss would feel disrespected.

Situation 24:

Most Effective - A: Budget cuts will affect everyone in the unit. Talking to peers can offer solutions that may not have been previously discovered.

Least Effective - B: Do not blame subordinates. This will erode trust in the unit.

Situation 25:

Most Effective - D: Keeping the drivers informed of the delay will help with them understand the situation. Accommodating them will help build rapport for future deliveries.

Least Effective - C: This would frustrate the drivers even more and may have an effect on future deliveries.

Situation 26:

Most Effective - D: HR is in the best position to determine the most appropriate response to your supervisor's activities outside of work. Choice A, confronting your supervisor, may or may not be effective and could negatively affect your working relationship with your supervisor. Choice C, taking your concerns to your supervisor's boss, is inappropriate when HR is available to deal with the situation.

Least Effective - E: Publicly condemning your supervisor and posting clips online will bring attention to the podcast and could harm the relationship between your home country and the country you are assigned to, which is exactly what you are trying to avoid. It is also a passive-aggressive and ineffective communication technique which could make others question your suitability for advancement.

Situation 27:

Most Effective - B: Helping the janitor and his brother find appropriate social services is a compassionate response that will also address the problem of missing food. If social services are not available in the country you are assigned to, Option E, organizing a food drive, would be an excellent backup option. However, this would require you to reveal that the janitor is the one that has been stealing the food.

Least Effective - A: While stealing generally is a cause for firing an employee, this option does not take the janitor's difficult situation into consideration and would be unnecessarily cruel.

Situation 28:

Most Effective - A: Privately explaining the importance of the dress code is the best way to address the problem. It gives your team member a chance to correct their behavior and also demonstrates your willingness and ability to effectively lead the members of your team.

Least Effective - D: Recommending that your team member be fired without even trying to resolve the situation is unnecessarily harsh, as well as demonstrating a lack of leadership ability on your part. Choice

B is also very ineffective, but it will most likely have fewer permanent consequences for your team member than being fired, and others in the meeting also have the opportunity to hold you accountable for your extremely poor leadership style.

English Expression

1. B: Move the sentence so that it comes before the preceding sentence. For this question, place the underlined sentence in each prospective choice's position. To keep it as-is is incorrect because the father "going crazy" doesn't logically follow the fact that he was a "city slicker." Choice *C* is incorrect because the sentence in question is not a concluding sentence and does not transition smoothly into the second paragraph. Choice *D* is incorrect because the sentence doesn't necessarily need to be omitted since it logically follows the very first sentence in the passage.

2. D: Choice *D* is correct because "As it turns out" indicates a contrast from the previous sentiment, that the RV was a great purchase. Choice *A* is incorrect because the sentence needs an effective transition from the paragraph before. Choice *B* is incorrect because the text indicates it *is* surprising that the RV was a great purchase because the author was skeptical beforehand. Choice *C* is incorrect because the transition "Furthermore" does not indicate a contrast.

3. B: This sentence calls for parallel structure. Choice *B* is correct because the verbs "wake," "eat," and "break" are consistent in tense and parts of speech. Choice *A* is incorrect because the words "wake" and "eat" are present tense while the word "broke" is in past tense. Choice *C* is incorrect because this turns the sentence into a question, which doesn't make sense within the context. Choice *D* is incorrect because it breaks tense with the rest of the passage. "Waking," "eating," and "breaking" are all present participles, and the context around the sentence is in past tense.

4. C: Choice *C* is correct because it is clear and fits within the context of the passage. Choice *A* is incorrect because "We rejoiced as 'hackers'" does not give a reason why hacking was rejoiced. Choice *B* is incorrect because it does not mention a solution being found and is therefore not specific enough. Choice *D* is incorrect because the meaning is eschewed by the helping verb "had to rejoice," and the sentence suggests that rejoicing was necessary to "hack" a solution.

5. A: The original sentence is correct because the verb tense as well as the meaning aligns with the rest of the passage. Choice *B* is incorrect because the order of the words makes the sentence more confusing than it otherwise would be. Choice *C* is incorrect because "We are even making" is in present tense. Choice *D* is incorrect because "We will make" is future tense. The surrounding text of the sentence is in past tense.

6. B: Choice *B* is correct because there is no punctuation needed if a dependent clause ("while traveling across America") is located behind the independent clause ("it allowed us to share adventures"). Choice *A* is incorrect because there are two dependent clauses connected and no independent clause, and a complete sentence requires at least one independent clause. Choice *C* is incorrect because of the same reason as Choice *A*. Semicolons have the same function as periods: there must be an independent clause on either side of the semicolon. Choice *D* is incorrect because the dash simply interrupts the complete sentence.

7. C: The rules for "me" and "I" is that one should use "I" when it is the subject pronoun of a sentence, and "me" when it is the object pronoun of the sentence. Break the sentence up to see if "I" or "me" should be used. To say "Those are memories that I have now shared" is correct, rather than "Those are memories that me have now shared." Choice D is incorrect because "my siblings" should come before "I."

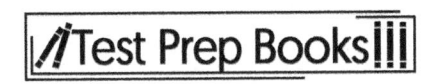

8. D: Choice D is correct because Fred Hampton becoming an activist was a direct result of him wanting to see lasting social change for Black people. Choice A doesn't make sense because "In the meantime" denotes something happening at the same time as another thing. Choice B is incorrect because the text's tone does not indicate that becoming a civil rights activist is an unfortunate path. Choice C is incorrect because "Finally" indicates something that comes last in a series of events, and the word in question is at the beginning of the introductory paragraph.

9. C: Choice C is correct because there should be a comma between the city and state, as well as after the word "Illinois." Commas should be used to separate all geographical items within a sentence. Choice A is incorrect because it does not include the comma after "Illinois." Choice B is incorrect because the comma after "Maywood" interrupts the phrase, "Maywood of Chicago." Finally, Choice D is incorrect because the order of the sentence designates that Chicago, Illinois is in Maywood, which is incorrect.

10. C: This is a difficult question. The paragraph is incorrect as-is because it is too long and thus loses the reader halfway through. Choice C is correct because if the new paragraph began with "While studying at Triton," we would see a smooth transition from one paragraph to the next. We can also see how the two paragraphs are logically split in two. The first half of the paragraph talks about where he studied. The second half of the paragraph talks about the NAACP and the result of his leadership in the association. If we look at the passage as a whole, we can see that there are two main topics that should be broken into two separate paragraphs.

11. B: The BPP "was another activist group that ..." We can figure out this answer by looking at context clues. We know that the BPP is "similar in function" to the NAACP. To find out what the NAACP's function is, we must look at the previous sentences. We know from above that the NAACP is an activist group, so we can assume that the BPP is also an activist group.

12. A: Choice A is correct because the Black Panther Party is one entity; therefore, the possession should show the "Party's approach" with the apostrophe between the "y" and the "s." Choice B is incorrect because the word "Parties" should not be plural. Choice C is incorrect because the apostrophe indicates that the word "Partys" is plural. The plural of "party" is "parties." Choice D is incorrect because, again, the word "parties" should not be plural; instead, it is one unified party.

13. C: Choice C is correct because the passage is told in past tense, and "enabled" is a past tense verb. Choice A, "enable," is present tense. Choice B, "are enabling," is a present participle, which suggests a continuing action. Choice D, "will enable," is future tense.

14. D: Choice D is correct because the conjunction "and" is the best way to combine the two independent clauses. Choice A is incorrect because the word "he" becomes repetitive since the two clauses can be joined together. Choice B is incorrect because the conjunction "but" indicates a contrast, and there is no contrast between the two clauses. Choice C is incorrect because the introduction of the comma after "project" with no conjunction creates a comma splice.

15. C: The word "acheivement" is misspelled. Remember the rules for "*i* before *e* except after *c*." It should be spelled "achievement." Choices B and D, "greatest" and "leader," are both spelled correctly.

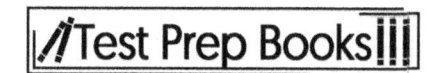

16. B: Choice *B* is correct because it provides the correct verb tense and verb form. Choice *A* is incorrect; Hampton was not "held by a press conference"—rather, he held a press conference. The passage indicates that he "made the gangs agree to a nonaggression pact," implying that it was Hampton who was doing the speaking for this conference. Choice *C* is incorrect because, with this use of the sentence, it would create a fragment because the verb "holding" has no helping verb in front of it. Choice *D* is incorrect because it adds an infinitive ("to hold") where a past tense form of a verb should be.

17. A: Choice *A* is correct because it provides the most clarity. Choice *B* is incorrect because it doesn't name the group until the end, so the phrase "the group" is vague. Choice *C* is incorrect because it indicates that the BPP's popularity grew as a result of placing the group under constant surveillance, which is incorrect. Choice *D* is incorrect because there is a misplaced modifier; this sentence actually says that the FBI's influence and popularity grew, which is incorrect.

18. B: Choice *B* is correct. Choice *A* is incorrect because there should be an independent clause on either side of a semicolon, and the phrase "In 1976" is not an independent clause. Choice *C* is incorrect because there should be a comma after introductory phrases in general, such as "In 1976," and Choice *C* omits a comma. Choice *D* is incorrect because the sentence "In 1976." is a fragment.

19. C: Choice *C* is correct because the past tense verb "provided" fits in with the rest of the verb tense throughout the passage. Choice *A*, "will provide," is future tense. Choice *B*, "provides," is present tense. Choice *D*, "providing," is a present participle, which means the action is continuous.

20. D: The correct answer is Choice *D* because this statement provides the most clarity. Choice *A* is incorrect because the noun "Chicago City Council" acts as one, so the verb "are" should be singular, not plural. Choice *B* is incorrect because it is perhaps the most confusingly worded out of all the answer choices; the phrase "December 4" interrupts the sentence without any indication of purpose. Choice *C* is incorrect because it is too vague and leaves out *who* does the commemorating.

21. B: Choice *B* is correct. Here, a colon is used to introduce an explanation. Colons either introduce explanations or lists. Additionally, the quote ends with the punctuation inside the quotes, unlike Choice *C*.

22. A: The verb tense in this passage is predominantly in the present tense, so Choice *A* is the correct answer. Choice *B* is incorrect because the subject and verb do not agree. It should be "Education provides," not "Education provide." Choice *C* is incorrect because the passage is in present tense, and "Education will provide" is future tense. Choice *D* doesn't make sense when placed in the sentence.

23. D: The possessive form of the word "it" is "its." The contraction "it's" denotes "it is." Thus, Choice *A* is wrong. The word "raises" in Choice *B* makes the sentence grammatically incorrect. Choice *C* adds an apostrophe at the end of "its." While adding an apostrophe to most words would indicate possession, adding 's to the word "it" indicates a contraction.

24. C: The word *civilised* should be spelled *civilized*. The words "distinguishes" and "creatures" are both spelled correctly.

25. B: Choice *B* is correct because it provides clarity by describing what "myopic" means right after the word itself. Choice *A* is incorrect because the explanation of "myopic" comes before the word; thus, the meaning is skewed. It's possible that Choice *C* makes sense within context. However, it's not the best way to say this because the commas create too many unnecessary phrases. Choice *D* is confusingly worded. Using "myopic focus" is not detrimental to society; however, the way D is worded makes it seem that way.

26. C: Again, we see where the second paragraph can be divided into two parts due to separate topics. The paragraph's first main focus is education addressing the mind, body, and soul. This first section, then, could end with the concluding sentence, "The human heart and psyche ..." The next sentence to start a new paragraph would be "Education is a basic human right." The rest of this paragraph talks about what education is and some of its characteristics.

27. A: Choice A is correct because the phrase "others' ideas" is both plural and indicates possession. Choice B is incorrect because "other's" indicates only one "other" that's in possession of "ideas," which is incorrect. Choice C is incorrect because no possession is indicated. Choice D is incorrect because the word "other" does not end in *s*. Others's is not a correct form of the plural possessive word.

28. D: This sentence must have a comma before "although" because the word "although" is connecting two independent clauses. Thus, Choices B and C are incorrect. Choice A is incorrect because the second sentence in the underlined section is a fragment.

29. C: Choice C is the correct choice because the word "their" indicates possession, and the text is talking about "their students," or the students of someone. Choice A, "there," means at a certain place and is incorrect. Choice B, "they're," is a contraction and means "they are." Choice D is not a word.

30. B: Choice B uses all punctuation correctly in this sentence. In American English, single quotes should only be used if they are quotes within a quote, making Choices A and C incorrect. Additionally, punctuation should go inside quotation marks with a few exceptions, making Choice D incorrect.

31. B: Choice B is correct because the conjunction "and" is used to connect phrases that are to be used jointly, such as teachers working hard to help students "identify salient information" and to "think critically." The conjunctions *so*, *but*, and *nor* are incorrect in the context of this sentence.

32. A: Choice A has consistent parallel structure with the verbs "read," "identify," and "determine." Choices B and C have faulty parallel structure with the words "determining" and "identifying." Choice D has incorrect subject/verb agreement. The sentence should read, "Students have to read…identify…and determine."

33. D: The correct choice for this sentence is that "they are…shaped by the influences." The prepositions "for," "to," and "with" do not make sense in this context. People are *shaped by*, not *shaped for, shaped to,* or *shaped with*.

34. A: To see which answer is correct, it might help to place the subject, "Teachers," near the verb. Choice A is correct: "Teachers…must strive" makes grammatical sense here. Choice B is incorrect because "Teachers…to strive" does not make grammatical sense. Choice C is incorrect because "Teachers must not only respect…but striving" eschews parallel structure. Choice D is incorrect because it is in past tense, and this passage is in present tense.

35. C: Choice C is correct because it uses an em-dash. Em-dashes are versatile. They can separate phrases that would otherwise be in parenthesis, or they can stand in for a colon. In this case, a colon would be another decent choice for this punctuation mark because the second sentence expands upon the first sentence. Choice A is incorrect because the statement is not a question. Choice B is incorrect because adding a comma here would create a comma splice. Choice D is incorrect because this creates a run-on sentence since the two sentences are independent clauses.

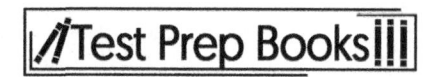

36. B: The best place for this sentence given all the answer choices is at the end of the first paragraph. Choice A is incorrect; the passage is told in chronological order, and leaving the sentence as-is defies that order, since we haven't been introduced to who raised George. Choice C is incorrect because this sentence is not an introductory sentence. It does not provide the main topic of the paragraph. Choice D is incorrect because again, it defies chronological order. By the end of paragraph two we have already gotten to George as an adult, so this sentence would not make sense here.

37. D: Out of these choices, a semicolon would be the best fit because there is an independent clause on either side of the semicolon, and the two sentences closely relate to each other. Choice A is incorrect because putting a comma between two independent clauses (i.e. complete sentences) creates a comma splice. Choice B is incorrect; omitting punctuation here creates a run-on sentence. Choice C is incorrect because an ellipsis (…) is used to designate an omission in the text.

38. B: This is another example of parallel structure. Choice A is incorrect because the verbs in the original sentence are "growing," "depleting," and "results," the last of which has a different form than the first two. Choices C and D add "depletes" and "grows," both of which abandon the "-ing" verbs.

39. C: Choice C is correct because it keeps with the verb tense in the rest of the passage: past tense. Choice A is in present tense, which is incorrect. Choice B is present progressive, which means there is a continual action, which is also incorrect. Choice D is incorrect because "was returning" is past progressive tense, which means that something was happening continuously at some point in the past.

40. C: The correct choice is the subordinating conjunction, "When." We should look at the clues around the phrase to see what fits best. Carver left his money "when he died." Choice A, "Because," could perhaps be correct, but "When" is the more appropriate word to use here. Choice B is incorrect; "Although" denotes a contrast, and there is no contrast here. Choice D is incorrect because "Finally" indicates something at the very end of a list or series, and there is no series at this point in the text.

41. A: There should be no change here. Both underlined sentences are complete and do not need changing. Choice B is incorrect because there is no punctuation between the two independent clauses, it is considered a run-on. Choice C is incorrect because placing a comma between two independent clauses creates a comma splice. Choice D is incorrect. The underlined portion could *possibly* act with a colon. However, it's not the best choice, so omit Choice D.

42. D: Choice D is correct. The text before this underlined phrase talks about the difference between "discovery" and "exploration," so making a decision on what term to label Columbus would be the best choice. The other three choices may be true to the historical narrative of Columbus; however, they do not fit within the surrounding text.

43. B: Choice B is the most clear, straightforward sentence out of all the answer choices. Choice A is inverted and is therefore a bit awkward. Choice C is unorganized and very confusing to follow. It also uses the second person "you," so this is incorrect. Finally, Choice D is incorrect; the sentence incorrectly uses the plural verb "are" rather than "is."

44. A: The comma is properly placed after the introductory phrase "In May of 2015." Choice B mixes present tense "is" with a sentence that should be written in past tense, as it is discussing something that occurred in the past. Choice C does not separate the introductory phrase from the rest of the sentence. Choice D places an extra, and unnecessary, comma prior to 2015.

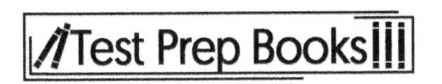

45. D: Choice D is correct, since it eliminates the unnecessary *as well* and adds a comma to separate the given example, making the sentence more direct. Choice A seems repetitive with *as well*, since it has *including*, and at the least needs punctuation. Choice B is poorly constructed, taking out the clearer *including*. Choice C also makes little sense.

46. D: Choice D is correct because the interrupting phrase, "seventeen years later," is separated by commas. Choice A is incorrect because putting a period between "later" and "The" causes the first sentence to become a fragment. Choice B is incorrect because of the same reason: the semicolon should have an independent clause on either side of it, and the first half of the sentence is not an independent clause. Choice C needs commas to separate the interrupting phrase or else the words become mashed together, causing confusion.

47. B: Choice B is correct because it adds the two commas needed to clarify key subjects individually and establish a better flow to the sentence. Since *destroying mountains*, *defeating scores of giants*, and *lifting up the world's largest creature* are separate feats, commas are needed to separate them. Also, because *the world's largest creature* can stand alone in the sentence, a comma needs to proceed its name; *the Midgard Serpent* is not necessary to the sentence but rather provides extra information as an aside. Choice A is unclear and thus incorrect. Choice C is still missing a comma, while Choice D put an extraneous one in an incorrect place.

48. B: In this sentence, the word *ocean* does not require an *s* after it to make it plural because "ocean levels" is plural. Therefore, Choices A and C are incorrect. Because the sentence is referring to multiple – if not all ocean levels – *ocean* does not require an apostrophe ('s) because that would indicate that only one ocean is the focus, which is not the case. Choice D does not fit well into the sentence and, once again, we see that *ocean* has an *s* after it. This leaves Choice B, which correctly completes the sentence and maintains the intended meaning.

49. A: Choice C can be eliminated because creating a new sentence with *not* is grammatically incorrect and throws off the rest of the sentence. Choice B is incorrect because a comma is definitely needed after *devastation* in the sentence. Choice D is also incorrect because "while" is a poor substitute for "although." *Although* in this context is meant to show contradiction with the idea that floods are associated with devastation. Therefore, none of these choices would be suitable revisions because the original was correct.

50. D: In the sentence, *is caused* is an awkward use of the verb here, so Choice A is incorrect. Choice B is incorrect because it does not agree with the subject, "flooding." *Causing*, Choice C, is a verb and it is in the present continuous tense, which appears to agree with the verb flooding, but it is incorrectly used without a helping verb. This leaves Choice D, *causes*, which does fit because it is in the indefinite present tense. Fitting each choice into the sentence and reading it in your mind will also reveal that Choice D, *causes*, correctly completes the sentence. Apply this method to all the questions when possible.

51. A: To *project* means to anticipate or forecast. This goes very well with the sentence because it describes how new technology is trying to estimate flood activity in order to prevent damage and save lives. "Project" in this case needs to be assisted by "to" in order to function in the sentence. Therefore,

Answer Explanations #1 | English Expression

Choice *A* is correct. Choices *B* and *D* are the incorrect tenses. Choice *C* is also incorrect because it lacks *to*.

52. A: Choice *D* is incorrect; *concealing* is the improper tense and it throws off the sentence. Choice *B* is a possibility, but the "be" is ultimately unnecessary in the context of the sentence, so it can be eliminated. Choice *C* is incorrect because "conceals" is the third-person present form of conceal, therefore it would not be congruent with the tense of the rest of the sentence. This makes Choice *A*, NO ERROR, the best option.

53. B: Choice *B* is correct because it uses the present tense of *understand* instead of the past tense *understood*. *Continues* emphasizes something ongoing. Therefore, the present tense of *understand* is needed. Choice *A* therefore has tense disagreement. Choice *C* uses an extraneous comma. While Choice *D's* use of the gerund is a better option, *in* would need to be added before *understanding* for correctness.

54. C: Choice *C* is correct. The subject and verb agree with each other (accounts describe), and there is no apostrophe because no possession is being shown. Choices *B* and *D* are incorrect because there is no possession—"accounts" is simply plural. Choice *A* is incorrect because the subject and verb do not agree with each other (accounts describes).

55. D: Choice *D* uses the correct punctuation. American English uses double quotes unless placing quotes within a quote (which would then require single quotes). Thus, Choices *A* and *C* are incorrect. Choice *B* is incorrect because the period should go outside of the parenthesis, not inside.

56. C: Choice *C* is the correct answer. The first sentence that stands out as the topic sentence is Sentence 3, because it speaks in general terms about what the following sentences will explain more in detail: "When selecting a career path, it's important to explore the various options available." Then, Sentence 1 is the best choice because it gives an expanding detail on the topic sentence: "Many students entering college may shy away from a major because they don't know much about it." Then, we get an example for this sentence from Sentence 2: "For example, many students won't opt for a career as an actuary, because they aren't exactly sure what it entails." Finally we end with Sentence 4, which wraps up the previous three sentences: "They would be missing out on a career that is very lucrative and in high demand."

57. A: The correct answer Choice is *A*. Again, the topic sentence tells us in general about the topic: "Hard water has a high mineral count, including calcium and magnesium." Then we are told *about* hard mineral deposits in Sentence 4: "The mineral deposits from hard water can stain hard surfaces in bathrooms and kitchens as well as clog pipes." With Sentence 3 we get more information on staining, including examples: "Hard water can stain dishes, ruin clothes, and reduce the life of any appliances it touches, such as hot water heaters, washing machines, and humidifiers." Finally, we can end with the solution in Sentence 1: "One solution is to install a water softener to reduce the mineral content of water, but this can be costly." This is a classic problem-solution structure.

58. D: Sentences 1 and 2 flow easily right away: Sentence 1 gives a topic sentence—it introduces an author and gives a situation. Sentence 2 tells about the author, her history, and the new novel, which are introduced in Sentence 1. Sentence 4 goes more into detail and tells us about the new novel and how it's praised even more than the children's series. Finally, Sentence 3 gives an example of Sentence 4: "In fact, her new novel was nominated for the prestigious Albert J. Beveridge Award but still isn't selling like her children's books, which fly off the shelves because of her name alone," which completes the paragraph.

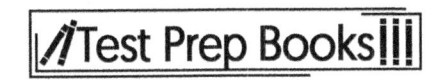

59. B: Sentence 4 is the topic sentence because it describes what the paragraph will be about: cigarettes. We see the word "addictive" in Sentence 4, so Sentence 1 is the next logical sentence because it defines *what addiction is*. Sentence 3 is also a logical next sentence because it should come before Sentence 2, which expands on Sentence 3. Thus, we have: "Cigarettes contain a drug called nicotine, one of the most addictive substances known to man. Addiction is defined as a compulsion to seek the substance despite negative consequences. According to the National Institute on Drug Abuse, nearly 35 million smokers expressed a desire to quit smoking in 2015. However, more than 85 percent of those who struggle with addiction will not achieve their goal."

60. B: This paragraph is in order from Sentence 1 through 4. The topic sentence says "It has recently been brought to my attention that most people believe that 75% of your body heat is lost through your head," outlining the main idea of the paragraph. Sentence 2 depicts what the author thinks about that statement. Sentence 3 expands on Sentence 2, saying: "It is natural to be gullible to anything said with enough authority." Sentence 4 refutes the idea in Sentence 1, "But the "fact" that the majority of your body heat is lost through your head is a lie," effectively concluding the paragraph.

61. B: This sentence is most likely to be placed after Sentence 2. In Sentence 2, we see the author introduce the notion of a "colony," and then in Sentence 3 we see the author give an example of one of those colonies, on Bird Island.

62. C: "the plume hunters who do not dare to raid the guarded rookeries" is the best choice here. Read each choice in the blank and see which one sounds the best. This is the choice that works with the agreement with the plural subject, "plume hunters." We would say "plume hunters" *do*, not *does*. *Whom* is used to refer to the object of a verb or preposition.

63. D: This sentence is most likely to be placed after Sentence 4. Sentence 4 says "This is more than a preference." In order to understand *how* Cynthia's being vegetarian is more than a preference, we would need this new sentence, which explains that "her body has never developed the enzymes to process meat or fish, so she becomes violently ill if she accidentally eats any of the offending foods." This sentence goes best after Sentence 4.

64. A: Choice *A* is the best answer. The sentence is correct as-is. "Cynthia keeps" is appropriate subject-verb agreement and establishes that the tense is in the present. The other choices are incorrect. Say each answer choice aloud in the blank and you will see how awkward Choices *B, C,* and *D* sound.

65. B: "Keeping this diet is part of her religion." Choice *B* is the correct answer. Again, read each answer choice in the blank to see which one sounds the best. Choice *B* has the correct subject/verb agreement and keeps the tense within the paragraph.

Practice Test #2

Job Knowledge

1. Which governing body is known to have the "power of the purse" within the U.S. government?
    a. Supreme Court
    b. Department of Commerce
    c. Congress
    d. Department of Labor

2. What is the name of the central bank that controls the value of money in the United States?
    a. Commodity Reserve
    b. Central Reserve
    c. Federal Reserve
    d. Bank Reserve

3. Which tone is most appropriate for an email to a supervisor requesting additional time to complete a project?
    a. Frantic and upset
    b. Colloquial and confident
    c. Calm and explanatory
    d. Appeasing and relaxed

4. Which of these is NOT a factor in which education can influence behavior?
    a. A school's rules and regulations
    b. Bullying establishing a system of social ranking
    c. School regulated social situations
    d. Grading

5. Which ONE of the following was NOT a cause of World War I?
    a. Communism
    b. Imperialism
    c. Militarism
    d. Nationalism

6. Who delivered the first televised political speech?
    a. Harry Truman
    b. Dwight Eisenhower
    c. John F. Kennedy
    d. Franklin D. Roosevelt

7. Which of the following military technologies did NOT play a role in World War I from 1914 to 1918?
    a. The atomic bomb
    b. Poison gas
    c. Armored tanks
    d. Aircraft

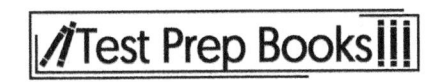

8. Which of the following is the best definition for a pure monopoly?
    a. When there is only one seller of a particular product or commodity, and the sole seller attempts to restrict firms from exiting and entering the industry at will
    b. When prices are determined by consumer demand, and no supplier maintains any significant influence over prices
    c. When people are completely free to buy the goods and services they want/need
    d. When a few large firms become the major sellers/distributors of an industry

9. The variable y is directly proportional to x. If $y = 3$ when $x = 5$, then what is y when $x = 20$?
    a. 10
    b. 12
    c. 14
    d. 16

10. Which of the following actions is considered an implied power of the presidency rather than an explicit power?
    a. Treaty signings
    b. Vetoes
    c. Pocket vetoes
    d. Executive orders

11. Which feature in Microsoft Word resembles the primary type of work that can be done in Microsoft Excel?
    a. Spell-check
    b. Font selection
    c. Thesaurus
    d. Tables and charts

12. The country of Blueland is negotiating a trade agreement with the country of Greenistan. The Greenistan dignitary remains unconvinced by the Blueland ambassador's arguments. What should the Blueland ambassador try next?
    a. Repeating his arguments again with renewed fervor
    b. Threatening a military attack if Greenistan does not accept
    c. Increasing the benefits that Greenistan receives in the deal
    d. Removing Blueland's advantages from the deal

13. A facilitator needs to consider all EXCEPT which of the following?
    a. The time available for meetings
    b. The structure of the meeting
    c. Which goals to set
    d. The number of team members

Questions 14-15 refer to the map below.

Mercosur Membership

Legend
- Full members
- Associate members

14. Mercosur is which of the following types of organizations?
    a. Customs union
    b. Environmental protection organization
    c. International lending agency
    d. Supranational union

15. Based on the map, which of the following roles does geography likely play in the formation of Mercosur?
    a. South American countries sought a way to pool their considerable natural resources.
    b. Political rivalries are less likely to arise between neighboring states.
    c. Significant economic cooperation and coordination is possible between neighboring states.
    d. Regional countries are influenced by the same climatic conditions.

Practice Test #2 | Job Knowledge

16. Which is NOT an indicator of economic growth?
    a. GDP (Gross Domestic Product)
    b. Unemployment
    c. Inflation
    d. Theory of the Firm

17. Which of the following is NOT one of the checks that individual branches have over another branch of government?
    a. The president may veto a bill passed by Congress
    b. The Supreme Court can try and remove the president for high crimes and misdemeanors committed in office
    c. Congress must approve all of the president's appointments to the Supreme Court
    d. Congress can pass a budget that limits what the president has to spend on defense

18. The period of business and industrial growth from 1876 through the turn of the twentieth century was deemed by author Mark Twain as what?
    a. Manifest Destiny
    b. The Columbian Exchange
    c. The New Deal
    d. The Gilded Age

19. For the following similar triangles, what are the values of x and y (rounded to one decimal place)?

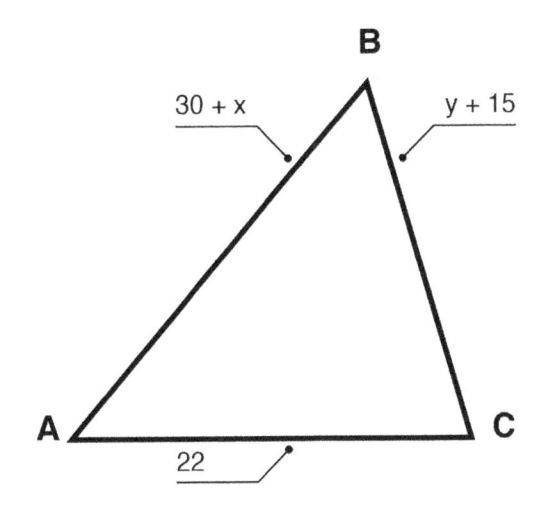

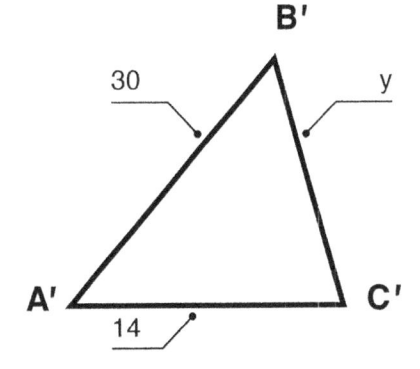

    a. $x = 19.5, y = 24.1$
    b. $x = 17.1, y = 26.3$
    c. $x = 26.3, y = 17.1$
    d. $x = 24.1, y = 19.5$

20. What is another name for public diplomacy?
    a. Elevator diplomacy
    b. People's diplomacy
    c. Open-forum diplomacy
    d. Streetside diplomacy

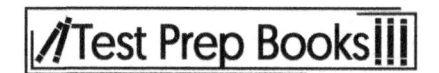

21. Michael leads an HR department at a federal agency. He is in the planning stage for the new fiscal year and is thrilled that he has created initiatives that are highly detailed and comprehensive and use the resources of contracts his agency currently has in place. He is very attached to the outcomes of these initiatives. However, a presidential election is taking place in one month that will likely affect the contracts that are awarded to his agency. What can Michael do to protect his new fiscal year plans?
    a. Ensure that there is leftover money from the previous fiscal year to serve as a cushion should he not receive expected contracts
    b. Create backup plans for all the contracts that may be affected, while calmly accepting that some changes may be unanticipated and out of his control
    c. Nothing, he has already distributed them to employees and archived them on the organization's servers
    d. Find a new job

22. Social contract theory developed in which one of the following intellectual contexts?
    a. The Enlightenment
    b. Humanism
    c. Modernism
    d. The Renaissance

23. What are The Federalist Papers?
    a. Anonymous articles supporting ratification of the Constitution..
    b. A document identifying basic liberties.
    c. A document which articulated America's system of government.
    d. A document that required the colonists to pay a tax on legal documents, newspapers, magazines and other printed materials.

24. Who is in control in a command economy?
    a. The consumer
    b. Private businesses
    c. The government
    d. Manufacturers

25. A six-sided die is rolled. What is the probability that the roll is 1 or 2?
    a. $\frac{1}{6}$
    b. $\frac{1}{4}$
    c. $\frac{1}{3}$
    d. $\frac{1}{2}$

26. Which of the following social media websites focuses primarily on short-form text posts, occasionally accompanied by images or short video clips?
    a. Instagram
    b. Twitter
    c. Imgur
    d. YouTube

Practice Test #2 | Job Knowledge

Question 27 refers to the picture below.

Packaged Coffee

27. Which of the following best describes how this product was produced?
    a. Production occurred on a local family farm that prioritizes environmental sustainability.
    b. Production occurred through a partnership with a worker-owned cooperative.
    c. Production met environmental sustainability standards and included reasonable compensation to workers.
    d. Production abided by free-trade rules, resulting in reduced costs for consumers.

28. Four people split a bill. The first person pays for $\frac{1}{5}$, the second person pays for $\frac{1}{4}$, and the third person pays for $\frac{1}{3}$. What fraction of the bill does the fourth person pay?
    a. $\frac{13}{60}$
    b. $\frac{47}{60}$
    c. $\frac{1}{4}$
    d. $\frac{4}{15}$

29. Which of the following was NOT an issue contributing to the American Revolution?
    a. Increased taxes on the colonies
    b. Britain's defeat in the French and Indian War
    c. The stationing of British soldiers in colonists' homes
    d. Changes in class relations

30. Which of the following techniques would help Mr. Johnson, a business executive, connect better with his audience during his next sales presentation?
    a. Practicing his speech with a natural intonation
    b. Repeating the key points every few minutes
    c. Making brief eye contact
    d. Inserting an appropriate joke

31. What is the relationship between diversity and inclusion in the workplace?
    a. Diversity reflects legally-mandated equal opportunity hiring practices, while inclusion reflects company culture.
    b. Diversity refers to only hiring employees from underrepresented groups, while inclusion refers to hiring employees from all demographics.
    c. Diversity involves hiring employees with a variety of backgrounds, personalities, and working styles, while inclusion involves making sure those differences are heard and represented in the workplace.
    d. Diversity means respecting and encouraging workers to retain their individuality in the workplace, while inclusion means integrating all workers into one shared corporate culture.

32. In an office, there are 50 workers. A total of 60% of the workers are women, and the chances of a woman wearing a skirt is 50%. If no men wear skirts, how many workers are wearing skirts?
    a. 12
    b. 15
    c. 16
    d. 20

33. Which ONE of the following best describes an economic benefit of free trade agreements?
    a. Free trade agreements increase international trade by reducing barriers to trade.
    b. Free trade agreements reduce the cost of reparations.
    c. Free trade agreements allow countries to protect domestic iron and steel production.
    d. Free trade agreements facilitate imperialism and the creation of lucrative empires.

34. The presidential cabinet has which of the following duties?
    a. Advise the president.
    b. Act as spokesperson for the U.S. government administration.
    c. Solicit donations for the president's re-election campaign.
    d. Preside over the Senate.

35. Genghis Khan founded which of the following empires?
    a. Golden Horde
    b. Mongol Empire
    c. Timurid Empire
    d. Yuan dynasty

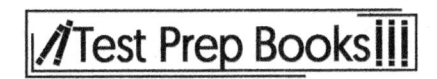

36. A truck is carrying three cylindrical barrels. Their bases have a diameter of 2 feet, and they have a height of 3 feet. What is the total volume of the three barrels in cubic feet?
   a. 3π
   b. 9π
   c. 12π
   d. 15π

37. The establishment clause deals with which of the following?
   a. The relationship between government and labor unions
   b. The relationship between government officials and lobbyists
   c. The relationship between government and the creation of new federal courts
   d. The relationship between government and religion

38. Which of the following were characteristics of the American economy after World War II?
   a. A return to the Great Depression.
   b. Increased use of computers.
   c. The decline of the Sun Belt.
   d. The fall of the stock market.

39. Economies of scale result in reduced costs as agricultural production increases. Which of the following best describes the negative consequences of this trend?
   a. Economies of scale have removed incentives for developing agricultural innovations.
   b. Economies of scale have disrupted global commodity chains, shifting the costs of production onto consumers.
   c. Economies of scale have spurred the corporatization of agriculture, bankrupting small family farms.
   d. Economies of scale have prevented the development of new food production and consumption movements.

40. Which of these advantages is the best reason for a library to switch to a digital database?
   a. Keyword searches
   b. Advertising the library
   c. Increasing library capacity
   d. Saving on costs

41. Calvin gives a long presentation with many anecdotes and examples. Some of them have little to do with the original idea, making it difficult to follow along with his speech. What is his audience most likely feeling?
   a. Excitement
   b. Disagreement with the original idea
   c. Confusion
   d. Anticipation

42. What term best describes a feeling of personal worth or value?
   a. Self-identity
   b. Self-concept
   c. Self-efficacy
   d. Self-esteem

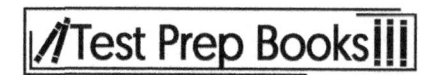

43. If Mr. Steele is preparing a report about his company intended for a general, non-specialist audience, and he wants to add something to help visually depict his company's budget. Which of the following would he be mostly likely to add to the document?
    a. An additional paragraph explaining the allocation of funds
    b. Highlighting on the sentences that explain the budget
    c. A pie chart showing the allocation of funds
    d. A selection from the accounting ledgers

Questions 44-45 refer to the passage below:

> It hath been shewn to have been the constant Opinion of there being a North-west Passage, from the Time soon after which the South Sea was discovered near the Western Part of America, and that this Opinion was adopted by the greatest Men not only in the Time they lived, but whose Eminence and great Abilities are revered by the present Age. That there is a Sea to Westward of Hudson's Bay, there hath been given the concurrent Testimony of Indians; and of Navigators and Indians that there is a Streight which unites such Sea with the Western Ocean. The Voyage which lead us into these Considerations, hath so many Circumstances relating to it, which, now they have been considered, shew the greatest Probability of its being authentick; which carry with them as much the Evidence of a Fact, afford as great a Degree of Credibility as we have for any Transaction done a long Time since, which hath not been of a publick Nature and transacted in the Face of the World, so as to fall under the Notice of every one, though under the Disadvantage that the Intent on one Part must have been to have it concealed and buried in Oblivion.

Excerpt from *The Great Probability of a Northwest Passage* by Thomas Jefferys, 1768

44. Which of the following events most directly triggered increased interest in the maritime route described in the passage?
    a. Vasco da Gama sailing around the Cape of Good Hope in 1488.
    b. Christopher Columbus reaching the Caribbean in 1492.
    c. Ferdinand Magellan's expedition circumnavigating the world in 1522.
    d. Henry Hudson exploring the Hudson Bay in 1611.

45. Which of the following was a long-term consequence of explorers looking for a "North-west passage"?
    a. European powers gained a faster route to the Pacific Ocean.
    b. European powers abandoned international trade networks.
    c. European powers forged alliances with Amerindian empires.
    d. European powers colonized the Americas.

46. Multiply $1,987 \times 0.05$.
    a. 9.935
    b. 99.35
    c. 993.5
    d. 93.95

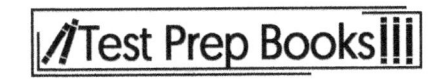

47. Which of the following situations would more than likely warrant a written employment contract?
   a. An employee who is a salesperson
   b. A full-time telecommuting employee
   c. An employee who is a department manager
   d. An employee who is a graphic artist

48. Which of the following is NOT a characteristic of contractionary monetary policy?
   a. Increases the money supply
   b. Possibly increases unemployment due to slowdowns in economic growth
   c. Decreases consumer spending
   d. Decreases loans and/or borrowing

49. After the ratification of the Constitution, which power held by the states under the Articles of Confederation was ceded to the federal government?
   a. Power to levy taxes
   b. Power to establish courts
   c. Power to coin money
   d. Power to regulate trade

50. The country of Blueland is establishing an embassy in the allied country of Greenistan. Mr. Redd is appointed as the embassy's media relations manager. Whom should he contact to start developing a positive image of Blueland in Greenistan?
   a. The owner of a local steel mill
   b. The head journalist of the Greenistan Times
   c. A random sample of citizens on the street
   d. The top general of Greenistan's military

51. Which event was the last major armed conflict between U.S. forces and Native Americans?
   a. Trail of Tears
   b. Tecumseh's War
   c. Massacre at Wounded Knee
   d. Battle of the Little Big Horn

52. Which of the following best describes how culture is transmitted across society?
   a. Culture is almost always transmitted through hierarchical relationships, and it has a trickle-down effect.
   b. Culture is primarily transmitted through religion, economic activities, and government policies.
   c. Cultural exchanges on the internet have given rise to a global popular culture in recent years.
   d. Culture can be transmitted through an endless variety of activities, and the transmission can either be intentional or spontaneous.

53. Differences in race, gender, sexual orientation, economic status, and language can be denoted as what?
   a. Behaviorism
   b. Peer pressure
   c. Adaptation
   d. Diversity

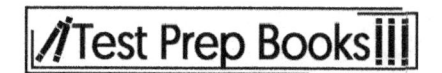

54. What is one advantage the South have over the North during the Civil War?
    a. The South was fighting far away from their homes.
    b. The South lacked free labor at home.
    c. The South had a more soldiers.
    d. The South had more experienced military leaders.

55. $3\frac{2}{3} - 1\frac{4}{5} =$
    a. $1\frac{13}{20}$
    b. $\frac{14}{15}$
    c. $\frac{4}{5}$
    d. $1\frac{13}{15}$

56. What organization helped Ronald Reagan win the White House in 1980?
    a. Great Awakening
    b. Moral Majority
    c. Know-Nothings
    d. Anti-Defamation League

57. Which type of information is probably NOT stored in a pharmacy's database?
    a. Medical history
    b. The location of medications
    c. Prescription information
    d. Financial transfer information

58. An advertisement for a new park and play area in a city newspaper would most likely be read by which of these people?
    a. Dr. Stevens, a traveling veterinarian specialist
    b. Mr. Takamoto, a visiting foreign dignitary
    c. Ms. Chandler, a young college student
    d. Ms. Lindenhurst, a member of the school board

59. Which of the following items is NOT a covered provision under the Fair Labor Standards Act (FLSA)?
    a. Overtime pay
    b. Employee classification
    c. Child labor
    d. Hazard pay

60. Which of the following is NOT covered under one of the federal government's enumerated powers?
    a. Borrowing money to pay off debt from a war abroad
    b. Passing a law to place a tax on sodas
    c. Banning the possession of firearms in churches
    d. Passing regulations on the sale of California grapes to other states

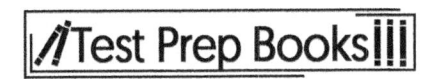

Situational Judgment

The Situational Judgment Test (SJT) is designed to determine an individual's ability to select the most and least effective way to handle a situation.

Situation 1

You are giving a press conference to reassure civilians during a state of emergency. You don't have much information, but you are repeatedly asked questions about what's going on. The audience is in a state of nervous distress, looking to you for answers.

What would you do?
- a. Ignore questions about the emergency and field other ones.
- b. Continue to offer the same reassuring statements of protection.
- c. End the press conference prematurely.
- d. Calmly explain that you will provide updates as soon as more information is available.
- e. Ask your aides to bring you more information.

Situation 2

You have been reassigned from the American embassy in Germany to the one in Japan. You've spent the past five years working and living in Germany but are unfamiliar with the cultural customs in Japan. A colleague tells you that the Japanese are polite and hard-working, but that's all you've heard. You have a week until you make the transition.

What would you do?
- a. Continue to work and assume you'll figure it out when you get there.
- b. Spend time learning what you can about Japanese culture.
- c. Request that higher-ups reconsider the move.
- d. Prepare a dossier to introduce yourself to your future colleagues.
- e. Take work off and party until the move.

Situation 3

Your team is putting together a multimedia presentation about life in various foreign countries. All that's left to compile is a section on an African country, but nobody else on the team has been to Africa. However, when you were younger, you worked with a volunteer organization in Kenya and have some experience living there.

What would you do?
- a. Volunteer yourself to work on this section.
- b. Suggest that someone else research this section.
- c. Drop this section and replace it with one about a country with which you are all familiar.
- d. Keep quiet and wait for someone else to volunteer.
- e. Randomly pick from a list of African countries and do the best you can putting this section together.

Situation 4

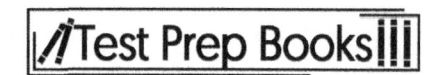

You've been invited to a meeting of several foreign leaders taking place in your host country. They plan to initiate a new economic policy and want you to give your opinion about its effects on your home country. However, you only have a basic understanding of your home country's economy and worry that your opinion may not be very well informed.

What would you do?
    a. Suggest that someone else with more knowledge of your home country's economy replace you.
    b. Take notes at the meeting and offer your opinion later.
    c. Do as much research on your home country's economy as you can to prepare.
    d. Decline to attend the meeting.
    e. Make a rough guess based on what you know.

Situation 5

Your team is putting the finishing touches on a new media campaign. The last step is to reach out to an organization that will implement a test run. It's the end of the week, and everyone on the team is exhausted. However, it's very important that the test run begin as soon as possible so the full plan can be implemented on schedule.

What would you do?
    a. Nominate a random team member to reach out to an organization.
    b. Reach out to an organization yourself as the team leader.
    c. Encourage the team to decide who will reach out.
    d. Let the team take a break and implement the plan next week.
    e. Let the rest of the team decide the next step.

Situation 6

You are meeting with your supervisor and his boss to discuss the scope of tasks in your next assignment. His boss wants to give you many tasks, more than you've ever handled before. After the meeting, your supervisor pulls you aside, says he understands that this will be a lot of work for you, and asks if there's anything he can do to help you.

What would you do?
    a. Sigh and say you'll manage somehow.
    b. Confidently say you can handle all of it.
    c. Ask if he can convince his boss to assign the work to someone else.
    d. Tell him which tasks you can't do.
    e. Figure out what you can manage yourself and ask for help with the rest.

Situation 7

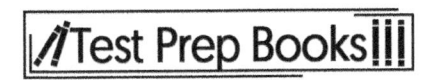

You are writing performance reviews for each member of your team. One team member has done an excellent job on all their work, but you don't care for their attitude in unrelated conversations. Your boss wants your honest opinion on every performance review so that he can make sure all teams are working together smoothly.

What would you do?
- a. Say that the member isn't a team player.
- b. Recommend a punishment for the member's attitude.
- c. Focus your review on the quality of the member's work.
- d. Focus your review on the member's attitude in casual conversation.
- e. Describe the team member as acceptable and average.

Situation 8

You want to propose a new idea to your boss. He appreciates thorough explanations, but his time is often taken up by other meetings or work obligations. You finally manage to schedule a half-hour meeting with him, so now you must prepare your presentation of the idea.

What would you do?
- a. Prepare a long and extensive explanation with examples.
- b. Prepare a short and simple explanation.
- c. Prepare basic talking points about the idea.
- d. Prepare a concise and detailed presentation.
- e. Passionately improvise your explanation when the time comes.

Situation 9

You are giving a presentation with slides and handouts. As you reach a critical moment of the presentation, the projector crashes and the slides are no longer visible.

What would you do?
- a. Continue with the presentation like nothing happened.
- b. Apologize and try to get the projector restarted.
- c. Borrow a handout and continue, using it as a reference.
- d. Stop the presentation and open the floor to questions.
- e. Pause the presentation and take a break.

Situation 10

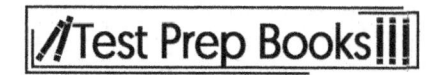

You are supervising a team meeting in which you and your colleagues are discussing how to handle an upcoming press conference. One team member consistently interrupts others to voice his opinions. Several other members are becoming visibly frustrated.

What would you do?
  a. Politely mediate the conversation and allow other team members to speak.
  b. Reprimand the interrupting team member and tell him to stop.
  c. Encourage everyone to speak up more and provide input.
  d. Let the meeting continue and handle the issue later.
  e. Jokingly mention that the interrupting member's ideas must be better if he keeps interrupting to talk about them.

Situation 11

A businessman from your home country meets with you abroad. He wants to open a new chain of businesses in the foreign country where you're stationed and explains his business model to you. However, you know that according to this country's laws, a significant amount of his business model will be denied.

What would you do?
  a. Refer him to one of the foreign government's agencies instead.
  b. Tell him to go ahead with his expansion plan.
  c. Try to work with the foreign country's government to get an exception.
  d. Explain why his business model won't work in this country.
  e. Explain the conflicts with foreign law and suggest a solution.

Situation 12

A citizen of your home country has been arrested in your assigned foreign country for violating the law. When you arrive at the detention center to speak with them, the local police state that you cannot visit, and their legal representation is not guaranteed.

What would you do?
  a. Declare your position and explain that you must ensure their receipt of legal counsel.
  b. Leave and try again tomorrow.
  c. Loudly disagree and insist that they allow you to visit.
  d. Threaten to publicize their treatment of your home country's citizen.
  e. Appeal to higher foreign governmental authorities for permission to visit.

Practice Test #2 | Situational Judgment

Situation 13

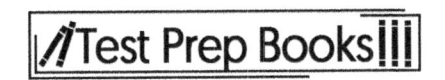

A tsunami strikes the country to which you've been assigned. Disaster relief efforts are struggling to reach everyone, and the region is a popular global tourist destination. The foreign government officials assure you that they're doing their best but must prioritize their own citizens.

What would you do?
    a. Publicly blame the foreign government for failing to provide sufficient relief.
    b. Demand increased effort from the foreign government to secure the safety of your home country's visiting citizens.
    c. Work independently from local relief efforts to evacuate your home country's visiting citizens.
    d. Coordinate with local relief efforts to ensure the safety of your home country's visiting citizens.
    e. Work with local relief efforts to increase efficiency so they can get to your home country's citizens sooner.

Situation 14

You've been assigned to a small foreign country that is looking to grow its economy as much as possible within two years. Reports indicate that this country has a comparatively lower rate of education among its citizens, many easily accessible natural resources, and only a simple shipping and transportation industry.

What would you do?
    a. Recommend investing in education and technical training.
    b. Recommend increasing production and refining the natural resources into products.
    c. Recommend importing materials and utilizing skilled labor to refine them.
    d. Recommend focusing solely on facilitation of trade between other nations.
    e. Recommend investing in infrastructure and exporting natural resources.

Situation 15

The president of your home country and the president of the foreign country to which you're assigned have decided to meet and discuss mutual agreements in foreign policy. The aides of both presidents reach out to you and request assistance with scheduling and facilitating the meeting.

What would you do?
    a. Set a meeting date at the embassy and inform both aides to make time for it.
    b. Coordinate between the two presidents' schedules and host the meeting at the embassy.
    c. Find a colleague to organize the meeting in your stead.
    d. Work with your home country's president to schedule the meeting and pass the timing along to the foreign country's president.
    e. Coordinate between the two presidents' schedules and host the meeting at a third-party location.

Situation 16

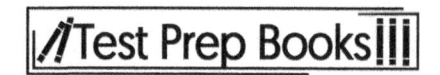

Your assigned foreign country is undergoing a revolution. They have recently earned their freedom from another country's rule and are hesitant to accept foreign aid. The people are restructuring their government to ensure more representation but seem to be struggling with implementation. You are reporting to your home country about the current situation to recommend a course of action.

What would you do?
   a. Advise staying neutral and avoid commentary about their development.
   b. Recommend sending a team of political experts to assist in the implementation of their new government.
   c. Caution against direct interference but recommend a meeting between the two countries to suggest options to the foreign country.
   d. Recommend inviting the newly freed country to form an alliance with your home country.
   e. Suggest praising the foreign country's newfound independence and sending a gift.

Situation 17

A foreign diplomat offers you a financial bonus to make a favorable recommendation to your home country's government in support of a new policy the foreign country has just implemented.

What would you do?
   a. Ignore him and proceed with your work as originally intended.
   b. Accept the bonus and recommend the policy to your home country.
   c. Reject the bonus and inform your supervisors.
   d. Accept half the bonus up front but tell him you'll have to see how the policy affects the foreign country before recommending it to your home country.
   e. Bargain with him to increase the bonus.

Situation 18

You are evaluating a project in your assigned foreign country that is being constructed by a contractor from your home country. Over the course of the evaluation, you learn that the contractor from your home country is intentionally doing low-quality work. A failure on this project could have extremely negative consequences on the relationship between the two countries.

What would you do?
   a. Consult with your supervisors and discuss how to inform all parties involved.
   b. Warn the contractor and remind them of the importance of their work.
   c. Tell the contractor you'll go public with the report if they don't improve the quality of their work immediately.
   d. Ignore this information and let the contracted project proceed.
   e. Privately inform your home country's government and suggest they change contractors immediately.

Situation 19

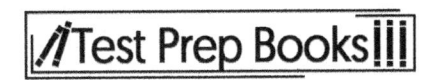

You are preparing a list of choices with a recommended option to send to an official from your home country. Your supervisor dismisses your recommendation and changes it to their own recommendation instead. You strongly disagree with the change.

What would you do?
    a. Go to your supervisor's boss and complain about the decision.
    b. Loudly disagree with your supervisor and insist that they change it back to your recommendation.
    c. Change it back to your recommendation before finally submitting it.
    d. Disagree but allow your supervisor to make the change.
    e. Politely disagree with your supervisor and present the reasoning for your recommendation.

Situation 20

While relaxing in the employee break room, you overhear two colleagues making inappropriate comments about a new team member who isn't in the room.

What would you do?
    a. Offer your own unfiltered opinion of the new team member.
    b. Stay quiet and keep to yourself.
    c. Report these comments to HR or a supervisor.
    d. Interrupt and tell them that their comments are inappropriate.
    e. Find the new team member and tell them what others are saying.

Situation 21

In your assigned country, recreational drug use is allowed. However, business policy at the embassy requires all team members to remain sober and clean on the job. As you pass a colleague in the hallway, you can smell alcohol and marijuana on them.

What would you do?
    a. Ignore them and return to work.
    b. Report their condition to HR or a supervisor.
    c. Help them sober up now.
    d. Ask to meet them after work.
    e. Warn them and remind them to stay sober.

Situation 22

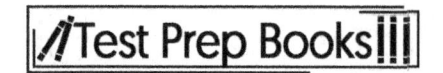

A close colleague tells you that one of their family members recently passed away. Understandably, they are very upset. You want to be a good friend by listening and helping when needed. Lately, they have been interrupting you for emotional help so often that it is hurting your productivity at work. Today, they knock on your door at the beginning of your shift asking to talk to you.

What would you do?
  a. Ask them to come back in a few minutes, then report them to your supervisor.
  b. Try to multitask and work while listening to them.
  c. Tell them you're very busy and can't listen right now.
  d. Drop what you're working on and help them.
  e. Politely explain that you want to help, but you must focus on work now and can meet with them after work.

Situation 23

A foreign student has been accepted to a university in your home country. Classes will begin soon, but the student will not receive their visa in time. They ask you to help expedite the process.

What would you do?
  a. Consult with your supervisor and see what can be done to help.
  b. Promise to get their visa in time and tell your supervisor what needs to be done.
  c. Expedite their visa personally.
  d. Tell them to ask someone else in your department because you're busy.
  e. Tell them to work with the university to attend classes remotely until the visa arrives.

Situation 24

A group has gathered outside of your embassy to protest a recent change in your home country's policy on climate change efforts. You don't want the situation to escalate and would prefer to resolve it as amicably as possible.

What would you do?
  a. Ask for increased security around the embassy.
  b. Demand that the protestors calm down and leave.
  c. Tell the protestors that you have no say in the policymaking decisions of your home country.
  d. Convey the situation and protestor's opinions to your home country's government.
  e. Try to ignore the protestors.

Situation 25

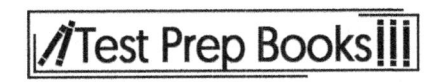

A citizen of your home country has gone missing while visiting your assigned country. Their family members, who are also visiting the country, are worried and ask you for help.

What would you do?
    a. Contact the relevant local authorities and help initiate an investigation.
    b. Start a private investigation conducted by the embassy.
    c. Tell the family to get in touch with the relevant local authorities.
    d. Return the family to your home country immediately.
    e. Ignore the family and continue with your regular work.

Situation 26

You are supervising a collaborative project. One team member privately reports to you that another member has repeatedly made statements containing sexual innuendos, which are making the reporting member uncomfortable. You are familiar with the other member and believe that they are simply intending to make jokes and do not mean harm.

What would you do?
    a. Tell the reporting team member that the other member is just joking.
    b. Openly reprimand the offending team member and remind all team members not to make these statements.
    c. Privately converse with the offending team member and ask them to refrain from making these statements.
    d. Remove the offending team member from the project.
    e. Do nothing and see if the problem goes away.

Situation 27

A citizen of your home country reaches out to you because they have become engaged to a citizen of your assigned country and wish to emigrate and live with their fiancée. They would like your assistance to make the procedure as painless as possible.

What would you do?
    a. Tell them to travel now and handle the whole process for them.
    b. Ask them if they're sure about their decision to emigrate.
    c. Suggest that the fiancée emigrate to your home country instead.
    d. Explain the foreign country's immigration process and send them any relevant documents.
    e. Refer them to a foreign agency to help with the process instead.

Situation 28

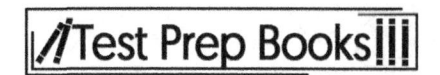

Your embassy is overwhelmed with visa requests. While on break, you learn one that of your colleagues is dealing with the increased volume by randomly rejecting every fourth application.

What would you do?
- a. Tell them they shouldn't be doing that.
- b. Pretend not to hear and return to work.
- c. Offer to handle the visa applications instead.
- d. Begin doing the same thing to speed up your workload.
- e. Inform your supervisor immediately.

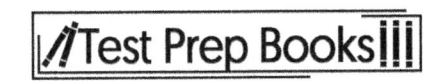

English Expression

For the answer choices below in response to the passages, choose the option that is most consistent with standard English in the underlined section.

Read the following passage and answer Questions 1–15.

On September 11th, 2001, a group of terrorists hijacked four American airplanes. The terrorists crashed the planes into the World Trade Center in New York City, the Pentagon in Washington D.C., and a field in Pennsylvania. Nearly 3,000 people died during the attacks, which propelled the United States into a (1) "War on Terror".

About the Terrorists

(2) Terrorists commonly uses fear and violence to achieve political goals. The nineteen terrorists who orchestrated and implemented the attacks of September 11th were militants associated with al-Qaeda, an Islamic extremist group founded by Osama bin Laden, Abdullah Azzam, and others in the late 1980s. (3) Bin Laden orchestrated the attacks as a response to what he felt was American injustice against Islam and hatred towards Muslims. In his words, "Terrorism against America deserves to be praised."

Islam is the religion of Muslims, (4) who live mainly in south and southwest Asia and Sub-Saharan Africa. The majority of Muslims practice Islam peacefully. However, fractures in Islam have led to the growth of Islamic extremists who strictly oppose Western influences. They seek to institute stringent Islamic law and destroy those who violate Islamic code.

In November 2002, bin Laden provided the explicit motives for the 9/11 terror attacks. According to this list, (5) Americas support of Israel, military presence in Saudi Arabia, and other anti-Muslim actions were the causes.

The Timeline of the Attacks

The morning of September 11 began like any other for most Americans. Then, at 8:45 a.m., a Boeing 767 plane (6) crashed into the north tower of the World Trade Center in New York City. Hundreds were instantly killed. Others were trapped on higher floors. The crash was initially thought to be a freak accident. When a second plane flew directly into the south tower eighteen minutes later, it was determined that America was under attack.

At 9:45 a.m., (7) slamming into the Pentagon was a third plane, America's military headquarters in Washington D.C. The jet fuel of this plane caused a major fire and partial building collapse that resulted in nearly 200 deaths. By 10:00 a.m., the south tower of the World Trade Center collapsed. Thirty minutes later, the north tower followed suit.

While this was happening, a fourth plane that departed from New Jersey, United Flight 93, was hijacked. The passengers learned of the attacks that occurred in New York and Washington D.C. and realized that they faced the same fate as the other planes that crashed. The passengers were determined to overpower the terrorists in an effort to prevent the deaths of additional innocent American citizens. Although the passengers were successful in (8) <u>diverging</u> the plane, it crashed in a western Pennsylvania field and killed everyone on board. The plane's final target remains uncertain, (9) <u>but believed by many people was the fact that United Flight 93 was heading for the White House.</u>

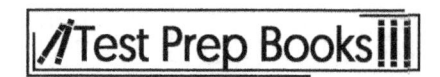

Heroes and Rescuers

(10) <u>Close to 3,000 people died in the World Trade Center attacks.</u> This figure includes 343 New York City firefighters and paramedics, 23 New York City police officers, and 37 Port Authority officers. Nevertheless, thousands of men and women in service worked (11) <u>valiantly</u> to evacuate the buildings, save trapped workers, extinguish infernos, uncover victims trapped in fallen rubble, and tend to nearly 10,000 injured individuals.

About 300 rescue dogs played a major role in the after-attack salvages. Working twelve-hour shifts, the dogs scoured the rubble and alerted paramedics when they found signs of life. While doing so, the dogs served as a source of comfort and therapy for the rescue teams.

Initial Impacts on America

The attacks of September 11, 2001 resulted in the immediate suspension of all air travel. No flights could take off from or land on American soil. (12) <u>American airports and airspace closed to all national and international flights.</u> Therefore, over five hundred flights had to turn back or be redirected to other countries. Canada alone received 226 flights and thousands of stranded passengers. (13) <u>Needless to say, as cancelled flights are rescheduled, air travel became backed up and chaotic for quite some time.</u>

At the time of the attacks, George W. Bush was the president of the United States. President Bush announced that "We will make no distinction between the terrorists who committed these acts and those who harbor them." The rate of hate crimes against American Muslims spiked, despite President Bush's call for the country to treat them with respect.

Additionally, relief funds were quickly arranged. The funds were used to support families of the victims, orphaned children, and those with major injuries. In this way, the tragic event brought the citizens together through acts of service towards those directly impacted by the attack.

Long-Term Effects of the Attacks

Over the past fifteen years, the attacks of September 11th have transformed the United States' government, travel safety protocols, and international relations. Anti-terrorism legislation became a priority for many countries as law enforcement and intelligence agencies teamed up to find and defeat alleged terrorists.

Present George W. Bush announced a War on Terror. He (14) <u>desired</u> to bring bin Laden and al-Qaeda to justice and prevent future terrorist networks from gaining strength. The War in Afghanistan began in October of 2001 when the United States and British forces bombed al-Qaeda camps. (15) The Taliban, a group of fundamental Muslims who protected Osama bin Laden, was overthrown on December 9, 2001. However, the war continued in order to defeat insurgency campaigns in neighboring countries. Ten years later, the United State Navy SEALS killed Osama bin Laden in Pakistan. During 2014, the United States declared the end of its involvement in the War on Terror in Afghanistan.

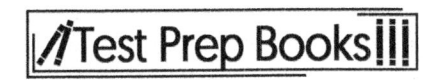

Museums and memorials have since been erected to honor and remember the thousands of people who died during the September 11th attacks, including the brave rescue workers who gave their lives in the effort to help others.

1. Which of the following would be the best choice for this sentence (reproduced below)?

Nearly 3,000 people died during the attacks, which propelled the United States into a (1) "War on Terror".

a. "War on Terror".
b. "war on terror".
c. "war on terror."
d. "War on Terror."

2. Which of the following would be the best choice for this sentence (reproduced below)?

(2) Terrorists commonly uses fear and violence to achieve political goals.

a. Terrorists commonly uses fear and violence to achieve political goals.
b. Terrorist's commonly use fear and violence to achieve political goals.
c. Terrorists commonly use fear and violence to achieve political goals.
d. Terrorists commonly use fear and violence to achieves political goals.

3. Which of the following would be the best choice for this sentence (reproduced below)?

(3) Bin Laden orchestrated the attacks as a response to what he felt was American injustice against Islam and hatred towards Muslims.

a. Bin Laden orchestrated the attacks as a response to what he felt was American injustice against Islam and hatred towards Muslims.
b. Bin Laden orchestrated the attacks as a response to what he felt was American injustice against Islam, and hatred towards Muslims.
c. Bin Laden orchestrated the attacks, as a response to what he felt was American injustice against Islam and hatred towards Muslims.
d. Bin Laden orchestrated the attacks as responding to what he felt was American injustice against Islam and hatred towards Muslims.

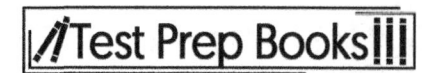

4. Which of the following would be the best choice for this sentence (reproduced below)?

Islam is the religion of Muslims, (4) who live mainly in south and southwest Asia and Sub-Saharan Africa.

   a. who live mainly in south and southwest Asia
   b. who live mainly in the South and Southwest Asia
   c. who live mainly in the south and Southwest Asia
   d. who live mainly in the south and southwest asia

5. Which of the following would be the best choice for this sentence (reproduced below)?

According to this list, (5) Americas support of Israel, military presence in Saudi Arabia, and other anti-Muslim actions were the causes.

   a. Americas support of Israel,
   b. America's support of israel,
   c. Americas support of Israel
   d. America's support of Israel,

6. Which of the following would be the best choice for this sentence (reproduced below)?

Then, at 8:45 a.m., a Boeing 767 plane (6) crashed into the north tower of the World Trade Center in New York City.

   a. crashed into the north tower of the World Trade Center
   b. crashes into the north tower of the World Trade Center
   c. crashing into the north tower of the World Trade Center
   d. crash into the north tower of the World Trade Center

7. Which of the following would be the best choice for this sentence (reproduced below)?

At 9:45 a.m., (7) slamming into the Pentagon was a third plane, America's military headquarters in Washington D.C.

   a. slamming into the Pentagon was a third plane,
   b. into the Pentagon slammed a third plane,
   c. a third plane slammed into the Pentagon,
   d. the Pentagon was slamming by a third plane,

8. Which of the following would be the best choice for this sentence (reproduced below)?

Although the passengers were successful in (8) diverging the plane, it crashed in a western Pennsylvania field and killed everyone on board.

   a. (No change; best as written.)
   b. Diverting
   c. Converging
   d. Distracting

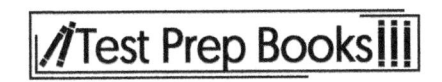

9. Which of the following would be the best choice for this sentence (reproduced below)?

The plane's final target remains uncertain, (9) but believed by many people was the fact that United Flight 93 was heading for the White House.

a. but believed by many people was the fact that United Flight 93 was heading for the White House.
b. but many believe that United Flight 93 was heading for the White House.
c. also heading for the white house United Flight 93 was believed to be.
d. then many believe that United Flight 93 was heading for the White House.

10. Which of the following would be the best choice for this sentence (reproduced below)?

(10) Close to 3,000 people died in the World Trade Center attacks.

a. Close to 3,000 people died in the World Trade Center attacks.
b. 3,000 people in the World Trade Center attacks died.
c. Dying in the World Trade Center attacks were around 3,000 people.
d. In the World Trade Center attacks were around 3,000 people dying.

11. Which of the following would be the best choice for this sentence (reproduced below)?

Nevertheless, thousands of men and women in service worked (11) valiantly to evacuate the buildings, save trapped workers, extinguish infernos, uncover victims trapped in fallen rubble, and tend to nearly 10,000 injured individuals.

a. (No change; best as written.)
b. valiently
c. valently
d. vanlyantly

12. Which of the following would be the best choice for this sentence (reproduced below)?

(12) American airports and airspace closed to all national and international flights.

a. American airports and airspace closed to all national and international flights.
b. American airports and airspace close to all national and international flights.
c. American airports and airspaces closed to all national and international flights.
d. American airspace and airports were closed to all national and international flights.

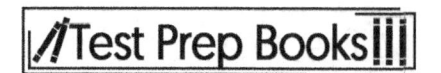

13. Which of the following would be the best choice for this sentence (reproduced below)?

(13) Needless to say, as cancelled flights are rescheduled, air travel became backed up and chaotic for quite some time.

a. as cancelled flights are rescheduled, air travel became backed up and chaotic for quite some time.
b. As cancelled flights are rescheduled, air travel became backed up and chaotic for quite some time.
c. Needless to say, as cancelled flights were rescheduled, air travel became backed up and chaotic for quite some time.
d. Needless to say, as cancelled flights are rescheduled, air travel became backed up and chaotic over a period of time.

14. Which of the following would be the best choice for this sentence (reproduced below)?

He (14) desired to bring bin Laden and al-Qaeda to justice and prevent future terrorist networks from gaining strength.

a. Desired
b. Perceived
c. Intended
d. Assimilated

15. Which of the following would be the best choice for this sentence (reproduced below)?

(15) The Taliban, a group of fundamental Muslims who protected Osama bin Laden, was overthrown on December 9, 2001. However, the war continued in order to defeat insurgency campaigns in neighboring countries.

a. The Taliban, a group of fundamental Muslims who protected Osama bin Laden, was overthrown on December 9, 2001. However, the war continued in order to defeat insurgency campaigns in neighboring countries.
b. The Taliban was overthrown on December 9, 2001. They were a group of fundamental Muslims who protected Osama bin Laden. However, the war continued in order to defeat insurgency campaigns in neighboring countries.
c. The Taliban, a group of fundamental Muslims who protected Osama bin Laden, on December 9, 2001 was overthrown. However, the war continued in order to defeat insurgency campaigns in neighboring countries.
d. Osama bin Laden's fundamental Muslims who protected him were called the Taliban and overthrown on December 9, 2001. Yet the war continued in order to defeat the insurgency campaigns in neighboring countries.

Read the following passage and answer Questions 16–24.

Practice Test #2 | English Expression

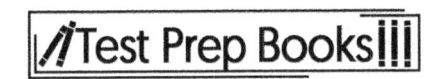

Since the first discovery of dinosaur bones, (16) scientists has made strides in technological development and methodologies used to investigate these extinct animals. We know more about dinosaurs than ever before and are still learning fascinating new things about how they looked and lived. However, one has to ask, (17) how if earlier perceptions of dinosaurs continue to influence people's understanding of these creatures? Can these perceptions inhibit progress towards further understanding of dinosaurs?

(18) The biggest problem with studying dinosaurs is simply that there are no living dinosaurs to observe. All discoveries associated with these animals are based on physical remains. To gauge behavioral characteristics, scientists cross-examine these (19) finds with living animals that seem similar in order to gain understanding. While this method is effective, these are still deductions. Some ideas about dinosaurs can't be tested and confirmed simply because humans can't replicate a living dinosaur. For example, a Spinosaurus has a large sail, or a finlike structure that grows from its back. Paleontologists know this sail exists and have ideas for the function of (20) the sail however they are uncertain of which idea is the true function. Some scientists believe (21) the sail serves to regulate the Spinosaurus' body temperature and yet others believe its used to attract mates. Still, other scientists think the sail is used to intimidate other predatory dinosaurs for self-defense. These are all viable explanations, but they are also influenced by what scientists know about modern animals. (22) Yet, it's quite possible that the sail could hold a completely unique function.

While it's (23) plausible, even likely that dinosaurs share many traits with modern animals, there is the danger of overattributing these qualities to a unique, extinct species. For much of the early nineteenth century, when people first started studying dinosaur bones, the assumption was that they were simply giant lizards. (24) For the longest time this image was the prevailing view on dinosaurs, until evidence indicated that they were more likely warm blooded. Scientists have also discovered that many dinosaurs had feathers and actually share many traits with modern birds.

16. Which of the following would be the best choice for this sentence (reproduced below)?

Since the first discovery of dinosaur bones, (16) scientists has made strides in technological development and methodologies used to investigate these extinct animals.

a. scientists has made strides in technological development and methodologies used to investigate
b. scientists has made strides in technological development, and methodologies, used to investigate
c. scientists have made strides in technological development and methodologies used to investigate
d. scientists, have made strides in technological development and methodologies used, to investigate

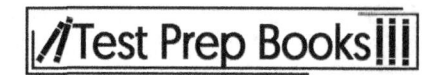

17. Which of the following would be the best choice for this sentence (reproduced below)?

However, one has to ask, (17) how if earlier perceptions of dinosaurs continue to influence people's understanding of these creatures?

a. how if earlier perceptions of dinosaurs
b. how perceptions of dinosaurs
c. how, if, earlier perceptions of dinosaurs
d. whether earlier perceptions of dinosaurs

18. Which of the following would be the best choice for this sentence (reproduced below)?

(18) The biggest problem with studying dinosaurs is simply that there are no living dinosaurs to observe.

a. The biggest problem with studying dinosaurs is simply that there are no living dinosaurs to observe.
b. The biggest problem with studying dinosaurs is simple, that there are no living dinosaurs to observe.
c. The biggest problem with studying dinosaurs is simple. There are no living dinosaurs to observe.
d. The biggest problem with studying dinosaurs, is simply that there are no living dinosaurs to observe.

19. Which of the following would be the best choice for this sentence (reproduced below)?

To gauge behavioral characteristics, scientists cross-examine these (19) finds with living animals that seem similar in order to gain understanding.

a. finds with living animals that seem similar in order to gain understanding.
b. finds with living animals to explore potential similarities.
c. finds with living animals to gain understanding of similarities.
d. finds with living animals that seem similar, in order, to gain understanding.

20. Which of the following would be the best choice for this sentence (reproduced below)?

Paleontologists know this sail exists and have ideas for the function of (20) the sail however they are uncertain of which idea is the true function.

a. the sail however they are uncertain of which idea is the true function.
b. the sail however, they are uncertain of which idea is the true function.
c. the sail however they are, uncertain, of which idea is the true function.
d. the sail; however, they are uncertain of which idea is the true function.

324

Practice Test #2 | English Expression

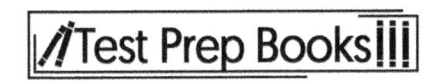

21. Which of the following would be the best choice for this sentence (reproduced below)?

Some scientists believe (21) the sail serves to regulate the Spinosaurus' body temperature and yet others believe its used to attract mates.

a. (No change; best as written.)
b. the sail serves to regulate the Spinosaurus' body temperature, yet others believe it's used to attract mates.
c. the sail serves to regulate the Spinosaurus' body temperature and yet others believe it's used to attract mates.
d. the sail serves to regulate the Spinosaurus' body temperature however others believe it's used to attract mates.

22. Which of the following would be the best choice for this sentence (reproduced below)?

(22) Yet, it's quite possible that the sail could hold a completely unique function.

a. Yet, it's quite possible
b. Yet, it's quite possible,
c. It's quite possible,
d. Its quite possible

23. Which of the following would be the best choice for this sentence (reproduced below)?

While it's (23) plausible, even likely that dinosaurs share many traits with modern animals, there is the danger of over attributing these qualities to a unique, extinct species.

a. plausible, even likely that dinosaurs share many
b. plausible, even likely that, dinosaurs share many
c. plausible, even likely, that dinosaurs share many
d. plausible even likely that dinosaurs share many

24. Which of the following would be the best choice for this sentence (reproduced below)?

(24) For the longest time this image was the prevailing view on dinosaurs, until evidence indicated that they were more likely warm blooded.

a. For the longest time this image was the prevailing view on dinosaurs
b. For the longest time this was the prevailing view on dinosaurs
c. For the longest time, this image, was the prevailing view on dinosaurs
d. For the longest time this was the prevailing image of dinosaurs

Read the following passage and answer Questions 25–33.

Everyone has heard the (25) idea of the end justifying the means; that would be Weston's philosophy. Weston is willing to cross any line, commit any act no matter how heinous, to achieve success in his goal. (26) Ransom is reviled by this fact, seeing total evil in Weston's plan. To do an evil act in order (27) to gain a result that's supposedly good would ultimately warp the final act. (28) This opposing viewpoints immediately distinguishes Ransom as the hero. In the

325

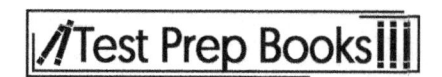

conflict with Un-man, Ransom remains true to his moral principles, someone who refuses to be compromised by power. Instead, Ransom makes it clear that by allowing such processes as murder and lying dictate how one attains a positive outcome, (29) the righteous goal becomes corrupted. The good end would not be truly good, but a twisted end that conceals corrupt deeds.

(30) This idea of allowing necessary evils to happen, is very tempting, it is what Weston fell prey to. (31) The temptation of the evil spirit Un-man ultimately takes over Weston and he is possessed. However, Ransom does not give into temptation. He remains faithful to the truth of what is right and incorrect. This leads him to directly face Un-man for the fate of Perelandra and its inhabitants.

Just as Weston was corrupted by the Un-man, (32) Un-man after this seeks to tempt the Queen of Perelandra to darkness. Ransom must literally (33) show her the right path, to accomplish this, he does this based on the same principle as the "means to an end" argument—that good follows good, and evil follows evil. Later in the plot, Weston/Un-man seeks to use deceptive reasoning to turn the queen to sin, pushing the queen to essentially ignore Melildil's rule to satisfy her own curiosity. In this sense, Un-man takes on the role of a false prophet, a tempter. Ransom must shed light on the truth, but this is difficult; his adversary is very clever and uses brilliant language. Ransom's lack of refinement heightens the weight of Un-man's corrupted logic, and so the Queen herself is intrigued by his logic.

Based on an excerpt from *Perelandra* by C.S. Lewis

25. Which of the following would be the best choice for this sentence (reproduced below)?

Everyone has heard the (25) idea of the end justifying the means; that would be Weston's philosophy.

   a. (No change; best as written.)
   b. idea of the end justifying the means; this is Weston's philosophy.
   c. idea of the end justifying the means, this is the philosophy of Weston
   d. idea of the end justifying the means. That would be Weston's philosophy.

26. Which of the following would be the best choice for this sentence (reproduced below)?

(26) Ransom is reviled by this fact, seeing total evil in Weston's plan.

   a. Ransom is reviled by this fact, seeing total evil in Weston's plan.
   b. Ransom is reviled by this fact; seeing total evil in Weston's plan.
   c. Ransom, is reviled by this fact, seeing total evil in Weston's plan.
   d. Ransom reviled by this, sees total evil in Weston's plan.

Practice Test #2 | English Expression

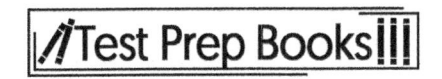

27. Which of the following would be the best choice for this sentence (reproduced below)?

    To do an evil act in order (27) to gain a result that's supposedly good would ultimately warp the final act.

    a. to gain a result that's supposedly good would ultimately warp the final act.
    b. for an outcome that's for a greater good would ultimately warp the final act.
    c. to gain a final act would warp its goodness.
    d. to achieve a positive outcome would ultimately warp the goodness of the final act.

28. Which of the following would be the best choice for this sentence (reproduced below)?

    (28) This opposing viewpoints immediately distinguishes Ransom as the hero.

    a. This opposing viewpoints immediately distinguishes Ransom as the hero.
    b. This opposing viewpoints immediately distinguishes Ransom, as the hero.
    c. This opposing viewpoint immediately distinguishes Ransom as the hero.
    d. Those opposing viewpoints immediately distinguishes Ransom as the hero.

29. Which of the following would be the best choice for this sentence (reproduced below)?

    Instead, Ransom makes it clear that by allowing such processes as murder and lying dictate how one attains a positive outcome, (29) the righteous goal becomes corrupted.

    a. the righteous goal becomes corrupted.
    b. the goal becomes corrupted and no longer righteous.
    c. the righteous goal becomes, corrupted.
    d. the goal becomes corrupted, when once it was righteous.

30. Which of the following would be the best choice for this sentence (reproduced below)?

    (30) This idea of allowing necessary evils to happen, is very tempting, it is what Weston fell prey to.

    a. This idea of allowing necessary evils to happen, is very tempting, it is what Weston fell prey to.
    b. This idea of allowing necessary evils to happen, is very tempting. This is what Weston fell prey to.
    c. This idea, allowing necessary evils to happen, is very tempting, it is what Weston fell prey to.
    d. This tempting idea of allowing necessary evils to happen is what Weston fell prey to.

31. Which of the following would be the best choice for this sentence (reproduced below)?

    (31) The temptation of the evil spirit Un-man ultimately takes over Weston and he is possessed.

    a. The temptation of the evil spirit Un-man ultimately takes over Weston and he is possessed.
    b. The temptation of the evil spirit Un-man ultimately takes over and possesses Weston.
    c. Weston is possessed as a result of the temptation of the evil spirit Un-man ultimately, who takes over.
    d. The temptation of the evil spirit Un-man takes over Weston and he is possessed ultimately.

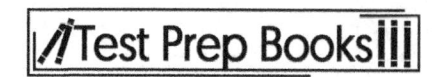

32. Which of the following would be the best choice for this sentence (reproduced below)?

Just as Weston was corrupted by the Un-man, (32) Un-man after this seeks to tempt the Queen of Perelandra to darkness.

a. Un-man after this seeks to tempt the Queen of Perelandra
b. Un-man, after this, would tempt the Queen of Perelandra
c. Un-man, after this, seeks to tempt the Queen of Perelandra
d. Un-man then seeks to tempt the Queen of Perelandra

33. Which of the following would be the best choice for this sentence (reproduced below)?

Ransom must literally (33) show her the right path, to accomplish this, he does this based on the same principle as the "means to an end" argument—that good follows good, and evil follows evil.

a. (No change; best as written.)
b. show her the right path. To accomplish this, he uses the same principle as the "means to an end" argument
c. show her the right path; to accomplish this he uses the same principle as the "means to an end" argument
d. show her the right path, to accomplish this, the same principle as the "means to an end" argument is applied

Read the following passage and answer Questions 34–42.

(34) What's clear about the news is today is that the broader the media the more ways there are to tell a story. Even if different news groups cover the same story, individual newsrooms can interpret or depict the story differently than other counterparts. Stories can also change depending on the type of (35) media in question incorporating different styles and unique ways to approach the news. (36) It is because of these respective media types that ethical and news-related subject matter can sometimes seem different or altered. But how does this affect the narrative of the new story?

I began by investigating a written newspaper article from the Baltimore Sun. Instantly striking are the bolded headlines. (37) These are clearly meant for direct the viewer to the most exciting and important stories the paper has to offer. What was particularly noteworthy about this edition was that the first page dealt with two major ethical issues. (38) On a national level there was a story on the evolving Petraeus scandal involving his supposed affair. The other article was focused locally in Baltimore, a piece questioning the city's Ethics Board and their current director. Just as a television newscaster communicates the story through camera and dialogue, the printed article applies intentional and targeted written narrative style. More so than any of the mediums, a news article seems to be focused specifically on a given story without need to jump to another. Finer details are usually expanded on (39) in written articles, usually people who read newspapers or go online for web articles want more than a quick blurb. The diction of the story is also more precise and can be either straightforward or suggestive (40) depending in earnest on the goal of the writer. However, there's still plenty of room for opinions to be inserted into the text.

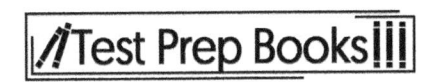

Usually, all news (41) <u>outlets have some sort of bias, it's just a question of how much</u> bias clouds the reporting. As long as this bias doesn't withhold information from the reader, it can be considered credible. (42) <u>However an over use of bias</u>, opinion, and suggestive language can rob readers of the chance to interpret the news events for themselves.

34. Which of the following would be the best choice for this sentence (reproduced below)?

(34) <u>What's clear about the news today is that the broader the media</u> the more ways there are to tell a story.

a. What's clear about the news today is that the broader the media
b. What's clear, about the news today, is that the broader the media
c. What's clear about today's news is that the broader the media
d. The news today is broader than earlier media

35. Which of the following would be the best choice for this sentence (reproduced below)?

Stories can also change depending on the type of (35) <u>media in question incorporating different styles and unique</u> ways to approach the news.

a. media in question incorporating different styles and unique
b. media in question; each incorporates unique styles and unique
c. media in question. To incorporate different styles and unique
d. media in question, incorporating different styles and unique

36. Which of the following would be the best choice for this sentence (reproduced below)?

(36) <u>It is because of these respective media types that ethical and news-related subject matter can sometimes seem different or altered.</u>

a. (No change; best as written.)
b. It is because of these respective media types, that ethical and news-related subject matter, can sometimes seem different or altered.
c. It is because of these respective media types, that ethical and news-related subject matter can sometimes seem different or altered.
d. It is because of these respective media types that ethical and news-related subject matter can sometimes seem different. Or altered.

37. Which of the following would be the best choice for this sentence (reproduced below)?

(37) <u>These are clearly meant for direct the viewer</u> to the most exciting and important stories the paper has to offer.

a. These are clearly meant for direct the viewer
b. These are clearly meant for the purpose of giving direction to the viewer
c. These are clearly meant to direct the viewer
d. These are clearly meant for the viewer to be directed

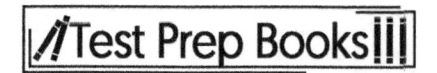

38. Which of the following would be the best choice for this sentence (reproduced below)?

(38) On a national level there was a story on the evolving Petraeus scandal involving his supposed affair.

   a. On a national level there was a story
   b. On a national level a story was there
   c. On a national level; there was a story
   d. On a national level, there was a story

39. Which of the following would be the best choice for this sentence (reproduced below)?

Finer details are usually expanded on (39) in written articles, usually people who read newspapers or go online for web articles want more than a quick blurb.

   a. in written articles, usually people who
   b. in written articles. People who usually
   c. in written articles, usually, people who
   d. in written articles usually people who

40. Which of the following would be the best choice for this sentence (reproduced below)?

The diction of the story is also more precise and can be either straightforward or suggestive (40) depending in earnest on the goal of the writer.

   a. depending in earnest on the goal of the writer.
   b. depending; in earnest on the goal of the writer.
   c. depending, in earnest, on the goal of the writer.
   d. the goal of the writer, in earnest, depends on the goal of the writer.

41. Which of the following would be the best choice for this sentence (reproduced below)?

Usually, all news (41) outlets have some sort of bias, it's just a question of how much bias clouds the reporting.

   a. outlets have some sort of bias, it's just a question of how much
   b. outlets have some sort of bias. Just a question of how much
   c. outlets have some sort of bias it can just be a question of how much
   d. outlets have some sort of bias, its just a question of how much

42. Which of the following would be the best choice for this sentence (reproduced below)?

(42) However an over use of bias, opinion, and suggestive language can rob readers of the chance to interpret the news events for themselves.

   a. However an over use of bias,
   b. However, an over use of bias,
   c. However, with too much bias,
   d. However, an overuse of bias,

Practice Test #2 | English Expression

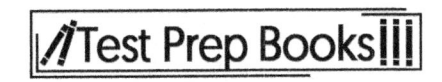

Sentence Selection: Select the one sentence that best meets the requirements of standard written English.

Questions 43–47

43.
   a. My grandparents have been traveling and have been sightseeing.
   b. My grandparents have been traveling and were sightseeing.
   c. My grandparents were traveling and have been sightseeing.
   d. My grandparents have been traveling and they're sightseeing.

44.
   a. The puppies enjoy chewing and to play tug-o-war.
   b. The puppies enjoy to chew and playing tug-o-war.
   c. The puppies enjoy to chew and to play tug-o-war.
   d. The puppies enjoy chewing and playing tug-o-war.

45.
   a. The moderator asked the candidates, "Is each of you prepared to discuss your position on global warming?".
   b. The moderator asked the candidates, "Is each of you prepared to discuss your position on global warming?"
   c. The moderator asked the candidates, 'Is each of you prepared to discuss your position on global warming?'
   d. The moderator asked the candidates, "Is each of you prepared to discuss your position on global warming"?

46.
   a. Carole is not currently working; her focus is on her children at the moment.
   b. Carole is not currently working and her focus is on her children at the moment.
   c. Carole is not currently working, her focus is on her children at the moment.
   d. Carole is not currently working her focus is on her children at the moment.

47.
   a. The rising popularity of the clean eating movement can be attributed to the fact that experts say added sugars and chemicals in our food are to blame for the obesity epidemic.
   b. The rising popularity of the clean eating movement can be attributed in the facts that experts say added sugars and chemicals in our food are to blame for the obesity epidemic.
   c. The rising popularity of the clean eating movement can be attributed to the fact that experts saying added sugars and chemicals in our food are to blame for the obesity epidemic.
   d. The rising popularity of the clean eating movement can be attributed with the facts that experts say added sugars and chemicals in our food are to blame for the obesity epidemic.

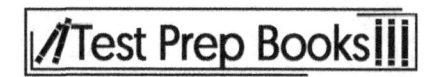

Sentence Correction: For the next eight questions, select the answer choice that needs to be used in place of the underlined text to make the sentence correct, or indicate that the underlined text is not in error.

Questions 48–55

48. An important issues stemming from this meeting is that we won't have enough time to meet all of the objectives.
    a. NO ERROR
    b. Important issue stemming from this meeting
    c. An important issue stemming from this meeting
    d. Important issues stemming from this meeting

49. She's looking for a suitcase that can fit all of her clothes, shoes, accessory, and makeup.
    a. NO ERROR
    b. clothes, shoes, accessories, and makeup.
    c. clothes, shoes, accessories, and makeups.
    d. clothes, shoe, accessory, and makeup.

50. Shawn started taking guitar lessons while he wanted to become a better musician.
    a. NO ERROR
    b. because he wants to become a better musician.
    c. even though he wanted to become a better musician.
    d. because he wanted to become a better musician.

51. Considering the recent rains we have had, it's a wonder the plants haven't drowned.
    a. NO ERROR
    b. Consider the recent rains we have had, it's a wonder
    c. Considering for how much recent rain we have had, its a wonder
    d. Considering, the recent rains we have had, its a wonder

52. Since none of the furniture were delivered on time, we have to move in at a later date.
    a. NO ERROR
    b. Since none of the furniture was delivered on time,
    c. Since all of the furniture were delivered on time,
    d. Since all of the furniture was delivered on time

53. It is necessary for instructors to offer tutoring to any students who need extra help in the class.
    a. NO ERROR
    b. for any students that need extra help in the class.
    c. with any students who need extra help in the class.
    d. for any students needing any extra help in their class.

54. The fact the train set only includes four cars and one small track was a big disappointment to my son.
    a. NO ERROR
    b. that the trains set only include four cars and one small track was a big disappointment
    c. that the train set only includes four cars and one small track was a big disappointment
    d. that the train set only includes four cars and one small track were a big disappointment

332

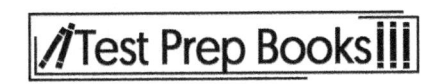

55. <u>Because many people</u> feel there are too many distractions to get any work done, I actually enjoy working from home.
   a. NO ERROR
   b. While many people
   c. Maybe many people
   d. With most people

Paragraph Organization: For each item in this section, select the ordering of sentences that results in the most organized paragraph.

Questions 56–60

56. Sentence 1: Leonardo da Vinci studied the flight of birds and began noting some basic principles of aerodynamics, which eventually led to the development of the steerable airship, or dirigible, in the late 18th century.

Sentence 2: It is said that kites existed in China around the fifth century B.C. that were capable of carrying a person into the air, making them the first man made "vehicles."

Sentence 3: The first recorded attempt at flight was made by a Spanish citizen who covered his arms in feathers and jumped.

Sentence 4: Aviation's history expands over 2,000 years.

   a. 2, 4, 3, 1
   b. 1, 3, 4, 2
   c. 3, 2, 1, 4
   d. 4, 2, 3, 1

57. Sentence 1: All of these areas are warm and wet areas within ten degrees of the equator.

Sentence 2: Tropical rainforests are found in five major areas of the world: Central America, South America, Central Africa, Asia stretching from India to islands in the Pacific Ocean, and Australia.

Sentence 3: They do not have a substantial dry season during the year.

Sentence 4: Rainforests cover approximately 6% of the Earth's surface.

   a. 1, 2, 3, 4
   b. 4, 2, 1, 3
   c. 3, 1, 2, 4
   d. 4, 1, 2, 3

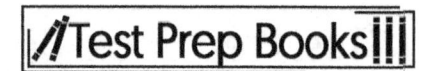

58. Sentence 1: At present, so I am told, the high gods of medicine have decreed that the first cries of the young shall be uttered upon the anesthetic air of a hospital, preferably a fashionable one.

Sentence 2: Whether this anachronism had any bearing upon the astonishing history I am about to set down will never be known.

Sentence 3: As long ago as 1860 it was the proper thing to be born at home.

Sentence 4: So young Mr. and Mrs. Roger Button were fifty years ahead of style when they decided, one day in the summer of 1860, that their first baby should be born in a hospital.

From *The Curious Case of Benjamin Button* by F.S. Fitzgerald, 1922

    a. 1, 3, 2, 4
    b. 3, 2, 1, 4
    c. 3, 1, 4, 2
    d. 4, 1, 3, 2

59. Sentence 1: Analogous features are those that have the same function but were not derived from a common ancestor.

Sentence 2: Cladograms are diagrams that classify organisms based on their proposed common ancestry but are focused on their common physical traits.

Sentence 3: Homologous features, on the other hand, have anatomical similarities, even if the function is no longer the same, due to a proposed common ancestor.

Sentence 4: Branching points on these diagrams represent when a group of organisms is thought to have developed a new trait.

    a. 2, 4, 1, 3
    b. 3, 2, 1, 4
    c. 2, 1, 4, 3
    d. 4, 2, 3, 1

Practice Test #2 | English Expression

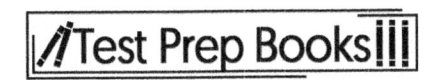

60. Sentence 1: How impious is the title of sacred majesty applied to a worm, who in the midst of his splendor is crumbling into dust!

Sentence 2: The Heathens paid divine honors to their deceased kings, and the Christian world hath improved on the plan, by doing the same to their living ones.

Sentence 3: It was the most prosperous invention the Devil ever set on foot for the promotion of idolatry.

Sentence 4: Government by kings was first introduced into the world by the Heathens, from whom the children of Israel copied the custom.

Excerpt from "Common Sense" by Thomas Paine

a. 1, 2, 3, 4
b. 2, 1, 3, 4
c. 4, 3, 2, 1
d. 3, 1, 2, 4

Paragraph Revision: This section consists of different paragraphs. Read each paragraph carefully, and then answer the questions that follow it.

Questions 61–65

Sentence 1: Practitioner of Ju-jitsu, and other martial arts, strive away from the act of total violence.

Sentence 2: We tend not to be violent individuals in the first place because of our training.

Sentence 3: The moves we learn are inherently harmful, so them should used sparingly and not to advance our own satisfaction.

Sentence 4: The lessons taught in Ju-jitsu urge people to be mindful of their capabilities while also being decisive when defense is required.

61. The writer discovers the following sentence has been left out of the paragraph: "From the first day on the mat, physical restraint is emphasized. " Which sentence is this sentence most likely to be placed after?

a. Sentence 1
b. Sentence 2
c. Sentence 3
d. Sentence 4

62. Choose the best choice for the underlined text in Sentence 1. If you think the text is correct as-is, choose Choice A.
a. Practitioner of Ju-jitsu, and other martial arts, strive away
b. Practitioners of Ju-jitsu, and other martial arts, strive away
c. Practitioners of Ju-jitsu, and other martial arts strive away
d. Practitioner of Ju-jitsu, and other martial arts, strives away

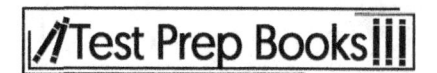

63. Choose the best choice for the underlined text in Sentence 3. If you think the text is correct as-is, choose Choice A.
   a. so them should used sparingly
   b. so them should be used sparingly
   c. so they should used sparingly
   d. so they should be used sparingly

Sentence 1: Most commonly, flooding is caused by excessive rain.

Sentence 2: Such rainfall may cause to overflow the water in rivers and other bodies of water.

Sentence 3: The excess water can cause dams to break.

Sentence 4: Such events can cause flooding of the surrounding riverbanks or coastal regions.

64. The writer discovers the following sentence has been left out of the paragraph: "The ground is not able to absorb all the water produced by a sudden heavy rainfall or rainfall that occurs over a prolonged period of time." Which sentence is this sentence most likely to be placed after?
   a. Sentence 1
   b. Sentence 2
   c. Sentence 3
   d. Sentence 4

65. Choose the best choice for the underlined text in Sentence 2. If you think the text is correct as-is, choose Choice A.
   a. may cause to overflow the water in rivers and other bodies of water.
   b. may been causing the rivers and other bodies of water to overflow.
   c. may cause the rivers and other bodies of water to overflow.
   d. may cause other bodies of water and water in rivers to overflow.

Written Essay #2

On the FSOT, you will be presented with multiple essay topics to choose from. The test allows you seven minutes to choose the topic before you get started. If you don't choose a topic before seven minutes, they will choose one for you. Then, you will have twenty-five minutes to develop and write your essay. Reviewers of your essay will look for a clear, organized essay with grammatically correct sentences. You will have 2800 characters, or spaces, to write your essay, then the screen will time out.

The following is an example topic essay:

> A common societal expectation is that high school students will pursue a college degree after they graduate. Some may argue that is hard to get a high-paying job or be successful without a college degree, but others disagree, saying that pursuing a vocational trade will make more money in the long run because training for such jobs is much more affordable than the traditional four-year degree. Even others may advocate for a gap year so that young adults can get work experience and determine what career path they would like to pursue.

Write an essay to someone who is considering whether to go to college. Take a side on the issue and argue whether or not he/she should pursue a college degree. Use specific examples to support your argument.

Answer Explanations #2

Job Knowledge

1. C: Article I, Section 8 of the U.S. Constitution grants Congress with the "power of the purse," which is the power to coin money and create a federal budget. All other governmental agencies must follow Congress's budget, including the Department of Labor and the Department of Commerce. The Supreme Court can deem the budget to be unconstitutional only if it violates constitutional law.

2. C: Federal Reserve. The Federal Reserve is the bank of banks. It is the central bank of the United States and controls the value of money. A commodity is the value of goods such as precious metals. While the Central Reserve and Bank Reserve may sound like good options, the term "bank reserve" refers to the amount of money a bank deposits into a central bank, and the Central Reserve is simply a fictitious name.

3. C: Choice C is correct because a calm and explanatory email makes the situation clear without adding distracting emotional or personal emphasis. Choice A is incorrect because a frantic and panicked tone would raise concern about whether the employee can complete the project at all. Choice B is incorrect because being overly colloquial and confident could make it seem as though the employee doesn't take the project seriously. Choice D is incorrect because apologizing and placating take the emphasis away from the objective facts; instead, the emphasis is placed on an unpleasant interpersonal transaction initiated by a wheedling employee who appears to view the supervisor as capricious and domineering.

4. B: While bullying may affect a person's life and often happens in schools, it does not establish ranking of any sort, and is not educational or part of the educational system. Choice A is correct because the rules established by the school help shape a sense of morals in students, or the lack thereof. Choice C is correct because the social situations foster sharing, patience, teamwork, and respect. Choice D is correct because grades establish a feeling of desire to meet expectations, as well as a fear of failing.

5. A: World War I had a number of interrelated causes. European powers were in an intense struggle over the colonization of Africa and Asia, so Choice B is incorrect. Imperialism was supported through intense militarization, particularly in terms of naval spending. Therefore, Choice C is incorrect. Governments stoked nationalist sentiments to justify their imperial conquests and aggressive militarization. Furthermore, Bosnian nationalist Gavrilo Princip assassinated the Archduke Franz Ferdinand of Austria, and it was the inciting incident that led the complex alliance systems into World War I. So, Choice D is incorrect. Although communism had begun to attract significant support during the latter half of the nineteenth century, it was not a primary cause of World War I. Communists didn't control the government of a major global power until the Russian Revolution overthrew the Czar in 1917. Thus, Choice A is the correct answer.

6: Choice A is correct. President Harry Truman delivered the first televised political speech in 1947. Choice B is incorrect because Dwight Eisenhower was the first to air campaign ads on television, not the first to air a televised speech. Choices C and D are incorrect, as John F. Kennedy was elected much later than the first televised speech and Franklin D. Roosevelt was elected much earlier.

7. A: The atomic bomb was created during World War II (1939–1945). Scientists and engineers did develop a number of other weapons in order to break through the heavily entrenched front lines during

Answer Explanations #2 | Job Knowledge

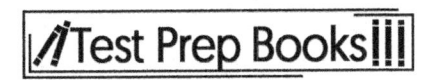

World War I. Poison gas killed or injured millions of men between 1914 and 1918. Aircraft were used to observe enemy positions and bombard enemy troops. Armored tanks were able to crush barbed wire fences and deflected machine gun bullets.

8. A: A pure monopoly is when there is only one seller of a particular product or commodity, and the sole seller attempts to restrict firms from exiting and entering the industry at will. Choices *B* and *C* describe a free enterprise economy. Choice *D* describes an oligopoly.

9. B: To be directly proportional means that $y = kx$. If x is changed from 5 to 20, the value of x is multiplied by 4. Applying the same rule to the y-value, also multiply the value of y by 4. Therefore:

$$y = 12$$

10. D: Executive orders are examples of the president's informal powers because they are not explicitly established as a responsibility of the president within the U.S. Constitution. All other answer options are explicitly granted as presidential powers by the U.S. Constitution.

11. D: Choice *D* is correct because Microsoft Excel is a spreadsheet program that stores and tracks data in a similar manner to tables or graphs from Microsoft Word, but with many more tools and features. Choices *A*, *B*, and *C* are incorrect because, although they are all features in both Microsoft Word and Microsoft Excel, they are not the core purpose of Excel.

12. C: Choice *C* is correct because increasing Greenistan's benefits is an increase in the reward offered for accepting the deal. Choice *A* is incorrect because the ambassador has already tried persuasion, with no success. Choice *B* is incorrect because threats of violent action aren't considered diplomacy. Choice *D* is incorrect because, although it does shift the balance of the deal toward Greenistan, it removes some of Blueland's own incentives for the agreement.

13. C: Goals are set by the team during the meeting, not solely by the facilitator. The allowed time, meeting structure, and members in the meeting are all responsibilities of the facilitator.

14. A: The map provides a visual representation of Mercosur member states. Mercosur is a customs union intended to promote free trade between members. In addition, the customs union jointly negotiates trade policies, which increases the members' bargaining power. Choice *B* is incorrect because Mercosur is much more concerned with free trade and economic development than environmental protection. Choice *C* is incorrect because although many individual members of Mercosur have longstanding relationships with international lending agencies, such as the International Monetary Fund, Mercosur doesn't specialize in lending programs. Choice *D* is incorrect because Mercosur doesn't feature a supranational government, meaning that member states are the sole sovereign authority within their territories.

15. C: Mercosur includes every country in South America, and therefore neighbors are jointly cooperating with this regional organization. Physical proximity facilitates economic cooperation and coordination. For example, neighboring states can easily share resources to be used in the implementation and enforcement of free-trade policies. If the members of Mercosur weren't neighboring states, it would have dramatically altered how Mercosur was formed and designed. Choice *A* is incorrect because Mercosur is a customs union, which doesn't require member states to pool natural resources. Choice *B* is incorrect because political rivalries frequently arise between neighboring states; in fact, there are numerous rivalries between Mercosur member states, such as the ongoing dispute between Venezuela and Brazil. Choice D is incorrect because South America is a relatively large region, and Mercosur extends across the entire continent. Consequently, the member states didn't develop under the same climatic conditions.

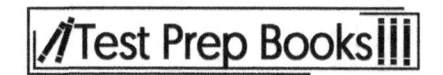

16. D: Theory of The Firm. Behaviors of firms is not an indicator of economic growth because it refers to the behavior that firms follow to reach their desired outcome. GDP, unemployment, and inflation are all indicators that help determine economic growth.

17. B: By design, there are many checks and balances among the branches of government. The president does have the power to veto any law passed Congress, which Congress can override. Congress also has the power to consider and approve all of the president's picks for the Supreme Court and federal courts. Congress also controls the budget, which can limit what the president has to spend on the military. However, the Supreme Court does not get to try the president for high crimes and misdemeanors; that job belongs to Congress. The Chief Justice of the Supreme Court, however, does preside over the hearings.

18. D: This period was called the Gilded Age since it appeared shiny and golden on the surface but was fueled by undercurrents of corruption led by big businessmen known as robber barons. Choice A, Manifest Destiny, is the concept referring to the pursuit and acquisition of new lands by the U.S., which led to the purchase of Alaska from Russia in 1867 and the annexation of Hawaii in 1898. The Columbian Exchange, Choice B, was an era of discovery, conquest, and colonization of the Americas by the Europeans. The New Deal, Choice C, was a plan launched by President Franklin Delano Roosevelt to help rebuild America's economy after the Great Depression.

19. B: Because the triangles are similar, the lengths of the corresponding sides are proportional. Therefore:

$$\frac{30+x}{30} = \frac{22}{14} = \frac{y+15}{y}$$

This results in the equation:

$$14(30 + x) = 22 \times 30$$

When solved, this gives:

$$x = 17.1$$

The proportion also results in the equation:

$$14(y + 15) = 22y$$

When solved, this gives:

$$y = 26.3$$

20. B: Choice B is correct because public diplomacy is sometimes called people's diplomacy, referring to its focus on a foreign country's public opinion of a different home country. Choices A, C, and D are incorrect because elevator, open-forum, and streetside are all fictional kinds of diplomacy.

Answer Explanations #2 | Job Knowledge

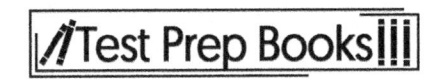

21. B: Even with the most diligent planning, HR leaders should expect the unexpected and never be too emotionally attached to outcomes. Michael should realize that all baseline plans are fluid and manage his expectations accordingly, while also preparing contingency plans for his operations. Most federal funds cannot roll over from fiscal years, and simply communicating information does not set them in stone.

22. A: Social contract theory developed during the Enlightenment in the eighteenth and nineteenth centuries. Along with John Locke and Thomas Hobbes, Jean Jacques-Rousseau was a prominent Enlightenment philosopher and social contract theorist. Thus, Choice A is the correct answer. Choice B is the second-best answer. Humanism is a philosophy that emphasizes individualism, human freedom, critical thinking, and rationalism, and Jean Jacques-Rousseau was heavily influenced by the humanist tradition. However, the Enlightenment better describes the intellectual context of the eighteenth and nineteenth centuries because humanism dates back to ancient times. So, Choice B is incorrect. Modernism is a philosophical and artistic movement that developed in the late nineteenth century based on the rejection of traditionalism, so Choice C is incorrect. The Renaissance was a cultural movement that revived humanism; however, the Renaissance lasted from the fourteenth century to the seventeenth century, which predates the Enlightenment. So, Choice D is incorrect.

23. A: The *Federalist Papers* were articles written anonymously under the pseudonym *Publius* that supported ratification of the U.S. Constitution. Choice B, a document identifying basic liberties, is the bill of rights. Choice C, a document which articulated America's system of government at the time of the Constitutional Convention, is the Articles of Confederation. After the Constitution was ratified, it would be the document described by this answer choice. Choice D, a document that required the colonists to pay a tax on legal documents, newspapers, magazines and other printed materials, is known as the Stamp Act.

24. C: In a command economy, the government controls the prices as well as what and how much of a product is produced.

25. C: A die has an equal chance for each outcome. Since it has six sides, each outcome has a probability of $\frac{1}{6}$. The chance of a 1 or a 2 is therefore $\frac{1}{6} + \frac{1}{6} = \frac{1}{3}$.

26. B: Choice B is correct. Twitter is a form of social media website that focuses on short text posts with a maximum of roughly 300 characters, and up to four images or a short video clip can be attached. Choices A, C, and D are all incorrect because in Instagram, Imgur, and YouTube the text is secondary.

27. C: The product in the image has a "Fair Trade" label. Trade organizations certify products as fair trade when they are produced in accordance with specific labor and environmental standards. The environmental standards always emphasize sustainability, and labor standards typically include reasonable compensation to workers. Choice A is incorrect because although environmental sustainability is part of the fair-trade movement, the production of these certified products doesn't necessarily occur on family farms. Choice B is incorrect because although many worker-owned cooperatives produce fair-trade agricultural products, this isn't a requirement for certification. Choice D is incorrect because fair trade isn't related to free trade, and consumers typically pay a premium for fair-trade products.

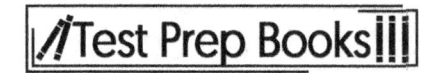

28. A: To find the fraction of the bill that the first three people pay, the fractions need to be added, which means finding the common denominator. The common denominator will be 60.

$$\frac{1}{5}+\frac{1}{4}+\frac{1}{3}=\frac{12}{60}+\frac{15}{60}+\frac{20}{60}=\frac{47}{60}$$

The remainder of the bill is:

$$1-\frac{47}{60}=\frac{60}{60}-\frac{47}{60}=\frac{13}{60}$$

29. B: Britain was not defeated in the French and Indian War, and, in fact, disputes with the colonies over the new territories it won contributed to the growing tensions. All other options were key motivations behind the Revolutionary War.

30. D: Choice D is correct because the use of appropriate humor helps the audience connect with the speaker on a more personal level. Choice A is incorrect because a natural intonation would help develop authenticity. Choice B is incorrect because although repetition would help keep audience attention, it does not improve connection. Choice C is incorrect because eye contact would help improve confidence.

31. C: Diversity involves hiring employees with a variety of backgrounds, personalities, and working styles, while inclusion involves making sure those differences are heard and represented in the workplace. Choice A is not the best answer because, while some aspects of an organization's diversity program may be guided by EEOC regulations, it does not include other diversity considerations like a variety of personality types, working styles, and backgrounds. Choice B is also incorrect because inclusion refers to integrating the contributions of diverse employees into the workplace. Finally, Choice D is not the best answer because diversity and inclusion are complementary rather than competing ideals.

32. B: If 60% of 50 workers are women, then there are 30 women working in the office. If half of them are wearing skirts, then that means 15 women wear skirts. Since none of the men wear skirts, this means there are 15 people wearing skirts.

33. A: Free trade agreements seek to increase international trade by limiting or eliminating tariffs and subsidies for domestic industries. Overall, international trade increased dramatically after the signing of the General Agreement on Tariffs and Trade (1947) and formation of the World Trade Organization (1995). Thus, Choice A is the correct answer. Although Keynes issued proposals to reduce German reparations and establish a Free Trade Union, they are separate proposals. Reparations aren't directly related to free trade agreements. As such, Choice B is incorrect. Choice C is incorrect because free trade agreements generally prohibit countries from subsidizing or protecting domestic industries. Free trade agreements don't facilitate imperialism, so Choice D is incorrect.

34. A: Although the Constitution makes no provisions for a presidential cabinet, President George Washington created one when he took office. Members of the cabinet advise the president on a wide variety of issues including, but not limited to, defense, transportation, and education. The White House Press Secretary acts as spokesperson for the U.S. government administration, Choice B. The cabinet members are not required to raise money for the president's re-election effort, Choice C. The Vice President, not the cabinet, is who presides over the Senate, Choice D.

Answer Explanations #2 | Job Knowledge

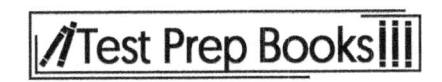

35. B: Genghis Khan was one of the most accomplished military generals in history. During the early thirteenth century, he united the five Mongol confederations and successfully invaded territory in present-day China, Central Asia, Eastern Europe, and the Middle East. These conquests marked the beginning of the Mongol Empire. At the time of Genghis Khan's death, the Mongol Empire held approximately twice as much territory as the Roman Empire. Thus, Choice *B* is the correct answer. Following the Mongol Empire's fragmentation at the end of the thirteenth century, a Mongol faction known as the Golden Horde assumed control of the Mongol Empire's former territory in Eastern Europe and Siberia. So, Choice *A* is incorrect. Kublai Khan completed the Mongol Empire's conquest of China. After declaring himself the emperor of China, he founded the Yuan Dynasty in 1271. So, Choice *C* is incorrect. Timur conquered the western half of the Chagatai Khanate and established the Timurid Empire in 1370. Therefore, Choice *D* is incorrect.

36. B: The formula for the volume of a cylinder is $\pi r^2 h$, where r is the radius and h is the height. The diameter is twice the radius, so these barrels have a radius of 1 foot. That means each barrel has a volume of:

$$\pi \times 1^2 \times 3 = 3\pi \text{ cubic feet}$$

Since there are three of them, the total is:

$$3 \times 3\pi = 9\pi \text{ cubic feet}$$

37. D: The term "establishment clause" refers to the part of the First Amendment that applies to freedom of religion. It says: "Congress shall make no law respecting an establishment of religion." Choices *A*, *B*, and *C* do not describe the establishment clause.

38. B: World War II brought about an end to the Great Depression by switching over to wartime production. After the end of World War II, consumer demand remained high and unemployment was usually low. Computers began to become more powerful, efficient, and inexpensive in the latter part of the 20th century, and they became more common in business. The Sun Belt actually expanded after World War II as the traditional manufacturing base in the North and Midwest fell into decline. Land was cheaper in the South and West and wages were also lower too, so these regions were very attractive to businesses.

39. C: Economies of scale have encouraged farms to continually expand operations, and most recently, this had led to corporatization. Unlike corporations, small family farms don't have the capital to purchase more land and invest in the latest technological innovations. Due to this discrepancy, small family farms aren't able to compete with large-scale operations in terms of the prices they can offer customers. In the face of these challenges, many small family farms have declared bankruptcy. Choice *A* is incorrect because economies of scale incentivize the development of innovations due to the greater potential for profit. Choice *B* is incorrect because economies of scale are the central feature of contemporary global commodity chains, and this scheme generally drives down prices for consumers. Choice *D* is incorrect because many new food production and consumption movements have developed in response to the rise of large-scale agricultural operations, such as community-supported agriculture, local food movements, and urban farming.

40. A: Choice *A* is correct because keyword searching is an easy way to search a massive library inventory, making it the most advantageous reason to switch to a digital database. Choice *B* is incorrect because a digital database has minimal impact on public advertising and awareness. Choice *C* is incorrect because a digital database does not necessarily increase total capacity if a particular medium or resource exists only in physical format. Choice D is incorrect because a digital database also does not necessarily save on operating costs—it may even increase them instead.

41. C: Choice C is correct because having many unrelated tangents and ideas will confuse Calvin's audience and make it difficult for them to follow his presentation. Choices A and D are incorrect because they imply that the audience is following Calvin's presentation and the question says that they are not. Choice B is incorrect because in order to disagree, the audience would have to be following Calvin's presentation.

42. D: Self-esteem is the term that best describes a feeling of personal worth or value. Self-efficacy refers to a person's feelings of competency to perform or achieve a particular task. Self-identity and self-concept have to do with one's overall view of self.

43. C: Choice C is correct because pie charts can help represent information visually. Choice A is incorrect because an additional paragraph would not help represent the information visually, only explain it. Choice B is incorrect because highlighted sentences are a way to emphasize some parts of a text, not a form of visual representation. Choice D is incorrect because poring over the accounting ledgers may be too technical for the intended audience and a simpler addition would be better.

44. B: Jefferys is referencing the Northwest Passage. There were rumors about a Northwest Passage to Asia prior to Columbus reaching the Caribbean, and his voyage ignited a firestorm of interest. From 1492 to 1800, European powers sponsored many hundreds of expeditions to locate the route. Thus, Choice B is the correct answer. Vasco da Gama sailing around the Cape of Good Hope led to increased European trade with East Africa, India, and China, but his journey around Africa was unrelated to the Northwest Passage. So, Choice A is incorrect. Ferdinand Magellan's circumnavigation of the world didn't increase interest in a Northwest Passage because his expedition traveled to Asia across the southern portion of the Atlantic Ocean. So, Choice C is incorrect. Choice D is the second-best answer. European explorers believed the Northwest Passage was located to the west of Hudson Bay, and the passage mentions Hudson Bay. However, the voyage of Christopher Columbus was the inciting incident for the entire Age of Discovery, so Choice D is incorrect.

45. D: European explorers never found the Northwest Passage, but the search uncovered the Americas' economic potential. European colonization started almost immediately after Columbus reached the Caribbean, and it spread across both continents as explorers continued to search for the elusive route to Asia. Thus, Choice D is the correct answer. Although Ferdinand Magellan found a passage to Asia through the southern Atlantic, it was much slower than sailing around the Cape of Good Hope. So, Choice A is incorrect. The search for a Northwest Passage exponentially increased international trade, so Choice B is incorrect. European powers occasionally made strategic short-term alliances with individual Amerindian tribes, but alliances weren't a long-term consequence of European exploration in the Americas. As such, Choice C is incorrect.

46. B: 99.35

Set up the problem, with the larger number on top. Multiply as if there are no decimal places. Add the answer rows together. Count the number of decimal places that were in the original numbers (2).

Place the decimal in that many spots from the right for the final solution.

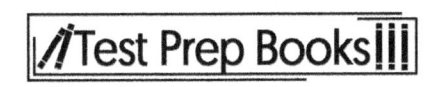

47. A: An employee who is a salesperson would more than likely warrant a written employment contract to outline information, such as salary (including guaranteed or discretionary bonuses), commission structure and payment processes, and clauses referencing non-compete agreements.

48. A: In contractionary monetary policy, the money supply is decreased. All of the other choices are characteristics of contractionary monetary policy.

49. C: Under the Constitution, the power to coin money is designated exclusively to the federal government, but both the states and the federal government maintain the power to collect taxes from the citizens under their jurisdictions and establish courts lower than the Supreme Court, though states may only establish regional courts within their states. The states reserve the right to regulate trade within their states (intrastate), while the federal government maintains the power to regulate trade between states (interstate).

50. B: Choice B is correct because organizations depend on positive relations with local media to maintain a positive view with the public. Choices A and D are incorrect because relations with local businesses or military are not relevant to media relations. Choice C is incorrect because public opinion is better affected via local media outlets rather than a random sample of citizens.

51. C: Massacre at Wounded Knee. The Massacre at Wounded Knee in 1890 left at least 150 Native Americans dead, including many women and children, and was the last major engagement between Indians and American soldiers. The Trail of Tears, Choice A, involved the forced relocation of tribes from the American Southeast in the 1830s. Although thousands of Native Americans died along the way, it was not a battle. Tecumseh launched his uprising in 1811, Choice B, and conflict between Native Americans and U.S. soldiers would continue for decades as the country expanded further west. The Battle of Little Big Horn in 1876, Choice D, was a great Native American victory that led to the death of General Custer and more than 200 men.

52. D: Culture can be transmitted in nearly endless ways, ranging from governmental policies to entertainment consumption. Furthermore, culture can be transmitted intentionally or spontaneously. For example, powerful institutions can sometimes unilaterally shift the culture to achieve a goal, but other times cultural change is a natural byproduct of social interactions that spirals in an unforeseen direction. Thus, Choice D is the correct answer. Culture is not always transmitted through hierarchical relationships. For example, relocation diffusion and contagious diffusion can occur outside of hierarchical relationships, so Choice A is incorrect. Religion, economic activities, and government policies play a powerful role in cultural development, but culture can be transmitted in other important ways, such as through social interactions and digital networks. Therefore, Choice B is incorrect. Choice C is a true statement, but it does not describe how culture is transmitted across society, so it's incorrect.

53. D: Diversity. Diversity refers to how everything and everyone is uniquely different. Choice A (behaviorism) is the study of how behavior influences the way human beings interact with their environment. Choice B (peer pressure) is when a group uses the majority vote to try to persuade the minority into changing their minds. Finally, Choice C (adaptation) is also incorrect because adaptation refers to how a human being adjusts to their surroundings to create a desired outcome. Therefore, Choice D (diversity) is correct.

54. D: The South had more experienced military leaders that the North due to their participation in the Mexican-American War. The South was defending their homes from damage, since most of the war happened in the South, so Choice A is incorrect. Because the South had free labor at home due to slavery, agricultural production could continue even when most of the men were away at war, so Choice B is incorrect. Finally, Choice C is incorrect because the North had a population of about 18.5 million while the South had only 5.5 million citizens and 3.5 million slaves. This meant the Union had more soldiers and could more easily replace them than the Confederacy could.

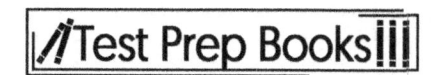

55. D: Convert these numbers to improper fractions: $\frac{11}{3} - \frac{9}{5}$. Then, convert the fractions to have a common denominator of 15, subtract, and convert the answer back to a mixed number.

$$\frac{11}{3} - \frac{9}{5} = \frac{55}{15} - \frac{27}{15} = \frac{28}{15} = 1\frac{13}{15}$$

56. B: Conservative evangelicals formed the Moral Majority in 1979 in an effort to address issues like abortion. Their enthusiasm helped carry Reagan into the White House and bring the U.S. Senate under Republican control for the first time in twenty-eight years. The First Great Awakening, Choice A, occurred in the 1700s and the Second Great Awakening began in the 1800s. These movements encouraged Protestants to have a more personal connection to Christ. The Know-Nothings, Choice C, opposed Catholic immigration during the 1800s. The Anti-Defamation League, Choice D, focused on combating anti-Semitism and Holocaust deniers.

57. D: Choice D is correct because financial transfer information is likely to be in a banking database, not in a pharmacy database. Choices A, B, and C are incorrect because medical history for patients, where medications are stored, and exact prescription information are all information that is likely to be in a pharmacy database.

58. D: Choice D is correct because newspapers are most effective at reaching a dedicated local audience of readers. Choices A and B are incorrect because the veterinarian specialist and foreign dignitary are only visiting temporarily and they may not bother to read local news. Choice C is also incorrect, as young college students may not read newspapers at all and are better reached by another medium.

59. D: Hazard pay is not a covered provision. The Fair Labor Standards Act (FLSA) establishes guidelines around Choice A, overtime pay, Choice B, employee classification (exempt and non-exempt status), minimum wage, on-call pay, record keeping, and Choice C, child labor.

60. C: The enumerated powers granted to Congress are the powers that the Constitution directly grants to them. Choice A is one of those powers, the power to create and borrow currency. Choice B is also one, as it falls under the power of Congress to both pass laws and levy taxes. Choice D also falls under the power of Congress to regulate interstate commerce. Choice C is not in the enumerated powers and is actually within the parameters of the case of US v. Lopez.

Situational Judgment

Situation 1

Most Effective - D: Remaining calm and promising to provide more information as it comes in would help the most to ease the fears of the audience.

Least Effective - C: Suddenly ending the press conference would make it seem like you lack confidence in your information or don't want to help the audience, increasing their panic and fear.

Answer Explanations #2 | Situational Judgment

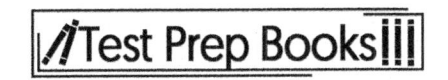

Situation 2

Most Effective - B: Taking the initiative to research unknown cultural customs shows adaptability and respect for different cultural environments.

Least Effective - E: Failing to take the impending cultural transition seriously shows a lack of respect for Japanese culture and a lack of cultural adaptability. Taking work off before such an important move in order to party also demonstrates a lack of respect for both your coworkers and your position.

Situation 3

Most Effective - A: Drawing inspiration from personal experience demonstrates initiative and an ability to leverage experience to excel at the job.

Least Effective - C: Not only does dropping the African portion of the presentation abandon an element of the project's criteria, but it also misses the opportunity to take advantage of personal experience to improve your work.

Situation 4

Most Effective - C: It would be rude to decline the invitation if the foreign leaders value your opinion, but it would be equally rude to be unprepared for the discussion. Learning more about your home country's economic systems and coming to the meeting prepared would be the best choice.

Least Effective - E: While not attending the meeting would be unhelpful, offering an uninformed opinion could influence the foreign country to make poor choices. This is possibly a worse situation than having no opinion at all.

Situation 5

Most Effective - B: Taking the lead lets the rest of your team rest, gets the project done in time, and demonstrates your responsibility as a team leader.

Least Effective - E: Failing to take the lead in this situation forces your team to make a decision in your absence, making your leadership both questionable and disappointing.

Situation 6

Most Effective - E: Recognizing your own limits shows good judgment. Determining a realistic amount of work that you can handle and asking for help on the more difficult tasks shows respect for the importance of the work while being cognizant of your own abilities and open to accepting help.

Least Effective - A: Showing a lack of confidence in your capabilities while simultaneously overstating your ability to carry out your assigned tasks is a sign of weak or poor judgment. Choice B, feigning confidence and failing to follow through, is also a poor option, but the passive-aggressive communication in Choice A makes it even less effective.

Situation 7

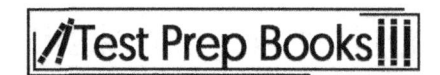

Most Effective - C: In this situation, it's important to be objective about a colleague's work. Reviewing them as an excellent worker without letting personal feelings about them interfere is the best choice.

Least Effective - B: Letting bias about a particular team member influence your review of their work performance gives the wrong impression to your boss and could raise concerns about your ability to avoid favoritism or subjectivity. Choice *D* is also ineffective because you have been asked to evaluate the team member's work performance, not his attitude outside of work; however, Choice *B* is even less effective because it recommends punishment for the member's attitude outside of work rather than simply reporting on it.

Situation 8

Most Effective - D: In this situation, a concise explanation that focuses on the key details will help convey the idea quickly and effectively.

Least Effective - E: Being improperly prepared will severely increase the risk of wasting your boss's time. It may fail to convey any idea at all, possibly even calling into question your ability to prepare for a presentation.

Situation 9

Most Effective - C: It's important to remain unfazed by unexpected circumstances. Borrowing a handout and continuing from there is a great demonstration of resourcefulness and flexibility.

Least Effective - D: Ending the presentation early because of an unexpected interruption would be confusing to the audience at best. At worst, you would display inability to adapt to changing situations.

Situation 10

Most Effective - A: If you keep the meeting flowing and give other team members a proper chance to speak, it will keep the team working together. Politely reprimanding the offending team member may be necessary afterwards; however, within the meeting itself, it's more important to keep things flowing and avoid unnecessary confrontation.

Least Effective - E: In this situation, a joke could have unintended consequences. The meeting might become more awkward or uncomfortable for all members, so a more serious approach is preferable.

Situation 11

Most Effective - E: The best course of action would be to explain the conflicts between business model and the law, then work with the businessman to find a compromise or solution that will allow him to expand.

Least Effective - B: Being aware of the problems and encouraging the businessman to walk into a situation where he is going to make an uninformed mistake is dishonest.

Answer Explanations #2 | Situational Judgment

Situation 12

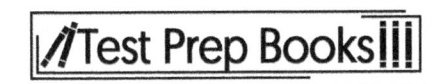

Most Effective - A: One of a foreign service officer's duties is to do their best to ensure that all citizens of their home country receive appropriate legal counsel. Politely but firmly explain the situation and work with foreign law enforcement to adhere to their procedures while ensuring that you carry out your own duty.

Least Effective - D: Threats of going public in this situation are not diplomatic and constitute an excessive escalation that could lead to unintended and negative consequences.

Situation 13

Most Effective - D: While a foreign service officer's efforts are focused on helping their home country's citizens first, working cooperatively with local relief efforts will improve the situation and ensure that everyone receives help.

Least Effective - A: Denouncing the efforts of local officials to provide relief without offering any help shows poor leadership and initiative. Choice *B* is also ineffective and rude; however, at least it encourages some sort of action and could potentially take place in private conversations. On the other hand, Choice *A* merely wastes time pointing fingers, and doing so publicly could undermine the relationship between your home country and your assigned country.

Situation 14

Most Effective - E: Given the timespan of only two years, the fastest economic growth would come from taking advantage of resources the country already has. In this case, expanding the existing shipping industry and exporting the available natural resources would allow for the quickest economic growth in two years.

Least Effective - A: While investing in education and technical skills does create economic growth, it takes longer than two years to feel the effects of that investment. In this case, it also ignores some of the readily available potential.

Situation 15

Most Effective - B: Coordinating the two schedules and hosting the meeting at a middle ground location like the embassy is the fairest way to facilitate the meeting. A third-party location as stated in Choice *E* might not have enough security, and your embassy is already a point of connection between the two countries. Therefore, Choice *B* is more effective.

Least Effective - A: Setting a meeting time without consideration for the presidents' busy and limited schedules is disrespectful and may be seen as a brute force approach.

Answer Explanations #2 | Situational Judgment

Situation 16

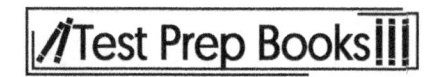

Most Effective - C: Offering help is good, especially if it can lead to positive relations with your home country. However, since these newly independent people are wary of foreign interference, a cautious approach is best.

Least Effective - B: Directly sending political aid to this country may be seen as invasive and unwarranted. Because they have recently earned their own political freedom and are wary of foreign interference, this action could have dangerous consequences.

Situation 17

Most Effective - C: Rejecting the bribe and warning other members of your team is the best and most honest choice.

Least Effective - B: Accepting the bribe is dishonest, illegal, and misleading. Choice E, bargaining to increase the bonus, is also an ineffective choice; however, in that scenario, the bribe has not actually been accepted, making it slightly less ineffective than Choice B.

Situation 18

Most Effective - A: Because much is at stake, the steps taken should be careful and involve all honest parties, including both countries' governments. Fixing the situation and getting all parties on the same page is the best option.

Least Effective - D: Allowing the project to continue would inevitably lead to failure, and the poor quality of the work will have negative political consequences.

Situation 19

Most Effective - E: You and your supervisor should work collaboratively to understand each other's reasonings for your differing recommendations. This is the most amicable and cooperative way to resolve the situation.

Least Effective - C: Subverting the chain of command and disregarding the suggestions of superiors is inappropriate and demonstrates a lack of respect for others.

Situation 20

Most Effective - C: Following proper procedure and informing HR or a supervisor for disciplinary action against the offending colleagues is the best choice.

Least Effective - A: Adding your own comments, even jokingly, is rude and inappropriate. All team members should be respectful of one another.

Situation 21

Most Effective - B: Regardless of the foreign country's policy, the embassy's rules are to remain sober on the job. Reporting the situation to HR or a supervisor is the most responsible choice.

Answer Explanations #2 | Situational Judgment

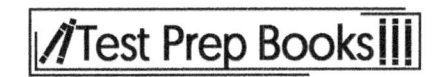

Least Effective - A: Ignoring the situation or not dealing with it immediately would not resolve the problem and could cause a serious incident depending on the situation.

Situation 22

Most Effective - E: Wanting to help a friend is admirable, but it can't get in the way of standard productivity. The best option would be to meet with them outside of work hours so that you can stay focused while on the clock.

Least Effective - D: Letting your own productivity fall behind to help someone else will just result in frustration or a worse situation like missing a deadline.

Situation 23

Most Effective - A: The best option is to see what can be done to expedite the process without overstepping the chain of command. A swift and positive outcome will help to improve the foreign student's view of your home country.

Least Effective - C: Overstepping the chain of command by personally expediting the visa could have negative repercussions for you and complicate the student's situation.

Situation 24

Most Effective - D: Even if you cannot professionally or personally do much to help, conveying the protestors' opinions to your home country is the best option.

Least Effective - B: Trying to disband the protestors with any kind of force is likely to be seen negatively and may lead to more intense protests in the future.

Situation 25

Most Effective - A: Helping citizens of your home country stay safe and working with local officials to facilitate that is one of the primary objectives of a foreign service officer.

Least Effective - E: Ignoring the situation would be directly shirking responsibility and could have serious repercussions.

Situation 26

Most Effective - C: Resolving the situation with minimal conflict is the most positive outcome and demonstrates effective leadership.

Least Effective - E: Choosing to ignore the issue will likely lead to increased internal conflict and more issues when collaborating on the project. It may also cause other team members to question your leadership abilities.

Situation 27

Most Effective - D: Using your knowledge of immigration law and procedures across both countries to help an engaged couple be together is the best choice.

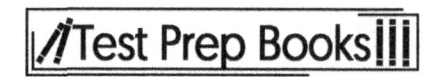

Least Effective - B: Questioning their choices is disrespectful and not your business. Choice C is also potentially disrespectful, but it could potentially be helpful in presenting them with all available options.

Situation 28

Most Effective - E: Immediately informing your supervisor of inappropriate and dishonest behavior is the best choice.

Least Effective - D: Engaging in such dishonest behavior yourself would be extremely inappropriate.

English Expression

1. D: The correct phrase should be "War on Terror." The phrase is capitalized because it was part of the campaign phrase that was launched by the U.S. government after September 11. Punctuation should always be used inside double quotes as well, making Choice *D* the best answer.

2. C: Terrorists commonly use fear and violence to achieve political goals. Choice *A* is incorrect because the subject *Terrorists* is plural while the verb *uses* is singular, so the subject and verb do not agree with each other. Choice *B* is incorrect because the word *Terrorist's* with the apostrophe *-s* shows possession, but the terrorists aren't in possession of anything in this sentence. Choice *D* is incorrect because the word *achieves* should be *achieve*.

3. A: No change is needed. Choices *B* and *C* utilize incorrect comma placements. Choice *D* utilizes an incorrect verb tense (*responding*).

4. B: The best answer Choice is *B*, *who live mainly in the South and Southwest Asia*. The directional terms *South Asia* and *Southwest Asia* are integral parts of a proper name and should therefore be capitalized.

5. D: This is the best answer choice because *America's* with the apostrophe *-s* shows possession of the word *support*, and *Israel* should be capitalized because it is a country and therefore a proper noun. Choice *A* does not show possession in the word *Americas*. Choice *B* does not capitalize the word *Israel*. Choice *C* does not show possession and does not include the necessary comma at the end of the phrase.

6. A: This sentence is correct as-is. The verb tense should be in the past—the other three answer choices either have a present or continuous verb tense, so these are incorrect.

7. C: Choice *C* is the most straightforward version of this independent clause, because it follows the "subject+verb+prepositional phrase" order which usually provides the most clarity.

8. B: Although *diverging* means to separate from the main route and go in a different direction, it is used awkwardly and unconventionally in this sentence. Therefore, Choice *A* is not the answer. Choice *B* is the correct answer because it implies that the passengers distracted the terrorists, which caused a change in the plane's direction. *Converging*, Choice *C,* is incorrect because it implies that the plane met another in a central location. Although the passengers may have distracted the terrorists, they did not distract the plane. Therefore, Choice *D* is incorrect.

9. B: Choice *B* is the best answer because it is straightforward and clear. Choice *A* is incorrect because the phrase *the fact that* is redundant. Choice *C* is inverted and doesn't make much sense because the subject comes after the verb. Choice D is incorrect because it does not have the appropriate transition, *but*, which is intended to show a contrast to the *uncertainty* phrase that comes before it.

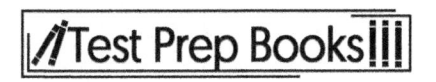

10. A: Choice A is the best choice for this sentence because it is the most straightforward and easiest to understand. Choice B is incorrect because it leaves out the hedging language. Choice C keeps the hedging language, but the sentence begins with a verb which is not the best decision for clarity. Choice D is incorrect because it begins with a preposition which is not the best choice for a straightforward presentation of the facts.

11. A: The word *valiantly* is spelled correctly in the original sentence.

12. D: Airspace and airports must be closed by people; they don't just close themselves, so it is proper to include an action to indicate that they were sealed off. Choice B is incorrect because the verb *close* is in the incorrect tense. Choice C is also incorrect because *airspace* does not need to become *airspaces* and the issue still remains: while there is action, it is not in the proper form to indicate human action. Choice D is correct because it correctly uses the helping verb *were*, which indicates human action.

13. C: This sentence contains improper verb agreement in the fragment *as cancelled flights are rescheduled*. *Are* is a present-tense verb while *rescheduled* is a past-tense verb. Because the attacks occurred in the past, both verbs need to be written in the past tense, as done in Choice C.

14. C: *Intended* means planned or meant to. *Intended* is a far better choice than *desired*, because it would communicate goals and strategy more than simply saying that Bush desired to do something. *Desired* communicates wishing or direct motive. Choices B and D have irrelevant meanings and wouldn't serve the sentence at all.

15. A: The original structure of the two sentences is correct. Choice B lacks the direct nature that the original sentence has. By breaking up the sentences, the connection between the Taliban's defeat and the ongoing war is separated by an unnecessary second sentence. Choice C corrects this problem, but the fluidity of the sentence is marred because of the awkward construction of the first sentence. Choice D begins well but lacks the use of *was* before *overthrown*.

16. C: Choice C is correct because it fixes the core issue with this sentence: the singular *has* should not describe the plural *scientists*. Thus, Choice A is incorrect. Choices B and D add unnecessary commas.

17. D: Choice D correctly conveys the writer's intention of asking if, or *whether*, early perceptions of dinosaurs are still influencing people. Choice A makes no sense as worded. Choice B is better, but *how* doesn't coincide with the context. Choice C adds unnecessary commas.

18. A: Choice A is correct, as the sentence does not require modification. Choices B and C implement extra punctuation unnecessarily, disrupting the flow of the sentence. Choice D incorrectly adds a comma in an awkward location.

19. B: Choice B is the strongest revision, as adding *to explore* is very effective in both shortening the sentence and maintaining, even enhancing, the point of the writer. To explore is to seek understanding in order to gain knowledge and insight, which coincides with the focus of the overall sentence. Choice A is not technically incorrect, but it is overcomplicated. Choice C is a decent revision, but the sentence could still be more condensed and sharpened. Choice D fails to make the sentence more concise and inserts unnecessary commas.

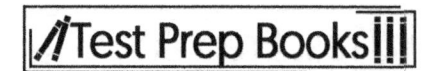

20. D: Choice D correctly applies a semicolon to introduce a new line of thought while remaining in a single sentence. The comma after *however* is also appropriately placed. Choice A is a run-on sentence. Choice B is also incorrect because the single comma is not enough to fix the sentence. Choice C adds commas around *uncertain* which are unnecessary.

21. B: Choice B not only fixes the homophone issue from *its*, which is possessive, to *it's*, which is a contraction of *it is*, but also streamlines the sentence by adding a comma and eliminating *and*. Choice A is incorrect because of these errors. Choices C and D only fix the homophone issue.

22. A: Choice A is correct, as the sentence is fine the way it is. Choices B and C add unnecessary commas, while Choice D uses the possessive *its* instead of the contraction *it's*.

23. C: Choice C is correct because the phrase *even likely* is flanked by commas, creating a kind of aside, which allows the reader to see this separate thought while acknowledging it as part of the overall sentence and subject at hand. Choice A is incorrect because it seems to ramble after *even* due to a missing comma after *likely*. Choice B is better but inserting a comma after *that* warps the flow of the writing. Choice D is incorrect because there must be a comma after *plausible*.

24. D: Choice D strengthens the overall sentence structure while condensing the words. This makes the subject of the sentence, and the emphasis of the writer, much clearer to the reader. Thus, while Choice A is technically correct, the language is choppy and over-complicated. Choice B is better but lacks the reference to a specific image of dinosaurs. Choice C introduces unnecessary commas.

25. B: Choice B correctly joins the two independent clauses. Choice A is decent, but "that would be" is too verbose for the sentence. Choice C incorrectly changes the semicolon to a comma. Choice D splits the clauses effectively but is not concise enough.

26. A: Choice A is correct, as the original sentence has no error. Choices B and C employ unnecessary semicolons and commas. Choice D would be an ideal revision, but it lacks the comma after *Ransom* that would enable the sentence structure to flow.

27. D: By reorganizing the sentence, the context becomes clearer with Choice D. Choice A has an awkward sentence structure. Choice B offers a revision that doesn't correspond well with the original sentence's intent. Choice C cuts out too much of the original content, losing the full meaning.

28. C: Choice C fixes the disagreement between the singular *this* and the plural *viewpoints*. Choice A, therefore, is incorrect. Choice B introduces an unnecessary comma. In Choice D, *those* agrees with *viewpoints*, but neither agrees with *distinguishes*.

29. A: Choice A is direct and clear, without any punctuation errors. Choice B is well-written but too wordy. Choice C adds an unnecessary comma. Choice D is also well-written but much less concise than Choice A.

30. D: Choice D rearranges the sentence to improve clarity and impact, with *tempting* directly describing *idea*. On its own, Choice A is a run-on. Choice B is better because it separates the clauses, but it keeps an unnecessary comma. Choice C is also an improvement but still a run-on.

31. B: Choice B is the best answer simply because the sentence makes it clear that Un-man takes over and possesses Weston. In Choice A, these events sounded like two different things, instead of an action

354

Answer Explanations #2 | English Expression

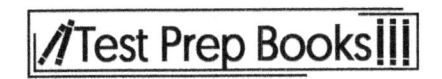

and result. Choices C and D make this relationship clearer, but the revisions don't flow very well grammatically.

32. D: Changing the phrase *after this* to *then* makes the sentence less complicated and captures the writer's intent, making Choice D correct. Choice A is awkwardly constructed. Choices B and C misuse their commas and do not adequately improve the clarity.

33. B: By starting a new sentence, the run-on issue is eliminated, and a new line of reasoning can be seamlessly introduced, making Choice B correct. Choice A is thus incorrect. While Choice C fixes the run-on via a semicolon, a comma is still needed after *this*. Choice D contains a comma splice. The independent clauses must be separated by more than just a comma, even with the rearrangement of the second half of the sentence.

34. C: Choice C condenses the original sentence while being more active in communicating the emphasis on changing times/media that the author is going for, so it is correct. Choice A is clunky because it lacks a comma after *today* to successfully transition into the second half of the sentence. Choice B inserts unnecessary commas. Choice D is a good revision of the underlined section, but not only does it not fully capture the original meaning, it also does not flow into the rest of the sentence.

35. B: Choice B clearly illustrates the author's point, with a well-placed semicolon that breaks the sentence into clearer, more readable sections. Choice A lacks punctuation. Choice C is incorrect because the period inserted after *question* forms an incomplete sentence. Choice D is a very good revision but does not make the author's point clearer than the original.

36. A: Choice A is correct: while the sentence seems long, it actually doesn't require any commas. The conjunction "that" successfully combines the two parts of the sentence without the need for additional punctuation. Choices B and C insert commas unnecessarily, incorrectly breaking up the flow of the sentence. Choice D alters the meaning of the original text by creating a new sentence, which is only a fragment.

37. C: Choice C correctly replaces *for* with *to*, the correct preposition for the selected area. Choice A is not the answer because of this incorrect preposition. Choice B is unnecessarily long and disrupts the original sentence structure. Choice D is also too wordy and lacks parallel structure.

38. D: Choice D is the answer because it inserts the correct punctuation to fix the sentence, linking the dependent and independent clauses. Choice A is therefore incorrect. Choice B is also incorrect since this revision only adds content to the sentence while lacking grammatical precision. Choice C overdoes the punctuation; only a comma is needed, not a semicolon.

39. B: Choice B correctly separates the section into two sentences and changes the word order to make the second part clearer. Choice A is incorrect because it is a run-on. Choice C adds an extraneous comma, while Choice D makes the run-on worse and does not coincide with the overall structure of the sentence.

40. C: Choice C is the best answer because of how the commas are used to flank *in earnest*. This distinguishes the side thought (*in earnest*) from the rest of the sentence. Choice A needs punctuation. Choice B inserts a semicolon in a spot that doesn't make sense, resulting in a fragmented sentence and lost meaning. Choice D is unnecessarily repetitive and creates a run-on.

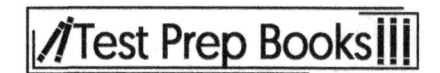

41. A: Choice A is correct because the sentence contains no errors. The comma after *bias* successfully links the two halves of the sentence, and the use of *it's* is correct as a contraction of *it is*. Choice B creates a sentence fragment, while Choice C creates a run-on. Choice D incorrectly changes *it's* to *its*.

42. D: Choice D correctly inserts a comma after *However* and fixes *over use* to *overuse*—in this usage, it is one word. Choice A is therefore incorrect, as is Choice B. Choice C is a good revision but does not fit well with the rest of the sentence.

43. A: The linking verbs *have been* are the same in both verb phrases, creating parallelism. Choice B is incorrect. *Have been traveling* does not match with *were sightseeing*. Choice C is incorrect. Again, *were traveling* does not match with *have been sightseeing*. Choice D is incorrect. The tenses of the verbs do not match. *Have been traveling* does not match with *they are sightseeing*.

44. D: To create parallelism, make both verbal gerunds. Choice A is incorrect. *Chewing* is a gerund and *to play* is an infinitive. Choice B is incorrect. *To chew* is an infinitive and *playing* is a gerund. Choice C is incorrect. *To chew* and *to play* are both infinitives, but they do not match with the verb *enjoy*.

45. B: Quotation marks are used to indicate something someone said. The example sentences feature a direct quotation that requires the use of double quotation marks. Also, the end punctuation, in this case a question mark, should always be contained within the quotation marks. Choice A is incorrect because there is an unnecessary period after the quotation mark. Choice C is incorrect because it uses single quotation marks, which are used for a quote within a quote. Choice D is incorrect because it places the punctuation outside of the quotation marks.

46. A: Choice A is correctly punctuated because it uses a semicolon to join two independent clauses that are related in meaning. Each of these clauses could function as an independent sentence. Choice B is incorrect because the conjunction is not preceded by a comma. A comma and conjunction should be used together to join independent clauses. Choice C is incorrect because a comma should only be used to join independent sentences when it also includes a coordinating conjunction such as *and* or *so*. Choice D does not use punctuation to join the independent clauses, so it is considered a fused (same as a run-on) sentence.

47. A: Choice A is the only option that uses the correct preposition and the correct verb form. Choices B and D both use the expression *attributed to the fact* incorrectly. It can only be attributed *to* the fact, not *with* or *in* the fact. Choice C incorrectly uses a gerund, *saying*, when it should use the present tense of the verb *say*.

48. C: In this answer, the article and subject agree, and the subject and predicate agree. Choice A is incorrect because the article (*an*) and the noun (*issues*) do not agree in number. Choice B is incorrect because an article is needed before *important issue*. Choice D is incorrect because the plural subject *issues* does not agree with the singular verb *is*.

49. B: Choice B is correct because it uses correct parallel structure of plural nouns. A is incorrect because the word *accessory* is in singular form. Choice C is incorrect because it pluralizes *makeup*, which is already in plural form. Choice D is incorrect because it again uses the singular *accessory*, and it uses the singular *shoe*.

50: In a cause/effect relationship, it is correct to use the word *because* in the clausal part of the sentence. This can eliminate both Choices *A and* C which don't clearly show the cause/effect relationship. Choice *B* is incorrect because it uses the present tense, when the first part of the sentence is in the past tense. It makes grammatical sense for both parts of the sentence to be in the past tense.

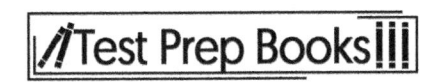

51. A: In Choice *B*, the present tense form of the verb *consider* creates an independent clause joined to another independent clause with only a comma, which is a comma splice and grammatically incorrect. Both *C* and *D* use the possessive form of *its*, when it should be the contraction *it's* for *it is*. Choice *D* also includes incorrect comma placement.

52. B: Choice *A* uses the plural form of the verb, when the subject is the pronoun *none*, which needs a singular verb. Choice *C* also uses the wrong verb form and uses the word *all* in place of *none*, which doesn't make sense in the context of the sentence. Choice *D* uses *all* again, and is missing the comma, which is necessary to set the dependent clause off from the independent clause.

53. A: Answer Choice *A* uses the best, most concise word choice. Choice *B* uses the pronoun *that* to refer to people instead of *who*. *C* incorrectly uses the preposition *with*. Choice *D* uses the preposition *for* and the additional word *any*, making the sentence wordy and less clear.

54. C: Choice *A* is missing the word *that*, which is necessary for the sentence to make sense. Choice *B* pluralizes *trains* and uses the singular form of the word *include*, so it does not agree with the word *set*. Choice *D* changes the verb to *were*, which is in plural form and does not agree with the singular subject.

55. B: Choice *B* uses the best choice of words to create a subordinate and independent clause. In Choice *A*, *because* makes it seem like this is the reason they enjoy working from home, which is incorrect. In *C*, the word *maybe* creates two independent clauses, which are not joined properly with a comma. Choice *D* uses *with*, which does not make grammatical sense.

56. D: Choice *D* is the correct answer. The text indicates a sequence throughout time. Sentence 4 introduces the topic of the paragraph: "Aviation's history expands over 2,000 years." Sentence 2 indicates the possibility of manmade vehicles as early as the fifth century B.C., which is the earliest time period among the sentences: "It is said that kites existed in China around the fifth century B.C. that were capable of carrying a person into the air, making them the first man made 'vehicles.'" Sentence 3 relates the very first recorded attempt at flight. Because it was recorded and because the sentence indicates that Spain existed as a nationality, we can safely assume it comes later than the fifth century B.C.: "The first recorded attempt at flight was made by a Spanish citizen who covered his arms in feathers and jumped." Finally, Sentence 1 addresses the latest chronological developments in these sentences: "Leonardo da Vinci studied the flight of birds and began noting some basic principles of aerodynamics, which eventually led to the development of the steerable airship, or dirigible, in the late 18th century."

57. B: Choice *B* is the correct answer. While both Sentence 4 and Sentence 2 could be a topic sentence, Sentence 4 is the better choice because it is a more general introduction to the topic of the paragraph whereas Sentence 2 provides more details and expands on the topic introduced by Sentence 4. Sentence 2, therefore, fits better as the second sentence in the paragraph. Sentence 1 is the next logical sentence because "All of these areas" clearly refers back to the areas listed in Sentence 2. Sentence 3 is the logical conclusion of the paragraph because it both provides further details in support of Sentence 1 and obliquely refers back to Sentence 4 and why the rainforests are so aptly named.

58. C: Choice *C* is the correct answer. While Sentence 3 or Sentence 1 could be the topic sentence, the "So" at the beginning of Sentence 4 sets up a connection with the sentence before it when it says "So, young Mr. and Mrs. Roger Button were fifty years ahead of style." Thus, the best order for these

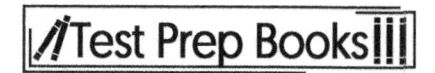

Sentences is Sentence 3, the normal situation for 1860; Sentence 1, the normal situation for "at present," which, for F.S. Fitzgerald, was in the 1920s; and then Sentence 4, which connects the Buttons' choice to have their baby in a hospital to what was fashionable "at present" and contrasts it to what was proper in 1860. Sentence 2 is the best choice for the final sentence in the paragraph because it clearly leads into the rest of the story.

59. A: Choice *A* is the correct answer. Sentence 2 clearly lays out the topic of the paragraph and is the only sentence that can function as a topic sentence. Sentence 4 is the logical choice for the next sentence because "these diagrams" refers back to the cladograms introduced in the first sentence. Sentence 1 or Sentence 3 could be the next sentence; however, based on the phrase "on the other hand" in Sentence 3, which makes it stand in contrast to the previous sentence, it makes the most sense for Sentence 1 to be the third sentence and Sentence 3 to be the final sentence in the paragraph.

60. C: Choice *C* is correct. Sentence 4 is the only sentence that stands out as the topic sentence of the paragraph, introducing the topic of "Government by kings" and its origins. Sentence 3 makes the most sense as the next sentence because it lays out the general problem with kingship, and the pronoun "It" can only refer back to "Government by kings" in Sentence 4. The next sentence is Sentence 2, explaining in more detail why Thomas Paine claims that government by kings is "the promotion of idolatry" and how it has developed over time. Sentence 1 makes the most sense as the final sentence because it builds on the foundation of the previous sentence to explain exactly why paying divine honors to living kings is such a bad idea.

61. B: This sentence is most likely to be placed after Sentence 2. In Sentence 2, the author introduces the training received in jiu-jitsu. This new sentence discusses physical restraint as a main point of that training, and then in Sentence 3 the author indicates why restraint is important.

62. B: Choice *B* is correct because it makes *Practitioners* plural, enabling it to agree with the verb *strive*. Making *Practitioners* plural also matches the context of the sentence. Therefore, Choice *A* is incorrect. Choice *C* is incorrect because it takes away a necessary comma. Choice *D* makes *Practitioner* and *strives* both singular, but without a modifier like *A* or *The* in front of *practitioner*, the sentence is not correct.

63. D: Choice *D* is the best answer because it corrects the two key errors in the section. *Them* is not the proper pronoun to use in this sentence. *They*, the third-person plural personal pronoun, should be used instead. Choices *A* and *B* are thus incorrect. Choice *D* also adds *be* to modify the main verb *used*, forming the appropriate compound verb. Choice *C* is missing this essential component.

64. A: Choice *A* is the best answer. Sentence 1 introduces the idea that flooding is most commonly caused by excessive rain, while Sentence 2 explains the effect of the excessive rain. This new sentence explains *why* the excessive rain in Sentence 1 causes the effect in Sentence 2, so it is best placed after Sentence 1.

65. C: Choice *C* is the best answer. Choice *A* is incorrect because *the water* is doing the overflowing, so it should come before the phrase *to overflow*. Choice *B* is incorrect because *may been causing* isn't an appropriate verb phrase. Choice *D* is incorrect because the word *water* is used repetitively.

Practice Test #3

Job Knowledge

1. Diplomacy is a form of negotiations between which two parties?
    a. Two different businesses
    b. Two different news channels
    c. Two different countries' governments
    d. Two different private citizens

2. Which statement is NOT true about a person's behavior?
    a. Behaviors change over time.
    b. Behaviors are influenced by a person's environment.
    c. A person will always have the same personal identity.
    d. Cultural changes influence a person's behavior.

3. Federalism is described as the relationship between the federal government and which of the following?
    a. The people
    b. State governments
    c. The branches of government
    d. The Constitution

4. Which of the following is NOT a feature of a typical word processor?
    a. Highlighting text
    b. Headers and footers
    c. Audio playback
    d. Automatic grammar correction

5. Divide, express with a remainder $1,202 \div 44$.
    a. $27\frac{2}{7}$
    b. $7\frac{2}{7}$
    c. $27\frac{7}{22}$
    d. $22\frac{7}{22}$

6. Frictional unemployment is best described by which of the following?
    a. When a person is no longer qualified for a job
    b. When a qualified person cannot be matched to a job
    c. When a person is laid off because of the business cycle
    d. When a person is unemployed for longer than six months

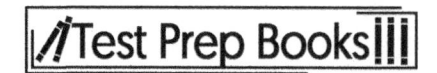

7. The NSA's surveillance of Americans' phones and data was underlined as a violation of which amendment of the Bill of Rights?
   a. The Fourth Amendment's protection of unlawful search and seizure
   b. The Fifth Amendment's due process clause
   c. The Fifth Amendment's protection against self-incrimination
   d. The Eighth Amendment's protection against "cruel and unusual punishment"

8. What was a concern that George Washington warned of in his Farewell Address?
   a. The danger of political parties
   b. To be prepared to intervene in Europe's affairs
   c. The abolition of slavery
   d. To protect states' rights through sectionalism

Questions 9-10 refer to the passage below.

> What is dangerous for Japan is, not the imitation of the outer features of the West, but the acceptance of the motive force of the Western nationalism as her own. Her social ideals are already showing signs of defeat at the hands of politics. I can see her motto, taken from science, "Survival of the Fittest," writ large at the entrance of her present-day history—the motto whose meaning is, "Help yourself, and never heed what it costs to others"; the motto of the blind man who only believes in what he can touch, because he cannot see. But those who can see know that men are so closely knit that when you strike others the blow comes back to yourself. The moral law, which is the greatest discovery of man, is the discovery of this wonderful truth, that man becomes all the truer the more he realizes himself in others. This truth has not only a subjective value but is manifested in every department of our life. And nations who sedulously cultivate moral blindness as the cult of patriotism will end their existence in a sudden and violent death.

Excerpt from the essay "Nationalism in Japan" by Rabindranath Tagore, 1917

9. According to the passage, why is nationalism so dangerous?
   a. Nationalism promotes the imitation of Western political structures.
   b. Nationalism encourages countries to pursue imperialism.
   c. Nationalism strengthens Japanese social ideals.
   d. Nationalism undermines Japan's traditional religious traditions.

10. Nationalism had the LEAST influence on which one of the following world events?
    a. German unification
    b. Latin American wars of independence
    c. Russo-Turkish War
    d. War of the Spanish Succession

Practice Test #3 | Job Knowledge

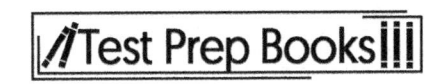

11. A homeowner hires a landscape company to mow the grass because he or she would like to use that time to do something else. The trade-off of paying someone to do a job to make more valuable use of time is an example of what?
    a. Economic systems
    b. Supply and demand
    c. Opportunity cost
    d. Inflation

12. Which event caused the second largest increase in unemployment in American history?
    a. Panic of 1893
    b. Depression of 1920
    c. Depression of 1929
    d. Great Recession of 2007

13. What is $\frac{420}{98}$ rounded to the nearest integer?
    a. 4
    b. 4.2
    c. 5
    d. 4.3

14. Which of the following agreements allowed territories to vote on whether or not they would become free or slave states?
    a. The Connecticut Compromise
    b. The Missouri Compromise
    c. The Compromise of 1850
    d. The Three-Fifths Compromise

15. Which of the following is NOT a form of mass media?
    a. Radio
    b. Billboards
    c. Social media
    d. Television

16. Which of the following is a quantitative method of job evaluation?
    a. Job ranking
    b. Paired comparison
    c. Factor comparison method
    d. Job classification

17. When did the use of connected commercial networks begin to reach a modern scale of use?
    a. 1990s
    b. 1980s
    c. 1970s
    d. 1960s

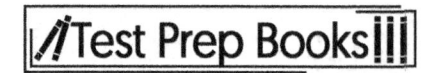

18. What is the y-intercept for $y = x^2 + 3x - 4$?
   a. $y = -4$
   b. $y = 3$
   c. $y = 4$
   d. $y = -3$

19. Which method is NOT a way that governments manage economies in a market system?
   a. Laissez-faire
   b. Absolute Monarchy
   c. Capitalism
   d. Self-interest

Questions 20-21 refer to the map below.

Overlapping Claims in the South China Sea

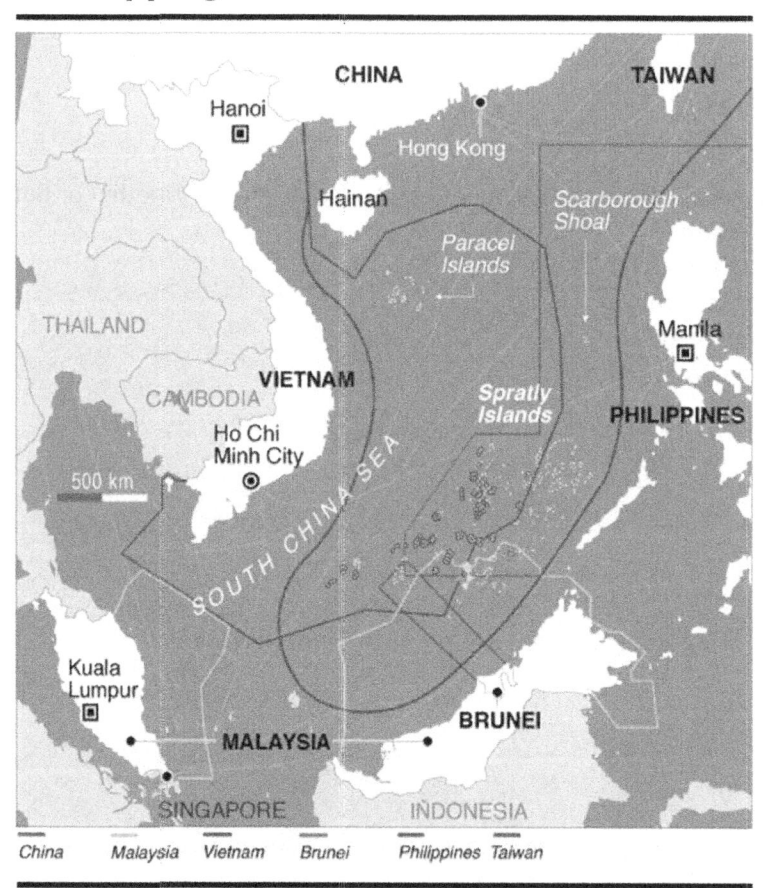

20. Based on the map, which of the following geographic areas likely involves the most complex series of competing sovereign claims?
   a. Hainan
   b. Spratly Islands
   c. Paracel Islands
   d. Scarborough Shoal

Practice Test #3 | Job Knowledge

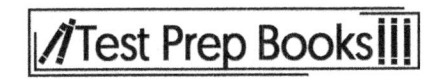

21. Which of the following international agreements is the most directly relevant for evaluating the claims expressed on the map?
    a. Association of Southeast Asian Nations (ASEAN)
    b. Convention on Facilitation of International Maritime Traffic (FAL Convention)
    c. International Convention for the Safety of Life at Sea (SOLAS)
    d. United Nations Convention on the Law of the Sea (UNCLOS)

22. Which of the following is NOT a purpose of the central bank?
    a. Manage interest rates
    b. Set the tax rate
    c. Backup the commercial banks
    d. Set reserve requirements

23. What is the primary function of Google Scholar?
    a. To learn about the latest news
    b. To keep up with friends and family
    c. To reach a global audience for help and awareness
    d. To search multiple library databases simultaneously

24. Which of the following is NOT a formal power of the presidency, but considered an informal power?
    a. Suspending Habeas Corpus during wartime
    b. Vetoing bills
    c. Appointing Cabinet members, ambassadors, consuls, Supreme Court judges, White House staff, and public ministers
    d. Acting as military "Commander in Chief"

25. Which of the following was an important development in the twentieth century?
    a. The United States and the Soviet Union officially declared war on each other in the Cold War.
    b. The League of Nations signed the Kyoto Protocol.
    c. World War I ended when the United States defeated Japan.
    d. India violently partitioned into India and Pakistan after the end of colonialism.

26. Which of the following best summarizes the Black Death's impact on European society?
    a. The Black Death increased the labor supply, resulting in wage increases for urban workers.
    b. The Black Death allowed governments to consolidate economic and political power.
    c. The Black Death reduced agricultural production and resulted in the Great Famine.
    d. The Black Death undermined governments and led to the scapegoating of vulnerable populations.

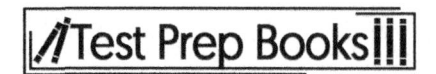

27. What is the area of the regular hexagon shown below?

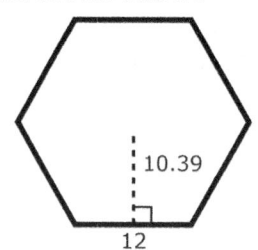

[Hexagon with apothem 10.39 and side 12]

    a. 124.68
    b. 374.04
    c. 748.08
    d. 676.79

Question 28 refers to the photograph below.

Old Faithful Geyser in Yellowstone National Park

28. Which of the following involves the commercialization of environmental features similar to the one depicted in the photograph?
    a. Ecotourism
    b. Growth poles
    c. Neoliberalism
    d. Sustainable development

Practice Test #3 | Job Knowledge

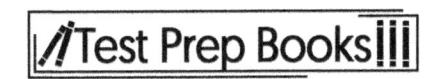

29. Which document established the first system of government in the United States?
    a. Declaration of Independence
    b. Constitution
    c. Articles of Confederation
    d. Bill of Rights

30. HR wants to organize a training program on cultural difference in the workplace. Whom should this training target?
    a. Managers and other employees in leadership positions, so they can communicate key practices to their subordinates
    b. Employees who have had problems with cultural misunderstandings in the past
    c. New employees because they are more likely to come from diverse backgrounds
    d. Employees from all levels of the organization

31. Dave gives an energetic speech to his fellow basketball players about their chances of winning the game tonight. However, many of his teammates don't share Dave's confidence afterward. What explains the lack of confidence among Dave's teammates?
    a. Dave's tone was too natural and dynamic.
    b. Dave didn't bring any visual aids.
    c. Dave's eyes darted all over the room during his speech.
    d. Dave didn't make any jokes and was too serious.

32. Which of the following are markets that establish a few large firms as the major sellers/distributors?
    a. Free enterprise economies
    b. Pure monopolies
    c. Oligopolies
    d. Command economies

33. A student gets an 85% on a test with 20 questions. How many answers did the student solve correctly?
    a. 15
    b. 16
    c. 17
    d. 18

34. Which one of the following most accurately describes a consequence of social contract theory?
    a. Social contract theory incentivized imperial conquests and colonization.
    b. Social contract theory contributed to an intense period of revolutions.
    c. Social contract theory incentivized an expansion of international trade networks.
    d. Social contract theory led to the growth of state power.

35. Which of these is NOT a protection within the Bill of Rights?
    a. Right to due process
    b. Freedom of speech
    c. Right to privacy
    d. Right to a speedy and fair trial

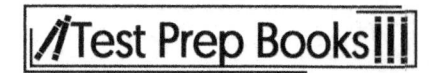

36. Which of the following would you add to a Microsoft Word document to display data recorded on each day of the week across several weeks?
    a. A bar chart
    b. A table
    c. A graph
    d. An equation

37. The action plan should include which of the following?
    a. Missing capacities
    b. Signatures of all team members
    c. Who, what, when, where, why and how
    d. A list of primary problem areas

38. Which statement is true about goods and services?
    a. The quantity of goods and services matters more than their value.
    b. The value of goods and services matters more than their quantity.
    c. The quality of goods and services matters more than their production.
    d. The production of goods and services matters more than their quality.

39. According to Maslow's hierarchy of needs, what is the highest level on the pyramid?
    a. Prestige
    b. Accomplishment
    c. Self-esteem
    d. Self-actualization

40. A ball is drawn at random from a ball pit containing 8 red balls, 7 yellow balls, 6 green balls, and 5 purple balls. What's the probability that the ball drawn is yellow?
    a. $\frac{1}{26}$
    b. $\frac{19}{26}$
    c. $\frac{14}{26}$
    d. $\frac{7}{26}$

41. Which of the following led to the American Revolution?
    a. The Stamp Act
    b. The Boston Massacre
    c. The Boston Tea Party
    d. All of the above

42. What sort of tone is most appropriate for a work-related email to a coworker who has been a friend for many years?
    a. Relaxed but work-focused
    b. Casual and discursive
    c. Formal and serious
    d. Apologetic and placating

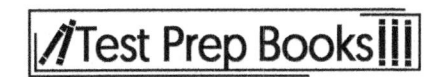

43. When is the most appropriate time to open the floor to questions during a speech?
    a. Before the speech begins
    b. Immediately after the introduction
    c. In the middle of the supporting arguments
    d. At the end of the speech

44. Which of the following best describes the process of acculturation?
    a. Acculturation occurs when a minority culture becomes nearly indistinguishable from a majority culture.
    b. Acculturation refers to how a minority culture adapts to a majority culture while still maintaining a unique cultural identity.
    c. Acculturation generally results in entirely new and unique forms of cultural expression.
    d. Acculturation is when multiple distinct cultures have significant impact on a population's cultural practices.

45. A rectangle has a length that is 5 feet longer than three times its width. If the perimeter is 90 feet, what is the length in feet?
    a. 10
    b. 20
    c. 25
    d. 35

46. Which of these is NOT one of the rights granted in the Sixth Amendment?
    a. The right to an impartial jury
    b. The right to legal counsel
    c. The right to not self-incriminate
    d. The right to a speedy trial

47. During the 1960s–1980s, deindustrialization in cities in the Industrial North (now called the "Rust Belt"), including hubs like Buffalo, Cleveland, Chicago, and Milwaukee, would be considered an example of which of the following?
    a. Political push factor
    b. Political pull factor
    c. Economic push factor
    d. Economic pull factor

48. A major news network wants to add a new form of internet media to reach a wider audience. Specifically, the network wants to make an audio-based prerecorded show focused on major events that listeners can freely listen to on their own time. What sort of media should the news network create?
    a. Podcast
    b. Wiki
    c. YouTube video
    d. Facebook page

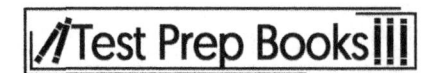

49. Which of the following caused America to join World War I in 1917?
    a. Germany's unrestricted submarine warfare
    b. The destruction of the USS Maine
    c. The Japanese attack on Pearl Harbor
    d. Franz Ferdinand's death in 1914

50. Which of the following is a medium used to conduct public diplomacy?
    a. A foreign student exchange
    b. A trade agreement
    c. A joint military exercise
    d. A public denouncement

51. Which group is more likely to succumb to or be influenced by peer pressure?
    a. Adolescents
    b. Senior Women
    c. Middle-aged men
    d. Small children

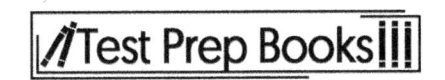

Question 52 refers to the table below.

Branch	Role	Checks & Balances on Other Branches	
Executive	Carries out the laws	Legislative Branch • Proposes laws • Vetoes laws • Calls special sessions of Congress • Makes appointments • Negotiates foreign treaties	Judicial Branch • Appoints federal judges • Grants pardons to federal offenders
Legislative	Makes the laws	Executive Branch • Has the ability to override a President's veto • Confirms executive appointments • Ratifies treaties • Has the ability to declare war • Appropriates money • Has the ability to impeach and remove President	Judicial Branch • Creates lower federal courts • Has the ability to impeach and remove judges • Has the ability to propose amendments to overrule judicial decisions • Approves appointments of federal judges
Judicial	Interprets the laws	Executive Branch • Has the ability to declare executive actions unconstitutional	Legislative Branch • Has the ability to declare acts of Congress unconstitutional

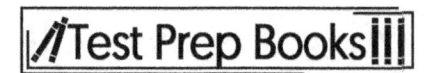

52. Using the table provided and your understanding of checks and balances, which of the following is true regarding legislation?
    a. Members of Congress debate and vote on legislation, although the president may request that legislators consider a certain proposal. The legislation will pass through Congress if it receives a three-quarters majority in both chambers, but the president can veto legislation that he or she disagrees with. The Supreme Court may review legislation and declare it unconstitutional.
    b. Members of Congress debate and vote on legislation, although the president may request that legislators consider a certain proposal. The legislation will pass through Congress if it receives a two-thirds majority in both chambers, but the president can veto legislation that he or she disagrees with. The Supreme Court may review legislation and declare it unconstitutional.
    c. Members of Congress debate and vote on legislation, although the president may request that legislators consider a certain proposal. The president may veto legislation that he or she disagrees with, but Congress can override the veto with a three-quarters majority in both chambers. The Supreme Court may review legislation and declare it unconstitutional.
    d. Members of Congress debate and vote on legislation, although the president may request that legislators consider a certain proposal. The president may veto legislation that he or she disagrees with, but Congress can override the veto with a two-thirds majority in both chambers. The Supreme Court may review legislation and declare it unconstitutional.

53. Which of the following provides the correct definition for multinational states?
    a. Multinational states contain multiple nation-states and transcend national boundaries.
    b. Multinational states have both a distinct cultural community and common system of government.
    c. Multinational states have sovereign control over multiple distinct communities of people.
    d. Multinational states feature autonomous regions to better integrate diverse cultural communities.

54. Which of the following is NOT a reason for an organization to use media relations?
    a. To put out a public service announcement
    b. To explain the reasons for firing several new staff hires
    c. To announce a new community service initiative
    d. To bring more awareness to the organization

55. Larry manages three HR employees. Jane oversees compensation and benefit tasks, Ira is in charge of risk management tasks, and Samir manages recruitment and hiring. Samir has an illness that takes him out of the office for six weeks, and during this time, all recruitment and hiring processes freeze. This majorly impacts two other departments that were waiting on new employees to begin. How could this situation have best been prevented?
    a. Larry should have cross-trained his three employees to fill in for each other should emergencies come up.
    b. Samir should have worked remotely to handle the candidates needed by the other two departments.
    c. Larry should have filled in for Samir's role for the entire duration of his absence.
    d. Ira should have analyzed Samir's workday operations to see if anything at work caused his illness.

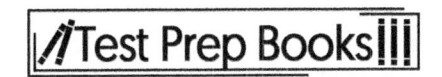

56. What type of digital system would allow four people from all over the world to collaborate on a project together?
   a. Internal database
   b. Cloud storage
   c. Email
   d. NoSQL

57. There are $4x + 1$ treats in each party favor bag. If a total of $60x + 15$ treats is distributed, how many bags are given out?
   a. 15
   b. 16
   c. 20
   d. 22

58. Which event helped sparked the gay and lesbian rights movement in 1969?
   a. The Stonewall Inn Riot
   b. The murder of Matthew Shepard
   c. The murder of Vincent Chin
   d. The emergence of AIDS

59. Which piece of legislation requires employers to pay employees for preliminary and postliminary tasks, such as job-related travel time that is outside of an employee's regular work commute and time spent in job-related training?
   a. Equal Pay Act
   b. Portal-to-Portal Act
   c. Fair Labor Standards Act (FLSA)
   d. Davis Bacon Act

60. Upon drafting the Constitution, which part of government did the Framers designate as the part MOST in touch with everyday Americans?
   a. The Senate
   b. The president
   c. The Supreme Court
   d. The House of Representatives

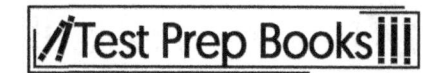

Situational Judgment

The Situational Judgment Test (SJT) is designed to determine an individual's ability to select the most and least effective way to handle a situation.

Situation 1

It's your first day on the job. When you go to the restroom, you see a message scrawled on the mirror "welcoming" you and using a derogatory slur.

What would you do?
 a. Ignore it and carry on with the day.
 b. Immediately report the situation to HR or a supervisor.
 c. Loudly ask who wrote it when you leave the bathroom.
 d. Consider asking for reassignment or quitting.
 e. Take pictures and post them online.

Situation 2

A protest has been going on outside your embassy for several days regarding a change in your home country's health care policies. On your way to work this morning, one protestor gets in your face and screams at you to do something about it.

What would you do?
 a. Angrily tell them it's not your job.
 b. Roll your eyes and step around them.
 c. Try to ignore them and go to work.
 d. Stand there and wait until they move.
 e. Politely tell them that you'll see what you can do.

Situation 3

Your supervisor always takes credit for the most difficult part of a project, even if you or other team members are the ones responsible for it. You would like some credit too. Your supervisor's boss is visiting today to meet with your team and observe your working environment.

What would you do?
 a. Do nothing and email the boss later.
 b. Interrupt the meeting to explain that you haven't been credited properly.
 c. Find a private moment to tell the boss that your supervisor often takes credit for the team's work.
 d. Try to get the boss's attention before the meeting starts.
 e. Confront your supervisor in front of the boss.

Situation 4

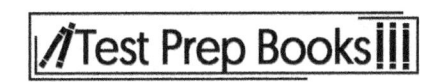

You are responsible for public relations between your home country's embassy and your assigned country. Your home country announces a new domestic policy that does not directly affect your assigned country. However, it is highly unpopular among both the public and the government officials of this foreign country. You have received several requests to do something about the new policy in your home country.

What would you do?
    a. Explain that the policy doesn't affect the foreign country but promise to convey their opinions to your home country's government.
    b. Tell them that the policy doesn't affect the foreign country, so they don't need to worry about it.
    c. Angrily tell them that there's nothing you can do about it.
    d. Ignore these requests and do other work.
    e. Write a report to your home country about increasing unrest in the foreign country.

Situation 5

Your assigned country is undergoing a civil war, and many refugees are seeking help from your home country's refugee program. One group of refugees asks you to do anything to get them out, even if it means falsifying information. You know they are in danger, and it is very likely that they may be injured or worse if they remain in the country much longer.

What would you do?
    a. Turn the group away.
    b. Tell them to submit their information to the refugee program as it is.
    c. Agree to falsify the information and get them evacuated.
    d. Ignore the refugees and hope they ask someone else for help.
    e. Warn the group that false information could disqualify them from the refugee program and warn your colleagues about the request.

Situation 6

At the end of an election cycle, most government staff of your assigned country are replaced with new staff. Many of your former contacts are no longer government employees, and those who are still there have no information on the new administration's plans regarding foreign policy.

What would you do?
    a. Ask the contacts who are still there to try to get information for you.
    b. Immediately reach out to the new staff members and try to form new contacts.
    c. Try to guess at their foreign policy plans based on their election platform.
    d. Wait and see what the new administration has planned.
    e. Demand that the administration tell you their foreign policy plans.

Situation 7

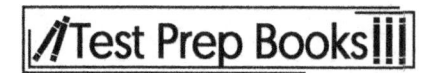

You are overseeing a construction project for a new dormitory on embassy grounds. Your home country wants you to contract only construction companies from home due to potential privacy concerns. However, working with suppliers from the foreign country would complete the construction much sooner. You are asked for a recommendation on how to proceed.

What would you do?
    a. Recommend hiring labor and using suppliers from your assigned country but screen them for privacy leaks every day.
    b. Recommend hiring labor and using suppliers exclusively from your home country.
    c. Recommend hiring labor from the foreign country and using suppliers from your home country.
    d. Recommend hiring labor from your home country and using suppliers from the foreign country.
    e. Recommend that the project is too much trouble and should be scrapped.

Situation 8

While working in your assigned country, a local news story breaks about a massive scam of counterfeit money. The country's economy is still stable, but the false money circulated deep into the economy before it was discovered, and there's no telling where the false money has ended up. You need to inform the people of your home country.

What would you do?
    a. Ask your colleagues to send emails and help spread the word.
    b. Send a report to your home country's government about the situation.
    c. Issue an updated travel advisory explaining and warning about the situation.
    d. Contact all current tourists from your home country to warn them directly.
    e. Try to buy an ad on prime-time television in your home country to warn people.

Situation 9

While checking your email one morning, you receive an anonymous email. The message threatens that something bad will happen at the embassy in one week if you don't immediately petition for a change to a particular travel policy from your home country. There is no sign of who sent it, and you are not aware of any active protests about the policy.

What would you do?
    a. Immediately meet with your supervisors and prepare to contact all relevant authorities.
    b. Do more research into active protests and this travel policy change and try to figure out who sent the email.
    c. Conduct your own investigation without informing anyone of the email.
    d. Assume that a co-worker sent it as a prank and carry on.
    e. Send a reply email asking for more information about the sender.

Situation 10

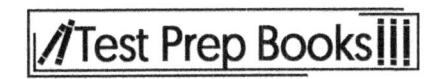

Your assigned country is expanding its solar power infrastructure. Within a year, they plan to have tripled their solar power output. You want to learn more about their plans and send a report recommending implementation of something similar in your home country.

What would you do?
    a. Research more about solar power and independently try to figure out how they're doing it.
    b. Wait and see if they publicize a report about the project's development.
    c. Ask if the project leaders can also implement this in your home country.
    d. Contact the project leaders, explain your situation, and ask for an opportunity to meet with them.
    e. Ask your contacts in the foreign country's government to get information for you.

Situation 11

Your assigned country is experiencing an outbreak of an uncommon flu variant. In your home country, it's common enough to be easily treatable, but hospital staff here are completely unfamiliar with it. The country's government declares an emergency and asks you for help.

What would you do?
    a. Try to advise them based on what you know of this flu variant.
    b. Send a report to your home country asking for medical personnel and supplies to help.
    c. Volunteer in your free time at a nearby hospital.
    d. Tell them that there's nothing you can do to help.
    e. Suggest to your supervisor that they enforce quarantines and distancing.

Situation 12

You are working on a report to be submitted to your home country's government. Due to changes in information, you will have to rewrite a significant portion of the report, delaying its submission. You will need to ask your supervisor for an extension of the due date.

What would you do?
    a. Send an apologetic email about the delayed report and ask for an extension.
    b. Work a massive number of overtime hours trying to meet the original deadline, even though it's extremely unlikely that you will be able to finish on time.
    c. Send a formal and polite email about the report that explains the reasons for requesting an extension.
    d. Send a quick and terse email letting your supervisor know it will be late.
    e. Don't bother with sending an email and just get it done when you can.

Situation 13

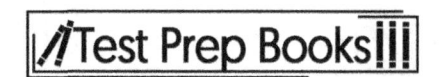

You are writing a speech to deliver on a special news broadcast in your assigned country. The topic is a recent polarizing policy change in your home country. You strongly disagree with the policy change, but the speech you are writing requires you to speak positively about it.

What would you do?
 a. Remove yourself from the project and ask for someone with a positive opinion to write it instead.
 b. Do your best to think about it from another angle and write the speech anyway.
 c. Try to stay neutral and write about both the pros and cons of the policy.
 d. Write a scathing negative critique of the policy instead.
 e. Tell your supervisor that you can't write a positive speech and ask to change the project's requirements.

Situation 14

You become aware that a colleague has posted disparaging remarks on social media about the government of your assigned country. Their settings are not private, so the post is publicly accessible. As of now, the local news media has made no comments about the post.

What would you do?
 a. Make your own social media post apologizing for and denouncing your colleague's statement.
 b. Ignore it and hope it doesn't become newsworthy.
 c. Contact the social media company and get the post removed.
 d. Write a public statement about the post and send it to the local news.
 e. Tell your colleague to remove the post and begin working on a statement about it with your supervisors.

Situation 15

A member of your home country's government makes negative public statements about your assigned country that are factually incorrect. You know that these comments will be damaging to your home country's relationship with this foreign country.

What would you do?
 a. Ignore the situation and hope it doesn't get worse.
 b. Publicly denounce the member of your home country's government who made the false comments.
 c. Alert your supervisors to the damaging comments and document their falsehood.
 d. Contact the foreign country's government immediately and offer an apology about the false statements.
 e. Try to correct the person who made the statements and get them to make a public apology.

Situation 16

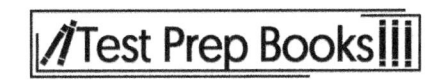

Your first overseas assignment is to a country where the living conditions do not meet the standards you are accustomed to. Many amenities are lacking, and the food makes you uncomfortable. You are dreading the assignment and are scheduled to leave in two weeks.

What would you do?
 a. Accept the assignment despite your hesitations about the living conditions.
 b. Ask to be reassigned somewhere else.
 c. Complain about the quality of living there and demand some guarantees of quality.
 d. Stay open to the assignment but voice your concerns and ask what can be done about them.
 e. Try to bring some things with you that will offset your concerns.

Situation 17

A country that neighbors your assigned country has been invaded. There is no indication that the invading force is interested in conquering more territory, but many visiting citizens from your home country are worried that the fighting could spread. You would like to offer some reassurance.

What would you do?
 a. Offer to expedite home any citizens who want to leave now.
 b. Caution your home country's citizens to be prepared and report to the embassy if they need help with evacuation.
 c. Tell your home country's citizens that the neighboring conflict probably won't spread.
 d. Share as much information as possible with your home country's citizens, including private information if needed, to dispel their fears.
 e. Arrange for additional security at the embassy to protect your home country's citizens.

Situation 18

An ambassador from your home country will be attending a formal dinner with other countries' dignitaries. The ambassador has asked you to help prepare some remarks for them to share in a short speech. You know that some of the ambassador's strong opinions on recent political events may not be viewed favorably by the other attending countries.

What would you do?
 a. Let the ambassador wing it during his speech.
 b. Advise the ambassador to avoid giving a speech if possible.
 c. Write a neutral speech about current events and strongly warn the ambassador to refrain from sharing their opinions.
 d. Get your supervisor's help with an appropriate speech topic.
 e. Keep the remarks positive and forward-thinking to avoid making a scene.

Situation 19

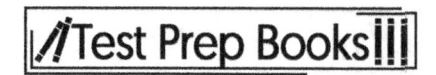

You are giving a speech in front of a crowd at the embassy. In the middle of a paragraph, the teleprompter cuts out and needs to be restarted to catch up to you. You pause for a moment, disguising it as a natural pause in the speech, to buy time for the teleprompter to catch up, but it looks like there will be a longer delay.

What would you do?
 a. Tell a relevant anecdote that would fit the speech.
 b. Repeat the previous paragraph with new emphasis.
 c. Skip towards the conclusion of the speech and wrap it up quickly.
 d. Pause and apologize to the audience for the wait.
 e. Try to continue from memory.

Situation 20

One of your reporting team members meets with you to discuss a raise. They do excellent work, mesh well with the team, and are clearly deserving of a raise. However, you just attended a budget meeting yesterday, and you are aware that for the next six months, money will be tight until new funding is arranged from your home country.

What would you do?
 a. Tell them you want to give them a raise but explain why you can't.
 b. Deny the raise and refuse to elaborate.
 c. Approve the raise and send a notice to the budgeting team.
 d. Ask them if they can wait on the raise for a few more months.
 e. Tell them that you want to give them a raise but need to discuss it with the budgeting team.

Situation 21

Due to health concerns in your assigned country, many workplaces are required to conduct business remotely. Your embassy's digital infrastructure is only designed to facilitate a few employees working from home, not everyone. It needs to be expanded to prevent everyone's work pace from slowing due to a digital holdup.

What would you do?
 a. Have half the team work from home and the other half work from the office to alleviate the digital slowdown.
 b. Research available data and communications solutions and quickly implement one.
 c. Have everyone go in to work anyway to keep productivity up.
 d. Go with the first solution you can find online and try to get it implemented as quickly as possible.
 e. Tell everyone that they'll have to deal with slow speeds when working from home.

Situation 22

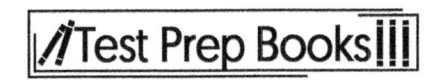

Your assigned country makes a major change to their domestic policy. It outlaws several behaviors related to public dress code, and the punishments are strict. Tourism in this country is uncommon, but you know that if any tourists visit from your home country, they would easily be caught off guard by these laws and would likely be arrested.

What would you do?
- a. Send a report to your home country's media outlets to warn the public about the policy change.
- b. Post an official at various entry points into the country to warn incoming tourists.
- c. Contact the country's government and ask for a tourist exemption clause.
- d. Post a travel warning online about the changed laws and advise tourists to read them closely or reconsider their travel plans.
- e. Use the embassy's social media channels to post warnings for tourists.

Situation 23

You are casually chatting with a colleague in the break room. On the job, they are polite, focused, and do excellent work. While talking to them, you learn that one of their hobbies is something for which you feel an extreme distaste. Later that week, you are asked to submit a performance review of that colleague.

What would you do?
- a. Stay objective and describe them as a great and positive worker.
- b. Describe both their performance and your opinion of them.
- c. Describe them as being distracted, unhelpful, and uncooperative because you dislike their hobby.
- d. Interject your thoughts about them in between comments about their positive attitude on the job.
- e. Say that you don't feel qualified to give a proper performance review.

Situation 24

You receive an email from a citizen of your home country. They would like to move to the country you work in but are unsure of the various legal procedures that they must complete. They explain that they contacted a lawyer who specializes in such information but were even more confused by their explanation. You are aware of several citizens from your home country who have gone missing recently, and while none have been found, reports suggest that they all planned to move to this country.

What would you do?
- a. Tell the citizen not to trust the lawyer and to reconsider moving at this time.
- b. Suggest that the citizen keep working with the lawyer and follow their instructions.
- c. Investigate the lawyer for connections to missing persons.
- d. Provide the citizen with the requested information and suggest that they contact the embassy or their lawyer with any further questions.
- e. Caution the citizen about the situation, recommend avoiding that lawyer in the future, and provide the requested information.

Situation 25

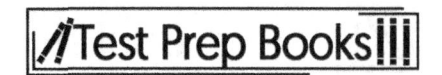

You are writing a performance review of a specific team member you supervise. They have solid potential, but they also have below-standard performance in several areas. They are contentious and will likely challenge any negative reviews of their work.

What would you do?
    a. Downplay their weaknesses to minimize the conflict later.
    b. Focus on their strengths and ignore their weaknesses.
    c. Review their strengths and weaknesses honestly.
    d. Focus entirely on their weaknesses and prepare to argue with them later.
    e. Ask someone else to write the review so that you don't have to deal with the team member's arguments.

Situation 26

You are serving as a translator for a prominent government official from your home country who is visiting your assigned country. An official from your assigned country makes insulting statements about your home country. Your home country's official looks to you for a translation.

What would you do?
    a. Lie and "translate" the insults as compliments.
    b. Downplay the insults but keep the context accurate.
    c. Translate the statements accurately even if they will upset your home country's official.
    d. Shrug and say you didn't understand.
    e. Tell your home country's official that he said something rude, but don't repeat it.

Situation 27

You meet with a confidential source from your assigned country to learn more about the political situation within their government. The source gives you information that your home country's government will be pleased to hear, but you suspect that the source is lying to you.

What would you do?
    a. Check with a different source that you know won't lie to you.
    b. Try to find out if your source is lying before you report anything.
    c. Report back to your home country's government that you couldn't find out anything useful.
    d. Trust your source completely and report the information to your home country's government.
    e. Report the information to your home country's government but explain why you suspect that it's false.

Situation 28

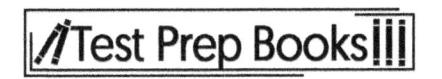

You are approached by a foreign official who wants advance information about a policy decision that your government has made but has not publicly announced yet. Giving the foreign official this information will help them and increase your influence with them, and you don't see any obvious way that it would harm your home country's interests.

What would you do?
- a. Accept the offer and share the information immediately.
- b. Try to negotiate with the foreign official to discern their intentions.
- c. Negotiate a deal on future policy information with the foreign official.
- d. Tell the official you will think about it, then inform your supervisors of the approach.
- e. Turn down the offer and tell the foreign official that you can't disclose the information.

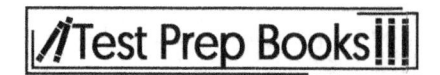

English Expression

For the answer choices below in response to the passages, choose the option that is most consistent with standard English in the underlined section.

Read the following passage and answer Questions 1–9.

I'm not alone when I say that it's hard to pay attention sometimes. I can't count how many times I've sat in a classroom, lecture, speech, or workshop and (1) been bored to tears or rather sleep. (2) Usually I turn to doodling in order to keep awake. This never really helps; I'm not much of an artist. Therefore, after giving up on drawing a masterpiece, I would just concentrate on keeping my eyes open and trying to be attentive. This didn't always work because I wasn't engaged in what was going on.

(3) Sometimes in particularly dull seminars, I'd imagine comical things going on in the room or with the people trapped in the room with me. Why? (4) Because I wasn't invested in what was going on I wasn't motivated to listen. I'm not going to write about how I conquered the difficult task of actually paying attention in a difficult or unappealing class—it can be done, sure. I have sat through the very epitome of boredom (in my view at least) several times and come away learning something. (5) Everyone probably has had to at one time do this. What I want to talk about is that profound moment when curiosity is sparked (6) in another person drawing them to pay attention to what is before them and expand their knowledge.

What really makes people pay attention? (7) Easy it's interest. This doesn't necessarily mean (8) embellishing subject matter drawing people's attention. This won't always work. However, an individual can present material in a way that is clear to understand and actually engages the audience. Asking questions to the audience or class will make them a part of the topic at hand. Discussions that make people think about the content and (9) how it applies to there lives world and future is key. If math is being discussed, an instructor can explain the purpose behind the equations or perhaps use real-world applications to show how relevant the topic is. When discussing history, a lecturer can prompt students to imagine themselves in the place of key figures and ask how they might respond. The bottom line is to explore the ideas rather than just lecture. Give people the chance to explore material from multiple angles, and they'll be hungry to keep paying attention for more information.

1. Which of the following would be the best choice for this sentence (reproduced below)?

   I can't count how many times I've sat in a classroom, lecture, speech, or workshop and (1) been bored to tears or rather sleep.

   a. been bored to tears or rather sleep.
   b. been bored to, tears, or rather sleep.
   c. been bored, to tears or rather sleep.
   d. been bored to tears or, rather, sleep.

Practice Test #3 | English Expression

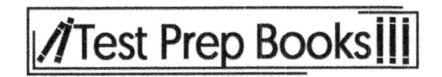

2. Which of the following would be the best choice for this sentence (reproduced below)?

   (2) Usually I turn to doodling in order to keep awake.

   a. Usually I turn to doodling in order to keep awake.
   b. Usually, I turn to doodling in order to keep awake.
   c. Usually I turn to doodling, in order, to keep awake.
   d. Usually I turned to doodling in order to keep awake.

3. Which of the following would be the best choice for this sentence (reproduced below)?

   (3) Sometimes in particularly dull seminars, I'd imagine comical things going on in the room or with the people trapped in the room with me.

   a. Sometimes in particularly dull seminars,
   b. Sometimes, in particularly, dull seminars,
   c. Sometimes in particularly dull seminars
   d. Sometimes in particularly, dull seminars,

4. Which of the following would be the best choice for this sentence (reproduced below)?

   (4) Because I wasn't invested in what was going on I wasn't motivated to listen.

   a. (No change; best as written.)
   b. Because I wasn't invested, in what was going on, I wasn't motivated to listen.
   c. Because I wasn't invested in what was going on. I wasn't motivated to listen.
   d. I wasn't motivated to listen because I wasn't invested in what was going on.

5. Which of the following would be the best choice for this sentence (reproduced below)?

   (5) Everyone probably has had to at one time do this.

   a. Everyone probably has had to at one time do this.
   b. Everyone probably has had to, at one time. Do this.
   c. Everyone's probably had to do this at some time.
   d. At one time everyone probably has had to do this.

6. Which of the following would be the best choice for this sentence (reproduced below)?

   What I want to talk about is that profound moment when curiosity is sparked (6) in another person drawing them to pay attention to what is before them and expand their knowledge.

   a. in another person drawing them to pay attention to what is before them
   b. in another person, drawing them to pay attention
   c. in another person; drawing them to pay attention to what is before them.
   d. in another person, drawing them to pay attention to what is before them.

383

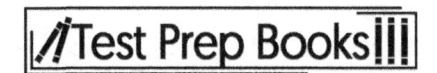

7. Which of the following would be the best choice for this sentence (reproduced below)?

(7) Easy it's interest.

a. Easy it's interest.
b. Easy it is interest.
c. Easy. It's interest.
d. Easy—it's interest.

8. Which of the following would be the best choice for this sentence (reproduced below)?

This doesn't necessarily mean (8) embellishing subject matter drawing people's attention.

a. embellishing subject matter drawing people's attention.
b. embellishing subject matter which draws people's attention.
c. embellishing subject matter to draw people's attention.
d. embellishing subject matter for the purpose of drawing people's attention.

9. Which of the following would be the best choice for this sentence (reproduced below)?

Discussions that make people think about the content and (9) how it applies to there lives world and future is key.

a. how it applies to there lives world and future is key.
b. how it applies to their lives, world, and future is key.
c. how it applied to there lives world and future is key.
d. how it applies to their lives, world and future is key.

Read the following passage and answer Questions 10–24.

In (10) "The Odyssey," Odysseus develops out of his experiences and the people he meets along his journey home. Many of his encounters involve female characters, some of whom offer Odysseus aid in his journey. (11) However, several of these characters deceive and even pose great danger to the hero. (12) This makes his journey home harder, it forces Odysseus himself to change and adapt in order to deal with the challenges. (13) For the time Odysseus reaches home, he has become notably distrustful of women and even those who have true intentions. It is this sense of caution that ultimately serves Odysseus in successfully defeating the suitors of Penelope upon his return home.

Odysseus would not have been able to defeat the suitors without stealth and deception. He had (14) to conceal himself in order to achieve revenge. This is something we see earlier in Odysseus' encounter with Polyphemus the Cyclops. While not female, Polyphemus displayed feminine qualities characterized by his "womb-like cave." (15) Entering into the dwelling Odysseus directly demanded hospitality Polyphemus instead butchered his men in spite of custom. In order to survive the encounter, Odysseus (16) relinquishes his true identity by telling Polyphemus his name is "Nobody." After the carnage of his men, he does not entrust the Cyclops with his true name. Rather,

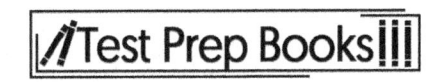

Odysseus uses disguise and cunning to trick Polyphemus into reopening the cave. When he emerges, he is then reborn again as "Odysseus."

This pattern is echoed again when Odysseus reaches Ithaca: "I look for endless ground to be spattered by the blood and brains of the suitors, these men who are eating all your substance away. But come now, let me make you so that no mortal can recognize you." Here, Athena reveals her plan to disguise Odysseus as he makes his move against the suitors. Why would Odysseus embrace the idea? With Polyphemus, Odysseus entered the cave trusting he would be received as a welcomed guest, but he wasn't. (17) Clearly, Odysseus isn't making the same mistake twice in trusting people to automatically abide by custom. Using a disguise allows Odysseus to apply strategy in a similar manner he had with Polyphemus. (18) This passage specifically described the suitors as eating away at Odysseus' substance, seeming to further the parallel with Polyphemus who devoured Odysseus' men. (19) Also like with Polyphemus, Odysseus only reveals his true identity when he knows his plan has succeeded. The disguise concept presents a strategic role, but it also sheds further light on the impact of Odysseus' travels. To conceal (20) ones identity is to withhold trust.

The Circe episode matches Odysseus against someone he already knows to be untrustworthy. It is known that Circe welcomes all men who (21) enter upon her island with food and drink, but this is a deception meant to ensnare them. This xenia, or hospitality, that Odysseus would have been accustomed to, turns out to be farce. She violates the trust of her guests by turning them into swine, thus making her a deceitful host and a woman Odysseus cannot trust. In order to (22) assure his and the crew's safety, Odysseus must look past her empty courtesy and deceive her in a way that will remedy the situation. With the knowledge of Circe's dark intentions (and Hermes' instructions), Odysseus attempts to out-maneuver Circe by making her think he will kill her. By doing this, he is taking on deceitful qualities so as to ensure he can bend her to proper behavior, which works. Still untrusting of Circe's submission, Odysseus makes her swear a formal oath: "I would not be willing to go to bed with you unless you can bring yourself, O goddess, to swear me a great oath that there is no other evil hurt you devise against me" (10:342-344). Even though Odysseus tames Circe, he is still distrustful. The oath becomes a final assurance that she is sincere. Until he knows for certain that no more treachery can befall him (the oath), he does not partake in showing any form of trust.

In the Land of the Dead, Odysseus encounters Agamemnon, who describes his own murder at the hand of his wife, Klytaimestra. Not only is this an example of a wife's betrayal, but a betrayal that appears close to Odysseus' own situation. Like Agamemnon, Odysseus (23) is returning home to his wife. However, Agamemnon didn't realize his wife had foul intentions, he trusted her to receive him with open arms:

> See, I had been thinking that I would be welcome to my children and thralls of my household when I came home, but she with thoughts surpassing grisly splashed the shame on herself and on the rest of her sex, on women still to come, even on the one whose acts are virtuous.

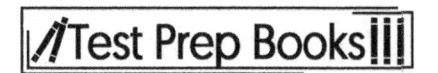

Clearly this is a cautionary story for Odysseus. After telling Odysseus of Klytaimestra's betrayal, Agamemnon warns Odysseus that all women are inherently distrustful. By this time, Odysseus has already been deceived and nearly killed by female/female-like characters. Agamemnon's logic seems to back up what he already experienced. (24) <u>As the text progresses, Odysseus</u> encounters the Sirens and Calypso, who seem to corroborate the idea that women are bad news. However, what is most impressionable on Odysseus is Agamemnon's distrust of even virtuous women, "even on the one whose acts are virtuous." Who is to say that they cannot turn against him like Klytaimestra did against Agamemnon. This seems to cement in Odysseus a fear of betrayal.

10. Which of the following would be the best choice for this sentence (reproduced below)?

    In (10) <u>"The Odyssey,"</u> Odysseus develops out of his experiences and the people he meets along his journey home.

    a. "The Odyssey,"
    b. 'The Odyssey'
    c. *The Odyssey*
    d. The Odyssey

11. Which of the following would be the best choice for this sentence (reproduced below)?

    (11) <u>However, several of these</u> characters deceive and even pose great danger to the hero.

    a. However, several of these
    b. However these
    c. However several of these
    d. Several of these

12. Which of the following would be the best choice for this sentence (reproduced below)?

    (12) <u>This makes his journey home harder, it forces Odysseus himself to change and adapt</u> in order to deal with the challenges.

    a. (No change; best as written.)
    b. This makes his journey home harder it forces Odysseus himself to change and adapt
    c. This makes his journey home harder which forces Odysseus to change and adapt
    d. This makes his journey home harder, forcing Odysseus to change and adapt

13. Which of the following would be the best choice for this sentence (reproduced below)?

    (13) <u>For the time Odysseus reaches home,</u> he has become notably distrustful of women and even those who have true intentions.

    a. For the time Odysseus reaches home,
    b. When the time Odysseus reaches home,
    c. By the time Odysseus reaches home,
    d. At the time Odysseus reaches home,

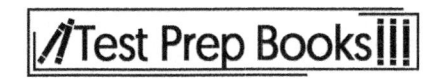

14. Which of the following would be the best choice for this sentence (reproduced below)?

He had (14) to conceal himself in order to achieve revenge.

a. to conceal
b. To be concealed
c. Conceals
d. Concealing

15. Which of the following would be the best choice for this sentence (reproduced below)?

(15) Entering into the dwelling Odysseus directly demanded hospitality Polyphemus instead butchered his men in spite of custom.

a. Entering into the dwelling Odysseus directly demanded hospitality Polyphemus instead butchered his men in spite of custom.
b. Entering into the dwelling, Odysseus directly demanded hospitality. Polyphemus instead butchered his men in spite of custom.
c. Entering into the dwelling, Odysseus directly demanded hospitality, Polyphemus instead butchered his men in spite of custom.
d. Entering into the dwelling; Odysseus directly demanded hospitality; Polyphemus instead butchered his men in spite of custom.

16. Which of the following would be the best choice for this sentence (reproduced below)?

In order to survive the encounter, Odysseus (16) relinquishes his true identity by telling Polyphemus his name is "Nobody."

a. relinquishes
b. Conceals
c. Withholds
d. Surrenders

17. Which of the following would be the best choice for this sentence (reproduced below)?
(17) Clearly, Odysseus isn't making the same mistake twice in trusting people to automatically abide by custom.

a. (No change; best as written.)
b. Clearly Odysseus isn't making the same mistake twice in trusting people to automatically abide by custom.
c. Clearly, Odysseus isn't making the same mistake twice; trusting people to automatically abide by custom.
d. Odysseus isn't making the same mistake twice in trusting people, clearly, to automatically abide by custom.

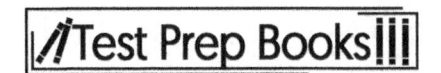

18. Which of the following would be the best choice for this sentence (reproduced below)?

    (18) This passage specifically described the suitors as eating away at Odysseus' substance, seeming to further the parallel with Polyphemus who devoured Odysseus' men.

    a. This passage specifically described
    b. This passages specifically describes
    c. This passage specifically describes
    d. These passage specifically describes

19. Which of the following would be the best choice for this sentence (reproduced below)?

    (19) Also like with Polyphemus, Odysseus only reveals his true identity when he knows his plan has succeeded.

    a. Also like with Polyphemus
    b. As he did with Polyphemus
    c. As he did before
    d. With the exact method as he had with Polyphemus

20. Which of the following would be the best choice for this sentence (reproduced below)?

    To conceal (20) ones identity is to withhold trust.

    a. ones
    b. One's
    c. Someone's
    d. Oneself

21. Which of the following would be the best choice for this sentence (reproduced below)?

    It is known that Circe welcomes all men who (21) enter upon her island with food and drink, but this is a deception meant to ensnare them.

    a. enter upon
    b. Land upon
    c. Arrive on
    d. Crash on

22. Which of the following would be the best choice for this sentence (reproduced below)?

    In order to (22) assure his and the crew's safety, Odysseus must look past her empty courtesy and deceive her in a way that will remedy the situation.

    a. assure
    b. Ensure
    c. Prevent
    d. Vindicate

Practice Test #3 | English Expression

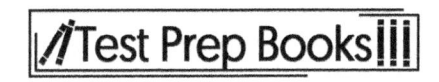

23. Which of the following would be the best choice for this sentence (reproduced below)?

    Like Agamemnon, Odysseus (23) is returning home to his wife.

    a. (No change; best as written.)
    b. returns
    c. returned
    d. was returned

24. Which of the following would be the best choice for this sentence (reproduced below)?

    (24) As the text progresses, Odysseus encounters the Sirens and Calypso, who seem to corroborate the idea that women are bad news.

    a. As the text progresses, Odysseus
    b. As the text progresses Odysseus
    c. The text progresses with Odysseus
    d. As Odysseus progresses in the text

Read the following passage and answer Questions 25–33.

In our essay and class discussion, (25) we came to talking about mirrors. It was an excellent class in which we focused on an article written by Salman Rushdie that compared the homeland to a mirror. (26) Essentially this mirror is an metaphor for us and our homeland. (27) When we look at our reflection we see the culture, our homeland staring back at us. An interesting analogy, but the conversation really began when we read that Rushdie himself stated that the cracked mirror is more valuable than a whole one. But why?

(28) After reflecting on the passage I found the answer to be simple. The analogy reflects the inherent nature of human individuality. The cracks in the mirror represent different aspects of our own being. Perhaps it is our personal views, our hobbies, or our differences with other people, but (29) whatever it is that makes us unique defines us, even while we are part of a big culture. (30) What this tells us is that we can have a homeland, but ultimately we ourselves are each different in it.

Just because one's (31) mirror is cracked, the individuals isn't disowned from the actual, physical homeland and culture within. It means that the homeland is uniquely perceived by the (32) individual beholding it and that there are in fact many aspects to culture itself. Like the various cracks, a culture has religion, language, and many other factors that form to make it whole. What this idea does is invite the viewer to accept their own view of their culture as a whole.

Like in Chandra's *Love and Longing in Bombay*, a single homeland has many stories to tell. Whether one is a cop or a retired war veteran, the individual will perceive the different aspects of the world with unduplicated eyes. (33) Rushdie, seems to be urging his readers to love their culture but to not be pressured by the common crowd. Again, the cracks represent differences which could easily be interpreted as views about the culture, so what this is saying is to accept the culture but accept oneself as well.

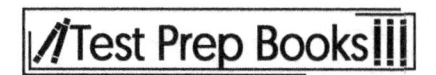

From the essay "Portals to Homeland: Mirrors"

25. Which of the following would be the best choice for this sentence (reproduced below)?

In our essay and class discussion, (25) we came to talking about mirrors.

a. we came to talking about
b. we were talking about
c. we talked about
d. we came to talk about

26. Which of the following would be the best choice for this sentence (reproduced below)?

(26) Essentially this mirror is an metaphor for us and our homeland.

a. Essentially this mirror is an metaphor for us and our homeland.
b. Essentially, this mirror is a metaphor for us and our homeland.
c. Essentially, this mirror is an metaphor for us and our homeland.
d. Essentially this mirror is an metaphor, for us and our homeland.

27. Which of the following would be the best choice for this sentence (reproduced below)?

(27) When we look at our reflection we see the culture, our homeland staring back at us.

a. (No change; best as written.)
b. When we look at our reflection we see our culture our homeland staring back at us.
c. When we look at our reflection we saw our culture, our homeland, staring back at us.
d. Looking at our reflection we see our culture as our homeland is staring back at us.

28. Which of the following would be the best choice for this sentence (reproduced below)?

(28) After reflecting on the passage I found the answer to be simple.

a. After reflecting on the passage I found the answer to be simple.
b. After reflecting on the passage; I found the answer to be simple.
c. After reflecting on the passage I finding the answer to be simple.
d. After reflecting on the passage, I found the answer to be simple.

Practice Test #3 | English Expression

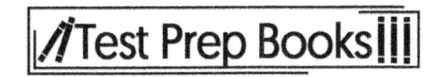

29. Which of the following would be the best choice for this sentence (reproduced below)?

    Perhaps it is our personal views, our hobbies, or our differences with other people, but (29) whatever it is that makes us unique defines us, even while we are part of a big culture.

    a. whatever it is that makes us unique defines us, even while we are part of a big culture.
    b. whatever it is, that makes us unique, defines us, even while we are part of a big culture.
    c. whatever it is that makes us unique also defines us, even while we are part of a bigger culture.
    d. whatever it is that makes us unique defines us, even though we are part of a big culture.

30. Which of the following would be the best choice for this sentence (reproduced below)?

    (30) What this tells us is that we can have a homeland, but ultimately we ourselves are each different in it.

    a. What this tells us is that we can have a homeland, but ultimately we ourselves are each different in it.
    b. What this tells us is that we can have a homeland, but ultimately, we ourselves are each different in it.
    c. What this tells us is that we can have a homeland, however, ultimately, we ourselves are each different in it.
    d. What this tells us is that we can have a homeland, ultimately we ourselves are each different in it.

31. Which of the following would be the best choice for this sentence (reproduced below)?

    Just because one's (31) mirror is cracked, the individuals isn't disowned from the actual, physical homeland and culture within.

    a. mirror is cracked, the individuals isn't disowned
    b. mirror is cracked, the individuals will not be disowned
    c. mirror is cracked, the individuals aren't disowned
    d. mirror is cracked, the individual isn't disowned

32. Which of the following would be the best choice for this sentence (reproduced below)?

    It means that the homeland is uniquely perceived by the (32) individual beholding it and that there are, in fact, many aspects of culture itself.

    a. individual beholding it and that there are, in fact, many aspects
    b. individual beholding it; and that there are in fact many aspects
    c. individual beholding it and that there is, in fact, many aspects
    d. individual beholding it and there's in fact, many aspects

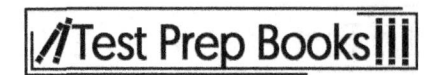

33. Which of the following would be the best choice for this sentence (reproduced below)?

(33) Rushdie, seems to be urging his readers to love their culture but to not be pressured by the common crowd.

a. Rushdie, seems to be urging his readers
b. Rushdie seemed to be urging his readers
c. Rushdie, seeming to urge his readers,
d. Rushdie seems to be urging his readers

Read the following passage and answer Questions 34–42.

Quantum mechanics, which describes how the universe works on its smallest scale, is inherently weird. Even the founders of the field (34) including Max Planck, Werner Heisenberg, and Wolfgang Pauli unsettled by the new theory's implications. (35) Instead of a deterministic world where everything can be predicted by equations, events at the quantum scale are purely probabilistic. (36) Every outcome exist simultaneously, while the actual act of observation forces nature to choose one path.

In our everyday lives, (37) this concept of determinism, is actually expressed in the thought experiment of Schrödinger's cat. Devised by Erwin Schrödinger, one of the founders of quantum mechanics, (38) it's purpose is to show how truly strange the framework is. Picture a box containing a cat, a radioactive element, and a vial of poison. (39) If the radioactive element decays, it will release the poison and kill the cat. The box is closed, so there is no way for anyone outside to know what is happening inside. Since the cat's status—alive and dead—are mutually exclusive, only one state can exist. (40) What quantum mechanics says however is that the cat is simultaneously alive and dead, existing in both states until the box's lid is removed and one outcome is chosen.

(41) Further confounding our sense of reality, Louis de Broglie proposed that, on the smallest scales, particles and waves are indistinguishable. This builds on Albert Einstein's famous theory that matter and energy are interchangeable. Although there isn't apparent evidence for this in our daily lives, various experiments have shown the validity of quantum mechanics. One of the most famous experiments is the double-slit experiment, which initially proved the wave nature of light. When shone through parallel slits onto a screen, (42) light creates a interference pattern of alternating bands of light and dark. But when electrons were fired at the slits, the act of observation changed the outcome. If observers monitored which slit the electrons travelled through, only one band was seen on the screen. This is expected, since we know electrons act as particles. However, when they monitored the screen only, an interference pattern is created—implying that the electrons behaved as waves!

34. Which of the following would be the best choice for this sentence (reproduced below)?

(34) Even the founders of the field <u>including Max Planck, Werner Heisenberg, and Wolfgang Pauli unsettled by the new theory's implications.</u>

a. (No change; best as written.)
b. including Max Planck, Werner Heisenberg, and Wolfgang Pauli; unsettled by the new theory's implications.
c. including Max Planck, Werner Heisenberg, and Wolfgang Pauli were unsettled by the new theories' implications.
d. including Max Planck, Werner Heisenberg, and Wolfgang Pauli were unsettled by the new theory's implications.

35. Which of the following would be the best choice for this sentence (reproduced below)?

(35) <u>Instead of a deterministic world where everything can be predicted by equations,</u> events at the quantum scale are purely probabilistic.

a. Instead of a deterministic world where everything can be predicted by equations,
b. Instead, of a deterministic world where everything can be predicted by equations,
c. Instead of a deterministic world where everything can be predicting by equations,
d. Instead of a deterministic world, where everything can be predicted by equations,

36. Which of the following would be the best choice for this sentence (reproduced below)?

(36) <u>Every outcome exist simultaneously,</u> while the actual act of observation forces nature to choose one path.

a. Every outcome exist simultaneously,
b. Each of these outcome exist simultaneously,
c. Every outcome, existing simultaneously,
d. Every outcome exists simultaneously,

37. Which of the following would be the best choice for this sentence (reproduced below)?

In our everyday lives, (37) <u>this concept of determinism, is actually expressed</u> in the thought experiment of Schrödinger's cat.

a. this concept of determinism, is actually expressed
b. this concept of determinism is actually expressed
c. this, concept of determinism, is actually expressed
d. this concept of determinism, is expressed actually

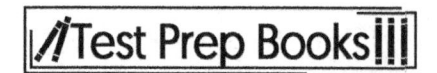

38. Which of the following would be the best choice for this sentence (reproduced below)?

Devised by Erwin Schrödinger, one of the founders of quantum mechanics, (38) it's purpose is to show how truly strange the framework is.

a. it's purpose is to show how truly strange
B. its purposes is to show how truly strange
c. its purpose is to show how truly strange
d. it's purpose, showing how truly strange

39. Which of the following would be the best choice for this sentence (reproduced below)?

(39) If the radioactive element decays, it will release the poison and kill the cat.

a. If the radioactive element decays, it will release the poison and kill the cat.
b. If, the radioactive element decays, it will release the poison and kill the cat.
c. If the radioactive element decays. It will release the poison and kill the cat.
d. If the radioactive element decays, releasing the poison and kill the cat.

40. Which of the following would be the best choice for this sentence (reproduced below)?

(40) What quantum mechanics says however is that the cat is simultaneously alive and dead, existing in both states until the box's lid is removed and one outcome is chosen.

a. What quantum mechanics says however is
b. What quantum mechanics says however, is
c. What quantum mechanics says. However, is
d. What quantum mechanics says, however, is

41. Which of the following would be the best choice for this sentence (reproduced below)?

(41) Further confounding our sense of reality, Louis de Broglie proposed that, on the smallest scales, particles and waves are indistinguishable.

a. Further confounding our sense of reality, Louis de Broglie proposed that, on the smallest scales, particles and waves are indistinguishable.
b. Further confounding our sense of reality Louis de Broglie proposed that on the smallest scales, particles and waves are indistinguishable.
c. Further confounding our sense of reality, Louis de Broglie proposed that on the smallest scales, particles and waves are indistinguishable.
d. Further, confounding our sense of reality, Louis de Broglie proposed that, on the smallest scales, particles and waves are indistinguishable.

Practice Test #3 | English Expression

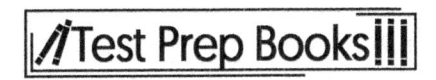

42. Which of the following would be the best choice for this sentence (reproduced below)?

When shone through parallel slits onto a screen, (42) light creates a interference pattern of alternating bands of light and dark.

a. (No change; best as written.)
b. light created an interference
c. lights create a interference
d. light, creating an interference,

Sentence Selection: Select the one sentence that best meets the requirements of standard written English.

Questions 43–47

43.
a. He is the clown who inflated balloons and honked his nose.
b. He is the clown who inflated balloons and who honked his nose.
c. He is the clown that inflated balloons and who honked his nose.
d. He is the clown that inflated balloons and that honked his nose.

44.
a. The building was sturdy and solid; it crumbled during the earthquake.
b. The building was study and solid although it crumbled during the earthquake.
c. Although the building was sturdy and solid, it crumbled during the earthquake.
d. Despite being sturdy and solid, the building crumbled during the earthquake.

45.
a. Jed was disatisfied with the acommodations at his hotel, so he requested another room.
b. Jed was dissatisfied with the accommodations at his hotel, so he requested another room.
c. Jed was dissatisfied with the accomodations at his hotel, so he requested another room.
d. Jed was disatisfied with the accommodations at his hotel, so he requested another room.

46.
a. The due date for the final paper in the course is Monday, May 16, 2016.
b. The due date for the final paper in the course is Monday, May 16 2016.
c. The due date for the final project in the course is Monday, May, 16, 2016.
d. The due date for the final project in the course is Monday May 16, 2016.

47.
a. It's often been said that work is better then rest.
b. Its often been said that work is better then rest.
c. It's often been said that work is better than rest.
d. Its often been said that work is better than rest.

Practice Test #3 | English Expression

Sentence Correction: For the next eight questions, select the answer choice that needs to be used in place of the underlined text to make the sentence correct, or indicate that the underlined text is not in error.

Questions 48–55

48. There were many questions <u>about what causes the case to have gone cold</u>, but the detective wasn't willing to discuss it with reporters.
    a. NO ERROR
    b. about why the case is cold
    c. about what causes the case to go cold
    d. about why the case went cold

49. <u>Because Shaun was used to playing guitar</u>, he needs to work much harder at playing bass.
    a. NO ERROR
    b. Even though Shaun is used to playing guitar,
    c. While Shaun was used to playing guitar,
    d. Because Shaun is used to playing guitar,

50. With such a <u>drastic range of traits, appearances and body types</u>, dogs are one of the most variable and adaptable species on the planet.
    a. NO ERROR
    b. drastic range of traits, appearances, and body types,
    c. drastic range of traits and appearances and body types,
    d. drastic range of traits, appearances, as well as body types,

51. Those animals with more of these traits, or better versions of these traits, gain an (7) <u>advantage over others of their species.</u>
    a. NO ERROR
    b. advantage over others, of their species.
    c. advantages over others of their species.
    d. advantage over others.

52. As with many romantic writers, Shelley invokes the classical myths and (49) <u>symbolism of Ancient Greece and Rome to high light core ideas.</u>
    a. NO ERROR
    b. symbolism of Ancient Greece and Rome to highlight core ideas.
    c. symbolism of ancient Greece and Rome to highlight core ideas.
    d. symbolism of Ancient Greece and Rome highlighting core ideas.

53. Looking deeper into the myth of Prometheus sheds light not only on the character of Frankenstein (50) <u>but also poses a psychological dilemma to the audience.</u>
    a. NO ERROR
    b. but also poses a psychological dilemma with the audience.
    c. but also poses a psychological dilemma for the audience.
    d. but also poses a psychological dilemma there before the audience.

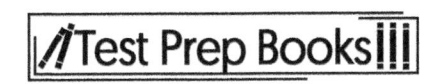

54. <u>Integrated into its core philosophy,</u> Jiu-Jitsu tempers the potential to do great physical harm with respect for that power, and for life.
   a. NO ERROR
   b. Integrated into its core philosophy,
   c. Integrated into it's core philosophy,
   d. Integrated into its' core philosophy,

55. Like in modern comics and movies, Thor was the god of thunder and wielded (4) <u>the hammer Mjolnir however there are several differences</u> between the ancient legend and modern hero.
   a. NO ERROR
   b. the hammer Mjolnir, however there are several differences
   c. the hammer Mjolnir. However there are several differences
   d. the hammer Mjolnir. However, there are several differences

Paragraph Organization: For each item in this section, select the ordering of sentences that results in the most organized paragraph.

Questions 56–60

56. Sentence 1: Phylogenetic trees are diagrams that map out the proposed evolutionary history of a species.

Sentence 2: The most recent proposed common ancestor between two species is the one before their lineages branch in the diagram.

Sentence 3: These diagrams do not attempt to include specific information about physical traits that were thought to be retained or disappeared during the evolutionary process.

Sentence 4: They are branching diagrams that make it easy to see how scientists believe certain species developed from other species.

   a. 1, 4, 2, 3
   b. 2, 3, 1, 4
   c. 3, 2, 1, 4
   d. 4, 1, 2, 3

57. Sentence 1: Finally, there are also fewer pests and diseases inside the greenhouse.

Sentence 2: There is more control of the temperature and humidity of the environment inside the greenhouse.

Sentence 3: Plants may grow better inside a greenhouse versus outside for several reasons.

Sentence 4: Additionally, the carbon dioxide produced by plants is trapped inside the greenhouse and can increase the rate of photosynthesis of the plants.

   a. 1, 2, 3, 4
   b. 2, 3, 1, 4
   c. 3, 2, 4, 1
   d. 4, 1, 2, 3

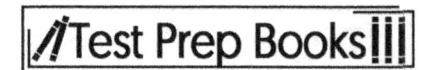

58. Sentence 1: William Shakespeare was the son of a glove-maker, he only had a basic grade school education, and he never set foot outside of England—so how could he have produced plays of such sophistication and imagination or written in such detail about historical figures and events, or about different cultures and locations around Europe?

Sentence 2: People who argue that William Shakespeare is not responsible for the plays attributed to his name are known as anti-Stratfordians (from the name of Shakespeare's birthplace, Stratford-upon-Avon).

Sentence 3: According to anti-Stratfordians, the depth of knowledge contained in Shakespeare's plays suggests a well-traveled writer from a wealthy background with a university education, not a countryside writer like Shakespeare.

Sentence 4: The most common anti-Stratfordian claim is that William Shakespeare simply was not educated enough or from a high enough social class to have written plays overflowing with references to such a wide range of subjects like history, the classics, religion, and international culture.

    a. 1, 2, 4, 3
    b. 2, 4, 1, 3
    c. 3, 1, 2, 4
    d. 4, 1, 2, 3

59. Sentence 1: Each cell contains organelles that are responsible for distinct functions and are essential for the organism's life.

Sentence 2: Organisms can be single-celled or multicellular.

Sentence 3: Because plants and animals have different necessities for generating energy and nutrients, their cells are similar but also have unique features.

Sentence 4: Cells are the smallest functional unit of living organisms.

    a. 1, 3, 2, 4
    b. 2, 4, 1, 3
    c. 3, 1, 2, 4
    d. 4, 2, 1, 3

60. Sentence 1: Three of the most common infecting agents are *Aspergillus, Histoplasma*, and *Candida*.

Sentence 2: Worldwide, fungal infections of the lung account for significant mortality in individuals with compromised immune function.

Sentence 3: Three tests used to identify specific markers for these mold species include ELISA (enzyme-linked immunosorbent assay), GM Assay (Galactomannan Assay), and PCR (polymerase chain reaction).

Practice Test #3 | English Expression

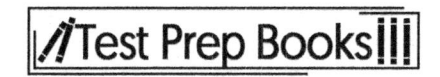

Sentence 4: Successful treatment of infections caused by these agents depends on an early and accurate diagnosis.

    a. 1, 3, 4, 2
    b. 2, 1, 4, 3
    c. 3, 1, 2, 4
    d. 4, 1, 2, 3

Paragraph Revision: This section consists of different paragraphs. Read each paragraph carefully, and then answer the questions that follow it.

Questions 61–65

Sentence 1: Our modern society <u>would actually look down on some</u> of Plato's ideas in *The Republic.*

Sentence 2: <u>Certainly his ideas could help create a more orderly and fair system, but at what cost?</u>

Sentence 3: The simple truth is that in many of his examples, we see that Plato has taken the individual completely out of the equation.

Sentence 4: To enforce these ideas, Plato seeks to use government to regulate and mandate these rules.

61. The writer discovers the following sentence has been left out of the paragraph: "Plato's ideal society is one that places human desire aside to focus on what will benefit the entire community." Which sentence is this sentence most likely to be placed after?
    a. Sentence 1
    b. Sentence 2
    c. Sentence 3
    d. Sentence 4

62. Choose the best choice for the underlined text in Sentence 1. If you think the text is correct as-is, choose Choice *A*.
    a. would actually look down on some
    b. would actually look down upon some
    c. would actually be looking down on some
    d. would actually look down on something

63. Choose the best choice for the underlined text in Sentence 2. If you think the text is correct as-is, choose Choice *A*.
    a. Certainly his ideas could help create a more orderly and fair system, but at what cost?
    b. Certainly, his ideas could help create a more orderly and fair system, at what cost?
    c. Certainly, his ideas could help create a more orderly and fair system, but at what cost?
    d. Certainly his ideas could help create a more orderly and fair system, at what cost?

Sentence 1: Flash flooding can occur without warning and without rainfall.

Sentence 2: Flash floods may be caused by a river being blocked by <u>a glacier; avalanche; landslide; logjam; a beaver's obstruction; construction; or dam.</u>

Sentence 3: Water builds behind such a blockage.

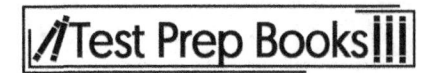

Sentence 4: Eventually, the mass and force of the built-up water become so extreme that it causes the obstruction to break.

64. The writer discovers the following sentence has been left out of the paragraph: "Thus, enormous amounts of water rush out towards the surrounding areas." Which sentence is this sentence most likely to be placed after?

   a. Sentence 1
   b. Sentence 2
   c. Sentence 3
   d. Sentence 4

65. Choose the best choice for the underlined text in Sentence 2. If you think the text is correct as-is, choose Choice A.
   a. a glacier; avalanche; landslide; logjam; a beaver's obstruction; construction; or dam.
   b. a glacier avalanche landslide logjam a beaver's obstruction construction or dam.
   c. a glacier, avalanche, landslide, logjam, a beavers obstruction, construction, or dam.
   d. a glacier, avalanche, landslide, logjam, a beaver's obstruction, construction, or dam.

Written Essay #3

On the FSOT, you will be presented with multiple essay topics to choose from. The test allows you seven minutes to choose the topic before you get started. If you don't choose a topic before seven minutes, they will choose one for you. Then, you will have twenty-five minutes to develop and write your essay. Reviewers of your essay will look for a clear, organized essay with grammatically correct sentences. You will have 2800 characters, or spaces, to write your essay, then the screen will time out.

The following is an example topic essay:

> Technology within education has had a dubious role in the past two decades. The use of cell phones and computers is debated regarding whether they may cause a distraction or help aid in learning. However, the conversation in recent years is that technology is hitting our society in full force and can no longer be ignored, especially in education. In fact, studies have found that technology, even the use of video games, may be a positive supplement to learning rather than hindering it. Still, ways in which to use technology are still debated, even the questions of *how much, when* and *what* technology can be used.

Write an essay to someone who is considering whether to use technology in teaching. Take a side on the issue and argue whether or not he/she should utilize technology within education. Use specific examples to support your argument.

Answer Explanations #3

Job Knowledge

1. C: Choice C is correct because diplomacy is a form of international negotiations between two countries' governments with militaristic, economic, environmental, or humanitarian goals. Choices A, B, and D are incorrect because negotiations between businesses, organizations, or private individuals—even if they are international in nature—do not involve two countries' governments.

2. C: A person will always have the same personal identity. Even though a person may identify with one subgroup or culture now, does not mean that they will agree with it in the future or that they have in the past. Personal identity will continue to change an individual's behavior throughout life.

3. B: Federalism, at least as it was put forth by the Founders, describes the relationship between the federal and state governments wherein the powers of government are divided between the two. Choice A is incorrect because Federalism does not refer to a relationship between the federal government and the people. Instead, the federal government interacts with the people through their state governments. Choice C is incorrect because the relationship between the branches of the federal government is defined by a system of checks and balances, not federalism. Choice D is incorrect because the Constitution lays out the system of federalism, but federalism does not describe the relationship between the federal government and the Constitution.

4. C: Choice C is correct because word processors focus on text, and audio playback is generally not a feature. Choices A, B, and D are all common word processor features—highlighting text, headers, footers, and automatic grammar corrections—so they are all incorrect.

5. C: $27\frac{7}{22}$

Set up the division problem.

$$44\overline{)1202}$$

44 does not go into 1 or 12 but will go into 120 so start there.

$$\begin{array}{r} 27 \\ 44\overline{)1202} \\ -88 \\ \hline 322 \\ -308 \\ \hline 14 \end{array}$$

The answer is $27\frac{14}{44}$.

Reduce the fraction for the final answer.

$$27\frac{7}{22}$$

Answer Explanations #3 | Job Knowledge

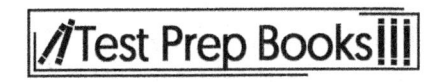

6. B: Frictional unemployment occurs when a qualified person is unable to find a job. Cyclical unemployment occurs as a product of the business cycle, such as during a time of recession. Structural unemployment occurs when a person is no longer qualified for that particular job.

7. A: The NSA's surveillance operation that began under the Patriot Act actually was found to violate only one part of the Bill of Rights. Due process wasn't that distinction, and neither was self-incrimination. Cruel and unusual punishment doesn't fit either. It was found to violate the unlawful search and seizure clause, as the government cannot look at your data without your knowledge.

8. A: George Washington was a slave owner himself in life, so he did not make abolition a theme in his Farewell Address. On the other hand, he was concerned that sectionalism could potentially destroy the United States, and he warned against it. Furthermore, he believed that Americans should avoid getting involved in European affairs. However, one issue that he felt was especially problematic was the formation of political parties, and he urged against it in his farewell.

9. B: The passage references the selfish nature of nationalism and how its violation of moral law leads to violent death. During the eighteenth and nineteenth centuries, nationalism motivated many bloody imperial conquests. Thus, Choice *B* is the correct answer. The passage mentions how Japan has imitated the "outer features of the West," which would include political structures. However, the passage draws a distinction between those features and nationalism because Tagore is urging Japan not to adopt nationalism. This wouldn't be possible if nationalism was an inherent part of the outer features. So, Choice *A* is incorrect. Choice *C* is incorrect because the passage asserts that nationalism is corrupting Japan's social ideals, not strengthening them. Tagore claims that nationalism violates moral law, but Japan's traditional religious practices are never specifically mentioned. So, Choice *D* is incorrect.

10. D: The Prussian political leader Otto von Bismarck leveraged nationalism to rally support for German unification, which occurred in 1871. So, Choice *A* is incorrect. Mexican nationalists defeated Spanish colonizers in the Mexican Revolution, and Simon Bolivar led nationalist revolts across South America during the early nineteenth century. So, Choice *B* is incorrect. The Russo-Turkish War was largely caused by nationalist revolts in Bulgaria, Montenegro, and Romania against the Ottoman Empire, so Choice *C* is incorrect. The War of the Spanish Succession was fought in the early eighteenth century, which predates the rise of nationalism in continental Europe. Thus, Choice *D* is the correct answer.

11. C: Opportunity cost. Opportunity cost can trade time, power, or anything else of value in exchange for something else. Economic systems determine what is being produced and by whom. Supply and demand refers to the quantity of goods and services that is produced or needed. Finally, inflation refers to how the cost of goods and services increases over time.

12. A: Choice *A* is correct. The Depression of 1929, commonly referred to as the Great Depression, is the largest increase to unemployment, but the question stem asks for the second-largest increase. According to the graph, the Panic of 1893 increased unemployment by approximately ten percent; the Depression of 1920 increased unemployment by approximately six percent; the Depression of 1929 increased unemployment by approximately fifteen percent; and the Great Recession of 2007 increased unemployment by approximately four percent. Thus, the Panic of 1893 marks the second-largest increase to unemployment. As a result, choices *B*, *C*, and *D* are incorrect.

13. A: Dividing by 98 can be approximated by dividing by 100, which would mean shifting the decimal point of the numerator to the left by 2. The result is 4.2 and rounds to 4.

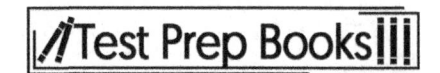

14. C: The Compromise of 1850. The Connecticut Compromise, Choice A, formed the basis for the Constitution by proposing a bicameral Congress. The Missouri Compromise, Choice B, banned slavery north of the 36°30' parallel in the Louisiana Territory. The Compromise of 1850 essentially undid the Missouri Compromise by introducing popular sovereignty, which allowed voters in territories to decide whether or not the state constitution would ban slavery. The Three-Fifths Compromise, Choice D, counted slaves as three-fifths of a human being when allocating representatives.

15. B: Choice B is correct because billboards are not a form of mass media. Choices A, B, and C are incorrect answers because they are all forms of mass media.

16. C: Factor comparison method. Quantitative job evaluation methods use a scaling system and provide a score that indicates how valuable one job is when compared to another job. The two specific examples noted are the point factor method and the factor comparison method. Choice A, job ranking, is when an organization defines the value of a specific job compared to other jobs in the organization. Choice B, paired comparison, is when an individual and their position is compared to another individual and their position. Choice D, job classification, is a system designed to evaluate the duties and authority levels of a job.

17. A: Choice A is correct because the modern commercial internet began to see widespread use in the 1990s. Choices B, C, and D are all incorrect as they are too early in time.

18. A: The y-intercept of an equation is found where the x-value is zero. Plugging zero into the equation for x allows the first two terms to cancel out, leaving -4.

19. B: Absolute monarchy, which is built on the vision of full government control over the economy, is a hallmark of command system economies. Laissez-faire, capitalism, and self-interest, in contrast, are all fundamental concepts behind the market system.

20. B: The Spratly Islands are one of the most hotly disputed geographic areas in the world. According to the map, Brunei, China, Malaysia, the Philippines, Taiwan, and Vietnam have overlapping claims over the Spratly Islands. Thus, Choice B is the correct answer. Choice A is incorrect because only Taiwan challenges China's sovereign claim over Hainan. Although China, Taiwan, and Vietnam all claim the Paracel Islands, more states claim the Spratly Islands. As such, Choice C is incorrect. China, the Philippines, and Taiwan all claim sovereignty over the Scarborough Shoal, but this is also slightly less competitive than the battle over the Spratly Islands. Therefore, Choice D is incorrect.

21. D: The map depicts overlapping claims on the South China Sea. Based on the territorial scope of these claims, it can be inferred that they involve exclusive economic zones (EEZs). The United Nations Convention on the Law of the Sea (UNCLOS) grants states the right to establish EEZs within 200 nautical miles of their coasts. As such, the states implicated in this territorial dispute would cite UNCLOS to defend their claims under international law. Thus, Choice D is the correct answer. Brunei, Malaysia, the Philippines, and Vietnam are members of the Association of Southeast Asian Nations (ASEAN), and this supranational political organization has backed its members' claims. However, ASEAN is not directly involved in asserting or evaluating those claims, so Choice A is incorrect. Choice B is incorrect because the Convention on Facilitation of International Maritime Traffic (FAL Convention) concentrates on safeguarding and optimizing maritime travel. Choice C is incorrect because the International Convention for the Safety of Life at Sea (SOLAS) focuses on setting safety standards for ships.

Answer Explanations #3 | Job Knowledge

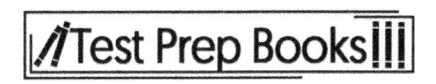

22. B: The central bank is responsible for all of these except for setting the tax rate. This is done by the government.

23. D: Choice D is correct because Google Scholar enables someone to search for information across many library databases all at once, providing a launching point to discover other information. Choices A, B, and C all describe functions of various social media websites, so they are all incorrect.

24. A: While suspending Habeas Corpus during wartime is not a formal power of the U.S. president, as stated by the U.S. Constitution, it is an informal power. For example, President Abraham Lincoln employed this extraconstitutional tactic to protect the nation during the Civil War.

25. D: It is important to realize that the Cold War was never an official war and that the United States and the Soviet Union instead funded proxy conflicts. The Kyoto Protocol was signed by members of the United Nations, as the League of Nations was long since defunct. While Japan was a minor participant in World War I, it was not defeated by America until World War II. The correct answer is D: India's partition between Hindu India and Islamic Pakistan led to large outbreaks of religious violence.

26. D: The Black Death had severe and long-lasting consequences due to the chaos it wreaked on European society. In the aftermath of this human tragedy, Europeans sought someone to blame. Given their poor performance in preventing the outbreak and spread of the disease, European governments suffered a fierce backlash from the incensed citizenry. For many European governments, the struggle to regain their legitimacy took nearly a century. Many vulnerable communities were also scapegoated and accused of maliciously spreading the Black Death. For example, vigilantes regularly expelled and/or massacred Jewish and Romani minority communities. Thus, Choice D is the correct answer. The Black Death caused a steep decline in the labor supply, which led to wage increases for urban workers. So, Choice A is incorrect. Likewise, Choice B is incorrect because the Black Death led to an even greater decentralization of economic and political power as angry communities agitated against the government. The Great Famine (1315–1317) occurred several decades before the Black Death (1347–1351), so Choice C is incorrect.

27. B: 374.04

The formula for finding the area of a regular polygon is $A = \frac{1}{2} \times a \times P$ where a is the length of the apothem (from the center to any side at a right angle), and P is the perimeter of the figure. The apothem a is given as 10.39, and the perimeter can be found by multiplying the length of one side by the number of sides (since the polygon is regular): $P = 12 \times 6 \rightarrow P = 72$. To find the area, substitute the values for a and P into the formula:

$$A = \frac{1}{2} \times a \times P$$

$$A = \frac{1}{2} \times (10.39) \times (72) \rightarrow A = 374.04$$

28. A: The photograph depicts Old Faithful Geyser in Yellowstone National Park, and the prompt mentions the commercialization of environmental features. Ecotourism is an economic activity in which people travel to relatively undisturbed locations in a natural environment, such as national parks. Choice B is incorrect because growth poles are economic sectors with higher rates of growth than the natural average. Choice C is incorrect because neoliberalism refers to policies related to free trade and free markets. Choice D is incorrect because ecotourism is a type of sustainable development, and the photograph specifically depicts a popular site of ecotourism.

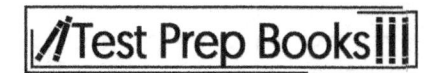

29. C: Articles of Confederation. Issued in 1776, the Declaration of Independence, Choice A, explained why the colonists decided to break away from England but did not establish a government. That was left to the Articles of Confederation, which were adopted in 1781. The Articles of Confederation established a very weak central government that was replaced by the Constitution, Choice B, in 1789. It established a stronger executive branch. In 1791, the Bill of Rights, Choice D, amended the Constitution by guaranteeing individual rights.

30. D: Employees from all levels of the organization should be included. Diversity and inclusion (D&I) should be part of an organization-wide policy that involves all employees. Choice A is not the best answer because key training messages may get lost in translation as they travel from leadership-level employees to their subordinates. Choice B is also not the best answer because it reacts to past problems rather than working to proactively create a workplace culture that avoids such conflict. Choice C is also not a good choice because long-standing employees also need training to adapt to changing workplace conditions.

31. C: Choice C is correct because a lack of eye contact conveys that the speaker does not have confidence in what he is saying. This could make Dave's teammates think that he does not actually have confidence about their chances of winning. Choices B and D are incorrect because visual aids and humor would help improve audience connection, not confidence. Choice A is incorrect because a natural and dynamic tone would be a positive sign of authenticity.

32. C: Oligopolies are markets that establish a few large firms as the major sellers/distributors. Free market economies, Choice A, allow for more competition, while command economies, Choice D, allow for greater government control. Choice B is incorrect because pure monopolies are typically dominated by one firm rather than a few.

33. C: 85% of a number means multiplying that number by 0.85. So:

$$0.85 \times 20 = \frac{85}{100} \times \frac{20}{1}$$

This can be simplified to:

$$\frac{17}{20} \times \frac{20}{1} = 17$$

34. B: Social contract theory directly contributed to an intense period of revolution. According to social contract theory, if the state fails to fulfill its obligations, then the contract is broken. Because the contract is broken, people are released and free to form a new state. For example, French revolutionaries claimed the monarchy had broken the social contract by denying citizens basic liberties and legal protections. In addition, in the Americas, more than a dozen new nation-states gained independence in the nineteenth century. Thus, Choice B is the correct answer. Social contract theory didn't incentivize imperialism or colonization; if anything, it did the opposite. So, Choice A is incorrect. International trade isn't directly related to social contract theory, so Choice C is incorrect. Although a firm social contract would theoretically strengthen the state, social contract theory didn't directly lead to the growth of power. So, Choice D is incorrect.

35. C: The Bill of Rights grants protections for almost all conceivable parts of life. The Framers were quite adamant that freedom was the ultimate right that the federal government could protect for its people, and so they worked hard to ensure that that was exactly what the federal government did. Right to privacy, however, is not considered one of these protections. While some have recently argued that it is implied, this protection is not explicitly given in the Bill of Rights. Choice *A* is incorrect because due process is one of those key pieces, guaranteeing every American gets equal protections under the law. Choice *B* is incorrect because freedom of speech grants this protection too, as one of the more well-known guarantees of the Constitution. Choice *D* is incorrect because the right to a fair and speedy trial is also one of those crucial protections.

36. B: Choice *B* is correct because a table can easily display an array of data organized into categories, in this case day of the week and the numbered week. Choice *A* is incorrect because a bar chart would be much less efficient since it can only compare data across one category. Choice *C* is incorrect because a graph would allow you observe trends in the data, not the data itself. Choice *D* is incorrect because an equation is not necessary to display the information clearly.

37. C: The action plan should always include the who, what, when, where, why and how. The action plan includes a list of existing capacities in order to *identify* missing capacities, so Choice *A* is incorrect. Choice *B* is incorrect because responsible parties, not member signatures, are an aspect of action plans. Problem areas are not determined by the action plan, so Choice *D* is incorrect.

38. B: The value of goods and services matters more than their quantity. For example, in the real estate industry, if a realtor sells ten houses valued at $200,000, their commission would be the same as a realtor who sells one house valued at $2,000,000. Even though one realtor sold more homes, the value of ten houses adds up to the same amount as the single home that the other realtor sold. Therefore, the number of goods and services produced does not determine economic growth—the value of the goods and services does.

39. D: The highest level of Maslow's hierarchy of needs is self-actualization, in which one achieves their full potential, including creative pursuits. Prestige, a feeling of accomplishment, and self-esteem are all part of the esteem needs, one level below the top and part of the psychological needs section.

40. D: The sample space is made up of:

$$8 + 7 + 6 + 5 = 26 \text{ balls}$$

The probability of pulling each individual ball is $\frac{1}{26}$. Since there are 7 yellow balls, the probability of pulling a yellow ball is $\frac{7}{26}$.

41. D: All three events led to increasing tension and conflict between the colonists and the British government, which finally exploded at the Battle of Lexington and Concord in 1775. The Stamp Act of 1765 imposed a tax on documents. It was repealed after colonists organized protests. The Boston Massacre resulted in the death of five colonists in 1770. The Boston Tea Party was a protest in 1773 against a law that hurt colonial tea merchants. The British responded to the tea party by punishing the colony of Massachusetts, which created fear among the other colonies and united them against the British government.

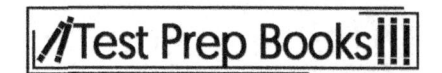

42. A: Choice A is correct because a relaxed, work-focused email is most appropriate for a coworker who has been a friend for many years. Choice B is incorrect because a discursive email is one that rambles, which may cause the important information about work to be overlooked. Choice C is incorrect because the coworker may feel that their years of friendship are being devalued by a cold, overly serious email. Choice D is incorrect because nothing in the question implies that apologizing is in order.

43. D: Choice D is correct because the most appropriate time to take questions is after the conclusion of the speech. Choices A, B, and C are incorrect because they are all poor times to take questions. Before your speech starts, the audience has no information to ask you questions about. During the introduction or supporting arguments, stopping to take questions breaks the flow of your speech and makes it harder to follow.

44. B: Acculturation occurs when the influence of a majority culture alters a minority culture's beliefs or practices, but the minority culture continues to be identifiable as a unique and distinct cultural entity. This differs from assimilation, which leads to the minority culture strongly resembling the majority culture. Thus, Choice B is the correct answer. Choice A is incorrect because it describes assimilation more than acculturation. Choice C is incorrect because it states the consequence of syncretism. Choice D is incorrect because it summarizes multiculturalism.

45. D: Denote the width as w and the length as l. Then, $l = 3w + 5$. The perimeter is:

$$2w + 2l = 90$$

Substituting the first expression for l into the second equation yields:

$$2(3w + 5) + 2w = 90$$

$$6w + 10 + 2w = 90$$

$$8w = 80$$

$$w = 10$$

Putting this into the first equation, it yields:

$$l = 3(10) + 5 = 35$$

46. C: The Sixth Amendment is a sweeping amendment that covers a lot of ground in terms of protections for those facing trial. The right to an impartial jury was key to be sure that no bias was in the process. Legal counsel also made sure there was representation for all. The right to a speedy trial was also in the protections. The right to not self-incriminate, however, was not, as that was covered in the previous amendment: the Fifth Amendment.

47. C: Deindustrialization in cities in the Industrial North during the 1960s–1980s pushed many residents away from industrial hubs like Buffalo, Cleveland, Chicago, and Milwaukee because the number of jobs dropped significantly. Thus, people needed to move elsewhere to find employment. This is an example of an economic push factor— pushing people out of the area because of an economic downturn. Choice A is incorrect because the situation described is an economic factor, not a political factor. Choice B is incorrect because the situation described is an economic factor, not a political factor, and because economic downturn is a push factor rather than a pull factor. Choice D is incorrect because an economic downturn is a push factor rather than a pull factor.

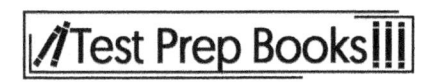

48. A: Choice A is correct because a podcast is a pre-recorded, audio-focused form of internet media. Choice C is incorrect because a YouTube video is a visual form of internet media. Choice D is incorrect because a Facebook page is also a visual form of internet media. Choice B is incorrect because a wiki is a text-based form of internet media.

49. A: Because the British naval blockade during World War I was so effective, Germany retaliated by using submarines to attack any ship bound for Britain or France. This led to the sinking of the RMS Lusitania in 1915, which killed more than 100 Americans. The destruction of the USS Maine, Choice B, sparked the Spanish-American War in 1898. The Japanese attack on Pearl Harbor in 1941, Choice C, brought America into World War II, not World War I. Franz Ferdinand's death in 1914, Choice D, sparked the outbreak of World War I, but America did not join the war until 1917.

50. A: Choice A is correct because educational exchange programs can expose students from different countries to new cultures and generate positive opinions of those cultures. Choices B and C are incorrect because trade agreements and military exercises are not used to conduct public diplomacy, which is a way of changing public opinion. Choice D is also incorrect because a public denouncement of one country by another would generate a negative reaction, which is the opposite of public diplomacy.

51. A: Adolescents are most likely to be influenced by pressure from their peers in making life decisions.

52. D: According to the system of checks and balances outlined in the Constitution, members of Congress debate and vote on legislation, although the president may request that legislators consider a certain proposal. The president may veto legislation that he or she disagrees with, but Congress can override the veto with a two-thirds majority in both chambers. The Supreme Court may review legislation and declare it unconstitutional. Choices A and B are incorrect because legislation requires a simple majority of both chambers to become a law. These options also do not mention the ability of Congress to override the President's veto, thus missing an important element of the checks and balances between the branches of government. Choice C is incorrect because Congress can override the President's veto with a two-thirds majority in both chambers, not a three-quarters majority.

53. C: As implied in the name, multinational states contain multiple nations within their borders. When used in this context, the concept of nations is referring to distinct communities of people that are bound by shared characteristics, such as language, religion, and connections to the land. Thus, Choice C is the correct answer. Choice A is incorrect because multinational states contain multiple nations, not nation-states. Choice B is incorrect because it states the definition of a nation-state. Choice D is incorrect because the incorporation of autonomous regions is only a possibility and not a defining characteristic.

54. B: Choice B is correct because internal decisions do not need to be addressed publicly, especially if they reflect poorly on the company. Choices A, C, and D are incorrect because they are all good reasons for an organization to reach out with media relations to widen the audience for their announcements.

55. A: Larry should have cross-trained his employees to fill in for one another in the case of emergencies. This allows normal business operations to continue, rather than halt, if an employee is absent. Samir should not have to work remotely when ill, and as a team leader, Larry should not be expected to step in and fulfill Samir's entire full-time job. Analyzing Samir's workday for causes of the illness is unnecessary unless Samir requests it.

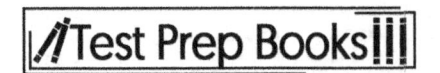

56. B: Choice B is correct because cloud storage allows a user to store many types of information online and access it anywhere that the user has an internet connection, so it is the best choice for a global collaborative project. Choice A is incorrect because an internal database may not have an external connection to the rest of the internet, making it limited and unavailable to anyone who cannot access it or is not near it locally. Choice C is incorrect because email may not be a convenient way to rely on every project member having access to the same files. Choice D is incorrect because a NoSQL database is designed to hold massive amounts of data from millions of users and would be excessively large for the number of project members.

57. A: Each bag contributes $4x + 1$ treats. The total treats will be in the form $4nx + n$ where n is the total number of bags. The total is in the form $60x + 15$, from which it is known $n = 15$.

58. A: The Stonewall Inn Riot in 1969 helped ignite the gay and lesbian rights movement when patrons fought back against a police raid. The site became a national monument in 2016. Although he became an icon of the gay and lesbian rights movement, Matthew Shepard was murdered in 1998. Thus, Choice B is incorrect. The murder of Vincent Chin, Choice C, in 1982, became a rallying cry for Asian American activists. The gay and lesbian rights movement was well established when activists campaigned to raise awareness of AIDS during the 1980s and 1990s, making Choice D incorrect.

59. B: The Portal-to-Portal Act deals with the preliminary and postliminary tasks of employees. The act requires employers to pay employees who are covered under the FLSA for time spent traveling to perform job-related tasks if that travel is outside of the employees' regular work commute. Additionally, employees are to be paid for hours spent in job-related training that is outside of their normal workday.

60. D: The Framers (Founding Fathers) had the idea that the higher an office gets, the more out of touch a representative could get from the American people. Members of the Supreme Court are appointed, so they are not the most in touch with everyday Americans. This goes for the Senate and the president as well, as both are elected to longer terms than Representatives. Additionally, the Framers originally set up the Senate such that Senators were chosen by state governments, rather than through direction election by the people. Likewise, the President is voted on by the Electoral College and not by the popular vote of the people.

Members of the House of Representatives are who the Framers had in mind to represent average Americans, both with their small districts and limited terms. Since they face election every two years, they have to consistently think about pleasing their constituents.

Situational Judgment

Situation 1

Most Effective - B: Harassment, whether directed at yourself or others, is unacceptable and should be reported immediately.

Least Effective - E: Posting pictures of the derogatory "welcome" online could cause an unnecessary stir on social media and is an inappropriate way of handling the situation.

Answer Explanations #3 | Situational Judgment

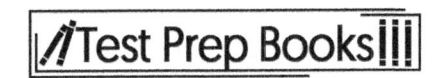

Situation 2

Most Effective - E: The protestor may be trying to get a rise out of you, so remaining calm and answering politely is the safest way to defuse the situation.

Least Effective - A: In this situation, getting angry at the protestor may escalate the situation and make it more dangerous.

Situation 3

Most Effective - C: It's important to make sure that everyone is credited fairly, but it would be best to mention this in a more private setting to avoid an unnecessary scene.

Least Effective - B: Interrupting the meeting would cause a distraction, confuse the boss, and upset everyone by diverging from the meeting's agenda.

Situation 4

Most Effective - A: You may not be able to do anything directly, but conveying the opinions of others to your home country's government does fall within your responsibilities and will help to ease the concerns of the foreign country's people.

Least Effective - C: Trying to push these concerns away will cause the foreign country's people to worry even more and become upset that you won't try to help.

Situation 5

Most Effective - E: Despite the danger, it is best to stay honest and warn the refugees about deceit in the evacuation process. You should also warn your colleagues to be alert for other groups that may attempt falsification.

Least Effective - C: Falsifying information is not only dishonest, but if it was discovered to be false, you could get fired and disqualify the refugees from the evacuation program. This would make the situation worse for everyone.

Situation 6

Most Effective - B: You will need new contacts to follow the new administration's plans, so you should reach out and form them immediately.

Least Effective - D: In this situation, any action is better than no action. Depending on which policies the new administration enacts, it may already be too late to formulate a response.

Situation 7

Most Effective - D: Hiring labor from your home country will help ease the privacy concerns while purchasing materials from local suppliers will keep the project moving at a faster pace, so a combination of efforts is the best approach.

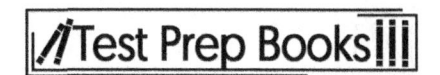

Least Effective - C: Hiring labor from the foreign country and importing supplies from your home country would be the worst of both approaches, requiring daily security screening and long wait times while supplies are in transit.

Situation 8

Most Effective - C: Travel advisories are easily accessible to tourists, so issuing one would be a great way to warn them about ongoing special circumstances.

Least Effective - A: Merely speaking with your colleagues doesn't inform any tourists who are currently visiting or planning to visit, so a different choice would be more effective.

Situation 9

Most Effective - A: Anything resembling a threat should be taken very seriously. Immediately informing supervisors and preparing to contact authorities for an investigation is the safest choice.

Least Effective - D: Dismissing the threat as a prank could have extremely dangerous consequences, making this the least effective option.

Situation 10

Most Effective - D: Being upfront and honest about your request will help the project leaders make a quick decision about sharing project information with you.

Least Effective - E: Attempting to gain information via indirect means could be misconstrued as some form of espionage and damage political relations.

Situation 11

Most Effective - B: While it does not guarantee a solution, sending a report and petitioning your home country's government for assistance is the best way to use your position to help this country stabilize.

Least Effective - D: Doing nothing in this situation is a poor decision when you can conceivably help in even a small way.

Situation 12

Most Effective - C: If an extension is required, then the best approach is to explain why it is required and politely request it from your supervisor.

Least Effective - E: Carrying on as normal without informing your supervisor will lead to confusion and frustration later when they expect a report that isn't ready yet.

Situation 13

Most Effective - A: In this situation, it would be best to find someone else who has a positive opinion of the policy and can write more naturally about it. Having your own negative opinion is fine, but you shouldn't force a disingenuous speech.

Answer Explanations #3 | Situational Judgment

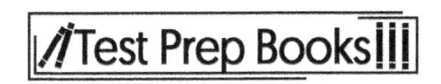

Least Effective - D: Writing a negative speech directly ignores the project's criteria and will make others question your ability to follow project directions.

Situation 14

Most Effective - E: An inappropriate social media post should be removed as quickly as possible. You should also formulate a statement in case it does break into local news so that you have a prompt and thought-out response.

Least Effective - B: Leaving the inappropriate social media post up will increase the risk of it getting publicized in the local news and could easily damage your home country's reputation with your assigned country.

Situation 15

Most Effective - C: Documenting the false claims and alerting your supervisors allows you to begin preparing a formal response that acknowledges the claims' falsehood. This is the best start towards mitigating the damage to foreign relations.

Least Effective - B: Publicly denouncing a member of your home country's government in response to the false claims is an overly blunt approach that could make the situation even more awkward and damaging. It also doesn't help to repair the damage to foreign relations.

Situation 16

Most Effective - D: Voicing your concerns is acceptable if you are willing to keep an open mind about cultural and situational differences.

Least Effective - C: Demanding specific accommodations is selfish and puts others in the awkward position of having to deal with your concerns. Refusing to accept the assignment could have negative consequences on your career because it indicates that you are not open minded or flexible enough to accept certain positions.

Situation 17

Most Effective - B: The most reassuring option is to offer what shareable information you can and explain the emergency procedures. Knowing what to do in advance will help many of your home country's citizens feel more at ease.

Least Effective - C: Unclear or uncertain information won't do much to reassure citizens. If the situation becomes worse and your assigned country is invaded too, then it will seem like a false prediction, and your home country's citizens may be less trusting of you in the future.

Situation 18

Most Effective - E: Keeping the ambassador's remarks focused on a positive future will provide encouragement to the attendees while avoiding situations that could cause embarrassment for the ambassador.

Least Effective - A: Letting the ambassador speak about whatever comes to their mind is dangerous, as they could end up focusing too much on their strong opinions and cause a scene at the dinner.

Answer Explanations #3 | Situational Judgment

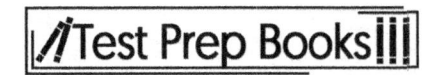

Situation 19

Most Effective - A: Smoothly transitioning into an anecdote relevant to the speech is a very resourceful way to buy time for the teleprompter to catch up without losing the audience in confusion.

Least Effective - D: Pausing everything while waiting for the teleprompter would be awkward and emphasize your dependence on it, which would weaken the speech's overall effectiveness.

Situation 20

Most Effective - E: An honest answer about their proposal and the budgeting concerns will show the team member that you are supportive of them while still considering the responsibilities of the organization.

Least Effective - B: Even if a raise cannot be worked out in the budget, the team member at least deserves to know why. Refusing to elaborate will make them more upset at you for denying it.

Situation 21

Most Effective - B: A prompt and effective upgrade will remove everyone's workflow slowdown and keep everyone as productive as possible. Choice D, which initially looks similar, does not adequately research the available options and could leave you paying for an ineffective or expensive solution, making it less effective than Choice B.

Least Effective - C: Making everyone go into work fixes the productivity problem, but it exposes everyone to an extreme health risk and should be avoided.

Situation 22

Most Effective - D: An online travel warning about the strict dress code changes is the best way to keep everyone informed and to avoid unnecessary arrests and legal action.

Least Effective - B: Low tourism makes a manpower approach too costly and doesn't help tourists who may have missed the officers or aren't prepared for the dress code.

Situation 23

Most Effective - A: What someone does outside of work has no bearing on their job performance. You should stay objective and focus on the quality of their work.

Least Effective - C: Lying about their job performance based on your feelings about what they do outside of work is dishonest and shows a lack of objectivity. This could cause others to have less trust in you.

Situation 24

Most Effective - E: With the knowledge you have of the ongoing missing persons situation, the best way to be helpful is to warn the citizen of the situation and provide accurate information so they can continue to prepare for their move with confidence.

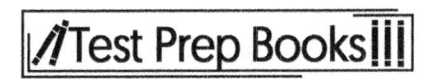

Least Effective - B: Pushing the citizen back towards the lawyer dodges the responsibility of helping them and potentially endangers them if the lawyer is fraudulent or involved in the missing persons situation.

Situation 25

Most Effective - C: Even if the team member argues against their weaknesses in the review, it's most important to be honest about all aspects of their performance to help them improve.

Least Effective - B: Writing a selective performance review just to avoid a confrontation or placate the team member's attitude will not help them grow professionally and will just delay dealing with the issue until later.

Situation 26

Most Effective - C: In this situation, your role is not to be a negotiator but to facilitate accurate conversation between two individuals. Translating the statements accurately is your responsibility regardless of how the person for whom you are translating will react.

Least Effective - A: Lying in translation gives the wrong impression to your home country's official and may lead to a larger misunderstanding later.

Situation 27

Most Effective - E: You should report what information you receive in case it is accurate, but you should also warn your home country's government about your concerns so that they exercise appropriate caution with the information.

Least Effective - D: If the source really is lying to you, then reporting the false information could have dangerous repercussions later. Therefore, you should exercise more caution.

Situation 28

Most Effective - D: The best approach is to keep the offer available in case it could lead to a positive outcome for your home country, but you should first discuss it with your supervisors to make sure that you are getting a fair deal and that there are no dangers of which you are unaware.

Least Effective - A: Even if it seems safe, it's possible that sharing this information with a foreign official could lead to a distinct disadvantage for your home country in the future, making this decision a risky choice.

English Expression

1. D: Choice *D* is the correct answer because "rather" acts as an interrupting word here and thus should be separated by commas. Choices *B* and *C* use commas unwisely, breaking the flow of the sentence.

2. B: Since the sentence can stand on its own without *Usually*, separating it from the rest of the sentence with a comma is correct. Choice *A* needs the comma after *Usually*, while Choice *C* uses commas incorrectly. Choice *D* is tempting, but changing *turn* to past tense goes against the rest of the paragraph.

Answer Explanations #3 | English Expression

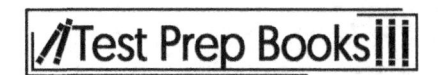

3. A: In Choice *A,* the dependent clause *Sometimes in particularly dull seminars* is seamlessly attached with a single comma after *seminars*. Choice *B* contains too many commas. Choice *C* does not correctly combine the dependent clause with the independent clause. Choice *D* introduces too many unnecessary commas.

4. D: Choice *D* rearranges the sentence to be more direct and straightforward, so it is correct. Choice *A* needs a comma after *on*. Choice *B* introduces unnecessary commas. Choice *C* creates an incomplete sentence, since *Because I wasn't invested in what was going on* is a dependent clause.

5. C: Choice *C* is fluid and direct, making it the best revision. Choice *A* is incorrect because the construction is awkward and lacks parallel structure. Choice *B* is incorrect because of the unnecessary comma and period. Choice *D* is close, but its sequence is still awkward and overly complicated.

6. B: Choice *B* correctly adds a comma after *person* and cuts out the extraneous writing, making the sentence more streamlined. Choice *A* is poorly constructed, lacking proper grammar to connect the sections of the sentence correctly. Choice *C* inserts an unnecessary semicolon and doesn't enable this section to flow well with the rest of the sentence. Choice *D* is better but still unnecessarily long.

7. D: This sentence, though short, is a complete sentence. The only thing the sentence needs is an em-dash after "Easy." In this sentence the em-dash works to add emphasis to the word "Easy" and also acts in place of a colon, but in a less formal way. Therefore, Choice *D* is correct. Choices *A* and *B* lack the crucial comma, while Choice *C* unnecessarily breaks the sentence apart.

8. C: Choice *C* successfully fixes the construction of the sentence, changing *drawing* into *to draw*. Keeping the original sentence disrupts the flow, so Choice *A* is incorrect. Choice *B*'s use of *which* offsets the whole sentence. Choice *D* is incorrect because it unnecessarily expands the sentence content and makes it more confusing.

9. B: Choice *B* fixes the homophone issue. Because the author is talking about people, *their* must be used instead of *there*. This revision also appropriately uses the Oxford comma, separating and distinguishing *lives, world, and future*. Choice *A* uses the wrong homophone and is missing commas. Choice *C* neglects to fix these problems and unnecessarily changes the tense of *applies*. Choice *D* fixes the homophone but fails to properly separate *world* and *future*.

10. C: Choice *C* is the correct answer. Shorter poems should be in quotation marks, but tiles of long, epic poems like *The Odyssey* should be written with italics.

11. A: Choice *A* is the best answer. *However* is an appropriate word to begin this sentence since it illustrates the idea of contrast: some of the females Odysseus encountered were helpful, *however* some were clearly not. Therefore, we can eliminate Choice *D*. Choice *B* is also incorrect because it eliminates the word *several*, which is also useful in distinguishing that, while some female characters were benevolent, several were deceptive and even harmful. Choice *C* is incorrect because it lacks the comma after *However*.

12. D: Choice *D* is the best answer because it uses a comma between an independent clause and a dependent clause and gets rid of the word *himself*, eliminating wordiness. Choice *A* is incorrect because the comma between two independent clauses causes a comma splice. Additionally, the word *himself* is repetitive. Choice *B* is incorrect because the absence of a semicolon or period after *harder* creates a run-on sentence.

Answer Explanations #3 | English Expression

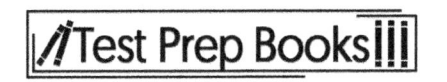

13. C: We would say *By the time Odysseus reaches* home to denote that one event occurs before the other. The other answer choices don't make this distinction.

14. A: Choice A is correct because it is in active voice rather than passive voice. Choice B is incorrect because *he had to be concealed himself* is passive voice and also creates wordiness with *himself*. Choice C makes the sentence grammatically incorrect. Choice D is incorrect because *concealing* does not go with the helping verb *had*. *Had concealing* is not a proper verb phrase.

15. B: Choice B is the best answer. Choice A is incorrect because it is a run-on sentence. Choice C is incorrect because the comma between two independent clauses creates a comma splice. Choice D is incorrect; semicolons should have independent clauses on either side of them, and the first phrase is not a complete sentence.

16. B: Choice B, *conceals,* is the best option because Odysseus does in fact hide (or conceal) his true identity behind a false name. Choice A is incorrect; *relinquishes* means to give up or to voluntarily cease control of something. This is not something Odysseus does because he does not surrender his true name—he just hides it. He does not *withhold* (Choice C) his true identity but offers an alternative. Choice D, *surrenders,* is synonymous with *relinquishes*.

17. A: Reading through the sentence, one can see that it flows and uses proper punctuation and grammar, which means that no change is necessary; Choice A is the correct answer. Choice B lacks the necessary comma after *Clearly*. Choice C utilizes an unnecessary semicolon. Choice D makes the sentence awkward by placing *clearly* in the middle of the sentence.

18. C: Choice C is the best answer choice. Choice A is incorrect because the author of the passage uses present tense when speaking about the text in question, so the verb should be *describes*. Choice B is incorrect because *passages* should be *passage*, singular. Choice D is incorrect because the word *These* should be *This*, describing a singular passage.

19. B: Choice B is the best answer because it avoids the wordiness of the original phrase *also like*, which makes Choice A incorrect. Choice C is compelling, but it lacks the necessary information that the original sentence has: we need to have Polyphemus still in the sentence. Choice D is a decent option, but much of it is unnecessary and already addressed in the remainder of the sentence that isn't underlined.

20. B: The issue with this word is that it lacks proper punctuation. *One* is referring to an individual, and it needs to show possession of *identity*. Therefore, *ones* must have an apostrophe to show ownership and to be correct. Thus, Choice B, *One's*, is the correct answer.

21. C: The current phrase repeats itself, so we can eliminate Choice A. Choices B and D are compelling but are somewhat specific. What must be communicated is that all men who reach the island, in whatever fashion, risk being seduced by Circe. Choice C is the most practical revision and is more direct, while allowing for other circumstances in which men come to Circe's island.

22. B: The best answer is Choice B, *ensure*, which means to make certain. Odysseus is trying to make certain that he and the crew will be safe by beating Circe at her own game. Choice A, *assure*, means to speak to someone in a way that eliminates doubt. This indirectly relates to what Odysseus wants to do, but to *assure* specifically refers to speaking to someone. Choices C and D are totally irrelevant. *Vindicate* means to free from blame, while *prevent* means to stop from happening.

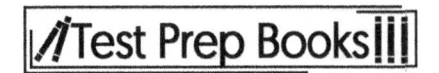

23. B: The best verb to use here is *returns*. When talking about text we use present tense verbs.

24. A: Choice *A* is the best answer. Choice *B* is incorrect because it is missing a comma after the introductory clause, *As the text progresses*. Choice *C* is incorrect; Odysseus is the subject of the sentence and must be outside of any phrases—Choice *C* has the subject *Odysseus* inside a prepositional phrase starting with the word *with*, so this is incorrect. Choice *D* is incorrect because again, our subject is inside a clause and therefore does not pair with the verb *encounters*.

25. C: Choice *C* is simple and straightforward, describing the event clearly for the reader to follow; talked is past tense, which is consistent with the rest of the passage. Choice *A* is incorrect, since we came to talking about confuses the tense of the sentence and the verb talk. Choices *B* and *D* are wordy and not as straightforward as Choice *C*.

26. B: Choice *B* is the correct answer because it adds a comma after *Essentially* and changes *an* to *a*. This is called the indefinite article, when an unspecified thing or quantity is referred to. However, *an* doesn't agree with *metaphor*, since *an* should only be used when the next word starts with a vowel. Choice *A* uses the article *an* and lacks the crucial comma after *Essentially*. Choice *C* is incorrect because it only provides the comma after *Essentially*, neglecting the indefinite article disagreement. Choice *D* is incorrect because neither issue is fixed and an unnecessary comma is introduced.

27. A: Choice *A* is correct because there are no errors present in the sentence. Choice *B* is a run on, because the clauses are not broken up by commas. Choice *C* has a verbal disagreement: *look* and *saw* are different tenses. Choice *D* changes the structure of the sentence but fails to add a transition to make this correct.

28. D: Choice *D* is correct because it uses a comma after the word *passage*, successfully connecting the dependent clause with its independent clause to form a complete thought/sentence. Choice *A* is therefore incorrect. Choice *B* uses a semicolon unwisely. The two clauses need to be connected to each other in order to make sense, otherwise they are just two fragments improperly combined. Choice *C* does not have the required comma and changes *found* to *finding*, an inappropriate tense for the verb in this sentence.

29. C: Choice *C* is correct because it fixes two major flaws in the original portion of the sentence. First, it inserts the adverb *also* to show the connection between *whatever it is that makes us unique* and *defines us*. Without this adverb, the sentence lacks clarity, and the connection is lost. Second, *big* is incorrect in this context. The sentence needs the superlative *bigger* in order to communicate the scope and scale of the author's assessment of how people relate to others on a grand scale. Choice *A* is therefore incorrect, Choice *B* inserts unnecessary commas, and Choice *D* subtly alters the original meaning.

30. B: Choice *B* is correct because a comma is correctly inserted after *ultimately*. This serves to express a side thought that helps transition into the rest of the sentence without having to break it apart. Choice *A* is incorrect because it lacks the comma after *ultimately*. Choice *C* uses too many commas and is overly complicated. Choice *D* lacks the necessary conjunction after the comma (*but*) before *ultimately*, making it a run-on sentence. It also lacks the important comma after *ultimately*.

31. D: Choice *D* corrects the subject-verb disagreement. *One's* is the possessive form of *one*, a single individual, not the plural *individuals*. *Isn't* is the singular contraction of *is not*, which conflicts with *individuals*. To correct this, either *isn't* must change to *aren't* or *individuals* should become the singular *individual*. The latter is correct because of the context of the sentence. Choice *A* is incorrect because of the subject-verb disagreement. Choice B uses the future tense, while Choice C's *aren't* conflicts with *one's*, which is possessive singular.

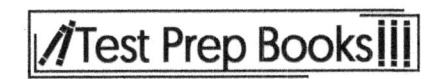

32. A: Choice A contains no grammatical errors and communicates the writer's message clearly. Choice B inserts an unnecessary semicolon. Choice C uses *is*, which disagrees with the plural *aspects. Are* must be used because it is plural. This is the same for Choice D, which uses *there's* (*there is*).

33. D: Choice D is the correct answer because it removes the comma after *Rushdie*. Adding a comma after the proper name in this case is incorrect because *Rushdie* is not being addressed directly. Rather, the writer is talking about Rushdie. Therefore, Choices A disrupts the construction of the sentence. Choice B is incorrect because *seemed*, in this context, should be present tense. The author is talking about a theme and idea that *Rushdie* had but that is still relevant and being actively studied. Choice C fails to remove the comma after Rushdie and applies the gerund *seeming* incorrectly.

34. D: Choice D is correct because it adds the helping verb *were* to modify *unsettled*. This allows the sentence to reflect that the founders were unsettled by the implications. Without *were* to connect the founders to *unsettled*, the sentence doesn't make sense. Choice A lacks the crucial helping verb, making it incorrect. Choice B is incorrect because of its unnecessary semicolon. Choice C changes *theory's*, which is singular possessive, to *theories'* (plural possessive), which isn't consistent with the sentence's context.

35. A: Choice A is correct because it contains no errors and requires no additional punctuation to form a coherent sentence. The single comma, used successfully, unites the two clauses and enables a solid grammatical structure. Choice B incorrectly places a comma after *Instead*, Choice C incorrectly changes *predicted* to *predicting*, and Choice D incorrectly separates *where everything can be predicted by equations* from the rest of the sentence.

36. D: Choice D is correct because it fixes the subject-verb disagreement with *Every outcome* and *exist*. *Exists* is third person present but also appropriate to reflect multiple outcomes, as indicated by *every outcome*. Choices A and B use *exist*, not *exists*, which makes them both incorrect. Choice C is fine on its own but does not fit with the rest of the sentence.

37. B: Choice B is correct because the comma after *determinism* isn't needed. Adding a comma in the selected area actually breaks up the independent clause of the sentence, thus compromising the overall structure of the sentence. Choices A, C, and D are therefore incorrect.

38. C: Choice C is the correct answer because it removes the contraction of *it is, it's*. Choice A, which is incorrect, originally used *it's*—note the apostrophe before *s*. *It's* simply means *it is*, while *its* (no apostrophe) shows possession. In this sentence, *its* is referring to the idea devised by Schrödinger, giving ownership of the purpose to the idea. Choice B is incorrect because *purpose* should remain singular. Choice D is incorrect because it uses *it's*.

39. A: Choice A is correct because the sentence is well-formed and grammatically correct. Choice B is incorrect because it adds an unnecessary comma after *if*. Choice C breaks the sentence apart, creating a sentence fragment. Choice D is incorrect because it changes *release* to a gerund and fails to make a coherent sentence, leaving only two dependent clauses.

40. D: Choice D is the correct answer. This is a tricky question, but Choice D is correct because, in the context of this sentence, it's important to have *however* flanked by commas. This is because the use of *however* is basically an aside to the reader, addressing an idea and then redirecting the reader to an alternative outcome or line of reasoning. Choice A is therefore confusing, with *however* floating in the sentence aimlessly. Choice B only uses one comma, which is incorrect. Choice C creates two incomplete sentences.

41. A: Choice A is correct. The sentence uses a lot of commas, but these are used effectively to highlight key points while continuing to focus on a central idea. Choice B is incorrect because the commas after *reality* and *that* are required. Choice C is incorrect because there should be a comma after *that* because *on the smallest scales* elaborates on the idea itself but not necessarily what Broglie said. Choice D puts a comma after *further*, which is unnecessary in this context.

42. B: Choice B correctly uses *an* instead of *a* to modify *interference*. The indefinite article *an* must be used before words that start with a vowel sound. The verb *created* is also in agreement with the tense of the story. Choice C incorrectly changes *creates* to *create* and pluralizes *light*, which is inconsistent with the rest of the sentence. Choice D modifies *creates* inappropriately and adds an incorrect comma after *light*.

43. B: Both verb phrases are introduced with the word *who*, creating parallelism. Choice A is incorrect. The introductory words for the verb phrases do not match. Choice C is incorrect. The introductory words for the verb phrases do not match and the word *that* would modify an object, not a person. Use *who* for a person. Choice D is incorrect. The word *that* in the sentence should be used to modify an object not a person, and the clown is a person.

44. D: To make *the building was sturdy and solid* subordinate to *the building crumbled in the earthquake*, create a dependent clause with the less important piece of information. Choice A is incorrect. It is two independent clauses joined with a semicolon and neither piece of information is subordinate to the other. Choice B is incorrect. This sentence implies that the building was still sturdy and solid after crumbling in the earthquake because the word *although* is misplaced. Choice C is incorrect because, even though it is a grammatically correct sentence, neither piece of information is subordinate to the other.

45. B: *Dissatisfied* and *accommodations* are both spelled correctly in Choice B. These are both considered commonly misspelled words. One or both words are spelled incorrectly in choices A, C, and D.

46. A: It is necessary to put a comma between the date and the year. It is also required to put a comma between the day of the week and the month. Choice B is incorrect because it is missing the comma between the day and year. Choice C is incorrect because it adds an unnecessary comma between the month and date. Choice D is missing the necessary comma between day of the week and the month.

47. C: This question focuses on the correct usage of the commonly confused word pairs of *it's/its* and *then/than*. *It's* is a contraction for *it is* or *it has*. *Its* is a possessive pronoun. The word *than* shows comparison between two things. *Then* is an adverb that conveys time. Choice C correctly uses *it's* and *than*. *It's* is a contraction for *it has* in this sentence, and *than* shows comparison between *work* and *rest*. None of the other answers choices use both of the correct words.

48. D: Choices A and C use additional words and phrases that are not necessary. Choice B is more concise, but uses the present tense of *is*. This does not agree with the rest of the sentence, which uses past tense. The best choice is Choice D, which uses the most concise sentence structure and is grammatically correct.

Answer Explanations #3 | English Expression

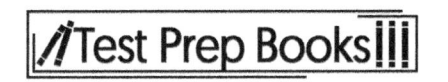

49. D: In a cause/effect relationship, it is correct to begin with the word *because*. This can eliminate both Choices *B* and *C*, which don't clearly show the cause/effect relationship. Choice *A* is incorrect because it uses the past tense, when the main clause is in the present tense. It makes grammatical sense for both parts of the sentence to be in present tense.

50. B: Choice *B* is correct because the Oxford comma is applied, clearly separating the specific terms. Choice *A* lacks this clarity. Choice *C* is correct but too wordy since commas can be easily applied. Choice *D* doesn't flow with the sentence's structure.

51. A: The sentence has no errors, so Choice *A* is correct. Choice *B* is incorrect because it adds an unnecessary comma. Choice *C* is incorrect because *advantage* should not be plural in this sentence without the removal of the singular *an*. Choice *D* is very tempting. While this would make the sentence more concise, this would ultimately alter the context of the sentence, which would be incorrect.

52. B: Choice *B* is correct, fixing the incorrect split of *highlight*. This is a polyseme, a word combined from two unrelated words to make a new word. On their own, *high* and *light* make no sense for the sentence, making Choice *A* incorrect. Choice *C* incorrectly decapitalizes *Ancient*—since it modifies *Greece* and works with the noun to describe a civilization, *Ancient Greece* functions as a proper noun, which should be capitalized. Choice *D* uses *highlighting*, a gerund, but the present tense of *highlight* is what works with the rest of the sentence; to make this change, a comma would be needed after *Rome*.

53. A: Choice *A* is correct, as *not only* and *but also* are correlative pairs. In this sentence, *but* successfully transitions the first part into the second half, making punctuation unnecessary. Additionally, the use of *to* indicates that an idea or challenge is being presented to the reader. Choice *B*'s *with*, *C*'s *for*, and *D*'s *there before* are not as active, meaning these revisions weaken the sentence.

54. A: Choice *A* is correct because the section contains no errors and clearly communicates the writer's point. Choice *B* is incorrect because it lacks a comma after *philosophy*, needed to link the first clause with the second. Choice *C* also has this issue but additionally alters *its* to *it's*; since *it is* does not make sense in this sentence, this is incorrect. Choice *D* is incorrect because *its* is already plural possessive and does not need an apostrophe on the end.

55. D: Choice *D* is correct since the sentence is lengthy as originally presented and should be split into two. Additionally, *however*, being a conjunction, needs a comma afterwards. Choice *A* is therefore incorrect due to missing punctuation. Choice *B* is an improvement but could separate the sentence's ideas better and more clearly. Choice *C* lacks the necessary comma after *However*.

56. A: Choice *A* is the correct answer. Sentence 1 introduces the topic of the paragraph, "phylogenetic trees." Sentence 4 is the next logical sentence because "They are branching diagrams" both refers back to the phylogenic trees introduced in the previous sentence and provides more information about the diagrams. While Sentence 2 or Sentence 3 could be the next sentence, Sentence 2 makes more sense because it gives the reader more information about what the phylogenetic trees do, whereas Sentence 3 shows the limits of the phylogenetic trees. Therefore, the best order for this paragraph is Sentence 1, Sentence 4, Sentence 2, and Sentence 3.

57. C: Choice *C* is the correct answer. Sentence 3 introduces greenhouses as the topic of the paragraph and indicates that the rest of the paragraph will discuss the reasons why "Plants may grow better inside a greenhouse versus outside." While the next three sentences expand on those reasons, Sentence 4 is the best choice for the third sentence because of the word "Additionally" – there must have been a reason introduced before this sentence, which means it cannot be the second sentence in the paragraph. Similarly, Sentence 1 makes the most sense as the final sentence because of the introductory word "Finally." That leaves Sentence 2 as the second sentence in the paragraph. The correct order, then, is Sentence 3, Sentence 2, Sentence 4, and Sentence 1.

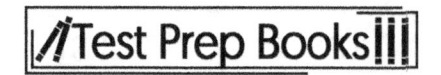

58. B: Choice *B* is the correct answer. The only sentence that works as a topic sentence for the paragraph is Sentence 2, introducing the reader to the group known as "anti-Stratfordians" and explaining the origin of that name. Sentence 4 makes the most sense as the next sentence because it explains the "most common anti-Stratfordian claim" – it expands on the topic sentence and provides a bridge to the rest of the paragraph. Sentence 1 is the best choice for the next sentence because it provides more detail to the argument laid out in Sentence 4. Sentence 3 is the logical conclusion to the paragraph because it sums up the overall argument of the paragraph. It is also a stronger ending that Sentence 1 because it does not end on a rhetorical question. The best order for this paragraph is Sentence 2, Sentence 4, Sentence 1, and Sentence 3.

59. D: Choice *D* is the correct answer. Sentence 4, "Cells are the smallest functional unit of living organisms," is the clear choice for a topic sentence. It is the broadest statement of the four sentences in this paragraph. Sentence 2 is the best choice for the next sentence because it introduces two types of living organisms, based on numbers of cells, which flows directly from the information introduced in the topic sentence. Sentence 1 is the logical choice for the next sentence because it provides more details about the cells themselves. Sentence 3 is the best choice for the final sentence because it builds on the concept of the previous sentence, that "cells contain organelles that are responsible for distinct functions," and explains why plants and animals would have cells that "are similar but also have unique features."

60. B: Choice *B* is the correct answer. Of the four sentences, only Sentence 2 can function as the topic sentence by laying out the topic that will be discussed in more detail in the remaining sentences. Sentence 1 then provides more details about the "fungal infections of the lung" introduced in the topic sentence. Sentence 4 is the next logical sentence because "these agents" clearly must refer back to the "most common infecting agents" in Sentence 1. Finally, Sentence 3 flows logically from Sentence 4 because it provides details about what tests would help provide the necessary "early and accurate diagnosis" from Sentence 4. Thus, the correct order of the sentences is Sentence 2, Sentence 1, Sentence 4, and Sentence 3.

61. C: This sentence is most likely to be placed after Sentence 3. In Sentence 3, the author introduces the idea that Plato takes the individual completely out of the equation. This new sentence explains why removing the individual is necessary, and then in Sentence 4 the author explains how Plato intended to enforce removing the individual. Because this new sentence explains why the idea in Sentence 3 must be enforced as described in Sentence 4, it is best placed after Sentence 3.

62. A: Choice *A* is correct because it contains no errors that mar the grammar or flow of the sentence. Choice *B* is incorrect because *upon* is incorrectly used to replace *on*. *Upon* refers specifically to a surface, which is not appropriate for this sentence. The preposition *on* is needed here. Choice *C* alters the sentence unnecessarily, confusing the tense and focus of the sentence by using *looking* instead of *look*. Choice *D* changes *some* to *something*, which makes no sense for the rest of the sentence.

63. C: Choice *C* is the correct answer because it adds a comma after *Certainly*. This is important because the author is addressing the audience before moving on to explore *his ideas*. Choice *A* is incorrect because the lack of a comma makes this sentence a run-on. Choices B and D are incorrect because, while the former applies the comma after *Certainly*, they both take away the *but* that modifies *at what costs*.

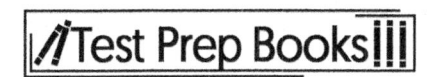

64. D: Choice D is correct. Sentence 4 discusses what happens due to the buildup of water in Sentence 3, and this new sentence describes the ultimate consequences of flash flooding. Because it is the logical culmination of the statements in Sentences 1-4, it is best placed after Sentence 4.

65. D: Choice A is incorrect; semicolons separate items in a list only when an item in the list contains a comma itself. Choice B is incorrect; items in a list should always be separated by commas. Choice C is incorrect because the word *beavers* is missing a possessive -'s at the end.

Index

Semicolon (, 42
1964 Civil Rights Act, 94
19th Amendment, 80, 88, 94
Abigail Adams, 94
Absolute Error, 147
Absolute Location, 106, 107, 240, 278
Absolute Number, 140
Absolute Phrase, 38
Abstract Noun, 12
Accuracy, 146
Active Voice, 15, 417
Acute Angle, 169, 173
Acute Triangle, 164
Adaptation, 217, 218, 305
Adjective Clause, 34
Adjective Phrase, 17
Adjectives, 16, 22
Adolf Hitler, 83, 101
Adverbs, 17
Affect and Effect, 24
Alexander Hamilton, 48, 71
Algebraic Expressions, 152
Alien and Sedition Acts, 71, 72
Alternate Exterior Angles, 176
Alternate Interior Angles, 176
Altitude, 176
Amendment I, 56, 57
Amendment II, 56
Amendment III, 56
Amendment IV, 56
Amendment IX, 57
Amendment V, 57
Amendment VI, 57
Amendment VII, 57
Amendment VIII, 57
Amendment X, 57
American War for Independence, 69
Andrew Jackson, 64, 72, 73
Angle-Angle-Angle (AAA), 175
Angle-Angle-Side (AAS), 175
Angle-Side-Angle (ASA), 175
Antecedent, 13
Anti-Defamation League, 91, 306, 346
Anti-Federalist Papers, 48

Apostrophe ('), 44
Appositive, 37
Arc, 182
Arc Measure, 182
Area Model, 144, 145
Articles, 16, 45, 46, 47, 48, 70, 305, 341, 365, 406
Articles of Confederation, 45, 46, 47, 48, 70, 305, 341, 365, 406
Asian Pacific American Heritage Month, 96
Assets, 119, 130, 215
Associative Property, 134
Attribution Theory, 219
Audience, 12, 25, 26, 27, 206, 207, 209, 219, 221, 223, 224, 302, 303, 304, 307, 342, 344, 346, 348, 363, 367, 378, 382, 396, 406, 408, 409, 414, 422
Bank Money, 125, 243, 281
Bar Graph, 190, 191
Barter System, 123
Bartering, 125
Base, 14, 86, 131, 132, 134, 153, 165, 167, 178, 179, 181, 184, 185, 343
Base-10 System, 131, 132
Battle of Saratoga, 69
Behavior of Firms, 122
Biased Estimators, 198
Bicameral, 46, 51, 55, 70, 404
Bilateral Agreements, 104
Bill of Rights, 49, 56, 70, 71, 360, 365, 403, 406, 407
Binomial Coefficient., 204
Binomial Distribution, 199
Binomial Experiment, 203
Biotechnology, 115
Bleeding Kansas, 77, 242, 281
Body Paragraphs, 29, 30
Booms, 119
Boston Tea Party In 1773, 68
Box Plot, 187, 191
British Raj, 99
Broadcasting, 209
Brown vs. Board of Education, 93, 241, 280
Brown vs. the Board of Education, 58

Index

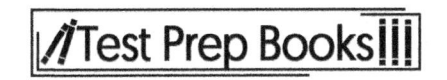

Business Cycle, 124, 125, 241, 243, 279, 282, 359, 403
Cabinet Members, 50, 51, 89, 342
Capital, 120, 122
Capital Resources, 122
Carel Germain, 217
Carl Stokes, 94
Caucuses, 61, 62
Causation, 200
Center of Dilation, 174
Central Angle, 182
Central Bank, 123, 126, 127, 296, 338, 363, 405
Central Intelligence Agency, 106
Central Limit Theorem, 202
Centroid, 176
Cesar Chavez, 95
Chemical Weathering, 109
Chi-Squared Goodness of Fit Test, 205
Chord, 182, 183
CIA World Factbook, 106
Circumscribed Angle, 182
Civil Liberty, 49, 56
   Civil Liberties, 48, 56, 57, 58, 59, 238, 276
Civil Rights, 56, 57, 64, 65, 66, 93, 97, 280, 289
Civil Rights Act of 1968, 94
Clauses, 24, 34, 38
Climate Change, 111, 116, 244, 314
Closed-Form Function, 148
Coercive Acts, 97
Coercive or Intolerable Acts, 69
Cognitive-Behavioral Group, 216
Cold War, 66, 84, 85, 86, 90, 100, 102, 103, 104, 105, 118, 276, 281, 363, 405
Colin Powell, 94
Collective Noun, 12, 21
Colons, 42, 290
Comma (,), 41
Command Economies, 120, 406
Commerce and Slave Trade Compromise, 46
Commodity Money, 125, 243, 281
Common Noun, 12
Community Development Theory, 219
Community-Level Change, 219
Commutative Property, 134
Comparative Adjectives, 16
Compass, 182
Complement, 22
Complementary, 173, 342
Complete Predicate, 19
Complete Subject, 19, 20
Complex Numbers, 132, 133
Complex Prepositions, 18
Complex Sentence, 39, 41
Composite Number, 134, 138, 139
Compound Predicate, 20
Compound Sentences, 38
Compound-Complex Sentence, 39
Conclusion, 29, 30, 32, 57, 117, 207, 357, 378, 408, 422
Concrete Noun, 12
Concurrent Powers, 47
Cone, 137, 167
Confidence Interval, 198, 203
Confidence Level, 199, 203
Conflict Theory, 214
Conformity, 219
Congruence, 173, 174, 175
Coniferous, 111
Conjugation, 14
Conjunctions, 18
Consecutive Interior Angle, 176
Constitution, 45, 60, 77, 404
Constitutional Union Party, 64, 275
Consumer Price Index (CPI), 124
Conversion Factor, 135, 148, 186
Coordinating Conjunctions, 18
Coping, 218
Correlation Coefficient (r), 200
Corresponding Angles, 176
Cosine, 173
Counter-Culture Movement, 85, 86
Database, 222, 303, 306, 343, 346, 371, 410
Deciduous, 110, 111
Declaration of Independence, 48, 69, 93, 97, 365, 406
Declaration of Rights and Sentiments, 58
Declarative Sentences, 39
Decolonization, 118
Definite Article, 16
Deflation, 123, 124
Degree of Freedom, 205
Degree of Freedom Value, 205
Degrees, 21, 107, 137, 166, 169, 171, 173, 175, 176, 177, 182, 198, 200, 203, 281, 333

Index

Degrees of Freedom, 198, 203
Deindividuation, 219
Delegated Powers, 47
Delegates, 49, 51, 62, 69, 70
Deltas, 109
Demand, 120, 121, 311, 314, 373
Democracy, 59, 61, 66, 83, 90, 97, 276, 278
Democratic Party, 61, 64, 77, 87, 90
Demography, 116
Demonstrative Pronouns, 13
Denial, 216
Density, 106, 116, 183, 236, 238, 274, 280
Dependent Clause, 24, 34, 39, 288, 357, 416, 418, 419, 420
Deposition, 109
Deserts, 110
Developmental Perspective, 215
Diagonals, 177
Dialects, 113
Diane Humetewa, 95
Difference of Squares, 153
Dilation, 174
Dimensional Analysis, 148
Diplomacy, 210, 239, 251, 359
Direct Object, 21, 22, 37
Direct Primaries, 60
Displacement, 215
Distribution of Income, 121
Distributive Property, 134
Domain, 149, 150, 224
East India Company Act, 99
Ecological Systems Perspective, 217
Economy, 58, 64, 76, 78, 79, 81, 82, 83, 86, 87, 90, 91, 92, 98, 100, 103, 104, 105, 113, 115, 116, 119, 121, 122, 123, 124, 125, 126, 127, 128, 129, 277, 279, 282, 283, 300, 303, 308, 311, 339, 340, 341, 374, 404
Electoral College, 50, 51, 61, 62, 71, 410
Electoral College System, 61
Electoral Process, 61
Electronic Mail, 223
Elizabeth Cady Stanton, 58
Ellipsis (...), 41, 292
Email, 223, 224, 226, 232, 246, 251, 284, 286, 296, 338, 366, 372, 374, 375, 379, 408, 410
Emancipation Proclamation, 57, 77, 240, 278
Em-Dash (—), 44

Emigration, 114
Emperor Franz Joseph I, 100
Entrepreneurs, 120
Entrepreneurship, 123
Equal Employment Practices (EEP), 221
Equator, 107, 108
Equiangular Polygons, 164
Equilateral Triangle, 164, 168, 176
Equinox, 108
Era of Good Feelings, 72
Erosion, 109
Ethnicity, 57, 58, 87, 113, 114
Exchange Rate, 127, 237, 275
Exclamatory Sentences, 40
Executive Branch, 45, 47, 49, 50, 51, 53, 89, 406
Experiment, 26, 86, 147, 197, 203, 392, 393
Exponent, 132, 134, 135, 137, 140, 153, 154, 155
Exponents, 132, 134, 139
Factor, 76, 79, 80, 83, 93, 98, 116, 123, 131, 132, 134, 136, 138, 139, 143, 152, 153, 154, 158, 174, 185, 195, 196, 238, 242, 276, 282, 296, 367, 404, 408
Fascism, 83, 237, 274
Federal Reserve, 126, 127, 237, 275, 296, 338
Federalism, 46, 47, 57, 117, 237, 359, 402
Federalist Papers, 48, 300, 341
Fiat Money, 125, 243, 281
Fifteenth Amendment, 57, 58
First Battle of Bull Run, 77
First Congress of the American Colonies, 97
First Continental Congress In 1774, 69, 97
First Great Awakening, 91, 346
First Person, 12
Fiscal Policy, 125
Five Civilized Tribes, 73
Fixed Exchange, 127
Flappers, 81
Floating (Flexible) Exchange Rates, 127
Foreign Policy, 66
Formal Regions, 108
Fourteenth Amendment, 57, 58
Fractional Exponents, 134
Franklin Chang-Diaz, 95
Franklin D. Roosevelt, 64, 82, 92, 296, 338
Franz Ferdinand, 83, 100, 338, 368, 409
French and Indian War, 67, 68, 302, 342

Index

Frequency Distributions, 192
Freshwater Ecosystems, 110
Function, 14, 34, 56, 66, 104, 129, 147, 148, 149, 150, 151, 152, 153, 154, 157, 199, 212, 216, 217, 218, 244, 256, 258, 280, 288, 289, 293, 323, 324, 325, 334, 356, 358, 363, 398, 422
Functional Regions, 109
Fundamental Attribution Error, 219
Gavrilo Princip, 100, 338
General Election, 62
Genetically Modified Organisms (GMOs), 115
  GMOs, 115
Geometric Distribution, 199
George Mason, 49
George Washington, 48, 69, 71, 264, 265, 360, 403
Gerund Phrase, 37
Gerunds, 36
Gilded Age, 79, 80, 299, 340
Girondists, 97
Glass Ceiling, 81
Globalization, 104, 115, 116
Goodness of Fit Tests, 205
GPS (Global Positioning System), 106
Great Depression, 64, 80, 82, 83, 86, 92, 101, 119, 236, 244, 274, 282, 303, 340, 343, 403
Great Leap Forward, 103
Great Migration, The, 81, 274
Great Society, The, 87
Green Revolution, 115
Gross Domestic Product (GDP), 121, 123, 124, 127
  Gross Domestic Products (GDP), 115
Group Polarization, 219
Gulf Stream, 111
Harlem Renaissance, 81, 274
Hemispheres, 107, 108, 277
Heptagon, 177
Hexagon, 177, 364
High Latitudes, 107
Hippies, 86
Histograms, 186, 187, 191
Holocaust, 84, 91, 101, 102, 346
Homer Plessy, 58
Homogeneity, 108
Homonyms, 23

House of Representatives, 46, 47, 51, 52, 54, 63, 70, 94, 371, 410
Human Relatedness, 218
Human Resources, 122
Humanistic Approach, 215
Hyphen (-), 43
Hypotenuse, 173, 175, 177, 179
Hypotenuse-Leg (HL), 175
I Have a Dream Speech, 93
Immigration, 48, 64, 72, 79, 91, 92, 106, 114, 237, 275, 315, 346, 351
Immigration and Nationality Act of 1965, 92
Imperative Mood, 16
Imperative Sentences, 39
Implied Powers, 47
Indefinite Articles, 16
Independent Clause, 18, 24, 34, 38, 39, 41, 42, 288, 289, 290, 291, 292, 293, 352, 354, 355, 356, 357, 416, 417, 418, 419, 420
Indicative Mood, 15
Indirect Object, 19, 22, 37
Infinitive, 37, 290, 356
Infinitive Phrase, 37
Inflation, 123, 124, 127, 128, 299, 361
Inherent Powers, 47
Inscribed Angle, 182
Interest Group, 59, 60, 65, 89, 90
Interjections, 18
Internal Migration, 114
International Trade, 127, 406
Internet, 60, 62, 87, 104, 106, 209, 224
Interpersonal Learning Groups, 216
Interquartile Range (IQR), 196
Interrogative Pronouns, 13
Interrogative Sentences, 40
Intolerable Acts, 69, 97
Introduction, 29, 30, 32, 207, 289, 357, 367, 408
Isosceles Trapezoid, 165
Isosceles Triangle, 164, 176
James Madison, 46, 48, 71
Jerry Falwell, 87
Jim Crow Laws, 58
John Adams, 48, 71, 94
John Jay, 48, 71
John Wilkes Booth, 78
Judicial Branch, 52, 53, 88
Know-Nothing Party, 64

Index

Labor, 79, 120, 267, 296, 306, 338, 346, 371
Land, 120, 238, 343, 385, 388
Latin American Wars of Independence, 98
Latitude, 106, 107, 108, 111, 278
Law of Large Numbers, 202
Legislative Branch, 47, 51, 55, 62
Liberator, The, 76
Life Stress, 217
Like Terms, 155
Line Graph, 188, 191
Line Plot, 189, 191
Line Segment, 161, 173, 174, 176, 182, 183
Linear Transformation, 195
Lobbyists, 65, 303
Location, 106, 240
Longitude, 106, 107, 108, 278
Lucy Stone, 58
Macroeconomics, 119, 122, 239, 277
Macrosystems, 217
Main Clauses, 34
Malcolm X, 58, 93, 281
Manifest Destiny, 73, 74, 299, 340
Mao Zedong, 102, 103
Marbury vs. Madison, 72, 241, 280
Margin of Error, 197, 203
Mark Twain, 79, 299
Market Economies, 120, 406
Martin Luther King Jr., 58, 93
Mass Media, 207, 208, 276
Massacre at Wounded Knee, 75, 95, 305, 345
McCullough vs. Maryland, 72
Mean, 133, 147, 175, 191, 192, 193, 194, 195, 196, 197, 198, 199, 200, 202, 203, 204, 279, 315, 382, 384, 402, 403
Media Relations, 208
Median, 165, 176, 187, 191, 192, 193, 194, 195, 196, 198, 204, 238, 267, 276, 279
Meridians, 106
Mexican-American War, 73, 76, 274, 276, 345
Mezzosystems, 217
Microeconomics, 119, 239, 277
Microsystems, 217
Midrange, 196
Missouri Compromise of 1820, 77
Mode, 25, 26, 27, 191, 192, 193, 194, 195, 196, 279
Molasses Act in 1731, 67

Money, 122, 123, 125, 129
Moral Majority, 87, 306, 346
Muckrakers, 80
Multilateral, 104, 210
Multiple, 38, 99, 134, 139, 142, 175, 194, 204, 209, 273, 279, 293, 337, 363, 367, 370, 382, 401, 409, 419
Mutual Aid Model, 216
Mutually Assured Destruction, 85
Mutually Bisecting Diagonals, 177
National Association for the Advancement of Colored People (NAACP), 58, 256, 258
National Hispanic Heritage Month, 95
National Socialist German Workers' Party, 101
National, State, and Municipal Elections, 60
Nation-State, 104, 117, 370, 406, 409
Native American Tribes, 56, 67, 70, 72, 73, 75, 95
Natural Number, 133, 134, 139
Natural Resources, 122
Negative Exponents, 135
New Deal, 64, 80, 82, 87, 92, 244, 282, 299, 340
New Jersey Plan, 46, 70
New Religious Movements, 91
New Women, 80
Newspaper, 209
Nonessential Clauses, 35
Non-Restrictive Clauses, 35
Non-Uniform Probability Model, 203
Normal Distribution, 191, 192, 193, 198, 199, 202
Normative Social Influence, 219
North Atlantic Treaty Organization (NATO), 102
Noun, 12, 13, 14, 16, 17, 18, 19, 20, 21, 22, 34, 35, 36, 37, 38, 290, 356, 421
Noun Phrase, 14, 35, 37
Number Line, 132, 133, 140, 143, 144, 156, 187, 189
Object of the Preposition, 17, 36, 37
Objective Pronouns, 13
Observational Study, 197
Obtuse Angle, 169
Obtuse Triangle, 164
Ocean Ecosystems, 110
Octagon, 168, 177
Old Lights, 91
One-Tailed Test, 198

Index

Open Primaries, 61
Order of Magnitude, 138
Order of Operations, 139
Orthocenter, 176
Oscar Hijuelos, 95
Out-Group, 219
Oxford Comma, 42, 416, 421
Panic of 1893, 81, 361, 403
Parallel Lines, 151, 160, 169
Parallels, 106
Parentheses, 43, 139
Participles, 14, 36
Patrick Henry, 49, 71
Pentagon, 177
Perestroika, 103
Perimeter, 177, 178
Perpendicular Bisecting Diagonals, 177
Perpendicular Bisectors, 177
Perpendicular Diagonals, 177
Personal Pronouns, 12
Phrase, 14, 17, 19, 31, 32, 34, 35, 36, 37, 41, 43, 289, 290, 291, 292, 293, 352, 354, 355, 358, 417
Physical Weathering, 109
Pitt's India Act, 99
Please Excuse My Dear Aunt Sally (PEMDAS), 140
  PEMDAS, 133, 135
Plessy Vs. Ferguson, 58, 93, 241, 280
Point Estimate, 198, 203
Political Action Committees, 90
Political Institution, 49, 278
Political Party, 61, 64, 101, 238, 244
Polygon, 161, 163, 164, 167, 168, 177, 178, 179, 180, 405
Population, 27, 46, 47, 51, 56, 62, 68, 70, 97, 100, 101, 106, 107, 112, 115, 116, 196, 197, 198, 199, 202, 203, 205, 236, 238, 275, 276, 280, 346, 367
Population Mean (μ), 197
Population Reference Bureau, 106
Population Reference Bureau (PRB), 106
Positive Linear Relationship, 200
Possessive Pronouns, 12
Power, 90, 218, 236, 274, 305
Power of 10, 132
Precision, 32, 146

Predicate, 14, 19, 20, 22, 356
Predicate Adjective, 22
Predicate Noun, 22
Prepositional Phrase, 36, 352, 418
  Prepositional Phrases, 17
Prepositions, 17
President, 40, 47, 48, 49, 50, 51, 52, 53, 55, 61, 62, 63, 64, 66, 70, 71, 72, 82, 88, 89, 94, 102, 275, 299, 302, 311, 318, 339, 340, 342, 370, 371, 405, 409, 410
President Dwight D. Eisenhower, 93
President Franklin D. Roosevelt, 80, 87, 282
President George Washington, 64, 90, 282, 342
President Harry Truman, 84, 208, 338
President James K. Polk, 73
President John Tyler, 73
President Lyndon B. Johnson, 87, 95
President Martin Van Buren, 73
President Richard Nixon, 95
President Woodrow Wilson, 83
Primary Purpose, 25, 27, 220
Prime Factorization, 134
Prime Meridian, 107
Prime Numbers, 134, 138, 139
Prism, 166, 173, 181
Product Markets, 121
Profits, 112, 116, 122, 129, 130
Projection, 216, 277
Pronoun, 12, 13, 14, 17, 18, 22, 23, 288, 357, 358, 420
Pronoun Reference, 13
Pronoun-Antecedent Agreement, 13
Proper Noun, 12, 40, 352, 421
Psychodynamic Theory, 215
Public Diplomacy, 210, 211
Public Opinion, 59, 66
Pull Factors, 114, 116
Puritans, 90
Push Factors, 114, 276
P-Value Approach, 203
Pyramid, 167, 181, 366
Pythagorean Theorem, 173, 177
Quadrilaterals, 165
Quartering Act, 68, 97
Quotation Marks (, 44
Race, 57, 58, 59, 60, 75, 78, 81, 85, 87, 93, 94, 103, 221, 241, 279, 305

Radius, 137, 178, 182, 183, 343
Random Sample, 197, 205, 305, 345
Randomized Experiment, 198
Range, 29, 149, 150, 186, 187, 191, 192, 194, 195, 196, 197, 198, 203, 206, 221, 238, 276, 396, 398
Rape of Nanking, 102
Rate of Change, 150
Rational Choice, 214
Rational Number, 132, 141, 142, 143, 144
Rationalization, 216
Ratios, 135, 136, 173
Ray, 161, 168
Reaction Formation, 216
Real Numbers, 132, 133
Recall Elections, 60
Reciprocal Pronouns, 13
Reconstruction, 57, 76, 78, 239
Rectangle, 144, 162, 163, 165, 168, 172, 173, 175, 178, 180, 181, 183, 186, 190, 243, 282, 367
Rectangular Arrays, 144
Referendums, 60
Regression Lines, 199, 200
Regular Polygon, 164, 168, 405
Reichstag, 101
Relationship, 23, 31, 36, 135, 136, 149, 156, 157, 173, 175, 177, 183, 188, 199, 200, 208, 209, 212, 220, 237, 244, 253, 287, 302, 303, 312, 349, 355, 356, 359, 376, 402, 421
Relative Adverb, 34
Relative Clause, 34, 35
Relative Error, 147
Relative Frequency Distribution, 192
Relative Pronoun, 34, 35
    Relative Pronouns, 13
Remainder Theorem, 154
Repression, 215
Republican Party, 61, 64, 71, 77, 87, 275
Required Reserve, 126
Reserved Powers, 47
Residual, 199
Restrictive Clauses, 35
Retirement, 52, 114, 130, 249, 285
Rewards Systems, 221
Rhombus, 165
Right Triangle, 164, 173, 175, 177, 179

Right-Angle, 169
Rigid Motion, 173, 174, 175
Robert E. Lee, 78
Roe vs. Wade, 94, 241
Role of Government, 45, 119
Sample, 191, 193, 194, 196, 197, 198, 199, 202, 203, 205, 240, 279, 407
Sample Surveys, 197
Samuel Adams, 49
Scale Factor, 136, 172, 174, 282
Scalene Triangle, 164, 176
Scarce, 119, 228
Scatter Plot, 188
Schlieffen Plan, 100
Scientific Notation, 137
Secant Line, 183
Second Great Awakening, 91, 346
Second Person, 12
Second Red Scare, 84
Secular, 114
Sediment, 109
Semi-Autonomous, 117
Senate, 46, 47, 49, 50, 51, 52, 54, 70, 76, 87, 89, 90, 94, 237, 275, 302, 342, 346, 371, 410
Severo Ochoa, 95
Sheryl WuDunn, 96
Side-Angle-Side (SAS), 175
Sides of the Angle, 168
Side-Side-Side (SSS), 175
Siege of Vicksburg in 1863, 78
Sigma, 196
Sigmund Freud's Psychoanalytic Theory, 215
Significance Value, 205
Simple Predicate, 20
Simple Sentence, 38
Simple Subject, 19, 20
Sine, 173
Social Constructionist Perspective, 215
Social Exchange Perspective, 214
Social Facilitation, 219
Social Learning Perspective, 215
Social Loafing, 219
Social Media, 222, 224, 361
Solid, 27, 28, 157, 162, 166, 181, 380, 395, 419, 420
Solid Figure, 162, 181
Solomon Asch, 219

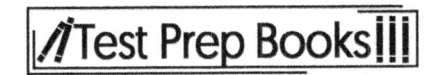

Index

Sonja Sotomayor, 95
Spatial Patterns, 113
Speaker of the House, 51, 54
Sphere, 167, 219
Spread of a Data Set, 191
Spreadsheets, 223
Square, 132, 134, 147, 150, 152, 154, 158, 165, 168, 169, 172, 173, 178, 180, 181, 183, 184, 185, 243
Square Root, 132, 134, 152, 158
Stamp Act of 1765, 68, 407
Standard Deviation, 192, 193, 196, 198
Standardizing, 193
Stanford Prison Experiment of 1971, 214
Star Spangled Banner, 72
State, 12, 14, 15, 16, 24, 45, 46, 47, 48, 49, 51, 52, 55, 56, 58, 59, 60, 61, 62, 63, 64, 66, 70, 71, 72, 75, 76, 77, 80, 90, 91, 103, 108, 110, 112, 114, 117, 118, 127, 148, 195, 207, 210, 226, 237, 239, 264, 271, 274, 275, 276, 289, 307, 310, 365, 392, 402, 404, 406, 409, 410
Statistics, 131, 186, 197, 198, 204, 267
Straight Angle, 169
Straightedge, 182
Strengths-Based Approach, 215
Subject, 14, 15, 18, 19, 20, 21, 22, 24, 27, 28, 30, 34, 35, 36, 37, 38, 39, 40, 77, 88, 109, 115, 117, 206, 223, 230, 286, 288, 290, 291, 293, 294, 295, 328, 329, 352, 353, 354, 356, 357, 382, 384, 418, 419
Subject Complement, 14, 22, 37
Subjective Pronouns, 13
Subject-Verb Agreement, 20, 295
Subjunctive Mood, 16
Sublimation, 216
Subordinate Clauses, 34
Subordinating ¬Conjunctions, 18
Subsistence Farming, 115, 282
Sugar Act, 68, 97
Summer Solstice, 107
Superlative Form, 17
Supplementary Angles, 176
Supply, 121, 124, 127, 239, 253, 277, 361, 403
Susan B. Anthony, 58
Systems Approach, 214
Systems Theory, 216
Systems-Centered Therapy Groups, 216

Taigas, 111
Talcott Parsons, 217
Tangent Line, 182
Tea Act In 1773, 68
Television, 209, 361
Tenth Amendment, 47, 55
    Tenth Amendment to the Constitution, 47
Test Statistic, 198, 203
Tetrahedron, 167
Theocracies, 114
Theory of the Firm, 122, 299
Thesis Statement, 29
Third Person, 12
Thirteenth Amendment, 57
Thirty-Eighth Parallel, 103
Thomas Jefferson, 48, 71
Three-Dimensional Figure, 163, 166, 180, 181
Three-Fifths Compromise, 46, 71, 361, 404
Title IX, 94
Topic Sentence, 29, 294, 295, 357, 358, 422
Toponyms, 108
Townshend Acts, 68
Trail of Tears, 73, 305, 345
Transversal, 176
Treaty of Paris, 70, 117
Tropic of Cancer, 107
Tropic of Capricorn, 107
Tropical Rain Forests, 111
T-Test, 198
Tundra, 110
Two-Dimensional Figure, 163, 178, 180
Two-Party System, 61, 65
Two-Tailed Test, 198
Ulysses S. Grant, 78
Unbiased Estimator, 198
Underground Railroad, 76
Unemployment, 82, 123, 124, 276, 299
Uniform Probability Model, 203
Uniformity, 108
Variability, 204
Verb, 13, 14, 15, 18, 19, 20, 21, 22, 24, 32, 34, 35, 36, 37, 38, 288, 289, 290, 291, 292, 293, 294, 295, 352, 353, 356, 357, 358, 417, 418, 419, 420
Verb Tense, 14
Verbals, 36
Vernaculars, 113

Index

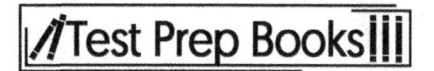

Vertex, 167, 168, 169, 170, 176, 181, 182
Vertex of the Angle, 168
Vertical Angles, 176
Vice President, 50, 51, 52
Vice President Andrew Johnson, 78
Vietnam Conflict, The, 103
Virginia Plan, 46, 70
Volume, 171, 172
Voter Initiatives, 60
Voting, 58, 60, 94
Voting Rights Act of 1965, 58, 94
Wagner Act of 1935, 82
Wall Street Crash of 1929, 119
Warsaw Pact, 84, 102
Weather, 109
Weathering, 109, 242, 281
William Patterson, 46
William Schwartz, 216
William T. Sherman, 78
Winter Solstice, 107

Dear FSOT Test Taker,

We would like to start by thanking you for purchasing this study guide for your FSOT exam. We hope that we exceeded your expectations.

Our goal in creating this study guide was to cover all of the topics that you will see on the test. We also strove to make our practice questions as similar as possible to what you will encounter on test day. With that being said, if you found something that you feel was not up to your standards, please send us an email and let us know.

We have study guides in a wide variety of fields. If you're interested in one, try searching for it on Amazon or send us an email.

Thanks Again and Happy Testing!
Product Development Team
info@studyguideteam.com

FREE Test Taking Tips Video/DVD Offer

To better serve you, we created videos covering test taking tips that we want to give you for FREE. **These videos cover world-class tips that will help you succeed on your test.**

We just ask that you send us feedback about this product. Please let us know what you thought about it—whether good, bad, or indifferent.

To get your **FREE videos**, you can use the QR code below or email freevideos@studyguideteam.com with "Free Videos" in the subject line and the following information in the body of the email:

    a. The title of your product

    b. Your product rating on a scale of 1-5, with 5 being the highest

    c. Your feedback about the product

If you have any questions or concerns, please don't hesitate to contact us at info@studyguideteam.com.

Thank you!

Made in the USA
Las Vegas, NV
16 November 2022